T0180843

Communications
in Computer and Information Science   2011

Harkeerat Kaur · Vinit Jakhetiya · Puneet Goyal ·
Pritee Khanna · Balasubramanian Raman ·
Sanjeev Kumar

Editors

Computer Vision and Image Processing

8th International Conference, CVIP 2023
Jammu, India, November 3–5, 2023
Revised Selected Papers, Part III

 Springer

Editors
Harkeerat Kaur
Indian Institute of Technology
Jammu, India

Vinit Jakhetiya
Indian Institute of Technology
Jammu, India

Puneet Goyal
Indian Institute of Technology
Ropar, India

Pritee Khanna
Indian Institute of Information Technology
Jabalpur, India

Balasubramanian Raman
Indian Institute of Technology
Roorkee, Uttarakhand, India

Sanjeev Kumar
Indian Institute of Technology
Roorkee, Uttarakhand, India

ISSN 1865-0929   ISSN 1865-0937 (electronic)
Communications in Computer and Information Science
ISBN 978-3-031-58534-0   ISBN 978-3-031-58535-7 (eBook)
https://doi.org/10.1007/978-3-031-58535-7

Preface

The 8th International Conference on Computer Vision & Image Processing (CVIP 2023), a premier annual conference focused on Computer Vision and Image Processing, was held during November 3–5, 2023 at Indian Institute of Technology Jammu (IIT Jammu), India. CVIP provides a great platform for students, academics, researchers and industry persons. Previous editions of CVIP were held at VNIT Nagpur (CVIP 2022), IIT Ropar (CVIP 2021), IIIT Allahabad (CVIP 2020), MNIT Jaipur (CVIP 2019), IIIT Jabalpur (CVIP 2018), and IIT Roorkee (CVIP 2017 and CVIP 2016). All editions of CVIP have been endorsed by the International Association for Pattern Recognition (IAPR).

This year we had paper submissions in two rounds. We received a total of 467 submissions, out of which 140 were accepted. CVIP 2023 set a benchmark as receiving the highest number of submissions in CVIP history till now. Submissions were received from almost all premier Indian institutions including IIT Kharagpur, IIT Guwahati, IIT Roorkee, IIT Delhi, IIT Bombay, IIT Kanpur, IIT Patna, IIT Goa, IIT Tirupati, IIT Varanasi, IIT Ropar, IIT Pallakad, IISC, ISI, IIIT Allahabad, IIIT Delhi, IIIT Gwalior, IIIT Jabalpur, IIIT Kanchipuram, and various NITs (Calicut, Warangal, Silchar, Delhi, Agartala) and various internationally renowned institutes such as Norwegian University of Science and Technology, Trinity College Dublin, NTU Singapore, New York University, etc. spanning over 10 different countries. A single-blind review policy was used with a minimum of three reviews per manuscript to decide acceptance or rejection. The selected papers cover various important and emerging aspects of image processing, computer vision applications and advance deep learning and machine learning techniques in the domain. The selected publications also address various practical and life-touching scenarios in the domain.

The technical program committee was led by Puneet Goyal, Pritee Khanna, Aparajita Ojha, Santosh Kumar Vipparthi (IIT Guwahati), Deepak Mishra (IIST Trivandrum), Ananda S. Chowdhury (Jadavpur University), Gaurav Bhatanagar (IIT Jodhpur), Deep Gupta (VNIT Nagpur), Ranjeet Kumar Rout (NIT Srinagar), Nidhi Goel (IGDTUW, Delhi), Rama Krishna Sai Gorthi (IIT Tirupati), Shiv Ram Dubey (IIIT Allahabad), Arvind Selwal (Central University Jammu) and Jagadeesh Kakarla (IIIT Kanchipuram). Apart from their roles as TPC members, their significant contribution along with IIT Jammu faculty members Karan Nathwani, Badri S. Subudhi, Yamuna Prasad, Ambika Shah, Gaurav Varshney, Shaifu Gupta, Samaresh Bera, Quleen Bijral, and Subhasis Bhattacharjee under the mentorship of Manoj Singh Gaur (General Chair and Director IIT Jammu) led to successful completion of the event.

CVIP 2023 was an incredible concoction of Academia, Industry and Entrepreneurship. Keynotes talks were delivered by Santanu Chaudhury (IIT Jodhpur), D. Ram Rajak (ISRO), Amal Chaturvedi (Roche), Tsachy Weissman (Stanford University), and Isao Echizen (University of Tokyo). For the first time in CVIP history a special session on Women in Computer Vision with keynote talks was given by Sushmita Mitra (ISI

Kolkata), Devi Parikh (Georgia Tech) and Geetha Manjunath (Niramai Health analytics), who have distinguished themselves in top research and entrepreneurial positions. The practical and real-life aspects of computer vision were demonstrated in special stalls set up by UNITY AR/VR, Niramai Health Analytics (a breast cancer detection device using AI and image processing), Asterbyte (emotion detection) and a special stall by IHUB Drishti (IIT Jodhpur). A challenge was also organized, Automatic Detection and Classification of Bleeding and Non-Bleeding frames in Wireless Capsule Endoscopy, with over 150 participants who took this challenge. Several technical workshops were also organized by Mathworks and UNITY AR/VR and a special tutorial on Learned Image Compression was delivered by Pulkit Tandon (Grancia) and Animesh Chaturvedi (Amazon).

CVIP 2023 presented high-quality research works with innovative ideas. To acknowledge and promote the spirit of research and participation, five different awards were announced: IAPR Best Paper Award, IAPR Best Student Paper, CVIP 2023 Best Paper Award, CVIP 2023 Best Student Paper Award and CVIP 2023 Best Poster Award. Three prizes were awarded to the challenge winners who secured first, second and third positions. Moreover, to celebrate outstanding work the committee nominated Umapada Pal, ISI Kolkata, for the CVIP 2023 Lifetime Achievement Award for his remarkable research in the field of Image Processing and Computer Vision. Also 75 travel grants were offered to partially support the travel of various participants who travelled to Jammu from near and far places.

We wish the CVIP conference series a grand success as the baton is passed to IIIT Kanchipuram for CVIP 2024 in high spirits!

November 2023

Harkeerat Kaur
Vinit Jakhetiya
Puneet Goyal
Pritee Khanna
Balasubramanian Raman
Sanjeev Kumar

Organization

Patron

B. B. Chaudhuri   ISI Kolkata, India

General Chairs

Manoj Singh Gaur	IIT Jammu, India
Santanu Choudhary	IIT Jodhpur, India
Isao Echizen	National Institute of Informatics, Japan

General Co-chairs

R. Balasubramanian	IIT Roorkee, India
Pritee Khanna	IIITDM Jabalpur, India
Yudong Zhang	University of Leicester, UK

Conference Chairs

Harkeerat Kaur	IIT Jammu, India
Vinit Jakhetiya	IIT Jammu, India
Puneet Goyal	IIT Ropar, India
Deep Gupta	VNIT Nagpur, India
Aparajita Ojha	IIITDM Jabalpur, India

Conference Co-chairs

Sanjeev Malik	IIT Roorkee, India
Partha Pritam Roy	IIT Roorkee, India
Naoufel Werghi	Khalifa University, UAE

Conference Conveners

Gaurav Bhatnagar	IIT Jodhpur, India
Subrahmanyam Murala	IIT Ropar, India
Satish K. Singh	IIIT Allahabad, India
Shiv Ram Dubey	IIIT Allahabad, India
Santosh Vipparthi	IIT Guwahati, India

Publicity Chairs

Jagadeesh Kakarla	IIITDM Kancheepuram, India
Arvind Selwal	Central University Jammu, India
Gaurav Varshney	IIT Jammu, India

Local Organization Committee

Yamuna Prasad	IIT Jammu, India
Shaifu Gupta	IIT Jammu, India
Badri Subudhi	IIT Jammu, India
Karan Nathwani	IIT Jammu, India
Samaresh Bera	IIT Jammu, India
Ambika Prasad Shah	IIT Jammu, India
Subhasis Bhattacharjee	IIT Jammu, India

Technical Program Committee

M. K. Bajpai	IIITDM Jabalpur, India
Deepak Mishra	IIST Trivandrum, India
Ananda S. Chowdhury	Jadavpur University, India
Rama Krishna Sai Gorthi	IIT Tirupati, India
M. V. Joshi	DA-IICT, India
Priyanka Singh	DA-IICT India
Ayan Seal	IIITDM Jabalpur, India
Abhinav Dhall	IIT Ropar, India
Durgesh Singh	IIITDM Jabalpur, India
Shreelekha Pandey	Thapar University, India
Nidhi Gupta	NIT Kurukshetra, India
Amal Chaturvedi	Roche, USA
Pulkit Tandon	Grancia, USA

Debashis Sen	IIT Kharagpur, India
M. Tanveer	IIT Indore, India
Surya Prakash	IIT Indore, India
Deepak Mishra	IIT Jodhpur, India
Basant Kumar	MNNIT Allahabad, India
Shubham Chandak	Amazon, USA
Ajay Mittal	UIET, Panjab University, India
Sumam David S.	NITK Surathkal, India
Shitala Prasad	IIT Goa, India
Anuj Mahajan	SMVDU Jammu, India
Mahesh R. Panicker	IIT Palakkad, India
Indukala Naladala	Apple Inc., India
Pankaj Pratap Singh	CIT Kokrajhar, India
Vishwas Rathi	NIT Kurukshetra, India

International Advisory Committee

Iman Behesti	University of Manitoba, Canada
Anil K. Jain	Michigan State University, USA
Kiran Raja	Nanyang Technological University, Singapore
Raghavendra Ramachandra	NTNU, Norway
Ondrej Krejcar	University of Hradec Kralove, Czech Republic
Bharat Biswal	New Jersey Institute of Technology, USA
Fabio Dell'Acqua	University of Pavia, Italy
K. P. Subbalakshmi	Stevens Institute of Technology, USA
Waleed H. Abdulla	University of Auckland, New Zealand
Yasushi Yamaguchi	University of Tokyo, Japan
Petia Radeva	Universitat de Barcelona, Spain
R. Venkatesh Babu	IISC Bangalore, India
Sharath Chandra Guntuku	University of Pennsylvania, USA
Shou Li	Case Western Reserve, University, USA
Gaurav Sharma	University of Rochester, USA
Rangaraj M. Rangayyan	University of Calgary, Canada
Yongmin Li	Brunel University London, UK
Phalguni Gupta	IIT Kanpur, India

Reviewers

Aashish Kumar	IIT Jammu, India
Abhimanyu Sahu	Motilal Nehru National Institute of Technology, India
Abhishek Singh Sambyal	Indian Institute of Technology Ropar, India
Aditi Palit	Indian Institute of Technology Tirupati, India
Ajay Mittal	Panjab University, India
Ajeet Verma	IIT Jammu, India
Amardeep Gupta	Amity University, India
Ambreen Sabha	Central University of Jammu, India
Amit Bhati	Indian Institute of Information Technology, Design and Manufacturing, Jabalpur, India
Amit Kumar	Indian Institute of Information Technology Kota, India
Amit Vishwakarma	Indian Institute of Information Technology, Design and Manufacturing, Jabalpur, India
Amitesh Rajput	Birla Institute of Technology & Science, Pilani, India
Angshuman Paul	Indian Institute of Technology Jodhpur, India
Anjali Gautam	Indian Institute of Technology Jodhpur, India
Ankit Bhurane	Visvesvaraya National Institute of Technology, India
Ankit Jain	National Institute of Technology Kurukshetra, India
Anuj Mahajan	Shri Mata Vaishno Devi University, India
Anuj Rai	Indian Institute of Technology Indore, India
Aravinda P. N.	Indian Institute of Technology Kharagpur, India
Arif Ahmed Sekh	XIM University, India
Arijit De	Jadavpur University, India
Arindam Sikdar	Jadavpur University, India
Arnav Bhavsar	IIT Mandi, India
Aroof Aimen	Indian Institute Of Technology Ropar, India
Arun Kumar Sivapuram	Indian Institute of Technology Tirupati, India
Ashish Gupta	Thapar University, India
Ashish Mishra	Indian Institute of Technology Madras, India
Ashish Phophalia	Indian Institute of Information Technology Vadodara, India
Ashish Tripathi	Malaviya National Institute of Technology Jaipur, India
Ashutosh Kulkarni	Indian Institute of Technology Ropar, India
Bala Venkateswarlu Isunuri	IIITDM, India

Basant Kumar	Motilal Nehru National Institute of Technology, India
Bharat Singh	Indian Institute of Information Technology Ranchi, India
Bhaskar Mukhoty	Mohamed bin Zayed University of Artificial Intelligence, UAE
Bhavana Singh	Maulana Azad National Institute of Technology Bhopal, India
Bhukya Krishna Priya	IIITDM Kancheepuram, India
Bindu Avadhani	IIITDM Kancheepuram, India
Bindu Avadhani	Amrita Vishwa Vidyapeetham, India
Chandranath Adak	Indian Institute of Technology Patna, India
Chinmaya Panigrahy	Thapar University, India
Debasis Samanta	Indian Institute of Technology Kharagpur, India
Deebha Mumtaz	IIT Jammu, India
Deep Gupta	Visvesvaraya National Institute of Technology, India
Deepak Mishra	Indian Institute of Space Science and Technology, India
Deepak Ranjan Nayak	Malaviya National Institute of Technology Jaipur, India
Deval Verma	Bennett University, India
Jagadeesh Kakarla	IIITDM Kancheepuram, India
Krishan Kumar	National Institute of Technology Kurukshetra, India
Mukesh Kumar	Indian Institute of Technology Patna, India
Palak Mahajan	Central University of Jammu, India
Rahul Nijhawan	Thapar University, India
Shiwangi Mishra	Asterbyte Software Systems Ltd., India
Soubhagya Barpanda	Vellore Institute of Technology, India
Arvind Selwal	Central University of Jammu, India
B. Surendiran	National Institute of Technology Puducherry, India
Chandra Prakash	National Institute of Technology Delhi, India
Debanjan Sadhya	Atal Bihari Vajpayee - Indian Institute of Information Technology & Management, India
Irshad Ahmad Ansari	Atal Bihari Vajpayee - Indian Institute of Information Technology & Management, India
Kirti Raj Bhatele	Rustamji Institute of Technology, India
Mohammed Javed	Indian Institute of Information Technology Allahabad, India
Parveen Kumar	National Institute of Technology Kurukshetra, India

Soumendu Chakraborty	Indian Institute of Information Technology Lucknow, India
Tusar Kanti Mishra	Manipal Institute of Technology, Manipal Academy of Higher Education, India
Vikram Pudi	Indian Institute of Technology Tirupati, India
Vishwas Rathi	Thapar University, India
Ayan Seal	IIITDM Jabalpur, India
Durgesh Singh	IIITDM Jabalpur, India
Gaurav Bhatnagar	Indian Institute of Technology Jodhpur, India
Gian Luca Foresti	University of Udine, Italy
Gorthi Rama Krishna Sai Subrahmanyam	Indian Institute Of Technology Tirupati, India
Gourav Siddhad	IIT Roorkee, India
Gulshan Sharma	Indian Institute of Technology Ropar, India
Gurinder Singh	Cleveland State University, USA
Gyan Singh Yadav	IIIT Kota, India
Hadia Kawoosa	Indian Institute of Technology Ropar, India
Harkeerat Kaur	Indian Institute of Technology Jammu, India
Indukala Naladala	Apple Co., USA
Ishrat Nazeer	National Institute of Technology Srinagar, India
Jagannath Sethi	Jadavpur University, India
Jasdeep Singh	Indian Institute of Technology Ropar, India
Jayant Mahawar	Indian Institute of Technology Jodhpur, India
Joohi Chauhan	Indian Institute of Technology Ropar, India
Joy Dhar	Indian Institute of Technology Ropar, India
Kailash Kalare	Motilal Nehru National Institute of Technology Allahabad, India
Kanchan Kashyap	VIT Bhopal University, India
Kanishka Tyagi	UHV Technologies Inc., USA
Kapil Rana	Indian Institute of Technology Ropar, India
Karan Nathwani	Indian Institute of Technology Jammu, India
Katta Ranjith	Indian Institute of Technology Ropar, India
Komuravelli Prashanth	Indian Institute of Technology Tirupati, India
Krishan Sharma	Scaledge India Pvt. Ltd., India
Krishna Kumar Mohbey	Central University of Rajasthan, India
Krishna Sumanth Vengala	Indian Institute of Technology Tirupati, India
Kushall Singh	Malaviya National Institute of Technology Jaipur, India
K. V. Sridhar	National Institute of Technology Warangal, India
Lalit Kane	MIT World Peace University, India
Mahapara Khurshid	IIT Jodhpur, India
Mahendra Gurve	Indian Institute of Technology Jammu, India

Mahesh Raveendranatha Panicker	Indian Institute of Technology Palakkad, India
Manisha Sawant	Visvesvaraya National Institute of Technology Nagpur, India
Manjunath Joshi	Dhirubhai Ambani Institute of Information and Communication Technology, India
Manoj Kumar	GLA University, India
Massimo Tistarelli	University of Sassari, Italy
Mayank Sharma	IIT Jammu, India
Meghna Kapoor	Indian Institute of Technology Jammu, India
Mohit Dua	National Institute of Technology Kurukshetra, India
Monika Khandelwal	National Institute of Technology Srinagar, India
Monika Mathur	IGDTUW, India
Monu Verma	University of Miami, USA
Mrinal Kanti Bhowmik	Tripura University, India
Muhammad Kanroo	Indian Institute of Technology Ropar, India
Mukesh Mann	Indian Institute of Information Technology Sonepat, India
Muzammil Khan	Maulana Azad National Institute of Technology, India
Nand Yadav	Indian Institute of Information Technology Allahabad, India
Neeru Rathee	MSIT, India
Neha Gour	Indian Institute of Information Technology, Design and Manufacturing, Jabalpur, India
Nidhi Goel	IGDTUW, India
Nidhi Gupta	National Institute of Technology Kurukshetra, India
Nikita Yadav	Maulana Azad National Institute of Technology, India
Nirmala Murali	IIST, India
Nitigya Sambyal	Thapar University, India
Nitin Kumar	Punjab Engineering College Chandigarh, India
Nitin Kumar	National Institute of Technology Uttarakhand, India
Nitish Kumar Mahala	Maulana Azad National Institute of Technology, India
Palak H.	Delhi Technological University, India
Palak Verma	IIT Jammu, India
Pankaj Kumar Sa	National Institute of Technology Rourkela, India
Pankaj P. Singh	Central Institute of Technology Kokrajhar, India
Partha Pratim Das	Indian Institute of Technology Kharagpur, India

Pisharody Harikrishnan Gopalakrishnan	Indian Institute of Technology Palakkad, India
Poonam Kainthura	University of Petroleum and Energy Studies, India
Poornima Thakur	Indian Institute of Information Technology, Design and Manufacturing, Jabalpur, India
Pournami P. N.	National Institute of Technology Calicut, India
Prashant Patil	Deakin University, India
Prashant Patil	Indian Institute of Technology Ropar, India
Pritee Khanna	Indian Institute of Information Technology, Design and Manufacturing, Jabalpur, India
Priyanka Kokil	Indian Institute of Information Technology, Design and Manufacturing, Jabalpur, India
Priyanka Mishra	Indian Institute of Technology Ropar, India
Protyay Dey	Indian Institute of Technology Ropar, India
Puneet Goyal	Indian Institute of Technology Ropar, India
Pushpendra Kumar	Maulana Azad National Institute of Technology Bhopal, India
R. Malmathanraj	NIT Tiruchirappalli, India
Rahul Raman	IIITDM Kancheepuram, India
Rakesh Sanodiya	Indian Institute of Information Technology Sri City, India
Ram Padhy	IIITDM Kancheepuram, India
Ramesh Kumar Mohapatra	National Institute of Technology Rourkela, India
Rameswar Panda	MIT-IBM Watson AI Lab, USA
Randheer Bagi	Thapar University, India
Ranjeet Rout	National Institute of Technology Srinagar, India
Raqib Khan	Indian Institute of Technology, India
Ravi Shanker	Indian Institute of Information Technology Ranchi, India
Ridhi Arora	IIT Roorkee, India
Rishabh Shukla	Indian Institute of Technology Jammu, India
Rohit Kumar	The Captury, Germany
Rukhmini Bandyopadhyay	University of Texas MD Anderson Cancer Center, India
S. N. Tazi	RTU, India
S. H. Shabbeer Basha	Indian Institute of Information Technology Sri City, India
Sachin Kansal	Thapar Institute of Engineering Technology, India
Sadbhawna	Indian Institute of Technology Jammu, India
Sadbhawna Thakur	Indian Institute of Technology Jammu, India
Samir Jain	IIITDM Jabalpur, India
Samridhi Singh	NIT Hamirpur, India
Sandeep Kumar	National Institute of Technology Delhi, India

Sania Bano	Indian Institute of Technology Ropar, India
Sanjay Kuanar	GIET University, India
Sankar Behera	Indian Institute of Technology Jammu, India
Santosh Vipparthi	Indian Institute of Technology Ropar, India
Santosh Mishra	Indian Institute of Technology Patna, India
Saquib Mazhar	IIT Guwahati, India
Sevakram Kumbhare	Jadavpur University, India
Shanti Chandra	Indian Institute of Information Technology Allahabad, India
Shehla Rafiq	Islamic University of Science & Technology, India
Shitala Prasad	NTU, Singapore
Shiv Ram Dubey	Indian Institute of Information Technology Allahabad, India
Shounak Chakraborty	Indian Institute of Information Technology Design and Manufacturing Kurnool, India
Shree Prakash	IIITDM Kancheepuram, India
Shruti Phutke	Indian Institute of Technology Ropar, India
Shubham Chandak	Amazon, USA
Snehasis Mukherjee	Shiv Nadar University, India
Soumi Dhar	NIT Silchar, India
Sree Rama Vamsidhar S.	Indian Institute of Technology Tirupati, India
Subin Sahayam	Shiv Nadar University, India
Sukrit Gupta	Hasso Plattner Institute, Germany
Sumam David S.	National Institute of Technology Karnataka, India
Surabhi Narayan	PES University, India
Surbhi Madan	Indian Institute of Technology Ropar, India
Surinder Singh	Central University of Jammu, India
Sushanta Sahu	Jadavpur University
Swalpa Kumar Roy	Alipurduar Government Engineering and Management College, India
Tajamul Ashraf	Indian Institute of Technology Delhi, India
Tanisha Gupta	Central University of Jammu, India
Tasneem Ahmed	Integral University Lucknow, India
Usma Bhat	Indian Institute of Technology Ropar, India
Vaishnavi Ravi	Indian Institute of Technology Tirupati, India
Vinayak Nageli	DRDO, India
Vipin Kamble	Visvesvaraya National Institute of Technology Nagpur, India
Vishal Satpute	VNIT Nagpur, India
Vishnu Srinivasa Murthy Yarlagadda	Manipal Institute of Technology Bengaluru, India

Vivekraj K.   Indian Institute of Information Technology
                               Dharwad, India
Watanabe Osamu   Takushoku University, Japan
Ximi Hoque   Indian Institute of Technology Ropar, India

Contents – Part III

Face Image Inpainting Using Context Encoders and Dynamically Initialized Mask

Sahil Maurya[✉] and Tushar Sandhan

Perception and Intelligence Lab, Department of EE, Indian Institute of Technology,
Kanpur, Kanpur, India
{sahilm,sandhan}@iitk.ac.in

Abstract. The problem of recovering missing data has garnered considerable attention due to its significance and challenges in recent times. In particular, the ability to recover clear face images from occluded face images has found applications in various domains. One prominent approach in this context is the utilization of autoencoders within the framework of Generative Adversarial Networks (GAN), such as the Context Encoder (CE). The CE is an unsupervised algorithm that leverages an autoencoder as its generator. It is designed to inpaint missing areas in an image based on the information present in the surrounding areas. By learning a compressed representation of the input image, the autoencoder can generate plausible and visually coherent predictions for the missing regions. We found that the initial values of the pixels in the missing area have a significant effect on the quality of the generated images. Careful selection of these initial values proved crucial in achieving accurate and visually appealing inpainted results. Furthermore, we explored various useful loss functions that can be employed within the model. We discovered that the choice of loss function also has a substantial effect on the visual quality of the generated images.

Keywords: Generative Adversarial Networks · Autoencoders · Context encoders · Inpainting · Face images

1 Introduction

The field of facial image analysis and manipulation has undergone a significant transformation because of the progress made in computer vision and image processing techniques in recent times. One area of particular interest is facial image inpainting, which involves the reconstruction and completion of missing or damaged facial regions. The ability to accurately inpaint face images has numerous practical applications, ranging from image restoration [9] to face recognition [5] and virtual reality [12]. Advancements in this domain also impact various other domains of facial image analysis and manipulation, such as emotion recognition [15], facial morphing [13], and facial movement tracking [20], by improving the quality of face images available to them.

H. Kaur et al. (Eds.): CVIP 2023, CCIS 2011, pp. 1–13, 2024.
https://doi.org/10.1007/978-3-031-58535-7_1

Traditional inpainting methods often rely on patch-based or texture synthesis techniques, which attempt to match surrounding image content to complete the missing regions. Examples include exemplar-based inpainting and patch-based approaches [4]. While these methods have shown promising results, they often struggle to generate realistic and coherent completions for complex images, especially in scenarios involving face images with intricate structures and fine details.

The Generative Adversarial Networks (GAN) were initially introduced in [11]. GAN consist of two fundamental components: a generator and a discriminator. The objective of the generator is to produce lifelike samples, whereas the discriminator's job is to distinguish between actual and generated samples. By training these networks in an adversarial setting, GAN learn to generate high-quality samples that resemble the training data. Context encoders are deep neural networks that learn to reconstruct omitted or obscured portions of an image based on its context. They are types of GAN in which the generator is an autoencoder [22]. Autoencoders are neural network architectures used for unsupervised learning and feature extraction. They consist of an encoder and a decoder, which involve the encoder transforming the input data to an abstraction in lower-dimensional space and the decoder recreating the input from the abstraction [2].

This paper examines the novel approach of using context encoders for facial image inpainting. It is illustrated in Fig. 1. By leveraging the power of deep learning, this technique aims to generate realistic and visually coherent facial inpaintings that seamlessly blend with the existing information.

2   Related Work

A number of approaches have been put forward in recent years aimed at solving the issue of facial image inpainting, aiming to generate visually plausible and semantically meaningful completions of missing facial regions. In this section, we provide an overview of the essential works that are closely associated with our suggested method and their contributions.

Image inpainting methods traditionally relied on techniques that tried to replicate the surroundings with some added stochasticity, such as texture synthesis techniques. [4] used a patch-based inpainting method. It considers the texture and structure of the neighbouring regions to inpaint the masked region. In [14], a method is proposed for recreating a partially damaged face. It used linear combinations of shape and texture to model faces. [29] uses pixel and feature level similarity for the reconstruction of photos.

There has been a significant shift towards using neural networks for image inpainting tasks since the advent of deep learning. [28] uses a cascaded approach to the problem. It first identifies the occluded region in the face image. It then parses the face by segmenting it into different elements and then uses the occlusion detection map and the face parsing map to reconstruct the face. [18] uses a generated occlusion face dataset added in a real environment and trains the YOLO v5 [30] deep learning model to identify occluded faces.

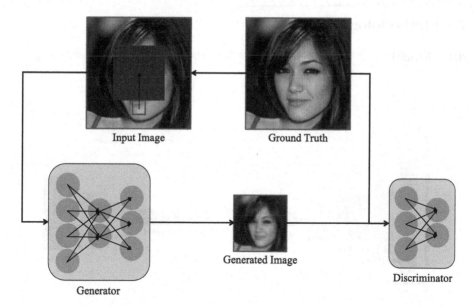

Fig. 1. A flowchart of a context encoder with a dynamic mask being used. The generator takes in face images with a masked region, where the masked region is initialized with the channel-wise average of the red box. It then generates images with the masked region inpainted. (Color figure online)

GANs have gained popularity due to their ability to capture complex image distributions. [10] uses GAN to restore degraded face images. [26] used Deep Convolutional GAN (DCGAN) to de-occulate face images. It first generated a mask where the obstructing objects were, and then it used DCGAN to inpaint the mask region based on surrounding pixels.

[3] proposed the Occlusion-Aware GAN (OA-GAN), which learns in a semi-supervised way. It begins by predicting an occlusion mask, which is then used to obtain feature maps for de-occlusion. The features are then used for face regeneration by filling the occluded regions based on nearby pixels.

Autoencoders have also been utilized to generate realistic and visually coherent results. [25] uses a sparse encoder for face occlusion detection. [23] used a Variational AutoEncoder (VAE) for facial generation from an occluded face image.

[21] introduced a new paradigm of generative models in which a GAN consisted of an encoder as the generative model. It was called a CE. If given an image with an arbitrary region missing, it was able to generate the content of the masked region based on neighbouring regions. [6] used a CE to generate part of a face based on some other part of the face. The proposed method extracts image features using multiple image scales. The features are then aggregated and used by the decoder to create images.

3   Methodology

3.1   Model

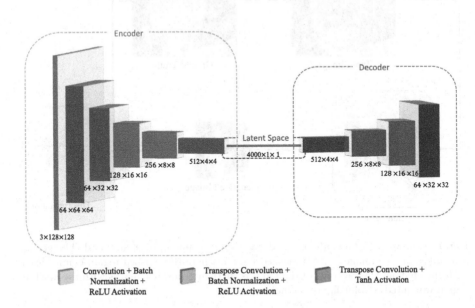

Fig. 2. The architecture of the generator that is used to generate the images. The decoder creates the image with the masked areas inpainted after the encoder transforms the image into latent space.

The neural network model was inspired by the context encoder [21], and it is a GAN model. It takes images with some missing regions as inputs and then inpaint the missing region appropriately according to its surroundings. Two components comprise the model: a generator and a discriminator. The generator consists of an encoder and a decoder linked by a bottleneck layer.

Generator: The generator is an encoder-decoder pair based on CNN as shown in Fig. 2. The encoder converts the input image into a representation in latent state. This latent representation is then used by the decoder to reproduce the image along with the missing parts of the image. The encoder uses six convolutional layers to compute the latent representation, while the decoder uses five transpose convolutional layers to upsample the features in order to generate images.

Discriminator: It is a CNN based binary classifier that predicts whether the input image is a real image or an image generated by the generator. The output is used in the loss function for the generator so that the generator can

Table 1. Detailed generator model architecture. It is also shown in Fig. 2.

Input	Layer	Channels	Filters	Activation	Output
$3 \times 128 \times 128$	2D Conv	3	64	LeakyReLU	$64 \times 64 \times 64$
$64 \times 64 \times 64$	2D Conv	64	64	LeakyReLU	$64 \times 32 \times 32$
$64 \times 32 \times 32$	2D Conv	64	128	LeakyReLU	$128 \times 16 \times 16$
$128 \times 16 \times 16$	2D Conv	128	256	LeakyReLU	$256 \times 8 \times 8$
$256 \times 8 \times 8$	2D Conv	256	512	LeakyReLU	$512 \times 4 \times 4$
$512 \times 4 \times 4$	2D Conv	512	4000	LeakyReLU	$4000 \times 1 \times 1$
$4000 \times 1 \times 1$	2D Transpose Conv	4000	512	ReLU	$512 \times 4 \times 4$
$512 \times 4 \times 4$	2D Transpose Conv	512	256	ReLU	$256 \times 8 \times 8$
$256 \times 8 \times 8$	2D Transpose Conv	256	128	ReLU	$128 \times 16 \times 16$
$128 \times 16 \times 16$	2D Transpose Conv	128	64	ReLU	$64 \times 32 \times 32$
$64 \times 32 \times 32$	2D Transpose Conv	64	3	Tanh	$3 \times 64 \times 64$

learn the difference between a real and a generated image. The generator and the discriminator are alternately trained for one epoch each, so that they train simultaneously.

During training, a mask is applied in the center of the image, covering up 25% of the image. The channel-wise value of the mask is the average of that channel across the whole dataset. Tables 1 and 2 present the complete network architectures of the generator and the discriminator, respectively. The kernel size in each of the layers is (4×4).

Dynamic Mask: The mask used in the baseline method is a constant mask applied across all the images. It is the channel-wise average of all the images across the dataset. In this method, we used a dynamic mask, i.e., a mask with different values for each individual image. It was observed that the model performs better if the initial color of the masked region is closer to the image that it is going to produce. So it helps if the mask is the same color as that of the skin of the person.

Table 2. Detailed discriminator model architecture.

Input	Layer	Channels	Filters	Activation	Output
$3 \times 64 \times 64$	2D Conv	3	64	LeakyReLU	$64 \times 32 \times 32$
$64 \times 32 \times 32$	2D Conv	64	128	LeakyReLU	$128 \times 16 \times 16$
$128 \times 16 \times 16$	2D Conv	128	256	LeakyReLU	$256 \times 8 \times 8$
$256 \times 8 \times 8$	2D Conv	256	512	LeakyReLU	$512 \times 4 \times 4$
$512 \times 4 \times 4$	2D Conv	512	1	Sigmoid	$1 \times 1 \times 1$

To determine the approximate color of the skin, a small box of size ($L/8 \times W/8$) right below the masked region was considered, where L and W are, respectively, the length and width of the image. This region generally consists of the chin and neck areas of the person. Hence, it can give an idea of the skin color of the person. The channel-wise average of this region was used to initialize the color of the masked region.

3.2   Loss Functions

The loss function is a joint loss function between a reconstruction (L2) loss and an adversarial loss. The reconstruction loss preserves the overall structure and coherence of the absent region relative to its context. However, it tends to produce averaged predictions that blur multiple modes together. The adversarial loss encourages the predictions to look more realistic and leads to the selection of a particular mode from the distribution of possible outputs.

Let x be the original image, z be the masked input image, $\mathcal{L}$ be the loss function, F be the generator, D be the discriminator, and M be the mask array, whose value is 1 where the mask is applied and is 0 where the mask is not applied. $\mathcal{X}$ is the real data distribution.

Reconstruction Loss: It is the normalized L2 distance between two images. The generated image is produced by passing the masked input image z given in Eq. (1) into the generator F. The reconstruction loss is taken between the masked regions of the original image and the generated image, as given in Eq. (2).

$$z = (1 - M) \odot x \tag{1}$$

$$\mathcal{L}_{rec}(x) = ||M \odot (x - F(z)||_2^2 \tag{2}$$

Adversarial Loss: It is used the discriminator. The discriminator distinguishes between generated and real images, while the generator tries to produce such images that they are all perceived as real images by the discriminator. This loss encourages the whole generated image to look real rather than just the masked region. It is given as,

$$\mathcal{L}_{adv}(x) = \max_{D} \mathbb{E}_{x \in \mathcal{X}}[\log(D(x)) + \log(1 - D(F(z)))] \tag{3}$$

Joint Loss Function: It is a weighted sum of the two losses. Here, λ_{adv} and λ_{rec} are the weight coefficients. λ_{adv} was taken to be equal to 0.001. It is given as,

$$\mathcal{L} = \lambda_{rec}\mathcal{L}_{rec} + \lambda_{adv}\mathcal{L}_{adv} \tag{4}$$

Discriminator Loss Function: The output of the discriminator is a real number between 0 and 1 used to classify between generated and real images. The binary cross entropy is therefore used as a loss function. It is given as,

$$\mathcal{L}_{disc}(x) = -[\log(D(x)) + \log(1 - D(F(z)))] \tag{5}$$

Different Adversarial loss functions were also tried in conjunction with the above method.

Least Squares GAN Loss (LSGAN): It [19] uses the least squares loss function in both the discriminator and the adversarial loss functions as given in Eqs. (6) and (7). It provides a continuous and non-saturating gradient in the discriminator.

$$\mathcal{L}_{adv}^{LSGAN}(x) = \max_D \mathbb{E}_{x \in \mathcal{X}}[(D(x) - 1)^2 - (D(F(z))^2)] \tag{6}$$

$$\mathcal{L}_{disc}^{LSGAN}(x) = 0.5[(D(x) - 1)^2 + D(F(z))^2] \tag{7}$$

Wasserstein GAN and Gradient Penalty (WGAN-GP): It [1] uses a loss function based on Wasserstein distance [7]. To impose the Lipschitz constraint [27], which is a requirement for the Wasserstein distance, the gradient penalty technique is employed. By adding a penalty term to the loss function, the gradient penalty regularises the discriminator.

$$\mathcal{L}_{adv}^{WGAN}(x) = -\max_D \mathbb{E}_{x \in \mathcal{X}} D(F(z)) \tag{8}$$

$$R = \mathbb{E}_{x \in \mathcal{X}}[(||\nabla D(\alpha x + (1 - \alpha(F(z)||_2 - 1)^2] \tag{9}$$

$$\mathcal{L}_{disc}^{WGAN}(x) = -[D(x) - D(F(z))] + \lambda R \tag{10}$$

where, λ is a weighting factor, α is a hyperparameter, and R stands for regularization.

Deep Regret Analytic GAN (DRAGAN) Loss: It [17] incorporates a penalty term in the traditional GAN loss that encourages the discriminator to be locally Lipschitz continuous. This helps in preventing the generator from generating unrealistic samples and helps improve the convergence properties of the training process.

$$\mathcal{L}_{adv}(x) = \max_D \mathbb{E}_{x \in \mathcal{X}}[\log(D(x)) + \log(1 - D(F(z)))] \tag{11}$$

$$R = \mathbb{E}_{x \in \mathcal{X}, \delta \in \mathcal{N}(0,c)}[(||\nabla D(F(z) + \delta)|| - 1)^2] \tag{12}$$

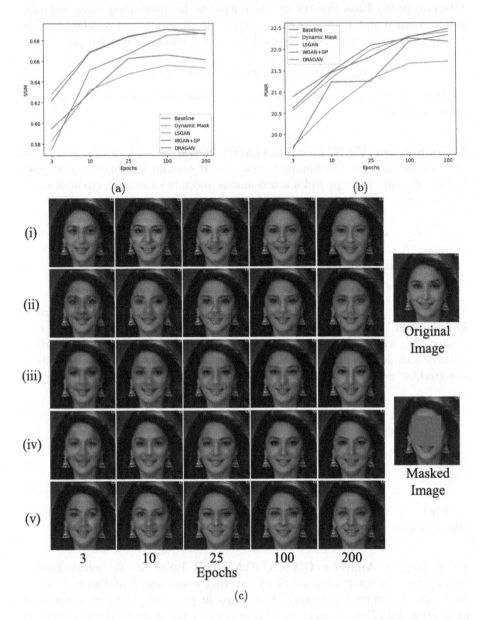

Fig. 3. (a) SSIM plotted against the number of training epochs. (b) PSNR plotted against the number of training epochs. (c) Improvement in the quality of face images plotted against the number of training epochs, (i) Reconstructed Images (Baseline) [21]; (ii) Reconstructed Images (Dynamic Mask); (iii) Reconstructed Images (Least Squared GAN loss) [19]; (iv) Reconstructed Images (Wasserstein GAN Loss and Gradient Penalty) [1]; (v) Reconstructed Images (Deep Regret Analytic GAN loss) [17].

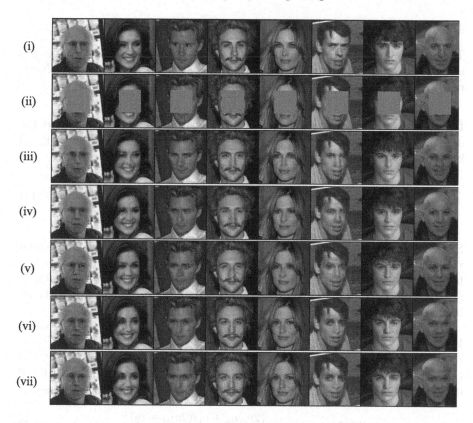

Fig. 4. Comparision between results produced by different methods on the celebA-HQ dataset, (i) Original Images; (ii) Masked Images; (iii) Reconstructed Images (Baseline) [21]; (iv) Reconstructed Images (Dynamic Mask); (v) Reconstructed Images (LSGAN) [19]; (vi) Reconstructed Images (WGAN+GP) [1]; (vi) Reconstructed Images (DRAGAN) [17].

$$\mathcal{L}_{disc}(x) = -[\log\left(D(x)\right) + \log\left(1 - D(F(z))\right)] + \lambda R \qquad (13)$$

where, λ is a weighting factor, c is a hyperparameter, and R stands for regularization.

4   Experiment

4.1   Dataset

The dataset used for the experiment is called the Celebrity Attributes - High Quality (celebA-HQ) dataset [16]. It contains 30,000 images of celebrities. The dataset was separated into 28000 training and 2000 test datasets.

4.2   Evaluation Metrics

The metrics used to evaluate the performances of image generation models are L1 loss, SSIM (Structural Similarity) [24] and PSNR (Peak Signal-to-Noise ratio) [8].

L1 Loss: It is the absolute difference between the generated image and the original image. The lower it is, the closer is the generated image to the original image. It is given as,

$$L1 = \sum_{i=1}^{n} |y_{true} - y_{predicted}| \tag{14}$$

SSIM: It is a technique used for estimating the visual quality of images and videos. It estimates the quality of the image by comparing it with a distortion free image. This method takes human perception into account, which other methods fail to consider. It evaluates the similarity based on three components: contrast, luminance and structure.

It is given by the Eq. (15) where, l and m are the two images being compared. Here, μ_l and μ_m represent the respective averages of l and m. σ_l^2 and σ_m^2 are, respectively the variances of l and m, while c_1 and c_2 correspond $(k_1 S)^2$ and $(k_2 S)^2$, respectively. k_1 and k_2 are constant values, which are equal to 0.01 and 0.03, respectively by default. S represents the dynamic range of pixel values.

$$SSIM(l, m) = \frac{(2\mu_l \mu_m + c_1)(2\sigma_{lm} + c_2)}{(\mu_l^2 + \mu_m^2 + c_1)(\sigma_l^2 + \sigma_m^2 + c_2)} \tag{15}$$

PSNR: It gauges how well an image or video signal has been compressed or reconstructed in comparision to the original version. The higher the PSNR value, the lower the amount of distortion or error between the two versions. It is typically expressed in decibels (dB). It is given as,

$$PSNR = 10 log_{10} \left(\frac{R^2}{MSE} \right) \tag{16}$$

where, $R = 255$ and MSE represents the mean square error of the two images being compared.

4.3   Results

The Nvidia(R) GeForce(TM) RTX(TM) 3060 GPU and the 11th generation Intel(R) Core(TM) i7 processor was used to conduct all the experiments. The results from the evaluation metrics can be seen in Table 3. The variation of SSIM and PSNR along with visual quality improvement, is plotted against the number of epochs in Fig. 3. It can be observed that the initial value of the masked region in an image has an adverse effect on the visual quality of the inpainted image produced. The model prefers the mask to be the same for each sample, even if the color of that mask is farther than the color it is expected to produce. The loss function used also has a significant effect on the inpainted image quality. While the L1 loss is similar for different methods, PSNR and SSIM show significant differences for the different methods. PSNR is better for WGAN-GP than for LSGAN and DRAGAN. However, SSIM is better for LSGAN than the others. Hence, it can be seen that among both of these methods, none of them is universally better, and they are both better at optimizing different criteria as per the evaluation metrics. The improvement in visual quality is depicted in Fig. 4.

Table 3. Results of various methods based on the quantitative metrics.

Metric	Baseline	Dynamic Mask	LSGAN	WGAN-GP	DRAGAN
L1	**0.11**	0.12	**0.11**	**0.11**	**0.11**
PSNR	22.2	21.8	22.4	**22.47**	22.23
SSIM	0.661	0.656	**0.689**	0.686	0.679

5   Conclusion

In this paper, a face image inpainting method using dynamic masks is proposed. It showed the significance of carefully choosing the initial color for the region to be inpainted. To enhance the performance of our approach, we explore the integration of different loss functions in conjunction with the dynamic masks. Specifically, we investigate the efficacy of three prominent loss functions: the least squares GAN loss, the Wasserstein GAN loss with a gradient penalty, and the Deep Regret Analytic GAN loss.

Both the LSGAN and WGAN loss functions, when used in conjunction with the dynamic masks, yield significantly improved results compared to the previous approaches.

References

1. Arjovsky, M., Chintala, S., Bottou, L.: Wasserstein gan (2017)
2. Bank, D., Koenigstein, N., Giryes, R.: Autoencoders. CoRR (2020)
3. Cai, J., Han, H., Cui, J., Chen, J., Liu, L., Zhou, S.K.: Semi-supervised natural face de-occlusion. IEEE TIFS **16**, 1044–1057 (2021)
4. Criminisi, A., Perez, P., Toyama, K.: Region filling and object removal by exemplar-based image inpainting. IEEE Trans. Image Process. **13**, 1200–1212 (2004)
5. Deng, J., Guo, J., Xue, N., Zafeiriou, S.: Arcface: additive angular margin loss for deep face recognition. In: IEEE/CVF CVPR (2019)

6. Do, T.D., Nguyen, Q.K., Nguyen, V.H.: A multi-scale context encoder for high quality restoration of facial images. In: International Conference on Multimedia Analysis and Pattern Recognition (MAPR), pp. 1–6 (2020)
7. Edwards, D.: On the Kantorovich-Rubinstein theorem. Int. J. Biol. Macromolec. (2011)
8. Erfurt, J., Helmrich, C.R., Bosse, S., Schwarz, H., Marpe, D., Wiegand, T.: A study of the perceptually weighted peak signal-to-noise ratio (WPSNR) for image compression. In: IEEE International Conference on Image Processing (2019)
9. Fang, W., Gu, E., Yi, W., Wang, W., Sheng, V.S.: A new method of image restoration technology based on WGAN. In: Computer Systems Science and Engineering, pp. 689–698 (2022)
10. Ghosh, S.S., Hua, Y., Mukherjee, S.S., Robertson, N.M.: Improving detection and recognition of degraded faces by discriminative feature restoration using GAN. In: IEEE International Conference on Image Processing (ICIP), pp. 2146–2150 (2020)
11. Goodfellow, I., et al.: Generative adversarial nets. In: Advances in Neural Information Processing Systems (2014)
12. Gupta, S., Shetty, A., Sharma, A.: Facial de-occlusion network for virtual telepresence systems (2022)
13. Hamza, M., Tehsin, S., Humayun, M., Almufareh, M.F., Alfayad, M.: A comprehensive review of face morph generation and detection of fraudulent identities. Appl. Sci. **12**, 12545 (2022)
14. Hwang, B.W., Lee, S.W.: Reconstruction of partially damaged face images based on a morphable face model. IEEE Trans. Pattern Anal. Mach. Intell. **25**, 365–372 (2003)
15. Jain, N., Kumar, S., Kumar, A., Shamsolmoali, P., Zareapoor, M.: Hybrid deep neural networks for face emotion recognition. Pattern Recogn. Lett. **115**, 101–106 (2018)
16. Karras, T., Aila, T., Laine, S., Lehtinen, J.: Progressive growing of GANs for improved quality, stability, and variation (2017)
17. Kodali, N., Abernethy, J., Hays, J., Kira, Z.: On convergence and stability of GANs (2017)
18. Luo, Y.: Research on occlusion face detection method in complex environment. In: IEEE IMCEC, pp. 1488–1491 (2022)
19. Mao, X., Li, Q., Xie, H., Lau, R.Y., Wang, Z., Smolley, S.P.: Least squares generative adversarial networks. In: IEEE ICCV (2017)
20. Paier, W., Hilsmann, A., Eisert, P.: Example-based facial animation of virtual reality avatars using auto-regressive neural networks. IEEE Comput. Graph. Appl. **41**, 52–63 (2021)
21. Pathak, D., Krähenbühl, P., Donahue, J., Darrell, T., Efros, A.A.: Context encoders: feature learning by inpainting. In: IEEE CVPR, pp. 2536–2544 (2016)
22. Schmidhuber, J.: Deep learning in neural networks: an overview. Neural Netw. **61**, 85–117 (2015)
23. Tu, C.T., Chen, Y.F.: Facial image inpainting with variational autoencoder. In: 2nd International Conference of Intelligent Robotic and Control Engineering (2019)
24. Wang, Z., Bovik, A.C., Sheikh, H.R., Simoncelli, E.P.: Image quality assessment: from error visibility to structural similarity. IEEE Trans. Image Process. **13**(4), 600–612 (2004)
25. Wu, B.F., Wu, Y.C.: Masked neural sparse encoder for face occlusion detection. In: IEEE International Conference on Systems, Man, and Cybernetics (2020)

26. Xu, L., Zhang, H., Raitoharju, J., Gabbouj, M.: Unsupervised facial image de-occlusion with optimized deep generative models. In: Eighth International Conference on Image Processing Theory, Tools and Applications (IPTA), pp. 1–6 (2018)
27. Zhang, C., Bengio, S., Hardt, M., Recht, B., Vinyals, O.: Understanding deep learning requires rethinking generalization. Commun. ACM **64**, 107–115 (2016)
28. Zhang, N., Liu, N., Han, J., Wan, K., Shao, L.: Face de-occlusion with deep cascade guidance learning. IEEE Trans. Multimedia **25**, 3217–3229 (2022)
29. Zhang, S., He, R., Sun, Z., Tan, T.: Demeshnet: blind face inpainting for deep meshface verification. IEEE TIFS **13**, 637–647 (2018)
30. Zhao, Z.Q., Zheng, P., Xu, S.T., Wu, X.: Object detection with deep learning: a review. IEEE Trans. Neural Netw. Learn. Syst. **30**, 3212–3232 (2019)

A Comparative Study on Deep CNN Visual Encoders for Image Captioning

M. Arun[✉], S. Arivazhagan, R. Harinisri, and P. S. Raghavi

Department of Electronics and Communication Engineering, Mepco Schlenk Engineering College, Sivakasi, Tamil Nadu, India
{arun,sarivu}@mepcoeng.ac.in

Abstract. Captioning an image is the process of describing it with syntactically and semantically meaningful terms. An image caption generator is developed by the integration of computer vision and natural language processing technology. Despite the fact that numerous techniques for generating image captions have been developed, the result is inadequate and the need for research in this area is still a demanding topic. The human process of describing any image is by seeing, focusing and captioning, which is equivalent that of feature representation, visual encoding and language generation for the image captioning systems. This study presents the construction of a simple deep learning-based image captioning model and investigates the efficacy of different visual encoding methods employed in the model. We have analyzed and compared the performance of six different pre-trained CNN visual encoding models using Bilingual Evaluation Understudy (BLEU) scores.

Keywords: Image Captioning · Flickr8K · Visual Encoding · BLEU · Flickr30K

1 Introduction

The field of image caption creation has garnered significant attention in recent years within the realm of computer vision and natural language processing research and also has a wide range of practical applications such as image retrieval based on text, info access for visually impaired, social robots etc.… Captioning images is a challenging task than object identification and image categorization. Humans can naturally locate visual objects and determine the image relationships in the images, thus they can create image captions after observing them. The art of human brain processes an image and organizes it into a caption is still unclear. Image captioning systems should use the data from the full image to provide human-like visual descriptions. High-level image description requires the ability to analyze objects, understand their states and relationships, and scene recognition to generate a semantically and syntactically accurate sentence. In short, captioning an image requires a complete understanding of the world and its components (Liu et al., 2018). Despite these challenges, imagine captioning research has advanced in recent years due to deep learning algorithms. Most image captioning systems fall into three categories. The first category uses retrieval-based approaches to find the closest matched photos and use their captions (Delvin et al., 2015). The second category is based on template-based approaches which construct descriptions with established syntactic rules and split phrases. Multiple classifiers recognize the objects in an image and their relationships before applying a rigid sentence template to generate a complete phrase (Fang et al., 2015). Since deep learning is so popular, neural networks based imagine captioning systems form the third category in current scenario. Most research uses encoder-decoder architectures (Cho et al., 2014) to generate image captions using a Convolutional Neural Network (CNN) as the encoder and a Recurrent Neural Network (RNN), especially Long Short-Term Memory (LSTM), as the decoder to maximize sentence likelihood given the image visual features. CNN encodes the input image into a 1-D array, whereas RNN or LSTM generates the caption. Figure 1 shows a schematic block diagram of the encoder-decoder based image captioning model.

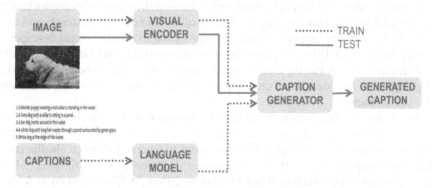

Fig. 1. A schematic diagram of an image captioning model (encoder-decoder based)

Finding suitable CNN and RNN models for this image captioning system is very challenging. This work is aimed to find out the optimal visual encoder model for generic image captioning systems. The research contributions of this work are as follows:

- A simple encoder-decoder image captioning model is created using pre-trained CNN models as visual encoders and a basic LSTM network as decoder
- Visual encoding ability of six pre-trained networks (ResNet50, VGG16, EfficientNetB0, EfficientNetB4, EfficientNetB7, and InceptionV3) for automatic image captioning using Flickr8K dataset is compared based on BLEU score.
- Validation of the optimal visual encoder is validated using Flickr30K dataset

2   Related Works

Using template-based methodologies, Farhadi et al. (2010) created an automated system to assess images and sentences. This score can be used to match descriptive sentences to images or identify images that illustrate them. The score is calculated by comparing the image's meaning to the statement. Girish Kulkarni et al. (2011) developed a system that automatically generates natural language descriptions from images based on the statistics from parsing massive volumes of text data and computer vision algorithms. This technology efficiently generates image-related statements.

Hodosh et al. (2013) created Flickr8K, a dataset of photos with various descriptive captions, for captioning tasks using retrieval-based approaches. They also presented the powerful KCCA-based baseline systems for description and search and examined them in detail. Their findings imply that ranking-based task automation evaluation metrics are more accurate and robust than generation-based image description metrics. A DTRNN model by Socher et al. (2014) embeds phrases in vector space using dependency trees to retrieve images. Unlike RNN-based models that used constituency trees, DT-RNNs organically focus on sentence action and agents. They can better abstract from word order and syntax. DT-RNNs beat other recursive and recurrent neural networks, kernelized CCA, and a bag-of-words baseline when finding an image that matches a sentence and vice versa. They also supplied more standard representations for image-describing sentences. Gong et al. (2014) embedded images and descriptive phrases in a shared latent space to study and tens of millions or hundreds of thousands of examples taught these embeddings. The new approach Stacked Auxiliary Embedding transfers knowledge from millions of poorly annotated photos to improve retrieval-based image description accuracy. Sun et al. (2015) introduced an autonomous visual concept discovery algorithm that filters text phrases based on the visual discriminative power of the related images and groups them into ideas based on visual and semantic similarities using parallel text and visual datasets.

Despite the fact that convolutional neural networks were not widely adopted after the emergence of LeNet, (Lecun et al., 1998) the increase in computing power in the 2010s has paved the way for more CNN networks to emerge for image classification (Ahila Priyadharshini et al, 2019), segmentation (Redmon et al, 2016), etc... More custom designed CNNs such as ResNet (He et al, 2016), VGGNet (Simonyan & Zisserman, 2015), InceptionNet (Szegedy et al, 2015), EfficientNet (Tan and Let, 2019), DIGINet (Madakannu & Selvaraj, 2019), etc.... are designed for specific tasks. The era of deep learning has spawned extensive research in the field of image captioning also. To mention few works in encoder-decoder based captioning model, Google researchers have presented a generative model based on a deep recurrent architecture that can be used to generate natural sentences describing an image. Experiments on multiple datasets demonstrate the model's precision and the fluency of the language it acquires exclusively from image descriptions (Vinyals et al, 2015). Amritkar & Jabade (2018) have designed a neural model which is regenerative for image captioning. This model generates natural sentences that can describe an image and it is composed of both Convolutional Neural Network (CNN) and Recurrent Neural Network (RNN). CNN is used to derive image features while RNN is used to generate sentences. A language model that learns from visual descriptions is tested on several datasets for precision and fluency. Recurrent models were tested for image captioning using visual or non-visual sequences by Donahue et al (2017). They also described end-to-end trainable recurrent convolutional networks for large-scale visual understanding tasks and showcased its use in activity recognition, image captioning, and video description. Recurrent convolutional models learn compositional representations in space and time, making them "doubly deep" compared to prior models that assumed a fixed visual representation or conducted simple tempo-ral averaging for sequential processing. Network state updates with nonlinearities can learn long-term dependencies. Bayoudh et al. (2021) investigated how to construct deep models that integrate and combine diverse visual cues across sensory modalities to help the computer vision community understand deep multimodal learning principles and techniques. The current literature on deep multimodal learning covers six perspectives: multimodal data representation, multimodal fusion (traditional and deep learning-based), multitask learning, multimodal alignment, multimodal transfer learning, and zero-shot learning. Kumari et al. (2020) used CNN and RNN to caption Flickr8K. Advanced region-based CNN (RCNN) technology identified the image's regions and recognised their items. RNN is utilised to generate the most relevant image caption in this study. The Bilingual Evaluation Understudy (BLEU) score evaluates. Zhang et al. (2022) presented a semantic-based image captioning system to improve accuracy and fluency. Veena et al. (2022) evaluated CNN pre-trained models VGG16, RESNET50, Xcep-tion, and INCEP-TION to see which captions images better. Ahamad et al. (2023) proposed a CNN-GRU encoder decode architecture for picture captioning that considers semantic context and time complexity. An encoder and decoder-based fast unsupervised image captioning model (RF-UIC) by Yang et al. (2023) helps visually impaired learners and supports.

3   Materials and Methods

In this research work we have used two datasets namely Flickr8K and Flickr30K for the image captioning task. Since Hodosh et al (2013) have introduced Flickr8K; this dataset has become the benchmark dataset which contains collection a collection of approximately 8K images along with five sentence-based image descriptions for every image. These descriptions provide clear explanations of the salient entities and events associated with the images. These images were hand-picked from six separate Flickr groups to depict a variety of scenes and situations. They do not contain any well-known people or locations. Some sample images and its associated captions from Flickr8K dataset are depicted in Fig. 2.

Flickr30k is also a prominent benchmark for sentence-based image description intro-duced by Young et al (2014). The dataset consists of 31,783 images of individuals par-ticipating in daily activities and events. Each image has 5 accompanying descriptions provided by human annotators.

The design of the image captioning system uses the concept based on encoder and decoder. For the encoding part, we have used the pre-trained networks such as Incep-tionv3, ResNet50, EfficientNet and VGGNet16. These models are already trained on ImageNet dataset. The decoder part uses an LSTM network for the generation of cap-tions. When we send an image through the visual encoding CNN, we obtain the encoded form of the image as 1-D array. Now the decoder is a combination of LSTM and single-layer feed-forward neural network (the input to this feed-forward network is the state vector and the output is the distribution coming out of the softmax function), which decodes the encoded information one word at a time to generate the output from the encoded image.

Sample images of Flickr8K dataset

5 captions for the respective images

1. A man belaying down a waterfall
2. a man in a harness wearing a white hat climbing down a waterfall
3. A man in a red shirt rappelling down a waterfall with a red rope
4. A man in red is climbing a waterfall with a red rope
5. The man in red is propelling down the waterfall

1. A group of young boys fight over a bag of trash
2. Three boys are struggling with one another and reaching for bag of litter
3. Three boys standing in a yard with a bunch of paper
4. Three people are outside with something on the grass
5. Two boys, surrounded by paper pieces , hold a third boys shirt to prevent him from grabbing a bag

Fig. 2. Sample images and its associated captions from Flickr8K

The architecture used in this work for caption generation is shown in Fig. 3. In Fig. 3, the texts which are highlighted in red are the variable parameters in this work. The input images, texts and the generated captions change based on the images and its corresponding text. The input image size (A) is changed to match the visual encoder. The input text size (B) is based on the longest sentence available in the captions. In all the visual encoders, the last layer is chopped off as we require only the visual representations and not the classification. The output size of the visual encoder (X) is also varied based on the CNN used. The other layers are not changed and the output layer size (Y) is based on the vocabulary size of the dataset used. The different visual encoders used in this work and the size of the input, outputs are mentioned in Table 1.

To measure the performance of the proposed captioning model, BLEU is the metric used and other measures are not taken into consideration in this research work. This BLEU metric is determined by the n-gram score, when one word is considered at a time, BLEU-1 score is obtained. However, when a pair of words, called bigram, is considered at a time, the calculated metric is called the BLEU-2 score. Similarly, trigrams and 4-g help in the computation of the BLEU-3 score and BLEU-4 score, respectively and is calculated by the formula mentioned in Eqn-1.

$$BLEU_k = BP.e^{\sum_{k=1}^{N} w_k log B_n} \qquad (1)$$

where, BP is the brevity penalty, k is the number of words, N = 4 (default), w_k is the weight for precision and is 0.25 (default), B_n denotes the precision.

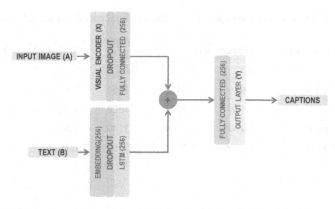

Fig. 3. Block diagram of the proposed encoder-decoder architecture for image captioning

Table 1. Details of Visual Encoders Used

Visual Encoder CNNs	Input size (A)	Total learnable parameters	Output shape (X)
Inceptionv3	299 × 299	5,468,453	2048
EfficientNet B0	224 × 224	5,271,845	1280
EfficientNet B4	380 × 380	5,402,917	1792
EfficientNet B7	600 × 600	5,599,525	2560
ResNet50	224 × 224	5,468,453	2048
VGG16	224 × 224	5,992,741	4096

4 Results and Discussion

The entire experimentations are conducted on a Dell Precision 7820 Tower with an NVIDIA Quadro RTX 5000 GPU and a RAM of 32 GB of memory. The evaluation was performed using the TensorFlow deep learning framework in Anaconda platform. Initially the experimentations are done extensively on the Flickr8K dataset to find out the best visual encoder for image captioning. The train test ratio maintained for this work is 70:30 on all the datasets. Cross entropy loss is used for training the network and Table 2 and Fig. 4 shows the training loss for different epochs for different visual encoders for the Flickr8K dataset.

As this training loss might not give full details about the performance of the system, the test dataset is fed into the captioning system and the BLEU-N (N1 to 4) scores are evaluated for the different visual encoders and the performance measure is shown in Table 3, 4, 5, 6, 7 and 8.

Table 2. Training loss for different epochs for different visual encoders for the Flickr8K dataset

Epoch	Inceptionv3	EfficientNet			ResNet50	VGG16
		B0	B4	B7		
25	2.1934	1.934	1.8442	1.7956	2.1311	2.0696
50	1.8053	1.5780	1.5021	1.4622	1.7829	1.7041
75	1.6200	1.4100	1.3500	1.3140	1.6039	1.5063
100	1.5107	1.3200	1.2572	1.2262	1.4821	1.3858

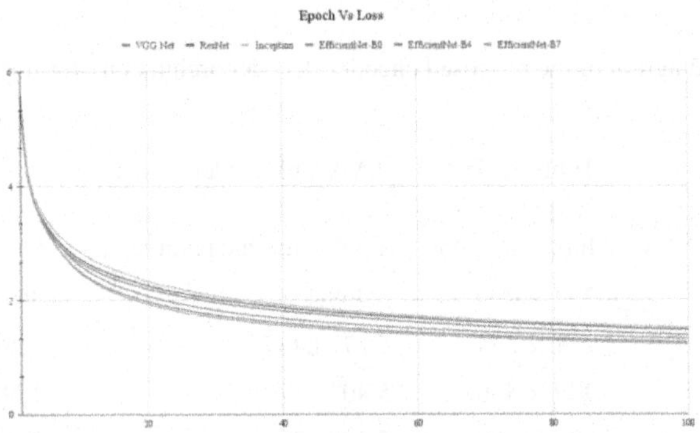

Fig. 4. Training loss for different epochs for various visual encoders for the Flickr8K dataset

From Table 3, 4, 5, 6, 7 and 8, we can observe that the BLEU-1 score of all the visual encoders are nearly the same and has only very little variations and all the models have score more than 0.5 which is a better score. The same holds true for the other BLEU scores also. Analyzing these results from the trained models, overall the EfficientNets serves well as a visual encoder than the other CNNs. This might be due to the fact that EfficientNet models have consistently achieved higher accuracy than VGGNet, Inception and ResNet50 models on a variety of image classification datasets, including ImageNet, CIFAR-100, and Flowers. So, the visual encoding is much better in EfficientNets for the Flickr8K dataset. More specifically the EfficientNetB4 is much better in terms of BLEU scores as the input size (380 × 380) of this visual encoder which matches nearly the input size of the images (500 × 300) in dataset. Training the model for 25 epochs is better than training the model for higher epochs. The sample predictions obtained for the same image from different visual encoders is mentioned in Fig. 5.

Table 3. BLEU scores for Inceptionv3 as visual encoder for the Flickr8K dataset

Metrics		Epochs			
		25	50	75	100
BLEU	1	0.5620	0.5411	0.5280	0.5218
	2	0.3380	0.3715	0.3029	0.2985
	3	0.2164	0.1990	0.1876	0.1845
	4	0.1332	0.1174	0.1115	0.1081

Table 4. BLEU scores for EfficientNetB0 as visual encoder for the Flickr8K dataset

Metrics		Epochs			
		25	50	75	100
BLEU	1	0.5613	0.5380	0.5402	0.5366
	2	0.3382	0.3713	0.3175	0.3123
	3	0.2161	0.2017	0.2003	0.1952
	4	0.1309	0.1220	0.1203	0.1164

Table 5. BLEU scores for EfficientNetB4 as visual encoder for the Flickr8K dataset

Metrics		Epochs			
		25	50	75	100
BLEU	1	0.5863	0.5617	0.5521	0.5388
	2	0.3636	0.3398	0.3302	0.3164
	3	0.2370	0.2186	0.2114	0.1981
	4	0.1464	0.1337	0.1293	0.1172

Table 6. BLEU scores for EfficientNetB7 as visual encoder for the Flickr8K dataset

Metrics		Epochs			
		25	50	75	100
BLEU	1	0.5720	0.5461	0.5270	0.5220
	2	0.3465	0.3234	0.3044	0.2944
	3	0.2231	0.2049	0.1862	0.1795
	4	0.1374	0.1248	0.1063	0.1041

Image	
Original Captions	1. baby girl has the contents of red pot all over her face 2. a baby girl holding red plastic box in one hand and eating from it with the other some of it on her face 3. little girl in highchair has food all over her lower face and her finger in her mouth 4. toddler with pudding all over her face and hands from eating with her fingers 5. the little girl is in her high chair eating jello
Inceptionv3	little girl in blue is sitting on her back eating eating
EfficientNetB0	women curve neck ice out neck theater pirate
EfficientNetB4	baby in yellow shirt is sitting on blue plastic toy and is eating with chopsticks
EfficientNetB7	little girl sitting in the grass and smiling
ResNet50	baby in blue shirt holding book on white and yellow toy
VGGNet16	baby in blue shirt holding book on white and yellow toy

Fig. 5. Sample predictions while using different Visual Encoders

Table 7. BLEU scores for ResNet50 as visual encoder for the Flickr8K dataset

Metrics		Epochs			
		25	50	75	100
BLEU	1	0.5414	0.5407	0.5298	0.5230
	2	0.3209	0.3160	0.3091	0.3024
	3	0.2004	0.1962	0.1931	0.1887
	4	0.1179	0.1150	0.1140	0.1118

Table 8. BLEU scores for VGGNet16 as visual encoder for the Flickr8K dataset

Metrics		Epochs			
		25	50	75	100
BLEU	1	0.5391	0.5121	0.5082	0.4982
	2	0.3121	0.2875	0.2863	0.2738
	3	0.1926	0.1733	0.1770	0.1657
	4	0.1121	0.0989	0.1044	0.0963

From Fig. 5, it is clearly observed that VGGNet16 and ResNet50 performs very similar in terms of visual encoding as the results are nearly the same, but not close enough to the original description. EfficientNetB0 totally predicts the image in wrong sense and this might be due to the input size of the image. EfficientNetB7 predicts the little girl but it predicts the scenario totally absurd as the input image size is more than that of the image size. Inceptionv3 does a better job but still it's not accurate. Considering the prediction from EfficientNetB4, its prediction is much better and the scenario is well understood but, the object detection is poor (finger is wrongly predicted as chopstick). So, according to our experimentations, we are suggesting that even with nearly the same number of learnable parameters, EfficientNetB4 architecture serves as a better visual encoder for image captioning tasks. It is also observed that with fewer samples, the model might memorize the training data rather than learning general patterns, limiting the model's ability to generate accurate and diverse captions.

Table 9. BLEU scores for EffcientNetB4 as visual encoder for the Flickr30K dataset

Metrics		EffcientNetB4
BLEU	1	0.4813
	2	0.2773
	3	0.1627
	4	0.0909

So, just to validate the performance of the EfficientNetB4 as visual encoder, we have used the Flickr30K dataset to evaluate the performance. The number of epochs is limited only to 25. The BLEU scores of for this experiment is shown in Table 9. Despite the BLEU score is less than 0.5, this network is able to generalize the captions for the images beyond the test set images also. Sample predictions for EfficientNetB4 as visual encoder trained on Flickr8K and Flickr30K is shown in Fig. 6.

From Fig. 6, it is evident that EfficientNetB4 trained on Flickr30K generalizes better and the actions and minute details are also captured well (blue shirt, walking). Still the model is not very perfect as it misses out on some details.

Image	Prediction based on Flickr8K Model	Prediction based on Flickr30K Model

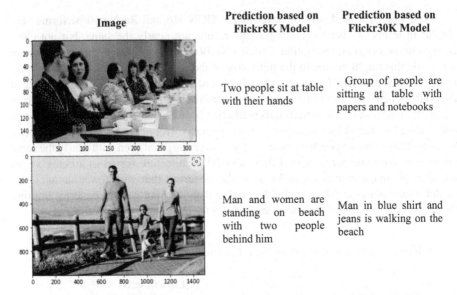

Two people sit at table with their hands — . Group of people are sitting at table with papers and notebooks

Man and women are standing on beach with two people behind him — Man in blue shirt and jeans is walking on the beach

Fig. 6. Sample predictions of images beyond dataset while using EfficientNetB4

5 Conclusion and Future Research Directions

In this work, we have designed a simple encoder-decoder based image captioning system and we have verified the effectiveness of six different visual encoders for this task. It is noted that the EfficienNetB4 performs better than the other pre-trained CNNs and gets generalized much better when trained on Flickr30K dataset. Still the model is not predicting the scene accurately. In future, a segmentation based CNN can be used along with the visual encoder for extracting the object based details and can be used for training. Captioning based systems for native languages can also be taken as a research path.

References

Ahila Priyadharshini, R., Arivazhagan, S., Arun, M., Mirnalini, A.: Maize leaf disease classification using deep convolutional neural networks. Neural Comput. Appl. **31**(12), 8887–8895 (2019). https://doi.org/10.1007/s00521-019-04228-3

Amritkar, C., Jabade, V.: Image caption generation using deep learning technique. In: 2018 Fourth International Conference on Computing Communication Control and Automation (ICCUBEA) (2018). https://doi.org/10.1109/iccubea.2018.8697360

Anitha Kumari, K., Mouneeshwari, C., Udhaya, R.B., Jasmitha, R.: Automated image captioning for Flickr8k dataset. In: Proceedings of International Conference on Artificial Intelligence, Smart Grid and Smart City Applications, 679–687 (2020). https://doi.org/10.1007/978-3-030-24051-6_62

Bayoudh, K., Knani, R., Hamdaoui, F., Mtibaa, A.: A survey on deep multimodal learning for computer vision: advances, trends, applications, and datasets. Vis. Comput. **38**(8), 2939–2970 (2021). https://doi.org/10.1007/s00371-021-02166-7

Cho, K., et al.: Learning phrase representations using RNN encoder–decoder for statistical machine translation. In: Proceedings of the 2014 Conference on Empirical Methods in Natural Language Processing (EMNLP) (2014). https://doi.org/10.3115/v1/d14-1179

Devlin, J., et al.: Language models for image captioning: the quirks and what works. In: Proceedings of the 53rd Annual Meeting of the Association for Computational Linguistics and the 7th International Joint Conference on Natural Language Processing (Volume 2: Short Papers) (2015). https://doi.org/10.3115/v1/p15-2017

Donahue, J., et al.: Long-term recurrent convolutional networks for visual recognition and description. IEEE Trans. Pattern Anal. Mach. Intell. **39**(4), 677–691 (2017). https://doi.org/10.1109/tpami.2016.2599174

Fang, H., et al.: From captions to visual concepts and back. In: 2015 IEEE Conference on Computer Vision and Pattern Recognition (CVPR) (2015). https://doi.org/10.1109/cvpr.2015.7298754

Farhadi, A., et al.: Every picture tells a story: generating sentences from images. In: Daniilidis, K., Maragos, P., Paragios, N. (eds.) Computer Vision – ECCV 2010. LNCS, vol. 6314, pp. 15–29. Springer, Heidelberg (2010). https://doi.org/10.1007/978-3-642-15561-1_2

Gong, Y., Wang, L., Hodosh, M., Hockenmaier, J., Lazebnik, S.: Improving image-sentence embeddings using large weakly annotated photo collections. In: Fleet, D., Pajdla, T., Schiele, B., Tuytelaars, T. (eds.) Computer Vision – ECCV 2014. LNCS, vol. 8692, pp. 529–545. Springer, Cham (2014). https://doi.org/10.1007/978-3-319-10593-2_35

He, K., Zhang, X., Ren, S., Sun, J.: Deep residual learning for image recognition. In: 2016 IEEE Conference on Computer Vision and Pattern Recognition (CVPR) (2016). https://doi.org/10.1109/cvpr.2016.90

Hodosh, M., Young, P., Hockenmaier, J.: Framing image description as a ranking task: data, models and evaluation metrics. J. Artif. Intell. Res. **47**, 853–899 (2013). https://doi.org/10.1613/jair.3994

Kulkarni, G., et al.: Baby talk: understanding and generating simple image descriptions. In: CVPR 2011 (2011)https://doi.org/10.1109/cvpr.2011.5995466

Lecun, Y., Bottou, L., Bengio, Y., Haffner, P.: Gradient-based learning applied to document recognition. Proc. IEEE **86**(11), 2278–2324 (1998). https://doi.org/10.1109/5.726791

Liu, S., Bai, L., Hu, Y., Wang, H.: Image captioning based on deep neural networks. In: MATEC Web of Conferences, vol. 232, p. 01052 (2018). https://doi.org/10.1051/matecconf/201823201052

Madakannu, A., Selvaraj, A.: DIGI-net: a deep convolutional neural network for multi-format digit recognition. Neural Comput. Appl. **32**(15), 11373–11383 (2019). https://doi.org/10.1007/s00521-019-04632-9

Redmon, J., Divvala, S., Girshick, R., Farhadi, A.: You only look once: Unified, real-time object detection. In: 2016 IEEE Conference on Computer Vision and Pattern Recognition (CVPR) (2016). https://doi.org/10.1109/cvpr.2016.91

Yang, R., Cui, X., Qin, Q., Deng, Z., Lan, R., Luo, X.: Fast RF-UIC: a fast unsupervised image captioning model. Displays **79**, 102490 (2023). https://doi.org/10.1016/j.displa.2023.102490

Simonyan, K., Zisserman, A.: Very deep convolutional networks for large-scale image recognition. In: 3rd International Conference on Learning Representations (ICLR 2015) (2015). https://arxiv.org/pdf/1409.1556.pdf

Socher, R., Karpathy, A., Le, Q.V., Manning, C.D., Ng, A.Y.: Grounded compositional semantics for finding and describing images with sentences. Trans. Assoc. Comput. Linguist. **2**, 207–218 (2014). https://doi.org/10.1162/tacl_a_00177

Sun, C., Gan, C., Nevatia, R.: Automatic concept discovery from parallel text and visual corpora. In: 2015 IEEE International Conference on Computer Vision (ICCV) (2015). https://doi.org/10.1109/iccv.2015.298

Szegedy, C., et al.: Going deeper with convolutions. In: 2015 IEEE Conference on Computer Vision and Pattern Recognition (CVPR) (2015). https://doi.org/10.1109/cvpr.2015.7298594

Tan, M., Le, Q.V.: EfficientNet: rethinking model scaling for convolutional neural networks. In: 36th International Conference on Machine Learning, pp. 6105–6114 (2019). https://arxiv.org/abs/1905.11946

Veena, S., Ashwin, K.S., Gupta, P.: Comparison of various CNN encoders for image captioning. J. Phys: Conf. Ser. **2335**(1), 012029 (2022). https://doi.org/10.1088/1742-6596/2335/1/012029

Vinyals, O., Toshev, A., Bengio, S., Erhan, D.: Show and tell: a neural image caption generator. In: 2015 IEEE Conference on Computer Vision and Pattern Recognition (CVPR) (2015). https://doi.org/10.1109/cvpr.2015.7298935

Young, P., Lai, A., Hodosh, M., Hockenmaier, J.: From image descriptions to visual denotations: new similarity metrics for semantic inference over event descriptions. Trans. Assoc. Comput. Linguist. **2**, 67–78 (2014). https://doi.org/10.1162/tacl_a_00166

Zhang, Z., Zhang, H., Wang, J., Sun, Z., Yang, Z.: Generating news image captions with semantic discourse extraction and contrastive style-coherent learning. Comput. Electri. Eng. **104**, 108429 (2022). https://doi.org/10.1016/j.compeleceng.2022.108429

Robust Semi-supervised Medical Image Classification: Leveraging Reliable Pseudo-labels

Devesh Kumar[1]([✉]), Geeta Sikka[2], and Samayveer Singh[1]

[1] Department of Computer Science and Engineering, Dr. B. R. Ambedkar National Institute of Technology, Jalandhar, Punjab, India
{deveshk.cs.21,samays}@nitj.ac.in
[2] Department of Computer Science and Engineering, National Institute of Technology, Delhi, Delhi, India
sikkag@nitdelhi.ac.in

Abstract. The field of semi-supervised learning (SSL) has fostered new techniques to increase the performance of machine learning models in interpreting medical images. This paper introduces a groundbreaking approach for medical image classification, which combines pseudo-loss approximation and adversarial distortion. Our model improves the learning process by offering a more accurate evaluation of pseudo-labels attached to unlabeled data. It uses pseudo-labeled data that are both trustworthy and meaningful, resulting in higher categorization accuracy. Moreover, adversarial distortion is added to unlabeled data through a cross pseudo-loss approximation strategy. This unique technique allows us to unlock the hidden value in previously ignored data, thereby further boosting our model's performance. We have conducted extensive experiments on two medical datasets, including the NCT-CRC-HE, to illustrate our model's efficacy and adaptability under various test scenarios. Comparative results, showing a consistent performance improvement over other SSL methods, underline the potential of our approach in redefining boundaries in semi-supervised medical image classification tasks, highlighting its promise to significantly contribute to the medical image analysis field.

Keywords: pseudo-label approximation · medical image analysis · Semi-supervised learning · adversarial distortion

1 Introduction

Deep learning has made significant progress in computer vision tasks, including, but not limited to, analyzing medical images. The advances have enabled real-world applications in areas like disease detection, lesion spotting, and treatment mapping [1–3]. However, annotating large quantities of medical images is a time-consuming, expensive task that needs specialist knowledge. This issue translates into a shortage of labeled data, which hinders the training of precise and stable deep-learning models in the medical field.

H. Kaur et al. (Eds.): CVIP 2023, CCIS 2011, pp. 27–38, 2024.
https://doi.org/10.1007/978-3-031-58535-7_3

SSL techniques have emerged as a possible solution to this problem because they are good at working with a very few amount of labeled data. SSL works by utilizing both labeled and unlabelled data, aiming to improve the accuracy of a classification and reduce the necessity of data annotation [4,5]. Unlabelled data, being more readily available from clinical sites, can provide useful inputs to enhance the training of models.

In a semi-supervised learning framework, making effective use of unlabeled data becomes crucial for gaining more insights. Two commonly used strategies in semi-supervised learning are pseudo-labeling and consistency regularization. Pseudo-labeling involves finding confident labels for re-training the model, while consistency regularization improves the model's stability by ensuring consistent predictions even with various disturbances [6,7].

Nevertheless, as illustrated in Fig. 1 conventional SSL approaches face obstacles in two primary aspects. First, identifying reliable pseudo-labeled data becomes a complex task when probability-based threshold methods are used. Confirmation bias often leads to incorrect pseudo-labels, which can adversely affect the performance of the model. This problem is evidenced by similar probability distributions seen in both accurate and incorrect pseudo-labels [8,9]. Secondly, unlabeled data samples, which often possess crucial information, are typically underutilized, especially those with low probabilities that generally cluster near the decision boundary. Articles [10,11] have indicated that during the training process, neural networks initially adapt to clean data and subsequently memorize the noisy data. Consequently, the loss associated with clean data is reduced in the early stages of training, while the loss connected with noisy data increases. Semi-supervised learning with adversarial distortion has demonstrated its ability to effectively extract knowledge from low-quality pseudo-labeled data [12].

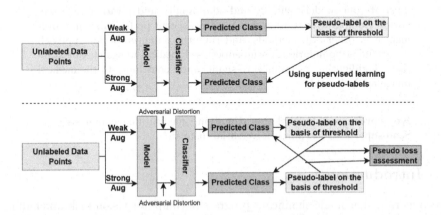

Fig. 1. Comparison of conventional Semi-Supervised Pseudo-Labeling techniques with adaptive approach.

This study introduces a method for medical image analysis with pseudo-loss approximation. It incorporates adversarial distortion based on cross-pseudo loss approximation in the calculation of pseudo labels. This innovative SSL approach is explicitly devised for medical image classification. The presented method addresses the hurdles conventional SSL methods encounter and offers two significant enhancements.

Our approach involves a method for choosing high-quality pseudo-labeled data using loss distribution approximation. We utilize the Gaussian Mixture Model (GMM) for the evaluation the loss distribution, a departure from solely relying on probability thresholds. This approach, with the implementation of cross pseudo-loss approximation, allows us to determine reliable pseudo-labeled data through posterior probabilities. This approach overcomes the limitations associated with threshold-based selection methods, facilitating the collection of high-quality pseudo-labeled data.

In addition, our method involves the implementation of adversarial distortion based on the calculated cross-pseudo loss that augments representation learning and contributes to decision boundary smoothing. This scheme involves the introduction of adversarial distortions at the feature level, enhancing the exploration of informative patterns in both selected pseudo-labeled data and unlabeled data. The strategy promotes more effective usage of available unlabeled samples and aids the model in capturing complex decision boundaries. The main contributions of the proposed method are summarized as follows:

1. This study introduces to choose pseudo-labeled data (data labeled by the model itself) based on an estimate of how errors are distributed. We use a model called a two-component Gaussian Mixture Model to find pseudo-labeled data that we can trust. This approach helps us get past the limitations of methods that rely on fixed probability levels.
2. The introduction of adversarial distortion, based on calculated cross-pseudo loss, is another major contribution of this study. It fosters enhanced representation learning and facilitates decision boundary smoothing. By incorporating adversarial distortions at the feature level, we stimulate the discovery of informative patterns in both chosen pseudo-labeled data and unlabeled data.
3. Comprehensive tests carried out on two medical image datasets NCT-CRC-HE [13] and Chest X-Ray14 [14] demonstrate the proposed method's edge over other advanced SSL techniques. It provides notable enhancements in classification performance, underlining its potential to boost medical image analysis.

In summary, the approach presented herein effectively tackles the issues inherent to semi-supervised medical image categorization. With the implementation of pioneering techniques for pseudo-labeled data selection and the introduction of adversarial distortion, our proposed approach exhibits enhanced performance. It thus opens up exciting prospects for future developments in SSL techniques for medical image analysis.

The rest of this article is organized as follows: Sect. 2 talks about previous studies on SSL techniques, pseudo-labeling, and consistency regulation. In Sect. 3, we introduce our new method, called cross-pseudo approximation with adversarial distortion. In Sect. 4, we present the outcomes we obtained when we tested our new method on two datasets. Lastly, in Sect. 5, we conclude the article and discuss our future plans.

2   Related Work

The realm of Medical Image Analysis has witnessed a considerable surge of interest in SSL, a technique that aims to augment the efficacy of machine learning models by utilizing both labeled and unlabeled data. While active learning targets samples based on their informativeness (how uncertain or ambiguous they are for the current model) and representativeness (how well they represent the underlying data distribution) [15], semi-supervised learning can capitalize on the inherent structure of the data without explicitly querying for new labels. Thus, semi-supervised learning might be more efficient when labeling costs are high or when it's challenging to iteratively access an oracle for annotations. This section offers an in-depth review of the pertinent literature in two primary areas: SSL medical image classification and SSL medical image segmentation in Sect. 2.2.

2.1   Methods in Semi-supervised Image Classification

The various SSL techniques employed fo image classification can be primarily bifurcated into three categories: pseudo-labeling, consistency regularization, and graph-based methods.

a. Pseudo-labeling: Methods grounded on pseudo-labeling allocate pseudo-labels to unlabeled data which are then incorporated during the training phase of the model. The Adaptive Confidence Pseudo-Labeling method [8] uses classifiers collectively to enhance the accuracy of pseudo-labels while implementing an anti-curriculum training strategy. Boosting with Multiple Instance Selection [16] takes into account the learning capability of the model at various training stages and proposes an adaptive pseudo-labeling strategy. Noise Student [17] follows an iterative training approach where pseudo-labels are generated by an updated teacher network, which then guide the learning process of the student network. Despite their successful application, these methods depend on probability thresholds to select reliable pseudo-labeled data, which can present challenges when the data comprises both correct and incorrect pseudo-labels.

b. Consistency Regularization: The objective of consistency regularization methods is to minimize the variance between predictions made on diverse views of unlabeled data. Self-Relation Consistency with Temporal Ensembling (SRC-MT) [6] introduces a data-driven consistency approach through self-ensembling learning. Virtual Adversarial Training [7] utilizes virtual adversarial perturbations to regularize the model's predicted outcomes, thereby enhancing its resilience to small input perturbations. AlphaMatch [18] implement alpha-divergence and optimizes the model similarly to Expectation-Maximization. In contrast, our proposed method injects adversarial distortions at the feature level, capitalizing on the benefits of discriminative information mining and incorporating complementary information between augmented views.

2.2   SSL Medical Image Segmentation

The challenge of acquiring labeled medical image data has prompted the rise of semi-supervised medical image segmentation research. Many methods in this area, such as those proposed in [1–3], are heavily reliant on pseudo-labeling techniques. In contrast, other researchers, including those cited in [6,7,18], have focused on the application of consistency regularization. Notably, studies [7,18] have made significant efforts to achieve model invariance to samples subjected to varying perturbations, while the study in [19] explores the consistency between different tasks.

Our study proposes a method for pseudo-labeled data selection using a two-component Gaussian Mixture Model and a unique adversarial distortion process based on calculated cross-pseudo loss to stimulate informative pattern discovery. Comprehensive testing across various datasets showcases its superiority over existing SSL techniques, highlighting its potential to enhance medical image analysis.

3   Methodology

In SSL, labeled dataset $\mathcal{D}_l = \{(x_i, y_i)\}_{i=1}^{n_l}$ and an unlabeled dataset $\mathcal{D}_u = \{(u_i)\}_{i=1}^{n_u}$ are available, where n_u significantly outweighs n_l; here, n_u and n_l denote the count of unlabeled and labeled data sets respectively. It is presumed that both datasets originate from a similar distribution, and the objective is to model the problem in such a way that labeled $\mathcal{D}_l$ and unlabeled $\mathcal{D}_u$ data both can be employed simultaneously, with methods varying in how they utilize the unlabeled dataset $\mathcal{D}_u$.

Our approach as demonstrated in the Fig. 2, starts with classifier initialization using the entire training dataset. We use GMM to model the loss distribution, computed specifically on labeled images, which helps us understand the loss distribution connected with these images.

To engage the unlabeled data, we implement a cross pseudo-loss approximation technique with the fitted GMM. This technique assists to identify the dependable pseudo-labeled data by inputting the cross pseudo-loss, subsequently aiding in the selection of accurate pseudo-labeled data for further training.

Moreover, we incorporate an adversarial consistency regularization strategy to take advantage of the remaining unlabeled data, not chosen as pseudo-labeled data. The introduction of adversarial distortions at the feature level encourages the model to learn from this useful yet unchosen data. Importantly, this strategy is not confined to unselected data and also applies to pseudo-labeled data selection.

Sections 3.1, 3.2 and 3.3 offer a comprehensive understanding of the loss distribution modeling process, and the high-quality pseudo-labeled data selection, and incorporate the adversarial distortion that improves the model's availity to learn from the unlabeled data.

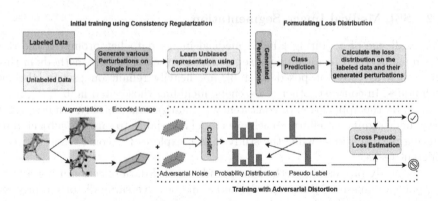

Fig. 2. An illustration of the proposed method initially trains the model using consistency regularization on the labeled data, which helps to create an unbiased representation. After that, the loss on the available labeled data is calculated. Cross pseudo-loss approximation generates reliable pseudo-label data for the unlabeled data. Additionally, we infuse adversarial distortion in the feature space to better utilize the unlabeled data.

So, our approach improves the effectiveness of semi-supervised medical image classification by combining techniques such as modeling loss distribution, selecting high-quality pseudo-labeled data, and using adversarial distortion.

3.1   Forming Loss Distribution

The process of pseudo-labeling-based SSL is typically organized into three steps: (1) the creation of a model, f_ϑ, with parameters ϑ, using the labeled data, $Ð_l$; (2) the pseudo-labels for the unlabeled dataset are calculated, $Ð_u$, and the formation of a collection of high-confidence pseudo-labeled examples, $\hat{Ð}_l = \{(u_i, f_\vartheta(u_i))\}_{i=1}^{N_u}$; (3) the retraining of the model, f_ϑ, using the combined labeled dataset, $Ð_l$, and the chosen pseudo-labeled dataset, $\hat{Ð}_u$. Yet, this framework possesses certain drawbacks. It relies heavily on the initial model's performance on the labeled dataset, $Ð_l$, and the quality of the generated pseudo-labeled data in $\hat{Ð}_l$. In numerous scenarios, the model, f_ϑ, initialized through this warm-up process, demonstrate confirmation bias [2] or partial distribution in $Ð_l$, combined with a huge quantity of inaccurately labeled samples for retraining.

Preliminary Training via Consistency Regularization. Our SSL structure is built upon the principle of consistency regularization. We enforce different perturbations on a particular input and mandate consistency in model predictions to unveil the invaluable feature information concealed in the unlabeled data. Contrastive loss is a loss function based on distance, mainly used in tasks such as metric learning and embedding spaces. It is generally employed when training a neural network to learn data encoding. This loss function punishes instances where similar samples are distanced in the encoding space, and unlike samples are positioned closely.

For a pair of samples (x_i, x_j) and a label y_{ij}, where $y_{ij} = 1$ if x_i and x_j belong to the same class and $y_{ij} = 0$ otherwise, the contrastive loss for this pair can be described as follows in the Eq. 1:

$$L(x_i, x_j, y_{ij}) = \frac{1}{2} * y_{ij} * D_w^2 + \frac{1}{2} * (1 - y_{ij}) * max(0, m - D_w)^2 \qquad (1)$$

Here, D_w signifies the distance between the pair of samples (x_i, x_j) in the embedding space, as determined by a metric like the Euclidean distance, m denotes the margin imposed between dissimilar pairs and is a hyperparameter that needs to be manually established. The total contrastive loss is subsequently computed as the sum or average of the loss for all pairs in your dataset.

The contrastive loss's goal is to minimize the distance D_w for similar pairs (where $y_{ij} = 1$) and to exceed the margin m for dissimilar pairs (where $y_{ij} = 0$) as given in Eq. 2. This prompts the network to learn embeddings where similar instances are positioned closely, and unlike instances are spread apart. Therefore, the preliminary loss is the sum of the contrastive loss across the entire data and the cross-entropy loss on the labeled data.

$$min_\theta \sum_{i=1}^{n_l} \mathcal{L}_s(f(x_i; \vartheta), y_i) + \xi \mathcal{L}_u(\{x_i\}_{i=1}^{n_l+n_u}) \qquad (2)$$

Loss Distribution: Defining a set of dependable pseudo-labeled data, $\hat{D}_u$, using predicted probabilities as a threshold is problematic due to the similarity in probability distributions between unlabeled samples with correct and incorrect pseudo-labels. To counter this, we take advantage of the fact that incorrect pseudo-labels tend to have high losses in the early training stages. This allows us to separate correct samples from incorrect ones based on their loss distribution. GMM opt over other loss distribution models due to its capability to capture complex multi-modal distributions, which can be particularly beneficial when dealing with varying degrees of labeling noise [23, 24]. To do this, we propose that the total loss distribution given in Eq. 3, is made up of two normal distributions. We utilize the GMM to model the loss distribution on D_l, which aids in differentiating between clean and noisy pseudo-labels as illustrated in Eq. 4.

$$\mathcal{L}(D_l | f_\vartheta) = \{-y_i \log(f_\vartheta(\hat{y}_i | x_i)), x_i \in D_l\} \qquad (3)$$

$$\mathcal{P}(l_i) = \sum_{g=0}^{\mathcal{G}-1} \Lambda_g \mathcal{I}_g \left(l_i | \gamma_g, \sum_g\right), l_i \in \mathcal{L}(D_l | f_\vartheta) \qquad (4)$$

Within this framework, $\mathcal{L}(D_l | f\vartheta)$ denotes the collection of losses on D_l. The weight for the $\mathcal{G}$-th Gaussian component is $\Lambda\mathcal{G} \geq 0$, ensuring that $\sum_{g=0}^{\mathcal{G}-1} \Lambda_g = 1$. For a particular loss value l_i, $\Lambda_g \mathcal{I}_g$ indicates the probability of l_i belonging to the

g-th Gaussian component. We use the Expectation Maximization (EM) method to adapt the GMM based on the losses observed in $Ð_l$. The optimization strategy is focused on maximizing the log-likelihood, which can be expressed as:

$$\hat{\vartheta}_{GMM} = \underset{\vartheta_{GMM}}{\arg\max}[\log \prod_{i=1}^{n_l} \mathcal{I}(l_i|\vartheta_{GMM})] \tag{5}$$

In the Eq. 5, $\vartheta_{GMM} = \Lambda_g, \gamma_g, \sum_g$ with $0 \le g \le \mathcal{G} - 1$. By observing the prior loss distribution on $Ð_l$, the GMM can distinguish reliable pseudo-labeled samples based on the distribution of pseudo-losses.

3.2   High-Quality Pseudo-label Selection

In SSL, the selection of reliable pseudo-labeled data is key to reaching the best performance from a model. In response to this challenge, Chen et al. [20] proposed a unique method known as cross pseudo-loss supervision. This technique leverages pseudo-loss approximations to assess the dependability and certainty of pseudo-labels assigned to unlabeled data. The goal of incorporating cross pseudo-loss supervision is to enhance the quality of the chosen pseudo-labeled data as given in Eq. 6 and Eq. 7, that are used for training. This method takes into account multiple perspectives of the unlabeled samples, utilizing the predictions from one perspective, ζ_{Aug1}, to approximate pseudo-loss for another view, ζ_{Aug2}. This process allows for a more precise and equitable evaluation of the model's predictions, thereby enhancing the overall learning process.

$$\hat{y}^{Aug1 \rightarrow Aug2} = \arg\max(f_\vartheta(\zeta_{Aug1}(u_i))) \tag{6}$$

$$\hat{y}^{Aug2 \rightarrow Aug1} = \arg\max(f_\vartheta(\zeta_{Aug2}(u_i))) \tag{7}$$

Cross entropy pseudo loss comes into play when assessing the performance of the model across various data augmentations, acting as an indicator of discrepancy between pseudo-labels and model predictions. This helps fine-tune the model's performance, ensuring robustness despite varying data augmentations.

$$l_i^{Aug1 \rightarrow Aug2} = -y_i^{\hat{Aug1} \rightarrow Aug2} \log(f_\vartheta(\zeta_{Aug1}(u_i))) \tag{8}$$

$$l_i^{Aug2 \rightarrow Aug1} = -y_i^{\hat{Aug2} \rightarrow Aug1} \log(f_\vartheta(\zeta_{Aug2}(u_i))) \tag{9}$$

Following the computation of Eq. 8 ($l_i^{Aug1 \rightarrow Aug2}$) and Eq. 9 ($l_i^{Aug2 \rightarrow Aug1}$) losses, the GMM is employed to aid in the selection of reliable pseudo-labels. In essence, this is a dual-phase strategy designed to enhance the quality of chosen pseudo-labeled samples within a SSL framework. The model uses the GMM for the loss distribution together with the cross pseudo-loss approximation. This helps improve the accuracy and reliability of the selected data points.

3.3 Training with Adversarial Distortion

To effectively harness the valuable information from unlabeled samples that weren't selected via Cross Pseudo-loss, we employ adversarial distortion grounded in the cross entropy loss. This approach entails the introduction of purposeful adversarial distortion at the feature level, facilitating the extraction of data from these instances. The tactical implementation of adversarial distortion serves to boost the model's resilience and capacity to uncover distinguishing information.

4   Result and Analysis

The proposed method has been evaluated using two distinct medical image classification datasets: NCT-CRC-HE [13] and Chest X-Ray14 [14]. The ChestX-ray8 dataset poses challenges due to its inherent class imbalance and potential label noise, while the NCT-CRC-HE dataset is complex because of histological variations and the subtle differences between benign and malignant tissue structures. The NCT-CRC-HE dataset is composed of 100,000 histology slides of colorectal cancer, categorized into nine different classes, forming a multi-class classification task. To align with previous studies [20–22] and ensure a balanced comparison, the dataset was divided into 70% for training, 10% for validation, and 20% for testing (Fig. 3).

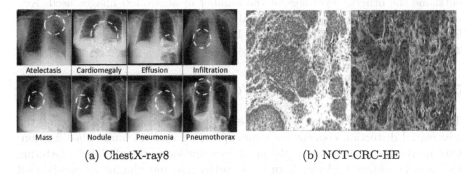

(a) ChestX-ray8   (b) NCT-CRC-HE

Fig. 3. Classes of the ChestX-ray8 dataset and the histopathology slides of NCT-CRC-HE dataset.

For both datasets, we built our model on the DenseNet121 architecture with an input size of 224 × 224. We used the Adam optimizer with an adaptive learning rate starting from 0.001 during the training process. Each mini-batch consists of 8 labeled and 24 unlabeled images. The model is trained for 100 epochs, where the first 20 epochs are used to warm up the model, and the following 30 epochs are for re-training.

Table 1. Method's Accuracy on particular Label Percentage for two datasets Chest X-Ray14 and NCT-CRC-HE

Chest X-Ray14				
Method	Label Percentage			
	2%	5%	10%	15%
Graph XNet [20]	55.62	59.14	64.13	69.68
NoTeacher [21]	71.15	78.60	77.86	78.35
SRC-MT [22]	77.52	78.83	79.23	81.75
Ours	77.65	80.01	80.65	82.15

NCT-CRC-HE dataset				
Method	Label Percentage			
	2%	5%	10%	15%
Base Model	78.64	80.06	82.47	86.38
Proposed	82.49	87.34	90.32	96.65

Hyper-parameters in our study, including ς (employed in calculating the cross-entropy loss on augmentation), ε (utilized to moderate the adversarial distortion), and ψ (applied to regulate the weight balance between the two pseudo-losses originating from image augmentation), were empirically established with values 0.05, 1, and 0.5 respectively. All the experiments were executed using the PyTorch framework on a 16GB NVIDIA Tesla V100 GPU.

Comparative Analysis: In this study, a comparison is made between our method and three recently proposed semi-supervised learning methods: Graph XNet [20], NoTeacher [21], and SRC-MT [22]. With identical network architectures and input image sizes used across all experiments, our method consistently outshone the others, regardless of the number of annotated images used. Key results, as summarized in Table 1, reveal that our method achieved superior performance gains, ranging from 0.13% to 1.40%, in accuracy when tested with the 2%, 5%, 10%, and 15% labeled data points.

5   Conclusion and Future Work

This paper proposes a pseudo-label loss approximation method leveraging the adversarial distortion concept for semi-supervised medical image classification. Our approach concentrates on the precise evaluation of pseudo-labels, fostering the model's ability to learn from trustworthy and meaningful pseudo-labeled data. Additionally, we advocate for the introduction of adversarial distortion to unlabeled data through a strategy called cross pseudo-loss approximation, thus efficiently harnessing the potential of valuable, yet overlooked, data. Comprehensive trials on two distinct medical datasets, NCT-CRCHE and Chest X-Ray14, validate our method's capability in enhancing classification accuracy and its adaptability across diverse experimental conditions. These promising results underline our method's potential to revolutionize semi-supervised medical image classification tasks.

Future research will focus on further optimization of our model, specifically tailoring it to various domains and effectively reducing data demands. We also anticipate incorporating emerging deep learning techniques into our model, ensuring it remains at the cutting edge of technology, while exploring its potential applications in fields with limited data availability.

References

1. Sun, W., Tseng, T.L., Zhang, J., Qian, W.: Computerized breast cancer analysis system using three stage semi-supervised learning method. Comput. Methods Programs Biomed. 1(135), 77–88 (2016)
2. Avni, U., Greenspan, H., Konen, E., Sharon, M., Goldberger, J.: X-ray categorization and retrieval on the organ and pathology level, using patch-based visual words. IEEE Trans. Med. Imaging 30(3), 733–46 (2010)
3. Li, X., Yu, L., Chen, H., Fu, C.W., Heng, P.A.: Semi-supervised skin lesion segmentation via transformation consistent self-ensembling model. arXiv preprint arXiv:1808.03887 (2018)
4. Arazo, E., Ortego, D., Albert, P., O'Connor, N., McGuinness, K.: Unsupervised label noise modeling and loss correction. In: International Conference on Machine Learning, 24 May 2019, pp. 312–321. PMLR (2019)
5. Kim, Y., Kim, J.M., Akata, Z., Lee, J.: Large loss matters in weakly supervised multi-label classification. In: Proceedings of the IEEE/CVF Conference on Computer Vision and Pattern Recognition, pp. 14156–14165 (2022)
6. Liu, Q., Yu, L., Luo, L., Dou, Q., Heng, P.A.: Semi-supervised medical image classification with relation-driven self-ensembling model. IEEE Trans. Med. Imaging 39(11), 3429–40 (2020)
7. Miyato, T., Maeda, S.I., Koyama, M., Ishii, S.: Virtual adversarial training: a regularization method for supervised and semi-supervised learning. IEEE Trans. Pattern Anal. Mach. Intell. 41(8), 1979–93 (2018)
8. Liu, F., Tian, Y., Chen, Y., Liu, Y., Belagiannis, V., Carneiro, G.: ACPL: Anti-curriculum pseudo-labelling for semi-supervised medical image classification. In: Proceedings of the IEEE/CVF Conference on Computer Vision and Pattern Recognition, pp. 20697–20706 (2022)
9. Hu, Z., Yang, Z., Hu, X., Nevatia, R.: Simple: similar pseudo label exploitation for semi-supervised classification. In: Proceedings of the IEEE/CVF Conference on Computer Vision and Pattern Recognition, pp. 15099–15108 (2021)
10. Battaglia, P.W., et al.: Relational inductive biases, deep learning, and graph networks. arXiv preprint arXiv:1806.01261 (2018)
11. Sharma, P., Ding, N., Goodman, S., Soricut, R.: Conceptual captions: a cleaned, hypernymed, image alt-text dataset for automatic image captioning. In: Proceedings of the 56th Annual Meeting of the Association for Computational Linguistics, vol. 1: Long Papers, pp. 2556–2565 (2018)
12. Xie, Y., Zhang, J., Xia, Y.: Semi-supervised adversarial model for benign-malignant lung nodule classification on chest CT. Med. Image Anal. 1(57), 237–48 (2019)
13. Kather, J.N., et al.: Predicting survival from colorectal cancer histology slides using deep learning: a retrospective multicenter study. PLoS Med. 16(1), e1002730 (2019)
14. Wang, X., Peng, Y., Lu, L., Lu, Z., Bagheri, M., Summers, R.M.: Chestx-ray8: hospital-scale chest x-ray database and benchmarks on weakly-supervised classification and localization of common thorax diseases. In: Proceedings of the IEEE Conference on Computer Vision and Pattern Recognition, pp. 2097–2106 (2017)

15. Settles, B.: Active learning literature survey. University of Wisconsin-Madison Department of Computer Sciences (2009)
16. Zhang, W., et al.: Boostmis: boosting medical image semi-supervised learning with adaptive pseudo labeling and informative active annotation. In: Proceedings of the IEEE/CVF Conference on Computer Vision and Pattern Recognition, pp. 20666–20676 (2022)
17. Xie, Q., Luong, M.T., Hovy, E., Le, Q.V.: Self-training with noisy student improves imagenet classification. In: Proceedings of the IEEE/CVF Conference on Computer Vision and Pattern Recognition, pp. 10687–10698 (2020)
18. Gong, C., Wang, D., Liu, Q.: Alphamatch: improving consistency for semi-supervised learning with alpha-divergence. In: Proceedings of the IEEE/CVF Conference on Computer Vision and Pattern Recognition, pp. 13683–13692 (2021)
19. Abuduweili, A., Li, X., Shi, H., Xu, C.Z., Dou, D.: Adaptive consistency regularization for semi-supervised transfer learning. In: Proceedings of the IEEE/CVF Conference on Computer Vision and Pattern Recognition, pp. 6923–6932 (2021)
20. Aviles-Rivero, A.I., et al.: GraphX small NET-NET-Chest X-Ray Classification Under Extreme Minimal Supervision. In: Shen, D., et al. (eds.) MICCAI 2019. LNCS, vol. 11769, pp. 504–512. Springer, Cham (2019). https://doi.org/10.1007/978-3-030-32226-7_56
21. Unnikrishnan, B., Nguyen, C.M., Balaram, S., Foo, C.S., Krishnaswamy, P.: Semi-supervised classification of diagnostic radiographs with noteacher: a teacher that is not mean. In: Martel, A.L., et al. (eds.) MICCAI 2020. LNCS, vol. 12261, pp. 624–634. Springer, Cham (2020). https://doi.org/10.1007/978-3-030-59710-8_61
22. Chen, X., Yuan, Y., Zeng, G., Wang, J.: Semi-supervised semantic segmentation with cross pseudo supervision. In: Proceedings of the IEEE/CVF Conference on Computer Vision and Pattern Recognition, pp. 2613–2622 (2021)
23. Singh, P.P., Garg, R.D.: A hybrid approach for information extraction from high resolution satellite imagery. Int. J. Image Graph. **13**(02), 1340007 (2013)
24. Singh, P.P., Garg, R.D.: Classification of high resolution satellite images using equivariant robust independent component analysis. In: Kumar Kundu, M., Mohapatra, D.P., Konar, A., Chakraborty, A. (eds.) Advanced Computing, Networking and Informatics- Volume 1. SIST, vol. 27, pp. 283–290. Springer, Cham (2014). https://doi.org/10.1007/978-3-319-07353-8_34

Semi-supervised Polyp Classification in Colonoscopy Images Using GAN

Darshika Verma$^{(\boxtimes)}$, Vanshali Sharma, and Pradip K. Das

Indian Institute of Technology Guwahati, Guwahati, Assam, India
{darshikaverma,vanshalisharma,pkdas}@iitg.ac.in

Abstract. Colorectal cancer (CRC) screening is carried out to appropriately identify and categorize the CRC precursors, called polyps. It is a crucial task for an effective treatment as unnecessary surgeries and ignorance of any potential cancer could be the situations of concern. Thus, classifying any detected lesion as an adenoma (with the potential to become cancerous) or hyperplastic (non-cancerous) is necessary. In recent years, such classification tasks are assisted by automated systems with promising outcomes. However, the extensive data needed for these systems to function satisfactorily have limited the widespread application of deep learning techniques in the medical field. To overcome this issue, in this paper, we employed a semi-supervised learning approach using GAN to classify polyps. Our approach needs limited labeled data while achieving enhanced classification performance. The experimental results show that the suggested semi-GAN approach, when applied to the PolypsSet and SUN datasets, produced a classification accuracy of 72.85% and 74.12% respectively. This represents a significant improvement over existing methods and highlights the potential of GANs in the medical image analysis field. These research findings have implications for improving the efficiency and accuracy of CRC screening and diagnosis, potentially leading to better patient outcomes.

Keywords: GAN · Semi-GAN · Polyp Classification · SUN Dataset

1 Introduction

The third most frequent cancer in the United States is colorectal cancer (CRC) [15]. It affects the colon or rectum and can be fatal if left untreated. Colonoscopy is a widely adopted medical procedure for detecting CRC precursors that are known as polyps. These polyps can be classified based on their appearance, location, and potential to become cancerous. The two most common types of colorectal polyps are Adenomatous and Hyperplastic polyps. Adenomatous polyps are flat or have a glandular appearance and can potentially become cancerous over time and therefore, have to be removed immediately. Hyperplastic polyps are usually small, non-cancerous growths and are generally not considered precancerous. Some sample images of these two types of polyps are shown in Fig. 1.

H. Kaur et al. (Eds.): CVIP 2023, CCIS 2011, pp. 39–51, 2024.
https://doi.org/10.1007/978-3-031-58535-7_4

Early detection and classification of such polyps are necessary for correct treatment. However, the manual diagnosis process depends on the operator's experience and can suffer from a high miss rate and misclassifications. To assist clinicians in CRC diagnosis, many automated systems have been developed which are expected to reduce clinicians' burden and miss rate.

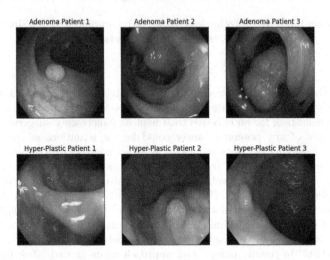

Fig. 1. The figure illustrates sample polyp images. The first row and the second row show adenoma and hyperplastic polyps, respectively, of different patients.

In the past few years, automated systems in healthcare settings are influenced by deep learning-based techniques due to their promising results reported in medical image analysis. Medical image detection, classification, and recognition tasks are becoming simpler [3], and these systems are anticipated to perform with more accuracy than a skilled professional or conventional image processing techniques. However, deep learning-based systems require large and diverse datasets and annotated samples for adequate outcomes which is a significant issue in the medical domain. Due to data security and privacy concerns, access to large and diverse datasets in the medical domain can be challenging. Additionally, the manual annotation of medical data is time-consuming and requires expert knowledge, making it difficult to create large annotated datasets. Thus, the aforementioned challenges prevent the development of healthcare deep learning models.

To overcome the issue of large annotated dataset availability, the concept of semi-supervised learning was introduced in many fields including medical imaging. In semi-supervised learning, pseudo-labeling is used with a large number of unlabeled samples and less labeled data. Inspired by this concept, Ordena [11] proposed semi-supervised GAN (semi-GAN) which is a modified version of the popular GAN for semi-supervised learning tasks. GANs generally have a generator network that creates synthetic data and a discriminator network that differentiates between fake and real data [4]. Semi-GAN includes an additional classifier network that learns to classify the synthetic data into different classes. This technique trains the generator and discriminator networks on labeled and unlabeled data, while only the labeled data is used to train the classifier network. The generator generates more realistic data, and the classifier network learns to classify the synthetic data into different categories, improving the model's overall accuracy.

In this paper, we propose a polyp classification approach that leverages the ability of semi-GAN to achieve enhanced classification results with fewer data requirements. Unlike the few existing works [12] in the literature, we used a small subset of the labeled dataset for training our model in a supervised manner while the results are enhanced using unlabeled data Thus, our approach eliminates the need to perform burdensome manual annotation procedures. We also carried out experiments with different settings to show how the medical datasets result in significantly biased results due to a high imbalance of sample distribution among different classes. Moreover, the existing techniques underperform if the majority class is undersampled to make a balanced distribution. On the other hand, using semi-GAN, we obtained improved results with the same count of minority class samples even after reducing majority class samples. The contribution of our proposed work is summarized below:

- We proposed a semi-supervised approach for polyp classification using semi-GAN, which still remains unexplored in the colonoscopy domain.
- We also investigate the issue of high data imbalance in the existing large datasets with annotated samples.
- We carried out exhaustive experiments with multiple settings and architectural variations. Our proposed approach outperformed the baseline method in all the different scenarios.

2   Related Work

2.1   Polyp Classification

Although polyp segmentation and detection have achieved tremendous progress, the classification of colon polyps is still a major challenge due to the limited availability of high-quality datasets. This is because classification algorithms require large datasets to train and test their models accurately.

Handcrafted feature-based approaches dominate the existing literature on polyp classification. Some utilize a pit pattern classification scheme to classify polyps into normal mucosa and hyperplastic classes, while others, such as Hafner et al. [5], employ a fractal dimension-based (LFD) strategy. Another approach proposed by Uhl et al. [16] is the blob-adapted local fractal dimension (BA-LFD) approach. However, the maximal-minimal filter bank strategy introduced by [19] has outperformed the BA-LFD-based approach. Some works combined the hand-crafted feature extraction process with machine learning methods. For example, Sasmal et al. [14] utilized PHOG and fractal weighted LBP techniques in combination with SVM and RUSBoosted tree to perform polyp classification. Wimmer et al. [18] proposed a maximal-minimal filter bank technique. Bora et al. [2] used the Least Square Support Vector Machine and Multi-layer Perceptron to perform classification along with different feature extraction approaches.

In recent years, there has been an increase in the availability of colonoscopy image datasets. Patel et al. [12] released the first large dataset for polyp classification purposes and presented a comparative analysis using CNN based models. Ribeiro et al. [13] first time explored different deep learning models and reported results on various model configurations (full training or transfer learning). Bhamre et al. [1] explored the advantage of using images acquired using narrow-band imaging (NBI) over white light (WL) images. They used Cycle-GAN to translate WL images into NBI images for better classification outcomes.

2.2 Semi-supervised Classification

In the colonoscopy domain, the exploration of semi-supervised learning is limited. However, several studies in the medical domain have adopted semi-supervised learning, aiming to improve classification accuracy and reduce reliance on manual annotations. In [20] semi-supervised colonoscopy polyp detection system was proposed that combines object detection methods with semi-supervised learning techniques. Another approach discussed in [8] was to introduce a semi-supervised learning framework using generative models. They employed a variational autoencoder (VAE) to generate synthetic polyp images and combined them with the labeled data for training a classifier. The VAE-based generation allowed for better utilization of the available data and improved classification accuracy. Other medical domains are also influenced by the semi-supervised learning technique. Wang et al. [17] utilized self-training and consistency regularization to extract the information contained in unlabeled data. Similarly, Liu et al. [9] used a sample relation consistency scheme to achieve the same with extra semantic details. These studies collectively demonstrate the potential of semi-supervised learning approaches in medical classification tasks.

3 Proposed Method

3.1 Overview

In this paper, we aim to perform polyp classification using limited labeled data. Our work is inspired by the semi-GAN approach due to its ability to achieve competitive outcomes with less data when compared to the supervised learning technique which underperforms when provided with limited data. A semi-GAN is a type of GAN that is trained using a combination of labeled and unlabeled data, where the labeled data is used to learn a supervised task, such as image classification, and the unlabeled data is used to improve the performance of the model by learning the underlying distribution of the data. In a typical GAN, the generator learns to produce realistic data by generating images similar to a training data set. However, in a semi-GAN, the model uses both labeled and unlabeled data to generate better images.

3.2   Architectural Details

The architecture of a semi-GAN is similar to that of a standard GAN, with the addition of a classifier network. The generator and discriminator networks are trained in an adversarial manner, while the classifier network is trained in a supervised manner. The generator takes as input a random noise vector and outputs a generated sample. Its goal is to generate samples similar to the real data. The discriminator is provided with a sample for which it outputs a probability score indicating whether the sample is real or generated. It aims to distinguish between real and generated samples. The classifier takes as input a sample and provides a probability distribution over the different classes. It targets to classify the labeled data.

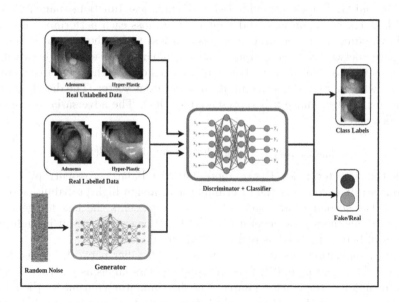

Fig. 2. Semi-Supervised GAN

The semi-GAN is trained in two phases as shown in Fig. 2. In the first phase, the generator and discriminator are trained in a standard GAN setup, using only the labeled data. Each iteration feeds a batch of labeled and unlabeled data into the network. The generator produces a batch of generated samples fed into the discriminator and the real samples. The discriminator produces a probability score for each sample, indicating whether it is real or generated. The adversarial loss is computed based on these scores, and the gradients are used to update the generator and discriminator networks.

In the second phase, the classifier is added to the architecture, the model is trained on both labeled and unlabeled data, and the classification loss is computed based on the predicted class probabilities and the true labels. The generator creates new samples, and the discriminator and classifier work together to identify the authenticity of the generated samples and label them appropriately. The gradients of the classification loss are used to update the classifier network. Finally, the regularization loss is computed based on the features extracted by the discriminator for the real and generated samples, and the gradients of the regularization loss are used to update the generator network.

During the training of semi-GAN, the generator instead of generating images similar to the original image, acts as a bad generator that generates images to create a decision boundary between the two classes of images. The generator learns from the labeled data to generate realistic samples, while the classifier uses the unlabeled data to improve its accuracy in identifying the generated samples. By using labeled and unlabeled data, the model can learn more about the underlying data distribution, leading to better performance.

The semi-GAN uses a weighted sum of three loss functions, namely, adversarial loss, classification loss, and regularization loss each performing a specific role in training the network. The adversarial loss trains the generator and discriminator networks. It is computed as the binary cross-entropy between the discriminator's output and the true label. Let us denote the generator's output as G(z), where z represents the input noise or latent vector. The discriminator's output for a given image x is represented as D(x). The adversarial loss can be described as:

$$L_{adversarial} = - \left[\log(D(x)) + \log(1 - D(G(z))) \right] \tag{1}$$

where the first term, $\log(D(x))$, represents the binary cross-entropy loss for real images. It encourages the discriminator to assign high probabilities to real images. The second term, $\log(1 - D(G(z)))$, represents the loss for generated images. It encourages the generator to produce images that result in high probabilities of being classified as real by the discriminator.

The classification loss is used to train the classifier network Let us denote the labeled data as x_i and their corresponding class labels as y_i, where i represents the index of the labeled sample. The discriminator's output for the labeled sample x_i is denoted as $D_c(x_i)$, which represents the predicted probability of x_i belonging to its true class. The classification loss, often computed using the cross-entropy loss and defined as:

$$L_{class} = - \sum_{i=1}^{N} y_i log(D_c(x_i)) \tag{2}$$

where N represents the total number of labeled samples in the training set. The term $y_i log(D_c(x_i))$ calculates the cross-entropy loss for each labeled sample, penalizing the discriminator if its prediction $D_c(x_i)$ deviates from the true class label y_i. The regularization loss encourages the generator to produce samples

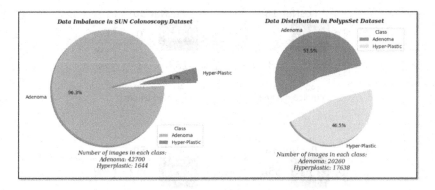

Fig. 3. Data Distribution of Datasets

consistent with the real data distribution. Let us denote the generated samples from the generator as G(z), where z represents the input noise or latent vector. The regularization loss is computed as the L2 distance between the features of the real and generated samples. It can be represented as:

$$L_{reg} = \lambda.||G(z)||_p \tag{3}$$

where λ is the hyper-parameter controlling the strength of regularization, and $||G(z)||_p$ represents the L1 or L2 norm of the generated samples G(z) generates using p-norm.

In semi-GAN, different architectures such as ResNet-18, ResNet-50 [6], and DenseNet-121 [7] are used as a classifier. ResNet architectures introduce residual connections, which enable the network to learn residual mappings, making it easier for the model to optimize and propagate gradients. ResNet-18 consists of 18 layers, whereas ResNet-50 contains 50 layers. DenseNet-121 is another deep CNN architecture that introduces dense connections. In DenseNet-121, each layer is connected to all subsequent layers in a feed-forward manner. This dense connectivity facilitates information flow across layers, enhances feature reuse, and helps alleviate the vanishing gradient problem.

4   Experiments and Results

4.1   Dataset and Training Details

We used two publicly available datasets to evaluate our approach: the SUN [10] and the PolypsSet [12] datasets. The SUN Dataset consists of video frames, out of which 42,700 contain adenoma polyps frames, while 1,644 frames belong to hyperplastic polyps. The PolypsSet dataset contains a total of 37,898 images, out of which 20,260 images depict adenoma polyps and 17638 images represent hyperplastic polyps. Figure 3 shows the data distribution of both datasets. The implementation is done using the PyTorch framework using TITAN Xp GPU. We used the Adam optimizer, and the learning rate is set to 0.002 with 200 epochs.

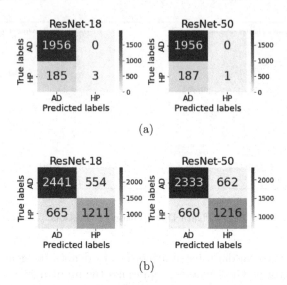

Fig. 4. Confusion matrix for (a) SUN Dataset and (b) PolypsSet. AD and HP refer to adenoma and hyperplastic cases, respectively.

Table 1. Classification Results on SUN dataset and PolypsSet

Metrics		SUN dataset		PolypsSet dataset	
		ResNet-18	ResNet-50	ResNet-18	ResNet-50
Test Accuracy		**0.9156**	0.9123	0.7286	**0.7497**
F1 Score	Adenoma	0.95	0.95	0.78	**0.80**
	Hyperplastic	0.00	0.00	0.65	**0.67**
Precision	Adenoma	0.91	0.91	0.78	**0.79**
	Hyperplastic	0.00	0.00	0.65	**0.69**
Recall	Adenoma	**1.00**	0.90	0.78	**0.82**
	Hyperplastic	0.00	0.00	0.65	0.65

4.2   Performance Evaluation

We carried out multiple experiments with different settings to evaluate the performance of our proposed approach. These experiments are case-wise discussed below in detail.

Case-1: In this experiment, we used all the samples of both datasets one at a time to train and evaluate our model. The results using the SUN dataset are shown in Table 1 and Fig. 4(a). It can be observed that the ResNet-18 and the ResNet-50 achieved an accuracy of 0.9156 and 0.9123, respectively. The F1 score, precision, and recall were also calculated and found to be between 0.87–0.92. However, these results are biased due to the data imbalance in the dataset,

Table 2. Classification Results on PolypsSet Dataset. AD and HP refer to adenoma and hyperplastic cases, respectively.

Metrics		ResNet-18	Semi-GAN+ ResNet-18	ResNet-50	Semi-GAN+ ResNet-50	DenseNet-121	Semi-GAN + DenseNet-121
Test Acc.		0.5617	**0.7285**	0.5789	0.6174	0.5763	0.6891
Validation Acc.		0.5680	**0.7152**	0.563	0.6000	0.5661	0.676
F1 Score	AD	0.6891	**0.7559**	0.6906	0.6650	0.6934	0.7345
	HP	0.1841	**0.6307**	0.2056	0.4933	0.2125	0.5317
Precision	AD	0.5257	**0.6490**	0.5286	0.5710	0.5419	0.6061
	HP	**1.0000**	0.8399	0.9672	0.6569	0.9877	0.8491
Recall	AD	**1.0000**	0.9049	0.9961	0.7961	0.9980	0.9320
	HP	0.1014	**0.5049**	0.1150	0.3949	0.1562	0.3870

Table 3. Classification Results on SUN Dataset. AD and HP refer to adenoma and hyperplastic cases, respectively.

Metrics		ResNet-18	Semi-GAN+ ResNet-18	ResNet-50	Semi-GAN+ ResNet-50	DenseNet-121	Semi-GAN + DenseNet-121
Test Acc.		0.6128	**0.7412**	0.6177	0.6647	0.5965	0.6891
Validation Acc.		0.5977	**0.7382**	0.6188	0.6328	0.5877	0.6589
F1 Score	AD	0.7114	**0.7549**	0.7071	0.7123	0.7024	0.6205
	HP	0.3306	0.6780	0.3628	0.5284	0.2698	**0.6793**
Precision	AD	0.5557	0.6764	0.5567	0.5992	0.5419	**0.6896**
	HP	0.9444	0.8000	0.8797	0.7649	**0.9877**	0.6262
Recall	AD	0.9883	0.8541	0.9688	0.8779	0.9980	0.5640
	HP	0.2004	0.5882	0.2285	0.4035	0.1562	**0.7421**

with a significantly larger number of adenoma cases (42700) than hyperplastic cases (1644). As a result, the model may have been trained more effectively on adenoma cases, leading to higher metrics scores for adenomas compared to hyperplastic cases. The results using the PolypsSet dataset are shown in Table 1 and Fig. 4(b). As the PolypsSet dataset has a balanced data distribution, the class-wise performance does not show any biased outcomes and provides an accuracy of 0.7286 and 0.7497 on the ResNet-18 and ResNet-50 model, respectively.

Case-2: The experiment aimed to evaluate the performance of different classifier architectures and also to present a comparative analysis between the baseline models. To establish a baseline model performance for the classification task, a subset of the PolypsSet dataset consisting of 100 labeled images (50 adenomas and 50 hyperplastic) was used for training the normal classification models. A set of 1000 images (500 adenomas and 500 hyperplastic) were used for testing, validation, and unlabeled training. Table 2 and Fig. 6 shows the associated results. It can be observed that our approach of semi-GAN outperformed the baseline models in each setting, with semi-GAN + ResNet-18 performing the best.

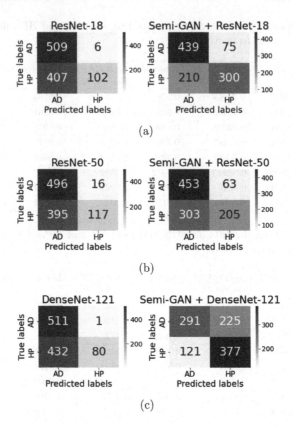

Fig. 5. Confusion matrix for SUN Dataset using (a) ResNet-18 and Semi-GAN+ResNet-18 (b) ResNet-50 and Semi-GAN+ResNet-50, (b) DenseNet-121 and Semi-GAN+DenseNet-121. AD and HP refer to adenoma and hyperplastic cases, respectively.

Case-3: Similar to Case-2, we experimented with the SUN dataset, using 100 labeled data points (50 for each class) and 500 data points each for validation, testing, and unlabelled tracing. Table 3 and Fig. 5 show the metric scores and confusion matrix, respectively. It can be observed that semi-GAN performed better in each setting and achieved the best outcome with ResNet-18.

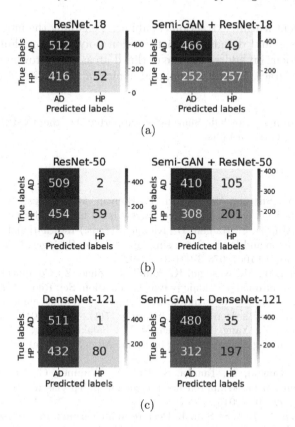

Fig. 6. Confusion matrix for PolypsSet Dataset using (a) ResNet-18 and Semi-GAN+ResNet-18 (b) ResNet-50 and Semi-GAN+ResNet-50, (b) DenseNet-121 and Semi-GAN+DenseNet-121. AD and HP refer to adenoma and hyperplastic cases, respectively.

5 Conclusion

In this paper, we proposed an approach for colon polyp classification using a semi-supervised GAN (semi-GAN) technique. Our method leveraged the ability of semi-GAN to perform with limited data. We used ResNet-18 combined with a semi-GAN. The experimental results demonstrate that our proposed approach achieved an overall accuracy of 72.85% and 74.12% using PolypsSet and SUN datasets, respectively, indicating its potential to aid in diagnosing and treating colon polyps. By incorporating the semi-GAN technique, we effectively utilized both labeled and unlabeled data to enhance the model's performance. This approach allowed us to overcome the limitations of the unavailability of a large number of labeled data samples, which is often the case in medical imaging datasets. The generated synthetic samples by the GAN model provided additional information for training, enabling the network to generalize better and improve its classification accuracy. Furthermore, the utilization of the ResNet architecture provided excellent feature extraction capabilities, enabling the model to capture intricate patterns and details within the colon polyp images. Future research efforts should focus on addressing the outlined areas of improvement to further enhance the accuracy, generalization, and clinical applicability of the proposed method.

Acknowledgements. Vanshali Sharma is supported by the INSPIRE fellowship (IF190362), DST, Govt. of India.

References

1. Bhamre, N.V., Sharma, V., Iwahori, Y., Bhuyan, M., Kasugai, K.: Colonoscopy polyp classification adding generated narrow band imaging. In: Gupta, D., Bhurchandi, K., Murala, S., Raman, B., Kumar, S. (eds.) International Conference on Computer Vision and Image Processing, pp. 322–334. Springer, Heidelberg (2022). https://doi.org/10.1007/978-3-031-31417-9_25
2. Bora, K., Bhuyan, M., Kasugai, K., Mallik, S., Zhao, Z.: Computational learning of features for automated colonic polyp classification. Sci. Rep. **11**(1), 1–16 (2021)
3. Ciompi, F., et al.: Towards automatic pulmonary nodule management in lung cancer screening with deep learning. Sci. Rep. **7**(1), 46479 (2017)
4. Dai, Z., Yang, Z., Yang, F., Cohen, W.W., Salakhutdinov, R.R.: Good semi-supervised learning that requires a bad gan. Adv. Neural Inf. Process. Syst. **30** (2017)
5. Häfner, M., Tamaki, T., Tanaka, S., Uhl, A., Wimmer, G., Yoshida, S.: Local fractal dimension based approaches for colonic polyp classification. Med. Image Anal. **26**(1), 92–107 (2015)
6. He, K., Zhang, X., Ren, S., Sun, J.: Deep residual learning. Image Recogn. **7** (2015)
7. Huang, G., Liu, Z., Van Der Maaten, L., Weinberger, K.Q.: Densely connected convolutional networks. In: Proceedings of the IEEE Conference on Computer Vision and Pattern Recognition, pp. 4700–4708 (2017)
8. Kingma, D.P., Mohamed, S., Jimenez Rezende, D., Welling, M.: Semi-supervised learning with deep generative models. Adv. Neural Inf. Proces. Syst. **27** (2014)
9. Liu, Q., Yu, L., Luo, L., Dou, Q., Heng, P.A.: Semi-supervised medical image classification with relation-driven self-ensembling model. IEEE Trans. Med. Imaging **39**(11), 3429–3440 (2020)
10. Misawa, M., et al.: Development of a computer-aided detection system for colonoscopy and a publicly accessible large colonoscopy video database (with video). Gastrointest. Endosc. **93**(4), 960–967 (2021)
11. Odena, A.: Semi-supervised learning with generative adversarial networks. arXiv preprint arXiv:1606.01583 (2016)
12. Patel, K., et al.: A comparative study on polyp classification using convolutional neural networks. PLoS ONE **15**(7), e0236452 (2020)
13. Ribeiro, E., Uhl, A., Wimmer, G., Häfner, M.: Exploring deep learning and transfer learning for colonic polyp classification. Comput. Math. Methods Med. **2016** (2016)
14. Sasmal, P., Bhuyan, M.K., Iwahori, Y., Kasugai, K.: Colonoscopic polyp classification using local shape and texture features. IEEE Access **9**, 92629–92639 (2021)
15. Society, A.: Key statistics for colorectal cancer (2021)
16. Uhl, A., Wimmer, G., Hafner, M.: Shape and size adapted local fractal dimension for the classification of polyps in HD colonoscopy. In: 2014 IEEE International Conference on Image Processing (ICIP), pp. 2299–2303. IEEE (2014)

17. Wang, X., Chen, H., Xiang, H., Lin, H., Lin, X., Heng, P.A.: Deep virtual adversarial self-training with consistency regularization for semi-supervised medical image classification. Med. Image Anal. **70**, 102010 (2021)
18. Wimmer, G., Uhl, A., Häfner, M.: A novel filterbank especially designed for the classification of colonic polyps. In: 2016 23rd International Conference on Pattern Recognition (ICPR), pp. 2150–2155. IEEE (2016)
19. Wimmer, G., Uhl, A., Häfner, M.: A novel filterbank especially designed for the classification of colonic polyps. In: 2016 23rd International Conference on Pattern Recognition (ICPR), pp. 2150–2155 (2016). https://doi.org/10.1109/ICPR.2016.7899954
20. Yao, L., He, F., Peng, H., Wang, X., Zhou, L., Huang, X.: Improving colonoscopy polyp detection rate using semi-supervised learning. J. Shanghai Jiaotong Univ. (Sci.) 1–9 (2022)

Towards Efficient Semantic Segmentation Compression via Meta Pruning

Ashutosh Mishra[1]([⊠]), Shyam Nandan Rai[2], Girish Varma[1],
and C. V. Jawahar[1]

[1] CVIT, KCIS, IIIT Hyderabad, Hyderabad, India
ashutosh.mishra@research.iiit.ac.in, {girish.varma,jawahar}@iiit.ac.in
[2] Politecnico di Torino, Turin, Italy

Abstract. Semantic segmentation provides a pixel-level understanding of an image essential for various scene-understanding vision tasks. However, semantic segmentation models demand significant computational resources during training and inference. These requirements pose a challenge in resource-constraint scenarios. To address this issue, we present a compression algorithm based on differentiable meta-pruning through hypernetwork: MPHyp. Our proposed method MPHyp utilizes hypernetworks that take latent vectors as input and output weight matrices for the segmentation model. L_1 sparsification follows the proximal gradient optimizer, updates the latent vectors and introduces sparsity leading to automatic model pruning. The proposed method offers the benefit of achieving controllable compression during the training and significantly reducing the training time. We compare our methodology with a popular pruning approach and demonstrate its efficacy by reducing the number of parameters and floating point operations while maintaining the mean Intersection over Union (mIoU) metric. We conduct experiments on two widely accepted semantic segmentation architectures: UNet and ERFNet. Our experiments and ablation study demonstrate the effectiveness of our proposed methodology by achieving efficient and reasonable segmentation results.

Keywords: Semantic segmentation · Hypernetworks · Pruning · Compression

1 Introduction

Semantic segmentation [2,3,23,37] is a dense prediction task of assigning class labels to each pixel in an image. It has been widely used in autonomous driving, medical imaging, and satellite imaging applications. However, semantic segmentation models such as DeepLabV1,V2 [2,3], DRN [37] generally have a large number of parameters. So deploying such models in environments with limited

A. Mishra and S. N. Rai—Equal contribution.

resources, such as mobile phones or embedded systems, can be challenging due to their large memory requirements during inference.

One potential approach to overcome the computational limitations is to adopt methods that reduce the model's complexity, like model compression, for instance, model pruning [7,14,24], or neural architecture search [8,32,34,40]. However, these methods above have their inherent problems. For instance, the method [32] is based on neural architecture search to find the best architecture within a predefined search space. The search space includes various architectural components, such as the number of layers, layer types (convolutional, recurrent, etc.), skip connections and other hyperparameters. However, it takes 8 Nvidia Turing GPUs with 24GB of VRAM to find such architectures, which is extremely expensive in terms of training complexity. On the other hand, pruning methods such as the lottery ticket hypothesis [7], a compression algorithm based on iterative pruning have shown a significant segmentation accuracy drop.

In order to efficiently prune semantic segmentation architectures, we propose a compression method based on differentiable meta pruning using hypernetworks MPHyp that substantially minimizes the training resources and simultaneously retains satisfactory segmentation performance. Our proposed technique is inspired from [19]. We call it meta-pruning since the parameters of the hypernetwork are responsible for generating weights of the segmentation model falling under the umbrella of meta-learning. The key concept behind the proposed approach is the hypernetwork that associates latent vectors for each layer in the segmentation network. This latent vector controls the output channel of the layer in consideration. Given the association of network layers, the latent vector serves as a controlling factor for the subsequent layer's input channel as well. During training, the hypernetwork receives the latent vectors from the current and preceding layers, which dictate the output and input channels of the current layer, respectively. The hypernetwork generates a weight matrix for the specific layer of the segmentation model. To achieve automatic pruning, we use the l_1 regularizer that helps in sparsification of the latent vectors. Subsequently, we employ proximal gradient algorithm to update and obtain the sparsified latent vectors. Together, this strategy leads to differentiability in the pruning mechanism. Once the compression ratio reaches the pre-determined level, the compression method stops. The sparsification of the latent vectors results in compressed outputs from the hypernetworks since the latent vectors and layers of the segmentation model are correlated. The proposed method offers the advantage of streamlining network pruning by focusing solely on the latent vectors, eliminating the need for additional complexities or human assistance. We find that our proposed method outperforms the baseline pruning method by a significant margin. We refrain from comparing with neural architecture search methods as they require huge training resources. To showcase the efficacy of our method, we performed extensive experimentation on IDD Lite [26]: a semantic segmentation dataset targeted for resource-constraint scenarios. In this context, resource-constraint means a lack of availability of better computing power. The images provided in this dataset are sampled and scaled from IDD [35], which are very different compared to other sophisticated semantic segmentation datasets like Cityscapes [5],

Mapillary [28]. We chose UNet [31] and ERFNet [30] as our semantic segmentation models due to the wide acceptability and application of these networks in various domains [21, 25].

The contribution of our work is summarized below:

1. We propose an efficient semantic segmentation pruning method MPHyp based on hypernetwork. Our proposed method preserves significant segmentation performance after pruning and efficiently trains while requiring minimal training resources (See Sect. 3).
2. We compare our method with the baseline method and a popular pruning algorithm on UNet and ERFNet architectures trained on the IDD Lite dataset (See Sect. 4).
3. We perform ablation studies and experimentation to show the efficacy of our method (See Sect. 6).

2   Related Work

2.1   Semantic Segmentation

Semantic segmentation methods [11,12] before deep learning utilize image features to perform segmentation. Fully Convolution Networks(FCN) [23] was the first deep learning-based method to output per pixel dense correspondences using a classification backbone for varying resolutions. The significant semantic segmentation performance gain of FCNs compared to non deep learning methods was due to the incorporation of skip connections between initial and final layers that combined coarse high features with fine low-level features. Subsequently, architectures such as Deeplabv1,Deeplabv2 [2,39] were proposed that improved semantic segmentation performance by a) using post-processing strategies, such as Conditional Random Fields (CRF) to refine the output, b) replacing normal convolutions with dilated convolutions to enlarge the receptive field to gather more context but at the cost of increased computational overhead [2,37], and c) increasing the field of view of the segmentation kernel by using features obtained from different strides and then aggregating them with average pooling and subsequent convolutional layers [13,38].

Concurrently, [3,4] proposed to use dilated convolutions inside the spatial pyramid pooling architecture to improve the accuracy along with increased training and inference time. Additionally, training the model on multiple scales and orientations of images, combined through pooling operations, was suggested for further accuracy improvement. Another work proposed attention-based methods to model long-range dependencies as well [15].

2.2   Semantic Segmentation Compression

To reduce the computation overload, neural architecture search (NAS) based methods have been adopted. It also helps to find lightweight models. Given a search space, neural architecture search-based methods help find a superior model. An example of NAS in semantic segmentation is [20]. This approach tries to find a repeatable cell structure along with the network architecture to improve the performance. However, it costs a huge amount of memory to reach the target architecture.

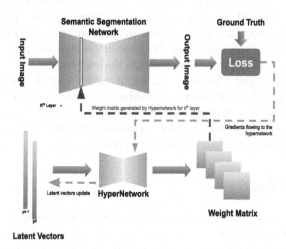

Fig. 1. Shows a pictorial representation of the proposed algorithm designed for compressing semantic segmentation networks using automatic differentiable pruning. Each layer of the segmentation network is associated with a latent vector. This latent vector is responsible for generating weights of the specific layer. While training, latent vectors get sparsified, leading to the pruning of the weights of the specific layer. The construction of the algorithm is such that the latent vector is covariant with its corresponding weight matrix. Weights produced by the hypernetwork generates the final output through the segmentation model.

A lot of compression methods tailoring to pruning have been proposed in the past. Architecture pruning, in general, aims to remove redundancies in the over-parameterized models for faster inference while maintaining most model non-redundant parameters. For instance, [10,27] tries to compress models using specific hardware architecture or library support. This is referred to as non-structured pruning. On the other hand, some approaches perform pruning on the entire architecture [14,24]. However, the performance of these pruning methods for complex tasks such as semantic segmentation has not been discussed.

2.3   HyperNetworks

Hypernetworks were first proposed in [9] that used a smaller network to generate weights for a bigger network. Hypernetworks have been widely used for neural architecture search [1], temporal forecasting [29], and also model compression [22]. The key idea behind hypernetwork is based on evolutionary methods that evolve smaller networks to generate weights of a larger network. A more efficient method to generate during the weight generation process, the search space is constrained within a smaller weight space [33]. Alternatively, the structure of the network can be kept fixed while weights are evolved through discrete cosine transform. This technique is referred to as a compressed weight search [18]. Similar to the aforementioned approach are Differentiable Pattern Producing Networks (DPPNs) that evolve the structure of the network while the weight parameters are learned [6]. Apart from evolutionary-based algorithms, CNN-based approaches such as [16] generate weights to apply a transformation to the images. [17] uses the concept of dynamic filters that are generated based on input for the task of spatial transformation and deblurring.

As discussed in prior related works, segmentation models are generally large, and compression techniques such as neural architecture search require extensive computational resources to extract efficient semantic segmentation models. Our proposed method overcomes the aforementioned problem by leveraging hypernetworks that require minimal training resources.

3   Methodology

In this section, we discuss the process of compression of semantic segmentation models using hypernetwork. This is a lossy compression technique since the pruned connections cannot be restored due to the removal of redundant weight connections. Figure 1 illustrates the overall design of the proposed method, which is discussed in subsequent sections in more detail.

3.1   Architectural Design

We now describe the process of adapting hypernetwork in a semantic segmentation network. The proposed hypernetwork architecture constructed for a single layer neural network has the following layers:

1. *Latent Layer*: that takes latent vectors as input and generates latent matrix.
2. *Embedding Layer*: is responsible for projecting latent matrix to embedding matrix.
3. *Output Layer*: transforms the embedding matrix to a final weight matrix of the corresponding layer.

As described above, we know the process of adapting single-layer neural network to hypernetwork, so we extend the same process for a semantic segmentation model. Suppose, we have a semantic segmentation model of K-layered network that requires to be pruned. Initially, we introduce a latent vector to all the layers that need to be pruned, as latent vectors are responsible for generating pruned weights. We keep the shape of the latent vector equal to the output channels for all the pruned layers to keep dimension consistency.

Assume for a given semantic segmentation layer k, the dimensionality of the weight matrix generated by k^{th} layer is $l \times m \times w \times h$, where l and m denote the output and input channels of kth semantic segmentation layer, and $w \times h$ denotes its corresponding kernel width and height. Also, consider the latent vector for the kth layer to be p^k. Since the size of the latent vector is equal to the number of output channels, the latent vector for k^{th} layer is $p^k \in R^l$. Thus, the dimensionality of the latent vector of the $k-1^{th}$ layer is $p^{k-1} \in R^m$.

Now, we pass latent vectors p^k and p^{k-1} as input to the hypernetwork corresponding to the kth layer to generate the latent matrix, given by,

$$\mathbf{P}^k = \mathbf{p}^k . \mathbf{p}^{k-1^T} + \mathbf{V}_0^k, \tag{1}$$

where,

$$\mathbf{P}^k, \mathbf{V}_0^k \in R^{n \times c}$$

$[T]$ represents the transpose of the matrix and $[.]$ denotes matrix multiplication. $\mathbf{V}_0$ is the bias matrix. Consequently, the latent matrix is further projected to an embedding dimension with the help of the embedding layer that is given by,

$$\mathbf{C}_{ij}^k = \mathbf{P}_{ij}^k . \mathbf{w}_1^k + \mathbf{v}_1^k \quad i = 1..l, j = 1...m, \tag{2}$$

$\mathbf{C}_{ij}^k, \mathbf{w}_1^k, \mathbf{v}_1^k \in R^e$, where e represents the embedding dimension. The elements of $\mathbf{w}_1^k$ and $\mathbf{v}_1^k$ are considered to be unique. We exclude the subscript (i,j) for ease of understanding. Now, we multiply $\mathbf{w}_1^k$, $\mathbf{v}_1^k$ and $\mathbf{P}_{ij}^k$ together to form a 3D matrix, given as $\mathbf{W}_1^k$, $\mathbf{V}_1^k$ and $\mathbf{C}_1^k \in R^{l \times m \times e}$ as formulated in Eq. (2). We generate the final output $\mathbf{G}_{ij}^k$ by passing the embedding matrix Eq. (2) through the output layer Eq. (3).

$$\mathbf{G}_{ij}^k = \mathbf{C}_{ij}^k . \mathbf{w}_2^k + \mathbf{v}_2^k \quad i = 1..l, j = 1...m, \tag{3}$$

where,

$$\mathbf{G}_{ij}^k, \mathbf{v}_2^k \in R^{wh}$$

and,

$$\mathbf{w}_2^k \in R^{wh \times e}$$

We can observe the vectors $\mathbf{w}_2^k$, $\mathbf{v}_2^k$ and $\mathbf{G}_{ij}^k$ generate the final weight of the segmentation layer k. The final dimensionality of variables involved in Eq. (3) are $\mathbf{W}_2^k \in R^{l \times m \times wh \times e}$ and $\mathbf{V}_2^k$ and $\mathbf{G}^k \in R^{l \times m \times wh}$.

In functional form, we can represent the output $\mathbf{G}^k$ as:

$$\mathbf{G}^k = h(\mathbf{p}^k, \mathbf{p}^{k-1}; \mathbf{W}^k, \mathbf{V}^k), \tag{4}$$

Here, h(.) indicates the overall transformation applied on the input latent vectors, parameterized by latent vectors and per layer weight tensors. In case of skip or residual connections present in the segmentation network, we handle it by concatenating the latent vector of the current layer and the associated skip connection layer to create the latent matrix using Eq. (1) and Eq. (3).

3.2 Sparsification of Latent Vectors

The next step of our proposed method is to introduce sparsification in latent vectors that are associated with layers of the semantic segmentation model. We introduce sparsity in latent vectors because all the latent vectors are connected to each other, and each latent vector is covariant with the output channels of the specific layer of the segmentation network. Sparsification of latent vectors leads to a reduction in the count of output channels, leading to compression of the network. We achieve this by constraining latent vectors under L_1-norm formulated as:

$$R(p) = \sum_{k=1}^{K} ||p^k||_1 \qquad (5)$$

where R is the regularization term. Now, we introduce differentiability with the help of the proximal gradient algorithm. In summary, the task of the proximal gradient algorithm is to sparsify and update the latent vectors. The latent vectors are updated using the proximal gradient algorithm given by,

$$\mathbf{p}[k+1] = \mathbf{prox}_{\lambda\mu R}(p[k] - \lambda\mu\nabla L(p[k])) \qquad (6)$$

3.3   Semantic Segmentation Network Pruning

After the sparsification of latent vectors by employing the L_1-norm followed by proximal operation, the latent vectors are forced to become sparse without any human assistance, leading to automatic pruning. The latent vector sparsification leads to the generation of pruned weights for the corresponding layer of the segmentation network. After the compression stage, we obtain sparse latent vectors p^k and p^{k-1} for k^{th} semantic segmentation layer. After this, we apply masks t^k, t^{k-1} on the pruned vectors that are near zero with a predefined threshold τ. If the value is greater than the threshold, the returned value is one else zero. The sparsified latent vector, $\bar{p}^k$ is pruned using mask (t^k).

After the desired compression ratio is met, we then finetune the pruned semantic segmentation network to improve the accuracy. We refer finetuning as converging stage. The hypernetwork defined earlier gets scrapped, followed by the onset of the normal training regime. It is important to note that if the compression ratio increases, then the number of compression epochs also increases.

4   Experiments

4.1   Models and Dataset

We employ UNet [31] and ERFNet [30] as the base semantic segmentation architectures on which all the experiments are performed. We use IDD Lite [26] for our experiments. IDD Lite is a custom dataset specifically designed for resource-constrained scenarios. This dataset contains 1400 training images and 400 validation images sampled and scaled from the updated IDD dataset [35], keeping the largest dimension to 320 while preserving the image's aspect ratio with the hierarchy of 7 coarse labels.

4.2   Training Detials

We use a single NVIDIA 1080Ti GPU for simultaneous training and compression through our proposed method using the Pytorch deep learning library. The initial learning rate is set to 0.1, and total epochs are set to 250. We employ a reduced learning rate on the plateau scheduler. The training batch size is kept at 32, and the validation batch size is 4. The embedding dimension is fixed to 8 in all the experiments. The sparsity regularization factor is fixed to be 0.5.

4.3 Performance Metric

We evaluate the performance of the pruned semantic segmentation model through mean Intersection over Union metric, given as:

$$IOU = \frac{TP}{TP + FP + FN} \qquad (7)$$

Here, TP, FP and FN are the number of true positives, false positives, and false negatives at the pixel level. For assessing the efficiency of pruning methods, we use the number of (a) floating point operations (GFlops), (b) parameters, and (c) flop ratio indicating the ratio of remaining flops and original flops.

Table 1. Shows the performance of our proposed method MPHyp on UNet and ERFNet. It can be observed that our method shows better performance than L1-pruning, with better accuracy and having a smaller network.

UNet					
Compression Ratio	Method	mIoU	GFlops	Params(M)	Flop Ratio
0.00	Un-Pruned	65.71	20.84	7.786	-
0.50	L1-Pruning [36]	43.18	10.42	3.897	0.5
	MPHyp	55.03	10.73	3.504	0.514
0.75	L1-Pruning [36]	26.71	5.212	1.951	0.25
	MPHyp	57.01	5.369	0.702	0.257
0.90	L1-Pruning [36]	19.09	2.098	0.778	0.10
	MPHyp	54.61	2.298	1.015	0.1102
0.95	L1-Pruning [36]	18.93	1.042	0.406	0.05
	MPHyp	52.9	1.361	0.76	0.065
ERFNet					
Compression Ratio	Method	mIoU	GFlops	Params(M)	Flop Ratio
0.00	Un-Pruned	58.06	3.72	2.063	-
0.50	L1-Pruning [36]	56.52	1.867	0.993	0.5
	MPHyp	55.49	1.794	0.959	0.482
0.75	L1-Pruning [36]	53.70	0.931	0.499	0.250
	MPHyp	55.14	0.937	0.408	0.251
0.90	L1-Pruning [36]	51.64	0.368	0.21	0.098
	MPHyp	52.24	0.403	0.128	0.118
0.95	L1-Pruning [36]	41.42	0.183	0.117	0.049
	MPHyp	51.63	0.256	0.109	0.068

5   Results

Quantitative Results: In this section, we discuss the results obtained from our proposed method: Meta-pruning based Hypernetwork (MPHyp) on UNet and ERFNet.

Table 1 shows the performance of MPHyp with L1-based channel pruning. We can observe that MPHyp preserves the segmentation accuracy at different compression ratios, whereas L1-pruning shows a significant drop in mIoU. Also, from the table, it is evident that for higher compression ratios, our proposed approach outperforms the L1-pruning technique, further decreasing the flops and parameter count. Simultaneously, MPHyp achieves a lower flop ratio and GFlops, resulting in faster network inference. We also show class-wise mIoU

Table 2. Shows the mIoU performance of MPHyp at various compression ratios for UNet architecture. We can observe that MPHyp significantly outperforms L1-Pruning with higher mIoU at a higher compression ratio and shows comparable performance with the Un-Pruned network. It is also important to note that MPHyp shows better performance (in Bold) than the un-pruned method on the Vehicles and Roadside-Objects class, which could be advantageous in autonomous applications.

Methods	Drivable	Non-drivable	Living Thing	Vehicles	Roadside-Objects	Far-objects	Sky	mIoU
Compression Ratio: 50 %								
Un-Pruned	92.51	36.89	49.97	69.79	43.19	72.96	94.67	65.71
L1-Pruning [36]	91.1	4.07	47.03	65.87	0.0	0.0	94.15	43.18
MPHyp	91.2	31.42	43.39	67.46	41.29	71.78	93.69	55.03
Compression Ratio: 75 %								
Un-Pruned	92.51	36.89	49.97	69.79	43.19	72.96	94.67	65.71
L1-Pruning [36]	90.16	3.34	0.0	0.0	0.0	0.0	93.5	26.71
MPHyp	92.61	33.26	47.06	**72.28**	**44.27**	72.72	93.92	57.01
Compression Ratio: 90 %								
Un-Pruned	92.51	36.89	49.97	69.79	43.19	72.96	94.67	65.71
L1-Pruning [36]	40.12	0.00	0.00	0.00	0.00	0.00	93.51	19.09
MPHyp	91.61	28.87	43.48	67.07	41.93	70.38	93.51	54.61
Compression Ratio: 95 %								
Un-Pruned	92.51	36.89	49.97	69.79	43.19	72.96	94.67	65.71
L1-Pruning [36]	40.15	0.00	0.00	0.00	0.00	0.00	92.36	18.93
MPHyp	91.06	22.34	41.64	66.00	40.34	68.86	92.97	52.90

Table 3. Shows the MPHyp performance at various embedding dimensions. We can observe as the embedding dimension increases, the semantic segmentation decreases. However, on the other hand, we have improved the flop ratio with increasing embedding dimension. We keep the pruning ratio fixed at 0.5.

Method	Embedding Dimension	mIoU	Flop Ratio
MPHyp	8	55.03	0.5114
MPHyp	16	54.22	0.5196
MPHyp	32	53.82	0.5042

Table 4. Shows the MPHyp performance for different sparsity regularization formulations at a pruning ratio of 0.5.

Method	Proximal Regularization	mIoU	Flop Ratio
MPHyp	L1	55.03	0.5114
MPHyp	L2	53.81	0.5293

results for various pruning methods Table 2 at different compression ratios. It can be observed that MPHyp significantly outperforms L1-Pruning with higher mIoU at a higher compression ratio and shows comparable performance with an Un-Pruned network. Interestingly, MPHyp shows better performance than the un-pruned method on the Vehicles and Roadside-Objects class, which are important classes in autonomous applications. On average, the training time of MPHyp at different compression ratios was around 1Hr on 1080ti, which is significantly lower than existing neural architecture search methods and L1-pruning, which has an average training time of 3Hrs.

Qualitative Results: Figure 2 displays the qualitative results obtained from our proposed approach and the baseline pruning algorithm. The first row demonstrates the prediction of classes *rider* and *bike*, and the second row focuses on the model's prediction for *car* class. The third and fourth rows illustrate classes *sidewalk* and *sky*, respectively. As it can be observed, MYHyp predictions have better fine details compared to L_1-pruning.

MYHyp-0.75 and MYHyp-0.90 predictions have finer details compared to MYHyp-0.95. L_1-pruning based approach's performance has very coarse boundaries for the objects of interest.

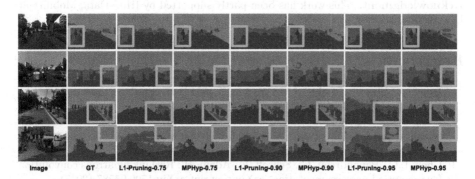

Fig. 2. Qualitative results at higher compression ratios 0.75, 0.9, and 0.95 comparing L1-pruning [36] and our proposed method is based on UNet architecture. Segmentation results enclosed in green boxes show that MPHyp is able to preserve segmentation results at higher pruning rates for different classes. (*Best viewed when zoomed*).

6   Ablations

We perform two ablations to see the performance of our proposed approach.

Embedding Dimension: We increase the embedding dimension from the default value of 8 to 16 and 32 in Table 3. We see that there is a trade-off between the mIoU value and the flop ratio. Though the flop ratio is marginally better for the higher embedding dimension, the mIoU metric follows a downward trend.

Proximal Gradient Regularizer: Now, we compare the effect of $L2$ regularizer and $L1$ regularizer to sparsify the latent vector, keeping the same pruning strategy in Table 4. We can observe that $L1$ regularizer shows better mIoU and flop ratio compared to $L2$ regularizer. It is also important to note that to have a reasonable convergence speed λ used for $L2$ regularizer must be significantly larger than that $L1$ regularizer.

7   Conclusion

In this paper, we propose an automatic pruning method with the added advantage of differentiability with the help of hypernetworks for semantic segmentation architectures. The proximal gradient algorithm and L1 sparsification, along with the proposed hypernetwork design, help to find the compact representation of the architecture in hand. We use two widely accepted semantic segmentation architectures to show the effectiveness of our proposed approach at different compression ratios. Our method opens a new direction of research toward an efficient pruning method for semantic segmentation.

Acknowledgment. This work has been partly supported by IHub-Data, Mobility at IIIT Hyderabad.

References

1. Brock, A., Lim, T., Ritchie, J.M., Weston, N.: SMASH: one-shot model architecture search through hypernetworks. In: ICLR 2018
2. Chen, L.C., Papandreou, G., Kokkinos, I., Murphy, K., Yuille, A.L.: Deeplab: semantic image segmentation with deep convolutional nets, atrous convolution, and fully connected crfs. IEEE Trans. PAMI **40**, 834–848 (2017)
3. Chen, L.C., Papandreou, G., Schroff, F., Adam, H.: Rethinking atrous convolution for semantic image segmentation. arXiv preprint arXiv:1706.05587 (2017)
4. Chen, L.C., Zhu, Y., Papandreou, G., Schroff, F., Adam, H.: Encoder-decoder with atrous separable convolution for semantic image segmentation. In: ECCV, pp. 801–818 (2018)
5. Cordts, M., et al.: The cityscapes dataset for semantic urban scene understanding. In: IEEE CVPR (2016)
6. Fernando, C., et al.: Convolution by evolution: differentiable pattern producing networks. In: Proceedings of the GECC 2016, pp. 109–116 (2016)

7. Frankle, J., Carbin, M.: The lottery ticket hypothesis: finding sparse, trainable neural networks. In: ICLR 2019
8. Gong, C., Jiang, Z., Wang, D., Lin, Y., Liu, Q., Pan, D.Z.: Mixed precision neural architecture search for energy efficient deep learning. In: IEEE/ACM ICCAD (2019)
9. Ha, D., Dai, A.M., Le, Q.V.: Hypernetworks. In: In Proceedings of ICLR 2017
10. Han, S., Pool, J., Tran, J., Dally, W.: Learning both weights and connections for efficient neural network. In: NeuRIPS (2015)
11. Hassner, T., Liu, C.: Dense Image Correspondences for Computer Vision. Springer, Heidelberg (2016). https://doi.org/10.1007/978-3-319-23048-1
12. Hassner, T., Mayzels, V., Zelnik-Manor, L.: On sifts and their scales. In: IEEE CVPR (2012)
13. He, K., Zhang, X., Ren, S., Sun, J.: Spatial pyramid pooling in deep convolutional networks for visual recognition. IEEE Trans. PAMI **37**(9), 1904–1916 (2015)
14. He, Y., Zhang, X., Sun, J.: Channel pruning for accelerating very deep neural networks. In: IEEE ICCV, pp. 1389–1397 (2017)
15. Ho, J., Kalchbrenner, N., Weissenborn, D., Salimans, T.: Axial attention in multidimensional transformers. arXiv preprint arXiv:1912.12180 (2019)
16. Jaderberg, M., Simonyan, K., Zisserman, A., et al.: Spatial transformer networks. In: NeuRIPS, vol. 28 (2015)
17. Jia, X., De Brabandere, B., Tuytelaars, T., Gool, L.V.: Dynamic filter networks. In: NeuRIPS, vol. 29 (2016)
18. Koutnik, J., Gomez, F., Schmidhuber, J.: Evolving neural networks in compressed weight space. In: Genetic and Evolutionary Computation, pp. 619–626 (2010)
19. Li, Y., Gu, S., Zhang, K., Van Gool, L., Timofte, R.: DHP: differentiable meta pruning via hypernetworks. In: Vedaldi, A., Bischof, H., Brox, T., Frahm, J.-M. (eds.) ECCV 2020. LNCS, vol. 12353, pp. 608–624. Springer, Cham (2020). https://doi.org/10.1007/978-3-030-58598-3_36
20. Liu, C., et al.: Auto-deeplab: hierarchical neural architecture search for semantic image segmentation. arXiv preprint arXiv:1901.02985 (2019)
21. Liu, X., Qi, J., Zhang, W., Bao, Z., Wang, K., Li, N.: Recognition method of maize crop rows at the seedling stage based on ms-erfnet model. Comput. Electron. Agric. **211**, 107964 (2023)
22. Liu, Z., et al.: Metapruning: meta learning for automatic neural network channel pruning. In: IEEE ICCV (2019)
23. Long, J., Shelhamer, E., Darrell, T.: Fully convolutional networks for semantic segmentation. In: IEEE CVPR (2015)
24. Luo, J.H., Wu, J., Lin, W.: Thinet: a filter level pruning method for deep neural network compression. In: IEEE ICCV, pp. 5058–5066 (2017)
25. McGlinchy, J., Johnson, B., Muller, B., Joseph, M., Diaz, J.: Application of unet fully convolutional neural network to impervious surface segmentation in urban environment from high resolution satellite imagery. In: IGARSS 2019
26. Mishra, A., et al.: Semantic segmentation datasets for resource constrained training. In: Babu, R.V., Prasanna, M., Namboodiri, V.P. (eds.) NCVPRIPG 2019. CCIS, vol. 1249, pp. 450–459. Springer, Singapore (2020). https://doi.org/10.1007/978-981-15-8697-2_42
27. Molchanov, D., Ashukha, A., Vetrov, D.: Variational dropout sparsifies deep neural networks. In: ICML, pp. 2498–2507. PMLR (2017)
28. Neuhold, G., Ollmann, T., Rota Bulo, S., Kontschieder, P.: The mapillary vistas dataset for semantic understanding of street scenes. In: IEEE ICCV (2017)

29. Pan, Z., Liang, Y., Zhang, J., Yi, X., Yu, Y., Zheng, Y.: Hyperst-net: hypernetworks for spatio-temporal forecasting. arXiv preprint arXiv:1809.10889 (2018)
30. Romera, E., Álvarez, J.M., Bergasa, L.M., Arroyo, R.: Erfnet: efficient residual factorized convnet for real-time semantic segmentation. IEEE T-ITS **19**, 263–272 (2017)
31. Ronneberger, O., Fischer, P., Brox, T.: U-Net: convolutional networks for biomedical image segmentation. In: Navab, N., Hornegger, J., Wells, W.M., Frangi, A.F. (eds.) MICCAI 2015. LNCS, vol. 9351, pp. 234–241. Springer, Cham (2015). https://doi.org/10.1007/978-3-319-24574-4_28
32. Shaw, A., Hunter, D., Landola, F., Sidhu, S.: Squeezenas: fast neural architecture search for faster semantic segmentation. In: Proceedings of the IEEE ICCVW (2019)
33. Stanley, K.O., D'Ambrosio, D.B., Gauci, J.: A hypercube-based encoding for evolving large-scale neural networks. J. Artif. Life **15**, 185–212 (2009)
34. Tan, M., et al.: Mnasnet: platform-aware neural architecture search for mobile. In: IEEE CVPR (2019)
35. Varma, G., Subramanian, A., Namboodiri, A., Chandraker, M., Jawahar, C.: Idd: a dataset for exproceedings of the eccvploring problems of autonomous navigation in unconstrained environments. In: 2019 IEEE WACV (2019)
36. Yang, C., et al.: Structured pruning of convolutional neural networks via l1 regularization. IEEE Access **7**, 106385–106394 (2019)
37. Yu, F., Koltun, V., Funkhouser, T.: Dilated residual networks. In: Proceedings of the IEEE CVPR, pp. 472–480 (2017)
38. Zhao, H., Shi, J., Qi, X., Wang, X., Jia, J.: Pyramid scene parsing network. In: IEEE CVPR, pp. 2881–2890 (2017)
39. Zheng, S., et al.: Conditional random fields as recurrent neural networks. In: IEEE ICCV, pp. 1529–1537 (2015)
40. Zoph, B., Le, Q.V.: Neural architecture search with reinforcement learning. arXiv preprint arXiv:1611.01578 (2016)

Cross-Domain Feature Extraction Using CycleGAN for Large FoV Thermal Image Creation

Sudeep Rathore[1]([✉])[iD], Avinash Upadhyay[1][iD], Manoj Sharma[1][iD], Ajay Yadav[1],
G. Shyam Chand[2], Amit Singhal[2][iD], Prerana Mukherjee[3][iD], and Brejesh Lall[4]

[1] Bennett University, Greater Noida, UP, India
`sudeep.nehu@gmail.com, manoj.sharma1@bennett.edu.in`
[2] Netaji Subhas University of Technology, New Delhi, India
`shyamchandg1@cet.ac.in`
[3] Jawaharlal Nehru University, New Delhi, India
[4] Indian Institute of Technology Delhi, New Delhi, India

Abstract. Thermal images are extensively utilized in defense operations due to their ability to capture thermal radiation. However, the limited Field of View (FoV) in thermal imaging systems often results in insufficient and fragmented large Field of View (FoV) simulation data, thereby compromising the effectiveness of defense applications using large Field of View (FoV) cameras. To address this challenge, we propose an innovative approach employing image stitching techniques to create comprehensive and detailed views. Traditional image feature extractors such as Scale-Invariant Feature Transform (SIFT) and Speeded Up Robust Features (SURF) are optimized for Red, Green, and Blue (RGB) images. Hence, their performance on thermal images is often sub-optimal as the thermal images contain low-resolution, reduced contrast and dynamic range, non-uniform thermal emissions, and the absence of color information, making identifying and matching robust features and descriptors difficult. To enhance feature extraction, we adopt the Cycle Generative Adversarial Network (CycleGAN) technique to convert thermal images into their RGB counterparts prior to feature extraction. This enables us to leverage the robustness of RGB-optimized feature extractors and amalgamate them with the features obtained from the original thermal images, resulting in a richer and more comprehensive feature set. The performance of this proposed network has been demonstrated and validated on various datasets, showing promising results for large Field of View (FoV) thermal image creation.

Keywords: Thermal Image stitching · Panorama · Feature Matching · Image Blending · CycleGAN · Deeplearning

1 Introduction

The defense sector has always been at the forefront of technological advancements, leveraging cutting-edge tools to gain strategic advantage. One such tech-

H. Kaur et al. (Eds.): CVIP 2023, CCIS 2011, pp. 65–77, 2024.
https://doi.org/10.1007/978-3-031-58535-7_6

nology is thermal imaging, which has become increasingly prevalent in defense applications due to its ability to operate in low-light conditions and penetrate smoke, haze, and fog. However, capturing real-world thermal images in live defense situations can be challenging due to the impracticality associated with sensitive defense operations.

To overcome this issue, the use of simulations has gained prominence. Simulations enable analysts to generate synthetic thermal data that can mimic real-life scenarios. A particularly important requirement in many defense applications is the need for large Field of View (FoV) thermal data. It's often challenging to obtain such large Field of View (FoV) data in real-world scenarios due to hardware limitations or risks associated with the exposure of expensive equipment. In such cases, a viable solution is the synthetic generation of large FoV thermal data from available smaller Field of View (FoV) thermal data. This process can be achieved through a stitching method, which involves combining multiple smaller FoV images to generate a larger Field of View (FoV) image that preserves the integrity of the original data.

Traditional image feature extractors, like Scale-Invariant Feature Transform (SIFT) and Speeded Up Robust Features (SURF), have been optimized for standard Red-Green-Blue (RGB) images. These algorithms have demonstrated excellent performance in detecting and describing local features in images, which is crucial for tasks like object recognition, image matching, and scene reconstruction. However, their application to thermal images has been limited due to the inherent differences between the two types of images.

To address this challenge, we propose using Cycle Generative Adversarial Networks (CycleGAN), a technique that has shown great promise in image-to-image translation. By leveraging this technique, we first convert the thermal image into an RGB equivalent. We can then utilize RGB-optimized feature extractors like SIFT and SURF to extract robust features from these images alongside the regular features obtained directly from the thermal image. This approach allows us to harness the power of these established feature extraction methods in a new domain.

This methodology has been tested using various datasets, showcasing the performance and versatility of the proposed approach. Through these extensive evaluations, we aim to underline the potential of our method to revolutionize the way thermal imaging is used in defense and other high-stakes applications.

2   Related Work

2.1   Feature Extractors

Scale Invariant Feature Transform (SIFT) [16] was introduced in 2004 by D.G. Lowe and is one of the most popular feature descriptor algorithms. Detection of feature points is done by finding Difference-of-Gaussians (DoG) on images. In the description stage, a 16*16 locality around the detected feature is extracted and subdivided into sub-blocks providing 128 bin values. Even though SIFT algorithm is invariant to operations like rotation and scaling, its high computational cost limits its usage in many situations.

In 2008, Speeded Up Robust Features (SURF) was put forward by Herbert Bay et al. [7], and the detector has an improved feature detection speed achieved by manipulating integral images by using the determinant of the Hessian Matrix. Each detected feature is described using 64 bin descriptors with Haar Wavelet responses. The computational cost of SURF is less than SIFT, which is a major advantage and is invariant to rotation and scaling.

KAZE feature descriptor was developed by P.F Alcantarilla et al. [3], which makes even blurred regions in an image locally adaptive in obtaining feature points with non-linear diffusion filtering. The functioning of the detector is by computing the normalized determinant of the Hessian matrix at many scales. KAZE is invariant to scaling and rotation, achieved by calculating dominance in orientation around selected features. Fast Explicit Diffusion (FED) [4], Binary Robust Invariant Scalable Keypoints (BRISK) [14] and Oriented FAST and Rotated BRIEF(ORB) [17] are also computationally efficient stitching algorithms.

Amanda Berg et al. [8] present a deep learning-based method for generating visible spectrum images from thermal infrared images. The proposed approach utilizes a cGAN framework and demonstrates promising results in improving thermal infrared imagery's visibility and color information. The method has the potential to enhance the usability and interpretation of thermal infrared images in various real-world applications.

Quincy G. Alexander et al. [5] proposes a deep learning-based approach that effectively combines thermal and RGB images for automated crack detection in civil infrastructure. The fusion of modalities improves the accuracy and reliability of crack detection, offering promising possibilities for real-world applications.

2.2 Feature Based stitching

Considering the recent developments in computer vision and image processing technologies in Fields ranging from national security and disaster management to entertainment applications in virtual reality, image stitching remains a hot research topic. Developing a more comprehensive view panorama by combining multiple images having overlapped FoV is termed image stitching [12,15]. It has highly impactful applications in aerial, marine, and space exploration to provide a single frame of subject data using successive images with an overlapping area of 30% or more for matching. Generally, significant operations in image stitching are key-point detection and feature description, defining transformation matrix, and image reconstruction followed by blending of seam lines [20].

In some instances, additional steps were taken to address issues like lens distortion, parallax, and exposure compensation to eliminate errors in the resultant panorama [9]. Detected features are generally in the form of lines, junctions, corners, blobs, edges, etc., which are further described in certain ways according to the specific patterns of their corresponding neighboring pixels; this entire process is termed feature description. Some commonly used feature descriptors are SIFT, SURF, KAZE, AKAZE, BRISK and ORB [20]. Elimination of outliers is carried out in outlier-rejection phase and some of the commonly used probabilistic models are Random Sample Consensus (RANSAC) [11,22], M-estimator Sample Consensus (MSAC) [21], and Progressive Sample Consensus (PROSAC) [10]. In general, the ORB feature extraction technique is computationally higher in efficiency than other feature descriptors, thus a popular choice in image stitching in infrared imagery.

3   Methodology

The methodology outlined in this paper describes a two-fold approach for generating Large Field of View (FoV) thermal images using cross-modality data. An overview of this process is depicted in Fig. 1, which illustrates the overall flow of thermal image stitching used for large Field of View (FoV) creation.

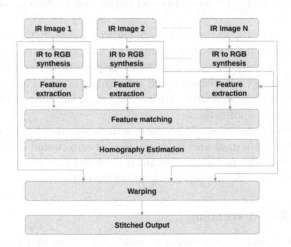

Fig. 1. Proposed flowchart for generating large FoV thermal image from small FoV image using stitching

3.1   Generation of RGB Pair Using CycleGAN

The Cycle Generative Adversarial Network (CycleGAN) [25] is a powerful technique for image-to-image translation. Our methodology used CycleGAN to transform thermal images into their RGB counterparts.

CycleGAN comprises two main components: Generator networks and Discriminator networks. Let's consider two domains, X (thermal images) and Y (RGB images). There will be two generator networks, G and F. G transforms images from X to Y ($G : X \rightarrow Y$), and F does the inverse, i.e., transforms images from Y to X ($F : Y \rightarrow X$).

On the other hand, there are two discriminator networks, D_X and D_Y. D_X aims to distinguish between images from domain X and images generated by F, while D_Y tries to distinguish between images from domain Y and images generated by G.

The unique aspect of CycleGAN is its incorporation of cycle consistency loss along with the traditional adversarial loss, which enforces a round-trip translation between the original and translated images. For instance, an image from domain X is translated to domain Y using generator G, and then translated back to domain X using generator F. The difference between the original image and the twice-translated image is minimized in the training process, which is the essence of cycle consistency loss.

The objective function used in our methodology is similar to the one proposed in CycleGAN [25].

The cycle consistency loss ensures that the learned translation does not deviate too much from the original content of the image, thereby preserving the integrity of the source domain while adapting it to the target domain. This balance between content preservation and style adaptation makes CycleGAN a powerful tool for domain adaptation problems (Fig. 2).

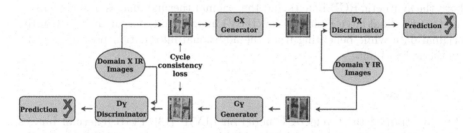

Fig. 2. CycleGAN architecture for the thermal image to RGB image conversion

3.2   Image Stitching

Once the RGB images and their corresponding feature sets are obtained, the next step involves stitching these images to create a large Field of View (FoV) image. This process consists of three main stages: feature extraction, homography estimation, and warping/stitching of the images.

In the feature extraction stage, we employ feature extractors such as SIFT, SURF, and ORB on both synthetic RGB and original thermal images. These algorithms work by detecting distinctive features in images that can align different views of a scene.

After extracting the features, we move on to homography estimation[12]. This process involves calculating the perspective transformation, or homography, that best aligns the features between images. The aligned feature for an image is shown in Fig. 3(a) for RGB image and Fig. 3(b) for thermal image. This step is crucial as it enables us to align the images accurately before they are stitched together.

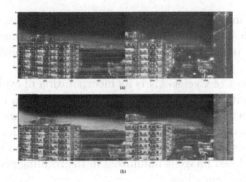

Fig. 3. RANSAC-based Features/Keypoints matching in (a) Synthetic RGB and (b) Thermal image

Finally, once the homography matrices are estimated, the images are warped or transformed to align correctly. After the images are warped, they are stitched together to create the final large Field of View (FoV) image. It is important to note that the stitching process takes into account the features extracted from both the synthetic RGB images and the original thermal images, thereby ensuring that the final large Field of View (FoV) image maintains the integrity of the original data while benefiting from the additional information provided by the synthetic RGB data.

3.3 Dataset

We have trained the CycleGAN model on LLVIP [13], FLIR Thermal Images Dataset [1], RoadScene [23] and TNO Multiband Image Data Collection [2]. We used a local dataset captured using the thermal camera with a FoV of 24 degrees, for evaluation purposes.

4 Results

This section presents the results obtained from the implementation of our methodology, demonstrating the effectiveness of the CycleGAN model in generating RGB images from thermal images, the superior performance of RGB-optimized feature extractors on synthetic RGB images, and the improved outcome of the stitching pipeline using amalgamated features.

Our results show that the CycleGAN model effectively translates thermal images into synthetic RGB images. The Fig. 4 provided demonstrates this by juxtaposing a thermal image and its corresponding synthetic RGB image generated using CycleGAN. The striking similarity in structural details between the two illustrates the model's competence in preserving the integrity of original features.

(a)   (b)   (c)   (d)

Fig. 4. Results of thermal to RGB image synthesis. (a) and (c) are the thermal images while (b) and (d) are its corresponding synthetic RGB image respectively. (a) is a thermal image from out local dataset, and (c) is a thermal image from FLIR ADAS dataset.

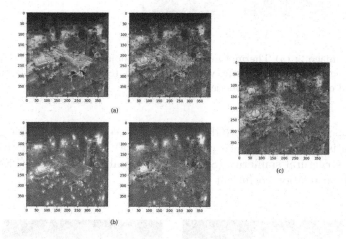

Fig. 5. For image 1: (a) Thermal image and its keypoints (b) Synthetic RGB of the corresponding thermal image along with its keypoints (c) Amalgamated features from thermal and corresponding synthetic RGB image.

We found that feature extractors, namely SIFT, SURF, and ORB, which are trained and optimized for RGB images, perform substantially better on synthetic RGB images compared to their performance on original thermal images. This is evident from the Fig. 5 and 6 (for the first and second image to be stitched, respectively), which showcases identified features on three types of images: synthetic RGB, thermal, and thermal images with concatenated features from both synthetic RGB and thermal images. The synthetic RGB image with the amalgamated features clearly indicates a higher density and variety of detected features, affirming our hypothesis.

Table 1 represents the number of features in the NIR image, the synthetic RGB image of the corresponding NIR image, combined features from NIR and corresponding synthetic RGB image, the number of matched features in NIR image (First image + Second image) and the number of matched features in NIR image and corresponding synthetic RGB image(for first image) + NIR image

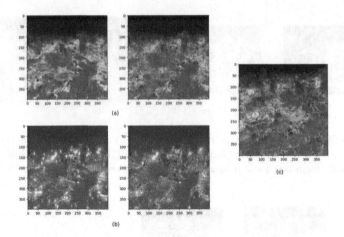

Fig. 6. For image 2: (a) Thermal image and its keypoints (b) Synthetic RGB of the corresponding thermal image along with its keypoints (c) Amalgamated features from thermal and corresponding synthetic RGB image.

and corresponding synthetic RGB image(for a second image). Table 2. shows the comparison of performance parameters of (a) CycleGAN and (b) pix-to-pix GAN, structural similarity (SSIM), peak signal-to-noise ratio (PSNR) and normalized correlation coefficient (NCC).

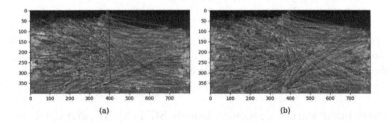

Fig. 7. Keypoints matching in image 1 and image 2: (a) Features from thermal images only (b) Amalgamated features from thermal image and corresponding synthetic RGB image.

The results of our stitching pipeline further establish the superior performance of amalgamated features extracted from thermal and corresponding synthetic RGB images. A comparison of the stitching output using features extracted solely from thermal images and those using amalgamated features reveals that the latter provides better performance in image stitching, as shown in Fig. 9. The figure demonstrates the more seamless and accurate alignment achieved with the amalgamated features, underscoring their importance in enhancing the quality of stitched thermal images. Table 3 shows a comparison between state-of-the-art methods and our proposed method (Figs. 7 and 8).

Table 1. Number of feature in thermal image, synthetic RGB image and amalgamated features from thermal image and corresponding synthetic RGB image

Image	Number of features
IR (First thermal image)	1439
Synthetic RGB image of first IR image	923
IR (Second thermal image)	1320
Synthetic RGB image of second IR image	904
Amalgamated features from IR and corresponding synthetic RGB image (First case)	2362
Amalgamated features from IR and corresponding synthetic RGB image (Second case)	2224
Number of matched feature in IR images only (First image and Second image)	719
Number of matched feature in IR image and corresponding synthetic RGB image (First case) and IR image and corresponding synthetic RGB image (Second case)	1587

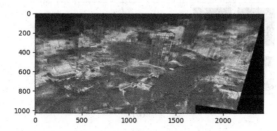

Fig. 8. Stitched output of thermal images (for image 1 and image 2).

Table 2. Performance comparison of (a) CycleGAN, and (b) Pix-to-pix GAN. Evaluation metrics to compare the models are SSIM, PSNR and Normalized Correlation Coefficient (NCC)

Ground Truth Image	Generated Image	SSIM	PSNR	NCC
		0.93748	32.61848	0.99824
		0.913215	30.28436	0.996110
		0.936806	33.51752	0.98792
		0.83039	25.12636	0.98937

(a)

Ground Truth Image	Generated Image	SSIM	PSNR	NCC
		0.60032	19.06486	0.97346
		0.64098	20.98029	0.97317
		0.57224	20.36890	0.85566
		0.25150	15.93882	0.91811

(b)

Table 3. Performance comparison of state-of-the-art methods with our proposed model

Method	PSNR	SSIM
Aslahishahri et al. [6]	31.21	0.93
Yuan et al. [24]	–	0.93
Sun et al. [19]	–	0.90
Soria et al. [18]	22.99	0.72
Proposed	**33.51**	**0.93**

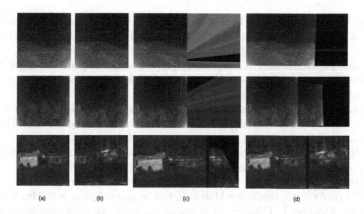

Fig. 9. Some more stitching results (a) First thermal image (b) Second thermal image (c) Using features of thermal images only and (d) Using Amalgamated features from thermal and corresponding synthetic RGB images.

5   Conclusion

The proposed research delved into synthetically generating Large field-of-view (FoV) thermal image data from existing smaller field-of-view (FoV) data. We presented an innovative approach for converting thermal images to RGB format using unpaired thermal-RGB data, a process that subsequently facilitated robust feature extraction for efficient thermal image stitching. We demonstrated the efficacy of Cycle Generative Adversarial Networks (CycleGAN) in transforming thermal images into their RGB equivalents, thereby paving the way for the deployment of established RGB-optimized feature extractors, such as SIFT, SURF and ORB, in this new arena. This transformation not only expanded the array of available feature extraction methodologies for thermal images but also considerably enhanced the overall effectiveness of feature extraction from these images.

References

1. Flir thermal starter dataset. https://www.kaggle.com/datasets/deepnewbie/flir-thermal-images-dataset?select=FLIR_ADAS_1_3, Accessed 22 Sep 2023
2. The tno multiband image data collection. Accessed 22 Sep 2023. https://figshare.com/articles/dataset/TNO_Image_Fusion_Dataset/1008029?backTo=/collections/The_TNO_Multiband_Image_Collection/3860689
3. Alcantarilla, P.F., Bartoli, A., Davison, A.J.: KAZE Features. In: Fitzgibbon, A., Lazebnik, S., Perona, P., Sato, Y., Schmid, C. (eds.) ECCV 2012. LNCS, vol. 7577, pp. 214–227. Springer, Heidelberg (2012). https://doi.org/10.1007/978-3-642-33783-3_16
4. Alcantarilla, P.F., Nuevo, J., Bartoli, A.: Fast explicit diffusion for accelerated features in nonlinear scale spaces. In: Burghardt, T., Damen, D., Mayol-Cuevas,

W.W., Mirmehdi, M. (eds.) British Machine Vision Conference, BMVC 2013, Bristol, UK, 9–13 September 2013. BMVA Press (2013). https://doi.org/10.5244/C.27. 13

5. Alexander, Q.G., Hoskere, V., Narazaki, Y., Maxwell, A., Spencer, B.F., Jr.: Fusion of thermal and RGB images for automated deep learning based crack detection in civil infrastructure. AI Civil Eng. **1**(1), 3 (2022)

6. Aslahishahri, M., et al.: From RGB to NIR: predicting of near infrared reflectance from visible spectrum aerial images of crops. In: Proceedings of the IEEE/CVF International Conference on Computer Vision, pp. 1312–1322 (2021)

7. Bay, H., Ess, A., Tuytelaars, T., Gool, L.V.: Speeded-up robust features (surf). Comput. Vis. Image Understand. **110**(3), 346 – 359 (2008).https://doi.org/ 10.1016/j.cviu.2007.09.014, http://www.sciencedirect.com/science/article/pii/ S1077314207001555, similarity Matching in Computer Vision and Multimedia

8. Berg, A., Ahlberg, J., Felsberg, M.: Generating visible spectrum images from thermal infrared. In: Proceedings of the IEEE Conference on Computer Vision and Pattern Recognition Workshops, pp. 1143–1152 (2018)

9. Chen, J., Wan, Q., Luo, L., Wang, Y., Luo, D.: Drone image stitching based on compactly supported radial basis function. IEEE J. Sel. Top. Appl. Earth Observ. Remote Sens. 1–10 (2019). https://doi.org/10.1109/JSTARS.2019.2947162

10. Chum, O., Matas, J.: Matching with prosac - progressive sample consensus. In: 2005 IEEE Computer Society Conference on Computer Vision and Pattern Recognition (CVPR 2005), vol. 1, pp. 220–226 (2005). https://doi.org/10.1109/CVPR.2005.221

11. Fischler, M.A., Bolles, R.C.: Random sample consensus: a paradigm for model fitting with applications to image analysis and automated cartography. Commun. ACM **24**(6), 381-395 (1981). https://doi.org/10.1145/358669.358692

12. Hartley, R., Zisserman, A.: Multiple View Geometry in Computer Vision, 2nd edn. Cambridge University Press, New York, NY, USA (2003)

13. Jia, X., Zhu, C., Li, M., Tang, W., Zhou, W.: LLVIP: A visible-infrared paired dataset for low-light vision. CoRR **abs/2108.10831** (2021). https://arxiv.org/ abs/2108.10831

14. Leutenegger, S., Chli, M., Siegwart, R.: Brisk: binary robust invariant scalable keypoints. In: Computer Vision (ICCV), 2011 IEEE International Conference on, pp. 2548–2555 (2011). https://doi.org/10.1109/ICCV.2011.6126542

15. Li, A., Guo, J., Guo, Y.: Image stitching based on semantic planar region consensus. IEEE Trans. Image Process. **30**, 5545–5558 (2021). https://doi.org/10.1109/TIP. 2021.3086079

16. Lowe, D.G.: Distinctive image features from scale-invariant keypoints. Int. J. Comput. Vision **60**(2), 91-110 (2004). https://doi.org/10.1023/B:VISI.0000029664. 99615.94

17. Rublee, E., Rabaud, V., Konolige, K., Bradski, G.: Orb: An efficient alternative to sift or surf. In: 2011 International Conference on Computer Vision, pp. 2564–2571 (2011). https://doi.org/10.1109/ICCV.2011.6126544

18. Soria, X., Sappa, A.D., Hammoud, R.I.: Wide-band color imagery restoration for RGB-NIR single sensor images. Sensors **18**(7), 2059 (2018)

19. Sun, T., Jung, C., Fu, Q., Han, Q.: Nir to RGB domain translation using asymmetric cycle generative adversarial networks. IEEE Access **7**, 112459–112469 (2019)

20. Tareen, S.A.K., Saleem, Z.: A comparative analysis of sift, surf, kaze, akaze, orb, and brisk, March 2018.https://doi.org/10.1109/ICOMET.2018.8346440

21. Torr, P.H., Zisserman, A.: Mlesac: a new robust estimator with application to estimating image geometry. Comput. Vis. Image Underst. **78**(1), 138–156 (2000)

22. Wang, H., Mirota, D., Hager, G.D.: A generalized kernel consensus-based robust estimator. IEEE Trans. Pattern Anal. Mach. Intell. **32**(1), 178–184 (2010). https://doi.org/10.1109/TPAMI.2009.148
23. Xu, H., Ma, J., Le, Z., Jiang, J., Guo, X.: Fusiondn: a unified densely connected network for image fusion. In: proceedings of the Thirty-Fourth AAAI Conference on Artificial Intelligence (2020)
24. Yuan, X., Tian, J., Reinartz, P.: Generating artificial near infrared spectral band from RGB image using conditional generative adversarial network. ISPRS Ann. Photogrammetry Remote Sens. Spatial Inf. Sci. **3**, 279–285 (2020)
25. Zhu, J.Y., Park, T., Isola, P., Efros, A.A.: Unpaired image-to-image translation using cycle-consistent adversarial networks. In: 2017 IEEE International Conference on Computer Vision (ICCV), pp. 2242–2251 (2017). https://doi.org/10.1109/ICCV.2017.244

Classification of Insect Pest Using Transfer Learning Mechanism

Parveen Malik$^{(\boxtimes)}$ and Manoj Kumar Parida

KIIT Deemed to Be University, Bhubeneswar 751024, Odisha, India
{parveen.malikfet,manoj.paridafet}@kiit.ac.in

Abstract. Classification of Insects is one of the most vital and essential research, which needs to be done for, various factors like, for the protection of crops in the agricultural sector. The identification of crop pests is a difficult problem since, pest infestations cause significant crop damage and quality degradation. The majority of insect species are quite similar to one another that makes the task of detection of the insect on field crops like rice, soybeans, and other crops more challenging than a normal detection of objects. Currently, classifying insects manually is the major method used to distinguish them in crop fields, but this is a time - consuming and expensive operation. Considering the advancements in the field of deep learning, we propose to use a pre-trained network model trained on a millions of images of ImageNet dataset to do the classification task using transfer learning mechanism. An extensive experimentation was done using various pretrained models like VGG, inception, xception, ResNet, MobileNet, DenseNet and efficient net. Various insect datasets were used for classification task and model was fined tuned using transfer learning. The EfficientNet B7 model has achieved the highest accuracy 70%, 98% and 99% on IP102 (102 classes), Xie (40 classes) and Kaggle village Synthetic dataset (10 classes) respectively.

Keywords: IP102 · Transfer Learning · Pretrained Neural Networks · Xception · Inception · ResNet50 · VGG16 · VGG19 · DenseNet121 · EfficientNetB7 · CNN

1 Introduction

Insect classification enables us to comprehend and record the remarkable biodiversity of insects, providing vital insights into their species composition, distribution, and abundance within ecosystems [3]. This understanding is crucial for evaluating ecosystem health, monitoring changes, and identifying potential biodiversity threats [16]. Moreover, insect classification plays a pivotal role in the discovery and description of new species, expanding our knowledge of biodiversity and evolutionary connections. It also facilitates ecological research by allowing us to investigate food webs, species interactions, and ecosystem dynamics. In agricultural contexts, accurate classification of pest species is vital for developing

H. Kaur et al. (Eds.): CVIP 2023, CCIS 2011, pp. 78–89, 2024.
https://doi.org/10.1007/978-3-031-58535-7_7

Fig. 1. All the images belong to IP102 Dataset having 102 classes [30]

effective pest management strategies, while identifying disease-carrying insects is key for disease surveillance and prevention. Furthermore, insect classification supports conservation efforts by identifying endangered species and guiding conservation actions [21]. Insect classification is a challenging task due to the vast diversity of insect species and their intricate morphological characteristics as shown in Fig. 1. Deep learning, a sub-field of machine learning, has emerged as a powerful technique for automatically recognizing patterns and features in complex data, making it a promising approach for insect classification. Deep learning algorithms, particularly convolutional neural networks (CNNs), have shown remarkable success in various image recognition tasks, including object recognition and classification. These networks are designed to learn hierarchical representations of input images by stacking multiple layers of interconnected neurons. Each layer extracts increasingly abstract features, allowing the network to capture intricate details and patterns. To classify insects using deep learning, a large labeled dataset is essential. This dataset should consist of diverse images of insects from different species, with accurate labels indicating their respective classifications. In this paper, we have deployed various deep neural network models like VGG, ResNet, Inception, Xception, MobileNet, DenseNet and EfficientNet as a base model and modified the architecture along with customization of final layers transfer learning. Finally hyper parameter tuning is done to verify the efficacy of the proposed model on various standard set of databases. The paper is organized as follows. In Sect. 2, extensive literature review has been done while proposed framework is given in Sect. 3. Further results and discussion has been illustrated in Sect. 4 with a conclusion in Sect. 5.

2   Related Work

Several methods have been developed on the insect classification field whose underlying model is either machine learning or deep learning techniques. Authors in Wang et al [28] used textual and visual clues as features, and then used Bayesian inference generative model to classify the different butterflies with 54.4% accuracy. A separate dataset was made by Wang et al. in [27] with 225 specimens from different orders of Insecta class. The method used SVM as anatomical feature extractor and artificial neural network (ANN) to do the classification. The best accuracy is shown to be 93%. Further authors in Z.Liu et al. [15] used a dataset with 5136 samples images clustered in 12 insect classes. The saliency features and DNN model was used for classification task with micro average precision of 0.951. In another work by Ghazi et al. [5], authors used AlexNet [11], GoogleNet [22], VGG net [20] as a base model for transfer learning and achieved the accuracy of 80% on dataset of Life CLEF 2015. C. Xie et al. in [31] created a dataset of 4500 images with 10 classes and classification was done using multiple level fusion framework with sparse coding & predefined dictionary. The accuracy on the dataset is reported to be around 89%. Ahmed et al. in [1] collected 4511 images using different language search engines and used CaffeNet model which was pre-trained on Image Net dataset(1000 classes) The accuracy of the model is around 87%. In order to enable deep learning models to effectively generalize to real-world scenarios, X. Wu et al. [30] made significant progress by introducing the IP102 dataset. This dataset consists of an extensive collection of insect images, comprising 102 distinct classes and a total of 75,222 images. Furthermore, a subset of 18,983 images within the dataset has been meticulously annotated for object detection purposes. The IP102 dataset incorporates a hierarchical taxonomy of insects, which allows for grouping certain insect pests together under common parent nodes, reflecting their shared impact on specific crops. One notable limitation of the IP102 Dataset is its inherent imbalance, as the distribution of images across different classes is uneven. To address this issue, the authors of the dataset employed various performance metrics such as precision, recall, F-measure, G-mean, and micro-average area under the curve (M_{AUC}) for the classification task. To explore the effectiveness of handcrafted features, SVM and KNN classifiers were utilized. The best accuracy achieved using handcrafted features was 19.5% with the SVM classifier using speeded up robust features (SURF) features, while the KNN classifier with Gabor features achieved an accuracy of 19.2%. For deep features, the ResNet architecture yielded the highest accuracy, reaching approximately 49.5%. In a similar vein to the previously mentioned large-scale dataset, L. Liu et al. [14] introduced a novel dataset called PestNet. This dataset consists of 88,670 images that belong to 16 different classes of pests. To enhance the performance of their model, the authors proposed incorporating a channel-spatial attention (CSA) layer into the convolutional neural network (CNN) backbone. The authors achieved their best results by using ResNet101 as the backbone architecture, achieving a mean average precision (mAP) of 75.46%. Authors in Y. Li et al. [13] used VGGNet [20], ResNet [6]and GoogleNet (Inception-V3) model [23] with K- fold cross validation to select the best model and find tuned it. After 5 cross validation, GoogleLeNet was found to give best accuracy of 93.29%. It was selected for further tuning. An accuracy of 98.91% was achieved with Adagrad optimizer and a learning rate Of 0.0001. Another research done by J. Kong et al. [10] introduced the usage of graphical higher order network with feature aggregation enhancement. Author used it with cross scale partial network stage as a backbone to get multi-scale features which can discriminate local portions of the image. The proposed model has achieved the identification accuracy of around 7.1% on IP102 dataset [30]. The paper by H. T. Ung. et al. [26] examined several CNN-based approaches, namely the Residual-Attention Network (RAN), Feature Pyramid Network (FPN), and the multi-branch and multi-scale attention network (MMAL-Net), for identifying insect pests. Out of these methods, MMAL-Net was found to be the most accurate, achieving a recognition accuracy of 72.15% on the IP102 dataset [30] and 99.78% on the C. Xie dataset [31]. In this research by E. Ayan et al [2], the GAEnsemble method achieved high classification accuracy for C. Xie [31] (98.81%) and IP102 (67.13%) datasets based on the test results. K. Thenmozhi et al. [25] used transfer learning mechanism used pretrained neural networks like AlexNet, ResNet, GoogLeNet, and VGGNet. In the experiments conducted, the CNN model achieved the highest classification accuracy of 96.75%, 97.47%, and 95.97% for the NBAIR insect dataset (consisting of 40 classes) [17], Xie insect dataset (consisting of 24 classes) [32], and Xie insect dataset (consisting of 40 classes) [31] respectively.

3 Proposed Framework

The underlying principle of the proposed methodology is transfer learning that refers to the process of leveraging knowledge gained from pre-trained models and applying it to new tasks or domains. By transferring learned representations or weights from one model to another, transfer learning enables faster training, improved performance, and better generalization. As we can infer from the Fig. 2, instead of starting from scratch and randomly initializing the model parameters, transfer learning allows us to initialize the network with weights learned from pretrained models. These initial weights are already optimized on a similar task or domain, providing a head start for the model. Consequently, the model requires fewer iterations to reach a good solution, which significantly reduces training time and computational resources. In the proposed method, we have used pretrained models like VGG16, VGG19, Inception, Xception, MobileNet, DenseNet, ResNet, and EfficientNet [4,6,9,18,20,22,24], trained on the ImageNet dataset is a smart and efficient approach to transfer learning. These models have been pretrained on a vast collection of images from the ImageNet dataset, which contains millions of labeled images across thousands of categories. During initial implementation of our proposed method, we have frozen the neural network model weights and removed the output layer. Next process involves addition of one global average pooling layer, dense layer (1024 neurons) and output layer with softmax activation function. The initial learning rate was kept at 0.0001

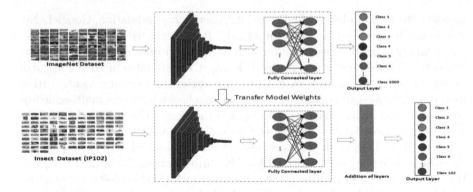

Fig. 2. Transfer Learning pipeline in which the pre-trained neural network weights trained on Imagenet dataset are freezed and then with addition of some layers are leveraged to classify the images on the other dataset.

with Adam as an optimizer. A brief review of the neural network modes used in proposed methodology are explained in subsequent sections.

3.1   VGG Network (VGG16 and VGG19)

VGG network proposed in [20] expanded the idea of AlexNet with max pooling layer sand-witched between the convolution layers (3 by 3 filters). As shown in Fig. 3, VGG 19 architecture has 19 layers (only learnable weight parameters) deep architecture.

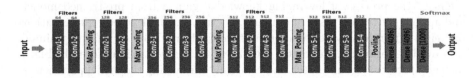

Fig. 3. VGG19 Architecture trained on ImageNet dataset [20]

3.2   Inception & Xception

Inception model (GoogLeNet) was proposed in C. Szegedy et al. [22] with 22 layer deep architecture. The Inception models employ the concept of "inception modules," which enable efficient multi-scale feature extraction. Inception module shown in Fig. 4 (a) employed convolutional filters with varying size to capture global & local information and pooling layer to reduce data dimensions. Then, concatenation of outputs is done afterwards. The latest iteration of inception V3 has been used in proposed model. Another variation of Inception called Xception (extreme inception) was proposed by F. Chollet [4] and used the depth

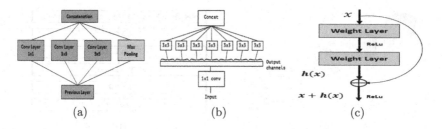

Fig. 4. (a) Inception Module (b) Xception Module (c) Residual Learning block [6]

wise convolution scheme which has two separate blocks of points-wise (1×1) and depth-wise (3×3) convolution filters (Fig. 4(b)). These filters reduced the computational cost by reducing number of parameters.

3.3 Residual Network (ResNet)

H. Kaiming et al. in [6] introduced the Residual Neural network (ResNet) with the key innovation in leveraging the residual (skip) connections which allowed learning of differentials between input and output. A residual learning block is shown in Fig. 4(c) and it also contain batch normalization with rectified linear activation function. Moreover, ResNet incorporates bottleneck blocks in its deeper layers, which consist of three convolutional layers. The first 1×1 convolutional layer reduces input feature map dimensionality. The subsequent 3×3 convolutional layer performs the primary computation, capturing detailed patterns. The final 1×1 convolutional layer increases output feature map dimensionality, enabling complex relationship representation. Bottleneck blocks efficiently handle deep networks, reducing computational burden and addressing the vanishing gradient problem.

3.4 DenseNet

Huang et al. [9] in 2016 presented Dense Convolutional Network (DenseNet) with distinctive connection pattern shown in Fig. 5 (a) which tackled the problem of gradient vanishing problem. In a DenseNet, each layer receives direct inputs from all preceding layers, not just the one below it. The feature maps of all previous layers are concatenated and used as inputs to the current layer, forming a dense block. This dense connection ensures maximum information flow between layers and facilitates gradient propagation.

3.5 MobileNet

A. G. Howard et al [8] created MobileNets considering difficulties in deploying models on low power devices. MobileNets employ depth-wise separable convolutions, illustrated in Fig. 5(b), to significantly reduce the number of parameters and operations required, as compared to traditional CNNs. The incorporation of

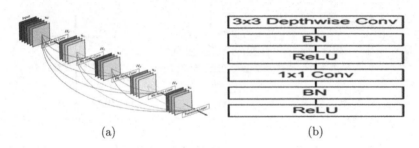

(a)   (b)

Fig. 5. (a) A 5 layer dense block [9] (b) The Depth-wise separable Convolution block use in [18]

depth-wise separable convolution was done owing to its ability to curtail the number of parameters and aggregation of channels feature representation in higher dimensional space. In proposed model, we have considered the recent iteration of MobileNet i.e. MobileNetV3 [7] which is more effective and precise.

3.6   EfficientNet

M. Tan et al. [24] introduced the efficientnet family (B0-B7) whose objective was to create model with high computational efficiency as well as state of the art performance. this was achieved by compound scaling the neural network in terms of depth, breadth and resolution. These parameters were optimized using grid-search algorithm. EfficientNet also incorporates other efficiency-boosting techniques, such as:

- Swish activation function: A non-linear activation function that is smoother than the commonly used ReLU function and has been shown to improve accuracy.
- Squeeze-and-Excitation (SE) blocks: A module that learns to selectively emphasize informative features and suppress uninformative ones, leading to better feature representation.
- Efficient channel attention (ECA): A module that efficiently models channel interactions to capture long-range dependencies in feature maps.

When evaluating these architectures, VGG models are characterized by their straightforward architectures but come with high computational costs. ResNet enables the training of exceptionally deep networks, although it can be memory-intensive. MobileNet focuses on efficiency, primarily designed for mobile devices. DenseNet emphasizes feature reuse and gradient flow. Inception and Xception employ parallel convolutions with distinct strategies, while EfficientNet aims to optimize both efficiency and accuracy. The selection of an architecture depends on the specific task requirements and the computational resources at hand (Fig. 6).

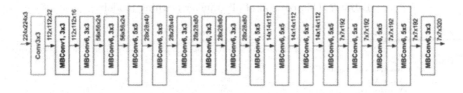

Fig. 6. Baseline Network which is designated as EfficientNetB0 [24]

4   Results and Discussion

In this paper, we have done performance analysis of various neural network models using Transfer learning against databases which are listed in Table 1. As we can see in Table 1, most of the dataset are unbalanced except Kaggle Village synthetic Insect Dataset [12]. We have performing benchmarking against C. Xie et al. [31], kaggle village synthetic insect dataset [12] and IP102 provided by X. Wu et al. [30]. In the proposed model, the weights of base layer of standard neural network model trained on ImageNet dataset except output layer are freezed while Global average layer, dense layer (1024 neurons) and output layer with neurons equal to number of classes of dataset (e.g. IP102 - 102 classes) is added in a sequential manner. Then, model is trained on dataset splitted in the ratio of 6:3:1 (train:test:validation) with learning rate of 0.0001 and Adam as an optimizer. In the fine-tuning process, the base layer weights are unfreezed and model is again trained. The model checkpoint was also considered while training. Data augmentation with rotation, width shift, shearing, zoom and flipping using Image data generator function of tensor-flow library. was also done in order to increase the effectiveness of training model and control the overfitting.

Table 1. Different Datasets used in classification of Insect Pest

Dataset	Availability	No. of samples	Samples range per class	Distribution	Classes	Year
J. Wang [28]	Yes	832	55–100	Uneven	10	2009
Ziyi Liu [15]	No	5136	183–50	Uneven	12	2016
Chengjun Xie [31]	Yes	4500	87–150	Uneven	40	2018
Ahmad A. Alfarisy [1]	No	4511	110–708	Uneven	13	2018
Xiaoping Wu (IP102) [30]	Yes	75222	71–5740	Uneven	102	2019
L. Liu [14]	No	88670	5302–25364	Uneven	16	2019
R. Wang [29]	No	49707	208–12783	Uneven	14	2021
Kaggle Insect Dataset [12]	Yes	10000	300	Even	10	2022

Table 2. Comparison of all transfer learning models

Model	Performance Measure	C. Xie [31]				Kaggle Village Synthetic [12]				IP102 [30]			
		Precision	Recall	F1-score	Accuracy	Precision	Recall	F1-score	Accuracy	Precision	Recall	F1-score	Accuracy
VGG16	Macro Avg.	0.93	0.90	0.91	92	0.72	0.72	0.72	72	0.55	0.46	0.47	58
	Weighted Avg.	0.93	0.92	0.92		0.72	0.72	0.72		0.59	0.58	0.57	
VGG19	Macro Avg.	0.95	0.94	0.94	95	0.74	0.74	0.74	74	0.39	0.31	0.31	46
	Weighted Avg.	0.95	0.95	0.94		0.74	0.74	0.74		0.46	0.46	0.43	
InceptionV3	Macro Avg.	0.98	0.98	0.98	98	0.96	0.96	0.96	96	0.61	0.55	0.56	65
	Weighted Avg.	0.98	0.98	0.98		0.96	0.96	0.96		0.65	0.65	0.64	
Xception	Macro Avg.	0.99	0.99	0.99	**99**	0.97	0.97	0.97	97	0.63	0.60	0.61	68
	Weighted Avg.	0.99	0.99	0.99		0.97	0.97	0.97		0.69	0.68	0.68	
ResNet50	Macro Avg.	0.98	0.98	0.98	98	0.94	0.93	0.93	93	0.60	0.55	0.56	63
	Weighted Avg.	0.98	0.98	0.98		0.94	0.93	0.93		0.65	0.63	0.63	
MobileNetV2	Macro Avg.	0.98	0.97	0.97	98	0.95	0.95	0.95	95	0.57	0.53	0.53	61
	Weighted Avg.	0.98	0.98	0.98		0.95	0.95	0.95		0.65	0.61	0.62	
DenseNet121	Macro Avg.	0.99	0.99	0.99	**99**	0.96	0.95	0.95	95	0.60	0.57	0.57	65
	Weighted Avg.	0.99	0.99	0.99		0.96	0.95	0.95		0.67	0.65	0.65	
EfficientNetB7	Macro Avg.	0.99	0.98	0.98	**99**	0.98	0.98	0.98	**98**	0.64	0.63	0.63	**70**
	Weighted Avg.	0.99	0.99	0.99		0.98	0.98	0.98		0.70	0.70	0.70	

4.1   Comparison of All the Models W.r.t Each Database

As seen in Table 2 and Fig. 7, EfficientNetB7 stands out as the top-performing transfer learning model on the all Datasets, primarily because of its excellent balance between model complexity and efficiency. However, each model has its own set of strengths and weaknesses. Therefore, choosing the most appropriate model depends on various factors such as computational resources, dataset size, and task complexity. It is essential to consider these specific requirements when making a selection.

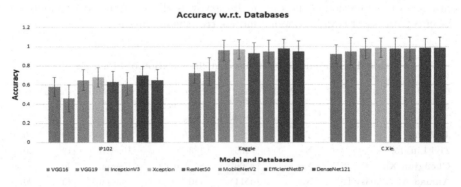

Fig. 7. Classification Accuracy for each database C. Xie [31], Village Synthetic [12] & IP102 dataset [30]

4.2   Explanation Through Grad-CAM

The Grad-CAM activation method [19] is employed to visually emphasize the regions in an input image that hold significant importance for the predictions made by deep learning models. This technique assists in interpreting and comprehending the inner workings of the model. By examining the Fig. 8, we observe that the EfficientNet model has effectively learned intricate patterns and features from the input data, with a particular emphasis on the region of interest. This indicates that the EfficientNet model is able to focus on and capture relevant information more effectively compared to other models.

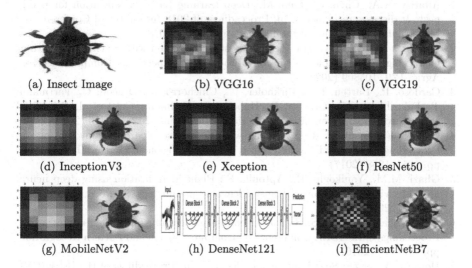

(a) Insect Image   (b) VGG16   (c) VGG19

(d) InceptionV3   (e) Xception   (f) ResNet50

(g) MobileNetV2   (h) DenseNet121   (i) EfficientNetB7

Fig. 8. (a) Original image while (b)-(i) depicts the heatmap along with the superimposed gradient activation map for each model.

5   Conclusion Ad Future Work

In this paper, a variety of deep learning models, including VGG16, VGG19, ResNet50, EfficientNetB7, MobileNetV2, InceptionV3 and Xception are used as base model for the task of classification using mechanism of transfer learning. Different dataset like Kaggle, Xie and IP102 are used for bench-marking the results with an objective of getting improvement in accuracy. After conducting extensive training and evaluation, the EfficientNet B7 model emerged as the top performer, surpassing the other architectures in terms of accuracy. This result underscores the effectiveness of the EfficientNet architecture, which incorporates advanced design principles and efficient scaling methods. However, it is essential to note that accuracy alone does not provide a comprehensive assessment of model performance. Additional considerations such as computational efficiency, model size, and inference speed should also be taken into account when selecting a model for real-world applications. Moreover, the IP102 dataset has quality issues as a lot of images are taken from slides, have no objects, presence of improper set of insect life cycles or have watermarks which is why the efficiency of various models is low. The future work entails the standardisation of dataset, data augmentation strategies exploration, usage of ensemble method and design of domain specific adaptation models.

References

1. Alfarisy, A.A., Chen, Q., Guo, M.: Deep learning based classification for paddy pests & diseases recognition. In: Proceedings of 2018 International Conference on Mathematics and Artificial Intelligence, pp. 21–25 (2018)
2. Ayan, E., Erbay, H., Varçın, F.: Crop pest classification with a genetic algorithm-based weighted ensemble of deep convolutional neural networks. Comput. Electron. Agric. **179**, 105809 (2020)
3. Cardoso, P., Barton, P.S., Birkhofer, K., Chichorro, F., Deacon, C., Fartmann, T., Fukushima, C.S., Gaigher, R., Habel, J.C., Hallmann, C.A., et al.: Scientists' warning to humanity on insect extinctions. Biol. Cons. **242**, 108426 (2020)
4. Chollet, F.: Xception: deep learning with depthwise separable convolutions. In: Proceedings of the IEEE Conference on Computer Vision and Pattern Recognition, pp. 1251–1258 (2017)
5. Ghazi, M.M., Yanikoglu, B., Aptoula, E.: Plant identification using deep neural networks via optimization of transfer learning parameters. Neurocomputing **235**, 228–235 (2017)
6. He, K., Zhang, X., Ren, S., Sun, J.: Deep residual learning for image recognition. In: Proceedings of the IEEE Conference on Computer Vision and Pattern Recognition, pp. 770–778 (2016)
7. Howard, A., et al.: Searching for mobilenetv3. In: Proceedings of the IEEE/CVF International Conference on Computer Vision, pp. 1314–1324 (2019)
8. Howard, A.G., et al.: Mobilenets: efficient convolutional neural networks for mobile vision applications. arXiv preprint arXiv:1704.04861 (2017)
9. Huang, G., Liu, Z., Van Der Maaten, L., Weinberger, K.Q.: Densely connected convolutional networks. In: Proceedings of the IEEE Conference on Computer Vision and Pattern Recognition, pp. 4700–4708 (2017)
10. Kong, J., Yang, C., Xiao, Y., Lin, S., Ma, K., Zhu, Q.: A graph-related high-order neural network architecture via feature aggregation enhancement for identification application of diseases and pests. Comput. Intell. Neurosci. **2022**, 1–16 (2022)
11. Krizhevsky, A., Sutskever, I., Hinton, G.E.: ImageNet classification with deep convolutional neural networks. Adv. Neural Inf. Process. Syst. **25**, 1–9 (2012)
12. Lanz, V.: Insect village synthetic dataset (2022). https://www.kaggle.com/dsv/4111904
13. Li, Y., Wang, H., Dang, L.M., Sadeghi-Niaraki, A., Moon, H.: Crop pest recognition in natural scenes using convolutional neural networks. Comput. Electron. Agric. **169**, 105174 (2020)
14. Liu, L., et al.: Pestnet: an end-to-end deep learning approach for large-scale multi-class pest detection and classification. IEEE Access **7**, 45301–45312 (2019). https://doi.org/10.1109/ACCESS.2019.2909522
15. Liu, Z., Gao, J., Yang, G., Zhang, H., He, Y.: Localization and classification of paddy field pests using a saliency map and deep convolutional neural network. Sci. Rep. **6**(1), 20410 (2016)
16. Miller, G.L., Foottit, R.G.: The taxonomy of crop pests: the aphids. In: Insect Biodiversity: Science and Society, pp. 627–639 (2017)

17. NBAIR: national bureau of agriculture insect research (2023). https://databases. nbair.res.in/insectpests/index.php

18. Sandler, M., Howard, A., Zhu, M., Zhmoginov, A., Chen, L.C.: Mobilenetv2: inverted residuals and linear bottlenecks. In: Proceedings of the IEEE Conference on Computer Vision and Pattern Recognition, pp. 4510–4520 (2018)

19. Selvaraju, R.R., Cogswell, M., Das, A., Vedantam, R., Parikh, D., Batra, D.: Grad-cam: visual explanations from deep networks via gradient-based localization. In: Proceedings of the IEEE International Conference on Computer Vision, pp. 618–626 (2017)

20. Simonyan, K., Zisserman, A.: Very deep convolutional networks for large-scale image recognition. arXiv preprint arXiv:1409.1556 (2014)

21. van der Sluijs, J.P.: Insect decline, an emerging global environmental risk. Curr. Opin. Environ. Sustainab. **46**, 39–42 (2020)

22. Szegedy, C., et al.: Going deeper with convolutions. In: Proceedings of the IEEE Conference on Computer Vision and Pattern Recognition, pp. 1–9 (2015)

23. Szegedy, C., Vanhoucke, V., Ioffe, S., Shlens, J., Wojna, Z.: Rethinking the inception architecture for computer vision. In: Proceedings of the IEEE Conference on Computer Vision and Pattern Recognition, pp. 2818–2826 (2016)

24. Tan, M., Le, Q.: EfficientNet: rethinking model scaling for convolutional neural networks. In: International Conference on Machine Learning, pp. 6105–6114. PMLR (2019)

25. Thenmozhi, K., Reddy, U.S.: Crop pest classification based on deep convolutional neural network and transfer learning. Comput. Electron. Agric. **164**, 104906 (2019)

26. Ung, H.T., Ung, H.Q., Nguyen, B.T.: An efficient insect pest classification using multiple convolutional neural network based models. arXiv preprint arXiv:2107.12189 (2021)

27. Wang, J., Lin, C., Ji, L., Liang, A.: A new automatic identification system of insect images at the order level. Knowl.-Based Syst. **33**, 102–110 (2012)

28. Wang, J., Markert, K., Everingham, M.: Learning models for object recognition from natural language descriptions. In: Proceedings of the British Machine Vision Conference (2009)

29. Wang, R., Liu, L., Xie, C., Yang, P., Li, R., Zhou, M.: Agripest: a large-scale domain-specific benchmark dataset for practical agricultural pest detection in the wild. Sensors **21**(5), 1601 (2021)

30. Wu, X., Zhan, C., Lai, Y.K., Cheng, M.M., Yang, J.: Ip102: a large-scale benchmark dataset for insect pest recognition. In: Proceedings of the IEEE/CVF Conference on Computer Vision and Pattern Recognition, pp. 8787–8796 (2019)

31. Xie, C., Wang, R., Zhang, J., Chen, P., Dong, W., Li, R., Chen, T., Chen, H.: Multi-level learning features for automatic classification of field crop pests. Comput. Electron. Agric. **152**, 233–241 (2018)

32. Xie, C., Zhang, J., Li, R., Li, J., Hong, P., Xia, J., Chen, P.: Automatic classification for field crop insects via multiple-task sparse representation and multiple-kernel learning. Comput. Electron. Agric. **119**, 123–132 (2015)

Federated Scaling of Pre-trained Models for Deep Facial Expression Recognition

P. V. N. Pooja Srihitha[ID], Mridula Verma[✉][ID],
and Munaga V. N. K. Prasad[ID]

Institute for Development and Research in Banking Technology, Hyderabad, India
{pvnpoojasrihitha,vmridula,mvnkprasad}@idrbt.ac.in

Abstract. Building an efficient deep learning-based Facial Expression Recognition (FER) system is challenging due to the requirements of large amounts of personal data and the rise in data privacy concerns. Federated learning has emerged as a promising solution for such problems, which however is communication-inefficient. Recently, pre-trained models have shown effective performance in federated learning setups regarding convergence. In this paper, we extend the traditional FER towards a new paradigm, where we study the performance of federated fine-tuning of standard vision pre-trained models for FER. More specifically, we propose a Federated Deep Facial Expression Recognition (FedFER) framework, where clients jointly learn to fuse the representations generated by pre-trained deep learning models rather than training a large-scale model from scratch without sharing any data. With the help of extensive experimentation using standard pre-trained vision models (ResNet-50, VGG-16, Xception, Vision Transformers) and benchmark datasets (CK+, FERG, FER-2013, JAFFE, MUG), this paper presents interesting perspectives for future research in the direction of federated Deep FER.

Keywords: Facial Expression Recognition · Deep Neural Networks · Federated Learning · Pre-trained vision models

1 Introduction

Facial expression recognition (FER) is imperative to human-centric computing applications, focusing on how well computers can recognize and understand human emotions and affective states. Real-world applications of automated FER include assistive robotics [8], healthcare [30], fatigue detection in drivers [21], advertisement recommendations [2], financial sector [22] and many more. A significant challenge for deep learning-based facial expression recognition (FER) methods is the requirement for vast amounts of data from diverse users and conditions. The traditional centralized data processing approach raises concerns about transparency and trust from end-users, particularly in light of privacy-sensitive facial expression data. Strict privacy regulations limit personal data collection without consent, making building a comprehensive FER model through

H. Kaur et al. (Eds.): CVIP 2023, CCIS 2011, pp. 90–101, 2024.
https://doi.org/10.1007/978-3-031-58535-7_8

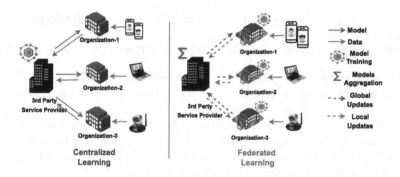

Fig. 1. Centralized machine learning framework vs. Federated learning framework for FER.

data integration challenging. Organizations often have limited data and supervision, further complicating the development of FER models.

Federated Learning (FL) [4,18] has gained significant attention as a solution to challenges posed by privacy and data management laws. Federated Learning has emerged as a promising solution that has captured the attention of both industry and academia while maintaining the privacy of individual datasets. FL is a decentralized collaborative learning technique where machine learning models are trained on multiple local datasets stored on various isolated devices such as smartphones, computers, and wearable devices without centralizing the training data [17]. The local training results, such as parameters or gradients, are then shared with a central server, which aggregates the results received by individual clients to calculate a global model.

Despite many successful efforts in federated learning and facial expression recognition, federated facial expression recognition is not a much-explored area. Some recent works include [32,37]. In [37], two models based on ResNet50V2 architecture (without pre-trained weights) are trained, one for the representation learning from unlabeled facial images to extract effective facial features, whereas the second for recognizing the facial expression in the few-shot learning setting. In [32], authors proposed an unsupervised personalization approach to learn a lightweight model with the MobileNetV2 architecture [33]. In this paper, a novel framework for Federated Facial Expression Recognition **FedFER** is proposed, which is based on scaling the state-of-the-art pre-trained computer vision models in a federated fashion (see Fig. 1). We are focusing on the cross-silo setup, where clients (organizations) utilize the facial expression recognition service to better understand their customers, with the help of a global third-party service provider, which captures and aggregates the facial dynamics knowledge from these silo-ed organizations without capturing the original face data. It is the first time pre-trained initialization is being explored for facial expression recognition tasks. We have selected four state-of-the-art pre-trained models, Resnet-50 [11], Vision Transformers [9], VGG-16 [38], and Xception [7], for the purpose of experimentation. The pre-trained weights with these models will help the FedAvg algorithm to converge faster.

The key aspects of this research work are as follows:

- This work presents Federated Facial Expression Recognition (FedFER) - an effort to examine the scalability of pre-trained vision models for facial expression recognition within a federated setting.
- Detailed experimentation with multiple CNN-backed pre-trained models and the recent popular Transformer-based vision model on benchmark datasets (CK+, FERG, FER-2013, JAFFE, and MUG). This study also demonstrates the impact of the number of clients on performance.
- The efficacy of the proposed FedFER framework is demonstrated by comparing the performance of pre-trained models for FER tasks in centralized and federated setups.

2 Related Works

2.1 Facial Expression Recognition

Deep learning-based end-to-end FER frameworks have recently been utilized to extract features that perform noticeably better than models that categorize facial expressions based on manually extracted features [19]. Following the re-usability concept, the current trend in deep learning is to utilize knowledge from pre-trained models for specific purposes. Pre-trained models are self-built networks trained on vast amounts of data from a general domain. A few examples of pre-trained models in computer vision include Alex-Net [1], VGG [38], VGG-face [15], ResNet [11], Xception [7]. According to [14], incorporating additional data can lead to developing models with high capacity and reduced overfitting, thereby enhancing performance in facial expression recognition. One good example is set in [16], where authors observed that pre-training on an enormous face or image dataset could improve expression recognition performance. Following this, several recent FER approaches utilize the pre-trained vision models [12,23]. However, all these approaches consider a centralized training approach, in which sensitive facial expression data has to be shared with a third-party FER service provider.

2.2 Federated Learning

Federated Learning [3,20] has emerged as a promising solution, which enables numerous edge devices to learn jointly while utilizing a global model. Following the principle of re-usability, the latest trend in federated learning approaches is to explore federated fine-tuning, where large-scale pre-trained models can be utilized for downstream tasks, for which the datasets need not to be shared with a centralized server [6]. This helps in reducing the adversarial effects of system and data heterogeneity [39,41,43]. A few works have focused on applying federated learning to biometrics, mainly face modality, as a new research area.

[35] demonstrated that incorporating face images can greatly improve the accuracy of pre-trained face recognition systems on commonly used face verification benchmark datasets. Additionally, [27] utilized a rigorous approach of differential privacy to securely transmit auxiliary embedding centers for federated face recognition. Recent works in federated facial expression recognition either do not focus on pre-trained models [37] or target federated pre-training [32]. In contrast, following the principle of re-usability, we consider pre-trained models that are learned to extract semantic representations from large, task-independent corpora and fine-tuned for FER tasks with datasets available at different clients (organizations).

3   FedFER: Federated Deep Facial Expression Recognition

3.1   Proposed Architecture

The proposed architecture of the FedFER aims to utilize pre-trained large models by extending their usability from a general domain to a specific domain of facial expression recognition in a privacy-preserved way. Organizations that are interested in making use of an efficient facial expression recognition solution for a better understanding of their user's or customer's emotions are the clients in the federated learning setup, and the server is a third-party service provider who is involved in providing a global deep-learning based FER solution to these clients. Our framework follows the regime of exploring new larger models with at least 25 million parameters (Resnet-50) in cross-silo federated learning. Thus, it is assumed that these clients have sufficient resources for performing computations (such as data collection from user and model training) on their own user/customer data. In contrast to the existing federated facial expression recognition methodologies, which consider training a FER model from scratch, we propose to utilize the pre-trained weights to be fine-tuned on the FER task in a privacy-preserved distributed fashion.

Our framework is based on three crucial considerations. First, due to privacy concerns, the datasets for FER are scarcely available. With insufficient datasets with multiple variations, the minimum requirement of creating a good generalized FER model is not satisfied. Secondly, random initialization usually leads to many communication rounds to achieve convergence and the cost of communication per round [29]. Thirdly, pre-training enables the learned global models to be more stable compared to the models with random initialization, reducing the impact of system heterogeneity [5]. The entire training set, obtained from all clients, is grouped, randomly shuffled, and then evenly divided among the same number of clients.

Consider having X number of clients, each having a unique private dataset D_a for $a \in \{1, \cdots, X\}$ and $\bigcup D_a = D$, $\forall a$. Each client c produces successive local pre-trained model $\mathbf{M}_{ar}$ by training it on D_a and sends their locally optimized $\mathbf{M}_{ar}$ to the server at every communication round r. The server uses the federated averaging algorithm (FedAvg) [25] to aggregate the individual models to obtain a global model $\mathbf{M}_r$ by performing,

$$\mathbf{M}_r = \sum_{c=1}^{X} \frac{D_a}{D} \mathbf{M}_{ar} \tag{1}$$

The aggregated weights (unified model) are then re-transmitted to each client, providing a unified summary of the FER at round r. Each client is presumed to be able to train the entire model without model breaking. The local training, updating, server aggregation, and broadcasting process are repeated multiple times until the global model converges to a satisfactory accuracy level. In place of sharing the initial model with random weights, in this work, we consider sharing the models with pre-trained weights so that convergence at a global optimum can be ensured. To facilitate easy reproduction of the results and comparison with other methods, unlike other studies in the field, this research utilizes publicly accessible pre-trained models - Resnet-50, VGG, Xception, and Vision-Transformer (ViT).

3.2 FedFER with Resnet-50, VGG, and Xception

In the proposed architecture, the pre-trained weights of the state-of-the-art vision model are shared among multiple clients to get fine-tuned on their own set of customer facial expressions. Each client has a local copy of the model (frozen layers of pre-trained models provided by the server) and a private facial expression dataset for fine-tuning. The fully connected dense layer is added at each client to match the number of classes according to the client task. The model with the new dense layer is trained on the task-specific local dataset while initially keeping the pre-trained layers fixed. After a predetermined number of epochs, the updates to the model will be transmitted to the server, which averages the model updates obtained from each device using a federated averaging algorithm. The procedure will be repeated multiple times through communication until either convergence is attained or the desired level of accuracy is achieved. We have experimented with Resnet-50, VGG-16, and Xception models, which are pre-trained on computer vision tasks, such as image classification, object detection, and image segmentation. All the three models Resnet50 [11] - a 50-layered deep residual network, VGG16 [38], and Xception [7] model that utilizes the depth-wise separable convolutions are trained on the ImageNet dataset. Though trained on the same Image Net dataset, they are all powerful architectures but have different trade-offs and are suited to different use cases.

3.3 FedFER with ViT

Vision Transformer [9] extracts the visual features using image initialization and patch embedding technologies. A pre-trained Vision Transformer model and private client data, such as individual frames of faces, would be near the multiple clients. Then, local dataset images are processed by a series of self-attention blocks, also known as Transformer blocks. These blocks extract features from the images by comparing each pixel to all other pixels. This step is performed locally on the clients. The local feature maps are then combined at a main server. A fully connected layer receives the aggregated feature map as input and generates the output values for each category of facial expressions. The clients are then provided with the revised model parameters for the following round of federated learning. Average the model updates from each device using a federated averaging algorithm. Repeated communication rounds several times until convergence or satisfactory accuracy is reached.

4   Experiments and Result Analysis

4.1   Datasets

A total of five benchmark FER datasets are utilized in this work. The **FER-2013** dataset[1] is considered the most complex dataset containing several challenging scenarios arising due to unconstrained data capturing. A few of these challenging scenarios are the low-resolution image (48 × 48) pixels, variation in head pose, and illumination, which significantly impact how well facial expression models function. 28,709 training images, 3,589 validation images, and 3,589 test images with seven expression labels are included in this dataset. The 4,113 training images and 881 test images in the Extended Cohn Kanade **CK+** dataset[2] each measure 170 × 170 pixels. A total of 55,767 images are included in **FERG**[3], of which 48,767 are used for training and the remaining 7000 are used for testing. JAFFE dataset[4] is made up of 213 grayscale photos of 10 Japanese female expressions, with each image having 256 × 256 pixels in size. The **MUG** dataset[5] images are of resolution 896 × 896. This dataset contains 800 training images and 21 test images.

4.2   Experimental Setup

The proposed method utilizes pre-trained vision models publicly available in Keras and TensorFlow. We used TensorFlow Federated (TFF) in our implementation, an open-source federated learning research library focused on distributed computing. In our experiments, we considered several remote clients having CPUs capable of handling low-scale training. These clients represent real-world scenarios where data may be distributed across different devices and network conditions. By leveraging these CPU-based clients, the proposed approach aims to evaluate the performance of a federated learning system in a practical setting and identify challenges and opportunities in real-world deployment. The experiments aim to demonstrate the system's effectiveness and provide insights

---

[1] https://www.kaggle.com/c/challenges-in-representation-learning-facial-expression-recognition-challenge/data.

[2] http://vasc.ri.cmu.edu/idb/html/face/facial_expression/.

[3] https://grail.cs.washington.edu/projects/deepexpr/ferg-2d-db.html.

[4] https://www.kasrl.org/jaffe_download.html.

[5] https://mug.ee.auth.gr/fed/.

into the impact of hyperparameter selection on model accuracy and convergence speed. We have utilized the Adam optimizer, which combines the stochastic gradient descent technique with individual learning rates for each parameter. The default number of clients is set as 10; 50 training epoch is set for each client. The initial learning rate is set as 0.001. A mini-batch size 32 is used, and the experiments are performed with 50 communication rounds between clients and the server. The metrics we used for comparison are accuracy, precision, recall, and F1-score.

4.3 Result Analysis

Our first set of experiments is focused on identifying the impact of federated fine-tuning for facial expression recognition in terms of precision, recall, and F1- score. We consider the FER-2013 dataset evenly distributed across ten clients in an iid fashion. Results are shown in Table 1. It can be observed that the VGG-16 model is performing better in terms of recall and F1 score with FedFER. This means that the VGG-16 model can accurately identify positive instances while having a low false positive rate. Higher recall is particularly important in scenarios where misclassification can have significant consequences in facial expression recognition datasets. In the federated fine-tuning, the Resnet-50 model has the highest precision score among the four models. The lower scores in the federated setting can be due to the added complexity and data heterogeneity compared to the centralized setting. These results indicate that while the federated fine-tuning approach improved the performance of the models compared to centralized fine-tuning, there is still room for improvement.

Table 1. Performance summary of Federated-FER and Centralised-FER for FER-2013 Dataset. Blue-colored values are best achieved for centralized-FER, whereas red-colored values are best achieved for Fed-FER.

Pre-trained models	Finetuning	Precision	Recall	F1-score
Resnet-50	Centralised	0.86	0.932	0.898
VGG-16	Centralised	0.958	0.840	0.895
Xception	Centralised	0.831	0.870	0.850
VIT	Centralised	0.885	0.913	0.899
Resnet-50	Federated	0.862	0.843	0.853
VGG-16	Federated	0.845	0.872	0.858
Xception	Federated	0.857	0.803	0.829
VIT	Federated	0.803	0.867	0.834

In the second set of experiments, five benchmark FER datasets are considered for centralized and federated fine-tuning, comprehensively evaluating the proposed method. Table 2 shows results in terms of accuracy. We also compared our results with multiple recent research works. The text in blue represents the best results on the corresponding dataset for centralized implementation, whereas the text in red represents the best results in federated setup. In this comparison, we only considered the datasets considered in the corresponding papers. The comparison between the centralized and federated learning approaches provides valuable insights into the effectiveness of the proposed federated fine-tuning app-roach for improving the performance of facial expression recognition tasks. The results show that different models perform best on different datasets, with some models achieving higher accuracy in centralized fine-tuning while others perform better in federated fine-tuning.

Table 2. Accuracy summary of federated averaging implementations and centralized implementations on facial expression datasets.

Pre-trained models	Fine tuning	Fer-2013	CK+	FERG	JAFFE	MUG
Resnet-50$_{ours}$	Centralized	85.37	96.8	99	94.3	99.8
Resnet-50 [10]	Centralized	73.40	89.56	–	–	–
Resnet-50 [42]	Centralized	74.08	98.52	99.83	–	–
Resnet-50 [24]	Centralized	–	95.40	90.50	98.70	–
VGG-16$_{ours}$	Centralized	84.07	95.0	99.04	93.8	95
VGG-16 [31]	Centralized	74.17	99.18	98.75	–	–
VGG-16 [28]	Centralized	78.00	98.00	98.00	–	–
VGG-16 [36]	Centralized	67.40	99.18	–	–	–
Xception$_{ours}$	Centralized	78.19	97.0	98.08	95.60	96.63
Xception [26]	Centralized	77.92	99.47	92.50	–	–
Xception [34]	Centralized	65.00	97.24	–	–	–
VIT$_{ours}$	Centralized	83.71	98.17	97.06	94.83	95.7
VIT [13]	Centralized	74.66	98.91	–	–	–
VIT [40]	Centralized	74.84	–	–	–	–
FedAffect [37]	Federated	84.9	–	97.3	–	–
Resnet-50	Federated	78.94	99.60	99.27	93.34	92.42
VGG-16	Federated	82.04	98.21	98.35	93.50	93.90
Xception	Federated	75.02	98.06	94.40	94.60	95.63
VIT	Federated	78.75	96.04	98.06	95.50	92.89

The impact of the varying number of clients on the FER-2013 dataset is shown in Table 3. It is observed that with an increasing number of clients, com-munication rounds are also increasing. Among other models, the number of communication rounds required between clients and the server is higher with Xception. Interestingly, with VIT 10 clients reduce the communication rounds compared to three and six clients.

Table 3. Number of training rounds required to reach 75% of accuracy on the FER-2013 dataset with varying number of clients.

Pre-trained models	3 Clients	6 Clients	10 Clients
Resnet-50	30	42	44
VGG-16	32	38	44
Xception	42	47	50
VIT	32	35	27

Figure 2 demonstrates the performance of the models for individual communication rounds. In the case of ResNet-50, the accuracy-communication round curves are much smoother with JAFFE and FERG datasets compared to MUG, CK+, and FER-2013 datasets. This also explains the inherent complexity of the FER-2013 dataset. Interestingly, the curves with the Xception model do not fluctuate with all the datasets. The accuracy-communication round curves for the VGG-16 model show a consistent progression when on the FER-2013 dataset compared to other datasets such as CK+, Jaffe, FERG, and MUG. The results were not consistently increasing or decreasing but showed slight fluctuations. However, overall, there was an upward trend in the performance. The initial stages of the VIT model performance were higher than other curves across all datasets, with the FERG dataset having high sharp spikes and occasional increases.

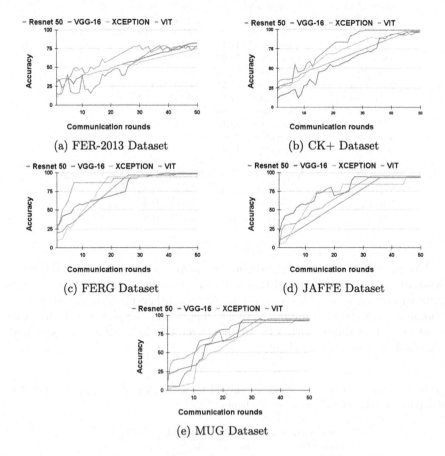

Fig. 2. Comparison of accuracy after each communication round for all FER Datasets.

5 Conclusion

This paper presented another view of utilizing federated learning for facial expression recognition in support of the claim that federated learning can perform just as well as centralized learning without needing to exchange or centralize private and sensitive data. It also showed that the proposed federated fine-tuning framework is resilient and performs on par with a centralized learning process despite the data distribution's decentralized data and asymmetrical aspects. Results of evaluations also indicate that the suggested approach is workable and outperforms the federated learning default configuration in terms of model correctness, stability, and communication effectiveness. We recognize that experimentation with multiple non-IID settings may be considered, which we will further investigate in future work.

References

1. Alom, M.Z., et al.: The history began from alexnet: a comprehensive survey on deep learning approaches. arXiv preprint arXiv:1803.01164 (2018)
2. Bandyopadhyay, S., Thakur, S.S., Mandal, J.K.: Online recommendation system using human facial expression based emotion detection: a proposed method. In: Mandal, J.K., Buyya, R., De, D. (eds.) Proceedings of International Conference on Advanced Computing Applications. AISC, vol. 1406, pp. 459–468. Springer, Singapore (2022). https://doi.org/10.1007/978-981-16-5207-3_38
3. Bonawitz, K., et al.: Towards federated learning at scale: system design. Proc. Mach. Learn. Syst. 1, 374–388 (2019)
4. Chen, F., Long, G., Wu, Z., Zhou, T., Jiang, J.: Personalized federated learning with graph. arXiv preprint arXiv:2203.00829 (2022)
5. Chen, H.Y., Tu, C.H., Li, Z., Shen, H.W., Chao, W.L.: On pre-training for federated learning. arXiv preprint arXiv:2206.11488 (2022)
6. Chen, J., Xu, W., Guo, S., Wang, J., Zhang, J., Wang, H.: Fedtune: a deep dive into efficient federated fine-tuning with pre-trained transformers. arXiv preprint arXiv:2211.08025 (2022)
7. Chollet, F.: Xception: Deep learning with depthwise separable convolutions. In: Proceedings of the IEEE Conference on Computer Vision and Pattern Recognition, pp. 1251–1258 (2017)
8. Deng, J., Pang, G., Zhang, Z., Pang, Z., Yang, H., Yang, G.: CGAN based facial expression recognition for human-robot interaction. IEEE Access 7, 9848–9859 (2019)
9. Dosovitskiy, A., et al.: An image is worth 16x16 words: transformers for image recognition at scale. arXiv preprint arXiv:2010.11929 (2020)
10. Gupta, S., Kumar, P., Tekchandani, R.K.: Facial emotion recognition based real-time learner engagement detection system in online learning context using deep learning models. Multimedia Tools Appl. 82(8), 11365–11394 (2023)
11. He, K., Zhang, X., Ren, S., Sun, J.: Deep residual learning for image recognition. In: Proceedings of the IEEE Conference on Computer Vision and Pattern Recognition, pp. 770–778 (2016)
12. Huang, Q., Huang, C., Wang, X., Jiang, F.: Facial expression recognition with grid-wise attention and visual transformer. Inf. Sci. 580, 35–54 (2021)

13. Ji, X., Dong, Z., Han, Y., Lai, C.S., Zhou, G., Qi, D.: EMSN: an energy-efficient memristive sequencer network for human emotion classification in mental health monitoring. IEEE Trans. Consum. Electron. **69**, 1005–1016 (2023)
14. Kahou, S.E., et al.: Emonets: multimodal deep learning approaches for emotion recognition in video. J. Multimodal User Interfaces **10** (2015). https://doi.org/10.1007/s12193-015-0195-2
15. Kim, T., Yu, C., Lee, S.: Facial expression recognition using feature additive pooling and progressive fine-tuning of CNN. Electron. Lett. **54**(23), 1326–1328 (2018)
16. Knyazev, B., Shvetsov, R., Efremova, N., Kuharenko, A.: Convolutional neural networks pretrained on large face recognition datasets for emotion classification from video. arXiv preprint arXiv:1711.04598 (2017)
17. Konečnỳ, J., McMahan, H.B., Ramage, D., Richtárik, P.: Federated optimization: distributed machine learning for on-device intelligence. arXiv preprint arXiv:1610.02527 (2016)
18. Li, L., Fan, Y., Tse, M., Lin, K.Y.: A review of applications in federated learning. Comput. Ind. Eng. **149**, 106854 (2020). https://doi.org/10.1016/j.cie.2020.106854, https://www.sciencedirect.com/science/article/pii/S0360835220305532
19. Li, S., Deng, W.: Deep facial expression recognition: a survey. IEEE Trans. Affect. Comput. **13**, 1195–1215 (2020)
20. Li, T., Sahu, A.K., Talwalkar, A., Smith, V.: Federated learning: challenges, methods, and future directions. IEEE Signal Process. Mag. **37**(3), 50–60 (2020)
21. Liu, Z., Peng, Y., Hu, W.: Driver fatigue detection based on deeply-learned facial expression representation. J. Vis. Commun. Image Represent. **71**, 102723 (2020)
22. Luo, C., Fan, X., Yan, Y., Jin, H., Wang, X.: Optimization of three-dimensional face recognition algorithms in financial identity authentication. Int. J. Comput. Commun. Control **17**(3) (2022)
23. Ma, F., Sun, B., Li, S.: Robust facial expression recognition with convolutional visual transformers. arXiv preprint arXiv:2103.16854 (2021)
24. Mandal, M., Verma, M., Mathur, S., Vipparthi, S.K., Murala, S., Kranthi Kumar, D.: Regional adaptive affinitive patterns (RADAP) with logical operators for facial expression recognition. IET Image Proc. **13**(5), 850–861 (2019)
25. McMahan, B., Moore, E., Ramage, D., Hampson, S., Arcas, B.A.V.: Communication-efficient learning of deep networks from decentralized data. In: Singh, A., Zhu, J. (eds.) Proceedings of the 20th International Conference on Artificial Intelligence and Statistics. Proceedings of Machine Learning Research, vol. 54, pp. 1273–1282. PMLR, 20–22 April 2017. https://proceedings.mlr.press/v54/mcmahan17a.html
26. Meena, G., Mohbey, K.K.: Sentiment analysis on images using different transfer learning models. Procedia Comput. Sci. **218**, 1640–1649 (2023)
27. Meng, Q., Zhou, F., Ren, H., Feng, T., Liu, G., Lin, Y.: Improving federated learning face recognition via privacy-agnostic clusters. arXiv preprint arXiv:2201.12467 (2022)
28. Mohan, K., Seal, A., Krejcar, O., Yazidi, A.: Facial expression recognition using local gravitational force descriptor-based deep convolution neural networks. IEEE Trans. Instrum. Meas. **70**, 1–12 (2020)
29. Nguyen, J., Malik, K., Sanjabi, M., Rabbat, M.: Where to begin? exploring the impact of pre-training and initialization in federated learning. arXiv preprint arXiv:2206.15387 (2022)
30. Pávez, R., Díaz, J., Arango-López, J., Ahumada, D., Méndez, C., Moreira, F.: Emotion recognition in children with autism spectrum disorder using convolutional

neural networks. In: Rocha, Á., Adeli, H., Dzemyda, G., Moreira, F., Ramalho Correia, A.M. (eds.) WorldCIST 2021. AISC, vol. 1365, pp. 585–595. Springer, Cham (2021). https://doi.org/10.1007/978-3-030-72657-7_56

31. Putro, M.D., Nguyen, D.L., Jo, K.H.: A fast CPU real-time facial expression detector using sequential attention network for human-robot interaction. IEEE Trans. Industr. Inf. **18**(11), 7665–7674 (2022)

32. Salman, A., Busso, C.: Privacy preserving personalization for video facial expression recognition using federated learning. In: Proceedings of the 2022 International Conference on Multimodal Interaction, pp. 495–503 (2022)

33. Sandler, M., Howard, A., Zhu, M., Zhmoginov, A., Chen, L.C.: Mobilenetv2: inverted residuals and linear bottlenecks. In: Proceedings of the IEEE Conference on Computer Vision and Pattern Recognition, pp. 4510–4520 (2018)

34. Shahzad, T., Iqbal, K., Khan, M.A., Iqbal, N., et al.: Role of zoning in facial expression using deep learning. IEEE Access **11**, 16493–16508 (2023)

35. Shao, R., Perera, P., Yuen, P.C., Patel, V.M.: Federated face presentation attack detection. arXiv preprint arXiv:2005.14638 (2020)

36. Shehada, D., Turky, A., Khan, W., Khan, B., Hussain, A.: A lightweight facial emotion recognition system using partial transfer learning for visually impaired people. IEEE Access **11**, 36961–36969 (2023)

37. Shome, D., Kar, T.: Fedaffect: few-shot federated learning for facial expression recognition. In: Proceedings of the IEEE/CVF International Conference on Computer Vision, pp. 4168–4175 (2021)

38. Simonyan, K., Zisserman, A.: Very deep convolutional networks for large-scale image recognition. arXiv preprint arXiv:1409.1556 (2014)

39. Sun, G., Mendieta, M., Yang, T., Chen, C.: Exploring parameter-efficient fine-tuning for improving communication efficiency in federated learning. arXiv preprint arXiv:2210.01708 (2022)

40. Sun, M., et al.: Attention-rectified and texture-enhanced cross-attention transformer feature fusion network for facial expression recognition. IEEE Trans. Ind. Inf. **19**, 11823–11832 (2023)

41. Weller, O., Marone, M., Braverman, V., Lawrie, D., Van Durme, B.: Pretrained models for multilingual federated learning. arXiv preprint arXiv:2206.02291 (2022)

42. Zang, H., Foo, S.Y., Bernadin, S., Meyer-Baese, A.: Facial emotion recognition using asymmetric pyramidal networks with gradient centralization. IEEE Access **9**, 64487–64498 (2021)

43. Zhang, L., Shen, L., Ding, L., Tao, D., Duan, L.Y.: Fine-tuning global model via data-free knowledge distillation for non-iid federated learning. In: Proceedings of the IEEE/CVF Conference on Computer Vision and Pattern Recognition, pp. 10174–10183 (2022)

Damage Segmentation and Restoration of Ancient Wall Paintings for Preserving Cultural Heritage

Hardaat Singh Baath[1], Soham Shinde[1], Jinam Keniya[1], Priyanshu Ranjan Mishra[1], Anil Saini[2,3], and Dhiraj[2,3(✉)]

[1] Birla Institute of Technology and Science, Pilani, India
{f20212662,f20212927,f20211622}@goa.bits-pilani.ac.in,
f20212259@hyderabad.bits-pilani.ac.in
[2] Academy of Scientific and Innovative Research (AcSIR), Ghaziabad, India
{anil,dhiraj}@ceeri.res.in
[3] CSIR-Central Electronics Engineering Research Institute, Pilani, India

Abstract. Rajasthani paintings are unique and intriguing art forms representing India's rich cultural heritage. However, these ancient master pieces are deteriorating due to the passage of time, environmental factors, and human actions. Preserving and Restoring these delicate artworks is crucial. One approach to aid their digital restoration is leveraging advanced technologies like deep learning. This study applies image segmentation and restoration techniques to restore the Rajasthani murals in the Mandawa region of rural rajasthan, India. The main objective is to segment the damaged murals, generate their corresponding binary masks and restore the corresponding areas of the damaged image. The research aims to achieve robust and accurate predicted masks for the murals by utilizing state-of-the-art deep learning models and using their outputs as inputs for image restoration as the final restored output image. Extensive comparisons with different segmentation models show that the proposed approach outperforms the rest with an mIOU of 0.892. The proposed method also demonstrates remarkable inpainting results with an SSIM score of 0.9812 on test images. Results show that the method achieves promising restoration of damaged ancient Indian Wall Paintings.

Keywords: Image segmentation · Ancient Indian murals · Restoration · Image Inpainting · Ensemble approach · STAPLE

1 Introduction

Rajasthani murals, a significant part of India's cultural heritage, depict vibrant narratives and are known for their exquisite craftsmanship. However, they have suffered various damages over time, including color fading, cracks, peeling, and vandalism. Restoring these murals poses unique challenges due to their complexity and fragility, requiring specialized techniques and expertise. Traditional restoration methods are time consuming, subjective, and may not capture the original nuances effectively.

H. Kaur et al. (Eds.): CVIP 2023, CCIS 2011, pp. 102–113, 2024.
https://doi.org/10.1007/978-3-031-58535-7_9

Deep learning models have emerged as powerful tools in computer vision, offering promising solutions for mural restoration. Multiple deep learning models such as UNet++ [1], DeepLabV3+ [2], PSPNet [3], and FPN [4] were used to accurately and comprehensively segment the murals. By combining the predictions of these models, segmentation accuracy was enhanced and addressed the challenges of damaged murals. An ensemble approach using the STAPLE [5] algorithm has been proposed to fuse the predictions from multiple models, resulting in a more robust and accurate segmentation outcome. Cluster wise training of PConvNet [6] for inpainting, specifically designed to handle the diverse patterns observed in Rajasthani murals, is proposed. To evaluate the performance of the proposed approach, the dataset was curated from the Havelis in the Mandawa region of rural Rajasthan, which serves as expansive galleries of Rajasthani art. The dataset comprises high resolution images capturing intricate details, style variations, and the observed damage of the murals.

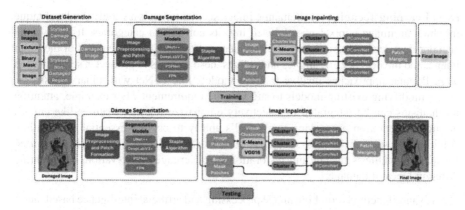

Fig. 1. Complete Pipeline of Proposed Work.

The proposed work focuses on the development of pipelines to enhance the training and performance of models in the context of damaged image processing as shown in Fig. 1:

- Firstly, a novel pipeline is presented for creating accurate synthetic damaged images from healthy image samples. Training models on these artificially generated damaged images can improve performance in handling real world damaged images.
- Secondly, a robust, non-redundant, and accurate damage detection and segmentation pipeline is introduced. By incorporating multiple models and algorithms, the reliability and effectiveness of the segmentation process are enhanced, ensuring its applicability across diverse scenarios.
- Lastly, an inpainting pipeline that utilizes edge based clustering to enhance the accuracy and specialization of the missing region restoration process is presented. This approach enables the generation of visually coherent and semantically consistent inpainted images, contributing to the overall improvement of the image restoration process.

2 Related Works

Segmentation and restoration of paintings are an active research field. In the following sections, recent development in the field is discussed.

Conventional Methods: Traditional methods for picture segmentation include unsupervised and semi-supervised machine learning methods such as Region Growing [7], which begins with a seed point or region and iteratively expands by adding neighboring pixels that fulfil predefined similarity criteria. It gradually builds coherent regions based on local similarity metrics, allowing picture regions with comparable properties to be segmented.

Watershed Transform [8], a region based segmentation algorithm that considers picture pixels as a topographic surface, segments regions by filling basins with water, is another frequently used method.

Deep Learning Techniques: Semantic image segmentation is a widely used technique in which an image is pixel wise labeled into its constituent categories. It involves an encoder decoder structure, where the encoder captures high level features of the input image, and the decoder up samples and refines these features to produce a segmentation map. Popular approaches involve training models like U-Net with binary masks [9, 10] or modifying existing models to suit specific requirements. For example, attention mechanisms can be integrated to selectively emphasize relevant features like cracks, during segmentation, improving the model's ability to capture essential information. Additionally, specialized masks, such as dusk like and jelly like masks [11], are used for texture synthesis testing and restoration in e-Heritage conservation, representing different types of damage.

Advanced methods combine image processing and artificial intelligence based methods such as such as Delaunay triangulation based interpolation and exemplar based inpainting [12]. These techniques drive innovation in the field and enhance the digital restoration of historical artefacts by improving the restoration of damaged areas.

3 Methodology

This section describes the pipeline used for the image segmentation process. A dataset of 488 high resolution clean images (6000 × 6000 pixels) was carefully collected for effective model training. These images were sourced from the ancient murals in the Havelis of the Mandawa region in rural Rajasthan. Additionally, damaged images and their corresponding binary masks were included in the dataset to facilitate the training process. The following sections will present further details on the data collection and preparation process, providing a comprehensive overview of the methodology employed.

3.1 Dataset Generation

Creating an adequate dataset is crucial for training and evaluating damage segmentation algorithms. This section focuses on two key aspects: masks which depict the regions of damage and textures which define the appearance of damage, and using them with clean images to create a synthesized damaged image. These processes were vital in generating the necessary data to train and test the proposed damage segmentation framework.

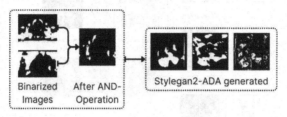

Fig. 2. Examples of masks generated.

Mask Generation: The mask generation process involves applying pixel wise AND operations on the initial mask set created using binarization of random images, creating random white patches resembling damage patterns. From these images, 897 binary masks were crafted. These binary masks were used as input for the Stylegan2ADA [13] framework to generate the final set of binary masks, as shown in Fig. 2. In total, 5,000 masks were generated for further processing, of which 90% was used as the training set and 10% was used as the test set.

Texture Generation: A total of 875 texture images were collected to generate the final textures. This collection included 205 diverse texture images from internet stock repositories, 220 AI-generated images for unique textures, and 450 images extracted from damaged sections of real murals for authentic and relevant samples. These texture images were then used as input data for the Stylegan2-ADA [13] framework to generate customized textures as shown in Fig. 3.

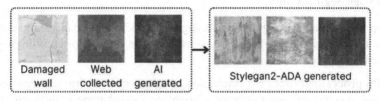

Fig. 3. Example of textures generated.

Damage Image Creation: Originally captured clean images (6000 × 6000 pixels) were divided into smaller grids (512 × 512 pixels) to augment the in-house dataset. To imitate real damage on clean images, dataset preparation pipeline includes the following steps: The following steps outline the pipeline as shown in Fig. 4:

– **Stylized Image Generation:** Two images with artistic filters or transformations were generated using clean images and a texture source. One image represents damaged patches, while the other represents non-damaged parts.

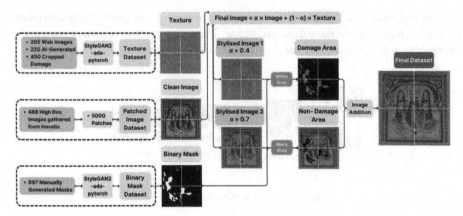

Fig. 4. Complete pipeline of Damage Generation

- **Segmentation and Separation:** By overlaying a binary mask, damaged and non-damaged regions in both stylized images were segmented and separated, ensuring an accurate representation of each area.
- **Result Combination:** Finally, the results were merged from the damaged and non-damaged stylized images, creating a synthesized damaged painting that mimics real instances of damaged artwork. This process captures the characteristics and appearance of actual damaged images.

Using these steps, 5,000 synthesized damaged paintings were created a dataset that accurately represent the desired characteristics for the research. These additional samples were used to train the models further.

3.2 Damage Segmentation

Next step in the pipeline is segmenting damaged regions from the damaged images and generate a binary mask using the proposed method. The steps followed is discussed in the subsequent sections.

Image Preprocessing: Before segmentation, images underwent crucial preprocessing. This included enhancing color saturation, brightness, and sharpness while introducing controlled noise levels as shown in Fig. 5. These improvements made the images visually appealing, representative of the scene, and captured finer details, thus facilitating better performance of the segmentation model. Controlled noise levels introduced variations that mimicked real world scenarios. The pre-processing workflow improved the dataset and segmentation model performance. Images were finally divided into 512x512 patches to preserve details during segmentation and inpainting.

Segmentation Models: The Segmentation model divides an input image into meaningful regions or objects and labels pixels or areas based on their category. In this study, four segmentation models were employed from Segmentation Models which are U-Net++

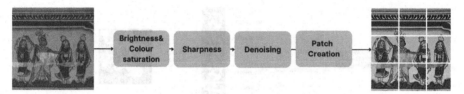

Fig. 5. Steps for data preprocessing.

[1], DeepLabV3+ [2], PSP Net [3] and FPN [4], and transfer learning was applied to harness the capabilities of pre-trained models by adapting them to new tasks or datasets.

- **UNet + +:** UNet + + [1] extends UNet with nested and dense skip connections, improving segmentation performance. It captures multiscale information and promotes feature fusion.
- **DeepLabV3 +:** It is an advanced segmentation model that enhances accuracy with dilated convolutions and atrous spatial pyramid pooling. It uses an encoder decoder architecture with skip connections to capture multiscale information and achieve precise delineation.
- **PSPNet:** It is a powerful image segmentation model that captures rich contextual information at different scales. It improves scene understanding and segmentation accuracy by incorporating comprehensive contextual details.
- **FPN:** FPN (Feature Pyramid Network) [4] is an image segmentation model that leverages feature pyramids to incorporate contextual information and enhance segmentation accuracy. By integrating it, multiscale features can be extracted, and precise segmentation of complex visual scenes can be achieved.

Loss Functions: In our scenario, the objective is to segment damaged areas within an image; two specific loss functions were employed: – *Cross-Entropy Loss (LCE), Dice Coefficient Loss (LDC).*

Final Loss: The same final loss function is used for all the models for ease of implementation. The loss term weights were determined by performing a hyper parameter search for the custom developed training dataset.

$$L_{final} = 0.4L_{CE} + 0.6L_{DC}$$

STAPLE Algorithm: STAPLE [5] (Simultaneous Truth and Performance Level Estimation) [5] is an unsupervised learning expectation maximization algorithm, it computes a probabilistic estimate of the accurate segmentation and measures the performance level of each segmentation in a collection. The algorithm considers segmentation masks combining them optimally to form a probabilistic estimate of the accurate segmentation.

Implementation (Segmentation): Unet++ [1], DeeplabV3+ [2], PSPNet [3], and FPN [4] were selected as the preferred models to detect and segment damaged regions in wall paintings. Paired with ResNet152 [14], ResNext10132x8d [15], timmResNeSt269e [16], and DenseNet161 [17] encoders, these models offer deep and efficient architectures capable of effectively capturing intricate visual patterns. Pretrained weights from Imagenet [18] were utilized for transfer learning, leveraging their learned feature representations.

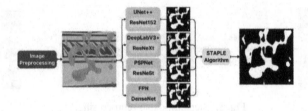

Fig. 6. The collected masks undergo further refinement using the STAPLE algorithm.

During training, damaged images and corresponding binary masks were used. The Adam optimizer, known for its versatility and efficiency, was employed, along with custom loss functions combining Cross Entropy Loss and Dice Loss. The training was performed on patches of size 512×512, with 100 epochs and a batch size of 8, adjusted as needed for different models. The STAPLE [5] algorithm, operating as an unsupervised procedure, iteratively refined the segmentation masks for improved accuracy.

The damaged image was fed into the four models in the testing phase, resulting in segmentation masks. These masks were processed through the STAPLE [5] algorithm to obtain a refined and improved final mask as shown in Fig. 6. The refined mask, along with the original image, was used for the inpainting procedure, allowing for intelligent restoration of the damaged regions based on the precise information provided by the refined mask

3.3   Image Inpainting

For inpainting., the PConvNet [6] was utilized as the preferred model. PConvNet [6] has shown strong performance in inpainting tasks involving irregular and variable damage patterns, making it highly suitable for the in-house dataset and research objectives. By integrating PConvNet [6] into the framework as shown in Fig. 7, our goal is to leverage its inpainting capabilities to restore the damaged regions of the murals based on the segmentation masks generated by the damage segmentation model. In the proposed approach, multiple PConvNet [6] models were trained separately on different clusters of datasets, where clusters are formed based on the type of patterns and style present in each patch. Further details on the clustering process are discussed in the subsequent section.

Visual Clustering: In the visual clustering step, the proposed approach uses VGG16 [19] for feature extraction and K-Means clustering to group similar patches.

K-Means [20] clustering partitions the dataset into distinct clusters, K=4 yielding the best results. These clusters inform the subsequent inpainting process, ensuring tailored treatment based on their specific characteristics. This approach enhances accuracy and produces realistic results in image inpainting. The clustered patches are then passed to the respective PConvNet [6] models for inpainting.

PConvNet: It applies partial convolution [6] on the damaged image, i.e., it only performs convolution operation on the non-missing pixels to get the contextual information of the image, which it later uses to in-paint damaged sections of the image.

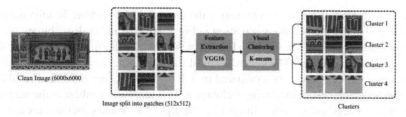

Fig. 7. Result of Visual Clustering of Patches (For k equals 4).

Loss Functions: Four loss functions were utilized: Pixel Reconstruction Loss(*Lvalid, Lhole*), Perceptual Loss(*Lperceptual*), Style Loss(*Lstyle*), Total Variation Loss(*Ltv*). The total loss as adapted from [6] is the combination of all the above loss functions and is shown below:

$$L_{total} = L_{valid} + 6L_{hole} + 0.05L_{perceptual} + 120(L_{style_{out}} + L_{style_{comp}}) + 0.1L_{tv}$$

Implementation (Inpainting): After segmenting the damaged patches, the image is divided into smaller patches of size 512 x 512 for inpainting. This ensures the preservation of finer details during the inpainting procedure. To extract subtle features, such as lines and repeating patterns, the VGG16 model is employed. The extracted features are the basis for clustering the patches into four distinct clusters using the K-Means algorithm. This clustering approach allows the inpainting model to specialize in recovering damages specific to each cluster. The PConvNet [6] model, known for its ability to address irregular and variable damage patterns, is adopted for the inpainting task. Four individual PConvNet [6] models are trained, each focused on recovering damages associated with its respective cluster.

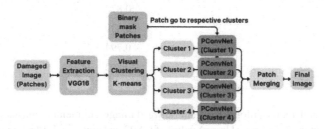

Fig. 8. Inpainting pipeline.

This cluster specific approach results in exceptional accuracy in the inpainting process. The restored patches are seamlessly stitched together, generating the final restored image with a resolution of 6000 × 6000 pixels as shown in Fig. 8.

4 Results

The algorithm development for the complete pipeline is performed in Python on an ubuntu machine with i7 processor, 32 GB RAM, and Nvidia GTX 1080Ti GPU. The proposed method represents a breakthrough in artificial dataset generation in the form of synthetic textures and masks for simulating the damaged regions from healthy images. As presented in the methodology proposed in Fig. 2, diverse and realistic binary masks were generated (Comparison shown in Fig. 9), including jelly like masks [13] resembling authentic damage patterns. The generated masks and their quality in terms of different performance indices have been compared in Table 1, with earlier published results to mark their effectiveness in inpainting techniques. This innovation enhances the dataset's comprehensiveness and accuracy. Integrating the alpha factor and generated textures, as shown in Fig. 4, is crucial in replicating realistic damage with fidelity, closely mimicking actual damage scenarios. To evaluate and assess the effectiveness of the proposed methodology for generating damage segmented masks, a comparison was conducted with other existing methods.

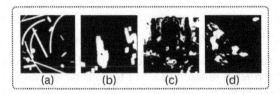

Fig. 9. Comparison: (a) Dynamic (b) Gated Convolution (c) cGAN [21] (d) Proposed

Table 1. Comparison of Mean Intersection over Union (mIOU) scores for different segmentation models.

Segmentation Model	mIOU
UNet + + [1]	0.851
DeepLabV3 + [2]	0.873
PSPNet [3]	0.820
FPN [4]	0.794
Proposed Approach	0.892

The proposed methodology for generating damage segmented masks achieved a mIoU (mean Intersection over Union) value of 0.892 as shown in Table 1, surpassing all other methods in the comparison. The mIoU value was calculated using the 500 images of the test dataset. This indicates remarkable efficiency and exceptional performance in accurately identifying damaged regions. The proposed approach's high accuracy and consistency make it suitable for practical applications where accurate damage identification is crucial. The generated inpainted regions seamlessly integrate with the surrounding undamaged areas while preserving the artistic attributes of the original mural. The proposed method demonstrates impressive performance with an SSIM score of 0.9812 when tested with 500 images of the test dataset.

As depicted in Fig. 10, the end to end pipeline excels in dataset generation, damage segmentation, and image inpainting, representing a significant advancement in mural restoration.

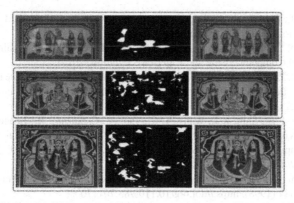

Fig. 10. (Left to Right) Damaged Image, Damage Segmentation, Inpainting Result

5   Conclusion

Art forms always played an essential role in human history. The murals present on walls of the old Havelis of Rajasthan represent a significant vibrant form of open art which are now in a deserted state. The proposed work presents a framework for the digital restoration of this art form through deep learning-based methods. The framework consists of an array of modules comprising synthetic damaged data generation, visual clustering, and inpainting as a whole. The proposed method advances the field by providing a more sophisticated and effective approach to artificial dataset generation. The utilization of diverse binary masks and the incorporation of the alpha factor and generated textures contribute to a higher level of realism in the simulated damage. Incorporating results of various segmentation models using the STAPLE algorithm ensures the robustness and accuracy of damage segmentation. Clustering the images and training PConvNet separately on each cluster helps us get tailored results for each cluster, ensuring better restoration. The future work includes the creation of a VRbased 3D model for walk-throughs and storytelling by using the restored mural images for presenting an enhanced 3D version of the Havelis targeting heritage preservation for coming generations.

Acknowledgement. The authors gratefully acknowledge the support of the Department of Science and Technology(DST), Government of India, for funding this project under grant No: DST/TDT/SHRI/48/2021.

References

1. Zhou, Z., Siddiquee, M.M.R., Tajbakhsh, N., Liang, J.: UNet++: redesigning skip connections to exploit multiscale features in image segmentation. IEEE Trans. Med. Imaging **39**(6), 1856–1867 (2020). https://doi.org/10.1109/TMI.2019.2959609
2. Chen, L.-C., Zhu, Y., Papandreou, G., Schroff, F., Adam, H.: Encoder-decoder with Atrous separable convolution for semantic image segmentation. In: Ferrari, V., Hebert, M., Sminchisescu, C., Weiss, Y. (eds.) Computer Vision – ECCV 2018. LNCS, vol. 11211, pp. 833–851. Springer, Cham (2018). https://doi.org/10.1007/978-3-030-01234-2_49

3. Zhao, H., et al.: Pyramid scene parsing network. In: Proceedings of the IEEE Conference on Computer Vision and Pattern Recognition (2017)

4. Lin, T.-Y., et al.: Feature pyramid networks for object detection. In: Proceedings of the IEEE Conference on Computer Vision and Pattern Recognition (2017)

5. Warfield, S.K., Zou, K.H., Wells, W.M.: Simultaneous truth and performance level estimation (STAPLE): an algorithm for the validation of image segmentation. IEEE Trans. Med. Imaging **23**(7), 903–921 (2004). https://doi.org/10.1109/TMI.2004.828354

6. Liu, G., Reda, F.A., Shih, K.J., Wang, T.-C., Tao, A., Catanzaro, B.: Image inpainting for irregular holes using partial convolutions. In: Ferrari, V., Hebert, M., Sminchisescu, C., Weiss, Y. (eds.) Computer Vision – ECCV 2018. LNCS, vol. 11215, pp. 89–105. Springer, Cham (2018). https://doi.org/10.1007/978-3-030-01252-6_6

7. Hojjatoleslami, S.A., Kittler, J.: Region growing: a new approach. IEEE Trans. Image Proc. **7**(7), 1079–1084 (1998). https://doi.org/10.1109/83.701170

8. Roerdink, J.B.T.M., Meijster, A.: The watershed transform: definitions, algorithms and parallelization strategies. Fundamenta informaticae **41**(1–2), 187–228 (2000)

9. Al-shaikhli, S., Bahrani, A.: Segmentation of Tumor tissue in Gray medical images using watershed transformation Method. Int. J. Adv. Comp. Techn. **2**, 123–127 (2010)

10. Singh, U., Maiti, S., Saini, A., Dhiraj: Ancient Indian murals digital restoration through image in painting. In: 2023 10th International Conference on Signal Processing and Integrated Networks (SPIN), Noida, India, pp. 635–640 (2023). https://doi.org/10.1109/SPIN57001.2023.10116111

11. Yu, T., et al.: End-to-end partial convolutions neural networks for Dunhuang grottoes wall-painting restoration. In: Proceedings of the IEEE/CVF International Conference on Computer Vision Workshops (2019)

12. Mol, V.R., Maheswari, P.U.: The digital reconstruction of degraded ancient temple murals using dynamic mask generation and an extended exemplar based regionfilling algorithm. Heritage Sci. **9**, 1–18 (2021)

13. Karras, T., et al.: Training generative adversarial networks with limited data. In: Advances in Neural Information Processing Systems, vol. 33, pp. 12104–12114 (2020)

14. He, K., Zhang, X., Ren, S., Sun, J.: Deep residual learning for image recognition. In: 2016 IEEE Conference on Computer Vision and Pattern Recognition (CVPR), Las Vegas, NV, USA, pp. 770–778 (2016). https://doi.org/10.1109/CVPR.2016.90

15. Xie, S., Girshick, R., Doll´ar, P., Tu, Z., He, K.: Aggregated residual transformations for deep neural networks. In: 2017 IEEE Conference on Computer Vision and Pattern Recognition (CVPR), Honolulu, HI, USA, pp. 5987–5995 (2017). https://doi.org/10.1109/CVPR.2017.634

16. Wightman, R., Touvron, H., Jégou, H.: ResNet strikes back: an improved training procedure in timm. CoRR abs/2110.00476 (2021)

17. Huang, G., Liu, Z., Van Der Maaten, L., Weinberger, K.Q.: Densely connected convolutional networks. In: 2017 IEEE Conference on Computer Vision and Pattern Recognition (CVPR), Honolulu, HI, USA, pp. 2261–2269 (2017). https://doi.org/10.1109/CVPR.2017.243

18. Deng, J., Dong, W., Socher, R., Li, L.-J., Li, K., Li, F.-F.: ImageNet: a large-scale hierarchical image database. In: 2009 IEEE Conference on Computer Vision and Pattern Recognition, Miami, FL, USA, pp. 248–255 (2009). https://doi.org/10.1109/CVPR.2009.5206848

19. Qassim, H., Verma, A., Feinzimer, D.: Compressed residual-VGG16 CNN model for big data places image recognition. In: 2018 IEEE 8th Annual Computing and Communication Workshop and Conference (CCWC), Las Vegas, NV, USA, pp. 169–175 (2018). https://doi.org/10.1109/CCWC.2018.8301729

20. Hartigan, J.A., Wong, M.A.: Algorithm AS 136: A K-Means clustering algorithm. J. Roy. Statist. Soc. Ser. C (Applied Statistics) **28**(1), 100–108 (1979). https://doi.org/10.2307/234 6830
21. Rakhimol, V., Uma Maheswari, P.: Restoration of ancient temple murals using cGAN and PConv networks. Comput. Graph. **109**, 100–110 (2022). https://doi.org/10.1016/j.cag.2022. 11.001

Colorization of Thermal Facial Images into Visible Facial Image Using RGB-GAN

Dnyaneshwar Bhadane and Soumendu Chakraborty[✉]

Department of Computer Science, Indian Institute of Information Technology
Lucknow, Lucknow 226002, Uttar Pradesh, India
soum.uit@gmail.com

Abstract. Images captured by thermal cameras are independent of lighting conditions. However, it can be challenging for human examiners to identify thermal face photos. Facial recognition technology enables automatic identification or verification of individuals in digital images or video frames extracted from video sequences. There are multiple methods employed by facial recognition systems, but they typically involve comparing the features extracted from a specific image with those stored in a database. This technology finds application in various areas, including access control and identification systems. It is worth noting that facial features can exhibit unique characteristics specific to an individual throughout their lifetime. In this paper, the process of colorizing thermal facial images into the visible spectrum based on Cycle GAN is undertaken. There are many variations of the GAN but to translate or map from the one domain image into another domain image the cycle GAN fits with its application. CycleGAN aims to acquire knowledge of the relationship between two distinct image collections originating from separate domains, each possessing unique styles, textures, or visual attributes. The RGB-GAN which is proposed in this paper refers to the red, green, and blue channel generative adversarial network that individually takes the independent images in the thermal format to colorize in the independent domain channel network-merging three generated channel results combined to make one RGB-colored image. One more generator network involves identifying and comparing the result with the original visible colored image to give feedback to the network. At last after training the final model, the classification task involves generating and classifying the correct person out group of persons when the thermal image is given as input. The output includes face recognition accuracy of generated images, comparative analysis with protocols and state-of-the-art techniques.

Keywords: Image translation · Cycle GAN · Colorization · Thermal Images · Facial data

1 Introduction

In recent years, Biometrics has garnered considerable interest from both academic and business circles. It has emerged as a favored method for human identification, primarily due to its ability to capture and analyze the unique physical

H. Kaur et al. (Eds.): CVIP 2023, CCIS 2011, pp. 114–127, 2024.
https://doi.org/10.1007/978-3-031-58535-7_10

characteristics of individuals. Among the various biometric applications, face recognition stands out as a prominent topic. What sets it apart is its ability to identify individuals without requiring their active cooperation, making it a user-friendly approach to human recognition. Face recognition technology holds immense significance in the domains of security and surveillance. It plays a pivotal role in security systems by facilitating efficient and precise identification of individuals. Widely utilized in access control systems, airports, public spaces, and other critical areas, it enables robust monitoring and accurate identification of people, thus bolstering overall security measures. By harnessing the power of face recognition, these systems can effectively detect and track individuals, strengthening surveillance efforts and aiding in the prevention and investigation of security breaches and criminal activities. These days when low light domains such as night vision and infrared thermal imaging. Night vision can be hindered by various conditions, including dust, smoke, overcast nights, rain, and fog. These factors negatively impact the effectiveness of traditional night vision systems. In contrast, thermal imaging remains unaffected by such conditions and can provide visibility even in complete darkness.

This paper investigates the application of conditional generative adversarial networks in our case Cycle GANs in image-to-image translation tasks of converting thermal facial images into visible colored images and identifying the correct person to be generated by the network with its correctly classified class. While traditional GANs learn a generative model of data, Cycle GANs specifically focus on learning a conditional generative model. By conditioning on an input image, cycle GANs enable the generation of a corresponding output image in the other domain. There is the use of multiple cycle GAN to generate the image from the thermal domain to specific images colored channel GANs such as Red/Green/Blue channel. Merge the generated images from the independent channel into one RGB-colored image. More discussion is being done as the paper progresses as follows.

1.1 Paper Organization

Section 1 describes the introduction and the state-of-the-art techniques in the fields of thermal, infrared, and image translation techniques. Section 2 outlines the system model followed by the problem statement and describes the methodology in detail. The experimental simulation and analysis of results for the proposed methodology are demonstrated in Sect. 4. Finally, Sect. 5 presents us with the conclusion and future scope of the work.

1.2 Related Work

The research on thermal-visible facial image translation is relatively limited compared to near infrared-visible facial image translation [8,13]. This is primarily attributed to the significant modality gap that exists between thermal and visible images, which poses additional challenges in the translation process.

Downsampling a high-resolution image thermal noisy image to produce a Super Resolution image [11], The connection between 2D images and 3D objects, commonly referred to as 3D object reconstruction from 2D images [12] using GAN. Generating the facial image from thermal image based on facial feature [14] tried to map the eye, nose, and lips position to predict the exact location on the face. In the thermal face images, a substantial amount of information about edge and texture is lost, while the face in near-infrared images exhibits notable being similar to visible light domain face images. Consequently, conducting face recognition tasks in the area of thermal imaging poses remarkably greater challenges compared to the near-infrared image domain. [4], Occlusion detection in thermal images [2].

The generic framework it proposes for using conditional GANs to handle various image translation jobs. The ability to learn extremely complicated mappings between several domains is demonstrated by them by explicitly supplying pairs of input and output images during training. The suggested technique shows promise in a number of applications, including colorizing grayscale photos, converting satellite images into maps, and improving images for use in medical imaging [6]. The paper [16] showed that CycleGAN is effective for a range of image translation tasks, including morphing images into paintings, turning horses into zebras, and altering daytime pictures into nighttime ones, among others. The outcomes demonstrated the model's capacity to produce excellent images with accurate and cogent translations [16]. The "pix2pix loss," which combines adversarial loss with the L1 distance between the generated and ground-truth images, is a new loss function proposed in the research. This loss function promotes sharpness while keeping tiny details in the translated images, producing visually appealing and highly perceptive results. This research [10] makes progress in the broader subject of unsupervised learning as well as the introduction of the image-to-image translation network. The authors overcame a fundamental restriction in prior methods by attacking the picture translation problem without relying on paired data, creating new opportunities for image manipulation and imaginative applications. The development of the Recycle-GAN architecture [3] and the advancement of unsupervised video modification are the paper's main contributions. The authors overcame a fundamental constraint in earlier video re-targeting methods by doing away with the requirement for paired data, making it more approachable and useful for real-world applications. The author [5] developed an innovative approach for achieving unsupervised picture translation using Generative Adversarial Networks (GANs) and a pre-trained encoder from StyleGAN. They were able to translate images from one domain to another without the need for paired training samples by using the StyleGAN encoder to map images from the source domain to the latent space and then decode them into the target domain [7].

1.3 Objectives and Contributions

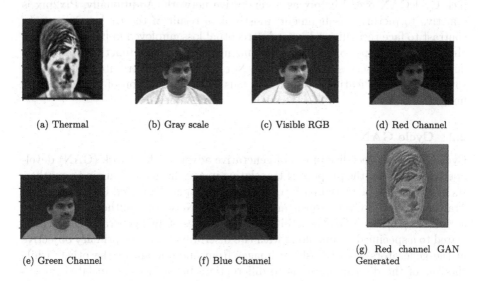

(a) Thermal   (b) Gray scale   (c) Visible RGB   (d) Red Channel

(e) Green Channel   (f) Blue Channel   (g) Red channel GAN Generated

Fig. 1. Images with color domain (Color figure online)

In this paper there are have two objectives, first generate the visible light image using RGB channel cycle GAN which is proposed in the paper, and to identify the correct facial person after generating an image from the thermal image the standard classification problem out of a set of faces trained on image classification model. The technique demonstrates the use of the RGB channel-based network of generative adversaries effectively to generate visible domain image RGB of the facial data set. a picture is typically loaded as a rank-3 array (height, width, color), where the last axis represents the image's color information. Each pixel in the RGB color space is represented by three values that describe the relative intensities of the channels in Red, Green, and Blue. Extracted all shades from the image and trained with cGAN for individual red, green, and blue channels.

2 Proposed Model

2.1 Model Overview

Our model comprises two main components: generative network and detector network. The generative network itself ability to convert thermal pictures into visual images; however, resulting translations may be relatively coarse. To achieve this translation task, we employ CycleGAN, a framework that enables bidirectional translation between thermal and visible images without the need for paired training data. This unsupervised learning approach leverages unpaired training images and benefits from a translation cycle, where the two translations mutually enhance each other during the training process.Pix2pix tends to be more prone to overfitting when trained on short datasets, hence we intentionally pick CycleGAN over Pix2pix as a generative network. Additionally, Pix2pix is sensitive to picture misalignment, mostly as a result of the L1 loss it uses. In contrast to face recognition loss and perceptual loss employed in [9] [10] with the aim of enhancing performance in recognizing faces, the loss function used in the detector network serves a dual purpose. Not only does it contribute to the preservation of identity features, but it also aids in the generation of photo-realistic images.

2.2   Cycle GAN

CycleGAN is a specialized form of generative adversarial network (GAN) developed explicitly for the purpose of translating images from one domain to another. Its inception can be traced back to the research paper "Unpaired Image-to-Image Translation using Cycle-Consistent Adversarial Networks" authored by Zhu et al. in 2017 [17]. CycleGAN's architecture comprises of dual generators, each dedicated to a specific domain, along with two discriminators. The primary objective of the generators is to transform images from one domain to the other, while the role of the discriminators is to differentiate between the translated images and authentic images belonging to the target domain. In the training process, the generators and discriminators engage in an adversarial learning scheme. The generators strive to deceive the discriminators by producing convincing translated images, whereas the discriminators endeavor to accurately classify real and translated images. Moreover, cycle consistency loss is employed to ensure that the original images and their reconstructions maintain consistent cyclic relationships.

CycleGAN Working: CycleGAN is a type of generative adversarial network (GAN) architecture designed for image-to-image translation tasks. It consists of two main components: generators and discriminators.

Generators: CycleGAN employs 2 generators: $G : X \rightarrow Y$ and $F : Y \rightarrow X$. Generator G learns to translate images from domain X to domain Y, while generator F performs the inverse translation from Y to X. The generators aim to generate realistic images that can fool the discriminators.

Discriminators: CycleGAN also utilizes two discriminators: D_X and D_Y. D_X discriminates between real images from domain X and images produced by F. Similarly, D_Y differentiates between real images from domain Y and images produced by G. The discriminators provide feedback to the generators by assessing the realism of the generated images.

Cycle GAN Loss: The loss function of CycleGAN consists of two main components: adversarial loss and cycle consistency loss.

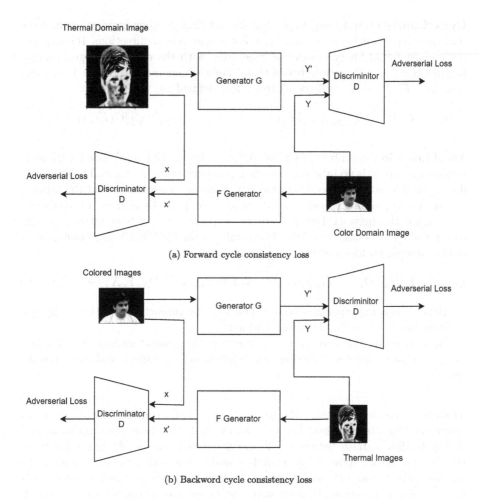

(a) Forward cycle consistency loss

(b) Backword cycle consistency loss

Fig. 2. Inside of Cycle GAN Architecture

Adversarial Loss: The adversarial loss is derived from the concept of generative adversarial networks (GANs). It involves training the generator and discriminator networks in an adversarial manner. The aim of the generator to produce pictures that are identical to the target domain, while the discriminator aims to differentiate between real images from the target domain and generated images. For the generator $G : X \rightarrow Y$, the adversarial loss is defined as:

$$\mathcal{L}_{\text{GAN}}(G, D_Y, X, Y) = \mathbb{E}_{y \sim p_{\text{data}}(y)}[\log D_Y(y)] + \mathbb{E}_{x \sim p_{\text{data}}(x)}[\log(1 - D_Y(G(x)))]$$

Similarly, for the generator $F : Y \rightarrow X$, the adversarial loss defined as:

$$\mathcal{L}_{\text{GAN}}(F, D_X, Y, X) = \mathbb{E}_{x \sim p_{\text{data}}(x)}[\log D_X(x)] + \mathbb{E}_{y \sim p_{\text{data}}(y)}[\log(1 - D_X(F(y)))]$$

Cycle Consistency Loss: As per Fig. 2a and 2b, Cycle consistency loss ensures that the translation between domains is consistent in both directions. It compares the reconstructed images from the generators with the original images, aiming to minimize the difference between them. For the generator $G : X \rightarrow Y$ and the generator $F : Y \rightarrow X$, cycle consistency loss defined as:

$$\mathcal{L}_{\text{cycle}}(G, F) = \mathbb{E}_{x \sim p_{\text{data}}(x)}[\|F(G(x)) - x\|_1] + \mathbb{E}_{y \sim p_{\text{data}}(y)}[\|G(F(y)) - y\|_1]$$

Total Loss: In the context of CycleGAN, the absence of paired data for training implies that there is no inherent correlation between the input x and the target y during the training process. Consequently, there is no assurance that the input x and the corresponding target y form a meaningful pair. To address this challenge and ensure the network learns accurate mapping, the authors introduced the concept of cycle consistency loss. The total loss for CycleGAN is a combination of the adversarial loss and the cycle consistency loss:

$$\mathcal{L}_{\text{total}}(G, F, D_X, D_Y) = \mathcal{L}_{\text{GAN}}(G, D_Y, X, Y) + \mathcal{L}_{\text{GAN}}(F, D_X, Y, X) + \lambda \mathcal{L}_{\text{cycle}}(G, F)$$

Here, λ is a hyperparameter that controls the importance of the cycle consistency loss relative to the adversarial loss.

By optimizing this combined loss function, the generators learn to translate images between the two domains while maintaining realism and cycle consistency.

Training: During training, the generators and discriminators engage in an adversarial learning process. The generators aim to minimize the discriminators' ability to differentiate between real and generated images. At the same time, the discriminators strive to accurately classify real and generated images. To ensure cycle consistency, an additional cycle consistency loss is employed. This loss compares the original image with the image reconstructed after a round-trip translation through both generators. By enforcing cycle consistency, the generators learn to maintain the original image content during translation.

CycleGAN facilitates unsupervised image-to-image translation by leveraging the adversarial learning framework and cycle consistency loss. It enables transformations between different domains without the need for paired training data. In a GAN architecture, there are two main components: the generator and the discriminator, which work collaboratively to solve a problem. In our specific setup, the generator model is designed to take a grayscale image (consisting of a single channel) as input and generate a 1-channel image. On the other hand, the discriminator model takes these generated channel images and discriminates the image with 1-channel input. It is important to note that the discriminator also needs exposure to authentic images (1-channel grayscale images) that are not produced by the generator. By learning from these real images, the discriminator can discern their authenticity.

2.3   RGB-GAN Methodology

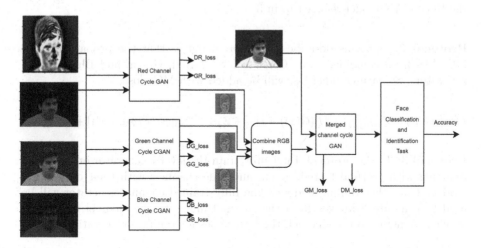

Fig. 3. RGB GAN Model Framework

There is two images are used during the training phase, where one thermal image (T) and one visible image (V) are taken. Now the Red, Green, and Blue intensities are extracted from the RGB visible domain image V. As shown in 3, Every channel is trained with a generator and discriminator mapping the thermal image with respected color domain channel and generate the grayscale image that described mapped intensities for the thermal image. Post the image generated from the 3 of the channel they are merged posing as a single image that has RGB Image. The combined image is passed to the next cycle GAN model where it is retrained with a mapped colored image.

The final generated image is evaluated and given the image classification task to identify the face of the person. During the training phase cycle GAN generate the loss, GR_loss (Generator-Red channel loss), DR_loss (Discriminator-Red channel loss), GG_loss (Generator-green channel loss), DG_loss (Discriminator-green channel loss), GB_loss (Generator-Blue channel loss), DB_loss (Discriminator-Blue channel loss), MG_loss (Merge channel generator loss) and MD_loss(Merge channel discriminator loss). So based on the loss propagation implemented 4 protocols on the basic architecture in 3,

3   Experiment

This section begins by outlining the implementation specifics and benchmarks. Next, we present the dataset and testing procedure. Lastly, An analysis is conducted based on an approach to the performance of different functions.

3.1   Four Modes of Protocol

Protocol 1: This protocol is the same as the described basic architecture of the RGB-GAN model referred to in 3.

Protocol 2: Same as describe 3, Just a change is that the propagating the MG_loss from combined cycle GAN to level 1 Red, Green, and Blue channel generators. So each channel loss will be added with MG_loss,

$$\mathcal{L}_{\text{cycle}}(G, F) = \mathbb{E}_{x \sim p_{\text{data}}(x)}[\|F(G(x)) - x\|_1] + \mathbb{E}_{y \sim p_{\text{data}}(y)}[\|G(F(y)) - y\|_1] + MG\_loss$$

Protocol 3: In the protocol, First fully train the level 1 generator on the given mapping with thermal to red, green, and blue channels with their cycle GAN models. Once the training is done. The fully trained channel generator will be used to generate 3 images from the thermal image to the channel image and applied to merge to the channel, the latter goes for the face recognition.

Protocol 4: In this approach, The input image 256*256 into 4 blocks 64*64 and trained each block on the respected colored channel and merged as a single image before the level 2 generator where the merged image is presented as a single image to mapped with original color RGB image. This way level 1 has 12 cycleGAN (3 for each block) merged all block results into the image before the level 2 generator.

4   Results and Discussion

4.1   Dataset

For evaluation purposes utilized the IRIS Thermal/Visible Face Database [1], which consists of thermal images captured by the FLIR SC6700 (3um to 7 um spectral range). The dataset included around 29 subjects and a total of 4,200 pairs of thermal and visible domain pair images. To ensure diverse poses, Images were not included with variations, extreme positions, attitudes, and repeated angles in illustration during experiments. Consequently, Approximately 690 pairs were obtained and they are roughly aligned or visible images, amounting to a total of 1,390 images (695 × 2) from the 29 subjects, which were utilized in our evaluation for all the methods.

4.2   Evaluation Measures

On the environment part, Google Colabs with a Tesla GPU T4 and 16 GB of RAM have been utilized. For each iteration, A random division of the dataset was performed. Eight subjects were selected for testing, while the remaining 21 subjects were used to train the transformation function f, resulting in approximately 500 images. It's important to note that the testing set only included the thermal faces of the eight subjects, and their corresponding visible faces were excluded from the experiment. Subsequently, The visible faces of all 29 subjects were enrolled into the VGG-Face model. However, it specifically excluded the visible faces of the eight subjects whose thermal faces were used by the TV-GAN to generate the visible images. This rigorous protocol ensured that none of the subject images were present in both the training and testing sets while training the transformation function f. In the context of image recognition, the term "rank" pertains to the position of a correctly identified image within a given list of potential candidates or classes. It serves as an evaluation measure to assess the accuracy of image recognition models. For instance, When 'Rank 1' is referred to, it implies that the correct class or label is the top prediction, while "Rank 5" indicates that the correct class is included among the top five predictions. As the rank increases, the evaluation metric becomes more lenient, allowing for a certain degree of flexibility in the predicted order.

The visible face gallery images utilized in this study had not been previously observed by the pre-trained face recognition model. The model was acquired from the VGG website for this purpose. The transformation functions for both RGB-GAN and Pix2Pix were trained on each separate training set split. To ensure a fair comparison, Implementation refrained from any data augmentation techniques such as horizontal flipping during the training process.

The evaluation process consisted of two protocols: Set A and Set B. In Set A, each subject in the gallery was represented by a single frontal face image. In contrast, Set B involved four images per person, capturing various stance angles. Multiple runs of the experiment were conducted, and the average performance was noted. Additionally, the performance at rank first, third, fifth, and seventh place was reported. For every iteration, the dataset was split into groups of random eight subjects for the testing and 21 participants were used to train the transformation function f, resulting in around 500 pictures for training purposes.

4.3   Baseline Models

Plain Mapping: No modifications or transformations were made to this fundamental. In simpler terms, regarding this particular baseline, function f simply performs a mapping identity, where the output Y is the same as the input X.

Patch-Based Approach: Previous research [9] has demonstrated the feasibility of training a transformation function f from the Near Infrared (NIR) domain to the Visible Light Domain (VLD) using a Convolutions Neural Network (CNN) with an encoder-decoder architecture. Building upon this knowledge, The same approach is applied to the conversion from thermal to visible images.

TV-GAN: Zhang et al. [15] have introduced a Thermal-to-Visible Generative Adversarial Network [15] designed specifically for converting thermal face images into their corresponding Visible Light Domain (VLD) counterparts. The

TV-GAN not only accomplishes this transformation but also ensures that crucial identity information is preserved. This preservation of identity information allows currently available VLD facial recognition models to effectively perform identification tasks using the generated VLD images.

4.4 Results

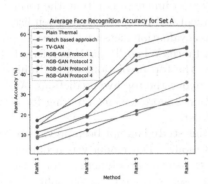 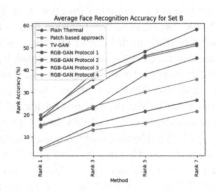

Fig. 4. Linear accuracy

Table 1. The average accuracy of face recognition (%) in a scenario where only a single visible frontal face image is available for each individual (Set A)

Method	Rank1	Rank3	Rank5	Rank7
Plain Mapping	3.6	12.3	21.8	27.8
Patch based approach	8.9	18.9	26.9	36
TV-GAN	13.9	33	46.8	53.4
RGB-GAN Protocol 1	11.2	19.4	42.2	49.8
RGB-GAN Protocol 2	**14.3**	**24.7**	**49.5**	52.9
RGB-GAN Protocol 3	**17.2**	**29.2**	**54.2**	**61.2**
RGB-GAN Protocol 4	8.34	15.12	20.2	29.5

The presented table data 1 showcases the accuracy of facial recognition on average, represented in percentages, in a specific scenario known as Set A. In Set A, only a single visible frontal face image is available for each individual. The table further provides the accuracy results at different ranks, namely 1, 3, 5, and 7 in order of importance. Several methods were evaluated in this scenario. The "Plain Thermal" method achieved an accuracy of 3.5% at Rank 1, gradually increasing to 27.2% at Rank 7. The "Patch-based Approach" exhibited better performance, with accuracy ranging from 8.9% at Rank 1 to 36% at Rank 7. The

"TV-GAN" method demonstrated even higher accuracy, starting from 13.9% at Rank 1 and reaching 53.4% at Rank 7. Comparatively, the "RGB-GAN" method, following different protocols labeled Protocol 1, Protocol 2, Protocol 3, and Protocol 4, achieved varying levels of accuracy across the different ranks. Overall, these results shed light on the performance of different methods in terms of face recognition accuracy in the given scenario with limited visible frontal face images available per individual.

Table 2. The average accuracy of face recognition (%) in the scenario where each person has four visible face images available (Set B)

Method	Rank1	Rank3	Rank5	Rank7
Plain Mapping	4.8	15.7	21.7	26.6
Patch based approach	14.6	23.5	30.1	35.7
TV-GAN	19.7	35.6	45.8	50.7
RGB-GAN Protocol 1	18.1	32.4	**46.3**	**51.8**
RGB-GAN Protocol 2	15.3	22.7	37.9	45.3
RGB-GAN Protocol 3	**18.2**	**38.2**	**48.2**	**58.2**
RGB-GAN Protocol 4	4.34	13.12	16.2	21.5

In the context of Set B, where each individual has four visible face images available, the average accuracy of face recognition is represented as a percentage in Table 2. The table provided illustrates the accuracy results at various ranks, including 1, 3, 5, and 7 in order of importance. The "Plain Mapping" method achieved an accuracy of 4.9% at Rank 1, gradually increasing to 26.5% at Rank 7. The "Patch-based Approach" exhibited improved performance, with accuracy ranging from 14.6% at Rank 1 to 35.7% at Rank 7. The "TV-GAN" method demonstrated even higher accuracy, starting from 19.9% at Rank 1 and reaching 50.9% at Rank 7. Similarly, the "RGB-GAN" method, following different protocols labeled Protocol 1, Protocol 2, Protocol 3, and Protocol 4, achieved varying levels of accuracy across different ranks. These results highlight the performance of different methods in terms of face recognition accuracy in the given scenario where each person has four available visible face images.

5   Conclusions

Facial images are particularly susceptible to aberrations and distortions. Therefore, it is desirable to have created images that seem photo-realistic. It is brought into the framework as the generative network and takes inspiration from Cycle-GAN, an unsupervised generating model. CycleGAN's core concept is to compare the cycle consistency of two distinct image distributions. In this instance, the visible face image distribution and the thermal facial image distribution are mapped using colorized channels. But we are as far as solving the real-world problem of accurately recognizing the face from the thermal camera.

When attempting to generate using the already trained Level 2 generator, a significant improvement in recognition accuracy is observed. In this study, good results were achieved for Rank 7 and Rank 5, but significant improvements are required to attain satisfactory results for Rank 1 and Rank 3 in real-world scenarios.

References

1. Iris thermal/visible face database. IEEE OTCBVS WS Series Bench (2012). https://vcipl-okstate.org/pbvs/bench/index.html
2. Alqudah, M., Mohamed, A.S.A., Lebai Lutfi, S.: Analysis of facial occlusion challenge in thermal images for human affective state recognition. Sensors **23** (03 2023). https://doi.org/10.3390/s23073513
3. Bansal, A., Ma, C., Ramanan, D.: Recycle-gan: Unsupervised video retargeting. In: Proceedings of the European Conference on Computer Vision (ECCV) (2018)
4. Dey, N., Ashour, A.S., Althoupety, A.: Thermal imaging in medical science, January 2017. https://doi.org/10.4018/978-1-5225-5204-8.ch046
5. Hu, Q., Wu, J., Zhang, H., Yu, Y.: Unsupervised image-to-image translation via pre-trained stylegan encoder. In: Proceedings of the European Conference on Computer Vision (ECCV) (2018)
6. Isola, P., Zhu, J.Y., Zhou, T., Efros, A.A.: Image-to-image translation with conditional adversarial networks. In: Proceedings of the IEEE Conference on Computer Vision and Pattern Recognition (CVPR) (2017)
7. Kounev, S.: Serverless computing revisited: evolution, state-of-the-art, and performance challenges. In: Companion of the 2023 ACM/SPEC International Conference on Performance Engineering, pp. 309–310 (2023)
8. Lezama, J., Qiu, Q., Sapiro, G.: Not afraid of the dark: NIR-VIS face recognition via cross-spectral hallucination and low-rank embedding. CoRR **abs/1611.06638** (2016). http://arxiv.org/abs/1611.06638
9. Lezama, J., Qiu, Q., Sapiro, G.: Not afraid of the dark: Nir-vis face recognition via cross-spectral hallucination and low-rank embedding (2016)
10. Liu, M.Y., Breuel, T., Kautz, J.: Unsupervised image-to-image translation networks. In: Advances in Neural Information Processing Systems (NIPS) (2017)
11. Mathur, A.N., Khattar, A., Sharma, O.: 2d to 3d medical image colorization. In: Proceedings of the IEEE/CVF Winter Conference on Applications of Computer Vision (WACV), pp. 2847–2856, January 2021
12. Noguchi, A., Harada, T.: Rgbd-GAN: unsupervised 3d representation learning from natural image datasets via RGBD image synthesis (2020)
13. Wang, N., Li, J., Tao, D., Li, X., Gao, X.: Heterogeneous image transformation. Pattern Recogn. Lett. **34**(1), 77–84 (2013). https://doi.org/0.1016/j.patrec.2012.04.005, extracting Semantics from Multi-Spectrum Video
14. Wang, Z., Chen, Z., Wu, F.: Thermal to visible facial image translation using generative adversarial networks. IEEE Signal Process. Lett. **25**(8), 1161–1165 (2018). https://doi.org/10.1109/LSP.2018.2845692
15. Zhang, T., Wiliem, A., Yang, S., Lovell, B.C.: Tv-GAN: generative adversarial network based thermal to visible face recognition (2017)

16. Zhu, J.Y., Park, T., Isola, P., Efros, A.A.: Unpaired image-to-image translation using cycle-consistent adversarial networks. In: Proceedings of the IEEE International Conference on Computer Vision (ICCV) (2017)
17. Zhu, J.Y., Park, T., Isola, P., Efros, A.A.: Unpaired image-to-image translation using cycle-consistent adversarial networks (2020)

Fusion of Handcrafted Features and Deep Features to Detect COVID-19

Koushik Gunda[1]([✉]), Soumendu Chakraborty[1], and Dubravko Culibrk[2]

[1] Indian Institute of Information Technology Lucknow, Lucknow, India
koushikgunda1434@gmail.com, soum.uit@gmail.com
[2] Institute of Artificial Intelligence, University of Novi Sad, Novi Sad, Serbia

Abstract. The COVID-19 pandemic's rapid growth has made it crucial to develop reliable and efficient diagnostic methods. In this study, we incorporate deep features and handcrafted features to provide a unique method for COVID-19 identification using chest X-rays. In order to extract high-level features from the chest X-ray pictures, we first use a convolutional neural network (CNN) that has already been trained to take advantage of deep learning. The discriminative information regarding COVID-19 infection is captured by the obtained deep features. In addition to the deep features, we also use manually created features that are meant to capture the unique features of COVID-19 in chest X-rays. Based on earlier study findings and domain understanding, these characteristics were manually constructed. They consist of statistical measures, shape-based characteristics, and texture descriptors. Comparing the performance of the classification with the standalone applications of convolutional and handcrafted features, we find that combining the features in our innovative framework enhances performance.

Keywords: COVID-19 · LGHP · Convolutional neural networks · LGB classifier · Feature level fusion

1 Introduction

The COVID-19 pandemic still has negative effects on the world's population, as shown by the rising number of demises that are primarily brought on by the unavailability of specific medications and boosters for this illness. Although the disease has a fatality incidence of between 2% and 3% [10], Significant concerns include its quick spread among people, difficulty in identifying it when dormant, and difficulty in distinguishing it from the ordinary flu. Antibody testing and reverse transcription polymerase chain reaction (RT-PCR) testing are currently regarded as the most accurate methods for addressing COVID-19 problems. However, Due to the ambiguity associated with antibody formation before a week is over since the first infection, the last technique does not offer protection against early diagnosis and containment. The former procedures requires a complex, expensive, and it takes a lot of time to eliminate human errors and health risks.

Since the disease's breakout, scientists have been seeking to develop quick, low-cost, and accurate detection approaches. Because the lungs are the first organs to be affected by COVID-19, issues there can be easily discovered., Medical imaging presents a key option. As a result, radiography scans may be able to reveal information about lung problems, which would therefore enable the detection of COVID-19.

Although they have the benefits of being affordable and low-risk when considering radiation threats to human health, X-ray modalities frequently require medical professionals to identify white areas that contain water and pus, that may not merely arise from COVID-19. Other thoracic conditions, like pulmonary tuberculosis, may be incorrectly classified as COVID-19 by radiologists [19]. Additionally, it is more challenging for radiologists to reach a consensus regarding the presence of COVID-19. Because of the resemblance between lung pictures that are affected by pneumonia, normal lung function, and COVID-19. More importantly, manual interpretations are significantly hampered by inter- and intra-radiologist variations as well as impacts from a variety of subjective criteria, such as the radiologist's level of expertise, emotions, and level of exhaustion. The high mistake rate associated with X-ray methods is not present in CT pictures, which offer a more accurate detection method [2].

Numerous researches in a variety of image-level disciplines have shown the promising potential of handcrafted features to provide the essential gradient, orientation, color, and pixel-based scale data. The ability of the resulting system to be generalized is constrained if only these features are used, as they might rely largely on local descriptors. Meanwhile, To gain significant information from an original dataset, Deep features may also be recovered as high-dimensional features. These findings motivate us to employ characteristics, that are considered to be crucial components in CXR images for the detection of COVID-19.

The remaining paper is as follows. In Sect. 1.1, we will talk about the related work. In Sect. 2, we will discuss the proposed methodology we implemented. In Sect. 3, we will talk about the experimental results obtained. In Sect. 4, we conclude with the conclusion.

1.1 Related Work

COVID-19 and other chest-related disorders are currently being studied utilizing image processing technologies because they all appear to have undergone a significant alteration. To attain the highest results, several researchers in computer vision and image processing use deep and machine learning methods [1]. These computer vision-based techniques have significant advantages for improving the detection of diseases that affect the chest or other ailments. Radiologists and patients can both benefit from these computer vision-based approaches in terms of technical understanding and case discussion. Due to some radiologists' lack of skill or their lack of experience in diagnosing certain chest diseases, manual diagnosis may undergo significant variances. These computer-based classifiers take into account these without the need for additional training on extra data from the specified classes.

To meet the growing demand for radiologists, more radiologists are needed. The National Health Services (NHS) claims that the demand for radiologists would rise by up to 30%, but the number of radiologists will only rise by 15%. In the COVID-19 pandemic, this gap ultimately results in a scarcity of radiologists. The rate of incorrect diagnoses also rises as a result of this increased burden on the radiologists who are still accessible. We discovered from the current situation that a research- and development-based tool is critical. Many patients who have COVID-19-like symptoms are given the diagnosis when they should not have been. Another prerequisite for intelligent systems to adequately assess the patient is the replacement of existing diagnosis systems. There aren't many studies that use Computed Tomography (CT) scans to identify disorders of the chest. Only 81 patients' CT scan data were used to report the 324 lung areas with 80% accuracy [25]. The authors of note pietka1994lung present a second study that suggested a framework for classifying disorders related to the chest using view-based radiography images. The authors [3] present a framework that makes use of projection-based profile traits and a deep neural network to categorize the radiography scans.

All of the suggested research focuses on the binary classification of whether the patient has a COVID-19 infection or not. A patient with COVID-19 may have a common cold, pneumonia, or another condition involving the chest. It is suggested to use a 3D CMixNet-based technique to categorize lung nodules and lessen false positive results. This approach makes use of a Gradient Boosting Machine-based Recurrent-CNN and 3D Customised Mixed Link Structure. The major connections between this approach and clinical biomarkers and physiological symptoms. Live body diagnosis is carried out via wireless body area networks (WBANS). Additionally, the LIDC-IDRI dataset is used to test this work [18].

Recent research [14,16,17] that has combined elements from different medical imaging areas strongly encourages the proposed study to do the same. However, recent advancements in deep features have also improved other fields, such as knee osteoarthritis [15]. The most recent research on ML [6] and DL [21] based methods for COVID-19 detection also encouraged the usage of an alternative tactic. As far as we are aware, no major and reliable method can precisely detect these disorders of the chest. The planned study sought to accurately identify the following groups of chest diseases: pneumonia, normal, and COVID-19.

2   Proposed Work

The classifier that we have proposed is tested and trained on 6,000 X-ray images. These images are categorized into three categories, namely: Covid-19, Pneumonia, and Normal images. Every image in the dataset is resized into 224×224 pixels. Later preprocessing is done on these images. Now we have extracted different deep-learning features and Handcrafted features from the images as shown in Fig. 1. After that, we applied max-pooling on it and fed it into a Light Gradient-Boosting Machine(LGB) classifier. The entire process is shown in Fig. 2.

2.1   Deep Features

To obtain deep features we have used Seven different CNN models: MobileNet, VGG, ResNet, DenseNet, InceptionV3, and Xception These models are been applied to the data set.

MobileNet. Although deeper and broader networks can be used to reach higher accuracy values, These networks are not suited for mobile applications since they cannot ensure efficiency concerning size and speed. However, a quick and accurate identification of COVID-19 is essential, making compact mobile deep learning systems more appealing. Due to its vast performance demonstrated in numerous application areas, such as the identification of medieval writers [8], the detection of live crabs [5], crowd counting in real-time [9], and wave gauging remotely [4], A strong and adaptable solution for mobile detection of COVID-19 may be provided by the MobileNetV2 [11], an upgrade of the MobileNetV1 technology. The usage of depthwise separable convolutions, which employs two 1D convolutions with two kernels rather than a single 2D convolution, is the key differentiating factor of MobileNetV2. Because of this, the training process can be completed with fewer parameters and less memory, creating a compact and effective model.

Depthwise convolution:

$$Z^{[l]} = \text{DepthwiseConv}(A^{[l-1]}, W^{[l]}) \tag{1}$$

$$A^{[l]} = ReLU(Z^{[l]}) \tag{2}$$

where 'l' stands for the layer index, 'A[l − 1]' stands for input activation of previous layers, 'W[l]' represents depthwise convolutional filters, 'Z[l]' stands for the layer's output,

Pointwise convolution:

$$Z^{[l+1]} = \text{PointwiseConv}(A^{[l]}, W^{[l+1]}) \tag{3}$$

$$A^{[l+1]} = ReLU(Z^{[l+1]}) \tag{4}$$

where W represents the pointwise convolutional filters, and Z represents the pointwise convolutional layer's output.

Depthwise separable convolution:

$$Z^{[l+1]} = \text{DepthwiseConv}(A^{[l]}, W^{[l]}) * \text{PointwiseConv}(A^{[l]}, W^{[l+1]}) \tag{5}$$

$$A^{[l+1]} = ReLU(Z^{[l+1]}) \tag{6}$$

VGG16. The VGG16 [22] is an extremely large CNN that has been pre-trained and was developed by the VGG(Visual Geometry Group) at the University of Oxford. In the classification problem of the 2014 ILSVR, the VGG16 came in first place. Simple 3×3 size kernels in convolutional layers are combined in a specific order in the VGG16 architecture to manage the effect of larger appropriate fields. The VGG16 architecture that has been constructed consists of 13 layers of convolutional, followed by 3 fully linked layers. Despite the VGG16 architecture's simplicity, its memory use and computational cost are astronomically large because of the kernels' exponential growth.

$$Z^{[l]} = W^{[l]} * A^{[l-1]} + b^{[l]} \qquad (7)$$

$$A^{[l]} = ReLU(Z^{[l]}) \qquad (8)$$

where '*' indicates the convolution operation, 'Z[l]' is the output of the convolutional layer, and 'A[l]' represents activation. Where 'l' denotes the layer index, 'W[l]' represents the weights, and 'b[l]' is the bias term.

$$A^{[l]} = \text{MaxPooling}(Z^{[l]}) \qquad (9)$$

Maxpolling indicates picking the maximum value within the pooling window

$$Z^{[l]} = W^{[l]} A^{[l-1]} + b^{[l]} \qquad (10)$$

$$A^{[l]} = ReLU(Z^{[l]}) \qquad (11)$$

where Z[l] is the output of the fully connected layer, W[l] is the weights, and A[l-1] is the input activation from the previous layer.

ResNet50 and ResNet101. The "skip connections" idea was first used in the ResNet DL models [13], which are a subclass of CNNs. In ResNets, batch normalization and non-linearities (ReLU) are used in combination with convolutional layer bypassing [20]. The "skip connections" in ResNet topologies provide the network the ability to simply move the activations from one ResNet block to another, keeping information as it passes through the layers, and they enable the training of even deeper networks [23]. The two ResNet family versions, ResNet50 and ResNet101, which have 49 and 100 layers, respectively, are used as deep feature extractors in the currently proposed COVID-19 diagnosis technique.

$$Z^{[l+1]} = W_2^{[l]} \cdot ReLU(W_1^{[l]} \cdot A^{[l]} + b_1^{[l]}) + b_2^{[l]} \qquad (12)$$

$$A^{[l+1]} = ReLU(Z^{[l+1]}) + A^{[l]} \qquad (13)$$

where 'l' denotes the block index, 'A[l]' is the input activation from the previous block, 'W[l]' represents the weights of convolutional layers, 'b[l]' is the bias terms, $Z[l+1]$ is the output of the block, The residual connection $\hat{A}[l]$ adds the input activation to the output of the league.

DenseNet. A dense convolutional neural network is called DenseNet-169 [12]. In a DenseNet architecture, every layer is connected to every layer below it. The number of connections in a network with N levels is $N(N+1)/2$. Initial convolutional and pooling layers make up DenseNet-169. It comprises four dense blocks, with a transition layer following each one and a classification layer with a softmax activation function at the network's end.

$$Z^{[l]} = [\text{concat}(A^{[l-1]}, A^{[l-2]}, ..., A^{[0]})] \cdot W^{[l]} + b^{[l]} \tag{14}$$

$$A^{[l]} = ReLU(Z^{[l]}) \tag{15}$$

where 'l' denotes block index, 'A' represents the activations from input layers or old blocks or output of dense block, 'W' represents the weight of the convolutional layer, 'b' denotes the bias,

InceptionV3. Sequentially ordered convolution layers are not employed in the InceptionV3 [24] instead, inception modules are used. These modules are repeatedly stacked together to construct a huge network. In the inception modules, a non-symmetric convolution structure is created by employing several filters of different sizes, producing an ever-increasing number of diverse spatial features. By utilizing numerous scale features, the employment of inception modules not only significantly reduces the number of parameters but also improves the network's capacity for recognition [26].

Xception. The Xception [7] technique uses depthwise separable convolutions as a better version of the inception architecture, allowing for more effective utilization of model parameters. The depthwise separable convolutions (improved inception modules) used in the Xception in place of the regular inception modules use spatial information and more channels. The strengthened characteristics, such as the depth of information, are the outcome of the improved inception modules.

2.2 Handcrafted Features

Handcrafted features use the information immediately present in each image to compute attributes that attempt to characterize each image. These manually created features are calculated for each image and sent into the LGB Classifier.

Local Gradient Hexa Pattern (LGHP). The LGHP is a feature extraction method used in image processing and computer vision. By examining the gradient magnitudes and orientations, it seeks to obtain the local texture data of a picture.

The image is divided into overlapping blocks or patches by LGHP. The algorithm calculates the gradient magnitudes and orientations for each patch. The gradient orientations are then quantized into six bins to create a hexa pattern. The local texture information is represented by the hexa patterns. To create a feature vector, the LGHP algorithm joins together the histograms acquired from various blocks or patches. The count or frequency of a given hexa pattern inside each block or patch is represented by each feature vector element. The local texture patterns contained in the image can be described by the LGHP feature vectors, which can then be used as texture descriptors. Applications for these descriptors include texture classification, object recognition, and image retrieval.

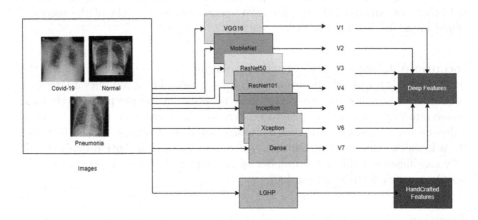

Fig. 1. Features Extraction

2.3   Max Pooling

We have handcrafted features and deep features with us right now. Now we need to concatenate them to classify them. so we need to apply max pooling on them

Let D represent Deep feature vector with(h, w, c1) values and H represent handcrafted features with (h, w, c2) values Now we need to max pool both the vectors individually:

$$P1 = MaxPool(D) \tag{16}$$

$$P2 = MaxPool(H) \tag{17}$$

max pool selects the maximum value in each pooling window. After applying the max pool individually we need to concatenate them:

$$C = Concatenate[P1, P2] \tag{18}$$

2.4 LGB Classifier

Decision trees are the foundation of the LGB gradient-boosting algorithm, which reduces memory utilization and increases model effectiveness. It employs the traditional XGB based on Exclusive Feature Bundling and Gradient-driven One Side Sampling (GOSS), two approaches. To increase estimation accuracy, GOSS randomly eliminates instances with tiny gradients while keeping examples with large gradients. GOSS filters out the data instances to determine an appropriate split value, making it faster than the XGB algorithm. This accelerates the procedure.

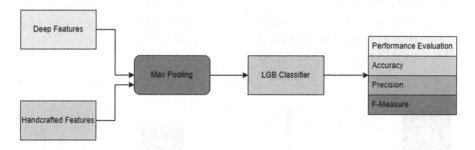

Fig. 2. Architecture of the Model

3 Results and Discussions

To evaluate the performance of the model proposed. Till now we have obtained the seven deep feature vectors with seven different CNN models. And also obtained the handcrafted feature vector of images by training using LGHP. Now we apply max pooling on them to get combined features. Now we need to classify using the LGB classifier. Now we have worked with handcrafted features plus deep features and seen the accuracy. The same process is worked without handcrafted features. Then we found that the accuracy that we are getting while including handcrafted features is high rather than just deep features. We not only performed this model for 7 CNN model architectures we have also tried with different combinations of 3 CNN models. There also we can see the same difference. When we include the handcrafted features we are getting better accuracy than when we are not including handcrafted features as shown in Table 1. We have performed this task for different sets of images. In every scenario, we have got the same result as above (Fig. 3).

Table 1. Accuracy of the models(%)

Models	Not Including handcrafted features	Including handcrafted features
INC+VGG+RES,	94	94.333333
DEN+INC+VGG	95.333333	95.666667
DEN+INC+RES	94.666667	95
DEN+INC+MOB	94.666667	95.333333
DEN+RES+MOB	94.666667	94.666667
INC+RES+MOB	93.666667	94
VGG+RES+MOB	95	95.333333
INC+VGG+MOB	94.333333	95.333333
DEN+VGG+RES	94.666667	95
DEN+VGG+MOB	95.333333	95.333333
7models	89.666667	90

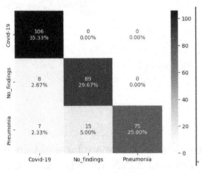
With handcrafted features

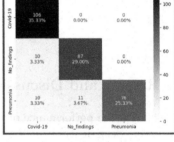
Without handcrafted features

Fig. 3. Confusion matrices

4   Conclusions

The work we have done so far reflects that including handcrafted features in the detection of COVID-19 is important. We have proved that adding handcrafted features signifies information added to the classifier with deep features obtained with different CNN models. The accuracy we have got With handcrafted features is more than without including handcrafted features. We performed this procedure with 1500 images initially but later we tried with 3000 images. In every scenario we have found that including handcrafted features plays a vital role in COVID-19 detection with good accuracy. The accuracy of the model is also increasing with more images but due to lack of resources, we are unable to get all the model results.

Acknowledgements. This work is supported by the "Research and Development Scheme of DST" under the project grant no "DST/ICD/Serbia/P-03/2021/(G)".

References

1. Albahli, S.: A deep ensemble learning method for effort-aware just-in-time defect prediction. Future Internet **11**(12), 246 (2019)
2. Alizadehsani, R., et al.: Risk factors prediction, clinical outcomes, and mortality in Covid-19 patients. J. Med. Virol. **93**(4), 2307–2320 (2021)
3. Boone, J.M., Seshagiri, S., Steiner, R.M.: Recognition of chest radiograph orientation for picture archiving and communications systems display using neural networks. J. Digit. Imaging **5**, 190–193 (1992)
4. Buscombe, D., Carini, R.J., Harrison, S.R., Chickadel, C.C., Warrick, J.A.: Optical wave gauging using deep neural networks. Coast. Eng. **155**, 103593 (2020)
5. Cao, S., Zhao, D., Liu, X., Sun, Y.: Real-time robust detector for underwater live crabs based on deep learning. Comput. Electron. Agric. **172**, 105339 (2020)
6. Chakraborty, C., Abougreen, A.: Intelligent Internet of Things and advanced machine learning techniques for Covid-19. EAI Endorsed Trans. Pervasive Health Technol. **7**(26) (2021)
7. Chollet, F.: Xception: deep learning with depthwise separable convolutions. In: Proceedings of the IEEE Conference on Computer Vision and Pattern Recognition, pp. 1251–1258 (2017)
8. Cilia, N.D., De Stefano, C., Fontanella, F., Marrocco, C., Molinara, M., Di Freca, A.S.: An end-to-end deep learning system for medieval writer identification. Pattern Recogn. Lett. **129**, 137–143 (2020)
9. Ding, Y., Zhu, Y., Feng, J., Zhang, P., Cheng, Z.: Interpretable spatio-temporal attention LSTM model for flood forecasting. Neurocomputing **403**, 348–359 (2020)
10. Guan, W., et al.: Clinical characteristics of coronavirus disease 2019, pp. 1708–1720 (2020)
11. Howard, A., Zhmoginov, A., Chen, L.C., Sandler, M., Zhu, M.: Inverted residuals and linear bottlenecks: mobile networks for classification, detection and segmentation (2018)
12. Huang, G., Liu, Z., Van Der Maaten, L., Weinberger, K.Q.: Densely connected convolutional networks. In: Proceedings of the IEEE Conference on Computer Vision and Pattern Recognition, pp. 4700–4708 (2017)
13. Jian, S., Kaiming, H., Shaoqing, R., Xiangyu, Z.: Deep residual learning for image recognition. In: IEEE Conference on Computer Vision & Pattern Recognition, pp. 770–778 (2016)
14. Lal, S., et al.: Adversarial attack and defence through adversarial training and feature fusion for diabetic retinopathy recognition. Sensors **21**(11), 3922 (2021)
15. Mahum, R., et al.: A novel hybrid approach based on deep CNN features to detect knee osteoarthritis. Sensors **21**(18), 6189 (2021)
16. Manzoor, K., et al.: A lightweight approach for skin lesion detection through optimal features fusion. Comput. Mater. Continua **70**(1), 1617–1630 (2022)
17. Meraj, T., et al.: Lung nodules detection using semantic segmentation and classification with optimal features. Neural Comput. Appl. **33**, 10737–10750 (2021)
18. Nasrullah, N., Sang, J., Alam, M.S., Mateen, M., Cai, B., Hu, H.: Automated lung nodule detection and classification using deep learning combined with multiple strategies. Sensors **19**(17), 3722 (2019)

19. Orioli, L., Hermans, M.P., Thissen, J.P., Maiter, D., Vandeleene, B., Yombi, J.C.: Covid-19 in diabetic patients: related risks and specifics of management. In: Annales d'endocrinologie, vol. 81, pp. 101–109. Elsevier (2020)

20. Pacheco, A.G., Krohling, R.A.: The impact of patient clinical information on automated skin cancer detection. Comput. Biol. Med. **116**, 103545 (2020)

21. Ravi, V., Narasimhan, H., Chakraborty, C., Pham, T.D.: Deep learning-based meta-classifier approach for Covid-19 classification using CT scan and chest X-ray images. Multimed. Syst. **28**(4), 1401–1415 (2022)

22. Simonyan, K., Zisserman, A.: Very deep convolutional networks for large-scale image recognition. arXiv preprint arXiv:1409.1556 (2014)

23. Somasundaram, K., Genish, T., et al.: An atlas based approach to segment the hippocampus from MRI of human head scans for the diagnosis of Alzheimers disease. Int. J. Comput. Intell. Inform. **5**(1) (2015)

24. Szegedy, C., Vanhoucke, V., Ioffe, S., Shlens, J., Wojna, Z.: Rethinking the inception architecture for computer vision. In: Proceedings of the IEEE Conference on Computer Vision and Pattern Recognition, pp. 2818–2826 (2016)

25. Yang, J., Zhang, M., Liu, Z., Ba, L., Gan, J., Xu, S.: Detection of lung atelectasis/consolidation by ultrasound in multiple trauma patients with mechanical ventilation. Critical Ultrasound J. **1**(1), 13–16 (2009)

26. Zhuang, X., Zhang, T.: Detection of sick broilers by digital image processing and deep learning. Biosys. Eng. **179**, 106–116 (2019)

An Improved AttnGAN Model for Text-to-Image Synthesis

Remya Gopalakrishnan[(✉)] [iD], Naveen Sambagni [iD], and P. V. Sudeep[(✉)] [iD]

Department of Electronics and Communication Engineering,
National Institute of Technology, Calicut, Kozhikode NIT Campus (PO), 673601,
Kerala, India
{remya_p210098ec,sudeep.pv}@nitc.ac.in

Abstract. Text-to-image generation models generate photo-realistic images from textual descriptions, typically using GANs and BiLSTM networks. However, as input text sequence length increases, these models suffer from a loss of information, leading to missed keywords and unsatisfactory results. To address this, we propose an attentional GAN (AttnGAN) model with a text attention mechanism. We evaluate AttnGAN variants on the MS-COCO dataset qualitatively and quantitatively. For the image quality analysis, we utilize performance measures such as FID score, R-precision, and IS score. Our results show that the proposed model outperforms existing approaches, producing more realistic images by preserving vital information in the input sequence.

Keywords: Context awareness · Deep learning · Image generation · Text encoder · Unified text attention

1 Introduction

Generative adversarial networks (GAN) [3] have revolutionized the field of image, video, and audio generation by effectively estimating the statistical properties of high-dimensional signals. Specifically, in the realm of text-to-image (TTI) generation, plausible images based on descriptions in natural language have been produced by GAN-based models [8,22]. This advancement opens up a variety of practical applications, including art creation, data visualization, graphic design, E-learning, data augmentation for image classifiers, and so on [8,11]. However, despite the promising progress made in GAN-based TTI generation, further exploration and research are necessary to fully understand the relationship between visual contents and natural languages.

To improve the fine-grained image generation process, GAN-based methods have utilized multiple generators [8,20,22], attention-guided refinement modules [9,21,24,26], and auxiliary architectures [23,25]. These methods involve extracting features from natural language text using a bidirectional LSTM recurrent neural network (RNN) [2]. However, natural language is ambiguous, and extracting relevant semantic features is crucial. LSTM has gained significant popularity in TTI research because of its proficiency in handling sequential data. However, a challenge in using LSTM is its vulnerability to longer-term dependency issues, which can lead to the loss of pertinent information [7,13,14]. Additionally, sequential text processing can lead to the omission of relevant keywords, further reducing output quality. To mitigate this issue, neural architecture with an attention mechanism can be employed to emphasize pertinent information in the input data. For this, a unified text attention architecture has been integrated into the TTI model, thereby reducing information loss in the model.

The integrated unified attention model, which incorporates the Multi Head Attention (MHA) mechanism, is an extension of the model present in [7]. The self-attention mechanism addresses the challenge of long-term dependencies by establishing global connections between each input word and every other word in pairs. In order to compute new representations for the input sequence, this process is iteratively repeated for each word. Moreover, MHA enables simultaneous attention to be applied to extracted features using different linear transformations of the same input. We experimented with the attentional GAN (AttnGAN) [21] model on the Microsoft common objects in context (MS-COCO) [17] dataset to assess the efficacy of text attention.

This work makes two main contributions to the AttnGAN-based TTI generation. Firstly, a unified text attention model is integrated with the AttnGAN [21] model to reduce information loss associated with LSTM networks. Secondly, the multi-head attention mechanism is utilized to learn different representations of the same text sequence by employing different linear transformations in each head. The rest of the paper is structured as follows. The relevant works in GAN-based TTI-generating models are covered in Sect. 2. Section 3 covers an explanation of the proposed architecture as well as the attention techniques used in natural language processing (NLP). Section 4 presents the experimental findings and comparisons to the base model. Section 5 is the conclusion of the work presented in this paper.

2 Literature Review

The primary objective of TTI synthesis is to produce high-quality images that align with the descriptions provided. The input descriptions are converted into semantic vectors by the text encoders and are subsequently fed into the generative network, often utilizing GAN [3] architecture for image generation. At the beginning stage, TTI synthesis primarily focused on improving the quality of the generated image. In 2016, the GAN-INT-CLS [18] model was introduced with a single-stage GAN network to generate plausible 64×64 resolution images. Following this, a two-stage network known as StackGAN [20] created images with higher resolution. Subsequent works [8,21–23] also adopted the stacked network approach, where the generation process is divided into multiple stages, generating more detailed and realistic images.

Then, the researchers recognized the importance of ensuring that the generated images align closely with the corresponding textual descriptions. For this, approaches such as [12, 23] have been developed. In [23] TTI generation is combined with image-to-text generation in the training process. Furthermore, visual-text multimodal attention mechanisms have played a crucial role in improving tasks related to images and text. For instance, the multimodal attention mechanism in AttnGAN [21] model enabled GANs to produce fine-grained, high-resolution images that closely correspond to natural language descriptions.

Furthermore, contrastive learning approaches, which aim to maximize the mutual information between text-image pairs, have been adopted in [25, 27, 30]. Additionally, the literature discusses simple and effective single stage TTI architectures such as [15, 16, 28]. The [16, 28] models incorporates a deep text-image fusion block for full fusion of textual and visual features. These developments reveal the growing trend in which researchers focus both on enhancing the image quality and alignment of the generated images and the input text in TTI generation.

In GAN models, images are typically generated based on text features extracted by an LSTM-based text encoder. However, LSTM networks have a limitation of information loss as the input sequence length increases [7, 13, 14]. This can lead to unsatisfactory results if important keywords are missed during sequence-by-sequence text processing in the LSTM network. To tackle this, we propose integrating a text attention mechanism into the text encoder. This attention mechanism helps the text encoder prioritize and preserve significant information within the input sequence, which the LSTM network can effectively utilize. Hence, the model can better capture and retain essential details from the input text, mitigating the longer-term dependency problem and improving the performance of the TTI synthesis system.

3   Methods and Materials

This work proposes the use of a text attention mechanism with AttnGAN [21] for fine-grained TTI generation. We incorporated the text attention mechanism with a unified model and integrated it into the text encoder of AttnGAN [21]. This mechanism creates contextual representations of the input sequence, which are subsequently applied to the LSTM network. This approach helps to reduce the information loss associated with the inherent sequential processing and enhances the output quality.

3.1   Attention in NLP

The fundamental concept underlying attention is the computation of weight distribution on the input sequence, which assigns more weight to more significant components. Thus, the neural architecture's attention mechanism makes it possible to dynamically highlight important information in the input data. NLP [10] generally uses textual elements as the input, either in their original input form or as a higher-level representation created from the input, upon which weights are assigned.

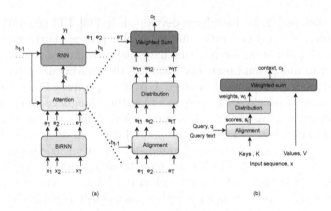

Fig. 1. Text attention architectures, (a) RNN search model with its attention network, and (b) Unified model.

RNN search is a classic attention architecture in NLP, used for machine translation from an input sequence $x = x_1, x_2, \ldots x_T$ to an output y. As Fig. 1 depicts, it consists of a BiRNN encoder and a decoder comprising an attention network and RNN. For each input sequence, the encoder computes the annotation term e. The attention network generates a context vector c_t for the input sequence at each time step t. For this, the alignment network takes as input the previous hidden state of the RNN h_{t-1} and the annotations to produce the scores s_{ti}. The scores represent the alignment between the inputs around position i and the outputs around position t. The distribution function normalizes these scores to obtain weights w_{ti}. The annotations are weighted and summed to produce the context vector c_t. Finally, the RNN computes a probability distribution over all possible output symbols and selects the most likely symbol from the embedding space as the output.

Further, the unified text attention model [7,10] eliminates the need for RNNs and condenses the entire encoder-decoder architecture into a single unit (see Fig. 1). This model maps a sequence of encoded data features, denoted as keys K, to a distribution of weights w. Additionally, a query element q, determines the attention weights of K that are deemed relevant to the task at hand. To compute the attention weights, the alignment function compares the q and the K, and from the derived scores s, the distribution function normalizes them into w. The computed attention weights are applied to the values V, which can be seen as a different representation of the input data. These weighted representations are then merged to produce the context vector c_t.

Moreover, the MHA mechanism [7] employs a self-attention that computes attention only based on the input sequence. Further, the input Q is a multidimensional element processed in parallel with K and V (see Fig. 2), which are different representations of the same data. The process involves applying multiple attention steps to each element of K, utilizing the same query at each step. This generates separate context embeddings, allowing each element of the new sequence to be influenced by the entire input,

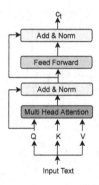

Fig. 2. The Multihead Attention Network architecture that uses a self-attention mechanism.

incorporating context without being constrained by local boundaries. This approach is particularly advantageous in capturing long-range dependencies, which RNNs struggle with [1,7]. Additionally, using different linear transformations of the same input in multiple attention heads enhances the model's ability to capture complex dependencies in the input sequence. The computational complexity of the attention head is $O(T^2d+Td^2)$, where T is the number of input elements of d dimension. The overall network architecture incorporates a feed-forward network layer with ReLu activation and layer normalization to improve learning.

3.2   Proposed Method

Our proposal involves incorporating a text attention mechanism with the unified text attention model into the text encoder of AttnGAN [21]. The AttnGAN [21] model is known for its ability to generate fine-grained TTI results through a multi-stage refinement. By integrating the text attention mechanism, we aim to generate contextual representations of the input sequence that reduce information loss associated with LSTM networks and thus improve AttnGAN [21].

The generator in AttnGAN utilizes a multimodal attentional network to generate specific sub-regions in the image by focusing on relevant words. Additionally, it encodes the natural language summary into a global sentence vector and each word into a word vector. The model also incorporates a deep attentional multimodal similarity model (DAMSM), which considers both global sentence-level details and fine-grained word-level information to calculate image-text similarity. DAMSM enhances the image-text matching loss, guiding the training of the generator for more accurate image generation.

Figure 3 illustrates the detailed architecture for the modified AttnGAN [21]. The text description is inputted into the text encoder integrated with an MHA mechanism. The text encoder produces the final hidden state, which represents the sentence feature s. The hidden states from all time steps also represent the word features w. After conditional augmentation (CA), which introduces variations in the generated images, the sentence features are combined with a

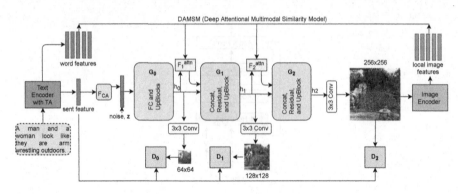

Fig. 3. The architecture of the proposed AttnGAN$_{\text{TA}}$ model.

noise vector z. The resulting input is then fed into the generator network G_0, which generates the image feature vector h_0.

$$h_0 = G_0(z, F^{ca}(s)) \tag{1}$$

The multimodal attention network inputs both the image feature vector and word features. It generates a word-context vector c for each subregion of the image.

$$c_i = F^{attn}(w, h_{i-1}) \tag{2}$$

where,

$$c_j = \sum_{i=0}^{T-1} \beta_{j,i} w_i \text{ and, } \beta_{j,i} = \frac{exp(h_j^T w_i)}{\sum_{k=0}^{T-1} exp(h_j^T w_k)} \tag{3}$$

The selection of specific words for generating particular regions of the final image depends critically on the word-context vector. Fine-grained images are generated in subsequent stages using the word-context vector and previous image features.

$$x_i, h_i = G_i(h_{i-1}, c_i) \text{ for } i = 1, 2 \tag{4}$$

The generator G and discriminator D are designed to minimize the minimax objective,

$$\min_{\text{G}} \max_{\text{D}} E_{x \sim p_x}[log D(x)] + E_{x \sim p_z}[log(1 - D(G(x)))]. \tag{5}$$

Here x is an actual data point sampled from the data distribution P_x, and the input z is sampled from a simple prior distribution P_z.

The objective function of the generator network is defined as the sum of the adversarial loss and DAMSM loss weighted with λ.

$$L_G = \sum_{i=0}^{2} L_{Gi} + \lambda L_{DAMSM} \tag{6}$$

where,

$$L_{G_i} = -\frac{1}{2}[E_{x \sim p_z} log D_i(G_i(x)) + E_{x \sim p_z} log D_i(G_i(x,s))] \tag{7}$$

Similarly, the discriminator network's objective function is to minimize discriminator loss.

$$
\begin{aligned}
L_{D_i} = -\frac{1}{2}[&E_{x \sim p_x} log D_i(x) + E_{x \sim p_z} log(1 - D_i(G_i(x))) \\
&+ E_{x \sim p_x} log D_i(x,s) + E_{x \sim p_x} log(1 - D_i(G_i(x,s)))]
\end{aligned}
\tag{8}
$$

G and D are updated to minimize the L_G and L_D loss, respectively.

4   Experiments

To verify the importance of text attention in TTI generation, we conducted experiments using the text attention mechanism in AttnGAN [21]. Additionally, we evaluated the performance of the proposed method qualitatively and quantitatively and compared it to the base model. We trained and tested AttnGAN [21] and AttnGAN$_{TA}$ on a local workstation with NVIDIA Quadro RTX 8000. The models are implemented using PyTorch, an open-source Python library.

4.1   Experimental Setup

We utilized the MS-COCO [17] dataset for our experiments, which includes 80K training images and 40K testing images, each with five textual descriptions. This dataset comprises images depicting complex everyday scenes that feature common objects in their natural contexts. It encompasses 91 categories of everyday objects, many of which have over 5,000 labeled instances. We can infer contextual information about the image by analyzing the average number of object categories and instances per image.

Using the same training parameters, the AttnGAN [21] and AttnGAN$_{TA}$ models are trained on the MS-COCO [17] dataset. A bidirectional LSTM text encoder with an embedding dimension of 256 is used for text embedding. Additionally, in the AttnGAN$_{TA}$ model, the MHA encoder network uses six attention heads with an embedding size of 300. The image encoder is a CNN based on the Inception-v3 model [19], which is pre-trained on the ImageNet dataset [4]. The local feature matrix, measuring 768×289, is obtained from the "mixed6e" layer of Inception-v3. On the other hand, the global feature vector, with a size of 2048, is extracted from its final average pooling layer.

The models combine the input noise vector with the sentence embedding to obtain a feature vector. This feature vector is gradually transformed into an image through refinement and a 3×3 convolution. The discriminators in the models have down-sampling layers to convert the input into a tensor and are fed to a sigmoid layer to classify the images as real or fake based on probabilities.

The models undergo training for 200 epochs with the given parameter values: Adam optimizer [29] with $\beta_1 = 0.5$, $\beta_2 = 0.999$, a learning rate of $\alpha = 0.0002$, and a batch size of 20. For DAMSM, the hyper-parameters $\gamma_1 = 4$, $\gamma_2 = 5$, and $\gamma_3 = 10$ are chosen, along with the balancing hyper-parameter $\lambda = 50$.

To evaluate the models, 30,000 images are generated by each model using randomly selected text descriptions that are not seen during training. The distance between the generated and real images in the feature space extracted from the pre-trained Inception v3 model is calculated for the FID [6] metric. The Inception model is applied to the generated image to obtain the conditional label distribution and the marginal distribution for IS [5] calculation. For R-precision [21], the evaluation involves selecting one ground truth description and 99 randomly chosen mismatching descriptions as candidate text descriptions for each query image.

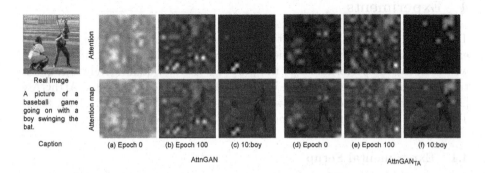

Fig. 4. Attention and attention maps of images during DAMSM pretraining for AttnGAN [21] and AttnGAN$_{TA}$ models on the MS-COCO [17] dataset. Columns: Attention map at epoch 0, attention map at epoch 100, and attention map for word "boy" for the given models.

4.2 Results

First, we examined the attention maps generated by AttnGAN [21] and AttnGAN$_{TA}$ models during the pretraining of DAMSM to assess the significance of text attention in the proposed model. For the given real input image and corresponding caption in Fig. 4, the top row represents the attention and the bottom row shows the attention maps for the given models. The attention maps are created by calculating the attention received from each word in the input caption and overlaying it on the given image. Further, the attention received from all words in the caption gives the overall attention. Figure 4(a) and 4(d) display the overall attention and attention map at epoch 0 for the AttnGAN [21] and AttnGAN$_{TA}$ models, respectively. It can be observed that the AttnGAN [21] model assigns equal attention to all the words, whereas the AttnGAN$_{TA}$ model focuses more on the relevant words. Figure 4(b) and 4(e) show the learned overall attention and attention maps at epoch 100 for the given models. The attention maps demonstrate that the proposed model significantly outperforms the AttnGAN [21] model in learning the semantic meaning of the text descriptions.

To further support this observation, Fig. 4(c) and 4(f) display the attention map for the word "boy" for the given models. The attention maps highlight the sub-regions of the image that receive the most attention based on the word "boy". It can be seen that the proposed model accurately maps the image of the boy and the base model fails to do so.

Further, we performed qualitative evaluations of the images generated by the AttnGAN [21] and AttnGAN$_{TA}$ models on the MS-COCO [17] dataset. Figure 5 displays the generated images by the respective TTI models for the input captions, with the real image provided in the first row for visual comparison. All TTI models can produce clean, realistic images. However, the proposed approach produces images with enhanced visual quality and is aligned with the given caption. The proposed model successfully generates a green van and outdoor scene, displayed in corresponding images in column 2 and column 6, respectively, that match the given caption, whereas the base model fails to do so. As displayed in column 4, even though the proposed model generates pillows on the bed instead of floor pillows, it successfully creates the interior of a straw hut. Qualitative evaluations on the MS-COCO [17] dataset indicate the superior performance of the AttnGAN$_{TA}$ model in generating complex scenarios.

To gain a deeper understanding of the knowledge acquired by the proposed model, we conducted an analysis of the attention maps generated by various models, as depicted in Fig. 6. The results obtained with the AttnGAN [21] model and the AttnGAN$_{TA}$ model are shown in the first and second rows, respectively. The left column of each row displays the generated image, and the following columns show the attention maps for the five top most attended words in the caption. These attention maps highlight the sub-regions of the image that receive the most attention based on the corresponding words in the caption. It can be

Fig. 5. Examples of generated images by AttnGAN [21] and AttnGAN$_{TA}$ models trained on MS-COCO [17] dataset.

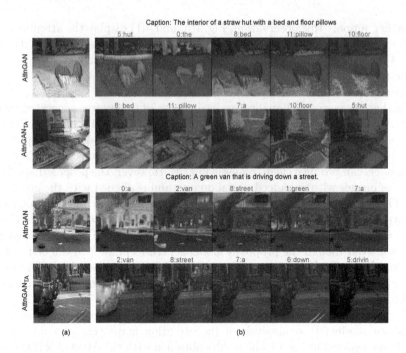

Fig. 6. Attention maps of images generated by AttnGAN [21] and AttnGAN$_{TA}$ models for the given captions with MS-COCO [17] dataset. Columns:(a) Generated image, and (b) attention map of top-5 most attended words.

observed that the AttnGAN$_{TA}$ model outperforms the AttnGAN [21] model in generating better images and understanding the semantic meaning of the text descriptions. The integration of text attention in the text encoder allows for the accurate detection of relevant features in the text description, resulting in improved image generation.

Table 1. Performance comparison of AttnGAN [21], and AttnGAN$_{TA}$ models in terms of quality evaluations metrics on the MS-COCO [17] dataset.

Dataset	Method	FID [6] ↓	IS [5] ↑	R-precision [21] ↑
MS-COCO [17]	AttnGAN [21]	26.03	26.40 ± 0.46	81.86 ± 0.61
	AttnGAN$_{TA}$ (Proposed)	**23.81**	**27.41 + 0.47**	**82.64 + 0.85**

We compared their FID [6], IS [5], and R-precision [21] values on the MS-COCO [17] dataset after training for 200 epochs to quantitatively evaluate the TTI models' performance. Table 1 presents the metric scores obtained with the AttnGAN$_{TA}$ and AttnGAN [21] models. It can be observed that the proposed model outperforms the base model in terms of all metric scores. This indicates that the proposed model generates higher quality and more diverse images that are matched with the given text descriptions. In summary, both qualitative and quantitative analyses demonstrate that the proposed model performs well and produces superior results compared to the base model.

5   Conclusions

In this paper, a variant of AttnGAN [21] is proposed by integrating text attention mechanisms into the text encoder network to enhance its performance. Our proposed AttnGAN$_{TA}$ model is able to preserve relevant information in the input sequence, reducing the risk of missing important keywords. Thereby, this integration improves the model's semantic understanding and visual quality. Furthermore, the use of an MHA mechanism allows the model to learn different representations of the same text sequence by utilizing various linear transformations in each head. Thus, the possibility of the proposed model for creating high-resolution images that accurately interpret input text can significantly enhance various aspects of human-computer interaction. To evaluate the effectiveness of our approach, we conducted experiments on the MS-COCO [17] dataset and compared it against the baseline model. Our quantitative results with FID [6], IS [5], and R-precision [21] metrics demonstrated how well our approach outperforms the baseline model. Notably, our approach achieves a significant 8.52 % improvement in the FID [6] score compared to AttnGAN [21].

References

1. Bengio, Y., Simard, P., Frasconi, P.: Learning long-term dependencies with gradient descent is difficult. IEEE Trans. Neural Netw. **5**(2), 157–166 (1994)
2. Schuster, M., Paliwal, K.K.: Bidirectional recurrent neural networks. IEEE Trans. Signal Process. **45**(11), 2673–2681 (1997)
3. Goodfellow, I., et al.: Generative adversarial nets. In: Advances in Neural Information Processing Systems, vol. 27, pp. 2672–2680 (2014)
4. Russakovsky, O., et al.: ImageNet large scale visual recognition challenge. Int. J. Comput. Vis. **115**(3), 211–252 (2015)
5. Salimans, T., Goodfellow, I., Zaremba, W., Cheung, V., Radford, A., Chen, X.: Improved techniques for training GANs. In: Advances in Neural Information Processing Systems, vol. 29 (2016)
6. Heusel, M., Ramsauer, H., Unterthiner, T., Nessler, B., Hochreiter, S.: GANs trained by a two time-scale update rule converge to a local nash equilibrium. In: Advances in Neural Information Processing Systems, vol. 30 (2017)
7. Vaswani, A., et al.: Attention is all you need. In: Advances in Neural Information Processing Systems, vol. 30 (2017)
8. Zhang, H., et al.: StackGAN++: realistic image synthesis with stacked generative adversarial networks. IEEE Trans. Pattern Anal. Mach. Intell. **41**(8), 1947–1962 (2018)
9. Li, B., Qi, X., Lukasiewicz, T., Torr, P.: Controllable text-to-image generation. In: Advances in Neural Information Processing Systems, vol. 32 (2019)

10. Galassi, A., Marco Lippi, M., Torroni, P.: Attention in natural language processing. IEEE Trans. Neural Netw. Learn. Syst. **32**(10), 4291–4308 (2020)
11. Naveen, S., Kiran, M.S.R., Indupriya, M., Manikanta, T.V., Sudeep, P.V.: Transformer models for enhancing AttnGAN based text to image generation. Image Vis. Comput. **115**, 104284 (2021)
12. Peng, D., Yang, W., Liu, C., Lü, S.: SAM-GAN: self-attention supporting multistage generative adversarial networks for text-to-image synthesis. Neural Netw. **138**, 57–67 (2021)
13. Andayani, F., Theng, L.B., Tsun, M.T., Chua, C.: Hybrid LSTM-transformer model for emotion recognition from speech audio files. IEEE Access **10**, 36018–36027 (2022)
14. Borji, A.: Pros and cons of GAN evaluation measures: new developments. Comput. Vis. Image Underst. **215**, 103329 (2022)
15. Zhang, Z., Schomaker, L.: DiverGAN: an efficient and effective single-stage framework for diverse text-to-image generation. Neurocomputing **473**, 182–198 (2022)
16. Jin, D., Li, G., Yu, Q., Yu, L., Cui, J., Qi, M.: GMF-GAN: gradual multi-granularity semantic fusion GAN for text-to-image synthesis. Digit. Signal Process. **140**, 104105 (2023)
17. Lin, T.-Y., et al.: Microsoft COCO: common objects in context. In: Fleet, D., Pajdla, T., Schiele, B., Tuytelaars, T. (eds.) ECCV 2014. LNCS, vol. 8693, pp. 740–755. Springer, Cham (2014). https://doi.org/10.1007/978-3-319-10602-1_48
18. Reed, S., Akata, Z., Yan, X., Logeswaran, L., Schiele, B., Lee, H.: Generative adversarial text to image synthesis. In: International Conference on Machine Learning, pp. 1060–1069. PMLR (2016)
19. Szegedy, C., Vanhoucke, V., Ioffe, S., Shlens, J., Wojna, Z.: Rethinking the inception architecture for computer vision. In: Proceedings of the IEEE Conference on Computer Vision and Pattern Recognition, pp. 2818–2826 (2016)
20. Zhang, H., et al.: StackGAN: text to photo-realistic image synthesis with stacked generative adversarial networks. In: Proceedings of the IEEE International Conference on Computer Vision, pp. 5907–5915 (2017)
21. Xu, T., et al.: AttnGAN: fine-grained text to image generation with attentional generative adversarial networks. In: Proceedings of the IEEE Conference on Computer Vision and Pattern Recognition, pp. 1316–1324 (2018)
22. Zhang, Z., Xie, Y., Yang, L.: Photographic text-to-image synthesis with a hierarchically-nested adversarial network. In: Proceedings of the IEEE Conference on Computer Vision and Pattern Recognition, pp. 6199–6208 (2018)
23. Qiao, T., Zhang, J., Xu, D., Tao, D.: MirrorGAN: learning text-to-image generation by redescription. In: Proceedings of the IEEE/CVF Conference on Computer Vision and Pattern Recognition, pp. 1505–1514 (2019)
24. Tan, H., Liu, X., Li, X., Zhang, Y., Yin, B.: Semantics-enhanced adversarial nets for text-to-image synthesis. In: Proceedings of the IEEE/CVF International Conference on Computer Vision, pp. 10501–10510 (2019)
25. Yin, G., Liu, B., Sheng, L., Yu, N., Wang, X., Shao, J.: Semantics disentangling for text-to-image generation. In: Proceedings of the IEEE/CVF Conference on Computer Vision and Pattern Recognition, pp. 2327–2336 (2019)
26. Zhu, M., Pan, P., Chen, W., Yang, Y.: DM-GAN: dynamic memory generative adversarial networks for text-to-image synthesis. In: Proceedings of the IEEE/CVF Conference on Computer Vision and Pattern Recognition, pp. 5802–5810 (2019)
27. Zhang, H., Koh, J.Y., Baldridge, J., Lee, H., Yang, Y.: Cross-modal contrastive learning for text-to-image generation. In: Proceedings of the IEEE/CVF Conference on Computer Vision and Pattern Recognition, pp. 833–842 (2021)

28. Tao, M., Tang, H., Wu, F., Jing, X.Y., Bao, B.K., Xu, C.: DF-GAN: a simple and effective baseline for text-to-image synthesis. In: Proceedings of the IEEE/CVF Conference on Computer Vision and Pattern Recognition, pp. 16515–16525 (2022)
29. Kingma, D.P., Ba, J.: Adam: a method for stochastic optimization. In: arXiv preprint arXiv:1412.6980 (2014)
30. Ye, H., Yang, X., Takac, M., Sunderraman, R., Ji, S.: Improving text-to-image synthesis using contrastive learning. In: arXiv preprint arXiv:2107.02423 (2021)

Analyzing the Impact of Instagram Filters on Facial Expression Recognition Algorithms

Jayshree Gupta[1], Sumeet Saurav[2]($\boxtimes$), and Sanjay Singh[2]

[1] Banasthali Vidyapith, Tonk, Rajasthan, India
[2] CSIR-Central Electronics Engineering Research Institute, Pilani, Rajasthan, India
sumeet@ceeri.res.in

Abstract. The human face conveys lots of information through facial expressions to other human beings and computers, sharing information about intentions, emotional health status, age, and ethnicity. This results in the criticality of Facial Expression Recognition (FER) systems in various applications, including emotion detection, behavior analysis, human-computer interactions, etc. However, the increasing prevalence of beauty filters in social media platforms like Instagram and other platforms has raised concerns about their potential impact on the accuracy and reliability of FER systems. The beauty filters could lead to a misalignment between the facial expressions captured by FER systems and the actual emotional state of the individual. In this research, we comprehensively analyze the influence of Instagram filters on FER systems using 30 commonly used Instagram Filters and their implications for research and application on the Real-world Affective Faces Database (RAF-DB) dataset. To assess the effectiveness of the suggested approach, we performed experiments employing three distinct FER models (EfficientFace, MA-Net, and POSTER) to validate the performance. We evaluated the performance of the proposed method by employing widely recognized evaluation metrics, including accuracy, precision, recall, and F1-score. This research highlights the challenges and implications associated with Instagram filters' influence on facial expression recognition, emphasizing the need for further research, algorithmic advancements, and ethical considerations in this evolving landscape.

Keywords: Facial expression recognition · Beauty filters · Instagram filters · Emotion detection

1 Introduction

Facial expressions are essential for human communication, and recognizing and understanding them has been extensively studied [14]. This research has practical applications in social interactions, robotics, medicine, and driver fatigue monitoring [7]. Advances in technology, such as cameras and machine learning, have contributed to the progress of Facial Expression Recognition (FER) systems [12].

H. Kaur et al. (Eds.): CVIP 2023, CCIS 2011, pp. 152–163, 2024.
https://doi.org/10.1007/978-3-031-58535-7_13

Deep learning techniques have become prominent in handling the challenges of emotion recognition in real-world settings, surpassing traditional methods that relied on handcrafted features [10]. Deep learning models have achieved state-of-the-art accuracy but face difficulties due to the substantial intra-class variability and inter-subject variations in facial expressions [9].

Existing facial expression databases are insufficient to train deep neural networks effectively, as they lack the diverse data required for robust recognition [11]. Challenges in FER include variations in pose, lighting conditions, occlusions, and biases related to individual identity [3]. Factors like variations in pose, image quality, and the use of Instagram filters can negatively impact FER accuracy [4]. Facial beautification techniques, popularized through social media platforms and smartphone applications, can alter the shape and texture of faces, posing challenges for facial expression recognition in security applications [1].

Filtered images, including those taken with smartphones, have gained popularity and can hinder face detection and recognition systems [5]. The ability to recognize individuals and detect faces can be impeded by filters that distort or conceal facial features. Methods need to be explored to mitigate the impact of these filters on face detection and recognition performance [2]. Some strategies involve training identity recognition systems using manipulated images [13], which has enhanced accuracy even with test images containing similar manipulations [6]. Further research is needed to understand the consequences of image manipulation and the effects of "beautification" filters on facial features [5]. This work aims to contribute to multiple aspects of the field and provide insights into these challenges.

2 Materials and Methods

2.1 Facial Expression Recognition Algorithms

Implementing the Facial Expression Recognition (FER) model for analyzing the impact of Instagram filters comprises several steps, as shown in Fig. 1. Initially, we employ transfer learning to train the model using a large dataset, and then we assess the model's performance using Instagram-filtered images to detect the seven fundamental expressions.

To accomplish this, we utilize three deep learning models: EfficientFace [16], MA-Net [15], and POSTER [17]. While these models share a common backbone architecture, they have been trained on different datasets to facilitate effective transfer learning. Each model provides unique insights into the impact of Instagram filters on FER performance.

To train the FER model, we incorporate pre-trained model checkpoints from each model mentioned above, specifically trained on the Real-world Affective Faces Database (RAF-DB) dataset. This integration enhances the accuracy and robustness of the FER system when analyzing filtered images. Next, we evaluate each filter's performance using the EfficientFace, MA-Net, and POSTER models. It allows us to measure the impact of each filter on FER accuracy and

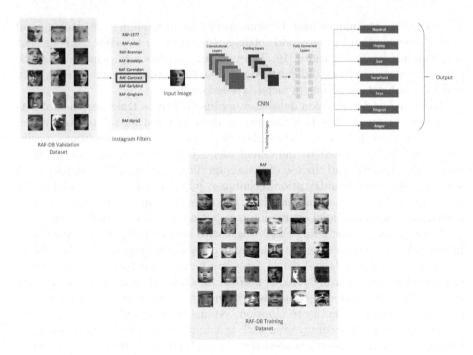

154   J. Gupta et al.

Fig. 1. Proposed FER pipeline for analysis

reliability. Through this analysis, we aim to uncover discrepancies or misclassifications between the captured facial expressions and the emotional states when filters are applied to the facial images.

2.2   EfficientFace

Figure 2 shows the internal details of the EfficientFace model. It is a robust facial expression recognition network that uses a local-feature extractor and a channel-spatial modulator to capture local and global-salient facial features. It also uses a label distribution learning method to handle the ambiguity and diversity of facial expressions. The model achieves state-of-the-art results on several benchmark datasets with fewer parameters than other methods [16].

EfficientFace is a lightweight facial expression recognition network that is designed to be both accurate and efficient. EfficientFace has demonstrated its efficacy on various facial expression recognition datasets, such as RAF-DB, CAER-S, and AffectNet-7, achieving accuracies of 88.36%, 85.87%, and 63.70%, respectively. Additionally, it has achieved a comparable performance on the AffectNet-8 dataset, with an accuracy of 59.89%. It achieves state-of-the-art accuracy on these datasets, while being significantly more efficient than other state-of-the-art methods [16].

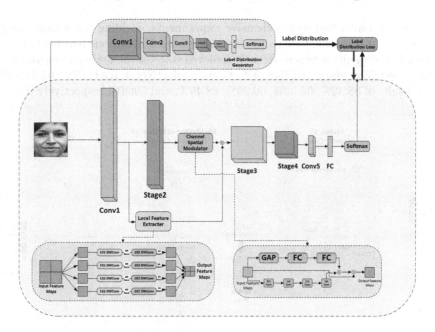

Fig. 2. Internal details of the EfficientFace model [16]

2.3   MA-Net

Figure 3 shows the internal details of the MA-Net model that is a deep learning model for facial expression recognition (FER) in the wild, which means recognizing facial expressions from unconstrained images with occlusion and pose variation. MA-Net stands for multi-scale and local attention network [15]. It comprises three primary components: a feature pre-extractor, a multi-scale module, and a local attention module. The feature pre-extractor is responsible for extracting middle-level features from the input images. The multi-scale module combines features with varying receptive fields, thereby reducing the sensitivity of deeper convolution layers to occlusion and variations in pose. The local attention module guides the network to concentrate on local salient features, mitigating the impact of occlusion and non-frontal pose on facial expression recognition.

MA-Net is a deep learning model for facial expression recognition in the wild. It is based on the ResNet architecture and introduces two novel attention modules to learn deep global multi-scale and local attention features. The global attention module uses a self-attention mechanism to learn global dependencies between different facial regions. The local attention module uses a spatial attention mechanism to learn local dependencies within each facial region [15]. The combination of global and local attention allows MA-Net to learn more discriminative features for facial expression recognition. This is especially important for recognizing facial expressions in the wild, where faces are often distorted or occluded.

MA-Net underwent comprehensive experiments, yielding outstanding outcomes and establishing itself as the leading approach in various real-world facial expression recognition benchmarks. It achieved state-of-the-art accuracies on several datasets including CAER-S, AffectNet-7, AffectNet-8, RAF-DB, and SFEW, with results of 88.42%, 64.53%, 60.29%, 88.40%, and 59.40% respectively [15].

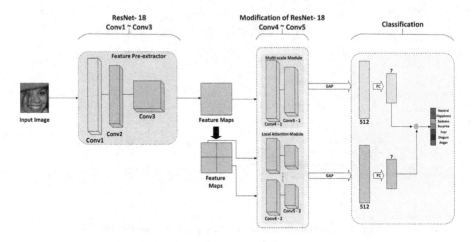

Fig. 3. Internal details of the MA-Net model [15]

2.4   POSTER

Figure 4 shows the internal details of the Pyramid crOss-fuSion TransformER network (POSTER). The POSTER model addresses three key issues: inter-class similarity, intra-class discrepancy, and scale sensitivity of the existing static-image-based FER models. It is a transformer-based cross-fusion method that consists of two main components: a two-stream module and a pyramid module. The two-stream module is used to fuse facial landmark and image features through a transformer-based cross-fusion paradigm, which enables effective collaboration of the two types of features and proper attention to salient facial regions. The pyramid module is used to promote scale invariance by extracting features at different scales and fusing them with another cross-fusion paradigm. The model uses MS-Celeb-1M pre-trained IR50 model as the backbone to extract image features from the facial images.

POSTER model is composed of two main components: a pyramid feature extractor and a transformer cross-fusion module. The pyramid feature extractor consists of a series of convolutional layers that extract features from the input image at different scales. The transformer cross-fusion module then fuses the features from different scales using a self-attention mechanism. This allows the model to learn to learn more discriminative features than previous methods, which makes it more robust to factors such as pose, expression, and illumination changes [17].

Extensive experiments were conducted to evaluate POSTER, which revealed its superior performance compared to state-of-the-art (SOTA) methods on various datasets. Specifically, on RAF-DB, it achieved an accuracy of 92.05%. On FERPlus, it achieved an accuracy of 91.62%. Additionally, on AffectNet with 7 classes, it achieved an accuracy of 67.31%, and on AffectNet with 8 classes, it achieved an accuracy of 63.34%. These results indicate a significant improvement over previous models [17].

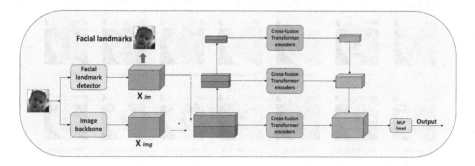

Fig. 4. Internal details of the POSTER model [17]

3   Experimental Results and Discussion

In this section, we discuss the details of our experimental configuration and the diverse experiments conducted on various FER datasets. Our experiments were conducted on an Ubuntu Linux operating system, utilizing PyTorch framework, and executed on NVIDIA GeForce RTX 3060 GPU to leverage its computational capabilities.

3.1   Datasets

In order to assess the effectiveness of our proposed approach, we conducted experiments using the RAF-DB dataset, supplemented with 30 Instagram filters applied to the dataset. These 30 filters, as shown in Fig. 5 were selected based on their popularity and include names such as 1977, Aden, Brannan, Brooklyn, Clarendon, Earlybird, Gingham, Hudson, Inkwell, Kelvin, Lark, Lofi, Maven, Mayfair, Moon, Nashville, Perpetua, Reyes, Rise, Slumber, Stinson, Toaster, Valencia, Walden, Willow, and Xpro2 [8].

For our experiment, we utilized a total of 12,271 images from the RAF-DB dataset for training purposes, while 3,068 images were reserved for validation. These images were categorized into a single-label subset, representing seven distinct classes corresponding to basic emotions: neutral, happy, sad, surprise, fear, disgust, and anger. To apply the 30 Instagram filters to the RAF-DB dataset, we called the respective functions from the "Pilgram- a python library for Instagram filters" against each filter [8].

158   J. Gupta et al.

Fig. 5. Sample Instagram filtered facial images

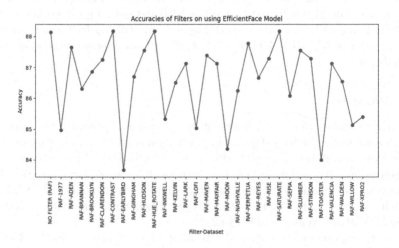

Fig. 6. Performance analysis result of the EfficientFace model

4   Results on EfficientFace Model

Figure 6 shows the performance comparison results of the EfficientFace model on the original and Instagram-filtered facial images from the test set of the RAF-DB dataset.

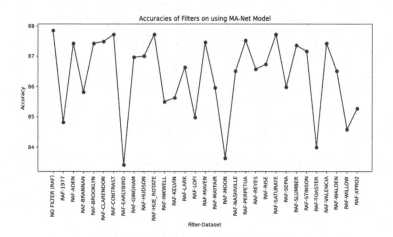

Fig. 7. Performance analysis result of the MA-Net model

Visualizing the results of Fig. 6, one can find that the EfficientFace model trained on the original facial images attained similar recognition accuracy on the original and RAF-CONTRAST, RAF-HUE_ROTATE AND RAF-SATURATE filtered facial images from the test set of the RAF-DB dataset. The results illustrate the robustness of the model against Instagram filters such as huerotate, saturate, and contrast. However, the model performed worst on the Earlybird-filtered facial images from the test set of the RAF-DB dataset.

5   Results on MA-Net Model

Line chart of Fig. 7 presents the performance analysis results of the MA-Net model on the Instagram-filtered facial images of the RAF-DB dataset. Looking at the results, we can find that the accuracy obtained by the MA-Net model on the original RAF-DB dataset is 87.842%. On comparing this accuracy with other filtered RAF-DB dataset, no filter is able to achieve the accuracy above this. Thus, robustness of the MA-Net model is slightly lower then the Efficient-Face model on the Instagram-filtered facial images from the RAF-DB dataset. Nevertheless, on the original test facial images of the dataset, the MA-Net model performed better than EfficientFace.

6   Results on POSTER Model

Figure 8 presents the performance analysis results of the POSTER model on the Instagram-filtered images from the RAF-DB dataset.

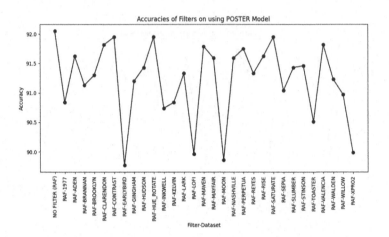

Fig. 8. Performance analysis result of the POSTER model

From the line chart of Fig. 8, we can found that the accuracy obtained by RAF-DB dataset on MA-Net Model is 87.842%. On comparing this accuracy with other filtered RAF-DB dataset, no filter is able to achieve the accuracy above this.

7   Comparison Results and Discussions

Our research paper explores an unexplored aspect in the field of Facial Expression Recognition (FER) by investigating the impact of Instagram filters on FER systems. This novel idea aims to analyze how popular image filters used in social media platforms, such as Instagram, affect the accuracy and performance of FER algorithms. By delving into this uncharted territory, we aim to make significant contributions to the advancement of FER systems and their applicability in real-world scenarios.

The impact of Instagram filters on FER systems has considerable implications for society. With the widespread use of social media platforms and the increasing demand for FER technology in various domains, understanding the influence of filters becomes crucial. By comprehensively analyzing this aspect, we can enhance the robustness and efficiency of FER systems, ultimately improving their accuracy in real-world settings.

This research addresses a critical gap in the existing literature. While many studies have focused on developing advanced FER algorithms, few have explored the specific influence of Instagram filters on FER performance. By examining this unique aspect, we are pioneering a new direction in FER research, opening avenues for further investigations and advancements in the field.

Through our analysis, we anticipate discovering valuable insights into how Instagram filters impact FER accuracy and recognition capabilities. The findings from our research can guide the development of more robust FER algorithms that can effectively handle images processed with Instagram filters. This knowledge will enable FER systems to better adapt to real-world scenarios and improve their performance in situations where filtered images are prevalent.

In our study, we employed three transfer learning models, namely Efficient-Face, MA-Net, and POSTER. To evaluate the impact of different filters on the accuracy of these models, we compared the results for each filtered dataset. Our findings revealed that only three filters, specifically RAF-Contrast, RAF-Hue_rotate, and RAF-Saturate, demonstrated a slight increase in accuracy of 0.032% when used with the EfficientFace model. However, for the other two models, no filtered dataset performed better than the unfiltered RAF dataset. Figure 9 provides a comprehensive understanding of the accuracy comparison for each filtered dataset across the different deep learning models for static-image-based FER.

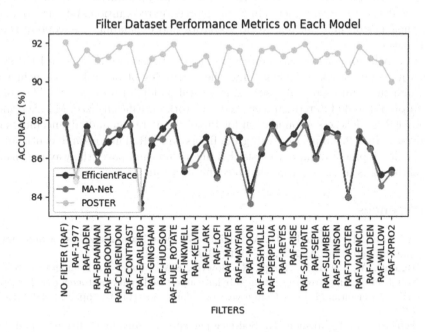

Fig. 9. Performance comparison results of the FER algorithms

8   Conclusion

This research study focuses on analyzing the impact of Instagram filters to the FER Systems. In addition to examining the influence of beauty filters on Facial Expression Recognition (FER) systems, our research study has significant positive implications for future research advancements. The insights gained from applying 30 Instagram filters to the RAF-DB Dataset have shed light on the attributes and characteristics of beautification achieved through these Instagram filters. This exploration opens up opportunities for researchers from various disciplines to delve deeper into the dynamics associated with the impact of beautification filters.

Our findings and contributions in this area offer valuable insights that were previously difficult to access. The 30 filtered datasets provide a comprehensive evaluation of the influence of Instagram filters on FER accuracy and reliability, enabling researchers to further investigate the specific effects of different filters and their impact on facial expression recognition. Additionally, our work on EfficientFace, MA-Net, and POSTER models demonstrates their efficacy and potential for advancing FER technology in the presence of Instagram filters. Researchers can build upon our findings to develop more robust and adaptive FER algorithms that account for the complexities introduced by beauty filters. This will lead to advancements in facial expression recognition systems, enhancing their performance in real-world scenarios and expanding the scope of their applications.

In conclusion, our research on the influence of Instagram filters on FER systems not only provides insights into the attributes of beautification achieved through these filters but also serves as a catalyst for future research. The combination of the 30 filtered datasets and our work on EfficientFace, MA-Net, and POSTER models sets a foundation for further exploration and advancements in understanding the impact of Instagram filters on FER. This research contributes to the development of more robust FER algorithms and paves the way for future breakthroughs in facial expression recognition technology.

References

1. Alzahrani, T., Al-Bander, B., Al-Nuaimy, W.: Deep learning models for automatic makeup detection. AI **2**(4), 497–511 (2021)
2. Bharati, A., Vatsa, M., Singh, R., Bowyer, K.W., Tong, X.: Demography-based facial retouching detection using subclass supervised sparse autoencoder. In: 2017 IEEE International Joint Conference on Biometrics (IJCB), pp. 474–482. IEEE (2017)
3. Felisberti, F.M., Musholt, K.: Self-face perception: individual differences and discrepancies associated with mental self-face representation, attractiveness and self-esteem. Psychol. Neurosci. **7**, 65–72 (2014)
4. Ferrara, M., Franco, A., Maltoni, D., Sun, Y.: On the impact of alterations on face photo recognition accuracy. In: Petrosino, A. (ed.) ICIAP 2013. LNCS, vol. 8156, pp. 743–751. Springer, Heidelberg (2013). https://doi.org/10.1007/978-3-642-41181-6_75

5. Fribourg, R., Peillard, E., Mcdonnell, R.: Mirror, mirror on my phone: Investigating dimensions of self-face perception induced by augmented reality filters. In: 2021 IEEE International Symposium on Mixed and Augmented Reality (ISMAR), pp. 470–478. IEEE (2021)

6. Hedman, P., Skepetzis, V., Hernandez-Diaz, K., Bigun, J., Alonso-Fernandez, F.: LFW-beautified: a dataset of face images with beautification and augmented reality filters. arXiv preprint arXiv:2203.06082 (2022)

7. Huang, G.B., Mattar, M., Berg, T., Learned-Miller, E.: Labeled faces in the wild: a database for studying face recognition in unconstrained environments. In: Workshop on Faces in 'Real-Life' Images: Detection, Alignment, and Recognition (2008)

8. Kamakura, A.: Pilgram. https://doi.org/10.5281/zenodo.6086991. https://github.com/akiomik/pilgram

9. Li, S., Deng, W.: Deep facial expression recognition: a survey. IEEE Trans. Affect. Comput. 13(3), 1195–1215 (2020)

10. Li, S., Deng, W., Du, J.: Reliable crowdsourcing and deep locality-preserving learning for expression recognition in the wild. In: Proceedings of the IEEE Conference on Computer Vision and Pattern Recognition, pp. 2852–2861 (2017)

11. Mare, T., et al.: A realistic approach to generate masked faces applied on two novel masked face recognition data sets. arXiv preprint arXiv:2109.01745 (2021)

12. Rathgeb, C., Dantcheva, A., Busch, C.: Impact and detection of facial beautification in face recognition: an overview. IEEE Access 7, 152667–152678 (2019)

13. Rathgeb, C., Satnoianu, C.I., Haryanto, N.E., Bernardo, K., Busch, C.: Differential detection of facial retouching: a multi-biometric approach. IEEE Access 8, 106373–106385 (2020)

14. Vasudeva, K., Biswas, S., Chandran, S.: Comparative analysis of techniques for recognising facial expressions. In: 2022 8th International Conference on Advanced Computing and Communication Systems (ICACCS), vol. 1, pp. 233–238. IEEE (2022)

15. Zhao, Z., Liu, Q., Wang, S.: Learning deep global multi-scale and local attention features for facial expression recognition in the wild. IEEE Trans. Image Process. 30, 6544–6556 (2021)

16. Zhao, Z., Liu, Q., Zhou, F.: Robust lightweight facial expression recognition network with label distribution training. In: Proceedings of the AAAI Conference on Artificial Intelligence, vol. 35, pp. 3510–3519 (2021)

17. Zheng, C., Mendieta, M., Chen, C.: Poster: a pyramid cross-fusion transformer network for facial expression recognition. arXiv preprint arXiv:2204.04083 (2022)

MAAD-GAN: Memory-Augmented Attention-Based Discriminator GAN for Video Anomaly Detection

Anikeit Sethi[1], Krishanu Saini[1], Rituraj Singh[1(✉)], Aruna Tiwari[1], Sumeet Saurav[2], Sanjay Singh[2], and Vikas Chauhan[3]

[1] Computer Science and Engineering, Indian Institute of Technology, Indore, Indore 452020, Madhya Pradesh, India
phd2001201002@iiti.ac.in
[2] Intelligent System Groups, CSIR-CEERI, Pilani, Pilani 333031, Rajasthan, India
[3] Electrical and Computer Science, National Taipei University of Technology, Taipei City 106, Taiwan

Abstract. The detection of anomalies in video data is of great importance in various applications, such as surveillance and industrial monitoring. This paper introduces a novel approach, named MAAD-GAN, for video anomaly detection (VAD) utilizing Generative Adversarial Networks (GANs). The MAAD-GAN framework combines a Wide Residual Network (WRN) in the generator with a memory module to learn the normal patterns present in the training video dataset, enabling the generation of realistic samples. To address the challenge of detecting subtle anomalies and those with motion characteristics, we propose the integration of self-attention in the discriminator model. Our proposed model MAAD-GAN enhances the ability to distinguish between real and generated samples, ensuring that anomalous samples are distorted when reconstructed. Experimental evaluations show the effectiveness of MAAD-GAN as compared to traditional methods on UCSD (University of California, San Diego) Peds2, CUHK Avenue, and ShanghaiTech datasets.

Keywords: Anomaly Detection · Generative Adversarial Networks · Deep Learning · Memory Network

1 Introduction

There has been a significant interest in the detection of anomalous events in video sequences, particularly within the context of surveillance systems deployed in the real world. Rare occurrences are termed anomalous events that deviate from the typical patterns of regular events. However, video anomaly detection (VAD)

The authors would like to thank the Ministry of Electronics and Information Technology (MeiTY) to grant this project titled "Resource Constrained Artificial Intelligence" with grant number: 4(16)/2019-ITEA.

poses a substantial challenge due to the subjective interpretation of behaviors in different scenarios. For instance, it might be uncommon to see a car on a sidewalk but typical to see the same car on a highway. Manual labeling of abnormal events is complex and time-consuming, leading to the adoption of unsupervised learning approaches in VAD. Furthermore, the high dimensionality of spatiotemporal video data adds to the complexity of unsupervised VAD.

The deep autoencoder (AE) is a widely used technique in unsupervised scenarios for modeling high-dimensional data [1,9]. It consists of an encoder that compresses input into a lower-dimensional encoding and a decoder that reconstructs data from the encoding. By minimizing the reconstruction error on normal data, AE-based AD detects abnormalities based on increased reconstruction error for abnormal input [33]. However, as dataset complexity increases, the generalization and accurate extraction of abnormalities by deep AE models become challenging. Additionally, the focus on reconstruction loss itself may hinder the model's robustness in properly reconstructing anomalies. GANs address limitations of Deep AE in various applications, excelling in tasks like data augmentation and high-quality image reconstruction [10,24]. Yu et al. [29] applied GANs in reconstruction-based AD, outperforming traditional AE models. GANs capture data distribution effectively, showing promise in enhancing AD [13].

The assumption that anomalies always lead to higher reconstruction errors is challenged by the ability of AE and AE-based generators to accurately reconstruct anomalous inputs, as observed in existing literature [33]. Anomalies lacking specific training samples and exhibiting unpredictable reconstruction behavior question the notion of higher reconstruction errors. Shared compositional characteristics with typical training data and an overly powerful decoder can enable the successful reconstruction of anomalies, undermining the reliability of reconstruction error as a reliable anomaly indicator. To address the aforementioned limitation, our proposed MAAD-GAN framework improves Video Anomaly Detection (VAD) by incorporating attention-based memory addressing. This mechanism allows for the retrieval of relevant memory items based on the input query, thereby enhancing the anomaly detection performance of the framework. Our main contributions to MAAD-GAN are summarized below:

1. We propose an adversarially trained MAAD-GAN consisting of a Wideresnet in the encoder to capture intricate patterns and enhance representation power.
2. We utilize the memory module in the bottleneck layers to effectively learn the regular events.
3. We also propose a novel discriminator with layer-wise self-attention to focus on the foreground for enhanced discrimination.
4. Experimental evaluation on benchmark datasets confirms the superiority of MAAD-GAN over state-of-the-art models, achieving higher AUC scores in UCSD Peds2, CUHK Avenue, and ShanghaiTech datasets.

In this work, we show the effectiveness and reliability of our proposed methods for detecting anomalies in surveillance videos. We conduct extensive tests and analyses to verify the performance of our approach. The remaining paper is organized as follows: Sect. 2 gives an overview of related work in the field, followed by Sect. 3 which details our proposed technique. In Sect. 4 we present the experimental results obtained from the proposed approach with a discussion on it in Sect. 5. Finally, Sect. 6 concludes our work.

2 Related Work

2.1 Video Anomaly Detection

The AD in video is a challenging task and the ambiguous definition of anomaly makes it further difficult to classify a video frame as normal or abnormal. Zhou et al. [31] proposed Anomaly Net which used the self-attention module in the AE as a generator following GAN-like architecture. Nguyen et al. [20] proposed a CNN model to map the object appearance with their motions. Yan et al. [26] proposed an R-VAE, a variational AE (VAE) based on a two-stream model consisting of both the appearance and motion streams to determine if there is an anomaly. STD [3], a reconstruction-based model which takes into account spatial-temporal information as input and reconstructs the frame using both. Liu et al. [13] proposed the prediction of frame based on the GAN method that is used to predict the future frame from the window of past frames. Lu et al. [15] proposed the Conv-VRNN model, a convolutional VAE architecture to predict the future frame. Liu et al. [12] proposed the MLEP model on compacting the normal distribution to create the gap between the normal and abnormal. Guo et al. [5] divide the video frames into pseudo-normal and abnormal frames and learn the features from the pseudo-normal frames to produce a prediction. Zhang et al. [30] proposed the NUFP model based on U-net architecture as a video frame prediction model. Li et al. [11] proposed a dual generator model which is based on both the foreground objects and their motion. Hao et al. [6] proposed the STCEN model, based on predicting the future frame using spatio-temporal features. Ye et al. [27] proposed AnoPCN which is based on both the spatial and motion features reconstruction.

2.2 Memory Based Methods

Luo et al. [16] proposed the ConvLSTM-AE model which utilizes the LSTM module with the convolutional layer to learn the motion from past frames. The main drawback of using LSTM, it requires more memory than other neural networks, as they have to store the state of the network at each time step. This can lead to longer inference times as the training samples increase. Gong et al. [4] proposed Mem-AE, a model that uses a memory module to learn the past normal events of video frames Park et al. [21] improved upon Mem-AE by automating the update of the memory module and carefully selecting the hyperparameters for training.

3 Methodology

This section introduces the MAAD-GAN method, designed for reconstruction-based VAD. The method comprises a Generator (G) and Discriminator (D), as illustrated in Fig. 1.

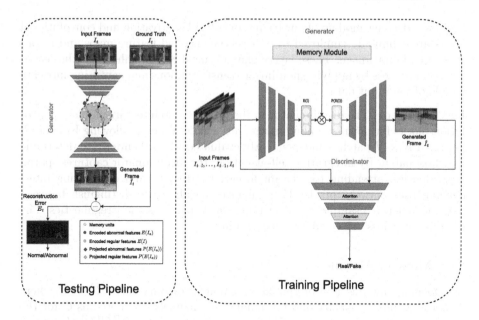

Fig. 1. Overview of Training and Testing of MAAD-GAN. The model follows adversarial training on normal samples whose representation is stored by a memory module (green). During testing, these anomalies (red) are mapped to normal features which results in improper reconstruction crucial for AD. (Color figure online)

3.1   Network Architecture

The MAAD-GAN framework leverages an AE architecture having an encoder (G_1) and a decoder (G_2). In MAAD-GAN, G_1 employs a Wide Residual Network (WRN) with a memory module in the latent space. G_2 utilizes the information encoded by G_1 to reconstruct the video frame.

Generator. The encoder and decoder in the generative network contain subblocks. Each sub-block comprises these layers: batch normalization [7], rectified linear unit (ReLU) [19], and a convolutional layer. To enhance the model's resilience in Video Anomaly Detection (VAD), MAAD-GAN incorporates the powerful Wide Residual Network (WRN) architecture [7,25]. WRN serves as the backbone for extracting spatial features and understanding the visual structure of the input sequence. With a widening factor (k) of 4, WRN can capture intricate and representative features, significantly improving the model's detection capabilities. Before feeding the output of G_1 to G_2, the lower-dimensional feature or latent space, denoted as E(I), is utilized to retrieve the relevant memory items. These memory items are retrieved by comparing the latent representation E(I) to the memory items stored in the memory module. The most similar memory items are then returned. The retrieved memory items are then used to obtain P(E(I)), representing the refined latent representation.

In the decoder module of our framework, ReLU activation and convolutional layers are commonly employed to process the encoded feature maps and reconstruct the input image. These layers play a crucial role in enhancing the reconstruction process by applying non-linear transformations and capturing intricate details of the input data.

Discriminator. The discriminator in the proposed architecture employs convolution blocks for down-sampling image into a $N \times N$ map, following Isola et al. [8]. Each $N \times N$ patch is independently evaluated for authenticity to determine real/fake patch. By integrating self-attention, the discriminator captures spatial dependencies, attending to relevant foreground regions and considering inter-dependencies between pixels. This enhances its ability to distinguish between real and generated samples by identifying subtle patterns and irregularities. The discriminator loss drives adversarial learning.

3.2   Memory Module

The memory module is represented as a matrix of dimension $\mathcal{R}^N \times C$ where N is the memory capacity and the number of channels is denoted as C for the features obtained from G_1 (z). The features vector $E(I) \in \mathcal{R}^{B \times H \times W \times C}$ where, batch-size is denoted as B, height is denoted as H and W is the width of the input layer of G_2 network. The similarity index for i^{th} frame between the $E(I)$ and the memory item $M = m_1, m_2, ..., m_N$ are shown in Eq. 1

$$P(\hat{E(I)})_i = \frac{\exp\left(m_i^T \cdot z\right)}{(||m_i||||z||)} \tag{1}$$

where $P(\hat{E}(I))_i$ is the similarity index between the ith memory item and latent feature z. The obtained $P(\hat{E}(I))$ is then normalized using the softmax function as shown in Eq. 2.

$$P(E(I))_i = \frac{\exp\left(P(\hat{E(I)})_i\right)}{\sum_{j=1}^{N} \exp\left(P(\hat{E(I)})_j\right)} \tag{2}$$

3.3   Loss Function for MAAD-GAN

The training is done in two parts, reconstruction learning, and adversarial learning. Reconstruction learning comprises the training of generator G through l_2 image similarity loss as depicted in Eq. 3.

$$\mathcal{L}_{sim}^G = ||I - \hat{I}||_2 \tag{3}$$

where the actual image is I and the reconstruction image is $\hat{I}$. The above distance function trains the generator to create resembling images. For a more robust and generalizable model, we combine reconstruction with adversarial learning. It utilizes a discriminator D, capable of separating real from fake image distributions, and utilizes its loss to learn the generation of sharp and realistic images. The adversarial loss is given below:

$$\mathcal{L}^D_{adv} = \mathrm{E}_{real}(D(I)) + \mathrm{E}_z(1 - D(\hat{I})) \tag{4}$$

where real is the actual distribution and z is the generated distribution. This loss trains D to learn to distinguish real frames to 0 and generated to 1. On the contrary, the goal of G opposite. It learns to make the discriminator's score on generated images to 0 (Eq. 5), trying to generate realistic samples.

$$\mathcal{L}^G_{adv} = \mathrm{E}_z(D(\hat{I})) \tag{5}$$

3.4 Anomaly Prediction

The MAAD-GAN framework is trained on video clips depicting normal events. Thus we expect our model to produce larger generation errors on irregular events. This feature can be measured by utilizing the Mean-squared error as our Anomaly Score (S_{ano}) as shown below:

$$S_{ano} = ||\hat{I}_t - I_t||_2 \tag{6}$$

where I_t is the frame being evaluated for anomaly during the testing phase.

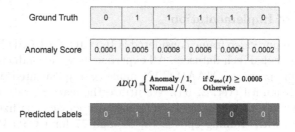

Fig. 2. The ground truth is the actual labels of the video, the anomaly score is obtained using MSE, and a suitable threshold is utilized for Anomaly detection (AD). The normal and irregular frames are labeled 0, and 1 respectively. The green-colored predicted labels conform with the ground truth, whereas the red one is incorrect. (Color figure online)

The anomaly score obtained is utilized to classify frames are regular or anomalous by defining a threshold. This thresholding technique is utilized to compute useful metrics such as AUC (Area under curve) to determine the performance of our model. Figure 2 shows the thresholding process.

4   Experimentation

The proposed MAAD-GAN framework demonstrates efficient real-time anomaly detection capabilities in video data. Here, we begin by describing the datasets used and the details of implementation employed for evaluating the framework's performance. We conduct a comprehensive qualitative and quantitative analysis to assess the effectiveness of MAAD-GAN in detecting anomalies.

4.1   Datasets

Our proposed methodology is evaluated on three benchmark datasets: CUHK Avenue, UCSD Ped2, and ShanghaiTech.

The CUHK Avenue dataset [14] contains 47 diverse types of anomalous activities captured in 16 training videos and 21 testing videos. It offers 15,328 training frames and 15,324 testing frames. The camera remains stationary, but subjects' sizes may differ due to varying distances from the camera.

The UCSD Ped2 dataset [18], comprises 12 testing movies and 16 training videos with 12 types of aberrant occurrences. It includes grayscale frames, 2010 testing samples, and 2550 training samples. Multiple anomalies occur in a single scene. The individuals have similar sizes, and the camera remains stationary.

The ShanghaiTech dataset [17] is specifically designed for crowd counting and analysis. It comprises two subsets, Part A and Part B, featuring highly congested areas. Part A focuses on stationary crowds, while Part B includes stationary and moving crowds. Part A consists of 482 images with 241,677 annotated individuals, while Part B comprises 716 images with 88,488 annotated individuals.

4.2   Details of Implementation

The size of the input video frame considered is 160×160 for UCSD Peds2, CUHK Avenue, and ShanghaiTech datasets. All experiments were conducted on a Tesla V100 GPU. Our proposed MAAD-GAN model is implemented on Tensorflow (ver. 2.13) in Xubuntu (ver. 22.04). We utilize the learning rate as 0.00026 in Adam optimizer on all the datasets. The memory capacity is fixed to 600 for all the datasets with training epochs 70, 80, and 77 for UCSD Peds2, CUHK Avenue, and ShanghaiTech datasets respectively.

MAAD-GAN's performance is assessed by calculating the AUC (Area Under Curve) values. The AUC value is calculated using the True Positive Rate (TPR) and the False Positive Rate (FPR) which is evaluated as shown in Eq. 7 and 8 respectively. By comparing the network's frame-level scores with ground truth labels, the TPR and FPR values are determined. The AUC value reveals the model's ability to detect anomalies and differentiate normal from abnormal events.

4.3   Evaluation Metrics

$$TPR = TP/(FN + TP) \tag{7}$$

$$FPR = FP/(FP + TN) \tag{8}$$

Anomalies were detected by the score comparison of the frame with a threshold value. This threshold value, indicated in Fig. 2, was adjusted iteratively to generate a confusion matrix. By evaluating the model's performance across various threshold settings, we assessed its ability to correctly identify anomalies.

4.4 Comparison Study

Here, we conduct a comparative analysis of the MAAD-GAN framework with related work in AD. We compare MAAD-GAN with traditional methods based on reconstruction and prediction, which have achieved benchmark results in recent years. We provide the Area Under the Curve (AUC) scores in Table 1 for benchmark datasets on various state-of-the-art models. This comparison enables us to assess the effectiveness and superiority of MAAD-GAN in detecting anomalies in comparison to existing approaches.

Table 1. Comparison on the benchmark datasets with other SOTA methods

Method	UCSD ped2	Avenue	ShanghaiTech
Mem-AE [4]	94.1%	83.3%	71.2%
Anomaly Net [31]	94.9%	86.1%	–
AM-CORR [20]	96.2%	86.9%	–
R-VAE [26]	92.4%	79.6%	–
STD [3]	96.7%	87.1%	73.7%
Frame-Prediction [13]	95.4%	84.9%	72.8%
Conv-VRNN [15]	96.1%	85.8%	
MLEP [12]	–	91.3%	75.6%
Attention-Prediction [32]	96.0%	86.0%	–
Self-training [5]	88.1%	86.6%	–
NUFP [30]	95.9%	85.2%	72.7%
Context-related Prediction [11]	96.3%	87.1%	73.6%
STCEN [6]	96.9%	86.6%	73.8%
AnoPCN [27]	96.8%	86.2%	73.6%
Prediction & Reconstruction [23]	96.3%	85.1%	73.0%
VEC-AM [28]	97.3%	89.6%	74.8%
VEC-AM (impl.) [28]	96.6%	88.3%	73.9%
Memory-guided [21]	97.0%	88.5%	72.8%
AMMC-Net [2]	96.6%	86.6%	73.7%
Ours	97.6%	89.3%	75.9%

5   Discussion

5.1 Visualization

To validate the practical application of MAAD-GAN for video surveillance systems, we visualize the performance of RGB abnormal frames. Figures 3 show the localization and performance of the generator for video-AD as frame level task. As shown in the image, on training for multiple epochs; Firstly, the anomaly score decreases, which represents that image generator quality of G has improved, and secondly, the score gap Δ_S, representing the difference between the mean anomaly scores for real and fake frames, increases. Thereby, showing the improvement in the abnormal-normal distinguishing capability of the model.

$$\Delta_S = |AS_{abnormal} - AS_{normal}| \tag{9}$$

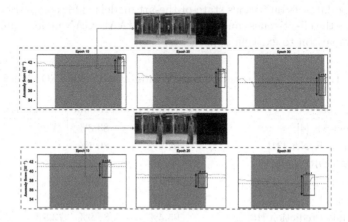

Fig. 3. The frame level anomaly score during training. Two instances of anomalies in the Avenue dataset are presented. The red line shows the average anomaly score of the video, and the score gap Δ shows the mean abnormal-normal difference (higher is better). (Color figure online)

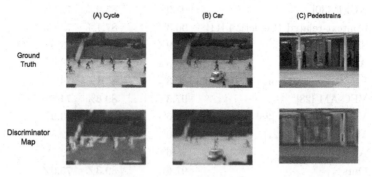

Fig. 4. Visualization of discriminator attention map using Grad-CAM. The intensity of the heatmap shows the enhanced focus on foreground features in video events.

5.2   Attention Maps

To understand the functionality of the attention module in D, as shown in Fig. 4, we demonstrate the attention maps acquired through Grad CAM [22] on various frames. We observe that this novel application of attention to discriminator enhances the ordinary adversarial learning, by focusing on relevant foreground objects. Thereby, considerably reducing the possibility of false alarms and the effect of background scenes.

6   Conclusion

In this work, we propose a Memory-Augmented Attention-based Discriminator Generative Adversarial Network (MAAD-GAN) for video anomaly detection. The obtained latent space after the encoder module is utilized to select the most similar memory item from the memory module. This ensures that the model is able to reconstruct the normal video frames effectively on the other hand as the memory item when not present in case of anomaly frame then the reconstruction error increases. MAAD-GAN is trained in an end-to-end manner with a self-attention-based Discriminator model which further improves the discrimination ability between the normal and anomaly frames. Experimental results demonstrate that it outperforms the other state-of-the-art models having different applications on various datasets proving its effectiveness ability. Further, we visualize the attention maps using Grad-CAM provides insights and interpretability to enhance the model's capabilities to understand anomaly detection.

References

1. Bengio, Y., Lamblin, P., Popovici, D., Larochelle, H.: Greedy layer-wise training of deep networks. In: Advances in Neural Information Processing Systems, vol. 19 (2006)
2. Cai, R., Zhang, H., Liu, W., Gao, S., Hao, Z.: Appearance-motion memory consistency network for video anomaly detection. In: Proceedings of the AAAI Conference on Artificial Intelligence, vol. 35, pp. 938–946 (2021)
3. Chang, Y., et al.: Video anomaly detection with spatio-temporal dissociation. Pattern Recogn. **122**, 108213 (2022)
4. Gong, D., et al.: Memorizing normality to detect anomaly: memory-augmented deep autoencoder for unsupervised anomaly detection. In: Proceedings of the IEEE/CVF International Conference on Computer Vision, pp. 1705–1714 (2019)
5. Guo, A., Guo, L., Zhang, R., Wang, Y., Gao, S.: Self-trained prediction model and novel anomaly score mechanism for video anomaly detection. Image Vis. Comput. **119**, 104391 (2022)
6. Hao, Y., Li, J., Wang, N., Wang, X., Gao, X.: Spatiotemporal consistency-enhanced network for video anomaly detection. Pattern Recogn. **121**, 108232 (2022)
7. Ioffe, S., Szegedy, C.: Batch normalization: accelerating deep network training by reducing internal covariate shift. In: International Conference on Machine Learning, pp. 448–456. PMLR (2015)
8. Isola, P., Zhu, J.Y., Zhou, T., Efros, A.A.: Image-to-image translation with conditional adversarial networks. In: Proceedings of the IEEE Conference on Computer Vision and Pattern Recognition, pp. 1125–1134 (2017)
9. Kingma, D.P., Welling, M.: Auto-encoding variational bayes. arXiv preprint arXiv:1312.6114 (2013)

10. Ledig, C., et al.: Photo-realistic single image super-resolution using a generative adversarial network. In: Proceedings of the IEEE Conference on Computer Vision and Pattern Recognition, pp. 4681–4690 (2017)
11. Li, D., Nie, X., Li, X., Zhang, Y., Yin, Y.: Context-related video anomaly detection via generative adversarial network. Pattern Recogn. Lett. **156**, 183–189 (2022)
12. Liu, W., Luo, W., Li, Z., Zhao, P., Gao, S., et al.: Margin learning embedded prediction for video anomaly detection with a few anomalies. In: IJCAI, pp. 3023–3030 (2019)
13. Liu, W., Luo, W., Lian, D., Gao, S.: Future frame prediction for anomaly detection–a new baseline. In: Proceedings of the IEEE Conference on Computer Vision and Pattern Recognition, pp. 6536–6545 (2018)
14. Lu, C., Shi, J., Jia, J.: Abnormal event detection at 150 fps in matlab. In: Proceedings of the IEEE International Conference on Computer Vision, pp. 2720–2727 (2013)
15. Lu, Y., Kumar, K.M., Shahabeddin Nabavi, S., Wang, Y.: Future frame prediction using convolutional VRNN for anomaly detection. In: 2019 16th IEEE International Conference on Advanced Video and Signal Based Surveillance (AVSS), pp. 1–8. IEEE (2019)
16. Luo, W., Liu, W., Gao, S.: Remembering history with convolutional LSTM for anomaly detection. In: 2017 IEEE International Conference on Multimedia and Expo (ICME), pp. 439–444. IEEE (2017)
17. Luo, W., Liu, W., Gao, S.: A revisit of sparse coding based anomaly detection in stacked RNN framework. In: Proceedings of the IEEE International Conference on Computer Vision, pp. 341–349 (2017)
18. Mahadevan, V., Li, W., Bhalodia, V., Vasconcelos, N.: Anomaly detection in crowded scenes. In: 2010 IEEE Computer Society Conference on Computer Vision and Pattern Recognition, pp. 1975–1981 (2010). https://doi.org/10.1109/CVPR.2010.5539872
19. Nair, V., Hinton, G.E.: Rectified linear units improve restricted Boltzmann machines. In: Proceedings of the 27th International Conference on Machine Learning (ICML 2010), pp. 807–814 (2010)
20. Nguyen, T.N., Meunier, J.: Anomaly detection in video sequence with appearance-motion correspondence. In: Proceedings of the IEEE/CVF International Conference on Computer Vision, pp. 1273–1283 (2019)
21. Park, H., Noh, J., Ham, B.: Learning memory-guided normality for anomaly detection. In: Proceedings of the IEEE/CVF Conference on Computer Vision and Pattern Recognition, pp. 14372–14381 (2020)
22. Selvaraju, R.R., Cogswell, M., Das, A., Vedantam, R., Parikh, D., Batra, D.: Grad-CAM: visual explanations from deep networks via gradient-based localization. In: Proceedings of the IEEE International Conference on Computer Vision, pp. 618–626 (2017)
23. Tang, Y., Zhao, L., Zhang, S., Gong, C., Li, G., Yang, J.: Integrating prediction and reconstruction for anomaly detection. Pattern Recogn. Lett. **129**, 123–130 (2020)
24. Tran, N.T., Tran, V.H., Nguyen, N.B., Nguyen, T.K., Cheung, N.M.: On data augmentation for GAN training. IEEE Trans. Image Process. **30**, 1882–1897 (2021)
25. Wu, Z., Shen, C., Van Den Hengel, A.: Wider or deeper: revisiting the resnet model for visual recognition. Pattern Recogn. **90**, 119–133 (2019)
26. Yan, S., Smith, J.S., Lu, W., Zhang, B.: Abnormal event detection from videos using a two-stream recurrent variational autoencoder. IEEE Trans. Cogn. Dev. Syst. **12**(1), 30–42 (2018)

27. Ye, M., Peng, X., Gan, W., Wu, W., Qiao, Y.: AnoPCN: video anomaly detection via deep predictive coding network. In: Proceedings of the 27th ACM International Conference on Multimedia, pp. 1805–1813 (2019)

28. Yu, G., et al.: Cloze test helps: effective video anomaly detection via learning to complete video events. In: Proceedings of the 28th ACM International Conference on Multimedia, pp. 583–591 (2020)

29. Yu, J., Lee, Y., Yow, K.C., Jeon, M., Pedrycz, W.: Abnormal event detection and localization via adversarial event prediction. IEEE Trans. Neural Netw. Learn. Syst. **33**(8), 3572–3586 (2021)

30. Zhang, Q., Feng, G., Wu, H.: Surveillance video anomaly detection via non-local U-net frame prediction. Multimed. Tools Appl. **81**(19), 27073–27088 (2022)

31. Zhou, J.T., Du, J., Zhu, H., Peng, X., Liu, Y., Goh, R.S.M.: Anomalynet: an anomaly detection network for video surveillance. IEEE Trans. Inf. Forensics Secur. **14**(10), 2537–2550 (2019)

32. Zhou, J.T., Zhang, L., Fang, Z., Du, J., Peng, X., Xiao, Y.: Attention-driven loss for anomaly detection in video surveillance. IEEE Trans. Circuits Syst. Video Technol. **30**(12), 4639–4647 (2019)

33. Zong, B., et al.: Deep autoencoding Gaussian mixture model for unsupervised anomaly detection. In: International Conference on Learning Representations (2018)

AG-PDCnet: An Attention Guided Parkinson's Disease Classification Network with MRI, DTI and Clinical Assessment Data

Sushanta Kumar Sahu[1,2]($\boxtimes$) and Ananda S. Chowdhury[1]

[1] Department of Electronics and Telecommunication Engineering,
Jadavpur University, Kolkata, India
{sksahu.etce.rs,as.chowdhury}@jadavpuruniversity.in
[2] School of Electronics Science, Odisha University of Technology and Research,
Bhubaneswar, India

Abstract. Parkinson's disease (PD) is the second most neurodegenerative disorder, which is prevalent worldwide. In this paper, we propose AG-PDCNet, an Attention Guided multi-class multi-modal PD Classification framework. In particular, we combine clinical assessments with the Neuroimaging data, namely, MRI and DTI. The three classes considered for this problem are PD, Healthy Controls (HC) and Scans Without Evidence of Dopamine Deficiency (SWEDD). Four CNNs, each boosted with an attention mechanism, are trained on gray matter (GM) and white matter (WM) from the MRI, and mean diffusivity (MD) and fractional anisotropy (FA) from the DTI. XGboost is employed for classification from the clinical data. At the decision level, the outputs of all the five models, four CNNs and the XGboost, are fused with an optimal weighted average fusion (OWAF) technique. Publicly available PPMI database is used for evaluation, yielding an accuracy of 96.93% for the three-class classification. Extensive comparisons, including ablation studies, are conducted to validate the effectiveness of our proposed solution.

Keywords: Attention mechanism · Multi-modal data · Multi-class classification · PD · SWEDD

1 Introduction

Parkinson's disease (PD) is a neurological condition that progressively impairs movement, causing tremors, stiffness, and bradykinesia [6]. The World Health Organization (WHO) reports PD as the second most prevalent neurodegenerative condition after Alzheimer's disease. Traditionally, PD classification has focused on distinguishing PD patients from healthy controls (HC). However, this approach overlooks a broader range of PD-related diseases, including Scans without Evidence of Dopamine Deficit (SWEDD) [24]. SWEDD describes people with Parkinson's-like symptoms but no dopamine impairments on neuroimaging scans. As a result, diagnosing Parkinson's disease becomes significantly more challenging.

Medical advancements spur interest in multimodal data for PD classification. Our research presents a classification scheme for the PD, SWEDD and HC groups. We aim to improve accuracy and reliability by considering the full spectrum of PD-related disorders. This work is different from our previous work, where only neuroimaging data was considered [22]. In particular, we have made two major changes as compared to [22]. First, we utilize additional clinical assessment data in addition to the neuroimaging data. In neuroimaging data, specifically MRI and diffusion tensor imaging (DTI) were considered, as they provide valuable structural and microstructural insights into PD pathology [9]. Secondly, to take full advantage of the neuroimaging data, an attention mechanism is included. So, the proposed model can focus on important properties and improve the discriminative power of the classification process. Our solution framework comprises four convolutional neural networks (CNNs) trained on gray matter (GM) and white matter (WM) from the MRI and mean diffusivity (MD) and fractional anisotropy (FA) from the DTI along with XGboost, a machine learning (ML) classifier for the clinical assessment data. The optimal weighted average fusion (OWAF) method [22] is used to integrate the outputs of all the five models at the decision level to produce a final classification. We evaluated our proposed framework (AG-PDCNet) for the classification of HC, SWEDD, and PD classes on the PPMI dataset and discovered an impressive accuracy of 96.93%. Furthermore, we conduct extensive comparisons and ablation studies to assess the effectiveness of the proposed solution. In summary, our paper presents a three-class classification framework for PD, incorporating an attention mechanism and utilizing a diverse range of clinical and neuroimaging features. Our approach improves upon existing two-class classification approaches by capturing a broader spectrum of PD-related conditions. The high accuracy achieved in classification task, highlights the potential of our framework for accurate and comprehensive PD diagnosis. We now summarize our contributions below:

1. We addresses the challenge of classifying PD, SWEDD and HC subjects. The inclusion of the SWEDD class significantly increases the complexity of the classification task.
2. Our framework integrates MRI, DTI and clinical assessments data to improve classification accuracy. We fuse the outputs of ML and DL based models trained on neuroimaging and clinical assessments data using late fusion.
3. We incorporate an attention mechanism to selectively focus on informative features or regions within the data. This enhances the discriminative power of the classification model by capturing subtle patterns and correlations necessary for accurate PD classification.

The remaining sections of this paper are structured as follows: Sect. 2 provides a review of related work in PD classification. In Sect. 3, we present our proposed methodology, incorporating an attention mechanism and a late fusion technique. Next in Sect. 4, we describe the experimental results in details. Finally, in Sect. 5, we conclude the paper and discuss some future directions of research.

2   Related Work

In this section, we present an overview of the existing literature on PD classification using sensory data, focusing on clinical, MRI, and DTI data individually. It also explores the combination of multiple modalities for PD classification. The use of attention mechanisms in medical image analysis is discussed. Studies encompass various sensory data sources, including voice [16], neuroimaging [7,11,24,25], gait [1], handwritten [4], and clinical data [29]. However, the primary emphasis of this work is on neuroimaging and clinical assessment data.

Neuroimaging techniques such as T1-W MRI and DTI are valuable for detecting PD-related brain changes [7,11]. Structural alterations in cerebellar, subcortical, and cortical regions affected by PD are investigated using MRI, specifically focusing on gray matter, white matter, and cortical thickness [11]. DTI provides greater sensitivity in detecting microstructural damage in white matter fiber integrity [7]. Many studies utilize machine learning (ML) and deep learning (DL) techniques with either MRI or DTI data. For instance, Templeton et al. [26] differentiate PD patients from healthy controls using ML classifiers on MRI data. Sivaranjini et al. [25] achieve an accuracy of 88.9% in detecting PD using AlexNet on MRI data. Rajanbabu et al. [21] achieve an accuracy of 97.8% in classifying PD with healthy controls using a DL-based ensemble learning technique.

We next mention some prominent works, incorporating multi-modal data for PD diagnosis. For instance, Gabrie et al. [11] employ GM, WM, and CSF volumes to classify PD and healthy control subjects, comparing seven ML classifiers. Park et al. [17] conducted multimodal ML studies and identified specific brain regions, such as the basal ganglia, thalamus and cerebellum affected by PD. Yang et al. enhance classification performance by integrating clinical assessments and MRI data [29]. Li et al. [14] utilize stacked sparse auto-encoders with DTI and MRI data for binary classifications, considering only MD data from DTI. Other works have explored the combination of GM and WM features, achieving promising classification accuracy [9,24]. The attention mechanism is used to extract high-level features from key regions of an image and to capture temporal dependencies and spatial relationships in images [10]. CNN models may significantly accelerate the learning process by highlighting critical information within feature maps by incorporating attention mechanisms. Although there are limited studies focusing on attention mechanisms and their impact on the detection and classification of neuroimaging diseases [13,31], they have proven to be valuable in allowing models to highlight salient features while disregarding irrelevant ones. Consequently, this leads to an improvement in the performance of classification tasks.

3   Proposed Method

We propose AG-PDCNet, an attention-guided multi-class, multi-modal PD Classification framework that integrates DL and ML-based models for accurate three-class classification. Our AG-PDCNet framework integrates multi-modal data, attention mechanisms and late fusion to improve the accuracy and robustness. All neuroimaging data are processed using CNN, while XGBoost focuses on clinical data. We employ attention mechanisms to fully leverage neuroimaging data in the classification task. This enables the model to focus on important properties and improve the discriminative power of the classification process. Based on multimodal data, each model generates a 3×1 probability vector. The probability vectors show the likelihood that the data belongs to one of three categories: HC, SWEDD or PD. The OWAF technique is then used to combine these probability vectors [22]. Figure 1 provides a schematic representation of our solution pipeline. In the subsequent subsections, we will describe the DL models, ML models and attention mechanisms used in our approach.

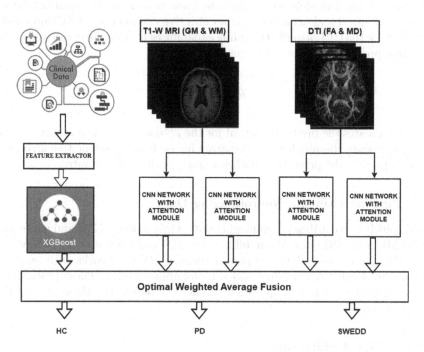

Fig. 1. AG-PDCNet architecture for multi-class multi-modal classification

3.1   Pipeline Utilizing Clinical Data

In the clinical data pipeline, we begin by extracting and selecting features from the input clinical assessment data using the ReliefF algorithm. MDS-UPDRS questionnaire, MoCA, GDS, and H & Y are a few features included in the clinical assessment data. Detailed descriptions about these features can be found in the PPMI database [15]. This allows us to identify the most informative features for PD classification. Once we have selected the relevant features, we process the data through XGBoost classifier. The XGBoost leverages the selected features to make accurate predictions.

3.1.1 Feature Extractor

The feature extractor is an essential component of an ML-based system since it is responsible for converting raw input into numerical values. The relief algorithm is a popular approach for selecting features. It calculates the best subset of features by assigning weights to each feature [28]. However The relief algorithm can only handle binary classification task. ReliefF, on the other hand, is an extension that can properly handle multi-class classification data [12].

3.1.2 XGBoost Classifier

The extreme gradient boosting (XGBoost) algorithm is an improved variant of the gradient boosting decision tree [8]. The XGBoost classifier integrates the outcomes of many models termed as base learners to make the final prediction. In terms of speed and accuracy, it is an effective classifier since XGBoost takes advantage of the CPU's multi-threading capabilities to minimize processing time. The final prediction can be represented in Eq. 1.

$$\overline{y}_i = y_i^0 + \eta \sum_{K=1}^{n} f_k(U_i) \tag{1}$$

Here $\overline{y}_i$ indicates the predicted output for the ith data with the parameter vector U_i, n represents the number of estimators for each independent tree structures f_k, y_i^0 represent the primary hypothesis and η is the learning rate.

3.2 Pipeline Utilizing Neuroimaging Data

In this pipeline, we utilize neuroimaging data. Gray matter (GM) and white matter (WM) from MRI data. Mean diffusivity (MD) and fractional anisotropy (FA) from DTI data. These data are passed through CNN networks with attention mechanism. Each CNN produce a 3×1 probability vector. These probabilities vectors utilizing a softmax operation predict the one of the three classes: HC, SWEDD and PD.

3.2.1 CNN Architecture

The CNN architecture used in this study is based on sushanta et al. [22] and draws inspiration from VGG-16 [23]. It consists of ten convolutional layers and four dense (fully connected) layers. The architecture utilizes small receptive fields (e.g., 3×3) in the convolutional layers. This CNN performs better for three-class classification on neuroimaging data [22]. The goal of this CNN architecture is to extract relevant features from neuroimaging data, capturing spatial patterns and structures that are indicative of Parkinson's disease classes. The input data is in nifti format and is normalized between 0 and 1 to ensure consistency across models. Preprocessing steps, including normalization, are implemented using the Nilearn and Scikit-learn packages [2,18]. Additionally, an attention mechanism is incorporated into the CNN network to enhance its performance. Finally, the last fully connected layers utilize a softmax operation to classify the data into three classes: PD, HC and SWEDD. In CNN, the cross-entropy loss is frequently used loss function to evaluate the model performance. The cross-entropy loss is given by the Eq. 2.

$$L_{CE} = -\sum_{k=1}^{K} p(y = k|\mathbf{x}) \log \widehat{p}(y = k|\mathbf{x}) \qquad (2)$$

Here, K represents the number of classes, where $K = 3$. $p(y = k|\mathbf{x})$ represents the true probabilities of the input $\mathbf{x}$ belonging to class k, while $\widehat{p}(y = k|\mathbf{x})$ represents the predicted probabilities for each class based on the model output.

3.2.2   Self-attention Module

The self-attention module is a crucial component of our model that captures dependencies among the input feature vectors. Our module is inspired from SAGAN architecture [30]. This module is a key component for capturing long-range dependencies in images. It allows the model to focus on important spatial locations and enhance the discriminative power of the network. Given an input feature map $\boldsymbol{F} \in \mathbb{R}^{H \times W \times C}$ the Self-Attention module generate a new feature map $\boldsymbol{G} \in \mathbb{R}^{H \times W \times C}$. Here H, W and C represent the height, width, and number of channels of the feature vector, respectively. The mathematical operations of the Self-Attention module can be summarized as follows:

$$\text{Query}(\boldsymbol{F}) = \boldsymbol{F} \cdot \boldsymbol{W}_Q \qquad (3)$$

$$\text{Key}(\boldsymbol{F}) = \boldsymbol{F} \cdot \boldsymbol{W}_K \qquad (4)$$

$$\text{Value}(\boldsymbol{F}) = \boldsymbol{F} \cdot \boldsymbol{W}_V \qquad (5)$$

Here, $\boldsymbol{W}_Q \in \mathbb{R}^{C \times C_Q}$, $\boldsymbol{W}_K \in \mathbb{R}^{C \times C_K}$, and $\boldsymbol{W}_V \in \mathbb{R}^{C \times C_V}$ represent learnable weight matrices, while C_Q, C_K, and C_V represent the dimensions of the query, key and value vectors, respectively. The attention map is computed as follows:

$$\text{Attention}(\boldsymbol{F}) = \text{softmax}\left(\frac{\text{Query}(\boldsymbol{F}) \cdot \text{Key}(\boldsymbol{F})^{\top}}{\sqrt{C_K}}\right) \qquad (6)$$

The attention map captures the importance of each spatial location by measuring the similarity between the query and the key vectors. Finally, the attended feature map $\boldsymbol{G}$ is obtained by combining the attention map with the value vectors:

$$\boldsymbol{G} = \text{Attention}(\boldsymbol{F}) \cdot \text{Value}(\boldsymbol{F}) \qquad (7)$$

The self-attention module enables our deep learning models to effectively capture dependencies and generate attention-based representations. This in turn enhances the discriminative power of Parkinson's disease classification tasks.

3.3   Late Fusion

Late fusion is a powerful ensemble technique that combines the outputs of multiple models or modalities at a later stage. In this study, we use the Optimal Weighted Average Fusion (OWAF) technique as late fusion [22]. The weights are generated in two stages: Modulated Rank Averaging (MRA) is used first, followed by grid search methods. These optimized weights integrate the probability vectors of all DL and ML-based models, leading to improved classification accuracy compared to using a single model in isolation. This approach enhances performance and provides more accurate predictions.

4   Experimental Results

We divide this section into four parts. We first present an overview of the preprocessing step, which comprises demographic information about the subjects and data balancing with ADASYN. We then describe the effects of different parameters used in ADASYN, CNN, XGBoost, and Attention Module. Next, we include a series of ablation studies that show the individual effects of multimodal data and the attention mechanism. Finally, we compare the performance of AG-PDCNet with a number of state-of-the-art (SOTA) techniques. All the experiments are carried out on a system with 16 GB of DDR4 RAM, a NVIDIA GeForce RTX 3060 GPU having 6 GB of memory, and an Intel i7-10750H processor having 2.60 GHz clock speed.

4.1   Data Pre-processing and Balancing

We have included 281 participants in our research. Each participant's clinical assessment data, MRI, and DTI are considered for experimentation purposes. We have collected both MRI and DTI data from their baseline visits, as can be found in the PPMI database [15]. The database contains FA and MD values, which are preprocessed DTI indices. WM and GM were generated from raw MRI data using SPM-12 tools and the DARTEL method [5]. The preprocessing steps for the DTI indices can be found in the PPMI database [15]. All the indices have distinct voxel representations for the PD and HC groups. In summary, five types of data are available for experimental analysis in the multi-class PD classification task. The demographic details of all participants used in this investigation are shown in Table 1.

For the experimental analysis, we randomly select 80 percent of the data from each class to create the training set, while the remaining 20 percent of each class is used for the test set. It is worth mentioning that the selected data for experimental analysis exhibits a highly unbalanced nature. To address this issue, we employ ADASYN, an oversampling strategy to enhance the number of samples for each minority class [20]. ADASYN generates synthetic samples for each minority class, based on the Euclidean distance of their k-nearest neighbors. As a consequence, the total number of data points in each class (PD, HC, and SWEDD) become equal.

Table 1. Demographic details of the participants

Attributes	HC	SWEDD	PD
Number of participants	67	37	177
Gender (F/M)	24/43	14/23	65/122
Age*	60.12 ±10.71	59.97 ±10.71	61.24 ±9.47

*mean ± standard deviation

4.2 Parameter Setting

The network parameters for both XGBoost and CNN models are manually set, as listed in Table 2. For the clinical assessment data, we use the ReliefF algorithm for feature selection and XGBoost as the classifier. The performance on clinical data is evaluated using different numbers of nearest neighbors (k). Through experimentation, we determine that k = 12 yields optimal results. The training parameters in each CNN model applied to different neuroimaging data are kept the same to avoid conflicts while combining the outputs of the models at the decision level. Three criteria are used to evaluate the performance of AG-PDCnet, namely, accuracy, precision, and recall. The Scikit-Learn package is used to compute all of the metrics [18].

Table 2. Hyper-parameter setting information

Hyper-parameter	Optimizer	Batch size	Learning rate	Number of epochs	Train-test split ratio	Kernel size	Stride
Value	ADAM	32	10^{-4}	100	80:20	3×3	1

4.3 Ablation Studies

We conduct ablation studies to investigate the contributions of multimodal data and attention mechanism on the proposed AG-PDCnet. MRI, DTI and clinical data are chosen in this work as our multimodal data sources. The results of the multi-class classification are presented in Table 3. This table clearly demonstrates that using multimodal data yields superior results as compared to that of a single modality in isolation. Additionally, Table 3 illustrates the effects of attention mechanism on neuroimaging data. We achieve best results when neuroimaging data boosted by the attention mechanism is combined with clinical assessment.

4.4 Comparisons with State-of-the-Art Methods

We compare our proposed solution with twelve state-of-the-art (SOTA) techniques. We consider methods which use single or multiple modalities for binary as well as three-class PD classification. Table 4 presents the comparison results

Table 3. Roll of different data modality and attention on classification

Data	Acc in (%)	Pre in (%)	Rec in (%)
Clinical (CD)	92.6	92.57	91.8
MRI (WM and GM)	90.02	90.17	90.02
DTI (FA and MD)	91.14	91.23	91.1
MRI and DTI	95.53	93.64	91.99
MRI-AT	91.19	91.27	90.88
DTI-AT	92.46	93.18	93.22
MRI-AT and DTI-AT	96.26	96.60	97.12
MRI, DTI and CD	96.07	94.88	94.45
MRI-AT, DTI-AT and CD	**96.93**	**96.88**	**97.27**

-AT, CD, Acc, Pre, and Rec Indicates Attention, Clinical Data, Accuracy, Precision, and Recall respectively.

Table 4. Performance comparisons of AG-PDCnet with other SOTA Methodologies

APPROACH	PD Vs. HC	PD Vs. SWEDD	HC Vs. SWEDD	PD Vs. HC Vs. SWEDD
Prashanth et al. [19]	95	-	-	-
Adeli et al. [3]	81.9	-	-	-
Cigdem et al. [9]	93.7	-	-	-
Singh et al. [24]	95.37	96.04	93.03	-
Gabriel et al. [11]	99.01(M) 87.10(F) 93.05 (A)	-	-	-
Yang et al. [29]	96.88	-	-	-
Li et al. [14]	85.24	-	89.67	-
Tremblay et al. [27]	88.3	-	-	-
Chakraborty et al. [6]	95.3	-	-	-
Sivaranjini et al. [25]	88.9	-	-	-
Rajanbabu et al. [21]	97.5	-	-	-
Sahu et al. [22]	97.8	94.5	95.7	95.53
Proposed method	**98.42**	**96.10**	**97.26**	**96.93**

M, F, A, - Indicates Male, Female, Average, and No *data* respectively. The percentage (%) is used to indicate the values.

for the twelve selected methods. Among these methods, six employ ML techniques, while the remaining six utilize DL techniques. Notably, four of the DL-based methods solely rely on MRI data, while one combines MRI and clinical data. Furthermore, nine out of the twelve methods concentrate on a binary classification between PD and HC, leaving out the more challenging SWEDD class.

Two of the remaining three methods [14,24] address the three-class classification. However, Li et al. [14] did not mention the classification result between PD and SWEDD. Finally, in a recent work [22], we addressed the three-class classification but did not consider clinical data and any attention mechanism.

To ensure fair comparisons, we also include three binary classifications results (PD vs HC, PD vs SWEDD and HC vs SWEDD) from our approach. Our proposed framework clearly outperforms eleven out of the twelve techniques compared. Only [21] demonstrates higher classification accuracy than our method. However, it only considers a single binary classification between HC and PD and ignores the SWEDD class altogether. Gabriel et al. [11] demonstrated better classification accuracy for males, but the average accuracy and accuracy for females are quite lower than ours. When the binary classification results of our system are taken into account, we exceed all twelve state-of-the-art counterparts.

5   Conclusion

In this paper, we proposed AG-PDCNet, an Attention Guided multi-class multimodal PD Classification framework. It uses neuroimaging data, namely, MRI and DTI along with the clinical assessment. Three classes, namely, PD, HC and SWEDD are considered for classification. We employ DL in form of four CNNs boosted by attention mechanism on WM, GM, FA and MD values; along with XGBoost, an ML classifier on the clinical data. The individual outcomes of the five classification models are fused to obtain the overall result. We have shown that our solution achieves a state-of-the-art three-class classification accuracy of 96.93%.

In the future, we plan to use a vision transformer (ViT) for modeling attention in a more comprehensive manner to further improve our classification accuracy. Furthermore, we will explore the integration of additional modalities, such as fMRI, and investigate the impact of incorporating longitudinal data to further enhance the performance of our model.

References

1. Abdulhay, E., Arunkumar, N., Narasimhan, K., Vellaiappan, E., Venkatraman, V.: Gait and tremor investigation using machine learning techniques for the diagnosis of parkinson disease. Futur. Gener. Comput. Syst. **83**, 366–373 (2018)
2. Abraham, A., Pedregosa, F., Eickenberg, M., Gervais, P., Mueller, A., et al.: Machine learning for neuroimaging with scikit-learn. Front. Neuroinform. **8**, 14 (2014)
3. Adeli, E., et al.: Joint feature-sample selection and robust diagnosis of parkinson's disease from MRI data. NeuroImage **141**, 206–219 (2016)
4. Afonso, L.C., et al.: A recurrence plot-based approach for parkinson's disease identification. Futur. Gener. Comput. Syst. **94**, 282–292 (2019)

5. Ashburner, J.: A fast diffeomorphic image registration algorithm. Neuroimage **38**(1), 95–113 (2007)
6. Chakraborty, S., Aich, S., Kim, H.C.: Detection of parkinson's disease from 3T T1 weighted MRI scans using 3D convolutional neural network. Diagnostics **10**(6), 402 (2020)
7. Chen, B., et al.: Detection of mild cognitive impairment in parkinson's disease using gradient boosting decision tree models based on multilevel dti indices. J. Transl. Med. **21**(1), 310 (2023)
8. Chen, T., Guestrin, C.: Xgboost: a scalable tree boosting system. In: Proceedings of the 22nd ACM SIGKDD International Conference on Knowledge Discovery and Data Mining, pp. 785–794 (2016)
9. Cigdem, O., Beheshti, I., Demirel, H.: Effects of different covariates and contrasts on classification of parkinson's disease using structural MRI. Comput. Biol. Med. **99**, 173–181 (2018)
10. Fu, J., et al.: Dual attention network for scene segmentation. In: Proceedings of the IEEE/CVF Conference on Computer Vision and Pattern Recognition, pp. 3146–3154 (2019)
11. Gabriel, S.L., Roberto, R.R.: Classification of PPMI MRI scans with voxel-based morphometry and machine learning to assist in the diagnosis of parkinson's disease. Comput. Methods Programs Biomed. **198** (2021)
12. Huang, Z., Yang, C., Zhou, X., Huang, T.: A hybrid feature selection method based on binary state transition algorithm and relieff. IEEE J. Biomed. Health Inform. **23**(5), 1888–1898 (2019)
13. Jin, D., et al.: Attention-based 3D convolutional network for alzheimer's disease diagnosis and biomarkers exploration. In: 2019 IEEE 16th International Symposium on Biomedical Imaging (ISBI 2019), pp. 1047–1051. IEEE (2019)
14. Li, S., Lei, H., Zhou, F., Gardezi, J., Lei, B.: Longitudinal and multi-modal data learning for parkinson's disease diagnosis via stacked sparse auto-encoder. In: 2019 IEEE 16th International Symposium on Biomedical Imaging (ISBI 2019), pp. 384–387. IEEE (2019)
15. [dataset] Marek, Jennings, D., Lasch, S., Siderowf, A., Tanner, C., et al.: The parkinson progression marker initiative (PPMI). Prog. Neurobiol. **95**, 629–635 (2011)
16. Moro-Velazquez, L., Gomez-Garcia, J.A., Arias-Londoño, J.D., Dehak, N., et al.: Advances in parkinson's disease detection and assessment using voice and speech: a review of the articulatory and phonatory aspects. Biomed. Signal Process. Control **66**, 102418 (2021)
17. Park, C.H., Lee, P.H., Lee, S.K., Chung, S.J., Shin, N.Y.: The diagnostic potential of multimodal neuroimaging measures in parkinson's disease and atypical parkinsonism. Brain Behav. **10**(11), e01808 (2020)
18. Pedregosa, F., Varoquaux, G., Gramfort, A., Michel, V., Thirion, B., Grisel, O., et al.: Scikit-learn: machine learning in Python. J. Mach. Learn. Res. **12**, 2825–2830 (2011)
19. Prashanth, R., Roy, S.D.: Early detection of parkinson's disease through patient questionnaire and predictive modelling. Int. J. Med. Informatics **119**, 75–87 (2018)
20. Pristyanto, Y., Nugraha, A.F., Dahlan, A., Wirasakti, L.A., et al.: Multiclass imbalanced handling using adasyn oversampling and stacking algorithm. In: 2022 16th International Conference on Ubiquitous Information Management and Communication, pp. 1–5. IEEE (2022)

21. Rajanbabu, K., Veetil, I.K., Sowmya, V., Gopalakrishnan, E.A., Soman, K.P.: Ensemble of deep transfer learning models for parkinson's disease classification. In: Reddy, V.S., Prasad, V.K., Wang, J., Reddy, K.T.V. (eds.) Soft Computing and Signal Processing. AISC, vol. 1340, pp. 135–143. Springer, Singapore (2022). https://doi.org/10.1007/978-981-16-1249-7_14

22. Sahu, S.K., Chowdhury, A.: Multi-modal multi-class parkinson disease classification using CNN and decision level fusion. In: 10th International Conference on Pattern Recognition and Machine Intelligence (acepted). arXiv preprint arXiv:2307.02978 (2023)

23. Simonyan, K., Zisserman, A.: Very deep convolutional networks for large-scale image recognition. arXiv preprint arXiv:1409.1556 (2014)

24. Singh, G., Samavedham, L., Lim, E.C.H., ADNI, PPMI, et al.: Determination of imaging biomarkers to decipher disease trajectories and differential diagnosis of neurodegenerative diseases. J. Neurosci. Methods 305, 105–116 (2018)

25. Sivaranjini, S., Sujatha, C.: Deep learning based diagnosis of parkinson's disease using convolutional neural network. Multimedia Tools Appl. 79(21), 15467–15479 (2020)

26. Templeton, J.M., Poellabauer, C., Schneider, S.: Classification of parkinson's disease and its stages using machine learning. Sci. Rep. 12(1), 14036 (2022)

27. Tremblay, C., Mei, J., Frasnelli, J.: Olfactory bulb surroundings can help to distinguish parkinson's disease from non-parkinsonian olfactory dysfunction. NeuroImage Clin. 28, 102457 (2020)

28. Xue, Y., Zhu, H., Neri, F.: A feature selection approach based on NSGA-II with relieff. Appl. Soft Comput. 134, 109987 (2023)

29. Yang, Y., Wei, L., Hu, Y., Wu, Y., Hu, L., Nie, S.: Classification of parkinson's disease based on multi-modal features and stacking ensemble learning. J. Neurosci. Methods 350 (2021)

30. Zhang, G., Kan, M., Shan, S., Chen, X.: Generative adversarial network with spatial attention for face attribute editing. In: Proceedings of the European Conference on Computer Vision (ECCV), pp. 417–432 (2018)

31. Zhang, J., Zheng, B., Gao, A., Feng, X., Liang, D., Long, X.: A 3D densely connected convolution neural network with connection-wise attention mechanism for alzheimer's disease classification. Magn. Reson. Imaging 78, 119–126 (2021)

Effective-LDAM: An Effective Loss Function to Mitigate Data Imbalance for Robust Chest X-Ray Disease Classification

S. Sree Rama Vamsidhar[1], Bhargava Satya Nunna[2], and Rama Krishna Gorthi[1(✉)]

[1] Indian Institute of Technology Tirupati, Tirupati, Andhra Pradesh, India
rkg@iittp.ac.in
[2] Andhra University, Visakhapatnam, Andhra Pradesh, India

Abstract. Deep Learning (DL) approaches have gained prominence in medical imaging for disease diagnosis. Chest X-ray (CXR) classification has emerged as an effective method for detecting various diseases. Among these methodologies, Chest X-ray (CXR) classification has proven to be an effective approach for detecting and analyzing various diseases. However, the reliable performance of DL classification algorithms is dependent upon access to large and balanced datasets, which pose challenges in medical imaging due to the impracticality of acquiring sufficient data for every disease category. To tackle this problem, we propose an algorithmic-centric approach called Effective-Label Distribution Aware Margin (E-LDAM), which modifies the margin of the widely adopted Label Distribution Aware Margin (LDAM) loss function using an effective number of samples in each class. Experimental evaluations on the COVIDx CXR dataset focus on Normal, Pneumonia, and COVID-19 classification. The experimental results demonstrate the effectiveness of the proposed E-LDAM approach, achieving a remarkable recall score of 97.81% for the minority class (COVID-19) in CXR image prediction. Furthermore, the overall accuracy of the three-class classification task attains an impressive level of 95.26%.

Keywords: Chest X-Ray · Classification · Imbalance · Loss function

1 Introduction

Data imbalance is a significant challenge encountered in the field of medical imaging, which can impact the accuracy and effectiveness of classification algorithms. In medical imaging, the imbalance arises when certain disease categories are underrepresented compared to others in the available dataset. This imbalance hampers the development of robust and reliable models for disease detection and diagnosis.

H. Kaur et al. (Eds.): CVIP 2023, CCIS 2011, pp. 188–198, 2024.
https://doi.org/10.1007/978-3-031-58535-7_16

With the advent of deep learning techniques there have been notable advancements in automating the analysis of medical images. However, the performance and generalizability of these models heavily depend on the availability of balanced and diverse data across different disease categories. Unfortunately, achieving a balanced distribution of medical images for each disease category is challenging due to factors like the rarity of certain diseases and limitations in data collection. Classifiers trained on imbalanced datasets tend to be biased towards the more prevalent disease categories, which can lead to inaccuracies in identifying and classifying less common diseases. In recent times, an imbalance in COVID-19 chest X-ray classification poses a significant challenge in medical imaging, impacting the accuracy and reliability of diagnostic algorithms. Chest X-ray (CXR) classification has emerged as a valuable tool for the detection and analysis of COVID-19 cases. However, due to various factors such as data availability and disease prevalence, imbalanced datasets are common in COVID-19 classification tasks.

To address the challenge of data imbalance in COVID-19 chest X-ray classification, researchers have explored various techniques and strategies. These include data over sampling, under sampling, methods [2,9,10,20], re-weighting loss functions [3,4], and employing advanced algorithms like [14], to handle imbalanced distributions. The aim is to ensure equitable consideration for both the majority and minority classes, thus improving the accuracy and reliability of COVID-19 classification models.

While data augmentation can be beneficial in certain computer vision applications, its application to medical imaging must be approached with caution due to the unique characteristics of medical images, ethical considerations, annotation requirements, limited data availability, and regulatory concerns. Hence, in this work, we focus on an algorithmic approach to mitigate the impact of data imbalance in COVID-19 chest X-ray classification, a three-class task using the COVIDx dataset [28].

In this paper, we propose an algorithmic approach to enhance the performance of diagnostic algorithms. Here, we propose a modified LDAM loss function with an effective number of class samples [5] to design the margin for each class, unlike the foundation work LDAM which considers the given class sample frequencies in the dataset and is termed as Effective LDAM (E-LDAM).

The major limitations of the LDAM loss function are it heavily relies on the presence of well-separated class boundaries, which may be challenging to achieve in datasets with overlapping or closely related classes, potentially leading to sub-optimal performance. Also, the LDAM loss struggles to handle extremely imbalanced datasets where the minority class has significantly fewer samples, leading to challenges in accurately representing and classifying the minority class.

Under the re-weighting techniques, the effective number of samples in Class Balanced loss [5] is a modified representation of class frequencies to provide a more accurate weighting scheme that accounts for the class imbalance. It is worth noting that the effective number of samples indirectly helps the learning objective in handling overlapping samples at the decision boundary. Therefore, in this work, we propose to modify LDAM using the effective number of samples. E-LDAM provides a robust and effective margin for the generalization of minority samples. By leveraging the classification ability of Heat Guided Convolution Neural Network (HG-CNN) [23] model to predict based on the fusion of global and local features of an image and the proposed E-LDAM loss function, a reliable classification model for COVID-19 detection from CXR images was developed. The main objective of this work is to achieve a superior recall score for COVID-19 (minority class) through enhanced loss function while also maintaining a consistent accuracy of the classification model.

The paper is organized as follows: Sect. 2 provides a review of related work in imbalanced data classification, particularly in the context of COVID-19 chest X-ray classification. In Sect. 3, we detail our proposed methodologies, covering data preprocessing, novel loss functions, and tailored model architectures for managing data imbalance in COVID-19 classification. Section 4 outlines our experimental setup, showcases results, and offers a thorough analysis. Finally, Sect. 5 presents the conclusion.

2   Related Work

This section provides an overview of the COVID-19 CXR imbalanced data classification works.

The wide variety of imbalanced data classification approaches in computer vision are discussed below.

To achieve an unbiased classification model, the approaches are broadly categorized into two categories. They are: 1. Data-centric approaches 2. Algorithmic-centric approaches.

Data-centric approaches are commonly employed to address the issue of imbalanced datasets, aiming to mitigate the disparity in the distribution of majority and minority classes. This mitigation involves two primary techniques: oversampling the minority class and undersampling the majority class. However, it's worth noting that while undersampling can help rectify bias, it also comes at the cost of discarding valuable and diverse information, ultimately resulting in a limited number of samples for model training. This limitation can be particularly problematic when dealing with deep learning models [8].

On the other hand, oversampling techniques, whether through data augmentation or data synthesis, predominantly rely on the existing samples from the minority classes [6,19,21]. An attempt has been made by Kim et al. [12] to bridge the diversity gap between majority and minority class data. However, it's essential to recognize that augmentation alone does not equate to an increase in genuinely diverse data. Instead, it may lead to overfitting on the limited number of minority samples, resulting in poor generalization, especially in scenarios of extreme class imbalance. In the context of COVID-19 detection, several studies have applied data re-sampling techniques, including works by Ozturk et al. [20], Bassi et al. [2], and Ismael et al. [10].

Algorithmic approaches aim to mitigate the inherent bias introduced by class-wise sample size disparities within a dataset. This bias is addressed through the re-weighting of the loss function, with weights being inversely proportional to the frequency of samples in a class-specific manner, as articulated in prior research [3]. While Categorical Cross-Entropy (CE) serves as the standard loss function for balanced datasets in classification tasks, its application to imbalanced datasets can lead to detrimental effects, particularly with respect to the minority class, potentially resulting in overfitting. To tackle dataset imbalance effectively, a body of work has emerged, either in conjunction with cross-entropy loss or independently, proposing specialized loss functions that enhance class separability. This is achieved through modifications to the similarity assessment term (final logits) or the inclusion of regularizers, yielding improved performance [13].

Some variants, such as the Class-Balanced Loss [5], introduce the concept of an "effective number" of samples to serve as alternative weights in the re-weighting process. The Focal loss [16], on the other hand, is designed to address class imbalance by down-weighting easily classified examples. Another line of research focuses on enhancing a model's ability to distinguish between classes by incorporating margins. The margin for class i is defined as the minimum distance of data belonging to the ith class from the decision boundary. Studies in the context of imbalanced data applications explore asymmetrical margins [11,15]. The Label Distribution Aware Margin loss (LDAM) [4] extends the existing soft margin loss [25] by assigning larger margins to minority classes. This learning objective promotes a simpler model for the minority class, facilitating increased generalization potential, while employing a more complex model for majority classes. Class label-dependent margins are incorporated into the CE loss function under this framework.

In the specific domain of COVID-19 detection, a limited number of algorithmic approaches have been explored. Wong et al. [28] introduced COVID-Net, while Li et al. [14] pursued discriminative cost-sensitive learning (DSCL) approach. DSCL incorporates a conditional center loss that enables the acquisition of deep discriminative representations from chest X-ray (CXR) data, allowing for adaptive adjustment of the cost associated with misclassifying COVID-19 instances within the classes. Additionally, Al-Rakhami [1] proposed a hybrid architecture that combines Convolutional Neural Networks (CNNs) and Recurrent Neural Networks (RNNs) with transfer learning techniques, leveraging CNNs for feature extraction from CXR images and RNNs for classification. Transfer learning, in which knowledge transfer occurs from one task to another with minimal training, is employed in this context. Furthermore, MM Rahman et al. [22] introduced a deep learning model based on the histogram of oriented gradients applied to input CXR images.

3 Proposed Method

In this section, we discuss the proposed E-LDAM in great detail.

3.1 Problem Formulation

In classification tasks, Cross entropy loss is a commonly used loss function that measures the dissimilarity between predicted class probabilities and the true class labels. It quantifies the error between the predicted probability distribution and the actual distribution using the logarithmic loss. In a k-class classification task, the CE loss function for an input sample is given as shown in Eq. 1.

$$\mathcal{L}_{ce} = -log\frac{e^{z_y}}{\sum_{j=1}^{k}e^{z_j}} \tag{1}$$

where z_j denotes the jth index value in the predicted output vector of the classification model.

However, the CE loss function alone cannot handle the imbalance in data. The works [25,26] proved that modifying the vanilla softmax cross-entropy loss, either by operating on CE loss term or by adding regularizers, can lead to improved performance since the class separation ability at the penultimate layer improves with the modified objectives [13].

Label Distribution Aware Margin Loss (LDAM) [4] is such a loss function that addresses the imbalance data classification. It introduces a margin-based formulation that enhances the discrimination between classes, particularly for minority classes with fewer samples. By assigning larger margins to minority classes, LDAM loss aims to alleviate the impact of data imbalance and improve their representation in the learned feature space.

Earlier works like Large-Margin Softmax [18], Angular Softmax [17], and Additive Margin Softmax [7] have been proposed to minimize intra-class variation in predictions and enlarge the inter-class margin. But, in contrast to the above loss functions with class-independent margins, LDAM supports using label-dependent margins which encourage bigger margins to minority classes over majority classes. The loss function equation of LDAM is given below.

$$\mathcal{L}_{ldam} = -log\frac{e^{z_y-\Delta_y}}{e^{z_y-\Delta_y} + \sum_{j\neq y}e^{z_j}} \tag{2}$$

where, for some constant C and number of samples present in class j i.e. n_j,

$$\Delta_j = \frac{C}{n_j^{1/4}} \ for \ j \in \{1,...k\} \tag{3}$$

Further, under reweighting techniques, **Class Balanced loss (CB loss)** [5] was proposed to mitigate the bias towards majority classes in imbalanced datasets. It dynamically adjusts the loss contribution of each class based on their respective frequencies to provide equal consideration to all classes during training. By reweighting the loss function, class-balanced loss ensures that each class contributes proportionally to the overall loss, effectively addressing the imbalance issue. CB loss is a re-weighting approach, specifically proposed to avoid the problem of data overlapping within the class. The effective number of samples can be described as a volume of a set of unique samples. The effective number of samples for each class could be calculated from the following equation.

$$E_n = \frac{1 - \beta^n}{1 - \beta} \tag{4}$$

where, n is the sample size of a particular class, and $\beta \in [0, 1)$ is a hyperparameter.

While cross-entropy loss is a standard choice, LDAM loss and class-balanced loss offer specific adaptations to handle imbalanced datasets. The incorporation of these loss functions in classification tasks helps to achieve fair and accurate predictions, particularly in scenarios where class distribution is uneven. We note a significant distinction between the re-weighting approach and LDAM. The scalar factor introduced in re-weighting is solely dependent on the class, while in LDAM, it also depends on the model's output.

3.2 Effective-LDAM (E-LDAM)

To optimize the decision boundary based on the effective number of samples in a class and mitigate the influence of similar samples, we propose a modified LDAM loss function. Instead of using the actual number of samples, we calculate the loss by considering the effective number of samples. Unlike the existing works [4,5] etc., which use E_n to re-weight the learning objective, the proposed approach makes use of E_n to design the decision boundary. By incorporating the concept of the effective number of samples, the LDAM loss function exhibits improved recall scores and precision for minority classes. This adjustment favors the minority classes by shifting the decision boundary optimally in favor of the minority class. The enhanced LDAM loss function, incorporating the effective number of samples, can be formulated as shown in the below equation.

$$\mathcal{L}_{e-ldam} = -log \frac{e^{z_y - \Delta_y}}{e^{z_y - \Delta_y} + \sum_{j \neq y} e^{z_j}} \tag{5}$$

$$\Delta_j = \frac{C}{E_{n_j}^{1/r}} \ for \ j \in \{1, ...k\} \tag{6}$$

E_n is the effective number of samples of class n, where E_n could be calculated by using $\frac{1 - \beta^n}{1 - \beta}$ and r is a positive integer.

4 Experimental Results

4.1 Architecture Details

In the experiments, we utilized a convolutional neural network model guided by heatmaps, consisting of three branches: global, local, and fusion. This model is known as the Heat guided Convolutional Neural Network (HG-CNN). It is designed to detect infections, especially those that appear as localized issues like COVID-19. HG-CNN combines information from the whole image and specific areas to improve accuracy and reduce errors caused by noise. HG-CNN uses a well-known architecture called DenseNet121 and operates in three stages, with each stage classifying images into one of three categories: COVID-19, Pneumonia, or Normal. The HG-CNN model's structure is given in Fig. 1.

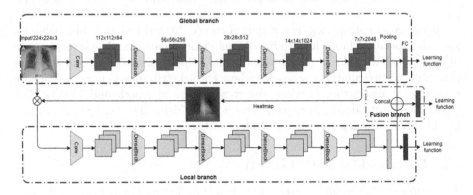

Fig. 1. HG-CNN for Chest X-ray image classification.

In the first stage (Stage 1), we prepare the input chest X-ray images by making them a standard size of 224×224 pixels and improving their quality using the histogram equalization technique. Then, we feed the processed image into the global branch for the three class classification i.e. Normal, Pneumonia, and COVID-19. From the trained global branch, we extract a heap map showing where the model should pay attention and the feature vector from the penultimate layer of dimension 1024×1. We resize and multiply the heap map with the original image and pass it to the local branch for the next stage (Stage 2). In Stage 2, the local branch produces another 1024-value feature vector at the penultimate layer. During training at the local branch, we focus on the parts of the image that matter the most, thanks to the attention map.

In the final stage (Stage 3), we combine the two feature vectors from Stages 1 and 2. We do this by putting them through a single layer called the fusion branch. This layer then tells us the probabilities of the image belonging to COVID-19, Pneumonia, or being Normal. It's essential to note that we train this model in stages: first the global branch, then the local branch, and finally, the fusion branch.

Working Mechanism: The way HG-CNN works is a lot like how a radiologist reads X-rays. First, we train the global branch, which is similar to a radiologist taking an initial look at the entire X-ray image. Then, we use heatmaps to find specific regions of interest, like areas with lesions, and include them in the X-ray image, making it weighted. This weighted image goes into the local branch, which is similar to a radiologist zooming in on the problem area after the initial assessment. Finally, we put together the global and local information to make a final decision, just like a radiologist who considers both the big picture and the details before making a diagnosis.

Also, it's important to mention that we train the model in two steps. First, we train the HG-CNN on the National Institutes of Health (NIH) dataset. Then, we fine-tune it for the specific 3-class classification task using the COVIDx dataset. We carefully adjust key settings like the number of training cycles, learning rates, how fast the learning rate decreases, and how many examples the model looks at in each training round, based on experiments at each stage of development.

4.2   Dataset

The dataset utilized for training and evaluating the proposed model comprises a total of 19,364 Chest X-ray (CXR) images sourced from the COVIDx dataset (version 8) by Wang et al. [28]. The COVIDx dataset is a compilation originating from five publicly available data repositories: (1) COVID-19 Image Data Collection, (2) ActualMed COVID-19 Chest X-ray Dataset Initiative [27], (3) RSNA Pneumonia Detection Challenge dataset, which utilized publicly available CXR data, (4) COVID-19 radiography database, and (5) RSNA International COVID-19 Open Radiology Database (RICORD) as reported in [24]. It's important to note that the dataset exhibits an imbalanced distribution of CXR images across various classes, as inherited from the COVIDx dataset. The distribution of samples for each class is detailed in Table 1.

Table 1. Sample distribution among the classes in COVIDx dataset.

COVIDx Dataset			
	COVID-19	Pneumonia	Normal
Train split	4649	5964	8751
Test split	274	105	100
Total	**4923**	**6069**	**8581**

4.3   Results

This section consists of details and results of experiments performed with the HG-CNN model on different loss functions. This section also includes the comparative results of various works with the proposed approach. The below Table 2 consists of the experiment results of each stage in the HG-CNN model Global, Local, and Fusion branches. Every stage in the HG-CNN model is experimented with different loss functions. The table below contains the overall accuracy of each stage and the recall score of COVID-19 obtained from experiments. From Table 2, we can also observe that effective loss functions have exhibited a better performance when compared to standard loss functions. The effective loss functions have increased the model's capability in handling the minority class COVID-19 at each phase of the model. They are able to improve the recall score for COVID-19 while maintaining the overall accuracy of the model.

Table 2. Results from the experiments performed on COVIDx dataset with proposed HG-CNN model across the standard loss functions & the proposed loss function.

Loss function	Metric	Global Branch	Local Branch	Fusion Branch
CE	Accuracy	91.86%	87.27%	93.74%
	Recall	90.51%	88.69%	93.43%
CB-CE	Accuracy	92.28%	84.76%	92.28%
	Recall	93.43%	88.32%	95.26%
LDAM	Accuracy	93.32%	86.22%	92.69%
	Recall	94.16%	86.86%	95.26%
E-LDAM	Accuracy	95%	88.10%	95.82%
	Recall	97.08%	87.96%	97.81%

E-LDAM loss function with the HG-CNN model has outperformed the various other significant contemporary works in detecting COVID-19 infection. The E-LDAM loss has enhanced the model's capability in detecting in handling the minority classes and has increased the recall score for the minority class like COVID-19 while maintaining a good accuracy when compared to other approaches. The comparative results of the proposed approach with various other approaches are shown in Table 3. The above table consists of other works in detecting COVID-19 infection by handling the imbalance in the dataset with algorithmic approaches.

Table 3. Comparison results on COVID-19 detection.

Method	Technique	Accuracy	Recall
Li, et al. [14]	Data augmentation	97.01%	97%
Rahman et al. [22]	Data augmentation	96.74%	96.5%
Proposed method	Loss function	95.82%	97.81%

5   Conclusion

In conclusion, our work introduces a novel loss function, E-LDAM, which incorporates the effective number of samples as weights for classification margin design, thereby enhancing the performance of a CXR classification model based on Heat Guided Convolutional Neural Network. Our study demonstrates that E-LDAM outperforms the existing LDAM loss function by > 3% in recall specifically for COVID-19 CXR images and > 2% in overall accuracy. These findings underscore the effectiveness of E-LDAM in mitigating data imbalance challenges, improving disease diagnosis accuracy in medical imaging, and facilitating the development of more reliable diagnostic systems. We aim to further advance our work by exploring additional algorithmic approaches and robust architectures to enhance the diagnosis of various data-scarce infections in the medical domain. We aim to further advance our work by exploring additional algorithmic approaches and robust architectures to enhance the diagnosis of various data-scarce infections in the medical domain.

References

1. Al-Rakhami, M.S., Islam, M.M., Islam, M.Z., Asraf, A., Sodhro, A.H., Ding, W.: Diagnosis of covid-19 from X-rays using combined CNN-RNN architecture with transfer learning. MedRxiv (2021)
2. Bassi, P.R., Attux, R.: A deep convolutional neural network for covid-19 detection using chest X-rays. Res. Biomed. Eng. **38**(1), 139–148 (2022)
3. Buda, M., Maki, A., Mazurowski, M.A.: A systematic study of the class imbalance problem in convolutional neural networks. Neural Netw. **106**, 249–259 (2018)
4. Cao, K., Wei, C., Gaidon, A., Arechiga, N., Ma, T.: Learning imbalanced datasets with label-distribution-aware margin loss. arXiv preprint arXiv:1906.07413 (2019)
5. Cui, Y., Jia, M., Lin, T.Y., Song, Y., Belongie, S.: Class-balanced loss based on effective number of samples. In: Proceedings of the IEEE/CVF Conference on Computer Vision and Pattern Recognition, pp. 9268–9277 (2019)
6. Cui, Y., Song, Y., Sun, C., Howard, A., Belongie, S.: Large scale fine-grained categorization and domain-specific transfer learning. In: Proceedings of the IEEE Conference on Computer Vision and Pattern Recognition, pp. 4109–4118 (2018)
7. Deng, J., Guo, J., Xue, N., Zafeiriou, S.: Arcface: additive angular margin loss for deep face recognition. In: Proceedings of the IEEE/CVF Conference on Computer Vision and Pattern Recognition, pp. 4690–4699 (2019)
8. He, H., Garcia, E.A.: Learning from imbalanced data. IEEE Trans. Knowl. Data Eng. **21**(9), 1263–1284 (2009). https://doi.org/10.1109/TKDE.2008.239
9. Islam, M.Z., Islam, M.M., Asraf, A.: A combined deep CNN-LSTM network for the detection of novel coronavirus (covid-19) using X-ray images. Informat. Med. Unlocked **20**, 100412 (2020)
10. Ismael, A.M., Şengür, A.: Deep learning approaches for covid-19 detection based on chest X-ray images. Expert Syst. Appl. **164**, 114054 (2021)
11. Khan, S., Hayat, M., Zamir, S.W., Shen, J., Shao, L.: Striking the right balance with uncertainty. In: Proceedings of the IEEE/CVF Conference on Computer Vision and Pattern Recognition, pp. 103–112 (2019)
12. Kim, J., Jeong, J., Shin, J.: M2M: imbalanced classification via major-to-minor translation. In: Proceedings of the IEEE/CVF Conference on Computer Vision and Pattern Recognition, pp. 13896–13905 (2020)
13. Kornblith, S., Lee, H., Chen, T., Norouzi, M.: What's in a loss function for image classification? arXiv preprint arXiv:2010.16402 (2020)

14. Li, T., Han, Z., Wei, B., Zheng, Y., Hong, Y., Cong, J.: Robust screening of covid-19 from chest X-ray via discriminative cost-sensitive learning. arXiv preprint arXiv:2004.12592 (2020)
15. Li, Z., Kamnitsas, K., Glocker, B.: Overfitting of neural nets under class imbalance: analysis and improvements for segmentation. In: Shen, D., et al. (eds.) MICCAI 2019. LNCS, vol. 11766, pp. 402–410. Springer, Cham (2019). https://doi.org/10. 1007/978-3-030-32248-9_45
16. Lin, T.Y., Goyal, P., Girshick, R., He, K., Dollár, P.: Focal loss for dense object detection. In: Proceedings of the IEEE International Conference on Computer Vision, pp. 2980–2988 (2017)
17. Liu, W., Wen, Y., Yu, Z., Li, M., Raj, B., Song, L.: Sphereface: deep hypersphere embedding for face recognition. In: Proceedings of the IEEE Conference on Computer Vision and Pattern Recognition, pp. 212–220 (2017)
18. Liu, W., Wen, Y., Yu, Z., Yang, M.: Large-margin softmax loss for convolutional neural networks. arXiv preprint arXiv:1612.02295 (2016)
19. Mikołajczyk, A., Grochowski, M.: Data augmentation for improving deep learning in image classification problem. In: 2018 International Interdisciplinary PhD Workshop (IIPhDW), pp. 117–122. IEEE (2018)
20. Ozturk, T., Talo, M., Yildirim, E.A., Baloglu, U.B., Yildirim, O., Acharya, U.R.: Automated detection of covid-19 cases using deep neural networks with X-ray images. Comput. Biol. Med. 121, 103792 (2020)
21. Perez, L., Wang, J.: The effectiveness of data augmentation in image classification using deep learning. arXiv preprint arXiv:1712.04621 (2017)
22. Rahman, M.M., Nooruddin, S., Hasan, K., Dey, N.K.: HOG+ CNN net: diagnosing covid-19 and pneumonia by deep neural network from chest X-ray images. SN Comput. Sci. 2(5), 1–15 (2021)
23. Sivapuram, A.K., Ravi, V., Senthil, G., Gorthi, R.K., et al.: Visal-a novel learning strategy to address class imbalance. Neural Netw. 161, 178–184 (2023)
24. Tsai, E.B., et al.: The RSNA international covid-19 open radiology database (RICORD). Radiology 299(1), E204 (2021)
25. Wang, F., Cheng, J., Liu, W., Liu, H.: Additive margin softmax for face verification. IEEE Signal Process. Lett. 25(7), 926–930 (2018)
26. Wang, H., et al.: Cosface: large margin cosine loss for deep face recognition. In: Proceedings of the IEEE Conference on Computer Vision and Pattern Recognition, pp. 5265–5274 (2018)
27. Wang, L., et al.: Actualmed covid-19 chest X-ray dataset initiative (2020). https:// github.com/agchung/Actualmed-COVID-chestxraydataset
28. Wang, L., Lin, Z.Q., Wong, A.: Covid-net: a tailored deep convolutional neural network design for detection of covid-19 cases from chest X-ray images. Sci. Rep. 10(1), 1–12 (2020)

Performance Elevation Using Augmented Pivot Point Rotation for Kidney Stone Detection

Gorli Santoshi$^{(\boxtimes)}$ and Ratnakar Dash

National Institute of Technology, Rourkela, Rourkela, India
iacr.santoshi@gmail.com, ratnakar@nitrkl.ac.in

Abstract. Kidney stone detection has been one of the key issues of healthcare professionals in the past. The recent development of deep learning-based models for kidney stone detection has reduced the time and workload of radiologists by assisting in the classification of kidney stone images. The contribution focuses firstly on generating the annotation of the publicly available dataset consisting of 1799 Non-Contrast Computerized Tomography (NCCT) coronal images collected from GitHub. Without manipulating the ratio of the training and testing samples, annotation of the images were carried out with bounding box instances of normal and kidney stone. A competent algorithm generates a new dataset using the augmented pivot point rotation (APPR) to the bounding box. The original and augmented datasets are trained on Single shot Detector (SSD), You Only Live Once (YOLOv7), and Faster Region-based Convolution Neural Network (RCNN) with backbones such as ResNet50, MobileNetv2, and ResNet101, and the results are compared. The result gives a trade-off between the single-stage and two-stage object detection models. The precision of YOLOv7 is 0.986 and 0.966 for normal and kidney stones, respectively, but the precision of the Faster RCNN for normal and kidney stones is balanced. Faster-RCNN training parameters are more compared to YOLOv7, resulting in an increase in training time. YOLOv7 surpasses the outcomes compared to other models with a mAP@0.5:0.95 of 0.933. An average mAP@0.5:0.95 scores for all the models trained on the augmented dataset is intensified by 18.9%. YOLOv7 and Faster-RCNN with ResNet50 provide promising results after training on augmented data. It is concluded that YOLOv7 and Faster RCNN with ResNet50 are suitable for localizing kidney stones with the proposed augmentation technique.

Keywords: Kidney stone detection · object detection · deep learning · augmentation

1 Introduction

Medical image analysis-based interpretation is dominantly used for early detection and diagnosis of diseases. Deep learning algorithms can automatically learn complex patterns and features from the images themselves, and they are especially well-suited for medical image analysis. Based on imaging data, these algorithms can segment anatomical components, detect and classify anomalies, and forecast clinical consequences.

Kidney stone symptoms can overlap with other diseases, including appendicitis or urinary tract infections. The exact diagnosis and suitable treatment are made possible by the proper detection of kidney stones by imaging examinations [1], such as CT scans or ultrasound, which helps distinguish kidney stones from other possible causes of symptoms. Automation algorithms assist healthcare professionals in early detection, potentially saving time and improving patient outcomes.

The conventional classification technique [2] guides healthcare professionals by determining the entire image belonging to a particular class. Object detection, conversely, oblige is detecting and classifying all the objects in the image with bounding boxes. A fully automated system will be effective if the model can predict the location of the kidney having the stone. A person can have one or two kidneys according to their health conditions. Stone can be present in both kidneys or only in one or none (normal). Localization of the renal calculi reduces the burden of the radiologist.

Medical professionals are under pressure to evaluate medical images as their use increases. Due to its excellent accuracy relative to conventional methods, deep learning has recently been increasingly used to support physicians in many medical imaging tasks. Deep learning performance often depends on the volume of training data [3]. However, compared to other areas, the availability of medical picture datasets [4] is typically constrained because of the production of the image ground truth and confidentiality information. Since there are typically fewer samples of medical anomalies than real-time data, numerous strategies to produce new positive samples have been proposed and employed to produce more training samples. However, creating a compelling data augmentation understanding [5] of the target dataset and its operation is necessary.

The objectives of the proposed work are:

- Fully automating the localization and classification of normal and kidney stone regions with bounding boxes.
- Comparison of standard deep learning object detection algorithms to find an end-to-end localization and classification of kidney stones.
- Apply relevant augmentation (APPR) to the target dataset, guiding the precise classification of the stone and normal kidney regions.

2   Literature Survey

Predicting the kidney stone can be carried out in two directions. The first direction is a classification of the kidney stones and the normal images of CT images. Tremendous works have been contributed by various authors in this direction. Yildirim et al. [6] proposed classifying kidney stones for Coronal Computed tomography (CT) images by using XResNet-50 with Grad-CAM to identify the area the model is concentrated to classify. The author used the 1799 images of normal and kidney stones images. The image consists of the whole abdomen, pelvis, and parts of the thorax. The accuracy of the model is 96.82%, but it concentrates on various locations in the image. Baygin et al. [7] used the same data as above by employing ExDARK19 as a transfer learning algorithm to decrease the training time of the model and extract the features. Iterative neighborhood component analysis (INCA) was used to select the feature vector, which concentrates on each location to correctly classify the stone images and finally fed to the k-nearest neighbors algorithm to classify the stone. The work could not show the location of the stone Patro el at. [2] proposed Kronecker Convolution-deep learning techniques by modifying the CNN algorithm to reduce the redundancy in feature maps without convolution overlapping, producing an efficient and accurate result. The classification accuracy was 98.56% and did not predict the location of the stone.

Recently, Authors have also made a novel contribution in the direction of using segmentation using deep learning algorithms like Regions with Convolutional Neural Networks (RCNN), U-Net, etc., and the stone burden is also calculated. Using a dataset of 465 CT scans, Langkvist et al. [8] used CNN and a probabilistic technique to locate the ureter stone. Although the dataset is 3D and contains some slices with stones, classifying and archiving 2.68 false positives per patient is insufficient to replace the radiologist's primary diagnostic reading. Reducing the number of pre-processing processes, like locating related components, binarizing, and choosing training data for class balance, is a challenge.

Liu et al. [9] use total variation (TV) flow for image noise reduction and Maximally Stable Extremal Regions (MSER) features for finding calculi candidates and computes a total of 7 texture and shape features to train a Support Vector Machine (SVM) for the task of identifying renal calculi in CT scans. The method was validated on a data set of 192 patients with a false positive rate of 8 per patient and a sensitivity of 69. The kidneys are segmented using a 3D U-Net model by Elton et al. [10] before being subjected to gradient-based anisotropic denoising, thresholding, and region-growing. Convolution Neural Network (CNN) is then used to separate kidney stones from spurious regions uses 180 CT colonography scans on 6185 patients for training and validation, yielding an AUC of 95%. By discriminating between kidney stones and plagues, the accuracy can be improved. Kaviani et al. [11] collected data from 4 Vendors containing 218 CT Scans, used threshold-based segmentation, and achieved a sensitivity of 79%. Li et al. [12] proposed a two-stage segmentation algorithm; in the first stage, coarse kidneys are detected, and the cropped kidney is obtained. U-net is used to segment the kidney stone from the cropped kidney. 500 unenhanced abdominal CT scans were collected among them, 260 were selected for annotation. The dataset contains 209 scans with stone and 50 without stone. The kidney stone dice score was 80.59.

With the rise in popularity of CNN and GPU-accelerated deep learning frameworks, new approaches to developing object detection algorithms were taken. Deep-learning object detection architectures are classified into two types. YOLOv7 [13] and SSD300 [14] are single-stage detectors that do away with the ROI extraction step and instead classify and regress the candidate anchor boxes directly. The object identification task is divided into two steps by two-stage detectors, which first extract ROI before classifying and regressing the ROIs using R-CNN [15], Fast RCNN [16], and Faster RCNN [17]. The localization of the kidney having renal calculi is not predicted in any of the contributions. As a result, we can evaluate the one-stage detector YOLOv7 and SSD300 compared to the two-stage Faster RCNN with other backbone networks. The categorization models were developed and tested using the backbone of deep learning architectures, including ResNet50, ResNet101, Mobilenetv2, and VGG16. To enhance the performance of image recognition models, suitable augmentation strategies [18] should be automatically designed in accordance with the target data and tasks. Image transformation operations like geometric transformation, photometric transformation, and their combinations are used for medical image classification [19], providing good results. Few works are contributed to augmenting the instances for object detection.

3   Methodology

3.1   Dataset Acquisition

The dataset is collected from the publicly available GitHub repository [6]. The dataset consists of 433 patients, with 268 patients reported having kidney stones and 165 patients with normal kidneys (no stones). A total of 1799 coronal CT images of the patients were collected, 790 images with kidney stones, and 1009 images of normal scans were obtained. The training and testing dataset was divided into an 80:20 ratio.

3.2   Data Annotation

A patient can have one or two kidneys according to their health conditions. Stone can be present in both kidneys or only in one or none (normal), so the image can have one or more instances. The proposed work categorizes the annotations into two classes: normal and kidney stone. The annotation is carried out using Roboflow online platform, which annotates the instances in the dataset using bounding boxes. The total instances generated for the 1799 images is 2738. Figure 1 presents the annotation of the normal and kidney stone images.

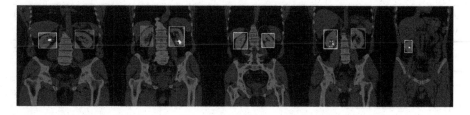

Fig. 1. The kidney stone and normal kidney with two different coloured bounding boxes, pink for kidney with stone and purple for normal kidney. (Color figure online)

3.3   Algorithm for Bounding Box Augmentation

The dataset is enhanced by using color transformations to increase the contrast of the images, as the input images are non-contrast coronal Images. The augmentation of the dataset is performed to generate a new dataset and add it to the existing dataset. The proposed method applies a bounding box pivot-point rotation randomly between $-15°$ to $+15°$. The algorithm first calculates the pivot point of the bounding boxes. Then, translates the bounding box such that the pivot point coincides with the coordinate origin. Anti-clockwise rotation is applied about the coordinate origin with a specified angle. Translate back the bounding box such that the pivot point is returned to its original position. The Algorithm 1 presents the steps to generate the dataset using augmentation.

The above algorithm is used for both the bounding boxes of the image, and new bounding boxes are generated to increase the size of the dataset. Figure 2 presents the augmented images with bounding boxes. The bounding box rotation helps in training the kidney more accurately; the visual images show that the angle of the kidney in coronal CT images is tilted. The contribution supports data generation as well as the tilt in the bounding boxes provides a more accurate classification of the kidney from other organs.

3.4   Proposed Architecture

Data augmentation is used to expand the dataset, various approaches are employed to increase the amount of data depending on the type of dataset. Data augmentation serves as a regularizer [20] during the training of machine learning models and aids in preventing overfitting. Data warping augmentations change existing images while retaining their label. This includes enhancements like random erasing, adversarial training, geometric and colour changes, and neural style transfer. Many geometric transformations exist, including noise injection, flip, crop, rotation, and translation. The label of the data is no longer preserved and requires post-transformation. Creating precise labels for every unsafe Data augmentation requires much processing time. There is no image processing function [18] that cannot result in a label-changing transformation along with augmentation. A non-label preserving transformation might make it easier for the model

Algorithm 1. Algorithm to find Augmented Pivot Point Rotation(APPR) within $[-15, 15]$ Degrees

---

1: **procedure** APPR($box[]$) **Input:Bounding box with four vertices as:** $(x_1, y_1), (x_2, y_2), (x_3, y_3), (x_4, y_4)$

2: $\theta \leftarrow$ random$[-15, 15]$

3: $rbox \leftarrow$ empty list   ▷ rbox is the new bounding box

4: $x_r \leftarrow \frac{x_1 + x_2 + x_3 + x_4}{4}$

5: $y_r \leftarrow \frac{y_1 + y_2 + y_3 + y_4}{4}$ ▷ x_r, y_r is the pivot point

6: **for each** (x, y) box vertices **do**

7:     $rotated_x \leftarrow (x - x_r) \cdot \cos((\theta)) - (y - y_r) \cdot \sin((\theta)) + x_r$

8:     $rotated_y \leftarrow (x - x_r) \cdot \sin((\theta)) + (y - y_r) \cdot \cos((\theta)) + y_r$

9:     $rbox$.append($(rotated_x, rotated_y)$)

10: **return** $rbox$ ▷ Returns New bounding box with rotation

---

Fig. 2. Sample augmented dataset of normal and kidney stone with bounding boxes.

to produce a response that is not confident about its prediction. To accomplish this, post-augmentation labels would need to be adjusted.

By directly applying the enhanced pivot point rotation to the bounding boxes rather than rotating the picture and then post-labeling to produce a reliable prediction, the proposed approach aims to overcome the post-augmentation of the labels. This is shown in Fig. 3, which presents the steps involved in generating the new dataset. The pivot point rotation is applied to the original dataset of 1799 images, and a new dataset is generated. Both the original and augmented datasets are combined to form a new dataset. The dataset is provided as input to the object detection algorithm for training.

Object detection algorithms provide an end-to-end localization of the objects in the image with the help of bounding boxes. More than one specific object can be detected using an object detection model. Deep learning architecture performs impressive results. The object detection task further localizes the kidney using a bounding box and related confidence score that expresses how confidently the object class-kidney stone or normal-is recognized within the bounding box.

R-CNN, Fast (R-CNN), Faster R-CNN, Region-based Fully Convolutional Network (R-FCN), single-shot detector (SSD), and You Only Live Once (YOLOv7) are some of the CNNs that have significantly raised the bar for performance on the field. Selecting an appropriate architecture depends on the size and complexity of the dataset and the resources available. In this contribution, YOLOv7 [17], SSD [14], and Faster RCNN [13] algorithms with the backbone as ResNet50, MobileNetV2, and YOLOv7 are selected as they achieved great

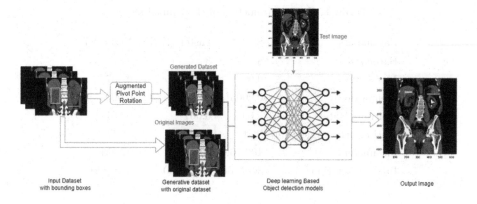

Fig. 3. Proposed Architecture to train Object detection algorithms.

success on large datasets, such as Pattern Analysis, Statistical Modelling, and Computational Learning Visual Object Classes (PASCAL VOC) [21], ImageNet [22], and Common Objects in Context (COCO) [23].

4   Experimental Setup

Various object detection techniques were used to validate the proposed pivot point rotation-based dataset. For experiments, we first evaluate how well YOLOv7, Faster RCNN with mobilenetv2, ResNet50 and ResNet101, and SSD300 locate the instances on original Coronal CT images. Using the augmented dataset, the above five models are retrained. Although the dataset is diverse, the same parameters are used to train the models. Pytorch is used to implement the experiments. The models are trained using an Intel® Xeon® Gold 6226R CPU running at 2.90GHz and an NVIDIA RTX A4000-GPU with 16GB of RAM. All five models are initialized using pre-trained parameters of the COCO dataset. The different hyperparameters used for training are provided in Table 1. The image size is adjusted according to the models used to train the dataset. The performance evaluation uses AP@0.5, AP@0.5:0.95, precision, and recall. These are explained in Sect. 5.1. The comparison of the object detection algorithm with respect to the original and generated dataset is presented in Sect. 5.

4.1   Evaluation Matrices

– **Intersection over Union (IoU)** The degree of overlapping between the instances ground truth (gt) and predicted instances (pd) is computed using Eq. 1

$$\text{IoU} = \frac{area(gt \cap pd)}{area(gt \cup pd)} \tag{1}$$

Table 1. Hyper parameters of the trained model

Parameters	SSD	Faster RCNN	YOLOV7
Batch size	8	8	8
Momentum	0.9	0.9	0.937
Weight decay	0.0005	0.0005	0.0005
Learning Rate	0.001	0.001	0.001
Optimization Algorithm	SGD	SGD	SGD
Parameters	103.76M	42M	37.2M
Image resolution	300*300	1333*800	320*320

True Positive (tp) is computed when IoU (gt,pd) is greater than the threshold, and False Positive (fp) is when IoU (gt,pd) is less than the threshold.

- **Precision and Recall**
Precision (P) is the ratio between samples correctly classifying those true samples as true and all samples the model properly identified as positive as in Eq. 2. Precision is high when ground truth samples are predicted accurately, and incorrect prediction of the other classes as true is low.

$$P = \frac{tp}{(tp + fp)} \tag{2}$$

Recall (R) is the ratio between the sample correctly classifying those ground truth samples as true and the total number of instances as in Eq. 3. The more positive samples that are classified, the larger the recall. Recall focuses on classifying the positive samples and ignores the negative samples.

$$R = \frac{tp}{(total instances)} \tag{3}$$

- **Mean Average Precision (mAP) @0.5** The average precision (AP) of each class is calculated using 11-point interpolation for all models. The mean Average Precision is calculated for each class, considering the IoU threshold value as 0.5. These AP values are averaged to find the mean Average Precision (mAP@0.5).

$$mAP@0.5 = \frac{1}{n} \sum_{r=1}^{n} AP_i, \tag{4}$$

- **Mean Average PrecisionmAP@0.5:0.95** The average of ten mAP scores was calculated with an IoU threshold of 0.5 to 0.95 with an increment of 0.05. The mAP score is the standard metric of COCO evaluation.

$$mAP@0.5:0.95 = \frac{1}{10} \sum_{r=1}^{10} mAP_i, \tag{5}$$

5   Experimental Results

The experiment presents the work to compare the five models trained on the original dataset as well as the performance of the same five models, trained on the proposed augmented dataset generated using the APPR algorithm. The results obtained by the ten models are categorized to address the trade-off regarding training and validation loss, comparing the Mean Average Precision (mAP@0.50) and mAP@0.5:0.95. The models perform for the IoU threshold@0.5 in terms of precision, and recall is also considered. The training and validation loss plots are obtained after training the models on the augmented dataset. The training and validation dataset ratio is 80:20, the same as provided in the publicly available dataset. Figure 4(a) shows that SSD300 generates over-fitting results on validating the new data for 100 epochs. Figure 4(b) and Figure 4(e) are of Faster-RCNN with ResNet50 and YOLOv7, produces good fitting for 50 epochs only. Faster-RCNN with Mobilenetv2 and ResNet101 in Figure 4(c) and (d) presents it is easier to predict the new data than the training dataset. The graphs contradict the results regarding evaluation parameters presented in Table 2.

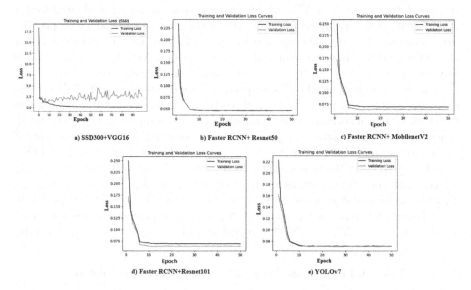

Fig. 4. Training and Validation loss plots of the five models trained on the augmented dataset.

Table 2. Mean Average Precision of five models on varied dataset

Object Detection Models	Backbone	Original Dataset		Augmented Dataset	
		mAP@0.5	mAP@.5:.95	mAP@0.5	mAP@.5:.95
SSD300	VGG16	0.965	0.602	**0.9866**	0.862
Faster-RCNN	Mobilenetv2	0.447	0.159	0.494	0.263
Faster-RCNN	ResNet50	0.977	**0.713**	0.980	0.893
Faster-RCNN	ResNet101	0.983	0.705	0.986	0.881
YOLOv7	–	**0.984**	0.706	0.984	**0.931**

Table 2 presents the mAP@0.5 and mAP@.5:0.95 results for the five object detection algorithms trained on the original dataset and augmented dataset. The results show that the Faster-RCNN with ResNet50 outperformed on the original dataset compared to Mobilenetv2 and ResNet101. Faster-RCNN also produces the best results when compared among the five models with mAP@0.5:0.95 score of 71.3%, whereas YOLOv7 performance is good for the threshold of 0.5.

After generating a new dataset by applying the APPR algorithm, YOLOv7 surpassed the result of mAP@0.5:0.95 with a spike of 22.5% and produced a magnificent result. Application of the APPR algorithm also produced a promising improvement with an average hike of 18.9% of all the five algorithms in terms of mAP@0.5:0.95, though a markable hike of 1% in mAP@0.5 results. SSD300 produces a better result of 98.66% when trained on the augmented dataset.

The precision and recall of the test dataset are computed for the IoU threshold value as 0.5. The precision is used to correctly classify the true samples as true rather than incorrectly classifying the negative samples as true. The recall concerns that every positive sample is correctly identified, but it is unconcerned if a negative sample is incorrectly labeled as positive. The performance of YOLOv7 is high in predicting the true samples more accurately than the negative sample as true with the original dataset. The precision value of the original dataset of YOLOv7 of kidney stones and normal instances is 98.7% and 96.4% respectively as in Table 3, whereas for the augmented dataset the precision score is reduced for the IoU threshold@0.5. SSD300 model identifies the true positive and false

Table 3. Precision and Recall of five models on Original dataset

Object Detection Models	Precision		Recall	
	Normal	Kidney-Stone	Normal	Kidney-Stone
SSD300 + VGG16	0.94	0.916	0.99	0.979
Faster-RCNN + MoblilenetV2	–	0.5869	–	0.9973
Faster-RCNN+ResNet50	0.9367	0.9470	0.9876	0.99
Faster-RCNN+ ResNet101	0.9610	0.9467	**0.9867**	**0.9920**
YOLOv7	**0.987**	**0.964**	0.981	0.979

negative samples correctly from the augmented dataset for an IoU threshold@0.5 as 98.4% and 99.7% for normal and kidney stones respectively as in Table 4. The recall of the Faster RCNN on both the original and augmented dataset is good, the true kidney stone and normal instances are correctly classified, but even some of the negative sample is also classified as true.

Table 4. Precision and Recall of five models on augmented dataset

Object Detection Models	Precision		Recall	
	Normal	Kidney-Stone	Normal	Kidney-Stone
SSD300 + VGG16	**0.9848**	**0.9818**	0.9848	0.9970
Faster-RCNN + MoblilenetV2	0.8681	0.9640	0.750	1.0
Faster-RCNN+ResNet50	0.9611	0.9746	0.9757	1.0
Faster-RCNN+ ResNet101	0.9477	0.9763	**0.9909**	**1.0**
YOLOv7	0.952	0.946	0.993	0.988

6   Conclusion and Future Scope

A new pivot point rotation-based augmentation technique has been proposed to enhance the performance of deep learning models for kidney stone detection. In this regards YOLOv7, SSD300, and Faster RCNN with the backbone models are trained with the original and augmented datasets. An average increase of 18.9% of mAP@0.5:0.95 is achieved by the use of an augmented dataset. We conclude that the proposed algorithm with pivot point rotation, enhances the performance of the models. The results of the work justify, YOLOV7 proves appreciating results in terms of mAP@0.5:0.95 with 93.1% when trained on the generated dataset, and the model training also results in a good fit. Faster-RCNN with ResNet50 performs skilfully at IoU threshold@0.5, confirmed by the results of mAP@0.5 as 0.980. SSD300 also produces promising results regarding the IoU threshold@0.5, but the graph presents that SSD300 convinces overfitting results. The need for a lightweight, accurate, and appropriate model with less time complexity is still a challenge in the medical field. The class imbalance problem must be addressed, as the original dataset had more normal than kidney stone instances. The contribution assists various researchers in evaluating multiple models and applying the appropriate model according to their requirements.

References

1. Renard-Penna, R., Martin, A., Conort, P., Mozer, P., Grenier, P.: Kidney stones and imaging: what can your radiologist do for you? World J. Urol. **33**, 193–202 (2015)
2. Patro, K.K., et al.: Application of kronecker convolutions in deep learning technique for automated detection of kidney stones with coronal CT images. Inf. Sci. **640**, 119005 (2023)
3. Ebrahimi, S., Mariano, V.Y.: Image quality improvement in kidney stone detection on computed tomography images. J. Image Graph. **3**, 40–46 (2015)
4. Kaur, J., Singh, W.: Tools, techniques, datasets and application areas for object detection in an image: a review. Multimedia Tools Appl. **81**(27), 38297–38351 (2022)
5. Garcea, F., Serra, A., Lamberti, F., Morra, L.: Data augmentation for medical imaging: a systematic literature review. Comput. Biol. Med. **152**, 106391 (2022)
6. Yildirim, K., Bozdag, P.G., Talo, M., Yildirim, O., Karabatak, M., Acharya, U.R.: Deep learning model for automated kidney stone detection using coronal CT images. Comput. Biol. Med. **135**, 104569 (2021)
7. Baygin, M., Yaman, O., Barua, P.D., Dogan, S., Tuncer, T., Acharya, U.R.: Exemplar Darknet19 feature generation technique for automated kidney stone detection with coronal CT images. Artif. Intell. Med. **127**, 102274 (2022)
8. Längkvist, M., Jendeberg, J., Thunberg, P., Loutfi, A., Lidén, M.: Computer aided detection of ureteral stones in thin slice computed tomography volumes using convolutional neural networks. Comput. Biol. Med. **97**, 153–160 (2018)
9. Liu, J., Wang, S., Turkbey, E.B., Linguraru, M.G., Yao, J., Summers, R.M.: Computer-aided detection of renal calculi from noncontrast CT images using TV-flow and MSER features. Med. Phys. **42**, 144–153 (2015)
10. Elton, D.C., Turkbey, E.B., Pickhardt, P.J., Summers, R.M.: A deep learning system for automated kidney stone detection and volumetric segmentation on non-contrast CT scans. Med. Phys. **49**, 2545–2554 (2022)
11. Kaviani, P., et al.: Performance of threshold-based stone segmentation and radiomics for determining the composition of kidney stones from single-energy CT. Jpn. J. Radiol. **41**(2), 194–200 (2023)
12. Li, D., et al.: Deep segmentation networks for segmenting kidneys and detecting kidney stones in unenhanced abdominal CT images. Diagnostics **12**(8), 1788 (2022)
13. Wang, C.Y., Bochkovskiy, A., Liao, H.Y.M.: Yolov7: trainable bag-of-freebies sets new state-of-the-art for real-time object detectors. arXiv preprint, arXiv:2207.02696 (2022)
14. Liu, W., et al.: SSD: single shot MultiBox detector. In: Leibe, B., Matas, J., Sebe, N., Welling, M. (eds.) ECCV 2016. LNCS, vol. 9905, pp. 21–37. Springer, Cham (2016). https://doi.org/10.1007/978-3-319-46448-0_2
15. Girshick, R., Donahue, J., Darrell, T., Malik, J.: Rich feature hierarchies for accurate object detection and semantic segmentation. In: Proceedings of the IEEE Conference on Computer Vision and Pattern Recognition, pp. 580–587 (2014)
16. Girshick, R.: Fast R-CNN. In: Proceedings of the IEEE International Conference on Computer Vision, pp. 1440–1448 (2015)
17. Ren, S., He, K., Girshick, R., Sun, J.: Faster R-CNN: towards real-time object detection with region proposal networks. In: Advances in Neural Information Processing Systems, vol. 28 (2015)

18. Shorten, C., Khoshgoftaar, T.M.: A survey on image data augmentation for deep learning. J. Big Data **6**(1), 1–48 (2019)
19. Goceri, E.: Medical image data augmentation: techniques, comparisons and interpretations. Artif. Intell. Rev. **56**, 1–45 (2023)
20. Golan, I., El-Yaniv, R.: Deep anomaly detection using geometric transformations. In: Advances in Neural Information Processing Systems, vol. 31 (2018)
21. Bird Boat Bottle Bus and Person Potted. PASCAL VOC-07
22. Deng, J., Dong, W., Socher, R., Li, L.J., Li, K., Fei-Fei, L.: Imagenet: a large-scale hierarchical image database. In: 2009 IEEE Conference on Computer Vision and Pattern Recognition, pp. 248–255. IEEE (2009)
23. Lin, T.-Y., et al.: Microsoft COCO: common objects in context. In: Fleet, D., Pajdla, T., Schiele, B., Tuytelaars, T. (eds.) ECCV 2014. LNCS, vol. 8693, pp. 740–755. Springer, Cham (2014). https://doi.org/10.1007/978-3-319-10602-1_48

MotionFormer: An Improved Transformer-Based Architecture for Multi-object Tracking

Harshit Agrawal, Agrya Halder, and Pratik Chattopadhyay[✉][iD]

Indian Institute of Technology (BHU), Varanasi, Varanasi, India
{harshitagrawal.cse18,agryahalder.rs.cse21,pratik.cse}@iitbhu.ac.in

Abstract. Multi-object tracking (MOT) is a crucial task in Computer Vision with numerous real-world applications. In recent years, Transformer-based models have shown promising results in MOT. However, existing methods still face challenges in scenarios involving short-term object occlusion, camera motion, and ambiguous detection especially in low frame-rate videos. In this work, we propose a novel variant of the TrackFormer model that addresses these limitations by integrating an online motion prediction module based on the Kalman Filter that incorporates the important temporal information present in the videos. The addition of the Kalman Filter helps the model study the tracked pedestrians' motion patterns and leverage them for effective association among targets across the video frames even in the case of short-term occlusions without adding much to the computational complexity of the overall framework. The proposed model is termed MotionFormer due to its inherent ability to utilize long-term motion information. Through extensive evaluations using popular tracking datasets, namely MOT-17 and MOT-20, we demonstrate the effectiveness of our approach over existing approaches. Results show that the MotionFormer provides reasonably good tracking accuracy with a much lesser identity switching rate as compared to the other models. Further, it significantly outperforms the base TrackFormer model in terms of tracking accuracy, F1-score, as well as identity switching rate for MOT-17 private and public and MOT-20 private data.

Keywords: Multi Object Tracking · Computer Vision · Motion Prediction · MotionFormer · Kalman Filter

1 Introduction

Multi-Object Tracking (MOT) involves following the trajectories of the various objects present in a video. These objects can be pedestrians, vehicles, animals, or birds. In this study, we focus on automated pedestrian tracking using Computer Vision algorithms. The problem is of immense significance, particularly in surveillance sites, for identification of suspicious activities, behavioral anomaly

H. Kaur et al. (Eds.): CVIP 2023, CCIS 2011, pp. 212–224, 2024.
https://doi.org/10.1007/978-3-031-58535-7_18

detection, etc., to provide improved public safety. Recently, there have been quite a few attempts to apply Transformers for Multi-Object Tracking, and practical models such as TrackFormer [10], TransTrack [18], etc., were developed. In this work, we improve the existing TrackFormer model [10] by including a motion prediction component in the form of a Kalman Filter for incorporating additional temporal information in addition to spatial information. This component is placed before the Trackformer decoder in the architecture for processing the bounding boxes and tracking queries propagating along the video. Further, an AutoEncoder-based decoder is leveraged for mapping the bounding boxes to track queries. It helps the model to study and learn the motion pattern of the pedestrians in the video which can then be used for effective data association from one frame to another by providing better clues to the Transformer decoder. Secondly, in case of short-term occlusion or poor illumination in a few frames, predicted bounding boxes contain enough information to form continuous trajectories and avoid fragmentation. Finally, the inclusion of a motion model can also aid in offsetting global camera motion which can potentially improve performance in videos recorded with a non-stationary camera. We term this improved TrackFormer model as MotionFormer.

In this paper, we present the architecture of our proposed MotionFormer model and compare its performance with that of TrackFormer using popular benchmark datasets. Results demonstrate that our model outperforms the Track-Former model in terms of standard MOT metrics. Further, we show that the real power of the motion model is leveraged if the videos are recorded at a low frame rate or in the presence of occlusion. The main contributions of our work are:

1. We improve the TrackFormer architecture for MOT through a joint tracking and detection model that incorporates spatial as well as temporal information by integrating a Kalman Filter-based motion model with TrackFormer.
2. We qualitatively show that our proposed model tracks better than Track-Former for partial and complete short-term occlusions in the video.
3. We achieve marginally better performance metrics on MOT-17 and MOT-20 public and private datasets than TrackFormer. Further, we show that on the low frame rate version of these datasets, there is a significant performance gain with our model due to the use of temporal information. We also make a comparative study with other existing Transformer-based models and the results demonstrate the superiority of our approach.

2   Related Work

Multi-Object Tracking, in essence, consists of two indispensable objectives: detecting objects in the video frames and associating the detections across the frames. Tracking by Detection (TBD) involves first detecting the objects and then establishing associations between these objects in different frames and forming continuous trajectories. Many MOT frameworks based on the TBD framework use pre-trained off-the-shelf object detectors to focus specifically on improving the tracking part [11,14,16,24]. Although TBD simplifies the MOT problem, it leads to dependence of the tracking process on the object detector used. To overcome this, models capable of detecting and tracking objects simultaneously have been proposed [13,19,22,23].

Transformers presented in [21] were originally proposed for Natural Language Processing tasks. Of late, these have been applied to various Computer Vision tasks as well owing to their performance and efficiency [7]. [17] formulates a Detection Transformer (DETR) for object detection as a prediction problem in which the model takes as input the image and outputs the location of targets. The approach in [33] proposed Deformable-DETR which uses deformable attention for faster convergence. In [2], Chu et al. introduce an end-to-end model termed TransMOT which employs a set of graph transformers to effectively model the spatio-temporal interactions among the objects.

TrackFormer [10] attempts to apply Transformers to the Multi-Object Tracking task by performing data association through learned queries in Deformable DETR. The encoder network converts each frame into queries which are carried over in different video frames preserving information about the target. The model computes attention between frames, trajectory, and target information, and the queries are converted into bounding boxes of objects using the decoder network of the Transformer. TransTrack [18] also extends the Deformable DETR by appending two decoder networks and utilizing the query-key methodology. It uses an attention module and works with two sets of queries: object query and track query. These are fed into the network to output two sets of bounding boxes after which Intersection over Union (IoU) is applied. This helps in learning from already detected objects in previous frames as well as detecting the new objects in the current frame simultaneously. TransCenter [27] introduces Query Learning Network (QLN) to take into account the positional correlation. Further, it explores different architectures of QLN which can lead to optimal performance with respect to efficiency and accuracy. TransMOT [2] merges graphs with Transformers resulting in a graph Transformer consisting of three parts: two encoders and a decoder for capturing both temporal and spatial information. MOTR [29] introduces Tracklet Aware Label Assignment and Temporal Aggregation Network which enables it to associate each query to a track and effectively model temporal relationship without any other post-processing. The resulting model is trainable in an end-to-end manner but is different from TransTrack [18] in the sense that it does not need any IoU loss. An improved version of MOTR, namely MOTRv2, has been proposed in [30] through bootstrapping an end-to-end multi-object tracking model with a pre-trained object detector.

Global Tracking Transformer (GTRT) [31] directly predicts object trajectories using queries from a short video sequence. Using cross-attention between track queries and targets, it performs global association in only one pass. Multi-Object Tracking With Memory (MeMOT) [1] tries to improve the long-range spatiotemporal association in [2,10,18,27,29] with memory encoding and decoding units built with attention and transformer modules respectively. The memory stores information about all the past detections and is updated by encoding information about the detections in the current frame. The decoding module is used to form associations among the detected objects and generate output trajectories. Other related work using Transformers for Multi-Object Tracking include [8,9,25,26,28], most of which do not give enough attention to the temporal information present in the videos. As a result, their tracking effectiveness degrades especially in case of object occlusion. We, therefore, propose a joint tracking and detection model that consists of a motion prediction component in addition to transformers for properly leveraging both spatial and temporal information. The model prediction component incorporated is lightweight and there is no noticeable increment to the computational complexity of the overall framework. At the same time, it boosts the tracking accuracy of the model, by learning critical motion cues which are especially helpful for tackling short-term occlusion and offsetting camera motion.

3   Proposed Model

Let us consider a video consisting of t frames I_1, I_2, ... I_t with M objects. The Multi-Object Tracking problem is formulated as a set prediction problem in which we have to determine the track T_i for each object $i \in 0, 1, 2, ..., M$. Each T_i is given as a sequence of bounding box coordinates $(bb^i_{x_1}, bb^i_{x_2}, bb^i_{x_3}...)$ where each of $x_1, x_2, ...$ belongs to 0 to t.

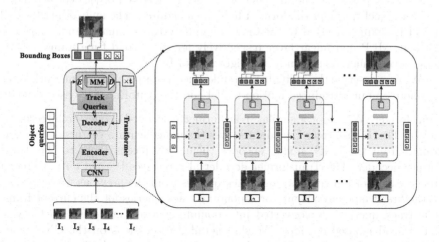

Fig. 1. Model architecture of MotionFormer

As shown in Fig. 1 (left part) our model consists of three main components:

- A CNN model followed by Transformer Encoder-Decoder adapted from [10],
- A Motion model (denoted by MM) to predict future bounding boxes.
- An AutoEncoder (with encoder denoted by E and decoder denoted by D) for mapping track queries to bounding boxes and class labels and vice-versa.

In the right part of Fig. 1, the process of tracking with MotionFormer is shown. The process begins with the very first video frame (I_1) being input into a CNN model to calculate its image features. This image feature vector is then fed into the Transformer encoder and the encoding is next passed on to the Transformer decoder. The decoder additionally receives object queries, i.e., a set of learned queries carrying information about the locations and appearances of objects and outputs a set of hidden embeddings called track queries through computation of the self-attention and cross-attention between encodings and object queries. These track queries are passed through an AutoEncoder-based encoder E consisting of two branches: one with an MLP and the other with a linear layer to get final bounding boxes and class logits of corresponding objects in the current frame.

Now, the bounding boxes are passed into a motion model, shown in Fig. 1 as *MM*, to predict the location of the corresponding objects in the next (i.e., second) time frame. The predicted bounding boxes are then converted back into the corresponding track queries lying in hidden embedding space using a decoder D. These predicted track queries along with the object queries are input to the Transformer decoder in the next (i.e., second) time frame. The decoder also receives the encodings corresponding to the second video frame I_2, and using these, the Transformer decoder computes self and cross-attentions. It then predicts the new location of the already detected object corresponding to each track query as well as the location of the newly detected object corresponding to each object query in the form of hidden embedding. The embedding for each object is again converted to the final bounding box coordinates and class logits with the MLP and linear layer respectively for the second time frame and the process continues, as shown in the right side of Fig. 1.

We now describe the individual modules incorporated in the framework focusing more on our introduced motion model and the AutoEncoder-based decoder.

Transformer: We adopt a similar Transformer Encoder-Decoder architecture as in [10]. The Transformer Encoder receives the image feature vectors of the video frames from the CNN model, encodes them, and passes them to the Transformer decoder. The Transformer decoder also receives learned output embeddings (called object queries) and track queries from the previous frame (except in the first frame) to output corresponding track queries for the current frame. The track queries are converted into bounding boxes and class labels by an AutoEncoder-based encoder. We skip detailed discussions on the CNN model and the Transformer architecture here since these are already discussed in [10].

Motion Model: The bounding boxes output by the above AutoEncoder-based encoder are passed to a motion model which maintains an independent state for each object detected up to the current frame. Based on its current location and already present state, the motion model gives an approximate prediction about the location of the object in the next frame. The Transformer decoder then refines the bounding box location by computing the encoder-decoder cross-attention with the next frame features and outputs the bounding box coordinates.

Specifically, in the first frame we feed in K object queries into the Transformer decoder and get L bounding box outputs with non-null classes called track queries. Each track query represents a unique object and carries relevant information about the location and appearance of the object along the temporal dimension in the video. These L track queries along with the K object queries are then fed in the next frame. The decoder now outputs $K+L$ bounding boxes and corresponding class information. For each object present in the previous frame, the corresponding track query from the L track queries is decoded. If a new object is detected in the current frame, then an object query from one of the K object queries is decoded. If an object detected in the previous frame disappears from the scene, the corresponding track query from K queries is decoded with a null value in class information to indicate this. This process is repeated with bounding boxes having non-null class information forming track queries again for the next frame as shown in Fig. 1.

The choice of motion model is critical in ensuring a fine balance between the accuracy and the efficiency of the model. Here, we choose Kalman Filter [6] as the motion model to predict the next bounding boxes, due to its inherent ability to estimate the state of a system accurately even in the presence of significant noise. Also, due to its recursive nature, Kalman Filter can update its bounding box estimate in real time. This makes it highly effective and well-suited for online applications. The use of the Kalman Filter as the motion model ensures that the predictions fed into the Transformer decoder are more reliable than those of the Trackformer [10]. Further, it is computationally quite efficient and does not increase the response time of the overall tracking framework substantially.

Mapping Track Queries to Bounding Boxes, Labels, and Vice-Versa: Track queries represented as plain bounding boxes cannot preserve the appearance information of the object which can bottleneck a model's performance. Thus, we use a d-dimensional hidden state embedding from the Transformer decoder as the track query for the next step. A three-layered Multi-Layer Perceptron Network (MLP) is used to obtain the desired bounding boxes with normalized center coordinates, height, and width of the box relative to the input image from the hidden embeddings. Another linear layer followed by softmax is used to predict the class label with a special value to indicate null class (i.e., background class) implying no object is detected corresponding to that object query. This MLP and the linear layer form the Encoder part of the AutoEncoder module.

Next, the motion model is used to convert the bounding boxes back to the hidden state embeddings which can be directly fed to the Transformer decoder in the next frame. The process is equivalent to learning an inverse operation of the MLP to convert the hidden state into the bounding boxes. Let z_t be the hidden state embeddings obtained from the Transformer decoder at time t. Further, let g be the function learned by the MLP that converts the hidden state embeddings into bounding boxes bb_t and h be the function transforming it into class logits c_t. So, we have $z_t \in \mathbb{R}^d$, $c_t \in \mathbb{R}^{CL}$ and $bb_t \in \mathbb{R}^4$. Typically, we have $d = 288$ and $CL = 21$ (20 classes and one null class). Also, let bb'_t be the bounding boxes predicted by the motion model. Then,

$$bb_t = g(z_t), \; c_t = h(z_t), \; \text{and} \; bb'_t = M(bb_t, bb_{t-1}, bb_{t-2}, \ldots). \tag{1}$$

Now, we need to learn a function to convert bb'_t to hidden embedding $z'_t \in \mathbb{R}$. For this, we additionally utilize the information in class logits c_t and z_t. This function is learned using an AutoEncoder (shown in Fig. 2) having the same MLP and linear layer used above as its encoder, and this is trained separately. The AutoEncoder's decoder then learns to convert the encodings (i.e., bounding boxes concatenated with class logits) back to the hidden state and weighted addition is done with z_t to get the hidden state embedding corresponding to the predicted bounding boxes, i.e., z'_t.

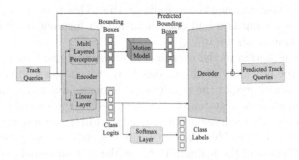

Fig. 2. AutoEncoder to convert bounding boxes to corresponding track queries

4   Implementation Details

For training and evaluation purposes, we have used the MOT-17 [12] and MOT-20 [3] datasets. Each of these datasets specifies a training and a test set for evaluation purposes, which we have also considered in this work to carry out all our experiments. MOT-17 provides 7 training and 7 test sequences whereas MOT-20 has 4 training and 4 test sequences captured in crowded scenarios. For MOT-17 public detections, we adopt the training methodology suggested in [10]. We train the model for 50 epochs with a learning rate 2×10^4 for the encoder network and 2×10^5 for the decoder network. The ResNet-50 [5] pre-trained on ImageNet data has been used as the backbone network for image feature extraction which is further fine-tuned using the training set of the MOT datasets for our experiments. Once trained, this network converts a $H \times W \times 3$ dimensional image into a lower dimensional feature tensor of size $\frac{H}{p} \times \frac{W}{q} \times r$, where H and W respectively denote the height and width of the image. For ResNet-50 architecture we have $p = 32$, $q = 32$, and $r = 2048$. This feature tensor represents the extracted image-level information from the video frame. A 1×1 convolution layer is further applied to lower the channel size to C ($C < 2048$). This feature tensor of size $H' \times W' \times C$ is then flattened along the first two dimensions to get a sequence of channels $H'W' \times C$, which is next input to the Transformer encoder.

Due to the prohibitively expensive computational cost and resource require-ment of training the model on the CrowdHuman dataset for private detections as suggested in [10], we do not train the model for private detections from scratch. Instead, we fine-tune the baseline model for MOT-17 and MOT-20 private detec-tions. We have done training on a single 24GB NVIDIA GeForce RTX 3090 GPU. Though we mainly focus on optimizing the Multi-Object Tracking Accuracy ($MOTA$), Identity F1 Scores ($IDF1$), and Identification Switches (IDs) which are widely regarded as three key metrics for measuring the object tracking cov-erage and identity preservation of any MOT system, we also report MT (Mostly Tracked), ML (Mostly Lost), FP (False Positives), and FN (False Negatives).

5   Experiments and Analysis

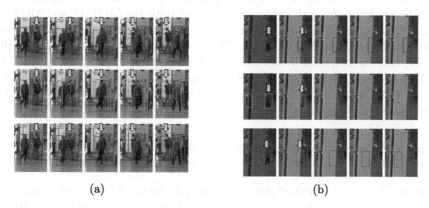

(a)   (b)

Fig. 3. Comparative tracking by TrackFormer and MotionFormer for (a) partial occlu-sion, (b) complete occlusion

We rigorously evaluate our model using the MOT-17 private and public datasets as well as the MOT-20 private dataset and compare its performance with that of TrackFormer [10]. First, we compare the quality of tracking by our MotionFormer and TrackFormer in the presence of occlusion. We have shown a few frames from MOT-20 data comparing the tracking performance of TrackFormer [10] and the proposed model MotionFormer against the ground truth for partial and complete occlusion in Figs. 3(a) and (b), respectively. We have manually identified the cases of partial and complete occlusion of the person pointed to by the yellow arrow in both figures for qualitative analysis. As the MOT videos are quite crowded containing dozens of people in a frame, the images have been cropped out to focus on the specific person under consideration for visualization purposes. Further to show meaningful displacement of persons in high frame rate MOT videos, every frame shown is 5 and 7 timestamps after the previous frame in Figs. 3(a) and (b), respectively. The person under consideration is moving toward the right in Fig. 3(a) and left in Fig. 3(b). In each comparison, the top row shows tracking by baseline TrackFormer model in blue bounding boxes, the middle row shows tracking by the proposed MotionFormer in green boxes, and the bottom row shows the ground truth in red boxes. In both cases, we can see that the TrackFormer either deviates or completely stops tracking the person in case of short-term occlusions, i.e., when the person is occluded by some other object or person in the scene. However, MotionFormer continues to track the person correctly for a few frames until the person becomes visible again or until the predictions of the motion model start becoming unreliable due to a lack of detections from the image (decided by inactive patience threshold).

We hypothesize that due to the high frame rate of MOT videos, the displacement of a person in any two successive frames is insignificant. The real benefit of integrating the motion model (MM) can be observed if the target video is captured at a low frame rate, or if the objects in the scene move very fast. To test this hypothesis, we design a low frame rate dataset by sampling every fifth image frame from the video sequences of both the MOT-17 and MOT-20 datasets. The resulting video sequence has a five times lesser frame rate as compared to the original MOT dataset. We report $MOTA$, $IDF1$, and IDs results of [10] and our proposed model using low frame rate MOT-17 private, MOT-17 public, and MOT-20 private datasets in Table 1. As observed, the improvement in the performance of the proposed model is significantly higher than [10] for low frame-rate datasets.

Table 1. Comparing TrackFormer with the proposed model on low frame rate MOT-17 private, MOT-17 public validation, and MOT-20 private test datasets

Model	MOT-17 Private			MOT-17 Public			MOT-20 Private		
	MOTA	IDF1	IDs	MOTA	IDF1	IDs	MOTA	IDF1	IDs
TrackFormer [10]	61.9	62.2	2799	51.2	55.1	3840	71.4	67.1	5848
MotionFormer (Ours)	**67.4**	**69.5**	**1488**	**54.9**	**57.8**	**2904**	**71.8**	**71.6**	**1951**

We next compare the performance of the proposed model with several recent Transformer-based models, namely [4,10,15,18,20,27,29,32], using the MOT-17 private, MOT-17 public, and MOT-20 private datasets and present the results in Table 2. The results of the compared approaches have been directly taken from the respective cited works. From Table 2, we can see that the proposed model performs incrementally better than the baseline TrackFormer model for almost all the evaluation metrics considered except the number of False Positives (FPs). We hypothesize that this slightly higher number of False Positives may be attributed to the setting of the hyper-parameters which controls the number of frames for which the model continues to track even when the object is not present in the video sequence. Since the Kalman Filter used here as the motion model works by assuming linear motion of the tracked object, the predicted position of the object begins to differ from its correct position for medium to

Table 2. Comparison of some recent Transformer-based MOT models with the proposed model using MOT-17 private dataset, MOT-17 public dataset, and MOT-20 private dataset. The best result in each column is shown in bold.

Dataset	Model	MOTA	IDF1	MT	ML	IDs	FP(10^4)	FN(10^4)
MOT-17 private	TrackFormer [10]	71.8	**74.1**	51.6	10.8	1446	**0.75**	7.79
	TransCenter [27]	73.2	62.2	40.8	18.5	4614	2.31	12.40
	TransTrack [18]	75.2	63.5	55.3	10.2	3603	5.02	8.64
	MOTR [29]	71.9	68.4	–	–	2115	2.11	13.60
	MO3TR_Plus [32]	**78.6**	72.4	47.9	16.9	2808	2.49	9.32
	STC_Tracker [4]	75.8	70.9	**53.6**	**7.6**	4533	4.50	8.70
	Swin_JDE [20]	72.3	70.7	37.7	22.8	2679	2.03	13.34
	MotionFormer (Ours)	71.9	**74.1**	53.6	9.8	**1386**	1.28	**7.31**
MOT-17 public	TrackFormer [10]	63.9	64.5	37.9	21.1	2553	**0.49**	11.20
	MOTR [29]	34.4	51.7	26.0	33.7	2824	17.26	19.45
	STC_Tracker [4]	**75.8**	**70.8**	**49.7**	**11.7**	3784	3.38	**9.90**
	TADN [15]	54.6	49.0	22.4	30.2	4869	3.63	21.49
	MotionFormer (Ours)	64.1	64.6	39.6	19.6	**2550**	0.82	10.87
MOT-20 private	TrackFormer [10]	68.6	65.7	14.9	4.0	1532	**2.03**	14.04
	TransCenter [27]	58.5	49.6	48.6	14.9	4695	6.42	14.60
	TransTrack [18]	65.0	59.4	50.1	13.4	3608	2.72	15.00
	STC_Tracker [4]	**73.0**	67.5	67.0	11.8	2011	3.02	**10.77**
	Swin_JDE [20]	70.4	**69.5**	58.8	13.4	2026	2.64	12.48
	MotionFormer (Ours)	65.8	67.8	**15.5**	**3.9**	**1515**	3.17	13.33

high occlusion, i.e., when the object remains occluded for several frames, and this problem becomes more apparent if the object motion is erratic. Still, our proposed MotionFormer has a reasonably low *FP* value for all three datasets. Further, in general, our MotionFormer has shown consistently better results than each of the other compared approaches for the different performance metrics used in the comparative study. It can be seen that MO3TR_Plus [32] performs better than each of the other techniques in terms of *MOTA* for the MOT-17 private dataset, whereas STC_Tracker [4] performs the best in terms of *MT* and *ML* for MOT-17 private dataset, in terms of *MOTA*, *IDF1*, *MT*, *ML* for MOT-17 public dataset, and in terms of *IDF1* and *FN* for MOT-20 private dataset. Despite the good performance of [4] in most of the metrics, its identity switching rate (*IDs*) is quite high. Moreover, the use of dense queries instead of sparse queries in [4] increases its computational complexity. Considering the above, our MotionFormer is indeed an effective MOT model which is robust against varying frame rates, occlusion, and walking speed and it provides reasonably good performance for the different performance metrics used in the study.

6   Conclusions and Future Work

In this work, we propose an improved MOT architecture termed MotionFormer that integrates a Kalman Filter-based motion model with TrackFormer. Our proposed model is more effective in handling short-term occlusions or low frame rate videos than the TrackFormer model and it has been seen to outperform TrackFormer in almost all the evaluation metrics considered for MOT-17 and MOT-20 datasets. This is because the introduction of the motion model helps MotionFormer in making more reliable bounding box predictions in the presence of challenges such as occlusion, fast-moving objects in the scene, or low frame rate videos. The main novelty of the work is utilizing a lightweight motion model to improve the performance of TrackFormer by a reasonable amount without increasing the computational overhead much. Our proposed model is quite simple and also performs better than several other Transformer-based tracking models in terms of most of the metrics used in the study. In the future, focus can be given to handling long-term occlusions, or situations in which objects re-enter a scene after several frames. Experimenting with non-linear motion models to handle erratic motions is also another promising future direction of work.

Acknowledgments. The authors acknowledge SERB-DST, Government of India for supporting their work with a project grant (ref. no. CRG/2020/005465).

References

1. Cai, J., et al.: MeMOT: multi-object tracking with memory. In: Proceedings of the IEEE/CVF Conference on Computer Vision and Pattern Recognition, pp. 8090–8100 (2022)
2. Chu, P., Wang, J., You, Q., Ling, H., Liu, Z.: TransMOT: spatial-temporal graph transformer for multiple object tracking. In: Proceedings of the IEEE/CVF Winter Conference on Applications of Computer Vision, pp. 4870–4880 (2023)
3. Dendorfer, P., et al.: MOT20: a benchmark for multi object tracking in crowded scenes. arXiv preprint arXiv:2003.09003 (2020)
4. Galor, A., Orfaig, R., Bobrovsky, B.Z.: Strong-transcenter: improved multi-object tracking based on transformers with dense representations. arXiv preprint arXiv:2210.13570 (2022)
5. He, K., Zhang, X., Ren, S., Sun, J.: Deep residual learning for image recognition. In: Proceedings of the IEEE Conference on Computer Vision and Pattern Recognition, pp. 770–778 (2016)
6. Kalman, R.: A new approach to liner filtering and prediction problems, transaction of ASME. J. Basic Eng. **83**(1), 95–108 (1961)
7. Khan, S., Naseer, M., Hayat, M., Zamir, S.W., Khan, F.S., Shah, M.: Transformers in vision: a survey. ACM Comput. Surv. (CSUR) **54**(10s), 1–41 (2022)
8. Li, Y., Lu, C.: Modeling human memory in multi-object tracking with transformers. In: Proceedings of the IEEE International Conference on Acoustics, Speech and Signal Processing, pp. 2849–2853 (2022)
9. Liu, Y., et al.: SegDQ: segmentation assisted multi-object tracking with dynamic query-based transformers. Neurocomputing **481**, 91–101 (2022)

10. Meinhardt, T., Kirillov, A., Leal-Taixe, L., Feichtenhofer, C.: TrackFormer: multi-object tracking with transformers. In: Proceedings of the IEEE/CVF Conference on Computer Vision and Pattern Recognition, pp. 8844–8854 (2022)
11. Miah, M., Bilodeau, G.A., Saunier, N.: Multi-object tracking and segmentation with a space-time memory network. In: Proceedings of the 20th Conference on Robots and Vision, pp. 184–193 (2023)
12. Milan, A., Leal-Taixé, L., Reid, I., Roth, S., Schindler, K.: MOT16: a benchmark for multi-object tracking. arXiv preprint arXiv:1603.00831 (2016)
13. Pang, B., Li, Y., Zhang, Y., Li, M., Lu, C.: TubeTK: adopting tubes to track multi-object in a one-step training model. In: Proceedings of the IEEE/CVF Conference on Computer Vision and Pattern Recognition, pp. 6308–6318 (2020)
14. Peri, N., et al.: Towards real-time systems for vehicle re-identification, multi-camera tracking, and anomaly detection. In: Proceedings of the IEEE/CVF Conference on Computer Vision and Pattern Recognition Workshops, pp. 622–623 (2020)
15. Psalta, A., Tsironis, V., Karantzalos, K.: Transformer-based assignment decision network for multiple object tracking. arXiv preprint arXiv:2208.03571 (2022)
16. Ristani, E., Tomasi, C.: Features for multi-target multi-camera tracking and re-identification. In: Proceedings of the IEEE Conference on Computer Vision and Pattern Recognition, pp. 6036–6046 (2018)
17. Rubin, J., Erkamp, R., Naidu, R.S., Thodiyil, A.O., Chen, A.: Attention distillation for detection transformers: application to real-time video object detection in ultrasound. In: Proceedings of the Machine Learning for Health, pp. 26–37 (2021)
18. Sun, P., et al.: TransTrack: multiple-object tracking with transformer. ArXiv abs/2012.15460 (2020)
19. Sun, S., Akhtar, N., Song, X., Song, H., Mian, A., Shah, M.: Simultaneous detection and tracking with motion modelling for multiple object tracking. In: Vedaldi, A., Bischof, H., Brox, T., Frahm, J.-M. (eds.) ECCV 2020. LNCS, vol. 12369, pp. 626–643. Springer, Cham (2020). https://doi.org/10.1007/978-3-030-58586-0_37
20. Tsai, C.Y., Shen, G.Y., Nisar, H.: Swin-JDE: joint detection and embedding multi-object tracking in crowded scenes based on swin-transformer. Eng. Appl. Artif. Intell. **119**, 105770 (2023)
21. Vaswani, A., et al.: Attention is all you need. In: Advances in Neural Information Processing Systems, vol. 30 (2017)
22. Voigtlaender, P., et al.: MOTS: multi-object tracking and segmentation. In: Proceedings of the IEEE/CVF Conference on Computer Vision and Pattern Recognition, pp. 7942–7951 (2019)
23. Wang, G., Wang, Y., Zhang, H., Gu, R., Hwang, J.N.: Exploit the connectivity: multi-object tracking with TrackletNet. In: Proceedings of the 27th ACM International Conference on Multimedia, pp. 482–490 (2019)
24. Weng, X., Wang, J., Held, D., Kitani, K.: 3D multi-object tracking: a baseline and new evaluation metrics. In: Proceedings of the IEEE/RSJ International Conference on Intelligent Robots and Systems (IROS), pp. 10359–10366 (2020)
25. Willes, J., Reading, C., Waslander, S.L.: InterTrack: interaction transformer for 3D multi-object tracking. In: Proceedings of the 20th Conference on Robots and Vision, pp. 73–80 (2023)
26. Xu, X., et al.: STN-track: Multiobject tracking of unmanned aerial vehicles by swin transformer neck and new data association method. IEEE J. Sel. Top. Appl. Earth Observ. Remote Sens. **15**, 8734–8743 (2022)
27. Xu, Y., Ban, Y., Delorme, G., Gan, C., Rus, D., Alameda-Pineda, X.: TransCenter: transformers with dense representations for multiple-object tracking. IEEE Trans. Pattern Anal. Mach. Intell. **45**(6), 7820–7835 (2022)

28. Yang, J., Ge, H., Su, S., Liu, G.: Transformer-based two-source motion model for multi-object tracking. Appl. Intell. **52**, 9967–9979 (2022)
29. Zeng, F., Dong, B., Zhang, Y., Wang, T., Zhang, X., Wei, Y.: MOTR: end-to-end multiple-object tracking with transformer. In: Avidan, S., Brostow, G., Cissé, M., Farinella, G.M., Hassner, T. (eds.) ECCV 2022. LNCS, vol. 13687, pp. 659–675. Springer, Cham (2022). https://doi.org/10.1007/978-3-031-19812-0_38
30. Zhang, Y., Wang, T., Zhang, X.: MOTRv2: bootstrapping end-to-end multi-object tracking by pretrained object detectors. In: Proceedings of the IEEE/CVF Conference on Computer Vision and Pattern Recognition, pp. 22056–22065 (2023)
31. Zhou, X., Yin, T., Koltun, V., Krähenbühl, P.: Global tracking transformers. In: Proceedings of the IEEE/CVF Conference on Computer Vision and Pattern Recognition, pp. 8771–8780 (2022)
32. Zhu, T., et al.: Looking beyond two frames: end-to-end multi-object tracking using spatial and temporal transformers. IEEE Trans. Pattern Anal. Mach. Intell. 1–14 (2022)
33. Zhu, X., Su, W., Lu, L., Li, B., Wang, X., Dai, J.: Deformable DETR: deformable transformers for end-to-end object detection. arXiv preprint arXiv:2010.04159 (2020)

Exploring the Feasibility of PPG for Estimation of Heart Rate Variability: A Mathematical Approach

Tejasv Bhatt[1], Abhishek Shrivastava[2], Santosh Kumar[2(✉)], and Shresth Gupta[2]

[1] United College of Engineering and Research, Prayagraj, Uttar Pradesh, India
[2] IIIT-Naya Raipur, Chattishghar Nava Raipur, India
abisheks@iitnr.edu.in, {santosh,shresth}@iiitnr.edu.in

Abstract. Smart monitoring of cardiovascular diseases (CVDs) is gaining popularity in the healthcare field due to a wide range of applications using electrocardiogram (ECG) and photoplethysmogram (PPG) based techniques. ECG-based estimation and analysis of Heart Rate Variability (HRV) is a prominent technique used to assess cardiovascular health. However, it is expensive and has little practical application for daily monitoring of HRV. To solve such an issue, we propose a mathematical model based on statistical measures using a based technique. The model preprocesses pulse sensor data to mitigate specific noise or artifacts using filtering and statistical signal processing techniques. The model performs statistical measures to calculate heart rate from the interbeat interval (IBI) between consecutive R-peaks of the pre-processed data. Moreover, the proposed model used time domain techniques to estimate HRV values using metrics including standard deviation of NN (SDNN) and root mean square of successive differences (RMSSD) for the proposed model and succeeded in achieving an accuracy of 89.19% for HRV and 99.89% for HR, which was then developed into a prototype for evaluating the accuracy of the proposed model.

Keywords: Inter Beat Interwell · Photoplethysmogram · Heart rate · Heart Rate Variability

1 Introduction

Cardiovascular diseases (CVDs) have become a significant global health issue, with the highest mortality rates recorded worldwide [1,2]. According to the World Health Organization (WHO) data, in 2016, approximately 17.9 million deaths were attributed to CVDs, among these deaths, 85% were caused by strokes and heart attacks [2]. It is important to note that underdeveloped and developing countries have reported a higher number of CVD-related deaths. These statistics highlight the urgent need for effective prevention and management strategies to combat this major health concern [2–4].

© The Author(s), under exclusive license to Springer Nature Switzerland AG 2024
H. Kaur et al. (Eds.): CVIP 2023, CCIS 2011, pp. 225–236, 2024.
https://doi.org/10.1007/978-3-031-58535-7_19

The impact of a large population on a country's societal resources is substantial. Lifestyle factors such as stress, hypertension, unhealthy diet, obesity, physical inactivity, diabetes, hyperlipidemia, and substance abuse, including alcohol consumption, contribute to the development of cardiovascular diseases (CVDs) [5–9]. Common symptoms of CVDs include congenital heart defects, coronary artery disease, cardiomyopathy, myocarditis, and mitochondrial infections. Early detection and diagnosis are crucial in the prevention and treatment of CVDs, and real-time monitoring of heart activity plays a vital role in accurately detecting these conditions [2,3]. ECG, EcoG, cardiac Catheterization, CT scan, and cardiac resonance images are popular techniques to detect CVDs, and amongst all of the above techniques ECG based system provides the best visual pattern of HRV to present the electrical and muscular function of the heart [9]. Being a noninvasive method, ECG avoids the perils of the invasive method. Although ECG is considered the gold standard for HRV estimation due to its accuracy, it is impractical and costly for continuous monitoring [9–11]. PPG, on the other hand, because of easy deployment, simplicity, and cost-effective, PPG is gaining significant attention and becoming an alternative technique to monitor and study vital body signs such as HRV PPG is convenient and can be integrated into wearable devices for everyday monitoring [12].

The framework offers a cost-effective, streamlined, and portable solution for monitoring individuals' heart health, Its ability to predict heart rate variability empowers healthcare professionals to take proactive measures and personalize treatment plans, thereby mitigating the impact of cardiovascular diseases on a global scale. The simultaneous analysis of PPG and ECG signals can enhance the accuracy and reliability of HRV estimation, providing valuable insights for healthcare professionals.

1.1   Motivation and Contibutions

ECG-based early diagnosis CVDs is a reliable method to diagnose and trace the electrical activity of a healthy heart [11], ECG is not only used to detect CVDs but also to detect various diseases in medical domains like pneumonia and respiratory diseases based on various types of waves form (P, Q, R, S, C, T). Continuous monitoring using ECG signals is a cumbersome task and it is more error-prone to misclassify the health diseases for early diagnosis therefore it is required to devise an automatic and robust system for early diagnosis of CVDs diseases based on HRV [13]. In this paper we address the problem of how to evaluate the HRV and HR values of individuals for early diagnosis of diseases to solve this problem, we proposed a mathematical approach based on statically major by using sensors to analyze multiple diseases of patients. The proposed system took raw sensor data from PPG and isolated micro factors that affect HRV and through careful study of the estimated micro-factors we have been able to estimate accurate HRV and HR [8]. This could then be used to estimate the overall Cardiovascular health of the tribal people of Chhattisgarh through PPG-based wearable devices, to minimize the need for medical experts in these tribal villages. The major contributions are highlighted as follows:

1. We propose a novel framework for the estimation of HRV and HR for early diagnosis and prediction of CVDs.
2. The proposed framework is evaluated on the prepared database using PPG through the connecting pulse sensor through Arduino.
3. we analyzed the health status of individual patient groups with different ages and severity of CVDs.
4. Compared and evaluated the efficiency of the proposed working prototype based on different benchmark settings in natural conditions.

2 Literature Survey

The Internet of Medical Things (IoMT) has attracted great attention for health-care monitoring with intelligent sensors subsequently addressing the issue of security and privacy risks involved with real-time assessment prototype [1], also addressing the energy-saving need for these real-time monitoring systems hence making prototype devices more resilient [2]. Subsequently, the emergence of PPG has enhanced its usage by providing a compact single sensor approach that can be used for daily real-time analysis [17] and through continuous efforts of researchers we have been able to achieve accuracy from PPG compatibility to ECG and others sophisticated, complex technology through utilizing the ratio at which sensor should be from various anatomical sites [3,9,10,14].

In recent studies, it has been proved that PPG for real-time analysis gives high accuracy, and utilizing this technology to extract HRV by utilizing a multi-modal approach and using sensors such as a pulse sensor along with a camera [5,7,8] through the accurate estimation of HRV and HR from wearable devices it is possible to monitor cardiovascular health of wearable [4], HR and HRV serve as essential indicators of cardiac health and overall well-being and even predict the CVDs [6] which can be prevented through small changes in lifestyle and prevention the risk of CVDs and strokes would be reduced significantly. This would contribute to increasing the life expectancy of individuals and significantly reducing the death ratios due to CVDs [10,11] with the potential to revolutionize healthcare by enabling continuous monitoring, personalized interventions, remote patient management, and advanced analytic. Future research and advancements in these areas will further enhance the capabilities of these technologies, leading to improved patient outcomes and well-being [12].

3 Materials and Model

In this section, we introduce our novel model for estimating heart rate variability (HRV) and provide an overview of the data preparation process and accurate prediction of CVDs. Our model utilizes statistical machine-learning techniques and non-invasive measurements to accurately estimate HRV. We carefully prepossess and analyze the sensor data to ensure reliable results for monitoring and predicting cardiovascular health.

228   T. Bhatt et al.

3.1 Proposed Model

In this section, the working of the proposed model is given in Fig. 1(a) and
Fig. 1(b). The proposed work is divided into two subsections estimation of HR
and estimation of HRV For the estimation of HR we first initialize control variables to zero and check the current pulse subsequently while updating a previous
pulse variable, Then we apply a condition, if the pulse is detected then calculate HR else exit subsequently updating the time variable, The second part of
the proposed approach deals with the estimation of HRV, we read and acquire
the raw PPG data based on acquired data we apply filtration such as baseline
wander To acquire a clean ppg signal we extract IBI by using a mathematical
formula for it, further, we calculate RMSSD and SDNN and by combining these
we estimate HRV. The proposed model is shown diagrammatically in Fig. 1:

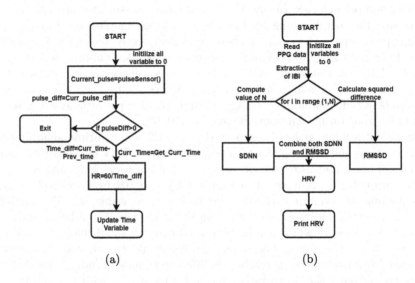

Fig. 1. Flowcharts: (a) Calculation of HR, (b) Estimation of HRV.

3.2 Data Preparation and Description

We conducted a data collection camp to provide awareness for healthy monitoring of heart disease in IIIT-Naya Raipur and nearby several villages such
as Uparawara, Rakhi, Nawagoan, and other villages along with medical experts
and professionals. In this data collection camp, we prepared a medical diagnostic-
related dataset of HRV and HR of participating individuals based on obtaining
consent and approval from them. To improve the size of the dataset, we also
conducted several sessions at the health center of IIIT-Naya Raipur with the
doctor's support and medical staff through various workshops. The prepared
dataset will be used for research purposes only. We accumulated the health data

of 20000 individuals which included 500 graduates, 200 staff, and 400 students. This was done in two phases and a total of 10 such paired phases were held hence totaling to 40000 individual readings of data were acquired using different sensors and compiled into the database which could be further used for various medical analysis and implementation of machine learning and deep learning models.

The proposed model captures various values of HR and HRV and stores them in CSV file, the model utilizes a simple Python code that efficiently acquires real-time data from the built hardware device and stores it simultaneously avoiding any loss in data and if the data bits are lost it is replaced by the median of the previous values while continuously storing the incoming values (Fig. 2).

Fig. 2. Preparation of database for the measurement of HRV and HR for early diagnosis of CVDs patients.

4   Hardware Required

The required hardware for the estimation of HRV is quite simple, cheap, and easy to build. The device's built-in accusation of PPG data is made up of only 3 parts which are explained in brief in Table 1.

A pulse sensor is a tool used to continuously measure and track a person's heart rate. It commonly makes use of optical or electrical sensors to find blood flow and record artery pulsations. Users can monitor their heart rate for a variety

Table 1. Description of hardware for PPG-based data acquisition

Hardware	Specification
Pulse Sensor	660nm super Green LED(Reflective)
Arduino UNO	I/O pins and 32 KB memory
USB power cable	Communication channel and power supply

of health and fitness goals with the help of the sensor, which offers a convenient and non-invasive approach to check heart rate. The sensor can be linked to wearable technology, fitness trackers, and healthcare monitoring systems [9].

The popular Arduino Uno microcontroller board is used frequently in DIY electronics projects and prototyping. It has a USB port for communication and programming, an Atmega328P microprocessor, and digital and analog input/output pins. An easy interface with sensors, actuators, and other electronic components is possible with Arduino Uno.

5   Experimental Setup

The end-to-end proposed Hardware framework is done with Photoplethysmography data through the aid of a pulse sensor, an Arduino UNO along a USB power cord which also acts as a communication channel between Arduino UNO and laptop the architecture is illustrated in the below block diagram in Fig. 3 along with working explained in brief.

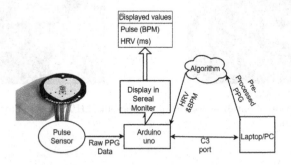

Fig. 3. Proposed framework for the assessment of HRV using pulse sensor.

The basic architecture of the above system is as follows:-

– In this setup, we provide input through a pulse sensor from the fingertip of the subject during the measurement trial.

Fig. 4. Preview of proposed hardware module

- The acquired data is transferred to Arduino UNO through jumper wires which are connected as such analog signal of the pulse sensor to the A0 pin of Arduino UNO, +ve pin of the pulse sensor to the 3.3V of Arduino UNO and lastly -ve pin to the ground of Arduino UNO to which is directly connected to our laptop through C3 port.
- We directly accessed Arduino UNO through an Arduino IDE, which provides us a platform to directly communicate with Arduino UNO and write our code on the provided sketch
- The code is then deployed to the Arduino UNO board and based on the algorithm it collects data from the pulse sensor and processes it to print output in the serial monitor connected with the Arduino output channel.
- This combined setup is then connected to the laptop through a USB type C cable which also acts as a communication channel(CO3) between Arduino UNO and the laptop. On a laptop, we wrote a code using the algorithm and uploaded it on our Arduino UNO (shown in Fig. 4).
- Estimated HRV and pulse are displayed in the serial monitor of Arduino IDE

5.1   HR Measurement

One of the challenging applications in the healthcare system is the continuous monitoring of heart rate using a wearable device for the early identification of cardiovascular disorders. Heart rate and HRV are typical indicators of a health state. The autonomic nervous system (ANS) of a human organism exhibits sympathetic and parasympathetic behavior, which can be used to determine HRV status [4,5,7]. The parasympathetic branches are associated with the body's resting and digesting phases, whereas the sympathetic branch is related to the body's active condition [17].

To accurately measure the heart rate of the volunteer, we utilized a pulse sensor which measures the pulsating blood flow in arteries by using a light source and a photo-detector, hence detecting changes in blood volume in the micro-vascular bed of skin. Through Heart Rate, we isolated IBI which is further used as a basis of estimation of HRV [16]. The following equations were used to accurately measure Heart Rate (shown in Eqs. (1, 2, 3, 4 and 5)).

$$rate[9] = IBI \tag{1}$$

$$RunningTotal = rate[9] + RunningTotal \tag{2}$$

$$BPM = 60000/RunningTotal \tag{3}$$

$$RunningTotal/ = 10 \tag{4}$$

$$HERATRATE = 60000/RunningTotal \tag{5}$$

5.2 Measuring Heart Rate Variability

We utilized the Inter Beat Interval (IBI) as a reference obtained by the PPG sensor (pulse sensor) and estimated the HRV of volunteers through the combination of RMSS, SDNN, and other small time-stamps and calibration algorithms to produce our required HRV [9]. The ANS is in balance and responds to both sympathetic and parasympathetic inputs in a subject with a high HRV.

Low HRV is a sign of stress or exhaustion and the sympathetic and parasympathetic nervous systems are over-represented in the body. A healthy body has a high HRV, but a low HRV suggests higher stress, which may raise the risk of cardiovascular disease [9,12]. In light of this, HRV analysis has emerged in recent years as a useful method for the early detection of cardiovascular illness. Therefore, to assess the state of cardiovascular health, both heart rate and HRV are used. By shining a light through the skin and detecting the volumetric change in blood during a heart cycle, HR and HRV can be calculated [8].

5.3 Estimation of HRV

For the estimation of HRV, instead of using the traditional method of calculating the normal to normal (N-N) interval of ECG waveform we instead deployed various mathematical equations and models [14]. We devised the mathematical equation for the estimation of HRV as follows:

$$SDNN = \sqrt{\frac{\sum_{i=1}^{n}(IBI_i - \overline{IBI})^2}{n-1}} \tag{6}$$

where IBI is an array of n inter-beat intervals,
$\overline{IBI}$ is the mean inter-beat interval,
$SDNN$ is the standard deviation of the inter-beat intervals.

$$RMSSD = \sqrt{\frac{1}{n-1}\sum_{i=2}^{n}(IBI_i - IBI_{i-1})^2} \tag{7}$$

$RMSSD$ is the root-mean-square of the successive differences between the inter-beat intervals.

$$HRV = \sqrt{SDNN^2 + RMSSD^2} \tag{8}$$

where HRV is the heart rate variability,

Table 2. Comparison between HRV calculated by the proposed model and Bioppac.

Group	Age	HRV (Model)	HRV(BIOpac)
1	20–35	117.31	121
2	25–30	80.83	88
3	55–60	42.33	48
4	18–25	120.67	112
5	30–35	111.55	128
6	60–70	35.73	39.5
7	35–40	80.83	85.5
8	20–25	100.89	94
9	25–30	67.73	55.5
10	35–40	114.23	100.5
11	70–80	97.73	87.5
12	70–80	58.73	65.5
13	65–70	33.73	31.5
14	40–45	70.73	75
15	35–40	77.23	83.5
16	35–40	98.73	88.5
17	14–18	108.73	117
18	14–18	116.73	106
19	14–18	111.53	121.5
20	70–80	54.37	61.5

6   Results and Analysis

The performance evaluation of the presented approach has been carried out using 20 different volunteers from IIIT-NR, Chhattisgarh. We have used 15-second individual samples for both HRV and BPM to cross-verify the integrity of the developed model with Biopac MP-36 4-channel data accusation device with variation psychological and environmental factors such as relaxed sitting, high mental workload sitting, and light physical stress sitting, marking data from BIOpac MP-36 as a reference.

Based on comparative analysis, the proposed approach achieved an overall accuracy of 89.19%. which is shown in Fig. 5 as the performance of proposed model. These comparison graphs further highlight the effectiveness of our model and open up a path for developing inexpensive and highly accurate ECG-free compact wearable devices.

Table 2 shows a side-by-side comparison of HRV collected from 20 volunteers for 15 s through the proposed model and Biopac MP-36 acquisition device.

1. Based on overall observation (Table 2), the average value of group 1,4,5,10 is extremely high as the group contains athletes.
2. Groups 11,12,20 contain individuals above the age of 70.
3. Group 2 consists of research scholars whose readings were taken in a relaxed, stress-free environment, whereas Group 9 consists of the same researchers but were taken after their presentation.
4. Groups 17–19 consist of physically active teenagers.
5. Groups 3,6,13 consist of patients suffering from cardiovascular diseases along with ages exceeding 55 years.
6. Groups 7,14,15,16 consist of staff of IIIT NR Chhattisgarh who were physically healthy with no current diseases.

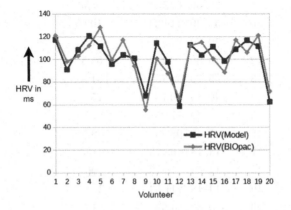

Fig. 5. Comparison of HRV estimation obtained from proposed hardware module and reference HRV obtained through Biopac acquisition device.

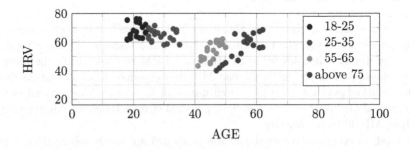

We used 20 volunteer data from each group randomly selected amongst the total of 40000 collected data. To manage the true HRV simultaneously, we used the Biopac MP-36 physiological acquisition device. The reference HRV calculation is done by placing three electrodes in standard anatomical sites to obtain ECG first. The simultaneous analysis of HRV is done and displayed in the student Biopac software interface. The estimated HRV from the proposed Hardware and the reference HRV from the Biopac device are provided in Table 2.

Advantages: Our lightweight, portable prototype offers a cost-effective real-time HRV monitoring system. We can enhance model accuracy for estimating CVD and neurophysiological diseases in user-friendly devices. By employing more powerful sensors, we can boost efficiency.

Limitations: Our model differs slightly from the standard BIOPAC device, making it susceptible to artifacts like motion and environmental factors. Medical experts don't endorse PPG for HRV extraction due to its sensitivity. To adopt this approach, we must enhance accuracy further, given PPg's extreme sensitivity.

7   Conclusion and Future Directions

An inexpensive and wearable approach to the daily analysis and estimation of HRV is confirmed in this work. This estimation is not done on the traditional ECG approach of calculating the time interval between R-R subsequent waveform but is based on purely mathematical calculation and process, which is also the major highlight of this work; this method holds vital importance in the prior estimation of psychological diseases, cardiovascular diseases and type-2 diabetes and above through the estimated HRV with an accuracy of 89.19% and HRV with an accuracy of 99.89%, We will be able to identify unhealthy lifestyle or environment. Through micro changes in these factors, the user can avoid the diseases mentioned above and significantly increase life expectancy and quality of life. However, there is much more work and upgrading to be done to this basic model. In the future, we hope to continue our work and make it an inexpensive and reliable tool for estimating mental and physical stress, diabetes, and cardiovascular diseases including predicting the possibility of heart attack and strokes.

References

1. Jiang, X., Zhang, J., Zhang, L.: FedRadar: federated multi-task transfer learning for radar-based internet of medical things. IEEE Trans. Netw. Serv. Manage. **20**, 1459–1469 (2023)
2. Reddy, G.N.K., Manikandan, M.S., Murty, N.N.: Evaluation of objective distortion measures for automatic quality assessment of processed PPG signals for real-time health monitoring devices. IEEE Access **10**, 15707–15745 (2022)
3. Kao, Y.H., Chao, P.C.P., Wey, C.L.: Design and validation of a new PPG module to acquire high-quality physiological signals for high-accuracy biomedical sensing. IEEE J. Sel. Top. Quantum Electron. **25**(1), 1–10 (2018)
4. Narciso, D., et al.: Using heart rate variability for comparing the effectiveness of virtual vs real training environments for firefighters. IEEE Trans. Vis. Comput. Graph. **29**(7), 3238–3250 (2022)
5. Yu, S.N., Wang, C.S., Chang, Y.P.: Heart rate estimation from remote photoplethysmography based on light-weight U-Net and attention modules. IEEE Access **11**, 54058–54069 (2023)

6. Beh, W.K., Wu, Y.H., Wu, A.Y.: Robust PPG-based mental workload assessment system using wearable devices. IEEE J. Biomed. Health Inf. **27**(5), 2323–2333 (2021)
7. Lv, W., et al.: Remote measurement of short-term heart rate with narrow beam millimeter wave radar. IEEE Access **9**, 65049–165058 (2021)
8. Umair, M., et al.: HRV and stress: a mixed-methods approach for comparison of wearable heart rate sensors for biofeedback. IEEE Access **9**, 14005–14024 (2021)
9. Sacha, J.: Interaction between heart rate and heart rate variability. Ann. Noninvasive Electrocardiol. **19**(3), 207–216 (2014)
10. Kamath, M.V., Mari ,W., Adrian, U. (eds.) Heart rate variability (HRV) signal analysis: clinical applications (2012)
11. Chakladar, D.D., Dey, S., Roy, P.P., Dogra, D.P.: EEG-based mental workload estimation using deep BLSTM-LSTM network and evolutionary algorithm. Biomed. Sig. Process. Control **60**, 101989 (2020)
12. Bhowmik, T., Dey, J., Tiwari, V.N.: A novel method for accurate estimation of HRV from smartwatch PPG signals. In: 2017 39th Annual International Conference of the IEEE Engineering in Medicine and Biology Society (EMBC), pp. 109-112. IEEE, July 2017
13. Reiss, A., et al.: Deep PPG: large-scale heart rate estimation with convolutional neural networks. Sensors **19**(14), 3079 (2019)
14. Kinnunen, H., et al.: Feasible assessment of recovery and cardiovascular health: accuracy of nocturnal HR and HRV assessed via ring PPG in comparison to medical grade ECG. Physiol. Measure. **41**(4), 04NT01 (2020)
15. Sandercock, G.R., Bromley, P.D., Brodie, D.A.: The reliability of short-term measurements of heart rate variability. Int. J. Cardiol. **103**(3), 238–247 (2005)
16. Loh, H.W., et al.: Application of photoplethysmography signals for healthcare systems: an in-depth review. Comput. Methods Program. Biomed. **216**, 106677 (2022)
17. ChuDuc, H., NguyenPhan, K., NguyenViet, D.: A review of heart rate variability and its applications. APCBEE Proc. **7**, 80–85 (2013)

Improved Multi-modal Image Fusion with Attention and Dense Networks: Visual and Quantitative Evaluation

Ankan Banerjee[1]([✉]) [ID], Dipti Patra[1] [ID], and Pradipta Roy[2] [ID]

[1] National Institute of Technology, Rourkela, India
ankan.banerjee95@gmail.com
[2] Integrated Test Range, DRDO, Candipur, India

Abstract. This article introduces a novel multi-modal image fusion approach based on Convolutional Block Attention Module and dense networks to enhance human perceptual quality and information content in the fused images. The proposed model preserves the edges of the infrared images and enhances the contrast of the visible image as a pre-processing part. Consequently, the use of Convolutional Block Attention Module has resulted in the extraction of more refined features from the source images. The visual results demonstrate that the fused images produced by the proposed method are visually superior to those generated by most standard fusion techniques. To substantiate the findings, quantitative analysis is conducted using various metrics. The proposed method exhibits the best Naturalness Image Quality Evaluator and Chen-Varshney metric values, which are human perception-based parameters. Moreover, the fused images exhibit the highest Standard Deviation value, signifying enhanced contrast. These results justify the proposed multi-modal image fusion technique outperforms standard methods both qualitatively and quantitatively, resulting in superior fused images with improved human perception quality.

Keywords: image fusion · attention · human perception · Convolutional Block Attention Module

1 Introduction

The field of image fusion has emerged as a thriving area of research, driven by the development of different sensors for image capturing. Image fusion techniques involve merging multiple source images to create a single, information-rich image that incorporates the unique features of each input. This integration process is particularly valuable when capturing a specific region of interest from different focal points, exposure settings, or sensors. By combining these diverse images with complementary properties, the resulting fused image exhibits enhanced information content, improved clarity, and increased interpretability. This advancement in image fusion technology holds great promise for a wide

H. Kaur et al. (Eds.): CVIP 2023, CCIS 2011, pp. 237–248, 2024.
https://doi.org/10.1007/978-3-031-58535-7_20

range of applications, empowering researchers and practitioners to extract more comprehensive insights and make informed decisions based on the fused image data in the domains of defense [26], remote sensing [10], medical [14,16], and many others.

This study focuses on fusing infrared (IR) and visible images, which capture complementary properties due to their distinct portions of the electromagnetic spectrum. IR images provide thermal profiles, valuable for temperature-based object detection, independent of illumination and weather conditions, while visible images offer superior resolution, texture, and visual details. On the other hand, visible images offer high-resolution visual details, aligning with human perception. The fusion process combines these strengths, resulting in a fused image that enables enhanced interpretability and human-centric analysis of the scene. The IR and visible image fusion finds application in the fields of surveillance [2], object detection [5], defense [26], etc.

The image fusion methods are classified on the domain basis as spatial and transform methods. The spatial domain methods perform fusion by applying basic mathematical operations like average, maximum, L_1 norm, etc. at the pixel level of the source images [11]. On the other hand, transform methods, also known as multi-scale transform (MST) methods, decompose the source images using various transform techniques such as wavelet transform [16], shearlet transform [27] or principal component analysis [14] . These transforms help extract features at different scales and orientations, facilitating a more comprehensive representation of the image content. After the fusion process, the fused image is reconstructed using the inverse transform method. After fusion, the fused image is reconstructed back using the inverse transform method.

The integration of deep learning techniques in image fusion research continues to advance the field, opening up new avenues for improved fusion performance and applications. Ram et al. [17] proposed the DeepFuse architecture, which was an unsupervised model for multi-exposure image fusion. Hui et al. [7] presented a VGG-19 as a feature extractor in their fusion network. A dense CNN-based fusion architecture was proposed by Hui et al. [6] which could handle the problem of vanishing gradient. Ma et al. [9] proposed image fusion based on the generative adversarial network, which could preserve the intensity of the IR image and the details of the visible image. Ruichao et al. [4] proposed the VIF-Net architecture for multi-modal image fusion based on dense networks. Zhengwen et al. [19] introduced a fusion model based on cross-attention for multi-modal, multi-exposure and multi-focal images. Han et al. [25] introduced a fusion model based on the saliency map classification of the source images.

Some of the CNN-based networks mentioned above have certain limitations. For example, in [4], the preservation of distinct features between infrared (IR) and visible images is not adequately considered, and the network architecture directly takes the source images as input without pre-processing these features. Moreover, models like VGG-19 in [7], which rely on transfer learning, are predominantly trained on visible images, making them ineffective for feature extraction from IR images. Additionally, networks solely based on CNN, such as DeepFuse

[17], encounter challenges related to the vanishing gradient problem. These limitations highlight the need for further research and development to improve the performance of CNN-based fusion networks. The key contributions of this article based on the shortcomings are listed below:

- Improved multi-modal image fusion technique based on CBAM and dense networks.
- The pre-processing steps has helped in preserving more features from the source image to the fused image.
- The qualitative and quantitative analysis showing the superior visual performance of the proposed method compared to various standard fusion techniques, as evident from the evaluation of brightness, background quality, human perception and contrast in fused images.

2   Materials and Methods

2.1   Attention Models

Attention is a fundamental cognitive function that holds great importance for the human visual senses. In the realm of human vision, it is notable that humans do not process all the information simultaneously, rather it is selective according to necessity. This ability to selectively attend to relevant stimuli enhances human cognitive efficiency by allocating resources effectively while focusing attention on specific elements of any scene or task [15]. Attention networks have become a prominent solution for tackling diverse challenges in deep learning like in the fields of medicine [18], facial expression recognition [29], image super resolution [12] and others. Attention can be classified as channel and spatial attention.

The extracted feature maps from any CNN consist of channel (C), height (H) and, width (W). The channel attention [23] focuses on the inter-channel relationship between the channels of the feature maps and performs squeezing in the spatial direction. The channel attention focuses on 'what' is meaningful in an input image. The channel attention block diagram is shown in Fig. 1.

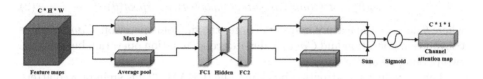

Fig. 1. Channel attention module

The channel attention module consists of both max and average pooling operation blocks, which operate individually on the spatial dimensions of the input feature map to generate feature descriptors. These descriptors are passed

on to the multi-layer perceptron (MLP) network, composed of two fully connected (FC1 and FC2) and one hidden layer. The feature vectors from the fully
connected layer is added and passed on to the sigmoid function to generate the
final channel attention map. Notably, the channel size in the feature map and
final channel attention map remains the same, while the height and width both
reduces to unity. Channel attention (M_C) can be mathematically depicted as in
Eq. 1.

$$M_C(\theta) = \sigma(MLP(avgpool(\theta)) + MLP(maxpool(\theta))) \tag{1}$$

where θ denotes the feature maps and σ denotes the sigmoid operation.

The spatial attention block [23] utilizes the inter-spatial relationship between
the feature maps and performs squeezing in the channel dimensions. Unlike the
channel attention module, spatial attention focuses on 'where' to look for in the
input image. The spatial attention block diagram is shown in Fig. 2.

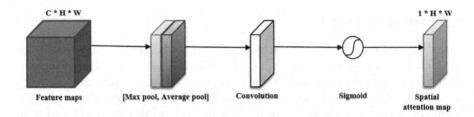

Fig. 2. Spatial attention module

The max and average pooling operations are performed along the channel axis
of the feature maps and the results are concatenated. The concatenated feature
descriptor is passed through a convolutional block and sigmoid layer to generate
the final spatial attention map. In the spatial attention map, the height and
width remain the same as in the input feature map, while the channel becomes
unity. Spatial attention (MS) can be mathematically depicted as in Eq. 2.

$$M_S(\theta) = \sigma(Conv(Concate[avgpool(\theta), maxpool(\theta)])) \tag{2}$$

where θ denotes the feature maps, σ denotes the sigmoid operation, $Conv$ denotes
convolution operation and $Concate$ denotes concatenation operation between the
two pooling results.

The convolutional attention block module (CBAM) [23] is an improved attention model, which can improve the feature representation of the CNNs. The
CBAM has a simple architecture in which the channel and spatial attention
blocks are connected in a cascade, thus both the 'what' and 'where' to look for
in an image are learned by the network and final attention map is generated
accordingly. The CBAM block diagram is presented in Fig. 3.

The CBAM takes the output from both the channel and spatial attention
modules; hence, the final output is the same size as the input feature map.

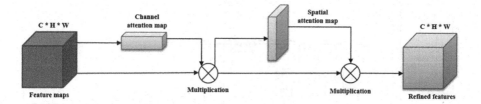

Fig. 3. Convolutional Attention Block Module

Initially, to the feature map with dimensions $C \times H \times W$ channel attention is applied, which results in a dimension of $C \times 1 \times 1$. This is followed by the spatial attention module, which results in dimension $1 \times H \times W$. The spatial map is multiplied element-wise to the previously multiplied result of the channel attention block and the original feature map. This is formulated in Eq. 3.

$$\hat{\theta} = M_C(\theta) \otimes \theta$$
$$\theta' = M_S(\hat{\theta}) \otimes \hat{\theta} \tag{3}$$

where $\hat{\theta}$ represents the output map after passing the input feature map θ through the channel attention module and θ' denotes the final feature map after passing through the CBAM network.

2.2 Datasets

The proposed image fusion model has been trained and tested on images from the TNO and RoadScene image datasets. The Netherlands Organization for Applied Scientific Research has prepared the dataset. [21]. It contains registered pairs of IR and visible images of military and surveillance scenarios. The RoadScene dataset contains 221 registered pairs of IR and visible image scenes of the resolution 1280×720 pixels [24]. The scenes were captured on roads containing cars, people, traffic lights, etc.

3 Proposed Method

3.1 Architecture

The proposed fusion model is shown in Fig. 4. The model consists of four major segments: the pre-processing part, the encoder part, the feature map fusion part and the decoder part. The CBAM block used in the architecture has been already discussed in Fig. 3. The numbers represent the number of channels at the output of the corresponding blocks. The block names CIi, CVi, and CFi $\forall i \in [1, 4]$ represents the convolutional block used for infrared, visible and reconstructed image respectively for all i in range 1 to 4.

As depicted in Fig. 4, the pre-processing part extracts the edges of the IR image and enhances the contrast of the visible image. For edge extraction, the

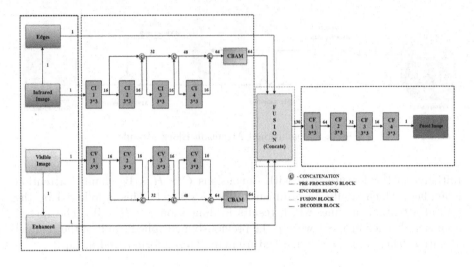

Fig. 4. Proposed fusion network architecture

basic morphological operations of erosion and dilation have been used. The eroded IR image is subtracted from the dilated IR image to obtain the IR edges. Similarly, for the visible image, the contrast is enhanced by the log transformation. These steps are performed so that the vital features of the source images are preserved before they 'vanish' in the CNN model. These pre-processed images are concatenated back later in the fusion block. The encoder block consists of four convolutional blocks connected in a dense architecture, to handle the vanishing gradient problem individually for the IR and the visible image. The kernel size of each filter is 3 × 3 for each CNN block, with a Rectified Linear Unit activation function. The output from both the IR pipeline and the visible pipeline is passed to the CBAM block for extracting more refined features and paying 'attention' to the important parts of the scene. The kernel size used in the convolution in the spatial attention block is 7 × 7. The encoder is followed by the fusion block, where the output from both the CBAMs and the pre-processing block is concatenated along the channel axis. The decoder finally reconstructs the fused image from the fused feature maps using four CNN blocks with kernel size 3 × 3.

3.2 Model Loss

The Structural Similarity Index Metric ($SSIM$) is a measurement technique used to quantify the structural similarity between two images. It takes into account the contrast, luminance, and structural information present in the images. The proposed model has been trained on a Modified $SSIM$ loss function. The Modified Structural Similarity Index Metric ($SSIM_M$) is a customized loss function specifically designed for infrared and visible image fusion, adapted from [4]. $SSIM_M$ is derived by eliminating the luminance component from the original SSIM function, as explained in [4]. The $SSIM_M$ is given as in Eq. 4.

$$SSIM_M(X,Y|W) = \frac{2\sigma_{XY} + C}{\sigma_X{}^2 + \sigma_Y{}^2 + C} \tag{4}$$

where W is the window of size 11×11, C is a constant with value 9×10^{-4}, σ gives the standard deviation of the image under consideration and σ_{XY} denotes the cross-correlation between the images.

$$E(I|W) = \frac{1}{m \times n} \sum_{i=1}^{m \times n} P_i \tag{5}$$

where $E(I|W)$ denotes the average intensity of an image I with size $m \times n$ within a window of size W and P_i indicates the value of ith pixel.

$$Score(I_v, I_i, I_f|W) = \begin{cases} SSIM_M(I_v, I_f|W), \\ \text{if } E(I_v|W) > E(I_i|W) \\ SSIM_M(I_i, I_f|W), \\ \text{if } E(I_v|W) \leq E(I_i|W) \end{cases} \tag{6}$$

$$L_{SSIM_M} = 1 - \frac{1}{N} \sum_{W=1}^{N} Score(I_v, I_i, I_f|W) \tag{7}$$

where N denotes the total number of sliding windows in the image. I_v, I_i and I_f refers to the visible, infrared and fused image respectively. The $SSIM_M$ loss is denoted by L_{SSIM_M} and given as in Eq. 7.

The Total Variation (TV) loss is computed by summing the absolute differences between adjacent pixels in the image. This loss function quantifies the variations or changes between neighboring pixels, taking into account both horizontal and vertical directions. By summing the absolute differences, the TV loss provides a measure of the overall smoothness or regularity of the image [22]. The TV loss between the visible and the fused image is given by L_{TV} as in Eq. 8.

$$L_{TV} = \sum_{i,j} ((D_{i,j-1} - D_{i,j})^2 + (D_{i+1,j} - D_{i,j})^2) \tag{8}$$

where $D(i,j)$ gives the pixel difference at (i,j) between visible and fused image given in 9.

$$D(i,j) = I_v(i,j) - I_f(i,j) \tag{9}$$

Finally, the total loss is defined by 10.

$$L_{total} = L_{TV} + \gamma \times L_{SSIM_M} \tag{10}$$

where γ is the regularization parameter for matching the magnitude of the two losses. The value γ has been tested for values 20, 100, 500, 800, 1000 and 1500. Experimentally, the image quality obtained at 800 was the best.

3.3   Model Training

The fusion network was trained using 21 images from the TNO dataset and 10 images from the RoadScene dataset. To prepare the data for training, the registered pairs of infrared (IR) and visible images were cropped and augmented into patches of size 64 × 64 pixels which resulted in a total of 17,500 images. The network parameters were fine-tuned during training for 100 epochs using the Adam optimizer, with a learning rate set to 0.0001. The optimization process involved minimizing both the $SSIM_M$ and TV losses to enhance fusion performance. The training and testing procedures were carried out in a PyTorch environment, utilizing a workstation equipped with an Intel(R) Xeon(R) Silver 4210R 2.40 GHz CPU, 16 GB RAM, and an NVIDIA Quadro RTX 5000 Ti GPU.

4   Results and Discussions

The results obtained from the model were compared both qualitatively and quantitatively with several standard image fusion methods. While qualitative analysis provides visual comparisons, it is important to supplement it with quantitative analysis using standard fusion metrics. These metrics enable a more objective evaluation of the fused image quality, taking into account various factors such as sharpness, contrast, and information preservation. By combining both qualitative and quantitative assessments, a comprehensive evaluation was performed.

4.1   Performance Evaluation

The fused images of the proposed method are compared with five standard fusion methods: fusion based on anisotropic diffusion Karhunen Loeve transform (ADF) [1], cross bilateral filter (CBF) [20], gradient transfer and total variation minimization (GTF) [8], VGG-19 [30], VIF-Net (VIF) [4]. The results for two images from the TNO dataset are shown in Figs. 5 and 6.

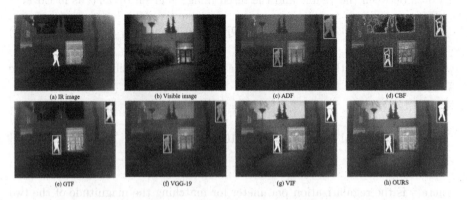

Fig. 5. Qualitative analysis of 'person' image from TNO dataset

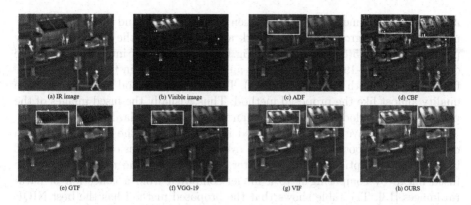

Fig. 6. Qualitative analysis of 'road' image from TNO dataset

The quantitative performance of the fused image was judged by comparing it with the standard fusion methods mentioned above. The metrics used were: natural image quality evaluator (NIQE) [13], mutual information (MI) [28], Chen-Varshney metric (Q_{CV}) [3], and standard deviation (SD) [28]. The values presented are the average values for the 21 images of the TNO dataset. The results are tabulated in Table 1. The best values are bolded for better understanding. + symbol denotes better performance for higher value and − symbol denotes beter performance for lower value.

Table 1. Quantitative analysis of the images of TNO dataset (average values)

Methods	NIQE(-)	MI(+)	Q_{CV}(-)	SD(+)
ADF	4.421	1.240	518.580	23.420
CBF	4.506	1.692	947.613	35.913
GTF	4.508	1.673	1281.277	31.579
VGG-19	3.647	1.368	403.818	25.626
VIF-Net	3.347	**2.783**	329.424	35.768
OURS	**3.305**	2.733	**327.592**	**36.138**

4.2 Discussion

This article introduces a multi-modal image fusion based on CBAM and dense networks that generate fused images having better human perceptual quality and information content. The qualitative analysis presented in Figs. 5 and 6, shows the performance of the proposed model. From Figs. 5(c) and 6(c), the brightness of the region of interest decreases and thus becomes unrecognizable in the ADF method. The quality of the background degrades because of the added noise in the CBF method as can be seen from Figs. 5(d) and 6(d). In the GTF method, the background becomes dark and the edges of the tree become very prominent in Fig. 5(e). Similarly, in Fig. 6(e) the region of interest has become dark. In the VGG-19 method, there is an overall decrease in the contrast in the fused image for both Figs. 5(f) and 6(f). The VIF-Net method shows good image quality almost like the proposed method. Thus, visually the fused images of the proposed method look much better than most of the standard fusion methods.

The quantitative analysis tabulated in Table 1 infers the better perception quality of the proposed fusion method over the standard fusion methods. NIQE is a human perception-based parameter, which defines the naturalness of the fused image by comparing it to a model computed from a collection of natural images [13]. The table shows that the proposed method has the best NIQE value. Mutual information is a measure that quantifies the amount of information shared between the source and the fused image. The proposed method has the second-best MI value among the standard fusion methods. Q_{CV} is another human perception-based metric, which gives the physical visual performance of the image [3]. The proposed method has the best Q_{CV} value, which indicates its better performance for human perception. SD measures the contrast in the fused image. The proposed method has the highest SD value. Overall, quantitatively the fused image has better human perception quality as evident from the discussion above.

The pre-processing part allowed better feature preservation, whereas the CBAM block resulted in extraction of more refined features. The contribution of each blocks is examined quantitatively as an ablation study tabulated in Table 2. It is obvious from Table 2, that the addition of the CBAM and the pre-processing block has improved the performance of the fusion model in terms of NIQE, Q_{CV} and the SD.

Table 2. Ablation study of various blocks on TNO dataset

Methods	NIQE(-)	MI(+)	Q_{CV}(-)	SD(+)
Without the preprocessing block	4.0663	**3.373**	1647.355	31.839
Without the CBAM block	3.402	2.716	347.613	35.771
OURS	**3.305**	2.733	**327.592**	**36.138**

5   Conclusion

In conclusion, this article presents a multi-modal image fusion method based on CBAM and dense networks, resulting in fused images with improved human perceptual quality and information content. The qualitative analysis demonstrates the superior performance of the proposed model compared to standard fusion methods. The proposed method preserves the region of interest brightness and enhances background quality, unlike other methods that suffer from decreased contrast, noise addition, or darkened backgrounds. The quantitative analysis further confirms the effectiveness of the proposed method, with lower NIQE values indicating a more natural fused image, higher mutual information values demonstrating substantial shared information between the source and fused image, and the best Q_{CV} value indicating better human vision comprehension. Additionally, the proposed method exhibits the highest SD value, indicating enhanced contrast in the fused image. Overall, the proposed method outperforms the standard fusion methods both qualitatively and quantitatively, providing fused images with superior human perception quality. These results underscore the practical utility of the proposed model in the realms of image fusion for object detection which can be extended for medical image fusion or designing self driving cars.

References

1. Bavirisetti, D.P., Dhuli, R.: Fusion of infrared and visible sensor images based on anisotropic diffusion and karhunen-loeve transform. IEEE Sens. J. **16**(1), 203–209 (2015)
2. Chen, C.Y., Lin, T.M., Wolf, W.H.: A visible/infrared fusion algorithm for distributed smart cameras. IEEE J. Sel. Top. Sig. Process. **2**(4), 514–525 (2008)
3. Chen, H., Varshney, P.K.: A human perception inspired quality metric for image fusion based on regional information. Inf. Fusion **8**(2), 193–207 (2007)
4. Hou, R., et al.: Vif-net: an unsupervised framework for infrared and visible image fusion. IEEE Trans. Comput. Imaging **6**, 640–651 (2020)
5. Li, G., Lai, W., Qu, X.: Pedestrian detection based on light perception fusion of visible and thermal images. Opt. Laser Technol. **156**, 108466 (2022)
6. Li, H., Wu, X.J.: Densefuse: a fusion approach to infrared and visible images. IEEE Trans. Image Process. **28**(5), 2614–2623 (2018)
7. Li, H., Wu, X.J., Kittler, J.: Infrared and visible image fusion using a deep learning framework. In: 2018 24th International Conference on Pattern Recognition (ICPR), pp. 2705–2710. IEEE (2018)
8. Ma, J., Chen, C., Li, C., Huang, J.: Infrared and visible image fusion via gradient transfer and total variation minimization. Inf. Fusion **31**, 100–109 (2016)
9. Ma, J., Yu, W., Liang, P., Li, C., Jiang, J.: Fusiongan: a generative adversarial network for infrared and visible image fusion. Inf. Fusion **48**, 11–26 (2019)
10. Ma, W., et al.: A novel adaptive hybrid fusion network for multiresolution remote sensing images classification. IEEE Trans. Geosci. Remote Sens. **60**, 1–17 (2021)
11. Marcello, J., Medina, A., Eugenio, F.: Evaluation of spatial and spectral effectiveness of pixel-level fusion techniques. IEEE Geosci. Remote Sens. Lett. **10**(3), 432–436 (2012)
12. Mei, Y., Fan, Y., Zhou, Y.: Image super-resolution with non-local sparse attention. In: Proceedings of the IEEE/CVF Conference on Computer Vision and Pattern Recognition, pp. 3517–3526 (2021)
13. Mittal, A., Soundararajan, R., Bovik, A.C.: Making a "completely blind" image quality analyzer. IEEE Sig. Process. Lett. **20**(3), 209–212 (2012)

14. Narmadha, M., Arthi, L., Narmatha, T.: Detection of human brain tumor by medical image processing and pca based image fusion. In: 2022 IEEE 2nd International Conference on Mobile Networks and Wireless Communications (ICMNWC), pp. 1–5. IEEE (2022)
15. Niu, Z., Zhong, G., Yu, H.: A review on the attention mechanism of deep learning. Neurocomputing **452**, 48–62 (2021)
16. Parmar, K., Kher, R.K., Thakkar, F.N.: Analysis of ct and mri image fusion using wavelet transform. In: 2012 International Conference on Communication Systems and Network Technologies, pp. 124–127. IEEE (2012)
17. Ram Prabhakar, K., Sai Srikar, V., Venkatesh Babu, R.: Deepfuse: a deep unsupervised approach for exposure fusion with extreme exposure image pairs. In: Proceedings of the IEEE International Conference on Computer Vision, pp. 4714–4722 (2017)
18. Shaik, N.S., Cherukuri, T.K.: Multi-level attention network: application to brain tumor classification. SIViP **16**(3), 817–824 (2022)
19. Shen, Z., Wang, J., Pan, Z., Li, Y., Wang, J.: Cross attention-guided dense network for images fusion. arXiv preprint arXiv:2109.11393 (2021)
20. Shreyamsha Kumar, B.: Image fusion based on pixel significance using cross bilateral filter. SIViP **9**(5), 1193–1204 (2015)
21. Toet, A.: The TNO multiband image data collection. Data Brief **15**, 249–251 (2017)
22. Wang, M., He, W., Zhang, H.: A spatial-spectral transformer network with total variation loss for hyperspectral image denoising. IEEE Geosci. Remote Sens. Lett. **20**, 1–5 (2023)
23. Woo, S., Park, J., Lee, J.Y., Kweon, I.S.: Cbam: convolutional block attention module. In: Proceedings of the European conference on computer vision (ECCV), pp. 3–19 (2018)
24. Xu, H., Ma, J., Jiang, J., Guo, X., Ling, H.: U2fusion: a unified unsupervised image fusion network. IEEE Trans. Pattern Anal. Mach. Intell. **44**(1), 502–518 (2020)
25. Xu, H., Zhang, H., Ma, J.: Classification saliency-based rule for visible and infrared image fusion. IEEE Trans. Comput. Imaging **7**, 824–836 (2021)
26. Xue, S., Liu, Y., Xu, C., Li, J.: Object detection in visible and infrared missile borne fusion image. In: 2022 International Conference on Image Processing, Computer Vision and Machine Learning (ICICML), pp. 19–23. IEEE (2022)
27. Yang, Y., Kong, X., Huang, S., Wan, W., Song, Z., Zhang, W.: Multi-sensor fusion of infrared and visible images based on modified side window filter and intensity transformation. IEEE Sens. J. **21**(21), 24829–24843 (2021)
28. Zhang, X., Ye, P., Xiao, G.: Vifb: a visible and infrared image fusion benchmark. In: Proceedings of the IEEE/CVF Conference on Computer Vision and Pattern Recognition Workshops, pp. 104–105 (2020)
29. Zhao, Z., Liu, Q., Wang, S.: Learning deep global multi-scale and local attention features for facial expression recognition in the wild. IEEE Trans. Image Process. **30**, 6544–6556 (2021)
30. Zhou, J., Ren, K., Wan, M., Cheng, B., Gu, G., Chen, Q.: An infrared and visible image fusion method based on VGG-19 network. Optik **248**, 168084 (2021)

Lightweight Learning Model for Speckle Denoising in Digital Holography

Vaishnavi Ravi(ORCID), Krishna Sumanth Vengala(ORCID), Rama Krishna Gorthi$^{(\boxtimes)}$(ORCID),
and Subrahmanyam Gorthi(ORCID)

Indian Institute of Technology, Tirupati, Andhra Pradesh, India
rkg@iittp.ac.in

Abstract. Digital holographic interference (DHI) is a well-known technique in optical metrology for recording and reconstructing 3D deformations. However, the interference patterns captured by DHI are usually affected by speckle noise, which can degrade the quality of the reconstructed deformations. In this work, we propose a lightweight, densely connected deep neural network(DNN) model that can effectively remove speckle noise from DHI images. To aid the DNN model to effectively learn the denoising task, we propose a structural similarity-based loss in addition to the popular L_2 loss. The outcomes of our experiments demonstrate that the proposed model outperforms three well-known conventional methods and existing deep learning methods. In addition, the quantitative results and the analysis plots show 58% and 121% higher PSNR and SSIM scores over the state-of-the-art conventional denoising method. Towards the end, the denoising results presented on a real sample depicts that the proposed model is able to generalize well to real DHI images even with synthetic sample training.

Keywords: Speckle Denoising · Digital Holography · Lightweight deep neural networks · depthwise separable convolutions

1 Introduction

Digital Holographic interference (DHI) is a popular optical imaging technique that can be used to record and reconstruct the three-dimensional deformation of an object. It has a wide range of applications, including industrial inspection, optical metrology, medical imaging, security, art, etc. [1]

DHI employs a coherent laser as a source to project an input reference beam and has a digital camera that captures the interference pattern between the reference beam and an object beam scattered by the object of interest. However, this interference pattern is significantly degraded by various random noises, including salt-and-pepper, gaussian and speckle noise. These noises can potentially corrupt the information in the signal captured, making it difficult to extract useful information from the image. In DHI, the interference pattern is predominantly corrupted by the speckle noise which is caused by coherence nature of

---

V. Ravi and K. S. Vengala—These authors contributed equally to this work.

H. Kaur et al. (Eds.): CVIP 2023, CCIS 2011, pp. 249–260, 2024.
https://doi.org/10.1007/978-3-031-58535-7_21

the laser light. Hence, speckle denoising becomes an important step for retaining image quality and estimating accurate absolute phase in DHI.

Several works have been proposed in the direction of speckle denoising in the literature [2,3]. Early methods for speckle noise reduction in digital holography relied on reducing the coherence of the light source or averaging multiple holograms with varying optical conditions [4–6]. However, these approaches involved rigorous and time-consuming experiments.

1.1 Motivation and Contribution

Nowadays, deep learning (DL) based models have demonstrated state-of-the-art performance over existing conventional algorithms in various low-vision tasks like such as image enhancement, restoration, object detection, and 3D reconstruction. The main motivation of this work is to employ learning-based techniques to address the speckle denoising problem in DHI as shown in Fig. 1 below.

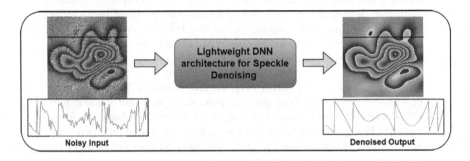

Fig. 1. Flow diagram of the proposed approach for removal of speckle noise

The main contributions of this work are:

- A Lightweight, densely connected Encoder-Decoder DNN model is proposed to address speckle denoising in DHI.
- A rich synthetic dataset of noisy and clean image pairs is created using smooth Gaussian Mixture Models (GMMs).
- Proposed lightweight DNN model's performance is compared with well-known denoising algorithms like median filtering (MedFilt) [7], Windowed Fourier Transform (WFT2D), Block matching algorithm (BM3D) [8] and also UNet [9] using the metrics Peak-Signal to Noise Ratio (PSNR) and Structural Similarity Index (SSIM).
- Results on a real DHI sample is presented which shows generalization ability of proposed method.

The remainder of the paper is structured as follows. Sect. 2 reviews the existing literature on speckle denoising. Sect. 3 describes the problem formulation, speckle data generation procedure and proposed lightweight DNN architecture and loss functions. Sect. 4 presents experiments and results. Following this, the conclusions are presented in Sect. 5.

2 Related Literature

Speckle denoising has been a very active area of research as it is very predominant in various techniques [10] [11] where coherence phenomenon occurs. In this section, we discuss various well-known works which attempted in this direction.

Speckle denoising algorithms in the literature can be broadly categorized into spatial filtering, transform domain filtering, and deep learning (DL)-based methods.

Spatial filtering methods typically apply conventional filters, such as median, Gaussian, [7] and adaptive filters [12], to the sine and cosine of the phase to preserve phase jumps. [13] employed a novel framework that combines multiple holograms and performed block grouping and collaborative filtering. In [14], the authors combined a multi-look approach with 3D block-matching numerical filtering to denoise the long-infrared hologram.

Montresor et al. discussed a detailed quantitative comparison of various algorithms for phase data de-noising in [15].

Among transform domain methods, the 2D windowed Fourier transform (WFT2D) method [8] is a specially designed denoising algorithm for phase filtering of speckle and holographic data. Other well-known transform domain methods employed Discrete Fourier Transform [2] and wavelet transform [3] for speckle denoising in DHI. Gabov et al. introduced BM3D [16], which is recognized as the state-of-the-art image denoising algorithm that works by grouping similar image patches and then jointly filtering them in the transform domain. BM3D is a complex algorithm with many parameters, but it has been shown to be very effective in removing noise from images.

In recent years, deep learning has demonstrated its potential for low-level vision tasks such as image denoising. [17], super-resolution, image segmentation etc. Following this trend, DL methods have been actively employed for speckle denoising in various modalities like Optical Diffraction Tomography, Ultrasound imaging, Optical Coherence Tomography and also DHI [10]. Jeon et al. [11] proposed UNet inspired DNN model to address speckle noising for holographic images. This model has 31M parameters and was trained on 800 synthetic data generated by following Rayleigh and Gaussian distribution. Following this, a DNN-based method(DnCNN) [1] is proposed o denoise interferograms obtained by digital holographic speckle pattern interferometry (DHSPI) which are essential for structural diagnosis of artworks. Recently, a deep learning-based algorithm has been proposed using a conditional generative adversarial network (cGAN). [10] for speckle denoising in DHI. However, cGANs are bulky models which are computationally expensive to train, and GANs, in general, are bulky and unstable as convergence is a problem. Hence, in this work, we proposed to develop a lightweight, densely connected DNN model for the task of speckle denoising in DHI.

3   Methodology

In this section, we elaborate on the principle of DHI and explain how we formulate the denoising task followed by the speckle dataset generation procedure. We then introduce the architecture of the lightweight DL model, and towards the end, we present the details of the loss functions employed to train the proposed lightweight model.

3.1   Principle of DHI

In DHI, a laser beam from the source is split into two beams: an object beam $O(x, y)$ and a reference beam $R(x, y)$. The object beam is scattered by the object to be imaged, and the reference beam is used to create an interference pattern. This interference pattern $I(x, y)$ is recorded by a digital camera and can be given by the equation below:

$$
\begin{aligned}
I(x, y) &= |R(x, y) + O(x, y)|^2 \\
&= |R(x, y)|^2 + |O(x, y)|^2 + (R(x, y)^* O(x, y) + R(x, y)O(x, y)^*)
\end{aligned}
\tag{1}
$$

The first two terms of the above equation represent the low-frequency amplitude, and the final term, which has the useful phase, is at high frequency. This high-frequency phase information can be extracted by applying Fourier transform as in Eq. 2 and performing frequency domain filtering. Following this, the inverse Fourier transform is computed on the remaining term $[G(m, n)]$ to retrieve the high-frequency component in the spatial domain i.e., $F^{-1}[G(m, n)]$.

$$
F[I(x, y)] = G_o(m, n) + G(m + \epsilon, n + \eta) + G^*(-m - \epsilon. - n - \eta)
\tag{2}
$$

where ϵ and η are the coefficients related to the projection angle of the reference wave and wavelength of the beam used in the DHI system. Finally, the phase of the object is obtained by applying the arctan function as given below.

$$
\phi(x, y) = tan^{-1} \left(\frac{Im(F^{-1}[G(m, n)])}{Re(F^{-1}[G(m, n)]} \right)
\tag{3}
$$

This principle is performed at multiple instances of time t_1 and t_2 where the interference patterns obtained are $I_1(x, y)$ and $I_2(x, y)$. From these interference patterns, phases ϕ_1 and ϕ_2 are extracted. If these t_1 and t_2 are the instances before and after object deformation, the phase difference $\Delta\phi(x, y)$ is related to the deformation of the opaque object surface given by:

$$
\Delta\phi(x, y) = \phi_1 - \phi_2
\tag{4}
$$

This phase difference $\Delta\phi$ is generally wrapped in the range of $[-\phi, \phi]$ due to the arctan function and is heavily corrupted by speckle noise, causing hindrance to extract the absolute phase.

3.2   Problem Formulation

The phase difference $\Delta\phi$ obtained in eq. 4 can be expressed as an exponential function and is decomposed as real cosine and imaginary sine parts by using the Euler formula as given in the eq. 5. These noisy real and imaginary parts have to be denoised to estimate the 3D deformation precisely.

$$exp[j\Delta\phi(x,y)] = cos[\Delta\phi(x,y)] + jsin[\Delta\phi(x,y)] \tag{5}$$

In this paper, we propose a learning-based approach to address the speckle denoising problem. We pose the denoising as a regression task and build a lightweight, densely connected DNN model. This DNN model is designed to take the real part and imaginary part of a noisy interference pattern and predict the denoised ones. Later, these denoised real and imaginary outputs are employed to retrieve the denoised wrapped phase with the help of Eq. 3. Once denoised wrapped phase is obtained, phase unwrapping and 3D deformation estimation can be done accurately.

3.3   Speckle Dataset Generation

It is well-known that DNN models are highly data-driven. As collecting real training samples time-consuming and expensive, we created synthetic samples to train the DNN model.

To mimic the absolute phase difference $\Delta\phi$ of the interference fringes given in Eq. 4, we generated Gaussian mixture models (GMMs), which are arithmetic combinations of different Gaussians with varying means and variances. Later, we computed $exp[j\Delta(x,y)]$ as in Eq. 5, then introduced speckle noise phenomenon by using MATLAB's *imnoise*, which performs the following operation.

$$S_n(x,y) = exp[j\Delta\phi(x,y)] + \eta(x,y)(exp[j\Delta\phi(x,y)]) \tag{6}$$

where $\eta(x,y)$ is the *speckle variance*. The real part and imaginary part of the wrapped phase are extracted from $S_n(x,y)$ as per Eq. 5, which serves as the input for the DNN model.

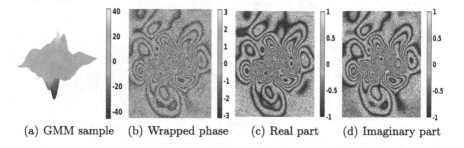

(a) GMM sample   (b) Wrapped phase   (c) Real part   (d) Imaginary part

Fig. 2. Synthetic sample generation.

We have created a dataset of 5000 samples using GMMs which has a dynamic range of [–150,150]. To bring generalization to the dataset, $\eta(x,y)$ is randomly chosen over the range (0,1]. One such absolute phase map is presented in Fig. 2(a), and the wrapped phase corresponding to them is in Fig. 2(b). The real part and imaginary part of noisy $S_n(x,y)$ are given in Fig. 2(c) and Fig. 2(d).

3.4   Proposed Lightweight Architecture

In this subsection, the architecture details of the proposed lightweight DNN model developed for speckle denoising task in DHI is explained. As it is a regression problem, we have considered the well-known encoder-decoder UNet++ [18] as the base model. Our aim is to build a lightweight model that can work better even in memory-constrained conditions and has limited inference time. Hence, we developed the lightweight version of the base model by employing depthwise separable convolutions in place of traditional ones.

Depthwise Separable Convolutions: This type of convolution can reduce the computational complexity of convolutional neural networks (CNNs). They work by decomposing a traditional convolution into two stages:

- A depthwise convolution, in which a single filter is applied to each input channel.
- A pointwise convolution, which fuses the depthwise convolutions' outputs.

The depthwise convolution allows the input channel to be processed independently and significantly reduces the number of parameters, whereas pointwise convolution fuses the depthwise convolutions's outputs and allows network to learn global features.

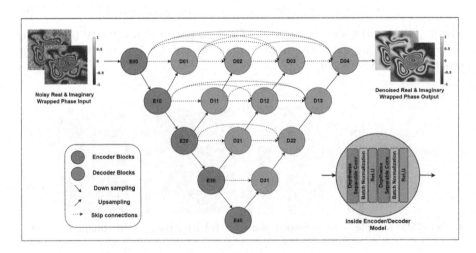

Fig. 3. Architecture diagram of the proposed approach.

The complete architecture is given in Fig. 3. There are a total of 15 convolution blocks in which 5 blocks constitute the encoder (Red circles), and the remaining is in the decoder block (Green circles). All these blocks are densely connected with each other, which enables better feature extraction. The operations performed inside each block are shown in the bottom-right of Fig. 3. Here, the traditional convolution block is replaced by depthwise separable convolution accompanied by batch norm and rectified linear activation unit (ReLU). This special type of convolution can increase the matrix operation efficiency by reducing the number of parameters per convolution, helping in reducing the overall model size by almost 80% and also in preventing overfitting. Hence, it is possible to achieve improved performance even with a significant reduction in the parameters.

Similar to UNet++, the proposed model has an encoder block in which the noisy real part and imaginary part of $S_n(x, y)$ are progressively downsampled by reducing its spatial resolution and also a decoder block where the upsampling layers gradually restore the spatial resolution of the feature maps. This downsampling, followed by upsampling, helps the network to learn features at multiple scales. Also, there are dense skip connections between the layers, which concatenate the features extracted from multiple UNet sub-networks on top of each other, with each sub-network capturing features at a different scale. Finally, the denoised real and imaginary parts of $S_n(x, y)$ obtained from the network are used to compute the denoised wrapped phase by using the equation given in Eq. 3.

3.5   Loss Function

In image denoising, two important factors to consider are the quality of the denoised image and its similarity to the ground truth clean image. To address both of these factors, we propose to use SSIM as a loss function in this work, along with regular L_2 loss function.

$$L_{mse} = MSE(x, y) = \frac{1}{mn} \sum_{i=1}^{m} \sum_{j=1}^{n} [x(i, j) - y(i, j)]^2 \qquad (7)$$

where x is the predicted image and y is the ground truth and m, n are the input image dimensions.

$$SSIM(x, y) = \frac{(2\mu_x \mu_y + c_1)(2\sigma_{xy} + c_2)}{(\mu_x^2 + \mu_y^2 + c_1)(\sigma_x^2 + \sigma_y^2 + c_2)} \qquad (8)$$

where μ_x, μ_y are the means and σ_x, σ_y, σ_{xy} are the variances of the input and output image. The variables c_1, c_2 are small values to stabilize the division with a weak denominator.

$$L_{ssim} = 1 - SSIM(x, y) \qquad (9)$$

Hence, the combined loss function $L_{combined}$ can be written as

$$L_{combined} = L_{mse} + L_{ssim} \tag{10}$$

4   Results

In this section, we presented the implementation details, followed by qualitative and quantitative results of the proposed denoising method. We compared our results with well-known conventional methods like median filtering(MedFilt), Windowed Fourier Transform (WFT2D) [8], BM3D [16] and DL method using UNet [10]. In addition, we investigated the performance of all the methods for varying values of η in terms of PSNR, SSIM, and, finally, an ablation study that validated the importance of combined loss function employed in this work. Towards the end, we showed the improved denoising results of the proposed and all other comparison methods on a real noisy wrapped phase captured using the DHI experimental set-up.

It is noteworthy that all the results presented in this section are the wrapped phases obtained using Eq. 3 over denoised real and imaginary parts of the interference pattern.

4.1   Experimental Analysis and Results on Synthetic Test Samples

The entire speckle noise dataset of 5000 samples is split into training, validation, and testing in the ratio 8:1:1. This dataset is used to train the proposed lightweight model for 60 epochs with an initial learning rate of 1×10^{-4} and Adam optimizer on two NVIDIA RTX 6000 GPUs.

Figure 4 shows the qualitative results on a noisy which has a synthetic test sample $\eta = 0.6$. The noisy sample is shown in Fig. 4(a) and the denoised wrapped phase maps of MedFilt, WFT2D, BM3D, UNet, and the proposed method, are shown in Fig. 4(c)-4(g) respectively. It is important to note that the UNet model compared in this work is trained with the same set of model parameters and loss function given in [10]for a fair comparison. It can be observed that the DL methods perform much better when compared to the conventional methods. Also, the results of both UNet and the proposed method look similar even though there is 97% reduction in the number of parameters.

Table 1. Quantitative metrics for performance comparison of denoising algorithms

Metrics	Comparison Methods					
	Noisy	MedFilt	WFT2D	BM3D	UNet	Proposed
PSNR(dB)	10.7	13.1	13.8	15.5	22.84	**24.58**
RMSE	3.3	1.95	1.64	1.11	0.21	**0.16**
SSIM	0.09	0.22	0.34	0.42	0.91	**0.93**
Inference Time	-	0.6 ± 0.1 s	22 ± 1 s	8 ± 1 s	0.25×10^{-3} s	**0.13×10^{-3} s**
Parameters	-	-	-	-	~32M	**~1M**

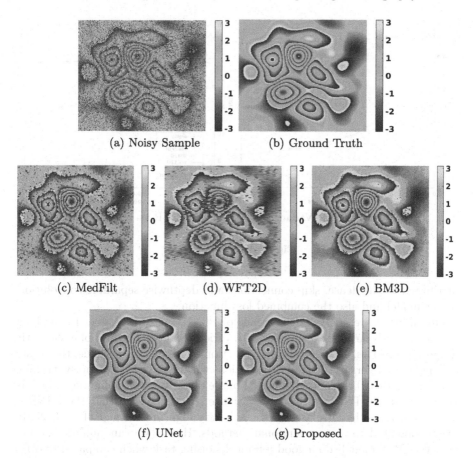

Fig. 4. Comparison results on a noisy sample with $\eta = 0.6$ by denoising methods

In order to quantify the performance of the proposed method better, we compared the results of all the methods in terms of PSNR, Root Mean Square Error (RMSE), and SSIM values and also presented the inference time and model complexity as given in Table 1.

Here, we observed that the PSNR value of the noisy sample is only 10.7 dB. The state-of-the-art conventional algorithm, BM3D could only improve the PSNR by a maximum of 5dB. However, UNet and the proposed method achieved 47% and 58% improved performance over BM3D itself. Interestingly, improved PSNR (in %) for the proposed method over UNet is 7.6% whereas cGAN given in [10] achieved only 4.7% improvement even with 97% more parameters. The same trend can be observed in SSIM also, with a 54% increase when compared to BM3D. This validates the superior performance of learning-based methods when compared to conventional ones. Moreover, the improved performance of the proposed method over UNet, even with 97% lesser learnable parameters, can be

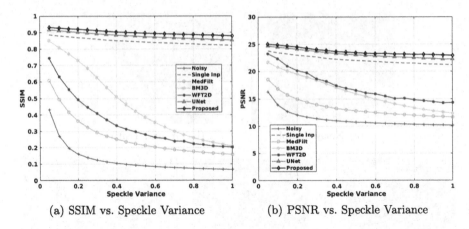

(a) SSIM vs. Speckle Variance   (b) PSNR vs. Speckle Variance

Fig. 5. Analysis plots.

attributed to the dense, skip connections and depthwise separable convolutions in our model and also the combined loss function.

In addition, we analyzed the trends of PSNR and SSIM values by applying all the methods on 100 test samples with varied η values. The first plot shows the graph for SSIM vs. speckle variance (η). Along with all the methods, the results of 'single inp' refers to the model predictions when it is trained on noisy wrapped phase to predict the denoised wrapped phase directly. In the same way, Fig. 5(b) shows trends for PSNR vs. speckle variance. It can be seen that the PSNR of samples denoised by DL-based methods is very high(in the range of 23dB-25dB) when compared to the conventional methods. Hence, we can validate the fact that the DNN models do a good job for denoising task when compared to other methods.

Table 2. Ablation Study

Metrics	L_{mse}	L_{ssim}	$L_{combined}$
SSIM	0.91	0.90	0.92
PSNR	23.921	23.718	24.141

For this final experiment, the proposed model is trained with L_{mse}, L_{ssim} and also $L_{combined}$ individually. The PSNR and SSIM values given in Table 2 validate that the combined loss function helps the proposed model to converge better when compared to individual ones.

4.2   Results on Real DHI Sample

In the actual experiment, a 632.8 nm He-Ne laser serves as the light source, while an aluminum foil is firmly clamped on all sides and subjected to rear-point loading via a screw thread. The digital holograms, corresponding to the states before and after the deformation, were recorded using a CCD camera. The procedure explained in Sect. 2.1 is performed to obtain the real and imaginary parts of $S_n(x,y)$ and are given as input to the denoising algorithm. The final denoised wrapped phase results are shown in Fig. 6 which demonstrate that the proposed model can generalize well to real data, even with synthetic sample training.

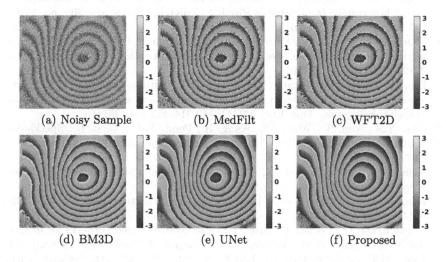

(a) Noisy Sample   (b) MedFilt   (c) WFT2D

(d) BM3D   (e) UNet   (f) Proposed

Fig. 6. Comparison results on a real noisy sample with various Denoising methods

5   Conclusion and Future Work

In this work, we proposed a lightweight, densely connected DL model to address speckle denoising in DHI. The proposed model is trained on the real and imaginary parts of synthetic noisy, clean interference pattern pairs to learn the denoising task. The qualitative and quantitative results show that the proposed model outperforms existing methods by a significant margin, with a 58% and 121% improvement in PSNR and SSIM, respectively over conventional BM3D method. Furthermore, the real results presented in this work demonstrate that the proposed model can generalize well to real data, even with synthetic sample training. In addition, the proposed method has a limited number of parameters which makes it suitable for implementation on memory constrained platforms. In our future work, we plan to implement the proposed model on an embedded platform to enable real-time measurements.

References

1. Yan, K., Chang, L., Andrianakis, M., Tornari, V., Yu, Y.: Deep learning-based wrapped phase denoising method for application in digital holographic speckle pattern interferometry. Appl. Sci. **10**(11), 4044 (2020)
2. Maycock, J., Hennelly, B.M., McDonald, J.B., Frauel, Y., Castro, A., Javidi, B., Naughton, T.J.: Reduction of speckle in digital holography by discrete fourier filtering. JOSA A **24**(6), 1617–1622 (2007)
3. Monaghan, D., Kelly, D., Hennelly, B., Javidi, B.: Speckle reduction techniques in digital holography. In: Journal of Physics: Conference Series, vol. 206, no. 1. IOP Publishing, p. 012026 (2010)
4. Memmolo, P., Bianco, V., Paturzo, M., Javidi, B., Netti, P.A., Ferraro, P.: Encoding multiple holograms for speckle-noise reduction in optical display. Opt. Express **22**(21), 25 768–25 775 (2014)
5. Leo, M., Piccolo, R., Distante, C., Memmolo, P., Paturzo, M., Ferraro, P.: Multilevel bidimensional empirical mode decomposition: a new speckle reduction method in digital holography. Opt. Eng. **53**(11), 112 314–112 314 (2014)
6. Kim, Y.S., Kim, T., Woo, S.S., Kang, H., Poon, T.-C., Zhou, C.: Speckle-free digital holographic recording of a diffusely reflecting object. Opt. Express **21**(7), 8183–8189 (2013)
7. Kemao, Q., Soon, S.H., Asundi, A.: Smoothing filters in phase-shifting interferometry. Opt. Laser Technol. **35**(8), 649–654 (2003)
8. Kemao, Q.: Windowed fourier transform for fringe pattern analysis. Appl. Opt. **43**(13), 2695–2702 (2004)
9. Ronneberger, O., Fischer, P., Brox, T.: U-net: convolutional networks for biomedical image segmentation. In: Navab, N., Hornegger, J., Wells, W.M., Frangi, A.F. (eds.) MICCAI 2015, Part III. LNCS, vol. 9351, pp. 234–241. Springer, Cham (2015). https://doi.org/10.1007/978-3-319-24574-4_28
10. Fang, Q., et al.: Speckle denoising based on deep learning via a conditional generative adversarial network in digital holographic interferometry. Opt. Express **30**(12), 20 666–20 683 (2022)
11. Jeon, W., Jeong, W., Son, K., Yang, H.: Speckle noise reduction for digital holographic images using multi-scale convolutional neural networks. Opt. Lett. **43**(17), 4240–4243 (2018)
12. Aebischer, H.A., Waldner, S.: A simple and effective method for filtering speckleinterferometric phase fringe patterns. Opt. Commun. **162**(4–6), 205–210 (1999)
13. Bianco, V., Memmolo, P., Paturzo, M., Finizio, A., Javidi, B., Ferraro, P.: Quasi noise-free digital holography. Light: Sci. Appl. **5**(9), e16 142–e16 142 (2016)
14. Bianco, V., Memmolo, P., Paturzo, M., Ferraro, P.: On-speckle suppression in IR digital holography. Opt. Lett. **41**(22), 5226–5229 (2016)
15. Montresor, S., Picart, P.: Quantitative appraisal for noise reduction in digital holographic phase imaging. Opt. Express **24**(13), 14 322–14 343 (2016)
16. Dabov, K., Foi, A., Katkovnik, V., Egiazarian, K.: Image denoising with blockmatching and 3d filtering, In: Image Processing: Algorithms and Systems, Neural Networks, and Machine Learning, vol. 6064. pp. 354–365. SPIE (2006)
17. Yan, K., Yu, Y., Huang, C., Sui, L., Qian, K., Asundi, A.: Fringe pattern denoising based on deep learning. Optics Commun. **437**, 148–152 (2019)
18. Zhou, Z., Siddiquee, M.M.R., Tajbakhsh, N., Liang, J.: Unet++: redesigning skip connections to exploit multiscale features in image segmentation. IEEE Trans. Med. Imaging **39**(6), 1856–1867 (2019)

Comparative Analysis of Stress Prediction Using Unsupervised Machine Learning Algorithms

Istuti Maurya[1], Anjali Sarvaiya[2], Kishor Upla[2(✉)],
and Raghavendra Ramachandra[3]

[1] Pandit Deendayal Energy University (PDEU), Gandhinagar, India
`istuti.mce21@sot.pdpu.ac.in`
[2] Sardar Vallabhbhai National Institute of Technology (SVNIT), Surat, India
`kishorupla@gmail.com`
[3] Norwegian University of Science and Technology (NTNU), Gjøvik, Norway
`raghavendra.ramachandra@ntnu.no`

Abstract. Stress has become prevalent in today's fast-paced lives, leading to numerous physical and mental health issues. Thus, its detection and intervention at the preliminary stage are crucial to protect a person from its adverse effects. Additionally, labelling of physiological signals collected during an experiment for supervised training is unfeasible owing to the high false-alarm rate. Hence, to mitigate the limitations of supervised methods that rely on labelled datasets and predefined stress thresholds, this study addresses the detection of stress by employing unsupervised machine learning (ML) approaches using heart rate data of patients. It allows for the automatic detection and characterization of stress patterns without prior knowledge or labelled data. Different ML algorithms, including K-mean clustering, spectral clustering, agglomerative clustering, and Density-Based Spatial Clustering of Applications with Noise (DBSCAN), were employed to extract meaningful patterns by performing experiments on the stress and well-being in the Early Life Knowledge Work (SWELL-KW) dataset. The analysis and results of this comparative study demonstrate the potential of unsupervised learning for the development of noninvasive, continuous, and robust methods for the detection and monitoring of stress using heart data.

Keywords: Stress Detection · Unsupervised Approach · Machine Learning · SWELL-KW dataset

1 Introduction

In recent years, there has been a noticeable rise in the prevalence of depression, anxiety, stress, and other stress-related diseases globally. Stress deteriorates a person's physical and mental health. The World Health Organization (WHO) defines stress as "a state of worry or mental tension caused by a difficult situation". In particular, chronic stress has been linked to adverse effects, such as compromised immune function, substance dependence, diabetes, cancer, stroke, and

H. Kaur et al. (Eds.): CVIP 2023, CCIS 2011, pp. 261–271, 2024.
https://doi.org/10.1007/978-3-031-58535-7_22

262   I. Maurya et al.

cardiovascular disorders. Hence, it is imperative to prioritize the advancement of robust techniques that are capable of continuous, real-time stress detection and monitoring. However, stress detection is complex, as it has physiological as well as psychological aspects. Furthermore, they are triggered by multiple factors and are difficult to capture. Remarkably, recent developments in wearable sensor technology have made it easier to collect different physiological parameters of stress in daily life. The physiological parameters frequently used for stress analysis are respiratory rate, heart rate, skin conductance, skin temperature, and galvanic skin response. Traditionally, stress assessment was performed by self-reporting, which is subjective and prone to bias, hindering their reliability and effectiveness. Consequently, there is a growing need to explore objective and real-time approaches for stress detection.

Recently, Machine Learning (ML) techniques have shown promise in various domains, including healthcare and behavioral analysis, by leveraging large datasets to uncover hidden patterns and make accurate predictions. Supervised ML algorithms have been widely employed in the field of stress detection by utilizing labelled training data to classify stress levels. However, the reliance on labelled data poses limitations, as acquiring such data in real-world settings can be time consuming, costly, and impractical. Several studies have reported the challenges of labelling the stress state and the importance of addressing these issues for further development of sensor-based stress monitoring systems [1,6]. The challenges of poor-quality reference data and human bias have encouraged the exploration of unsupervised ML techniques for stress detection and monitoring. Unsupervised learning offers a novel and powerful avenue for stress detection because it does not require labelled data for training. It identifies inherent patterns and relationships within the data, enabling the detection and characterization of stress without prior knowledge of the labelled instances. The primary objective of this study was to investigate the effectiveness of unsupervised ML algorithms in detecting and quantifying stress levels based on physiological signals and other relevant features. By leveraging these signals and employing unsupervised learning techniques, this study aimed to develop a robust and automated stress detection system. The main contributions of this study are as follows.

- The unsupervised methodology encompasses a range of feature selection techniques aimed at identifying and selecting relevant features from the dataset. By carefully selecting the most relevant features, this method enhances the accuracy and effectiveness of the unsupervised learning process, leading to improved stress detection and characterization.
- The study involves a comparative analysis of different unsupervised ML algorithms using the SWELL-KW dataset for stress detection. The experimental results demonstrate the superiority of the DBSCAN algorithm and suggest its potential for practical applications in real-life scenarios, facilitating timely interventions, and personalized stress management strategies.

The remainder of this paper is organized as follows. Section 2 describes the existing studies on stress detection. A block schematic representation of the proposed method is presented in Sect. 3. Section 4 reports the different unsupervised algorithms used for this comparative study. Finally, in Sect. 5, the experimental justification related to different unsupervised ML techniques is tabulated, along with details related to the dataset. Finally, conclusion of the study is drafted in Sect. 6.

2 Related Works

Numerous supervised ML algorithms have been utilized for the detection and classification of stress. These techniques include logistic regression, Gaussian Naive Bayes, Decision Tree (DT), Random Forest, AdaBoost, K-Nearest Neighbor (K-NN). The idea of supervised training was initially explored by Albaladejo-González et al. [2], achieved 88.64% accuracy. Furthermore, Fiorini et al. [3] compared the performance of different supervised learning algorithms, such as a Support Vector Machine (SVM), DT, and KNN, and obtained an accuracy of 85%. Moreover, Ramos et al. [8] determined the stress outside laboratory settings with the help of Naïve Bayes and logistic regression algorithms. The main drawback associated with supervised training is the requirement for true labels, which are mostly impractical. Therefore, unsupervised training is a useful alternative at this stage. Rescio et al. [9] applied the k-means clustering algorithm for stress classification with the help of features such as Heart Rate (HR), Galvanic Skin Response (GSR), and electrooculogram (EOG) signals collected from 11 volunteers. Furthermore, Huysmans et al. [4] proposed a mental stress detection model based on a self-organizing map (SOM) that uses Skin Conductance (SC) and electrocardiogram (ECG) features. Maaoui et al. [6] classified stress based on three unsupervised algorithms: K-mean, Gaussian Mixture Model (GMM), and SOM. Kavita Pabreja et al. [7] have reported the stress of students in educational institutions of India and by taking 25 features, they have obtained R-squared value of 0.8042. Motivated by these studies, here, we report a comparative analysis of different unsupervised methods for stress detection on stress and well-being in the Early Life Knowledge Work (SWELL-KW) dataset.

3 Methodology

A block diagram of the unsupervised ML approach is presented in Fig. 1. First, the input heart rate samples were passed through the preprocessing block. This removes unnecessary null values and examines statistics, such as the mean and variance present in the input dataset. Following the removal of null values, statistical measures, such as mean and variance, were computed to gain insight into the distribution and variability of the heart rate data. These statistics help to understand the characteristics of heart rate data and may contribute to feature selection or normalization techniques. The input data consisted of categorical data. Categorical variables contain non-numerical values that cannot be processed directly by most algorithms. By converting categorical data into label data, each unique category is assigned a numerical label, enabling algorithms to

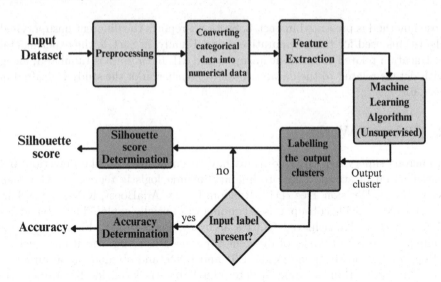

Fig. 1. The block diagram of the unsupervised machine learning approach.

effectively handle and analyze the data. The feature extraction block of the block diagram incorporates a variance threshold technique to select relevant features from the dataset. This block involves setting a threshold value for the variance of each feature and retaining only the features that surpass the threshold. Thus, it helps reduce dimensionality, enhance computational efficiency, and improve accuracy. Following the feature extraction stage, the extracted data are passed through several unsupervised ML techniques to generate outputs in a cluster form. Different unsupervised algorithms, such as k-means clustering, hierarchical clustering, and Density-Based Spatial Clustering of Applications with Noise (DBSCAN), group the data points based on their similarities and differences. The resulting output assigns each data point to a specific cluster, thereby enabling the identification of patterns and structures within the data. After the clustering process, the output clusters were labeled for further analysis. If the input data has corresponding labels available, the accuracy of the clustering results can be evaluated using supervised evaluation metrics and if corresponding labels are not available then Silhouette Score is normally calculated which indicates better clustering results, implying clear separation between clusters and well-assigned data points.

3.1   Feature Selection

Feature selection is an important technique for selecting only the features that are necessary for the model to analyze. Avoiding this increases the computational cost and delays the generation of output. Motivated by the literature, in this comparative analysis, we adopted a variance-based feature selection technique, which refers to the instability or variability of the feature selection methods.

This means that different runs or iterations of the feature selection process may lead to different subsets of selected features. The main factors contributing to the variance in feature selection are:

- Dependency on the training dataset: Feature selection methods rely on the information present in the training data. If the dataset is small or contains noisy or misleading features, different feature selection runs may result in different feature subsets.
- Sensitivity to feature ranking criteria: Many feature selection techniques rank features based on certain criteria, such as correlation with the target variable, mutual information, or statistical tests. Different ranking criteria can prioritize different features, leading to variability in the selected feature subsets.
- Interaction between features: Some feature selection methods consider interactions between features, such as recursive feature elimination. The presence of interactions can introduce variability into the selected feature subsets.
- Randomness in the algorithms: Some feature selection methods use randomization or sampling techniques during the selection process. This randomness can lead to different outcomes in each run of the algorithm, resulting in a variance in the selected feature subsets.

Following are some of the heart-related (i.e., Heart-Rate (HR)) features explained that we have selected after feature selection

- **HR statistical feature:** The HR measures the frequency of cardiac beats per minute. The heart rate from an ECG signal was determined by multiplying the time between RR intervals by one minute, the heart rate from an ECG signal is determined. The mean, median, and standard deviation are considered to be the first-order statistical aspects of physiological signals. Standard deviation is used to calculate the variance or dispersion of a signal.
- **HRV statistical features:** The temporal fluctuation between sequences of consecutive heartbeat intervals is known as the Heart Rate Variation (HRV). The interval between two consecutive R waves is known as RR or R-R spacing. The measuring units for RR intervals are milliseconds (ms) and Beats Per Minute (BPM).
- **HRV frequency domain features:** While frequency domain characteristics provide a spectral arrangement of the physiological information, time domain features are made possible by the magnitude of the autonomous heartbeat in temporal variations. The Power Spectral Density (PSD) of NN intervals typically serves as the basis for determining frequency-domain characteristics. Welch's approach [10] was used to perform non-parametric PSD analysis. This indicates that the amount of power is dispersed as a frequency function. Low-frequency (LF) and high-frequency (HF) bands were created from spectral components. The sums of the power spectra in the low (frequency range of 0.040.15 Hz) and high (0.150.40 Hz) bands show sympathetic and vagal fluctuations of cardiac activity. The LF/HF ratio is a useful metric for identifying the stress.

4 Unsupervised Machine Learning (ML) Algorithm

Unlike supervised learning, the unsupervised learning focuses on predicting outputs from unlabeled data without the need for explicit training. Thus, clustering is a key concept within unsupervised learning, wherein data points are grouped into clusters based on their similarities. In this research, several well-known unsupervised learning algorithms have been employed, including K-means clustering, Density-Based Spatial Clustering of Applications with Noise (DBSCAN), Spectral clustering, and Agglomerative clustering. Each of this algorithm employs a different approach to cluster formation and brings its own advantages and limitations to the analysis. The details associated to each of this are as follow:

- **K-Means Clustering:** K-means clustering aims to minimize sum of squares the within-cluster. It also known as inertia or distortion. It tries to create compact clusters where the data points within each cluster are similar to each other while being dissimilar to points in other clusters. One of the main considerations in using K-means clustering is determining the optimal value of K, the number of clusters. This can be determined using techniques such as the elbow method, silhouette analysis, or domain knowledge.
- **Spectral Clustering:** Spectral clustering is an unsupervised learning algorithm that groups data points based on their similarity. It constructs a similarity matrix, transforms it into a Laplacian matrix, and identifies the low-dimensional representation that separates clusters. It handles complex structures and non-convex clusters, making it useful for various applications. However, parameter tuning is crucial, and it captures both global and local structures in the data. Overall, spectral clustering is a powerful method for discovering patterns and clustering similar data points.
- **Agglomerative Clustering:** Agglomerative clustering is a hierarchical clustering algorithm. It starts with each data point as its own cluster and merges similar clusters iteratively until a desired number of clusters is obtained. It uses distance or similarity measures to determine cluster similarity and can handle various cluster shapes and sizes. The algorithm forms a dendrogram that helps to visualize the clustering hierarchy. However, it can be computationally expensive for large datasets, and it may be sensitive to outliers. Overall, agglomerative clustering is a flexible and effective method for grouping data into clusters.
- **Density-Based Spatial Clustering of Applications with Noise (DBSCAN):** It is a popular unsupervised machine learning algorithm used for clustering and discovering clusters of arbitrary shape in spatial data. It is particularly effective in handling datasets with irregular or non-linear structures and is robust to noise and outliers. Unlike traditional clustering algorithms like K-means, DBSCAN does not require the number of clusters to be specified in advance.

5   Experimental Analysis

This section describes the details related to dataset and results obtained using different unsupervised methods.

5.1   Dataset

The Stress and Wellbeing in Early Life Knowledge Work (SWELL-KW) is provided on the basis of the natural working conditions of 25 candidates [5]. Many sensors are used to record facial expressions from camera recordings, body postures from a Kinect 3D sensor and Heart Rate (HR) and skin conductance from body sensors. The data have been recorded with the following settings:

- No stress - Participates were given tasks with no time bound.
- Time pressure - Participates were given tasks with a deadline.
- Interruptions - Participants were given tasks with deadlines having email interruptions in between, some of the emails were related to the given task and some were just sent to compel them to reply.

During data collections, participants were required to fill out a feedback form between each condition and were given a brief break. Care was taken to ensure that none of the participants had pre-existing stress-related issues. The participants were not informed about the nature of the test beforehand, as the data collection aimed to capture responses under natural conditions. Specifically, heart-related features from the SWELL-KW dataset were utilized for analysis in this work, focusing solely on physiological measures associated with the participant's heart rates.

5.2   Training Details

The coding procedures, including null value removal, label encoding, and feature extraction, contribute to improving data quality, enhancing analysis, and selecting informative features for subsequent modeling and analysis. The Sklearn library was utilized for the implementation of various algorithms. The preprocessing stage of the dataset involved the removal of columns containing null values. Fortunately, actual output values are available, allowing for the comparison of derived outputs. The label encoder from Sklearn was employed to assign labels to the data, for evaluation and comparison are shown in Table 1. Feature extraction was performed using the Variance Threshold method from the Sklearn library. This technique facilitated the removal of features with low variance, resulting in a dataset with 25 columns after feature extraction, while 11 columns were removed. After preprocessing the data, various unsupervised algorithms from the Sklearn library were applied to the dataset. To optimize the results, the algorithm parameters were iteratively adjusted and fine-tuned to achieve higher accuracy. The parameter settings fine-tuned for different unsupervised algorithms are depicted in Table 2.

Table 1. Actual labels of classifications using label encoder.

Value of label y	Label defining which condition
0	Interruptions
1	No Stress
2	Time Pressure

Table 2. Parameter tuning for different unsupervised algorithms.

Algorithms	Parameter used
K-means clustering	N_clusters=3 init='k-means++'
Agglomerative Clustering	n_clusters=3
Spectral Clustering	n_clusters=3 affinity=nearest_neighbors n_neighbors=5 n_init=10 eigen_solver='lobpcg' assign_labels='kmeans'
DBSCAN	eps=1050 min_samples=2

In K-means clustering, we have used 3 parameter i.e., n_clusters, init and random_state. Here, n-clusters refers to The number of clusters (k). It is the predefined number of groups or clusters into which the data will be partitioned. Init is the initial centroid selection method, which determines how the initial cluster centroids are chosen. Common strategies include randomly selecting k data points as the initial centroids, using k-means++ to ensure diverse and well-distributed centroids, or providing a custom initialization. The random state parameter is used to specify the seed value for the random number generator. It controls the initialization of centroids and can affect the reproducibility of the clustering results. In both the algorithms Spectral Clustering and Agglomerative clustering n_clusters parameter specify the desired number of clusters to be generated by the algorithm. It determines the final number of clusters in the clustering solution. In Spectral clustering, affinity specifies the similarity measure or affinity matrix used to capture the pairwise similarities between data points. Common choices include "nearest_neighbors" for k-nearest neighbours, "rbf" for Gaussian kernel similarity, or "precomputed" if you provide your own affinity matrix. N_neighbors is defined as, if the affinity measure is set to "nearest_neighbors", this parameter determines the number of nearest neighbours to consider when constructing the affinity matrix. eigen_solver specifies the algorithm used to compute the eigenvectors and eigenvalues of the Laplacian matrix. Popular options include "arpack" for large sparse matrices, "lobpcg" for smaller problems, and "amg" for using Algebraic Multigrid. N_init represents the number of times the algorithm will be run with different initializations. The final clustering solution will be the best result achieved among all the runs. Further, DBSCAN algorithm was given 2 parameters - epsilon (eps) and min_samples rest of the parameters were default ones. Epsilon defines the radius within which neighbouring points are considered part of the same cluster. It determines the maximum distance between two points for them to be considered neighbours. The Min_samples specifies the minimum number of points that must be within the epsilon radius to form a dense region. Points with fewer than min_samples neighbours are considered outliers or noise.

5.3   Result Analysis

The comparison of different techniques are compared with accuracy and silhouette score which is tabulated in Table 3. The availability of actual output allowed for the comparison between the predicted output of the unsupervised algorithm and the ground truth, enabling the calculation of accuracy. On the other hand, the silhouette score, is derived using the present dataset (without true label) and the predicted clusters. It is a metric that ranges from 1 to -1, where a score closer to 1 indicates effective clustering with well-separated clusters. Thus, the accuracy metric provided insights into the agreement between the predicted and actual output, while the silhouette score offered a measure of the clustering effectiveness and the separation between clusters.

Accuracy: Accuracy is the most straightforward metric and measures the percentage of correct predictions made by the model. it is defined as,

$$Accuracy = \frac{true\ positive\ labels + true\ negative\ labels}{total\ readings} \qquad (1)$$

Silhouette Score: The silhouette score is a measure used to evaluate the quality of clustering results. It provides an indication of how well the data points within each cluster are separated from other clusters. The formula of silhouette score for a single data point is,

$$Silhouette\ Score = \frac{b(i) - a(i)}{max(a(i), b(i))}, \qquad (2)$$

where $s(i)$ represents the silhouette score for the data point i, $a(i)$ is the average distance between i and all other data points within the same cluster, and $b(i)$ is the average distance between i and all data points in the nearest neighboring cluster.

From Table 3, one can observe that Agglomerative Clustering obtains an accuracy of 41.67%, indicating that it correctly classified most of the data points. Its Silhouette Score of 0.409 suggests the clustering quality is moderate, with some overlaps between clusters. Similarly, K-means clustering performs slightly better with an accuracy of 48.03%. The Silhouette Score of this method is 0.464 implies a similar clustering quality as Agglomerative Clustering. The spectral

Table 3. The quantitative comparison of different unsupervised ML techniques in terms of accuracy and Silhouette score.

Classifiers	Accuracy (%)	Silhouette Score
Agglomerative Clustering	41.67	0.409
K-means clustering	48.03	0.464
Spectral Clustering	53.44	−0.134
DBSCAN	**53.57**	**0.683**

clustering demonstrated improved performance compared to the previous two algorithms, achieving an accuracy of 53.44%. However, the negative Silhouette Score of −0.134 signifies that poor clustering quality, with data points possibly assigned to incorrect clusters and significant overlap between clusters. On the other hand, DBSCAN technique shows promising results with an accuracy of 53.57%. The high Silhouette Score of 0.68 indicates a good clustering quality, with well-defined and compact clusters. In summary, among the evaluated algorithms, DBSCAN performs superior with the highest accuracy and a notable Silhouette Score, indicating clear separation between clusters. Thus, Agglomerative and K-means clustering exhibit poor performance, the Spectral Clustering obtained a relatively high accuracy; however, it suffers from poorer clustering quality as indicated by the negative Silhouette Score and performance of DBSCAN unsupervised technique is superior among all the unsupervised techniques.

6   Conclusion

There is a significant amount of ongoing research focused on stress-related studies. However, there has been relatively limited attention given to the prediction of stress. While numerous publications have utilized supervised models to forecast stress, acquiring labeled data is not always feasible. In this study, we have leveraged unsupervised algorithms utilizing the available features of the SWELL-KW dataset. Our analysis reveals that DBSCAN emerged as the most effective unsupervised algorithm for identifying stress conditions with an accuracy of 54.57%. Nonetheless, the accuracy achieved was relatively low. As a result, our future papers will aim to enhance the accuracy of the DBSCAN algorithm and further improve upon our findings.

References

1. Adams, P., et al.: Towards personal stress informatics: Comparing minimally invasive techniques for measuring daily stress in the wild. In: Proceedings of the 8th International Conference on Pervasive Computing Technologies for Healthcare, pp. 72–79 (2014)

2. Albaladejo-González, M., Ruipérez-Valiente, J.A., Gómez Mármol, F.: Evaluating different configurations of machine learning models and their transfer learning capabilities for stress detection using heart rate. J. Ambient Intell. Humanized Comput. **14**, 1–11 (2022). https://doi.org/10.1007/s12652-022-04365-z
3. Fiorini, L., Mancioppi, G., Semeraro, F., Fujita, H., Cavallo, F.: Unsupervised emotional state classification through physiological parameters for social robotics applications. Knowl.-Based Syst. **190**, 105217 (2020)
4. Huysmans, D., Smets, E., De Raedt, W., Van Hoof, C., Bogaerts, K., Van Diest, I., Helic, D.: Unsupervised learning for mental stress detection. In: Proceedings of the 11th International Joint Conference on Biomedical Engineering Systems and Technologies, vol. 4, pp. 26–35 (2018)
5. Koldijk, S., Sappelli, M., Verberne, S., Neerincx, M.A., Kraaij, W.: The swell knowledge work dataset for stress and user modeling research. In: Proceedings of the 16th International Conference on Multimodal Interaction, pp. 291–298 (2014)
6. Maaoui, C., Pruski, A.: Unsupervised stress detection from remote physiological signal. In: 2018 IEEE International Conference on Industrial Technology (ICIT), pp. 1538–1543. IEEE (2018)
7. Pabreja, K., Singh, A., Singh, R., Agnihotri, R., Kaushik, S., Malhotra, T.: Stress Prediction Model Using Machine Learning. In: Bansal, P., Tushir, M., Balas, V.E., Srivastava, R. (eds.) Proceedings of International Conference on Artificial Intelligence and Applications. AISC, vol. 1164, pp. 57–68. Springer, Singapore (2021). https://doi.org/10.1007/978-981-15-4992-2_6
8. Ramos, J., Hong, J.H., Dey, A.K.: Stress recognition-a step outside the lab. In: International Conference on Physiological Computing Systems, vol. 2, pp. 107–118. SCITEPRESS (2014)
9. Rescioa, G., Leonea, A., Sicilianoa, P.: Unsupervised-based framework for aged worker's stress detection. Work Artif. Intell. Ageing Soc. **2804**, 81–7 (2020)
10. Rogers, T., Worden, K., Fuentes, R., Dervilis, N., Tygesen, U., Cross, E.: A bayesian non-parametric clustering approach for semi-supervised structural health monitoring. Mech. Syst. Signal Process. **119**, 100–119 (2019)

A Fractional Order Derivative Based Active Contour Model for Simultaneous Image Despeckling and Segmentation

Ankit Kumar[✉][iD] and Subit K. Jain[iD]

Department of Mathematics and Scientific Computing, National Institute of
Technology Hamirpur, Hamirpur 177005, Himachal Pradesh, India
ankitkumar2675@gmail.com

Abstract. Image segmentation faces significant challenges due to the
presence of intensity heterogeneity and noise in real-world images. Specifically, medical ultrasound images are usually corrupted by speckle noise
and intensity heterogeneity. To address these challenges, we introduce a
new level set-based variational model by utilizing fractional edge terms.
Our model comprises two equations, one performing image segmentation and the second suppressing the speckle noise simultaneously. The
initial contour is guided towards the target boundaries by the segmentation equation, resulting in accurate segmentation. Simultaneously, the
despeckling equation diminishes the influence of speckle noise, thereby
improving the quality of segmentation. We perform comparison experiments on natural and medical images to demonstrate the efficiency of
the present fractional active contour model (FACM). These images, especially ultrasound images, are characterized by speckle noise and intensity
heterogeneity. Several segmentation measures are utilized to evaluate the
performance of our present model. Through experimental outcomes, we
demonstrate that our model surpasses most existing active contour models thus providing superior segmentation outcomes.

Keywords: Image segmentation · Speckle noise · Partial differential
equations · Variational model · Ultrasound imaging · Fractional order
differentiation

1 Introduction

Image segmentation is a vital and fundamental aspect of computer vision and
image processing, particularly in the area of medical image analysis [1,2]. Its
primary aim is to partition a given image into meaningful and analyzable components. Over time, numerous approaches have been developed for image segmentation, among them, geometric active contour models [3,4] employing the
level set method [5] have proven to be efficient and effective techniques. These
models offer a wide range of capabilities and have contributed significantly to
advancing image segmentation in various applications.

© The Author(s), under exclusive license to Springer Nature Switzerland AG 2024
H. Kaur et al. (Eds.): CVIP 2023, CCIS 2011, pp. 272–283, 2024.
https://doi.org/10.1007/978-3-031-58535-7_23

The snake model also known as the active contour model (ACM) [6], has demonstrated its efficiency in the area of image segmentation. This model delineate the target boundaries by utilizing dynamic contours driven by an energy-minimizing principle. Regrettably, this model is sensitive to initial conditions and faces challenges in dealing with topological changes, such as curve splitting and merging. Subsequent to the introduction of the ACM, extensive research efforts have been devoted to enhancing its performance. Researchers have made significant progress in addressing the limitations associated with initial conditions and topological changes, thereby improving the overall performance of the ACM. One of the notable and significant advancements in active contour models is the implicit ACM [5], which is expressed in the level set architecture. The main merit of this approach lies in its ability to automatically handle topological changes. This is a significant advantage compared to traditional parametric active contour models, which generally struggle to address such changes in an automatic manner. The implicit active contour model provides a more robust and versatile solution for image segmentation, allowing for more accurate and efficient results.

Among the ACMs, the Chan-Vese model [7] is a widely recognized segmentation model based on global fitting terms. The underlying assumption of this model is that the image regions possess piecewise-constant characteristics. However, this model can sometimes become trapped in local minima, limiting its effectiveness in certain scenarios. To address the challenges posed by intensity heterogeneity, several models [8–10] have been proposed. However, these models often exhibit sensitivity to noise and initialization, limiting their performance. More recently, coupled models [11,12] that integrate image denoising and segmentation have exhibited good performance in low noise. Regrettably, these coupled models neglect to take into account the noise distribution, leading to inaccuracies in both segmentation and denoising tasks.

Many researchers have investigated various techniques related to image segmentation and denoising. Fractional order differentiation has emerged as a particularly promising approach due to its superior performance in the presence of intensity heterogeneity and noise. Fractional order differentiation offers advantages by nonlinearly preserving low-frequency information while simultaneously smoothing or enhancing high-frequency information, depending on the specific values of the fractional order [13–15]. This characteristic has proven beneficial for effectively handling noise in image segmentation tasks.

To tackle the aforementioned challenges, we propose a new FACM that simultaneously addresses the image despeckling and segmentation. In brief, this study makes the following notable contributions:

- Introduction of a new FACM to eliminate the influence of speckle noise in inhomogeneous environments.
- Design of a despeckling equation in combination with a segmentation equation to reduce the effect of Rayleigh speckle noise which is commonly encountered in ultrasound images [16–18].

– Demonstration of superior performance of the proposed model through
  numerical evaluations on a diverse range of images, including natural and
  ultrasound images, surpassing the capabilities of existing ACMs.

The structure of this article is organized in the following manner: Sect. 2
presents a new FACM. The numerical experiments and corresponding discussions
are described in Sect. 3. Section 4 provides the concluding remarks and summary
of this study.

2   Methodology

This paper aims to accurately identify the target boundaries in noisy and inhomogeneous environments. To address these challenges simultaneously, we propose a new FACM inspired by the Jin-Yang model [19] and the distance regularized level set model [4]. Our proposed model combines the image denoising
equation with fractional order derivative based segmentation equation. This integration allows our model to effectively mitigate speckle noise in noisy images and
accurately identify target areas even in non-uniform intensity distribution.

2.1   The Proposed Fractional Active Contour Model

The energy functional proposed in this study is specifically designed to optimize
both the despeckling and segmentation tasks simultaneously. This joint optimization ensures the extraction of accurate and robust target boundaries. The
proposed energy functional is given as follows:

$$E^{Proposed}(\varphi, I) = \beta \int_{\mathbb{D}} e(|\nabla^{\alpha} I|) \, \delta_{\varepsilon}(\varphi) \, |\nabla \varphi| dx + \gamma \int_{\mathbb{D}} e(|\nabla^{\alpha} I|) \, \mathcal{H}_{\varepsilon}(-\varphi) dx$$
$$+ \frac{\mu}{2} \int_{\mathbb{D}} (|\nabla \varphi| - 1)^2 \, dx + \int_{\mathbb{D}} |\nabla I| dx + \lambda \int_{\mathbb{D}} \frac{(I_0 - I)^2}{I} dx, \tag{1}$$

where $\mathbb{D}$, I, I_0, and φ are the image domain, denoised image, observed image,
and level set function, respectively. Moreover, the regularized Heaviside func-
tion $\mathcal{H}_{\varepsilon}(.)$, regularized Dirac delta function $\delta_{\varepsilon}(.)$, and the edge function $e(.)$ are
described in Eq. (2), Eq. (3), and Eq. (4), respectively.

$$\mathcal{H}_{\varepsilon}(\tau) = \frac{1}{\pi} \left[\frac{\pi}{2} + \arctan \left(\frac{\tau}{\varepsilon} \right) \right]. \tag{2}$$

$$\delta_{\varepsilon}(\tau) = \frac{1}{\pi} \frac{\varepsilon}{\varepsilon^2 + \tau^2}. \tag{3}$$

$$e(\tau) = \frac{1}{\tau^2 + 1}. \tag{4}$$

The present energy functional in Eq. (1) incorporates five essential components, each playing a unique role in the segmentation procedure. The first component directs the initial curve toward the edges of the desired region of interest

(ROI). The second component further ensures that the curve aligns with the target boundaries, maintaining its direction accurately. To promote smoothness and prevent contour leakage, the third component acts as a regularizer. The fourth component serves as an image-smoothing factor which effectively eliminates image artifacts and thus enhances the quality of segmentation outcomes. Lastly, the final component focuses on suppressing multiplicative noise within the image. The parameters β, γ, μ, and λ are responsible for governing and controlling the evolution process of both segmentation and despeckling, as outlined in the proposed framework (1). These parameters manage the individual components as explained in the preceding text. In other words, they dictate how the segmentation and noise reduction procedures progress and interact within the framework. Hence, the present FACM offers the unique capability of simultaneously performing image despeckling and segmentation. This allows the elimination of speckle noise and the achievement of accurate boundary delineation of target boundaries.

To minimize Eq. (1) and find the optimal solution, we employ the Euler-Lagrange and gradient descent method. By treating all parameters as constant and minimizing Eq. (1) with respect to level set function φ and image I, we have the set of equations as follows:

$$\frac{\partial \varphi}{\partial t} = \beta \delta_\varepsilon \mathrm{div}\left(e\frac{\nabla \varphi}{|\nabla \varphi|}\right) + \gamma \delta_\varepsilon e + \mu \left(\nabla^2 \varphi - \mathrm{div}\left(\frac{\nabla \varphi}{|\nabla \varphi|}\right)\right), \qquad \text{in } \mathbb{D}_T, \quad (5a)$$

$$\frac{\partial I}{\partial t} = \mathrm{div}\left(\frac{\nabla I}{|\nabla I|}\right) + \lambda \left(\frac{I_0^2 - I^2}{I^2}\right), \qquad \text{in } \mathbb{D}_T, \quad (5b)$$

$$\varphi(x,0) = \varphi_0(x), \quad I(x,0) = I_0(x), \qquad \text{in } \mathbb{D}, \quad (5c)$$

$$\frac{\partial \varphi}{\partial n} = 0, \quad \frac{\partial I}{\partial n} = 0, \qquad \text{on } \partial \mathbb{D}_T, \quad (5d)$$

where $\mathbb{D}_T := \mathbb{D} \times (0,T)$, $\partial \mathbb{D}_T := \partial \mathbb{D} \times (0,T)$, and n is the outward normal direction at the boundary surface $\partial \mathbb{D}$. Furthermore, Eq. (5c) and Eq. (5d) describe the initial and boundary conditions of the present system.

2.2 Numerical Discretization

In the literature, there is a wide range of definitions available for fractional derivatives [20], offering diverse mathematical formulations to describe this concept. In our approach, we employed the Grünwald-Letnikov derivative [20] to address the fractional edge term. The definition of the Grünwald-Letnikov derivative can be expressed as follows:

$$_{GL}D_{a,t}^\alpha f(t) = \lim_{h \to 0} h^{-\alpha} \sum_{i=0}^{\frac{t-a}{h}} (-1)^i \binom{\alpha}{i} f(t - ih), \qquad (6)$$

where h represents the step size, and $h = 1$ considered in this study. To approximate the α-order spatial partial derivatives in the horizontal ($D_x^\alpha I$) and vertical

$(D_y^\alpha I)$ directions within the two-dimensional image domain. We utilize the following approach for the pixel location denoted as $x = (r, s)$.

$$D_x^\alpha I(r, s) \approx I(r, s) + (-\alpha)I(r-1, s) + \frac{(-\alpha)(-\alpha+1)}{2}I(r-2, s) + \dots$$
$$+ \frac{\Gamma(M - \alpha - 1)}{(M-1)!\Gamma(-\alpha)}I(r - M + 1, s), \tag{7}$$

$$D_y^\alpha I(r, s) \approx I(r, s) + (-\alpha)I(r, s-1) + \frac{(-\alpha)(-\alpha+1)}{2}I(r, s-2) + \dots$$
$$+ \frac{\Gamma(N - \alpha - 1)}{(N-1)!\Gamma(-\alpha)}I(r, s - N + 1), \tag{8}$$

where $M \times N$ represents the size of image I.

The Grünwald-Letnikov derivative given in Eq. (6) is utilized to approximate the fractional edge term. To reduce the computational burden, we consider only the first three terms in Eq. (7) and Eq. (8). Therefore, we define the fractional gradient as follows: $|\nabla^\alpha I| = \sqrt{(D_x^\alpha I)^2 + (D_y^\alpha I)^2}$. We have utilized the finite difference scheme to solve the proposed system. Among the available options, explicit schemes are the simplest but often require smaller time steps for stability [21]. So, we have employed the explicit finite difference scheme to showcase the superiority of the present FACM. Consequently, the numerical discretization of the present FACM is outlined as follows:

$$\varphi_{i,j}^k = \varphi_{i,j}^{k-1} + \Delta t D_1(\varphi_{i,j}^{k-1}), \tag{9a}$$
$$I_{i,j}^k = I_{i,j}^{k-1} + \Delta t D_2(I_{i,j}^{k-1}), \tag{9b}$$

where D_1 and D_2 in Eq. (9a) and Eq. (9b) are the approximated versions of right hand side of Eq. (5a) and Eq. (5b), respectively. In addition, the parameter values considered in this article are as follows: $\Delta t = 0.2$, $0 < \alpha < 2$, $\beta = [6, 10]$, $\gamma \in [-2, 2]$, $\mu \in [0.1, 0.2]$, $\varepsilon = 1.5$, $\lambda = 0.1$, and the maximum iteration limit set at 1500.

3   Experimental Results and Discussions

In this segment, we assess the performance of the present FACM by comparing its segmentation outcomes with those of other existing ACMs, using the evaluation metrics outlined in Table 1. In the context of achieving the best segmentation, ideally, the values for all these measures should approach 1, with the exception of GCE and HD. Since GCE and HD measure the error, they should approach a minimum value close to zero. Further, all experiments are performed using MATLAB (R2020b) on a Windows 10 (64-bit) laptop equipped with an Intel Core $i5$ processor operating at a speed of 1.60 GHz and 8 GB RAM.

In Table 1, the gold truth curve and the segmented curve are denoted by the symbols C_1 and C_2, respectively. In this context, True Positive (TP) represents the correctly labeled pixels within the ROI. True Negative (TN) denotes

Table 1. Segmentation evaluation measures for assessing the quality of image segmentation.

Metric	Abbreviation	Definition
Hausdorff distance [22]	HD	$\max\{\max_{a \in C_1} \min_{b \in C_2} \|a - b\|, \max_{b \in C_2} \min_{a \in C_1} \|a - b\|\}$
Dice coefficient [22]	DC	$\frac{2TP}{2TP+FN+FP}$
Accuracy [22]	A	$\frac{TP+TN}{FN+TN+FP+TP}$
Global consistency error [23]	GCE	$\frac{1}{|D|} \min\left\{ \frac{FN(FN+2TP)}{FN+TP} + \frac{FP(FP+2TN)}{FP+TN}, \frac{FP(FP+2TP)}{FP+TP} + \frac{FN(FN+2TN)}{FN+TN} \right\}$
Jaccard index [22]	JI	$\frac{TP}{TP+FP+FN}$
Matthews correlation coefficient [24]	MCC	$\frac{TN.TP-FN.FP}{\sqrt{(FN+TN).(FP+TN).(FN+TP).(FP+TP)}}$
Sensitivity [22]	S	$\frac{TP}{TP+FN}$

the accurately labeled pixels outside the ROI. False Positive (FP) signifies the mislabeled non-ROI pixels labeled as the ROI pixels. Conversely, False Negative (FN) represents the mislabeled ROI pixels classified as non-ROI pixels.

3.1 Segmentation Outcomes for Clean and Noisy Images

In our experimental setup, we considered three natural images, comprising two clean images and one noisy image, all of which were sourced from the dataset [25]. With a scale value of 0.6, Rayleigh speckle noise is used to degrade the noisy image. To check the performance of the present FACM, we consider four well-known ACMs specifically designed to handle speckle noise: adaptive variational level set model (AVLSM) [11], and robust variational level set model (RVLSM) [12], Ali-Rada-Badshah model (ARB) [26], hybrid and local fuzzy region-edge-based active contour model (HLFRA) [27]. We used the parameter values provided in the published implementations of these models.

Table 2. Quantitative evaluation of several assessment measures for natural images.

Model	Accuracy [22]			GCE [23]			Jaccard [22]			MCC [24]			Sensitivity [22]		
	Image1	Image2	Image3	Image1	Image2	Image3	Image1	Image2	Image3	Image1	Image2	Image3	Image1	Image2	Image3
ARB [26]	0.9828	0.9799	0.6455	0.0327	0.0389	0.4577	0.9010	0.8089	0.2304	0.9395	0.8833	0.2958	0.9997	0.8866	0.2430
HLFRA [27]	0.8068	0.7740	0.6006	0.2909	0.2970	0.4990	0.4537	0.2683	0.2394	0.5646	0.4103	0.3451	0.4712	0.2786	0.2413
AVLSM [11]	0.9841	0.8793	0.7491	0.0304	0.1760	0.3577	0.9084	0.4253	0.2134	0.9440	0.5931	0.2358	0.9996	0.4357	0.2648
RVLSM [12]	0.9770	0.7804	0.8294	0.0429	0.2877	0.2497	0.8677	0.2884	0.4076	0.9188	0.4496	0.5447	0.9997	0.2934	0.4251
Proposed FACM	0.9910	0.9910	0.9889	0.0176	0.0172	0.0216	0.9479	0.9044	0.9201	0.9683	0.9462	0.9523	0.9997	0.9988	0.9377

In Fig. 1, the first column clearly illustrates that the majority of the models, except for the present FACM, struggled to accurately delineate the target boundaries due to weak edges. Similarly, in the second and third columns, these models illustrate poor segmentation outcomes when faced with a cluttered and complex background. In contrast, the proposed model demonstrated its effectiveness by accurately locating target boundaries in all images with complex background and high noise as depicted in Fig. 1, surpassing the performance of the other models. These experimental outcomes highlight the the significant advantages of the present FACM when working with images that contains a variety of geometric

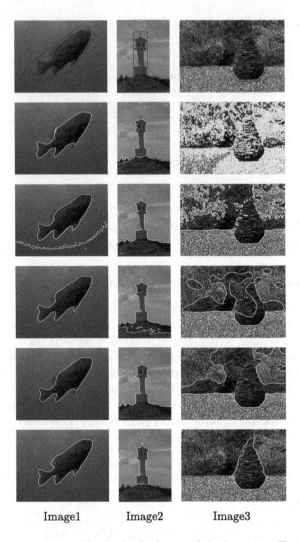

Image1   Image2   Image3

Fig. 1. The segmentation results for both clean and noisy images. From the first row to the last row: images with initial contours, segmented results of ARB [26], HLFRA [27], AVLSM [11], RVLSM [12], and present FACM, respectively.

regions, in both clean and noisy environments. Thus, the results unequivocally establish the superiority of the present FACM over existing models in terms of robustness and accuracy. Moreover, the numerical results depicted in Table 2, along with the bar graph depicted in Fig. 2, offers substantial evidence in favor of the assertion that the present FACM outperforms the existing ACMs examined in this section. Furthermore, the current model attains the highest scores for evaluation metrics including the accuracy, sensitivity, Matthews correlation coefficient, Jaccard index, and dice coefficient across several images. Moreover,

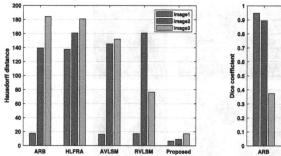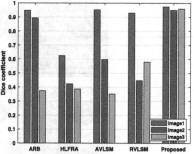

Fig. 2. Comparison of HD and DC metrics for different models on clean images.

it exhibits the lowest values for the global consistency error and Hausdorff distance among all algorithms examined in the study. These results serve as strong empirical support for the superior performance of our proposed model.

3.2   Segmentation Outcomes for Medical Images

To conduct a more thorough assessment of the efficacy of present FACM, we considered three medical ultrasound images from the dataset [28] for numerical experiments. As depicted in Fig. 3, the present FACM demonstrated remarkable success in accurately locating and delineating the desired ROI within the medical ultrasound images. Thus, during the application phase, the current FACM efficiently detects and delineates the areas with defective tissue in the ultrasound images. Conversely, the considered existing ACMs struggled to tackle the inherent challenges presented in these ultrasound images, including factors like speckle noise and intensity heterogeneity. These observations provide compelling evidence of the superior performance of the present FACM in handling complex ultrasound images with challenging characteristics.

The quantitative results for medical ultrasound images are visualized in Fig. 4 and described in Table 3. Notably, the current FACM achieved the highest values of evaluation measures such as accuracy, sensitivity, Matthews correlation coefficient, Jaccard index, and dice coefficient across different images. Additionally, it demonstrates the lowest values for the global consistency error and Hausdorff distance compared to the rest of the models considered in this sub-section. These findings indicate that the current model surpasses the performance of existing ACMs in relation to the considered evaluation metrics, highlighting its superior efficiency. Therefore, the numerical results showcased in the Table 3, along with the supporting bar graph in Fig. 4, offer robust support for the assertion regarding the present FACM's superior performance over the selected ACMs investigated in this paper.

Ultimately, the proposed FACM adeptly segments the desired ROI in both Fig. 1 and Fig. 3, outperforming the shortcomings observed in the rest of the ACMs assessed in this section. Consequently, the proposed FACM demonstrates

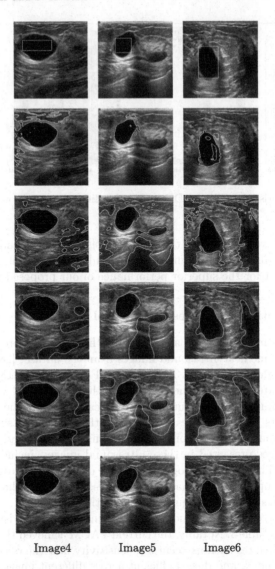

Image4   Image5   Image6

Fig. 3. The segmentation results for medical ultrasound images. From the first row to the last row: images with initial contours, segmented results of ARB [26], HLFRA [27], AVLSM [11], RVLSM [12], and present FACM, respectively.

a notable advantage in quantitative analysis over the alternative ACMs, as evidenced by the data presented in Table 2, Table 3, Fig. 2, and Fig. 4. Furthermore, the quantitative study demonstrates that the current FACM produces the best segmentation outcomes for the most of the cases. In summary, the current FACM demonstrates its superiority over the other ACMs discussed in this article by consistently delivering the most favorable segmentation results, both in

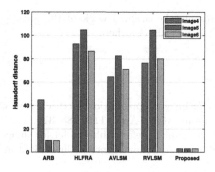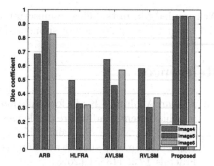

Fig. 4. Comparison of HD and DC metrics for different models on ultrasound images.

Table 3. Quantitative assessment of several evaluation measures for ultrasound images.

Model	Accuracy [22]			GCE [23]			Jaccard [22]			MCC [24]			Sensitivity [22]		
	Image4	Image5	Image6	Image4	Image5	Image6	Image4	Image5	Image6	Image4	Image5	Image6	Image4	Image5	Image6
ARB [26]	0.8860	0.9877	0.9682	0.1775	0.0234	0.0598	0.5193	0.8435	0.7048	0.6598	0.9097	0.8098	0.5329	0.8740	0.8036
HLFRA [27]	0.7566	0.7261	0.6248	0.3323	0.3299	0.4474	0.3282	0.1959	0.1909	0.4583	0.3607	0.3322	0.3378	0.1973	0.1911
AVLSM [11]	0.8667	0.8410	0.8665	0.2030	0.2080	0.1874	0.4756	0.2978	0.3977	0.6171	0.4899	0.5794	0.4917	0.3002	0.3996
RVLSM [12]	0.8294	0.6910	0.7001	0.2497	0.3662	0.3688	0.4076	0.1781	0.2282	0.5447	0.3346	0.3894	0.4251	0.1792	0.2285
Proposed FACM	0.9884	0.9940	0.9915	0.0223	0.0117	0.0167	0.9109	0.9140	0.9099	0.9477	0.9523	0.9483	0.9923	0.9841	0.9383

terms of visual quality and numerical performance. The precision of the present FACM is underscored by the minimal variation in the metrics values, indicating its robustness in a variety of imaging conditions. As a result, the present FACM consistently demonstrates its effectiveness in diverse image datasets.

4 Conclusion

This article presents a new level set-based variational model to simultaneously perform image despeckling and segmentation. The present despeckling equation effectively eliminates the effect of Rayleigh speckle noise from various images, including clean, noisy, and medical ultrasound images. The fractional order derivative-based edge term in the segmentation equation demonstrates superior performance in accurately locating the target boundaries, particularly in challenging scenarios characterized by inhomogeneity and noise. The experimental results provide strong evidence of the superior efficiency and performance of our current model compared to the majority of existing ACMs. The present study offers a significant enhancement in accurately delineating the target boundaries within the image, particularly in complex imaging situations. By effectively addressing issues such as noise, intensity heterogeneity, and other complexities, our model demonstrates remarkable capabilities in accurately delineating objects within images. Its superior performance and ability to handle challenging scenarios make it a valuable tool for various applications that rely on precise image segmentation.

Acknowledgements. This manuscript represents the original work of the authors and has not been published or submitted simultaneously elsewhere.

References

1. Kumar, A., Jain, S.K.: Deformable models for image segmentation: a critical review of achievements and future challenges. Comput. Math. Appl. **119**, 288–311 (2022)
2. Kumar, A., Majee, S., Jain, S.K.: CDM: a coupled deformable model for image segmentation with speckle noise and severe intensity inhomogeneity. Chaos Solitons Fractals **172**, 113551 (2023)
3. Caselles, V., Kimmel, R., Sapiro, G.: Geodesic active contours. Int. J. Comput. Vision **22**(1), 61–79 (1997)
4. Li, C., Xu, C., Gui, C., Fox, M.D.: Distance regularized level set evolution and its application to image segmentation. IEEE Trans. Image Process. **19**(12), 3243–3254 (2010)
5. Osher, S., Sethian, J.A.: Fronts propagating with curvature-dependent speed: algorithms based on Hamilton-Jacobi formulations. J. Comput. Phys. **79**(1), 12–49 (1988)
6. Kass, M., Witkin, A., Terzopoulos, D.: Snakes: active contour models. Int. J. Comput. Vision **1**(4), 321–331 (1988)
7. Chan, T.F., Vese, L.A.: Active contours without edges. IEEE Trans. Image Process. **10**(2), 266–277 (2001)
8. Li, C., Kao, C.-Y., Gore, J.C., Ding, Z.: Minimization of region-scalable fitting energy for image segmentation. IEEE Trans. Image Process. **17**(10), 1940–1949 (2008)
9. Zhang, K., Song, H., Zhang, L.: Active contours driven by local image fitting energy. Pattern Recogn. **43**(4), 1199–1206 (2010)
10. Li, C., Huang, R., Ding, Z., Gatenby, J.C., Metaxas, D.N., Gore, J.C.: A level set method for image segmentation in the presence of intensity inhomogeneities with application to MRI. IEEE Trans. Image Process. **20**(7), 2007–2016 (2011)
11. Cai, Q., et al.: AVLSM: adaptive variational level set model for image segmentation in the presence of severe intensity inhomogeneity and high noise. IEEE Trans. Image Process. **31**, 43–57 (2021)
12. Zhang, F., Liu, H., Cao, C., Cai, Q., Zhang, D.: RVLSM: robust variational level set method for image segmentation with intensity inhomogeneity and high noise. Inf. Sci. (2022)
13. Ren, Z.: Adaptive active contour model driven by fractional order fitting energy. Signal Process. **117**, 138–150 (2015)
14. Chen, B., Huang, S., Liang, Z., Chen, W., Pan, B.: A fractional order derivative based active contour model for inhomogeneous image segmentation. Appl. Math. Model. **65**, 120–136 (2019)
15. Li, M.-M., Li, B.-Z.: A novel active contour model for noisy image segmentation based on adaptive fractional order differentiation. IEEE Trans. Image Process. **29**, 9520–9531 (2020)
16. Aysal, T.C., Barner, K.E.: Rayleigh-maximum-likelihood filtering for speckle reduction of ultrasound images. IEEE Trans. Med. Imaging **26**(5), 712–727 (2007)
17. Wang, G., Xu, J., Pan, Z., Diao, Z.: Ultrasound image denoising using backward diffusion and framelet regularization. Biomed. Signal Process. Control **13**, 212–217 (2014)

18. Kang, M., Jung, M., Kang, M.: Higher-order regularization based image restoration with automatic regularization parameter selection. Comput. Math. Appl. **76**(1), 58–80 (2018)
19. Jin, Z., Yang, X.: A variational model to remove the multiplicative noise in ultrasound images. J. Math. Imaging Vision **39**(1), 62–74 (2011)
20. Podlubny, I.: Fractional Differential Equations. Mathematics in Science and Engineering, vol. 198 . Academic Press (1999)
21. Kumar, A., Jain, S.K.: A coupled system for simultaneous image despeckling and segmentation. In: Das, A.K., Nayak, J., Naik, B., Vimal, S., Pelusi, D. (eds.) CIPR 2022. LNNS, pp. 505–515. Springer, Singapore (2023). https://doi.org/10.1007/978-981-99-3734-9_41
22. Karunanayake, N., Aimmanee, P., Lohitvisate, W., Makhanov, S.S.: Particle method for segmentation of breast tumors in ultrasound images. Math. Comput. Simul. **170**, 257–284 (2020)
23. Taha, A.A., Hanbury, A.: Metrics for evaluating 3d medical image segmentation: analysis, selection, and tool. BMC Med. Imaging **15**(1), 1–28 (2015)
24. Chicco, D., Jurman, G.: The advantages of the Matthews correlation coefficient (MCC) over F1 score and accuracy in binary classification evaluation. BMC Genomics **21**(1), 1–13 (2020)
25. Alpert, S., Galun, M., Basri, R., Brandt, A.: Image segmentation by probabilistic bottom-up aggregation and cue integration. In: 2007 IEEE Conference on Computer Vision and Pattern Recognition, pp. 1–8 (2007)
26. Ali, H., Rada, L., Badshah, N.: Image segmentation for intensity inhomogeneity in presence of high noise. IEEE Trans. Image Process. **27**(8), 3729–3738 (2018)
27. Fang, J., Liu, H., Zhang, L., Liu, J., Liu, H.: Region-edge-based active contours driven by hybrid and local fuzzy region-based energy for image segmentation. Inf. Sci. **546**, 397–419 (2021)
28. Al-Dhabyani, W., Gomaa, M., Khaled, H., Fahmy, A.: Dataset of breast ultrasound images. Data Brief **28**, 104863 (2020)

Making Domain Specific Adversarial Attacks for Retinal Fundus Images

Nirmal Joseph[1]([✉]) [iD], P. M. Ameer[1] [iD], Sudhish N. George[1] [iD],
and Kiran Raja[2] [iD]

[1] National Institute of Technology, Calicut, Kattangal, India
{nirmal_p230136ec,ameer,sudhish}@nitc.ac.in
[2] Norwegian University of Science and Technology, Trondheim, Norway
kiran.raja@ntnu.no

Abstract. Adversarial attacks on deep neural networks (DNN) aim at creating perturbations that can lead to misclassification by intention, despite being imperceptible. This work presents a new approach for creating adversarial samples for retinal fundus images by not only introducing imperceptible noise, but make them visually realistic by introducing domain specific details. Specifically, we introduce exudates on to retinal fundus images to make a healthy image appear as a diabetic image. With such an approach, the work is intended to make both DNN based systems and human observers such as medical practitioners to misclassify a healthy image as a diabetic image. The generated images through new attack are further validated using a DNN based classifier and human observers (3 practitioners and 30 normal observers) to demonstrate the strength of the attacks. While the generated images are misclassified with 100% success in a DNN classifier, we also show that the images can realistically fool humans when domain specific details are added through a set of experiments conducted on a publicly available dataset. The evaluation indicates high degree of attacks for instance in insurance frauds, and demonstrates the need for better attack detection methods.

Keywords: Diabetic retinopathy · adversarial attacks · fundus images

1 Introduction

The comprehensive success of Deep Neural Networks (DNN) in the field of natural image processing and classification has paved the way to their applications in the field of medical image processing [1]. The detection of Diabetic Retinopathy (DR) from retinal fundus images is a typical application where DNN models are used and have shown promising results in recent research [2]. Recent works have shown that these models can achieve high accuracy in detecting DR, with some models achieving an accuracy of over 90% [3]. Motivated by such success, the US Food and Drug Administration (US FDA) approved AI-based detection of DR for clinical practices, making it the first system to be approved for clinical practice in 2018 [4].

H. Kaur et al. (Eds.): CVIP 2023, CCIS 2011, pp. 284–295, 2024.
https://doi.org/10.1007/978-3-031-58535-7_24

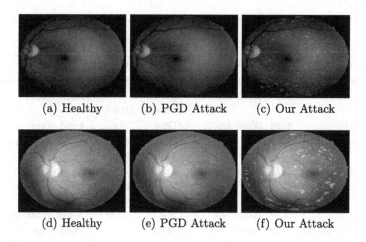

(a) Healthy   (b) PGD Attack   (c) Our Attack

(d) Healthy   (e) PGD Attack   (f) Our Attack

Fig. 1. Illustration of PGD attacks as compared to our proposed attack.

Along with the success of deep learning models improving in the performance have emerged the concerns of safety and robustness in practical applications [5]. A non-robust DNN can result in models that confidently arrive at incorrect conclusions, creating a significant problem [6]. Adversarial attacks are one example of such a problem and have received widespread attention in academia and industry [7]. Deep-learning systems in medical applications are also vulnerable to such attacks. In fact, compared to natural images, medical images are more vulnerable to such attacks with minimal perturbation required and can lead to catastrophic outcomes [8,9]. This vulnerability hinders the application of medical deep learning systems in clinical settings due to misdiagnosis of diseases and risks to patients [8–10].

Adversarial attacks on AI-based DR detection systems can disrupt practical applications if employed in clinical practices. By employing an adversarial attack, a normal image can be misclassified as a DR image leading to misdiagnosis and putting patient to risk [6]. Alternatively, adversarial attacks can be used for fraudulent purposes such as false insurance claims, leading to financial losses for insurance companies and potentially higher premiums for policyholders [14].

Various techniques are available for crafting adversarial attacks on medical images to influence the classification of such images by the system such as Fast Gradient Sign Method (FGSM), Iterative-FGSM (I-FGSM), and Basic Iterative Method (BIM) [11]. Such techniques introduce imperceptible adversarial perturbations into the image that can easily deceive classification models [6,8,12]. However, these attacks need to be practical in terms of posing threat to AI-based systems and at the same time visually appear realistic. Artificial perturbations need to account for domain-specific perturbations that can deceive human observers, especially in the case of medical images.

We present a new approach of crafting perturbations for fundus images by incorporating domain-specific perturbations in this work. Specifically, we introduce a new approach that can produce perturbed images with imperceptible

Table 1. Summary of Adversarial Attack works on fundoscopic medical images

Reference	Year	Attack scenario	Method	Data Modality
Paschali et al. [14]	2018	White box	FGSM, DeepFool	MRI, Fundoscopy
Finlayson et al. [6]	2018	White box	PGD, AdvPatch	Fundoscopy X-ray
Cheng et al. [16]	2020	White box	Adversarial Exposure Attack	Fundoscopy
Yoo et al. [17]	2020	White box	FGSM	Fundoscopy
Qi et al. [18]	2021	White box	Stabilized Medical Image Attack	CT, Fundoscopy
Shao et al. [19]	2021	White box	Multi-scale Attack	Fundoscopy, Dermoscopy
Yao et al. [12]	2021	White box	Hierarchical Feature Constraint	X-ray, Fundoscopy
Minagi et al. [22]	2022	White box	UAP	X-ray, Fundoscopy
Selvakkumar et al. [23]	2022	White box	FGSM	Fundoscopy
Bharath et al. [25]	2022	White box	FGSM, L-BFGS	Fundoscopy
Koga et al. [20]	2021	Black box	Black-box UAP	Dermoscopy, Fundoscopy
Pranava et al. [24]	2022	Black box	FGSM, BIM, PGD	CT, Fundoscopy
Shah et al. [15]	2018	No box	FGSM	Fundoscopy
Bortsova et al. [21]	2021	No box	FGSM, PGD	X-ray, Fundoscopy

noise and add exudates on fundus images. The addition of domain-specific details can make the fundus image with no indication of diabetes be classified as an image with diabetes. An example of the image from our approach compared to other perturbation approaches is provided in Fig. 1. As noted from Fig. 1, an image of a healthy retina is converted to an image showing diabetic retinopathy through the addition of exudates (c and f) unlike the other perturbation based on (Projected Gradient Descent) PGD which includes perturbation that is imperceptible. The proposed approach of generating domain-specific perturbation is tested on an algorithm to validate its ability to deceive the machine-driven algorithm. Further, we also test the human perception of those images with 30 regular observers and 03 medical practitioners.

In the rest of the paper, we first present a set of related works in Sect. 1.1 followed by details on the proposed approach in Sect. 2. We then present the details of the dataset used for experimental evaluation in Sect. 3. The strength of the perturbation attack is further measured through a dedicated algorithm and studying the human perception as discussed in Sect. 3.3 prior to conclusions in Sect. 5.

1.1 Related Works

Based on the level of knowledge of the attacker about the system being targeted, the adversarial attacks are classified into black box and white box attacks [11]. In a white-box attack scenario, the attacker has full knowledge of the target model and can access the target DNN's inference outputs an unlimited number of times. Black-box attacks rely on zeroth-order optimization techniques that involve querying the target DNN's output multiple times.

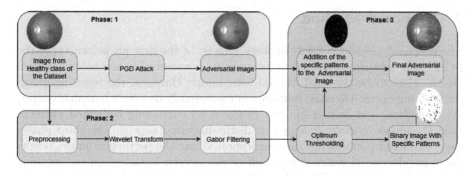

Fig. 2. Block diagram representation of the proposed method.

The majority of research on adversarial attacks for medical images concentrates on the white-box scenario. The attacker is capable of treating the target diagnosis DNN as a locally deployed model during the adversarial example generation process [11]. Table 1 presents a comprehensive overview of works on adversarial attacks for fundoscopic medical image analysis for the benefit of the reader[1]. Based on Table 1, it is evident that the majority of gradient-based attacks on retinal fundus images rely on the FGSM method. Although PGD is regarded as the strongest first-order attack, there are no methods exclusively designed to attack fundus images using PGD. Therefore, we present a new attack building on PGD for generating adversarial examples targeted on retinal fundus images.

1.2 Contributions

Motivated by missing works on adversarial attacks for fundus images, we propose a new approach to create perturbed images that can appear as realistic images with pathology. Our contributions from this work are therefore

- We propose a new approach to perturb the images with adversarial noise and domain-specific perturbations such as exudates for fundus images to make them appear as diabetic fundus images.
- We employ a DNN-based approach to classify fundus images into DR and healthy categories where we demonstrate the ability of newly generated attacks to deceive a well-performing algorithm.
- We further validate the ability of the images generated using a newly developed approach, we conduct human observer tests by employing medical practitioners and regular observers.

---

[1] Due to space constraints, we refrain from detailed discussions on individual works.

N. Joseph et al.

2 Proposed Method

The proposed method consists of three phases. In the first phase, we apply the PGD-based adversarial attack to generate an adversarial image belonging to a healthy class to be classified as a diabetic image. However, the resulting image contains imperceptible noise that does not necessarily deceive a human observer. We, therefore, add domain-specific exudates by extracting dedicated patterns from the image to make it appear realistic diabetic image. In the third phase, these extracted patterns are then incorporated into the perturbed image, resulting in an adversarial image that can effectively deceive both human and machine learning-driven models. The schematic of the proposed method is presented in Fig. 2 and each of the phases in our algorithm is further explained below.

2.1 Phase 1: PGD Attack

PGD [13] attack is a popular and powerful adversarial attack method in the field of machine learning, particularly for deep learning models. The idea behind PGD attack is to find the most effective perturbations to an input image that can cause the model to misclassify it with high confidence. The PGD attack is chosen since it is considered as a stronger and more robust attack compared to FGSM and other first-order gradient-based attacks.

Given a clean input example x and a classification model f, the PGD attack generates an adversarial example x_adv by iteratively perturbing the input in the direction of the gradient of the loss function with respect to the input, while ensuring that the perturbation is within a specified Lp-norm bound [8] as given by Eq. 1.

$$x_{adv} = \text{Clip}(x + \alpha * \text{sign}(\nabla_x J(f(x_{adv}), y)), x - \epsilon, x + \epsilon) \qquad (1)$$

where, Clip is a function that clips the values of the perturbed image to be within the range of the original input, α is the step size for the perturbation, $\Delta_x J(f(x_{adv}), y)$ is the gradient of the loss function J with respect to the input x_adv, and ϵ is the Lp-norm bound on the perturbation. The perturbation is iteratively applied T times, with the perturbed example at each iteration given by:

$$x_{adv,t} = \text{Clip}(x_{adv,t-1} + \alpha * \text{sign}(\nabla_x J(f(x_{adv,t-1}), y)), x - \epsilon, x + \epsilon) \qquad (2)$$

where, t is the iteration index.

2.2 Phase 2: Creation of Image-Specific Exudates

Our work makes a significant contribution in the generation of patterns that resemble exudates for each retinal fundus image. As shown in Fig. 3, a healthy retinal image is free of exudates, while an image with DR will have both features, which makes them distinguishable by human observers. As the perturbation is already generated using PGD attack to deceive a classification model and further fool human observers, we extract patterns from the original image and apply the same to the perturbed image making the adversarial attack robust to both machines and humans.

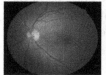  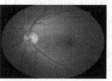 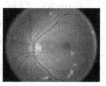

(a) Healthy fundus image   (b)   Perturbation added during PGD Attack   (c) Perturbed Image after PGD Attack   (d)   Unperturbed image with DR

Fig. 3. Example of an adversarial image created by using Gradient Based attack [8]. Both the original and perturbed image looks exactly the same for a human observer even though the system identifies the latter as a case with DR, whereas an unperturbed image with DR looks very different for a human observer.

Pre-processing. In the pre-processing steps, the images are converted to grayscale followed by adaptive histogram equalization. This approach can help to avoid the over-enhancement of large, homogeneous regions, which can occur with global histogram equalization. By using adaptive histogram equalization, we can enhance the contrast of the fundus image in a way that highlights the features we are interested in, such as exudates, while preserving the overall appearance of the image.

Performing Wavelet Transform and Gabor Filtering. After the pre-processing, we will perform Discrete Wavelet Transform (DWT) using the Haar Wavelet on the image. The mathematical equation for the Haar wavelet transform can be expressed as follows:

$$WT(j,k) = (1/sqrt(2))^j * \sum_{n=0}^{2^j-1} h_n^{j-1} * x_{k,n} \qquad (3)$$

This equation represents the Haar wavelet transform (WT) of a signal 'x'. The transform is computed at a specific scale 'j' and position 'k'. The equation calculates the weighted sum of the signal 'x' over a set of coefficients 'h' that depends on the scale 'j'. The result is a new representation of the signal 'x' that emphasizes certain features or patterns at different scales.

The subsequent step involves applying Gabor filtering to the image using a Gabor filter bank based on Gaussian-generated kernels. The 2D Gaussian Gabor filter can be defined as:

$$g_{\lambda,\theta,\psi}(x,y) = \frac{1}{2\pi\sigma^2} e^{-\frac{x'^2+\gamma^2 y'^2}{2\sigma^2}} \left[\cos(2\pi\frac{x'}{\lambda} + \psi) e^{-\frac{\theta^2}{2\sigma^2}} \right] \qquad (4)$$

where $x' = x \cos \theta + y \sin \theta$ and $y' = -x \sin \theta + y \cos \theta$. Here, λ is the wavelength of the sinusoidal factor of the filter, θ is the orientation of the normal to the parallel stripes of a Gabor function, ψ is the phase offset, and σ is the standard deviation of the Gaussian envelope. The parameter γ controls the ellipticity of the support of the Gabor function. A Gabor filter bank consists of a set of such filters with different values of λ, θ, and ψ. By performing Gabor filtering using a Gaussian generated kernel based Gabor filter bank, it is possible to enhance specific features in an image, such as blood vessels, exudates, and other lesions in retinal fundus images.

2.3 Phase 3: Optimum Thresholding and Generation of Final Adversarial Image

After enhancing specific features such as exudates, blood vessels, and lesions in the grayscale image through previous operations, the subsequent step is to convert it into a binary image via optimal thresholding. The resultant binary image contains particular patterns relative to the original image. These patterns' positions are identified and added to the PGD adversarial image from the original image at the exact locations, generating the final adversarial image.

3 Experiment

3.1 Dataset

The Kaggle 2015 database was used to obtain retinal fundoscopic images for this study[2]. The dataset includes $35,126$ retina scan images to detect diabetic retinopathy that are resized to a uniform size of 224×224 pixels. In the original dataset, the images were classified into five categories. However, for our work, we have only considered two classes, namely, Healthy and DR, by merging all the images from the original dataset into these two categories. Thus, the dataset used in this work contains 25810 images belonging to the healthy category and 9316 images belonging to the DR category.

3.2 Experimental Setup

DNN Model. We utilized the ResNet-50 [1] architecture pre-trained on the ImageNet dataset as our base network. The original top layer of the network was replaced with a new dense layer containing 128 neurons, followed by a dropout layer with a rate of 0.2, and another dense layer with a single neuron for binary classification. To improve the performance of the model and to prevent overfitting, we applied data augmentation techniques such as random rotations, width/height shifts, and horizontal flips. Additionally, all input images were center-cropped to a size of $224 \times 224 \times 3$. We train the healthy v/s DR classification network which is further used to study the attack strength of newly generated images from our proposed approach.

---

[2] https://www.kaggle.com/c/diabetic-retinopathy-detection/data, 2015.

PGD Attack and Addition of Exudates to Fool the Human Observer.
By conducting a normal PGD attack with a maximum perturbation of $\epsilon = 1/255$
all healthy images were validated to be misclassified into DR category. While the
perturbation can fool the DNN model, the noise is imperceptible to humans and
can easily be classified as healthy by practitioners. To make the attacks more
realistic, we perform the steps listed in Sect. 2.2, 2.3. The outcomes of each
stage are illustrated in Fig. 4, where the starting image is the same one utilized
to create the adversarial image through the PGD attack, and it belongs to the
healthy category of the dataset. We then apply thresholding to the grayscale
image obtained after wavelet transform and Gabor filtering, represented as image
c in Fig. 4, which ranges from 0 to 255. We threshold using a value above the
mean value of gray level (i.e., 128) such that exudates appear not synthetic[3].The
resulting image of these operations produces an image looking similar to exudates
as a binary image which is shown in Fig. 4(d).

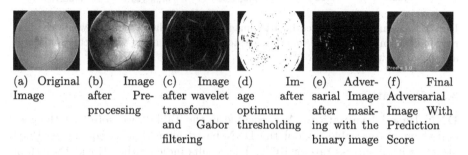

(a) Original Image (b) Image after Preprocessing (c) Image after wavelet transform and Gabor filtering (d) Image after optimum thresholding (e) Adversarial Image after masking with the binary image (f) Final Adversarial Image With Prediction Score

Fig. 4. Set of operations performed to create image-specific exudates to fool the human
observer. As it can be seen from image 'd' after the thresholding, some patterns similar
to exudates are generated. The same patterns extracted are shown in image 'e' and
image 'f' shows the final adversarial image.

Generation of Final Adversarial Image. The binary image containing the
desired patterns is then transferred to the adversarial image generated through
PGD attack in a manner that the resulting image appears normal to human
observers, resembling an image with DR. We, therefore, employ the binary image
as a mask, and based on the pixel positions in the binary image, the corresponding pixel values are added to the intermediate adversarial image to produce
the final adversarial image. Alternatively, a simpler approach is to multiply the
adversarial image with the inverted binary mask, which will set all the pixel values outside the desired pattern to zero, while keeping the pattern intact. Then,
a scaled version of the resulting image can be added to the original adversarial image to produce the final image. The final adversarial image generated is
again tested with the healthy v/s DR classification model to validate the ability

---

[3] Empirical results indicate a threshold value in the range of 190-200 to produce better
outcomes.

to deceive the model. As illustrated in the Fig. 4, the visual similarity can be observed compared to the final result of a sample image with a normal fundus image with DR as shown in Fig. 3(d). Additional results can further be seen in Fig. 5.

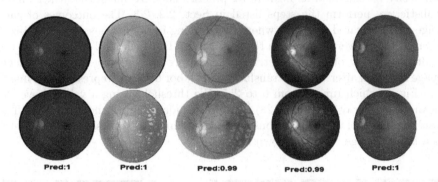

Pred:1   Pred:1   Pred:0.99   Pred:0.99   Pred:1

Fig. 5. Five randomly selected healthy images from the dataset are shown in the first row and the final adversarial image generated from them along with prediction scores are shown in the second row.

3.3   Evaluation

DNN-Based Evaluation. As presented in the Table 2, we note that the generated images are able to fool the DNN based algorithm as equally as PGD attacks with a success rate of 100%. The results indicate the attack strength of the images.

Table 2. COMPARISON OF THE PROPOSED ATTACK WITH OTHER ATTACKS

Attack Name	Attack Success (%)	Patterns resembles Exudates	Fooling Human Observer
BIM	100	No	No
FGSM	98.85	No	No
PGD	100	No	No
Proposed Attack	100	Yes	Practitioner - Kappa score -0.693
Proposed Attack	100	Yes	Normal Observer - Kappa score -0.705

Human Observer Evaluation. To further evaluate the visual quality of the generated images, we select a subset of 50 images where we include 10 newly generated perturbed images along with 15 diabetic and 25 healthy images. We conduct evaluations by employing 3 medical practitioners and 30 regular observers to classify the images into DR and healthy categories based on their perception. We measure the ability to fool human observers using the Kappa score (κ) [26]. An average $\kappa = 0.693$ is obtained from the observations of medical practitioners while an average kappa score of $\kappa = 0.705$ is obtained from the observations of regular observers, both indicate substantial agreement beyond chance on the generated images as DR images[4]. Further, we show the spread of average accuracy in identifying different categories (Healthy, diabetic and Perturbed) as presented in Fig. 6. As noted from Fig. 6, human observers classify the newly generated adversarial attack images as DR images 90% on an average while 10% of images are classified as healthy images suggesting high strength of images to deceive human perception.

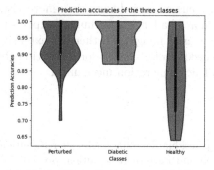 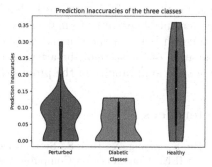

(a) Evaluation of observer classification accuracy in different scenarios: (a) Perturbed image classification into the DR class, (b) Classification of diabetic images into DR class and (c) Classification of healthy images into healthy class (No DR).

(b) Evaluation of observer classification inaccuracy in different scenarios: (a) Perturbed image classification into the DR class, (b) Classification of diabetic images into DR class and (c) Classification of healthy images into No DR class.

Fig. 6. Prediction accuracy and inaccuracy of regular observers on test set comprises of 10 Perturbed, 15 Diabetic and 25 normal images

4   Limitations of Current Work

Our current implementation of the method has been focused on one specific dataset. To ensure its effectiveness and generalizability, it is necessary to extend the evaluation to include other available datasets. Furthermore, conducting the evaluation with a larger number of medical practitioners will provide valuable insights into individual perceptual differences among experts. While our work has utilized the PGD adversarial attack method, it is important to note that the proposed method can generate similar outputs with most of the adversarial attacks employed in this field as long as the adversarial perturbations remain visually

---

[4] κ in the range $0.61 - 0.80$ shows substantial agreement beyond chance.

imperceptible to humans. By expanding the evaluation to multiple datasets and involving a larger group of medical practitioners, the reliability and applicability of the method in real-world scenarios should be studied in future works.

5   Conclusion

This paper proposes a new method for generating adversarial images from retinal fundus images that can deceive both human observers and DNN models simultaneously. The approach builds on PGD attack to introduce domain-specific details such as exudates to generate visually perceptible patterns to fool human observers to misclassify healthy fundus images. To the best of our knowledge, this is the first work in this area that aims to deceive both human and AI systems simultaneously. Future work should focus on introducing even more visually perceptible patterns to make it even more challenging for human experts to distinguish between the original and adversarial images. Further, an extensive evaluation of the state-of-the-art models needs to be studied for measuring the large-scale applicability of the proposed attack generation mechanism.

References

1. He, K., Zhang, X., Ren, S., Sun, J.: Deep residual learning for image recognition. In: IEEE Conference on Computer Vision and Pattern Recognition, pp. 770–778 (2016)
2. Gondal, W.M., Köhler, J.M., Grzeszick, R., Hirsch, M.: Weakly-supervised localization of diabetic retinopathy lesions in retinal fundus images. In: IEEE International Conference on Image Processing (ICIP), vol. 35, pp. 2069–2073 (2017)
3. Sebastian, A., Elharrouss, O.: A survey on deep-learning-based diabetic retinopathy classification. Diagnostics **13**, 345 (2023)
4. FDA. https://www.fda.gov/news-event/pressannouncements/fda-permits-marketing-artificial-intelligencebased-device-detect-certain-diabetes-related-eye
5. Qayyum, A., Qadir, J., Bilal, M., Al-Fuqaha, A.: Secure and robust machine learning for healthcare: a survey. IEEE Rev. Biomed. Eng. **14**, 156–180 (2020)
6. Finlayson, S.G., et al.: Adversarial attacks on medical machine learning. Science **363**(6433), 1287–1289 (2019)
7. Biggio, B., Roli, F.: Wild patterns: ten years after the rise of adversarial machine learning. In: ACM SIGSAC Conference on Computer and Communications Security, pp. 2154–2156 (2018)
8. Ma, X., et al.: Understanding adversarial attacks on deep learning based medical image analysis systems. Pattern Recogn. 107332 (2021)
9. Zhang, L., Wang, H., Li, Q., Zhao, M.-H.: Big data and medical research in China. Br. Med. J. **360** (2018)
10. IBIS (2023). https://www.ibisworld.com/industry-statistics/market-size/health-medical-insurance-united-states
11. Dong, J., Chen, J., Xie, X., Lai, J.: Adversarial attack and defense for medical image analysis: methods and applications. arXiv preprint arXiv:2303.14133 (2023)

12. Yao, Q., He, Z., Lin, Y., Ma, K., Zheng, Y., Zhou, S.K.: A hierarchical feature constraint to camouflage medical adversarial attacks. In: de Bruijne, M., et al. (eds.) MICCAI 2021. LNCS, vol. 12903, pp. 36–47. Springer, Cham (2021). https://doi.org/10.1007/978-3-030-87199-4_4
13. Madry, A., Makelov, A., Schmidt, L., Tsipras, D., Vladu, A.: Towards deep learning models resistant to adversarial attacks. arXiv preprint arXiv:1706.06083 (2017)
14. Paschali, M., Conjeti, S., Navarro, F., Navab, N.: Generalizability *vs.* robustness: investigating medical imaging networks using adversarial examples. In: Frangi, A.F., Schnabel, J.A., Davatzikos, C., Alberola-López, C., Fichtinger, G. (eds.) MICCAI 2018. LNCS, vol. 11070, pp. 493–501. Springer, Cham (2018). https://doi.org/10.1007/978-3-030-00928-1_56
15. Shah, A., Lynch, S., Niemeijer, M.: Susceptibility to misdiagnosis of adversarial images by deep learning based retinal image analysis algorithms. In: IEEE 15th International Symposium on Biomedical Imaging, pp. 1454–1457 (2018)
16. Cheng, Y., Juefei-Xu, F.: Adversarial exposure attack on diabetic retinopathy imagery. arXiv preprint arXiv:2009.09231 (2020)
17. Yoo, T.K., Choi, J.Y.: Outcomes of adversarial attacks on deep learning models for ophthalmology imaging domains. JAMA Ophthalmol. **138**(111), 1213–1215 (2020)
18. Qi, G., Gong, L., Song, Y., Ma, K., Zheng, Y.: Stabilized medical image attacks. arXiv preprint arXiv:2103.05232 (2021)
19. Shao, M., Zhang, G., Zuo, W., Meng, D.: Target attack on biomedical image segmentation model based on multi-scale gradients. Inf. Sci. **554**, 33–46 (2021)
20. Koga, K., Takemoto, K.: Simple black-box universal adversarial attacks on medical image classification based on deep neural networks. arXiv preprint arXiv:2108.04979 (2021)
21. Bortsova, G., González-Gonzalo, C., Wetstein, S.C., Dubost, F.: Adversarial attack vulnerability of medical image analysis systems: unexplored factors. Med. Image Anal. **73**, 102141 (2021)
22. Minagi, A., Hirano, H., Takemoto, K.: Natural images allow universal adversarial attacks on medical image classification using deep neural networks with transfer learning. J. Imaging **8**(2), 38 (2022)
23. Selvakkumar, A., Pal, S., Jadidi, Z.: Addressing adversarial machine learning attacks in smart healthcare perspectives. In: Suryadevara, N.K., George, B., Jayasundera, K.P., Roy, J.K., Mukhopadhyay, S.C. (eds.) Sensing Technology. LNEE, vol. 886, pp. 269–282. Springer, Cham (2022). https://doi.org/10.1007/978-3-030-98886-9_21
24. BMS, P.R., Anusree, V., Sreeratcha, B., Ra, P.K.: Analysis of the effect of black box adversarial attacks on medical image classification models,. In: 2022 Third International Conference on Intelligent Computing Instrumentation and Control Technologies (ICICICT), pp. 528–531 (2022)
25. Bharath Kumar, D.P., Kumar, N., Dunston, S.D., Rajam, V.M.A.: Analysis of the impact of white box adversarial attacks in ResNet while classifying retinal fundus images. In: Kalinathan, L., Priyadharsini, R., Kanmani, M., Manisha, S. (eds.) ICCIDS 2022. IFIP Advances in Information and Communication Technology, vol. 654, pp. 162–175. Springer, Cham (2022). https://doi.org/10.1007/978-3-031-16364-7
26. McHugh, M.L.: Interrater reliability: the kappa statistic. Biochem. Med. **22**, 276–282 (2012)

A Fast and Efficient Algorithm for Construction of Discrete Voronoi Diagram

Soumi Dhar[✉] and Shyamosree Pal

National Institute of Technology Silchar, Silchar, Assam, India
soumi.dhar92@gmail.com

Abstract. Unlike the cells of a Voronoi diagram in the real space the cells of a discrete Voronoi diagram in the discrete space has finite number of points. Hence in the literature we find a significant difference in the approach to the construction of the discrete voronoi diagram as compared to the construction of the Voronoi Diagram in the real space. In the discrete space the construction of discrete Voronoi diagram for a set of given sites is the process of assigning each pixel in the discrete space to its nearest site. Although there are many algorithms for the construction of discrete Voronoi diagram using the above mentioned approach, none of these algorithms found in the literature take into consideration the geometrical properties of the Voronoi Diagram while constructing it. We present a novel approach for the construction of discrete Voronoi Diagram for a given set of points based on a purely digital geometric approach taking into consideration its geometry. Since the circle is defined as the locus of a point that is equidistant from a given point, our algorithm constructs digital circles around each site, to assign the pixels that are nearest to that site using an iterative circle growing technique. The key idea of the proposed algorithm is that in the i-th iteration (initially $i = 1$) we assign pixels which are at a distance given by the open interval $(i - \frac{1}{2}, i + \frac{1}{2})$ from each site, provided, they are not already assigned to any other site. Thus, at any instant of time a pixel, p is assigned to a site s if and only if s is its nearest site in the digital space. Our algorithm terminates once all pixels have been assigned to the nearest site.

Keyword: Voronoi diagram, Discrete Circle and Missing pixels

1 Introduction

Voronoi diagram is considered as of the classical problems in Discrete and Geometry. [1, 2]. It is a partitioning scheme of the plane into subdivisions or regions corresponding to each site such that any point in a given region is nearest to the corresponding site contained in that region. It serves as the most widely used tools in computational geometry [3–6] as it has a wide range of applications in many scientific and engineering disciplines [7, 8]. It has applications in medical sciences like visualization of medical datasets [9], optimum mesh generation on a rabbit femur surface using Voronoi neighborhood [10], and others. Voronoi diagram can be used to solve the face detection problems as shown in [11, 12]. This diagram seems very powerful tool in robot path planning

© The Author(s), under exclusive license to Springer Nature Switzerland AG 2024
H. Kaur et al. (Eds.): CVIP 2023, CCIS 2011, pp. 296–308, 2024.
https://doi.org/10.1007/978-3-031-58535-7_25

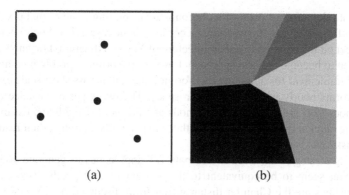

Fig. 1. (a) Input consisting of five sites. (b) Output Discrete Voronoi diagram for the given input.

[13], too. If the points are treated as obstacles in a given space, then restricting a robot to traverse the edges created by the Voronoi diagram will ensure that it is the maximum distance away from the nearest surrounding points at all times. The 3D Voronoi diagram [14]can be used for numerous and surprisingly different geometric problem [15, 16]. In computational geometry it tends to be the appropriate solution to the proximity queries [17, 18]. Voronoi diagrams together with farthest-point Voronoi diagrams [19] are used for efficient algorithms to compute the roundness of a set of points. Voronoi diagram can solve the problem of deriving the capacity of wireless sensor network [20].

So researchers have tried to develop algorithms for computing Voronoi diagram since the middle of 20th century. The most common algorithm available in the literature is the Incremental algorithm which is of $O(n^2)$ complexity [21] but relatively easy to implement, the Divide and Conquer approach with $O(nlogn)$ complexity [22] and the Fortune's algorithm with complexity $O(nlogn)$ [23] which is by far the optimal solution. But the problem with all the above mentioned algorithms is that they fail to perform with the same accuracy when applied to discrete space. This is because when we compute a Discrete Voronoi diagram we have to consider a finite domain (represented as a uniform grid) such that the Discrete Voronoi region of site is the finite set of cells closer to that site than any other.

Thus in our work we aim to find the discrete Voronoi Diagram of a given set of sites within a bounded space, I in Z^2, as shown in Fig. 1.

This paper is divided into the following sections as follows. In Sect. 2 where we mention the related work in discrete Voronoi diagram construction. In Sect. 4 we give our novel algorithm for the construction of the discrete Voronoi diagram based on assignment of each pixel to a given site. In Sect. 5 we discuss the results of our experimentation. Finally in Sect. 6 we conclude our paper.

2   Related Works

There are good numbers of theoretical as well as practical algorithms for computing Voronoi diagrams of real-space points in any dimension.. Fortune [17] was the first one to offer a mathematical geometry-based approach to the challenge. Every pixel site develops into the leftmost pixel of its Voronoi areas, putting it the primal pixel reached throughout from left to right sweeping, according to the researcher. Such interpretation has no effect on the compositional architecture of Voronoi diagram. Fortune's approach is often seen to become the best approach, however the primary problem being that it is difficult to implement for obtaining the Voronoi diagram across short scale executions, and it performs poorly in non - euclidean space. The two types of distance transform (DT) methods [24] are estimate DT methods and precise DT methods. Estimation DT methods are quicker than accurate DT methods in generally, although their results might involve mistakes.

Scanning strategies are used in estimate DT approaches to generate computation expenses that seem to be equivalent to the amount of grid pixels. Two extensively used approaches are the Chamfer distance transform discussed in [25] and sequential Euclidean distance mapping is reported in [26]. Either of the approaches mentioned to employ a mask matrix to read a full picture grid pixels twice. Many different types of precise Distance Transform methods have been discussed in the literature, including such preserving and ordering the front of the transmission, and recording numerous adjacent sites rather than only one. This screening sequence connects every one of the processes listed, with something like the values of an unit getting determined by that of the values of units scanned beforehand. As a result, the problems may emerge while parallelizing similar techniques. Some other time-consuming precise DT approach is to apply a mask to every unit the value of unit not get modified further [23], Although this method provides some concurrency, it is poor in terms of computing. [27] developed a concurrent approach for dividing the grids (discontinuous surface) into several subsections and processing those everyone at once utilizing multiprocessor computers. Such strategy should account for the effect of neighboring subsections. As a consequence of the absence of concurrency at the cell level, this approach is useless on GPU. But when it comes to the construction of discrete Voronoi diagram the approach totally changes as we shift our focus from the real domain to the discrete domain. Thus, to solve the discrete Voronoi diagram problem researchers have implemented various algorithms applicable to the discrete space. Most of these algorithms are GPU based random flooding of the discrete space with site information. In [28] the first such GPU algorithm was proposed. Jump Flood algorithms and various variants of Jump Flood algorithms [29,30], which are basically concerned with the finding of nearest site for each cell in the given finite discrete space are the most common and popular algorithms found in the literature. But JFA as well as its variants do not consider the geometric characteristics of the discrete space and uses a random flooding technique to compute the discrete Voronoi diagram which accounts for some excess computation as it resolves all clashes by calculating the Euclidean distance of the concerned pixel from the concerned sites.

3   Preliminaries

As mentioned earlier the geometric primitive used in this paper is the digital circle. There are several definitions of a digital circle available in the literature based on the fact that whether the center and radius of the circle have real or integer values. Here we are considering Bresenham's digital circle having integer values for center and radius

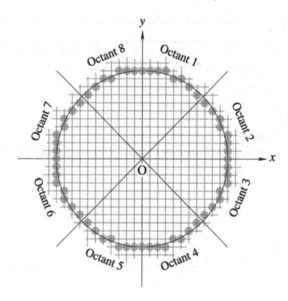

Fig. 2. A complete digital circle with radius 11 showing all the eight octant [20].

and its construction is as proposed in [31]. If Z represents the set of a nonnegative integers, then Z^+ is presented as the set of positive integers such that radius $r \in Z^+$. Let the center be $S = O(0,0)$, So the equation which provides the corresponding digital circle is denoted by Eq. 1

$$S_1^z(O,r) = \left\{ (i,j) \in Z^2 | 0 \le i \le j \le r \wedge |j - \sqrt{r^2 - l^2}| < \frac{1}{2} \right\} \tag{1}$$

Hence, octant 1 of any digital circle $S^z(P,r)$ which have $P(i_P, j_P) \in Z^2$ as the center and radius $r \in Z^+$ obtained is by the following equation: (2):

$$S_i^Z(P,r) = \{(i+i_P, j+j_P)|(i,j) \in S^Z(O,r)\}. \tag{2}$$

The digital circle possesses 8-octant symmetry [31], thus generating the set of points of a single octant of the circle (in Fig. 2) is only required to generate the complete circle can be formed by the reflection of the respective axes of symmetry. Figure 2 is an example of digital circle with center point at $O_i(0,0)$ where radius $r = 11$.

3.1 Construction of a Digital Circle

Utilizing the total count of perfect squares which falls in the intervals as mentioned in Fact 1, the authors has proposed i [31] a significant algorithm for the construction of digital circles which forms the basis of our discrete voronoi diagram construction algorithm. The digital circle construction algorithm given in [31]. Everything is not as smooth as it seems in this circle growing algorithm. As we construct digital circles of

---

Procedure MDCS

Input : r : *Radius of integer value,* s_i : *Center with integer points*
Output: *Pixels of digital circle of radius r along with absentee pixel if any*

1 **int** $i = 0, j = r, s = 0, w = r - 1, w1 = r$;
2 **int** $l = w, l1 = w1$;
3 **while** $j \geqslant i$ **do**
4   **while** $s \leqslant w$ **do**
5          $drawCircle(i, j)$ //*Function to put 8 symmetric pixels at subsequence points*;
6          $s = s + i$;
7          $i + +$;
8          $s = s + i$;
9   **end**
10   **if** $s \leqslant w1$ **then**
11         $drawCircle(i, j)$ //*Function to put 8 symmetric pixels at subsequence points*;
12   **end**
13     $s = w + l + l$;
14     $l = l - 1, l1 = l1 - 1$;
15 **end**

---

consecutive radii, starting with radius $r = 1$, we face the problem of absentee pixel generation. As given in the literature, in [32] the authors have shown that while constructing a digital disc of radius r by the circle growing technique (similar to our proposed work) there arises a set of pixels that are not included in the disc but lie well within the digital disc of radius r. In [33] Andres suggested that instead of using digital circles [31] as primitive, the use of arithmetical circle [34] would solve the problem of absentee pixels. But the problem with arithmetical circle is that it plots only one pixels at a time, whereas digital circle generation using the distribution of square numbers in discrete intervals is more efficient because it considers the run - length property. In our work we have come up with an idea to construct arithmetical circle using the run length properties of DCS. In order to do so, we have modified the algorithm which successfully generates a disc without any absentee pixels and the algorithm is termed as procedure *MDCS* (Fig. 3).

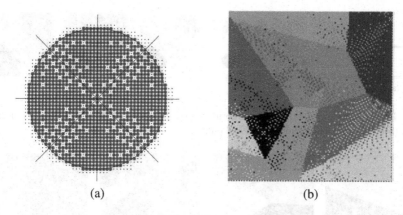

(a)   (b)

Fig. 3. (a) Absentee pixels in the digital disc of radius $r=20$ [32]. (b) Erroneous discrete Voronoi diagram construction where each absentee pixel is assigned to a site that is not its nearest site.

4 Proposed Method

In this work we propose a novel algorithm for the construction of discrete voronoi diagram for a given set of k sites in the discrete space of size $P \times Q$, where P and Q are the number of rows and columns of the discrete space, respectively. Since the discrete space is finite in nature the focus of our work is to assign each pixel in this $P \times Q$ discrete space to its nearest site from the given distribution of k sites, namely, $\{s_1, s_2, ...s_k\}$ using a digital circle growing algorithm. The circle suffices as the geometric primitive as it gives the locus of all points that are equidistant to a given point. For any real circle of radius r all its points are at a distance r from the center of the circle. But for a digital circle of radius r we cannot say that each of its points (pixels) are at a distance r from the center as is evident from the definition, (considering the Euclidean distance of the center of a pixel located on a digital circle and the center of the digital circle). Rather, the center of each pixel of a given digital circle is at a distance from the center of the circle contained in the open interval $(r - \frac{1}{2}, r + \frac{1}{2})$. Since the above interval is open we can conclude that if we construct two digital circles of radius r and $r+1$ about a given center B, then all points of the digital circle of radius r will be nearer to B (center), than all points of the digital circle of radius $r+1$. As stated earlier for a given set of k sites ($\{s_1, s_2, ...s_k\}$) all the points within the cell of site, s_i, in a Voronoi diagram are the points closer or equally closer to all other $k-1$ sites in the given distribution. So this property highly correlates with the general property of a digital circle and is used in our algorithm for Voronoi diagram construction. Hence, we propose an iterative circle growing algorithm to propagate the information of the sites and eventually generate the discrete Voronoi diagram.

The basic steps of are algorithm are as follows:

- In each iteration a digital circle of radius r is constructed around a site (as the center) and the points on this digital circle are assigned to that site if and only if it is not assigned to any other site. The iteration completes when a digital circle of radius r is considered around each site, $s_i (1 \leqslant i \leqslant k)$ as the center.

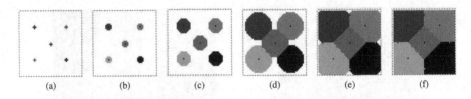

Fig. 4. Demonstration of the proposed algorithm. (a) Input having 5 sites in a 50×50 discrete space. (b)–(e) Intermediate outputs. (f) Final output.

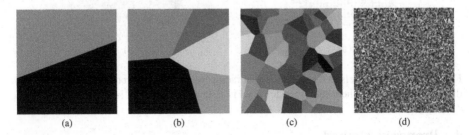

Fig. 5. Discrete voronoi diagram constructed by our algorithm for set of sites of size = (a) 2, (b) 10, (c) 100, (d) 10000

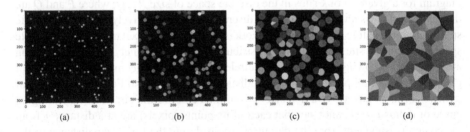

Fig. 6. Proposed discrete Voronoi diagram algorithm in action (a) r=2, (b) r=10, (c) r=20, (d) r-50

- The first iteration starts with $r = 1$ and in each successive iterations we increase the radius from r to $r + 1$ and keep on iterating until all points in the given discrete space are assigned to a site, $s_i \in \{s_1, s_2, ...s_k\}$.

Figure 5 gives the demonstration of the proposed algorithm (Fig. 4).

4.1 Proposed Algorithm(Serial Approach)

The proposed method for the construction of discrete voronoi diagram is given by Algorithm 1 which is described as follows. The input to the algorithm is a set of k sites (randomly generated). First we set a variable *Unassigned* equal to the total number of pixels in the discrete space that do not have any site information (step 2). In steps 3 and 4 of the algorithm all sites are set to a status of 1, signifying them as active sites. In step 6 we obtain the maximum radius of digital circle which has to be drawn for any site in any grid position as the floor of the diagonal distance of the given discrete space. This

---

Algorithm 1: Discrete Voronoi Diagram Construction

Input : k : *Set of sites* , P : *Total count of rows in the grid* and Q:*Total count of columns in the grid*

Output: *Discrete Voronoi diagram on* $P \times Q$ *grid*

1 int $d, r, i, stopgrowth, Status[i]$;
2 int $Unassigned = P \times Q - k$;
3 **for** $i \leftarrow 1$ **to** k **do**
4 | Initialize Status[i]=1
5 **end**
6 $d = \lfloor \sqrt{P^2 + Q^2} \rfloor$;
7 **for** $r \leftarrow 1$ **to** d **do**
8 | **for** $i \leftarrow 1$ **to** k **do**
9 | | **if** *(Status[i]==1)* **then**
10 | | | *stopgrowth*=MDCS() //pixels are assigned to site i only if they are not assigned to any other site;
11 | | | *Unassigned = Unassigned − stopgrowth*;
12 | | | **if** *(stopgrowth==0)* **then**
13 | | | | Status[i]=0;
14 | | | **end**
15 | | **end**
16 | **end**
17 | **if** *(Unassigned==0)* **then**
18 | | Exit;
19 | **end**
20 **end**

---

is the worst case situation when the site lies at one of the corners of the discrete space. Then we start the outer **for** loop whose loop variable r gives the radius for digital circle construction for each iteration (step 7–18). The inner **for** loop gives the different sites or centers around which the concentric digital circles are to be drawn (step 8–13). Inside the inner **for** loop it is checked whether the i-th site is active i.e., whether new pixels were assigned to this site in the previous iteration and its status is 1 (9). If its *status* is 1 it is still active or its cell has not been constructed completely, and the digital circle of radius r is constructed around this site i in step 10 by calling the *MDCS*() procedure.

The procedure *MDCS*() is almost the same as the *DCS* algorithm mentioned in [31]. The only difference being that we declare in the above mentioned procedure two additional variables w_1 and l_1 (step 1) required to keep track of the lookahead aspect for absentee finding. For each of the ordinate value j in the first octant we check whether the square number stored in s when it comes out of the inner **while** loop is $\leq w_1$. If it is so then it signifies that (i, j) is an absentee pixel. This pixel and its 8-symmetric pixels are then assigned to this site i if it is already not assigned to any other site. At the end of the procedure in steps 13 and 14 $w1$ and $l1$ are updated and made ready for the next value of j.

Finally in the inner loop the status of site i is set to 0 if *stopgrowth* is found to be zero, signifying that the voronoi cell for site i has been completely constructed and no more new assignments are possible. Also *Unassigned* is updated by deducting from it the total of all pixels assigned to site i in that iteration (step 11). In step 17 and 18 of the outer loop it is checked whether all pixels have been assigned to their respective sites. Since the number of pixels in the discrete space are finite our algorithm terminates (Fig. 6).

4.2 Correctness of the Proposed Method

The loop invariant of the proposed algorithm can be stated as

The jth iteration of the outer **for** loop starts with allocating all pixels, that are at a distance less than $(j-1)+\frac{1}{2}$ from any site are assigned to their nearest site.

To prove the above loop invariant we must show that it is correct in each of the three cases:

Initialization: It is true before the first iteration of the loop as at this point only the pixels that represent sites are assigned. and they are at a distance zero from their respective sites.

Maintenance: Now, after iteration $j-1$ all pixels at a distance less than $(j-1)+\frac{1}{2}$ from any site are assigned to their nearest site. In the j-th iteration we are constructing concentric circles of radius j around each sites $\in \{s_1, s_2, ...s_k\}$. By the property of the digital circle of radius j all the pixels on the digital circle are at a distance given by the open interval $(j-\frac{1}{2}, j+\frac{1}{2})$ from the respective center (or sites). Again, there are some pixels that belong neither to the digital circle of radius j nor to the digital circle of radius $j+1$. They arise due to the fact that the digital circle we are constructing using *DCS* are minimally connected in its 8-neighborhood. But there are pixels in the 4-connected neighborhood of a digital circle which also lie at a distance less than $j+\frac{1}{2}$) from the respective site center. Since these pixels cannot belong to a digital circle of radius $j+1$ they are assigned to the corresponding nearest site in the j-th iteration itself.

The lookahead technique used correctly finds all such pixel and assigns them to the corresponding site if it is not already assigned to some other nearer site. Thus after the j-th iteration all pixels that are at a distance less than $j+\frac{1}{2}$ have been assigned to its nearest site.

Since we do not change the previous assignment of pixels it guarantees the correctness of the algorithm. This is because a pixel assigned to a site in a previous assignment will always be at a distance less than $j-\frac{1}{2}$ to that particular site as it is obtained by constructing a digital circle of radius less than j from that site.

Termination: The algorithm terminates when there are no more pixels left unassigned. Since it correctly exits each iteration, at the end of the final iteration it will terminate with the correct output (Table 1).

Table 1. Time taken by our algorithm for different no. of input sites

No. of Sites	Time taken (in seconds)
10	0.006
100	0.019
500	0.021
1000	0.013
10000	0.026

5   Experimental Results and Discussions

The proposed algorithm has been implemented in Dev C++. The hardware platform is Intel(R) i5-8300H CPU clock rate 2.30GHz, Nvidia GeForce GTX 1650Ti Graphics card, warp size 32, maximum number of threads per block is 1024. For each run of our experiment, random generation of input sites for a discrete space of size 4096 × 4096 has been considered. The number of sites ranges from 2 to 10000.

We have compared our proposed solution with the most popular algorithm for discrete Voronoi diagram construction namely Jump flood algorithm. As the name suggests, it works by iteratively "jumping" between nearby pixels in a grid without taking into account the geometric characteristics of the discrete space. It finds the closest point to each pixel by calculating the euclidean distance. The JFA algorithm can produce errors [29] with the increased number of step size in the computation of the Voronoi diagram(See Fig. 10). In JFA each grid point permits many other seeds to temporarily be its nearest seeds in order to pass them on to other grid points. It can produce incorrect edges in the Voronoi diagram if the input points are closely spaced. On a contrary our proposed solution based on a modified variant of discrete circle generating algorithm(MDCS) which does not involve any jumping, which means once a pixel has been assigned to a particular site it never changes it position, so there is almost no error caused due the temporary placement of the pixels. It ensures the correctness of the algorithm. Moreover it has also been observed that the proposed algorithm performs similar or better results in terms of execution time. The time frame has been plotted in Fig. 9.

5.1   Empirical Analysis

The minimum radius of our digital circle is 1, whereas the maximum radius will be the diagonal distance of the discrete space in the worst case. If we consider a square grid of $n \times n$ its diagonal distance will be $\sqrt{2}n$. From emperical analysis it is clear that for k sites the worst case complexity of initiation of pixel assignment in our proposed algorithm is $O(kn^2)$. But experimental results show that as the number of sites increase the minimum and maximum radius to which digital circles, having site as its center, are to be grown decreases rapidly. This means for large number of input sites the incremental digital circle construction are stopped much earlier for each site, which increases the efficiency of the algorithm. Thus our algorithm performs much better than its worst case complexity in all practical cases.

6 Conclusion and Future Scope

In this present study the authors have proposed a novel algorithm for fast construction of discrete Voronoi diagram. The proposed approach is based on traditional serial execution of the code. Surprisingly this novel approach performs outstanding in terms of CPU times. The advantage of our algorithm is that we are obtaining the discrete Voronoi diagram considering geometric primitives that ensures that a pixel will be assigned to a site only if it is its nearest site and the pixel is unassigned. This ensures no distance calculation is required to resolve clashes because if the pixel is already assigned to a site in an earlier iteration then any other site trying to include it in its cell in a later iteration cannot be nearer than its already assigned site. This circle growing technique is an elegant feature of our both the algorithms which has been conceptualised using the digital geometric techniques. The novelty of this algorithm lies in the interesting fact that it uses digital geometric primitives which has not been used in any of the existing algorithms [29,30]. Also it terminates with the correct output as is evident from the experimental results without any additional steps. The accuracy of our algorithm is within a tolerance of $\delta \leqslant 0.5$ unit arising due to the discrete space constraints which can be tolerated in all practical applications. The parallelization of the proposed algorithm taking into account on GPUs can be treated as engrossing problem, and it would definitely bring down the time complexity of the construction algorithm. Also implementation of the proposed algorithm in some real applications like robot path planning, molecular structure analysis, face recognition etc. remain as an open problem.

Conflict of Interest. The authors declare that there is no conflict of interest.

References

1. Aurenhammer, F.: Voronoi diagrams-a survey of a fundamental geometric data structure. ACM Comput. Surv. **23**(3), 345–405 (1991). https://doi.org/10.1145/116873.116880
2. Klette, R., Rosenfeld, A.: Digital Geometry: Geometric Methods for Digital Picture Analysis. Morgan Kaufmann Publishers Inc., San Francisco (2004)
3. Wein, R., van den Berg, J.P., Halperin, D.: The visibility-voronoi complex and its applications, Computational Geometry 36(1), 66–87 (2007). special Issue on the 21st European Workshop on Computational Geometry. https://doi.org/10.1016/j.comgeo.2005.11.007. https://www.sciencedirect.com/science/article/pii/S0925772106000496
4. Wang, X., et al.: Intrinsic computation of centroidal Voronoi tessellation (CVT) on meshes, Comput.-Aided Des. **58**, 51–61 (2015). solid and Physical Modeling 2014. https://doi.org/10.1016/j.cad.2014.08.023. https://www.sciencedirect.com/science/article/pii/S0010448514001924
5. Kim, D.S.: A single beta-complex solves all geometry problems in a molecule, pp. 254–260 (2009). https://doi.org/10.1109/ISVD.2009.41
6. Pal, S., Dutta, R., Bhowmick, P.: Circular arc segmentation by curvature estimation and geometric validation. Int. J. Image Graph. **12**(04), 1250024 (2012). https://doi.org/10.1142/S0219467812500246
7. She, B., Zhu, X., ye, X., Su, K., Lee, J.: Weighted network Voronoi diagrams for local spatial analysis. Comput. Environ. Urban Syst. **52**, 70–80 (2015). https://doi.org/10.1016/j.compenvurbsys.2015.03.005

8. Dhar, S., Pal, S.: Surface reconstruction: roles in the field of computer vision and computer graphics. Int. J. Image Graph. **22**(01), 2250008 (2022). https://doi.org/10.1142/S0219467822500085

9. Lindow, N., Baum, D., Hege, H.-C.: Voronoi-based extraction and visualization of molecular paths. IEEE Trans. Visual Comput. Graphics **17**, 2025–34 (2011). https://doi.org/10.1109/TVCG.2011.259

10. Brown, K.Q.: Voronoi diagrams from convex hulls. Inf. Proc. Lett. **9**(5), 223–228 (1979). https://doi.org/10.1016/0020-0190(79)90074-7

11. Shivanasab, P., Ali Abbaspour, R.: An incremental algorithm for simultaneous construction of 2D Voronoi diagram and Delaunay triangulation based on a face-based data structure. Adv. Eng. Softw. **169**, 103129 (2022). https://www.sciencedirect.com/science/article/pii/S0965997822000400

12. Jida, S., Ouanan, M., Aksasse, B.: Color image segmentation using Voronoi diagram and 2D histogram. Int. J. Tomogr. Simul. **30**, 14–20 (2017)

13. Šeda, M., Pich, V.: Robot motion planning using generalised Voronoi diagrams. target 1 (2008) q2

14. Biswas, R., Bhowmick, P.: Construction of persistent Voronoi diagram on 3D digital plane, pp. 93–104 (2017). https://doi.org/10.1007/978-3-319-59108-7_8

15. Zhao, S., Evans, T.M., Zhou, X.: Three-dimensional Voronoi analysis of monodisperse ellipsoids during triaxial shear. Powder Technol. **323**, 323–336 (2018). https://doi.org/10.1016/j.powtec.2017.10.023. https://www.sciencedirect.com/science/article/pii/S0032591017308197

16. Surajkanta, Y., Pal, S.: Recognition of spherical segments using number theoretic properties of Isothetic covers. Multimedia Tools Appl., 1–24 (2022). https://doi.org/10.1007/s11042-022-14182-3

17. Fortune, S.: A sweepline algorithm for Voronoi diagrams. In: Proceedings of the Second Annual Symposium on Computational Geometry, SCG '86. Association for Computing Machinery, New York, pp. 313-322 (1986). https://doi.org/10.1145/10515.10549

18. Ferreira, N., Poco, J., Vo, H.T., Freire, J., Silva, C.T.: Visual exploration of big Spatiotemporal urban data: a study of New York city taxi trips. IEEE Trans. Visual Comput. Graphics **19**(12), 2149–2158 (2013). https://doi.org/10.1109/TVCG.2013.226

19. de Berg, M., Cheong, O., van Kreveld, M.J., Overmars, M.H.: Computational Geometry: Algorithms and Applications, 3rd ed. Springer Cham (2008). https://www.worldcat.org/oclc/227584184

20. Saha, D., Das, N., Pal, S.: A digital-geometric approach for computing area coverage in wireless sensor networks. In: Natarajan, R. (ed.) Distributed Computing and Internet Technology, pp. 134–145. Springer International Publishing, Cham (2014). https://doi.org/10.1007/978-3-319-04483-5_15

21. Allen, S.R., Barba, L., Iacono, J., Langerman, S.: Incremental Voronoi diagrams. CoRR abs/1603.08485 (2016). http://arxiv.org/abs/1603.08485

22. Sherbrooke, E., Patrikalakis, N., Brisson, E.: Computation of the medial axis transform of 3-D Polyhedra (1995). https://doi.org/10.1145/218013.218059

23. Albers, G., Guibas, L.J., Mitchell, J.S.B., Roos, T.: Voronoi diagrams of moving points. Int. J. Comput. Geom. Appl. **08**(03), 365–379 (1998). https://doi.org/10.1142/S0218195998000187

24. Meijster, A., Roerdink, J., Hesselink, W.: A general algorithm for computing distance transforms in linear time. In: Goutsias, J., Vincent, L., Bloomberg, D.S. (eds.) Mathematical Morphology and its Applications to Image and Signal Processing. Computational Imaging and Vision, vol. 18, pp. 331–340. Springer, Boston (2002). https://doi.org/10.1007/0-306-47025-X_36

25. Arora, S., Raghavan, P., Rao, S.: Approximation schemes for Euclidean k-medians and related problems. In: Proceedings of the Thirtieth Annual ACM Symposium on Theory of Computing, STOC '98, pp. 106-113. Association for Computing Machinery, New York (1998). https://doi.org/10.1145/276698.276718
26. Borradaile, G., Klein, P.N., Mathieu, C.: A polynomial-time approximation scheme for euclidean steiner forest (2015)
27. Sugihara, K., Iri, M.: A robust topology-oriented incremental algorithm for Voronoi diagrams. Int. J. Comput. Geom. Appl. **04**(02), 179–228 (1994). https://doi.org/10.1142/S0218195994000124
28. Hoff, K.E., Keyser, J., Lin, M., Manocha, D., Culver, T.: Fast computation of generalized Voronoi diagrams using graphics hardware. In: Proceedings of the 26th Annual Conference on Computer Graphics and Interactive Techniques, SIGGRAPH '99. ACM Press/Addison-Wesley Publishing Co., USA, pp. 277–286 (1999). https://doi.org/10.1145/311535.311567
29. Rong, G., Tan, T.-S.: Jump flooding in GPU with applications to Voronoi diagram and distance transform, vol. 2006, pp. 109–116 (2006). https://doi.org/10.1145/1111411.1111431
30. Masood, T.B., Malladi, H.K., Natarajan, V.: Facet-JFA: faster computation of discrete Voronoi diagrams. In: Proceedings of the 2014 Indian Conference on Computer Vision Graphics and Image Processing, ICVGIP '14. Association for Computing Machinery, New York (2014). https://doi.org/10.1145/2683483.2683503
31. Bhowmick, P., Bhattacharya, B.B.: Number-theoretic interpretation and construction of a digital circle. Discr. Appl. Math. **156**(12), 2381–2399 (2008). https://doi.org/10.1016/j.dam.2007.10.022. https://www.sciencedirect.com/science/article/pii/S0166218X07004817
32. Bera, S., Bhowmick, P., Bhattacharya, B.: On the characterization of absentee-voxels in a spherical surface and volume of revolution in F^3 z 3. J. Math. Imaging Vision **56** (2016). https://doi.org/10.1007/s10851-016-0654-8
33. Andres, E., Richaume, L., Largeteau-Skapin, G.: Digital surface of revolution with hand-drawn generatrix. J. Math. Imaging Vis. (2017). https://doi.org/10.1007/s10851-017-0708-6
34. Andres, E.: Discrete circles, rings and spheres. Comput. Graph. **18**(5), 695–706 (1994). https://doi.org/10.1016/0097-8493(94)90164-3

An Explainable Deep Learning Model for Fingerprint Presentation Attack Detection

Anuj Rai[✉] [iD] and Somnath Dey[iD]

Indian Institute of Technology Indore, Indore 453552, India
{phd1901201003,somnathd}@iiti.ac.in

Abstract. Automatic fingerprint recognition systems stand as the most extensively employed for person identification as compared with systems based on other biometric traits. Their usefulness in a variety of applications makes them vulnerable to presentation attacks which can be performed by presenting an artificial artifact of a genuine user's fingerprint to the fingerprint based recognition systems. Hence, presentation attack detection becomes essential to ensure the security of fingerprint-based recognition systems. This paper proposes a novel method that incorporates the concept of explainability for the enhancement of the classification performance of the deep learning model. The proposed method consists of two building blocks including a heatmap generator and a classifier. The heatmap generator highlights the key features and generates a heatmap that helps the classifier to learn its parameters in a better way. The proposed method is validated using benchmark LivDet 2011, 2013, and 2015 databases. The comparative analysis demonstrates the superior performance of the proposed model in terms of classification accuracy when compared to state-of-the-art methodologies.

Keywords: Fingerprint Biometrics · Presentation Attack · Deep Learning · Explainability

1 Introduction

The Automatic Fingerprint Recognition System (AFRS) stands as an easy-to-use and cost-effective biometric-driven solution for person recognition. Comparable to other biometric recognition systems, it verifies a person with less time and human effort. AFRS plays an important role in person verification or authentication within security-related applications, including airport security checks, Aadhar verification, international borders [4], and various commercial applications including Automated Teller Machines (ATM). However, due to its wide-ranging applications, AFRS is susceptible to an array of attacks, with Presentation Attacks (PAs) being a notable concern. PAs encompass fraudulent attempts to deceive AFRS sensors by presenting fabricated artifacts of a legitimate user's fingerprint. These attacks can manifest in two primary forms: cooperative method and non-cooperative method of spoofing. In non-cooperative spoofing, latent fingerprints left by individuals on smooth surfaces are photographed

H. Kaur et al. (Eds.): CVIP 2023, CCIS 2011, pp. 309–321, 2024.
https://doi.org/10.1007/978-3-031-58535-7_26

and subsequently digitized before being artificially reproduced using spoofing materials. On the other side, cooperative method relies on the subject itself to provide their finger impression for spoofing. In addition, the security of AFRS is severely hampered by the discovery of novel fabrication materials as they can be used by attackers to create more realistic spoofs. Fingerprint Presentation Attack Detection (FPAD) is a defense mechanism against such attacks. The FPAD methods are categorized as hardware-based methods and software-based methods. Hardware-based approaches are comparably expensive since they require extra sensors to assess the natural properties such as wetness, temperature, heart rate, etc. On the other hand, software-based solutions necessitate solely a fingerprint sample, rendering them not only user-friendly but also a cost-effective option for utilization by organizations.

The existing software-based methods can be further categorized as perspiration and pore-based based methods [20] [13], quality features-based methods [19] [18] [8], and deep learning-based methods [26] [3] [22]. Perspiration-based methods hinge on two key factors: the ambient temperature and the level of pressure applied to the fingertip. Calculating this feature frequently requires multiple impressions of the fingertip to ascertain whether the fingerprint is genuine or a spoof. Similarly, the extraction of pore-based features requires a high-resolution fingerprint sample (>1000 dpi), raising the cost of an FPAD model based on this feature. Recently, techniques reliant on quality-based features and deep learning have exhibited noteworthy robustness in identifying Presentation Attacks (PAs). Nonetheless, these approaches still confront challenges in achieving high classification accuracy when tested with spoof samples fabricated from unknown materials.

The proposed architectural framework consists of an integrated encoder-decoder system alongside a classifier, operating in an end-to-end manner. The encoder-decoder is responsible for highlighting the important pixels in an image which plays a vital role in the classification of the sample. This module transforms the input sample into a corresponding heatmap, which is subsequently employed as input for the second module comprising a CNN classifier. The proposed model is validated using benchmark fingerprint databases and it demonstrates superior performance compared to state-of-the-art methods in benchmark FPAD protocols. The subsequent sections of this paper are arranged as follows. Section 2 provides an overview of prior FPAD methods put forth by researchers. Section 3 elaborates on the design and other details of the proposed method. Sections 4 and 5 provide comprehensive insights into our experimental setup, results, and comparison of the proposed method with state-of-the-art methods. The paper is concluded in Sect. 6.

2   Related Work

The applications of AFRS in various security-related applications have made them prone to PAs. In recent times, researchers have suggested various methods for confronting PAs. Some of these methods are discussed in this section.

Abhyankar and colleagues [2] devised a wavelet-based approach for FPAD, leveraging fingerprint perspiration patterns to differentiate between real and spoof fingerprints. Similarly, Tan et al. (2015) [20] leveraged perspiration patterns in their work to detect Presentation Attacks (PAs). They adopted an intensity-based method to acquire both static and dynamic perspiration characteristics. The perspiration is caused by tiny holes which are present in the finger skin. Espinoza et al. [5] utilized the number of sweat pores as a key feature for the detection of PAs. In a similar way, Marcalis et al. [14] utilized the number of pores as a discriminating feature to develop an FPAD method. The fabrication of spoofs causes some irregularities in the spoofs samples which makes them separable from the live samples. The natural properties of the finger's skin, in contrast to the fabricated spoofs, exhibit distinctive qualities such as color, moisture content, and elasticity level, which manifest in the quality of the acquired fingerprint samples. Park et al. [17], in their study, employed a set of six statistical features, encompassing metrics like skewness, kurtosis, deviation, variance, hyper skewness, and hyper flatness, as part of their methodology for the detection of Presentation Attacks (PAs). The ATVSFFp database is used to validate the proposed method. Galbally et al. [6] proposed a novel approach for the detection of PAs in the face, iris, and fingerprint-based biometric systems, leveraging a comprehensive set of twenty-five quality features. Similarly, Sharma et al. [19] proposed an approach that makes use of diverse quality features, including Ridge Width Smoothness (RWS), Valley Width Smoothness (VWS), Ridge Valley Clarity (RVC), Frequency Domain Analysis (FDA), Gabor quality, etc. The proposed method is validated using the LivDet 2009, 2011, 2013, and 2015 databases. The evolution of Convolutional Neural Networks (CNN) attracted various researchers to utilize them for discriminating between live and spoof samples. The possession of convolutional filters enables CNNs to extract minute features from input samples which are hard for other handcrafted feature methods to extract. Arora et al. [3] proposed a model that utilizes VGG 16 classifier. The effectiveness of this method is demonstrated through validation using a range of benchmark databases, including ATVSFFp, LivDet 2013, and 2015 databases. Uliyan et al. [22] proposed an approach based on deep features for the detection of Presentation Attacks (PAs). It utilizes the Restricted Boltzmann Machine (RBM) for feature extraction and the Deep Boltzmann Machine (DBM) to explore intricate feature correlations. Zhang et al. [26] proposed a deep-learning model featuring a sequence of adapted residual blocks. This restructured design achieves the detection of PAs with reduced over-fitting and processing time. The validation of this approach is conducted on Livdet 2013 and 2015 databases. Nogueira et al. [16], in their work, utilized existing deep CNN architectures such as Alexnet, VGG, etc. The validation of the proposed method is carried out on LivDet 2009, 2011, and 2013 databases.

The detailed literature survey concludes that perspiration and pore-based methods are less user-friendly as well as cost-effective due to certain limitations. The quality feature-based methods perform better but deep learning-based methods outperform others due to the possession of convolutional filters. However, these methods needs to be improved in terms of classification accuracy.

3   Proposed Work

This paper proposes a novel architectural design, composed of two distinct components: an encoder-decoder block and a classifier, as illustrated in Fig. 1. The encoder-decoder block is responsible for generating heatmaps, which highlight important pixels within the input image sample. Subsequently, the generated heatmap serves as input for the classifier, tasked with determining the liveness of the input fingerprint sample. Importantly, both the encoder-decoder and the classifier blocks engage in collaborative parameter learning in an end-to-end approach. Detailed explanations of these blocks are provided in the ensuing sub-sections.

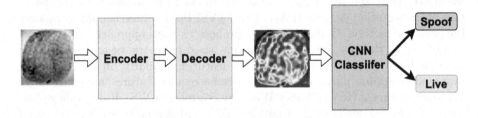

Fig. 1. Block diagram of the proposed architecture

3.1   Pre-processing

The fingerprint samples obtained using various sensing devices has different spatial dimensions with uneven widths and heights. The samples are resized to the nearest value of the power of two to their height. For example, the fingerprint sample, captured with the italdata sensor in LivDet 2011 database has a spatial dimension of 355×391 which is further resized as 512×512.

3.2   Encoder-Decoder Block

The encoder-decoder block highlights the important pixels in the input fingerprint sample by first down-sizing and then up-sizing the input sample. The encoder-decoder block, depicted in Fig. 2 is inspired by the method discussed in [21]. The encoder is composed of a convolutional operator followed by a max pool operator and again convolutional filter and max pool operation. In this way, the encoder down-sizes the input sample by two times. The decoder part up-sizes the output of the encoder by first applying the pair of convolutional and upsampling operators two times. The activation function applied to the last convolutional operator in tanh which generates values in the range of -1 to +1 and the number of output feature maps is kept as one. In this way, the encoder-decoder block generates a single-channel heatmap for an input fingerprint sample. The decoder block of the proposed models differs from the decoder of the method discussed in [21] as it uses the pair of upsampling and convolutional filter instead of the transposed convolutional operator utilized in [21]. This modification reduces the computational requirements as compared with [21].

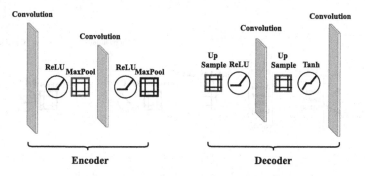

Fig. 2. Architectures of Encoder and Decoder

3.3 Classifier

The classifier block comprises the proposed Convolutional Neural Network (CNN), which encompasses a series of convolutional layers, subsequently followed by batch-normalization layers and max-pooling layers. This block takes a single-channel heatmap generated by the encoder-decoder block and generates a liveness score for an input fingerprint sample. The output feature maps generated by the first, second, third, fourth, fifth, and sixth convolutional filters are 8, 16, 32, 64, 128, and 256 respectively. The output of the last convolutional layer is fed as an input to the GlobalAveragePool layer which computes a single value for a corresponding feature map. In the last, two fully connected layers are added to perform the classification. The first fully connected layer consists of 256 neurons while the second layer has a single neuron to perform binary classification. The output from the classifier block yields a liveness score, which falls within the range of 0 to 1. A fingerprint sample with a liveness score below 0.5 is classified as a spoof, while those with a liveness score exceeding 0.5 are classified as live. A comprehensive depiction of the classifier block's architecture is presented in Fig. 3.

4   Experimental Setup

4.1   Database

To assess the efficacy of the proposed method, a series of experiments were conducted using the Liveness Detection Competition (LivDet) 2011, 2013, and 2015 databases. Table 1 outlines the details of the aforementioned databases.

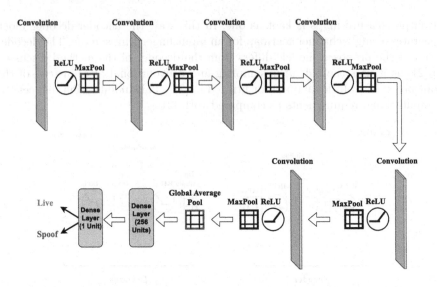

Fig. 3. Architecture of the classifier block

Table 1. Details of the utilized LivDet databases

Database	Sensor	Live	Spoof	Spoofing Materials
LivDet 2011	Biometrika	1000/1000	1000/1000	Ecoflex, Gelatine, Latex, Siligum, Woodglue
	Italdata	1000/1000	1000/1000	
	Digital Persona	1000/1000	1000/1000	Gelatine, Latex, Playdoh, Silicone, WoodGlue
	Sagem	1000/1000	1000/1000	
LivDet 2013	Biometrika	1000/1000	1000/1000	Ecoflex, Gelatine, Latex, Modsil, Woodglue
	Digital Persona	1000/1000	1000/1000	
LivDet 2015	Crossmatch	1000/1000	1473/1448	Body Double, Ecoflex, Playdoh, OOMOO, Gelatine
	Digital Persona	1000/1000	1000/1500	Ecoflex, Latex, Gelatine, Woodglue, Liquid Ecoflex, RTV
	Greenbit	1000/1000	1000/1500	
	Hi-Scan	1000/1000	1000/1500	

4.2   Performance Metrics

The performance of the proposed model undergoes evaluation in accordance with the ISO/IEC IS 30107 criteria [1]. Within this evaluation, the Attack Presentation Classification Error Rate (APCER) quantifies the rate of misclassification for spoof fingerprint samples, while the Bonafide Presentation Classification Error Rate (BPCER) measures the rate of misclassification for live fingerprint samples.

The formulations for BPCER and APCER are represented by Eq. (1) and Eq. (2), respectively.

$$BPCER = \frac{\# \text{ misclassified live samples}}{\text{Total live samples}} \times 100 \qquad (1)$$

$$APCER = \frac{\#\ \text{misclassified spoof samples}}{\text{Total fake samples}} \times 100 \tag{2}$$

The Average Classification Error (ACE) represents the aggregate error comprising APCER and BPCER, denoting the overall performance of the FPAD system. The formulation of ACE is denoted by Eq. (3).

$$ACE = \frac{BPCER + APCER}{2} \tag{3}$$

The ACE is subsequently employed to measure the classification accuracy of the FPAD model. The formulation of Accuracy in terms of ACE is denoted as Eq. (4).

$$Accuracy = 100 - ACE \tag{4}$$

4.3 Implementation Details

The proposed model is implemented using the PyTorch library in Python, with all training and testing procedures conducted on an NVIDIA TESLA P100 GPU. The initial values for the learning rate and batch size were configured as 0.0001 and 1, respectively. We have trained a separate model for every dataset present in the LivDet database from scratch for 300 epochs, which requires approximately 6–7 hours of training time for a single model. The training and testing datasets available in LivDet databases are utilized for the training and testing of the models respectively.

4.4 Ablation Study

To assess the influence of the heatmap-generator block on the CNN classifier's training, we conducted a separate evaluation of the classifier block using the LivDet 2015 database. The classifier exhibited classification accuracy of 94%, in comparison to the accuracy achieved by the entire model, which is reported in Table 6 as 95.32%. This study reveals the significance of the heatmap generated by the heatmap-generator block, indicating its role in facilitating more effective training of the classifier.

5 Experimental Results and Comparative Analysis

5.1 Experimental Results

Intra Sensor Known Spoofing Material. In this experimental protocol, both the training and testing samples are acquired utilizing the same sensing device. Specifically, fingerprint samples from the LivDet 2011 database are collected using a cooperative method of spoofing, while those from LivDet 2013 are obtained through a non-cooperative method of spoofing. The spoof samples of the training and testing datasets of both LivDet 2011 and 2013 databases are fabricated using the same spoofing materials. The proposed model's performance over LivDet 2011 and LivDet 2013 databases is reported in Table 2. Table 2 shows that the proposed model achieved an average APCER, BPCER, and ACE of 1.12%, 3.27%, and 2.25% respectively for the LivDet 2011 database. Similarly, it achieved an average APCER, BPCER, and ACE of 1.3%, 1.05%, and 1.12% for the LivDet 2013 database. Similarly, the column "BPCER" and "APCER (known)" reports the findings of the proposed method on the LivDet 2015 database. Table 3 shows that the proposed method achieves an average BPCER and APCER of 4.75% and 3.97% respectively on LivDet 2015 database.

Table 2. The performance in intra-sensor known-material protocol using LivDet 2011 and 2013 databases

Database	Sensor	BPCER	APCER	ACE (%)
LivDet 2011	Biometrika	5.61	2.9	4.25
	Digital Persona	0.30	0.10	0.20
	Italdata	7.0	1.0	4.0
	Sagem	0.20	0.87	0.55
	Average	**3.27**	**1.12**	**2.25**
LivDet 2013	Biometrika	0.80	0.40	0.60
	Italdata	1.30	2.20	1.65
	Average	**1.05**	**1.3**	**1.12**

Table 3. The performance in intra-sensor known and unknown materials protocols using LivDet 2015 database

Database	Sensor	BPCER	APCER (Known)	APCER (Unknown)	ACE (%)
LivDet 2015	Crossmatch	2.27	0.59	6.01	4.99
	Digital Persona	6.7	4.5	9.4	6.68
	Biometrika	5.1	1.2	7.4	4.0
	Greenbit	4.93	1.3	3.4	3.05
	Average	**4.75**	**3.97**	**6.55**	**4.68**

Intra Sensor Unknown Spoofing Material. In this experimental protocol, both training and testing images are acquired using the same sensing device. However, the spoof samples in the testing dataset are fabricated with materials distinct from those used in the training dataset. Evaluating the performance of an FPAD model under this protocol assesses its resilience in real-world scenarios, where attackers may employ novel fabrication materials for the fabrication of spoofs. Notably, the LivDet 2015 database partially falls into this category, with 33% of its testing spoof samples being generated using unknown materials. The results of our proposed method in this experimental setup are presented in the column labeled 'APCER(Unknown)' in Table 3. As illustrated in Table 3, our proposed method attains an APCER of 6.55% when subjected to testing with spoof samples fabricated using unknown materials.

5.2   Comparative Analysis

Comparison with State-of-the-art Methods on LivDet 2011 Database. Table 4 contains a comprehensive comparison of the performance of the proposed model with state-of-the-art approaches that are validated on LivDet 2011 database. Table 4 shows that the proposed method produces higher classification accuracy as compared with the methods discussed in [8,9,16,23–25], and [19]. The aforementioned comparison confirms that the proposed method performs better than the state-of-the-art methods while the fingerprint samples are captured with the cooperative method of spoofing.

Table 4. Comparison with state-of-the-art methods on LivDet 2011 database

Method	Accuracy (Biometrika)	Accuracy (Digital Persona)	Accuracy (Italdata)	Accuracy (Sagem)	Accuracy
Xia et al. [23]	93.55	96.2	88.25	96.66	93.37
Yuan et al. [24]	97.05	88.94	97.8	92.01	93.82
Gragnaniello et al. [8]	93.1	92.00	87.35	96.35	92.2
Yuan et al. [25]	91.8	98.1	94.91	95.36	95.04
Yuan et al. [24]	90.08	98.65	87.65	97.1	93.55
Jian et al. [9]	95.75	98.4	94.1	96.83	96.27
Sharma et al. [19]	92.7	94.4	88.6	93.3	92.25
Proposed Method	**95.75**	**99.80**	**96.00**	**99.45**	**97.75**

Comparison with State-of-the-art Methods on LivDet 2013 Database. Table 5 provides an extensive comparison of our proposed model's performance against state-of-the-art approaches validated on the LivDet 2013 database. As depicted in Table 5, our proposed method consistently achieves higher classification accuracy when contrasted with the methodologies mentioned in [7,10,12,24–26]. This comprehensive comparison substantiates the superiority of our proposed approach, particularly when spoofs with samples acquired through the non-cooperative method of spoofing.

Table 5. Comparison with state-of-the-art methods on LivDet 2013 database

Method	Accuracy (Biometrika)	Accuracy (Italdata)	Accuracy
Yuan et al. [24]	96.45	97.65	97.05
Zhang et al. [26]	99.53	96.99	98.26
Gottschlich et al. [7]	96.10	98.30	97.0
Johnson et al. [10]	98.0	98.4	98.20
Yuan et al. [25]	95.65	98.6	97.12
Jung et al. [12]	94.12	97.92	96.02
Proposed Method	**99.40**	**98.45**	**98.87**

Comparison with State-of-the-art Methods on LivDet 2015 Database.
Table 6 presents a comprehensive comparison of the performance of our proposed model against state-of-the-art methods when evaluated on the LivDet 2015 database. As observed in Table 6, our proposed method demonstrates superior performance in comparison to the approaches mentioned in [22] and [11]. Furthermore, it exhibits comparable classification accuracy to the methods outlined in [15].

Table 6. Comparison with state-of-the-art methods on LivDet 2015 database

Method	Accuracy (Crossmatch)	Accuracy (Greenbit)	Accuracy (Digital Persona)	Accuracy (Biometrika)	Accuracy
LivDet 2015 Winner [15]	98.10	95.40	93.72	94.36	95.39
Uliyan et al. [22]	95.00	–	–	–	95.00
Jung et al. [11]	98.60	96.20	90.50	95.80	95.27
Proposed Method	**95.01**	**96.95**	**93.32**	**96.00**	**95.32**

5.3 Evaluation of the Proposed Method in High-Security Constraint

An FPAD model's performance evaluation should extend beyond achieving minimal APCER, BPCER, and ACE values, especially when considering it for high-security systems. In this section, we present the results of the proposed model in high-security scenarios, employing the Detection Error Trade-off (DET) curve. The DET curve provides a graphical representation of error rates generated by a binary classification system at different threshold values. Figure 4 depicts the DET curves for the utilized databases of LivDet 2011, 2013, and 2015. Figure 4 illustrates that the proposed model attains a BPCER below 5% while maintaining an APCER of 1% when evaluated on sagem and digital persona sensors of LivDet 2011 database. Moreover, the BPCER remains below 10% for 1% of APCER when tested on biometrika and italdata sensors of the same database. When evaluated on LivDet 2013, our proposed model successfully achieves a BPCER below 1% while keeping the APCER at 1% when tested on the biometrika sensor. Similarly, when assessing the proposed model on italdata sensor of the same database, the model sustains a BPCER below 5% while maintaining an APCER of 1%. The proposed model obtains a BPCER of less than 10% while testing on crossmatch and greenbit sensors from the LivDet 2015 database, while it is in the 20% to 30% range for biometrika and digital persona sensors from the same database.

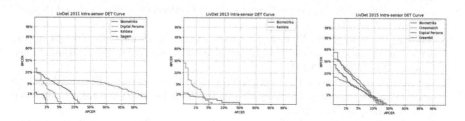

Fig. 4. Detection Error Trade-off (DET) curves for LivDet 2011, 2013, and 2015 databases

6   Conclusion

The AFRS, deployed across a wide spectrum of security and commercial applications, is susceptible to PAs. Within this study, we introduce an FPAD approach that exhibits competence in discerning spoof attempts generated through both cooperative and non-cooperative methods, encompassing known and unknown fabrication materials. Our research underscores the inadequacy of existing handcrafted and deep learning-based methods in effectively detecting PAs when subjected to benchmark testing protocols. One possible cause is the shortcomings of CNN-based classifiers in extracting features from fingerprint samples due to the limited amount of discriminating information present in them. The proposed method detects PAs by first converting the input fingerprint sample into a heatmap that highlights the minute features. The proposed method is tested on benchmark databases in different experimental protocols and it outperforms state-of-the-art methods. Furthermore, our future work will involve evaluating the proposed model's effectiveness in cross-sensor and cross-database validation scenarios.

References

1. 30107-3:2017(en), I.: Information technology - biometric presentation attack detection - part 3: Testing and reporting (2017)
2. Abhyankar, A., Schuckers, S.: Integrating a wavelet based perspiration liveness check with fingerprint recognition. Pattern Recogn. **42**, 452–464 (2009)

3. Arora, S.: Fingerprint spoofing detection to improve customer security in mobile financial applications using deep learning. Arab. J. Sci. Eng. **45**, 2847–2863 (2019)
4. Baishya, J., Tiwari, P.K., Rai, A., Dey, S.: Impact of existing deep CNN and image descriptors empowered SVM models on fingerprint presentation attacks detection. In: Sarkar, R., Pal, S., Basu, S., Plewczynski, D., Bhattacharjee, D. (eds.) Proceedings of International Conference on Frontiers in Computing and Systems. Lecture Notes in Networks and Systems, vol. 690, pp. 241–251. Springer, Singapore (2023). https://doi.org/10.1007/978-981-99-2680-0_22
5. Espinoza, M., Champod, C.: Using the number of pores on fingerprint images to detect spoofing attacks. In: 2011 International Conference on Hand-Based Biometrics, pp. 1–5 (2011)
6. Galbally, J., Marcel, S., Fierrez, J.: Image quality assessment for fake biometric detection: application to iris, fingerprint, and face recognition. IEEE Trans. Image Process. **23**, 710–724 (2014)
7. Gottschlich, C., Marasco, E., Yang, A.Y., Cukic, B.: Fingerprint liveness detection based on histograms of invariant gradients. In: IEEE International Joint Conference on Biometrics, pp. 1–7 (2014)
8. Gragnaniello, D., Poggi, G., Sansone, C., Verdoliva, L.: Fingerprint liveness detection based on weber local image descriptor. In: 2013 IEEE Workshop on Biometric Measurements and Systems for Security and Medical Applications, pp. 46–50 (2013)
9. Jian, W., Zhou, Y., Liu, H.: Densely connected convolutional network optimized by genetic algorithm for fingerprint liveness detection. IEEE Access **9**, 2229–2243 (2021)
10. Johnson, P., Schuckers, S.: Fingerprint pore characteristics for liveness detection. In: 2014 International Conference of the Biometrics Special Interest Group (BIOSIG), pp. 1–8 (2014)
11. Jung, H.Y., Heo, Y.: Fingerprint liveness map construction using convolutional neural network. Electron. Lett. **54**, 564–566 (2018)
12. Jung, H.Y., Heo, Y.S., Lee, S.: Fingerprint liveness detection by a template-probe convolutional neural network. IEEE Access **7**, 118986–118993 (2019)
13. Marasco, E., Sansone, C.: Combining perspiration- and morphology-based static features for fingerprint liveness detection. Pattern Recogn. Lett. **33**(9), 1148–1156 (2012)
14. Marcialis, G.L., Roli, F., Tidu, A.: Analysis of fingerprint pores for vitality detection. In: 2010 20th International Conference on Pattern Recognition, pp. 1289–1292 (2010)
15. Mura, V., Ghiani, L., Marcialis, G.L., Roli, F., Yambay, D.A., Schuckers, S.A.: LivDet 2015 fingerprint liveness detection competition 2015. In: 2015 IEEE 7th International Conference on Biometrics Theory, Applications and Systems (BTAS), pp. 1–6 (2015)
16. Nogueira, R.F., de Alencar Lotufo, R., Campos Machado, R.: Fingerprint liveness detection using convolutional neural networks. IEEE Trans. Inf. Forensics Secur. **11**(6), 1206–1213 (2016)
17. Park, Y., Jang, U., Lee, E.C.: Statistical anti-spoofing method for fingerprint recognition. Soft. Comput. **22**, 4175–4184 (2018)
18. Sharma, D., Selwal, A.: HyFiPAD: a hybrid approach for fingerprint presentation attack detection using local and adaptive image features. Vis. Comput. **38**, 2999–3025 (2021)
19. Sharma, R., Dey, S.: Fingerprint liveness detection using local quality features. Vis. Comput. **35**, 1393–1410 (2019)

20. Tan, B., Schuckers, S.: Comparison of ridge- and intensity-based perspiration liveness detection methods in fingerprint scanners. In: Proceedings of Biometric Technology for Human Identification III, pp. 94 – 103 (2006)
21. Tavanaei, A.: Embedded encoder-decoder in convolutional networks towards explainable AI. CoRR **abs/2007.06712** (2020)
22. Uliyan, D.M., Sadeghi, S., Jalab, H.A.: Anti-spoofing method for fingerprint recognition using patch based deep learning machine. Eng. Sci. Technol. Int. J. **23**(2), 264–273 (2020)
23. Xia, Z., Yuan, C., Lv, R., Sun, X., Xiong, N.N., Shi, Y.Q.: A novel weber local binary descriptor for fingerprint liveness detection. IEEE Trans. Syst., Man, Cybern.: Syst. **50**(4), 1526–1536 (2020)
24. Yuan, C., Sun, X., Wu, Q.M.: Difference co-occurrence matrix using BP neural network for fingerprint liveness detection. Soft. Comput. **23**(13), 5157–5169 (2019)
25. Yuan, C., et al.: Fingerprint liveness detection using an improved CNN with image scale equalization. IEEE Access **7**, 26953–26966 (2019)
26. Zhang, Y., Shi, D., Zhan, X., Cao, D., Zhu, K., Li, Z.: Slim-ResCNN: a deep residual convolutional neural network for fingerprint liveness detection. IEEE Access **7**, 91476–91487 (2019)

Multiscale Feature Fusion Using Hybrid Loss for Skin Lesion Segmentation

Rahul Verma and Tushar Sandhan[✉]

Perception and Intelligence Lab, Department of Electrical Engineering,
Indian Institute of Technology, Kanpur, Kanpur 208016, India
{rahulverma21,sandhan}@iitk.ac.in

Abstract. Skin cancer is prevalent these days but patients' chances of survival are significantly increased by its early diagnosis. Skin lesion segmentation is an important step in distinguishing skin cancer from malignant lesions in dermoscopic images. Despite the significant advancements made by deep models in enhancing the accuracy and resilience of image segmentation, the task of achieving segmentation outcomes with precise boundaries and accurate structures remains a formidable challenge. In this paper, we proposed a method that combines a CNN architecture and hybrid loss to achieve image segmentation results of high accuracy. The proposed methodology aims to enhance the lesion boundary and integrates low-level details and advanced levels of semantics through the utilisation of feature maps at a range of scales. It also learns hierarchical representations. The model also acquires hierarchical representations by utilising the entire aggregated feature maps. Here, The features of skin lesions are extracted from the segmented region in order to evaluate the lesion. To evaluate the various level of quality of the lesion segmentation, we utilised commonly used evaluation metrics such as the Jaccard Index, IOU, Precision, Dice Coefficient(F1-score), Recall, and Accuracy. Based on the results of the lesion segmentations experiment on ISIC-2018 dataset, we did a comparison of the above metrics with other state-of-the-art techniques. Our proposed method demonstrates exceptional performance across all metrics and achieved better results.

Keywords: Segmentation · Skin cancer · CNN · Deep learning · Hierarchical Feature Integration

1 Introduction

Cancer is considered a highly significant disease due to its characteristic of abnormal cellular proliferation, which possesses the potential to attack and spread to various regions of the human body. Cancer is defined as a disease caused by uncontrolled cell proliferation in many organs [8]. Various body parts, including the liver, lungs, blood, and others, can potentially be impacted by it. Skin cancer is a primary cause of disease and the top cause of death worldwide. The various dermoscopic images of skin cancer are shown in Fig. 1 which became one of the important

H. Kaur et al. (Eds.): CVIP 2023, CCIS 2011, pp. 322–336, 2024.
https://doi.org/10.1007/978-3-031-58535-7_27

concerns for society. The rate of skin cancer cases has undergone a substantial rise in recent years because of the impact of environmental factors. According to the organization American Cancer Society, there were a total of 115,320 newly diagnosed cases of melanoma which is the lethal variety of skin cancer in the United States in the year 2019. Additionally, the report states that there were 11,540 recorded deaths related to melanoma during the same time period [9]. Ultra-Violet (UV) radiation exposure is the primary cause of skin cancer. The increasing prevalence of skin cancer has been attributed to the growing number of individuals engaging in outdoor activities without adequate sun protection.

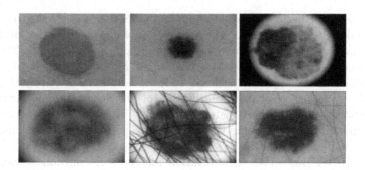

Fig. 1. Dermoscopic images of skin cancer lesions.

Asians are gradually getting prominence for these outdoor activities. Therefore, skin cancer is a major and serious risk for everyone. When an early diagnosis is made and the initiation of treatment takes place, the five-year survival rate is 92%. The success of skin cancer treatment depends on early diagnosis.

The segmentation of skin lesions is treated as an essential preliminary step in the diagnosis. This step is crucial because it relies heavily on segregating the lesion from the dermoscopic images provided. By extracting the necessary information accurately, correct diagnosis and other clinical aspects can be effectively tackled [1,4]. The main objective of our study is to perform segmentation of dermoscopic skin lesions which is a challenging task in its own right. The appearance, size, and texture of skin lesions vary greatly. A variety of techniques were studied, including learning-based [5,6] such as thresholding and level set methods. Additionally, non-learning approach such as thresholding and level set methodology [7,10] were studied as well.

Deep learning has emerged as an effective method for solving image processing problems such as image segmentation in recent years. In this particular context, CNNs(convolutional neural networks) [11,12] as shown in Fig. 2 have emerged as the most effective tools in image processing and computer vision [5].

Deep learning and relevant image processing algorithms have the capability to eliminate the human factor, thereby yielding outcomes that are more reliable compared to traditional approaches. One of the primary benefits of these techniques is their non-invasive nature, which significantly reduces the time required

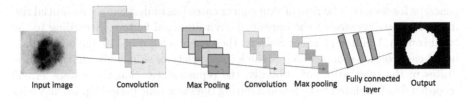

Fig. 2. General overview of the architectural design of a CNN (Convolutional Neural NetworK) used for the purpose of skin lesion segmentation.

for diagnosis. Furthermore, these techniques reduce diagnostic costs to near zero and mistake rates to near zero. The application of machine learning in different disease diagnoses has experienced significant growth in recent times [12].

There are numerous CNN-based techniques for skin lesions segmentation, one of which is the approach utilising fully convolutional-deconvolutional networks [5], approach involves the utilisation of deep convolutional networks in combination with the Jaccard distance metric [6]. However, the accuracy of skin lesion segmentation approaches is constrained, especially in low contrast, noisy, irregular shape regions of the lesions.

Here, U-Net [13] serves as motivation for our segmentation network. Segmenting the image by pixels rather than as a whole is effective. As a result, it increases the segmentation accuracy of medical images. Additionally, U-Net based techniques typically need less memory when performing training using a small training batch size. In this paper, a model is proposed that utilises the U-Net architecture as the fundamental structure. The U-Net network is chosen for its ability to promote effective information flow and achieve high performance. Later, the MultiResUnet deep learning segmentation model is utilised due to being known for being highly advanced and robust. Additionally, the Hybrid loss function is incorporated as an enhancement over the other U-Net, MultiResUnet, and other advanced models.

2   Methodology

In the domain of segmentation of medical images [13, 25, 26], the U-Net model is frequently employed because the entire convolution network's shown superiority over other popular segmentation techniques.

2.1   U-Net

The U-Net architecture is widely recognised in the field of a deep learning network that uses an encoder-decoder model. Deep neural network training with greater network depth can enhance accuracy. In order to enhance the quality of semantic segmentation, it is imperative to incorporate high-level semantic information while focusing on the low-level details [3, 13]. Training a deep neural network poses significant challenges, particularly when the number of available training datasets samples is limited. Then, We consider that the U-Net contributes to the reduction of the magnitude of the training challenges. By replicating the features at the low level to their corresponding features at the high level, the idea is that a path for information propagation is established. This makes it possible for signals to flow between the low and high levels in a much more straightforward manner and also compensates for finer details of semantic features.

An encoder-decoder configuration specific to the U-shaped architecture is used [13]. This can be achieved by the encoder, which simultaneously expands the channel's numbers while decreasing the spatial dimensions of individual layers. The decoder, however, performs a function where it increases the spatial dimensions while simultaneously decreasing the number of channels. The key breakthrough of U-Net architecture lies in its approach to upsampling within the network. In addition to upsampling the features, U-Net incorporates the higher-resolution feature maps from the encoder side network by concatenating them with the upsampled features. This strategy enhances the learning of representations through subsequent convolutions [3,13].

However, there are still weaknesses [24] in the traditional U-net design. MultiResUNet is modified architecture [27] of U-Net [13] which we utilised in this paper.

2.2   Proposed Method

Since the MultiResUNet [27] architecture as shown in Fig. 3 utilised in this paper which is the improved architecture of U-Net for the segmentation of the various medical images.

The architecture of the network U-Net can be enhanced by incorporating parallel convolution layers of different sizes, such as 3×3, 5×5, and 7×7, using the methodology employed in the Inception network [30]. This approach, illustrated in Fig. 4(a), represents a straightforward means of improving the U-Net's design. This is also the most effective strategy. We concatenated these three convolution blocks to extract the spatial characteristics from different levels of scales. The memory required will grow as a result of this operation, despite the fact that the concatenation of 5×5 and 7×7 convolution layers will result in an improvement in performance. We used a chain of convolution kernels with a size of 3×3 to replace the 5×5 and 7×7 kernels, which are shown in Fig. 4(b).

This allowed us to simplify the process. To avoid memory issues, the number of filters is gradually raised for each 3×3 layer. In order to provide more spatial information, we also included a residual connection and utilised 1×1 1 convolution layers. These structures were combined to create MultiResUnet Block as illustrated in Fig. 4(b).

It also involves implementing a shortcut connection within a convolutional layer circuit, which includes a deep residual connection which is known as the Res path demonstrated in Fig. 5. This integration is aimed at addressing the discrepancies in encoder-decoder characteristics within the U-Net architecture caused by skip connections.

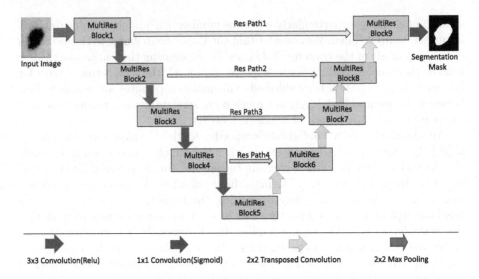

Fig. 3. The architectural design of the MultiResUnet model used for skin lesion segmentation.

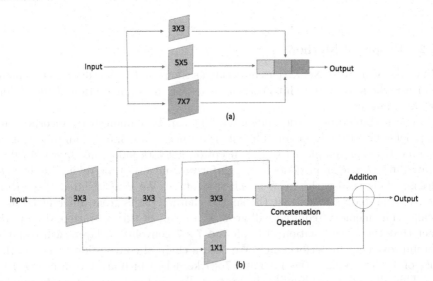

Fig. 4. MultiRes Block (a) Inception block (b) addition of residual connection to create MultiRes Block

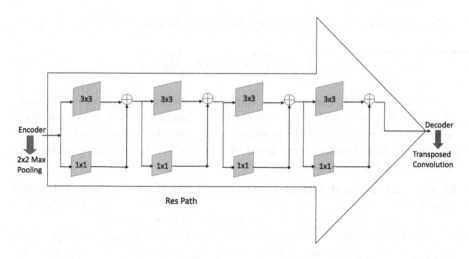

Fig. 5. Architecture of Res Path which follow the path from encoder to decoder as shown in Fig. 3.

Each level in the MultiResUNet model's encoder block which is referred to as the MultiRes block and is explained in Fig. 3, is made consisting of three convolution layers (Conv2D) of kernel size (3 × 3), the padding, and ReLU activation for each layer. The Concatenation layer was employed to merge the outputs generated by the three convolution layers, followed by the utilisation of the BatchNormalization layer(BN). The mappings of features from the part of the encoder to the section of the decoder are concatenated with the decoder feature after passing through a series of three convolution layers with residual connections as shown in Fig. 3.

The decoder blocks begin by performing a transposed convolution on the convolution results obtained from the previous encoder block. This is then followed by the Concatenation layer. At the last stage of the model, a single convolution process is employed, utilising a sigmoid which is an activation function. This process generates results of lesion segmentation, which consist of pixel values representation ranging from 0 to 1.

In this paper, we proposed a model with different Hybrid Loss functions as a brief introduction of models with different losses discussed below:

Model with BCE Loss: In this model, in the context of the network's loss function, took the binary cross-entropy(BCE) function [34] and made it as small as possible. Let's say that for image A, the model's predicted mask of lesion segmentation is B_x and the ground truth is B. Here, the network predicts $\hat{B}_{px}$ for a pixel px, and the value of the ground truth is B_{px}.

This image's binay Cross-Entropy (CE) loss is described as:

$$CE(A, B, \hat{B}) = \sum_{px \epsilon A} -(B_{px} log(\hat{B}_{px}) + (1 - B_{px})log(1 - \hat{B}_{px})) \qquad (1)$$

The loss function L becomes for a batch of N images:

$$L = \frac{1}{N} \sum_{k=1}^{N} CE(A_k, B_k, \hat{B}_K) \tag{2}$$

The loss of BCE (Binary Cross Entropy) is calculated on a per-pixel basis. The algorithm does not take into account the labels assigned to the neighborhood and assigns equal weight to both foreground and background pixels. This feature aids in achieving convergence on all pixels and ensures the attainment of reasonably favorable local optima.

Model with Hybrid Loss1: A collection of training images and their corresponding segmentations of ground truth are provided. Here, the objective is to accurately and reliably estimate the parameters of the network.

In order to significantly improve the skin lesion boundary, the loss function MS-SSIM (Multi-scale structural similarity index) [28] that assigns greater weights to vague boundaries. It encapsulates the information about the structure in an image and observes simply the contours of an object's borders. The SSIM Loss can be defined as:

$$FL_{ssim} = \frac{1 - (2\mu_a\mu_b + C_1)(2\sigma_{ab} + C_2)}{(\mu_a^2 + \mu_b^2 + C_1)(\sigma_a^2 + \sigma_b^2 + C_1)} \tag{3}$$

where a, and b are the pixel values of respective patches which are cropped from their predicted segmentation mask and ground truth respectively. C_1 and C_2 are non-zero small constant. μ_a, μ_b are mean and σ_a, σ_b are standard deviation of a and b.

The Focal Loss [29] developed in order to effectively address the issue of imbalanced background and foreground classes during the process of training in the one-stage object detection task scenario. So, in this scenario, the foreground class is significantly more numerous than the background class.

We defined focal loss as:

$$FL(x_t) = -(1 - x_t)^\alpha log(x_t) \tag{4}$$

where variable x_t represents the probability that is predicted for the class associated with the label in the model, $\alpha \geq 0$ and $(1 - x_t)^\alpha$ is modulating factor [29] to cross-entropy loss.

IOU loss [32] Performs well on data that is evenly balanced. Provides a greater accent on the extensive foreground sections. IOU loss can be defined as: where

$$L_{iou} = \frac{\sum_{x=1}^{N} \sum_{y=1}^{M} S(p,q)G(p,q)}{\sum_{p=1}^{N} \sum_{q=1}^{M} [S(p,q) + G(p,q) - S(p,q)G(p,q)]} \tag{5}$$

here S(p,q) is defined as the predicted segmentation mask, and G(p,q) is the ground truth of pixel (p,q).

By utilising the fusion of focal loss [29], MS-SSIM(Multi-scale structural similarity index) loss [33] and IoU(Intersection of Union) loss [32], a hybrid loss incorporating CNN is proposed for the purpose of segmentation at the pixel, patch, and map levels in a three-level hierarchy that has the ability to capture structures of varying scales, ranging from large-scale to fine, while maintaining clear and distinct boundaries.

The mathematical expression representing hybrid loss for the image segmentation is given by the following equation:

$$L_{seg} = L_{fl} + L_{ms-ssim} + L_{iou} \qquad (6)$$

where L_{fl}, $L_{ms-ssim}$, and L_{iou} denotes focal loss, MS-SSIM loss, and IoU loss respectively.

Model with Hybrid Loss2: We proposed a hybrid loss with CNN to provide high-quality regional segmentation and distinct borders, which is the combination of BCE loss [34], SSIM(Multi-scale structural similar- ity index) loss [33], and IoU(Intersection of Union loss) [32], respectively.

The hybrid loss, which is integrated with the CNN, is represented by the following equation as L_{seg}:

$$L_{seg} = L_{bce} + L_{ssim} + L_{iou} \qquad (7)$$

where L_{ssim}, L_{bce}, L_{iou} denotes SSIM loss, BCE loss, and IoU loss respectively. To get the best result, the three aforementioned losses are combined to form a hybrid loss. The BCE loss function is employed to ensure a uniform gradient across all pixels. On the other hand, the IoU metric is utilised to highlight the foreground. The SSIM (Structural Similarity Index) technique is employed to enhance the accuracy of background predictions by minimizing them to zero. Additionally, it promotes the preservation of the original input image's structure by applying a larger value of loss in the vicinity of the boundaries.

3 Experiments and Results

3.1 Datasets

The dermoscopic images of various skin lesions from the ISIC (International Skin Imaging Collaboration) challenge 2018 [20] dataset are utilised in our study. The dataset has a size of 10.4GB and comprises 2594 dermoscopic images and corresponding ground truth images which are provided by dermoscopic experts.

The dermoscopic images in the dataset are saved in the JPEG format and RGB colour while ground truth masks are saved in the PNG format. The original image size was maintained and this ensures optimal segmentation quality.

3.2 Evaluation Metrics

Dice Coefficient: The Dice coefficient metrics are utilised for evaluating the quality of the image segmentation task [14, 15]. The metric evaluates the quality of the generated segmentation results.

Jaccard: The Jaccard similarity [15,16] is related to the Dice coefficient. Its value increases proportionally with the quality of the segmentation result in the range of 0 to 1.

Accuracy: The accuracy(%) measurement reflects how effective a segmentation method accurately recognises.

3.3   Implementation and Results

We used the Keras framework [21] with Tensorflow 2.9.1 [22] as the backend. Training for models is being carried out on a system powered by the Nvidea RTX 3060 Geforce model with 12GB of memory, and LINUX is serving as the experimental environment. There are 1687 training images with a resolution of 1022×767 available for use in training, samples of input images, and their ground truth as shown in Fig. 6.

Our model in this paper is able to utilise images of unlimited size, but it will need a specific amount of GPU RAM in order to retain the feature mappings. We make use of training images of a uniform dimension 256×256 and a batch size of 16 was employed for the training process. We divided the image datasets into three parts for training, validation, and testing into 65%,15%, and 20% i.e., 1687, 389, and 518 respectively.

Table 1. The obtained results for the U-Net during the training process with varying epochs for the ISIC 2018 datasets.

Epoch	Dice coeff.	IOU	Loss	Precision	Recall
10	0.863	0.764	0.133	0.890	0.860
20	0.899	0.816	0.100	0.915	0.889
30	0.914	0.843	0.083	0.932	0.903
50	0.951	0.907	0.048	0.958	0.943
70	0.963	0.929	0.036	0.967	0.959
100	0.975	0.952	0.024	0.977	0.973

Table 2. The obtained results for the proposed model during the training process with varying epochs for the ISIC 2018 datasets.

Epoch	Dice coeff.	IOU	Loss	Precision	Recall
10	0.888	0.804	0.532	0.913	0.890
20	0.940	0.889	0.272	0.954	0.944
30	0.963	0.930	0.171	0.971	0.966
50	0.978	0.958	0.105	0.984	0.980
70	0.982	0.965	0.090	0.986	0.983
100	0.986	0.973	0.070	0.989	0.987

Both the U-net model and the Proposed model underwent training in multiple steps. The models in this paper were trained for 100 epochs with a learning rate of 0.1 which dynamically changes using the Adam optimizer. It was selected from the Keras library and is a method that utilises stochastic gradient descent (SGD). We observed the number of training parameters for the proposed model equals 7,269,294 which is approx 0.23 times(1/4 times) the total training parameters of U-net which is 31,055,297. Following are the results we observed after the implementation of both U-net and Proposed model for given datasets ISIC 2018.

Table 3. Comparison of results on ISIC 2018 datsets between both models in training process.

Model	Epoch	Dice	IOU	Loss	Precision	Recall	Parameters	Time(sec)
U-Net	100	0.975	0.952	0.024	0.977	0.973	31,055,297	34,100
our Model	100	**0.986**	**0.973**	**0.070**	**0.989**	**0.989**	**7,269,294**	**15,025**

The framework was assessed using the Dice Coefficient(F1-score), Accuracy, Jaccard Index, Precision, IOU, Sensitivity, and Recall metrics. It takes approximately 9.4 h for U-net and 5.1 h for the proposed model to train for 100 epochs. The results are presented in Tables 1 and 2, respectively for various evaluation metrics on ISIC 2018 for various epochs of model training. Table 3 presents a comprehensive analysis and comparison of the results obtained from the ISIC 2018 image dataset and our proposed model demonstrates superior performance compared to the U-Net model across all evaluation metrics during the training process.

We use the semantic segmentation technique after training. For the segmentation process, we randomly select 518 dermoscopic images, and we evaluated the score of the results. The average scores are used to evaluate how well one skin lesion segmentation method is compared to another method.

To make an evaluation of the quality of the obtained segmentations, we chose a set of challenging images as shown in Fig. 6. These images were specifically chosen for their characteristics, including the presence of noise, irregular shapes, and low contrast. Figure 6 shows the original dermoscopic images of the ISIC-2018 challenge dataset in the first column(i), the mask ground truth in the second column(ii), lesion segmentation results using the U-Net model in the third column(iii), and lesion segmentation using the proposed technique in the fourth column(iv).

It is clear that there is a difference between the segmentation results of lesions obtained by the proposed method in this paper and those obtained using the U-Net for the skin lesion area. The proposed methodology exhibited a higher degree of success compared to alternative models when applied to challenging image set which are labeled as images (a, b, c, d, e, f, g, h). We also visualised the qualitative result of segmentation by overlay of segmented images on input

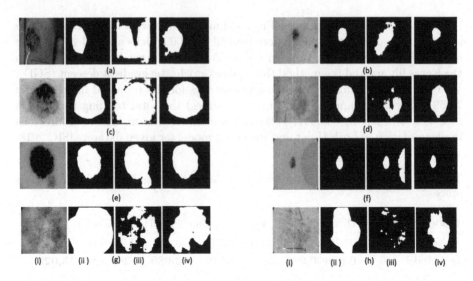

Fig. 6. Results for skin lesion segmentation for challenging image set (a,b,c,d,e,f,g,h) of dataset 2018.(i) Input dermoscopic Image (ii) Ground truth (iii) segmentation mask by U-net model (iv) Segmentation mask by Proposed model.

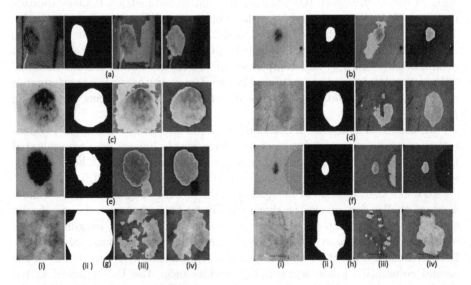

Fig. 7. Comparison of results by overlay the segmented images set (a,b,c,d,e,f,g,h) on top of the main input dermoscopic image (i) Input dermoscopic Image (ii) Ground truth (iii) overlay of segmented image by U-net model (iv) overlay of segmented image by Proposed model.

Table 4. The metrics results obtained in testing for challenging images set as shown in Fig. 6 or Fig. 7. For U-net

Image	Accuracy	F1-score	Jaccard	Precision	Recall
a	0.637	0.466	0.304	0.304	**0.999**
b	0.881	0.434	0.277	0.277	1
c	0.625	0.685	0.521	0.521	1
d	0.878	0.660	0.493	0.964	0.502
e	0.918	0.875	0.778	0.778	1
f	0.922	0.426	0.270	0.277	**0.914**
g	0.569	0.659	0.491	**0.995**	0.492
h	0.606	0.195	0.108	0.277	**0.985**

Table 5. The metrics results obtained in testing for challenging images set as shown in Fig. 6. or Fig. 7. for our model

Image	Accuracy	F1-score	Jaccard	Precision	Recall
a	**0.966**	**0.900**	**0.818**	**0.844**	0.963
b	**0.989**	**0.884**	**0.793**	**0.922**	1
c	**0.957**	**0.948**	**0.902**	**0.943**	0.953
d	**0.959**	**0.907**	**0.830**	**0.989**	**0.838**
e	**0.974**	**0.957**	**0.917**	**0.919**	1
f	**0.994**	**0.902**	**0.822**	**0.979**	0.836
g	**0.710**	**0.795**	**0.660**	0.989	**0.664**
h	**0.846**	**0.792**	**0.656**	**0.978**	0.666

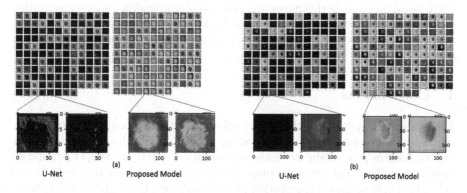

Fig. 8. Feature map for skin lesion segmentation for ISIC datasets 2018 by proposed model.

dermoscopic images as shown in Fig. 7. Which helps easily to compare the results and can be seen that our proposed model performed well.

Tables 4 and 5 present the average scores for the metrics F-1 score and Jaccard, as well as the accuracy, precision, and recall of each selected challenging image for the network U-Net model and our proposed method respectively. The acquired scores for our proposed method are very impressive.

Table 6. Comparison of scores between proposed model and other models for skin lesion segmentation.

Model	Accuracy	F1-Score	jaccard
FocusNet [23]	0.921	0.831	0.756
U-Net [13]	0.925	0768	0.651
Residual U-Net [2]	0.931	0.793	0.697
Attention U-Net [31]	0.925	0.768	0.682
MultiRes + BCE loss	0.945	0.842	0.756
Our MultiRes+Hybrid loss1	0.947	0.851	0.772
Our MultiRes+Hybrid loss2	**0.948**	**0.855**	**0.775**

The features of skin lesions are extracted from the segmented region in order to evaluate the lesion. In Fig. 8 the feature map was visualised by U-Net and our model for some challenging dermoscopic images. The above results show how our model is more powerful and complex in terms of extracting richer features to improve the segmentation of the skin lesion region. Our model gives results that are clearer, better and recovers more accurate boundary and corner details.

A comparison of the average scores of evaluation metrices of the proposed CNN-based methods in this paper and other comparable skin lesion segmentation models from the literature is shown in Table 6. For this comparison accuracy, F-1 scores and Jaccard scores of our proposed method demonstrated superior accuracy compared to the other models.

4 Conclusions

The proposed approach in this paper presents a methodology for dermoscopic skin lesion segmentation. It combines the use of CNN and a hybrid loss function to achieve precise and accurate segmentation of the images. The proposed method has the capability to capture fine structures, such as thin regions and holes. It is able to give segmentation probability maps that exhibit highly accurate boundaries. We produce a more precise position-specific and boundary-specific segmentation map. In order to evaluate the level of quality of the obtained segmentations of skin lesions, we have chosen a set of challenging images. These images were specifically chosen for their characteristics, including the presence of noise, irregular shapes, and low contrast and it has been demonstrated that the proposed model exhibits high effectiveness. In the future, we are going to perform tests on different datasets of skin lesion images and other medical image datasets to evaluate the proposed method.

Acknowledgement. This work is partially supported by the project TCS/EE/ 2019156 at IIT Kanpur.

References

1. Celebi, M.E., Wen, Q., Iyatomi, H., Shimizu, K., Zhou, H., Schaefer, G.: A state-of-the-art survey on lesion border detection in Dermoscopy images, pp. 97–129 (2015). https://doi.org/10.1201/b19107-5
2. Zhang, Z., Liu, Q., Wang, Y.: Road extraction by deep residual UNet. IEEE Geosci. Remote Sens. Lett. **15**(5), 749–753 (2018)
3. Long, J., Shelhamer, E., Darrell, T.: Fully convolutional networks for semantic segmentation. In: CVPR, pp. 3431–3440 (2015)
4. Burdick, J., Marques, O., Weinthal, J., Furht, B.: Rethinking skin lesion segmentation in a convolutional classifier. J. Digit. Imaging **31**, 435–440 (2018)
5. Yuan, Y., Lo, Y.-C.: Improving Dermoscopic image segmentation with enhanced convolutional-deconvolutional networks. IEEE J. Biomed. Health Inform. **23**(2), 519–526 (2019)
6. Yuan, Y., Chao, M., Lo, Y.-C.: Automatic skin lesion segmentation using deep fully convolutional networks with Jaccard distance. IEEE Trans. Med. Imaging **36**(9), 1876–1886 (2017)
7. Thanh, D.N., Erkan, U., Prasath, V.S., Kumar, V., Hien, N.N.: A skin lesion segmentation method for Dermoscopic images based on adaptive thresholding with normalization of color models. In: IEEE 2019 6th International Conference on Electrical and Electronics Engineering, pp. 116–120 (2019)
8. Baykara, O.T.: Current modalities in treatment of cancer. Balıkesir Health Sci. J. **5**, 154–165 (2016)
9. Siegel, R.L., Miller, K.D., Jemal, A.: Cancer statistic. CA Cancer J. Clin. **71**, 7–33 (2021)
10. Thanh, D.N.H., et al.: Automatic initial boundary generation methods based on edge detectors for the level set function of the Chan-Vese segmentation model and applications in biomedical image processing. In: Satapathy, S., Bhateja, V., Nguyen, B., Nguyen, N., Le, D.N. (eds.) Frontiers in Intelligent Computing: Theory and Applications. Advances in Intelligent Systems and Computing, vol. 1014, pp. 171–181. Springer, Singapore (2020). https://doi.org/10.1007/978-981-13-9920-6_18
11. Bi, L., Kim, J., Ahn, E., Feng, D.: Automatic skin lesion analysis using large-scale Dermoscopy images and deep residual networks. arXiv preprint (2017)
12. Gillmann, C., Saur, D.: How to deal with uncertainty in machine learning for medical imaging? In: Proceedings of the TREX 2021: Workshop on TRust and EXpertise in Visual Analytics, New Orleans, LA, USA (2021)
13. Ronneberger, O., Fischer, P., Brox, T.: U-net: convolutional networks for biomedical image segmentation. In: Navab, N., Hornegger, J., Wells, W., Frangi, A. (eds.) Medical Image Computing and Computer-Assisted Intervention - MICCAI 2015. Lecture Notes in Computer Science(), vol. 9351, pp. 234–241. Springer, Cham (2015). https://doi.org/10.1007/978-3-319-24574-4_28
14. Csurka, G., Larlus, D., Perronnin, F.: What is a good evaluation measure for semantic segmentation. In: The British Machine Vision Conference (2013)

15. Thanh, D.N.H., Prasath, V.B.S., Hieu, L.M., Hien, N.N.: Melanoma skin cancer detection method based on adaptive principal curvature, colour normalisation and feature extraction with the ABCD rule. J. Digit. Imaging **33**, 574–585 (2020)
16. Abdel, A.T., Allan, H.: Metrics for evaluating 3D medical image segmentation: analysis, selection, and tool. BMC Med. Imaging **15**, 1–29 (2015)
17. L'opez, A.R.: Skin lesion detection from Dermascopic images using convolutional neural networks. Semantic Scholar
18. Wang, Y., Rahman, A.: Optimizing intersection-over-union in deep neural networks for image segmentation. In: Bebis, G., et al. (eds.) Advances in Visual Computing. Lecture Notes in Computer Science(), vol. 10072. Springer, Cham (2016). https://doi.org/10.1007/978-3-319-50835-1_22
19. Baldi, P., et al.: Assessing the accuracy of prediction algorithms for classification: an overview. Bioinformatics **16**, 412–424 (2000)
20. DATASETS: https://challenge.isic-archive.com/data/2018
21. Li, A., et al.: Tensor flow and Keras-based convolutional neural network in CAT image recognition. In: Proc. 2nd Int. Conf. Comput. Modeling, Simulation Appl. Math. (CMSAM). Science and Engineering Research Center, p. 5 (2017)
22. Abadi, M., et al.: TensorFlow: a system for large-scale machine learning. In: Proc. USENIX Symp. OSDI, pp. 28–265 (2016)
23. Kaul, C., Manandhar, S., Pears, N.: FocusNet: an attention-based fully convolutional network for medical image segmentation. In: ISBI (2019)
24. Ibtehaz, N., Rahman, M.S.: MultiResUNet: rethinking the UNet architecture for multimodal biomedical image segmentation, pp. 74–87 (2019). arXiv:1902.04049
25. Baumgartner, C.F., et al.: An exploration of 2D and 3D deep learning techniques for cardiac MR image segmentation. In: Pop, M., et al. (eds.) Statistical Atlases and Computational Models of the Heart. ACDC and MMWHS Challenges. Lecture Notes in Computer Science(), vol. 10663, pp. 111–119. Springer, Cham (2017). https://doi.org/10.1007/978-3-319-75541-0_12
26. Alom, M.Z., et al.: Recurrent residual convolutional neural network based on u-net for medical image segmentation (2018). arXiv:1802.06955
27. Ibtehaz, N., Rahman, M.S.: MultiResUNet: rethinking the UNet architecture for multimodal biomedical image segmentation (2019)
28. Wang, Z., Simoncelli, E.P., Bovik, A.C.: Multiscale structural similarity for image quality assessment. In: The Thrity-Seventh Asilomar Conference on Signals, Systems & Computers (2003)
29. Lin, T.-Y., et al.: Focal loss for dense object detection, pp. 2980-2988. In: The IEEE International Conference on Computer Vision (2017)
30. Chen, L.C., Zhu, Y., Papandreou, G., Schroff, F., Adam, H.: Encoderdecoder with Atrous separable convolution for semantic image segmentation. In: Ferrari, V., Hebert, M., Sminchisescu, C., Weiss, Y. (eds.) Computer Vision – ECCV 2018. Lecture Notes in Computer Science(), vol. 11211. Springer, Cham (2018). https://doi.org/10.1007/978-3-030-01234-2_49
31. Oktay, O., et al.: Attention U-Net: learning where to look for the pancreas (2018). arXiv:1804.03999
32. Mattyus, G., et al.: Deep-RoadMapper: extracting road topology from aerial images. In: The IEEE International Conference on Computer Vision (2017)
33. Wang, Z., Simoncelli, E.P., Bovik, A.C.: Multiscale structural similarity for image quality assessment. In: ACSSC, vol. 2, pp. 1398–1402 (2003)
34. de Boer, P.-T., Kroese, D.P., Mannor, S., Rubinstein, R.Y.: A tutorial on the cross-entropy method. Ann. OR **134**(1), 19–67 (2005)

High Capacity and Reversible Steganographic Technique with Authentication Capability

Iffat Rehman Ansari[1]([✉]) [iD], Nasir N. Hurrah[1], Mohd Ayyub Khan[2], and Ekram Khan[1]

[1] Department of Electronics Engineering, Zakir Husain College of Engineering and Technology, AMU, Aligarh, India
iransari.uwp@amu.ac.in
[2] Electrical Engineering Section, University Polytechnic, AMU, Aligarh, India

Abstract. This paper proposes a high capacity and reversible DCT-based stegano-graphic technique with authentication capability for 8-bit grayscale general and medical images. The technique obtains 64 DCT coefficients by performing DCT on an (8×8) cover image block and only uses selected AC coefficients to hide the secret message. The proposed scheme embeds a fragile watermark using LSB substitution in the selected pixel of the (8×8) stego image block to verify the stego image's authenticity. The proposed scheme's performance is evaluated based on payload, imperceptibility, fragility, and image authentication analyses. Simulation results confirm that the steganographic technique is reversible, supports a good payload, and produces high quality watermarked images. The proposed technique outperforms state-of-the-art techniques in embedding capacity while maintaining good image quality. The fragility and authentication analysis confirm that our proposed scheme is fragile in nature and can detect various image processing and geometrical attacks. Our scheme can verify the stego image's authenticity and is also capable of detecting whether the message has been corrupted.

Keywords: Steganography · Fragile Watermark · DCT Coefficients · Embedding Capacity · Image Authentication

1 Introduction

Secure communication is the need of the hour as digital data is readily available on the internet due to the development and advancement in network communication technologies [1, 2]. Any confidential and secret information embedded in a digital image, such as data related to online voting, personal data hidden in smart cards, and data related to electronic patient records [3] needs content authentication at the receiver as the data may be attacked and altered intentionally or unintentionally. Many technologies, such as digital signatures and fingerprinting have been used for content authentication. Steganography [4–6], the ability to hide information within another file or message, is one of the best techniques to authenticate digital images. Moreover, steganography can also be used for forensic investigations to detect and analyze hidden evidence or smuggle information in digital media.

H. Kaur et al. (Eds.): CVIP 2023, CCIS 2011, pp. 337–349, 2024.
https://doi.org/10.1007/978-3-031-58535-7_28

The steganographic schemes are divided into spatial and frequency domains. The spatial domain steganography techniques embed the secret message in the cover image using Pixel Value Differencing (PVD) or directly in pixel's least significant bit (LSB). Hence, these approaches are simple, less complex but less robust [7, 8] while in the techniques based on the frequency domain, the information is hidden in the transformed coefficients of the cover image generated by Discrete Fourier Transform (DFT), Discrete Cosine Transform (DCT), Discrete Wavelet Transform (DWT), and Integer Wavelet Transform (IWT). These approaches provide robustness to different types of attacks, although they are computationally more complex [9, 10].

On the other hand, watermarking is a technique used to embed a visible or invisible mark or logo into a digital file, such as an image or audio file, to indicate its ownership, origin, or authenticity [11]. A watermark logo is generally of very small size. Watermarking can also be done in the spatial or frequency domains. In spatial domain techniques, the watermark is embedded in the LSBs of the cover image pixels without deteriorating the image quality [12, 13], while in the frequency domain, the watermark is embedded in the cover images modified transformed coefficients generated by DFT, DCT and DWT [14–16]. The spatial domain watermarking techniques are simple, providing high embedding capacity and easy detection and extraction compared to transform domain watermarking techniques.

In this paper, we propose a DCT based high capacity and reversible steganographic technique with authentication capability that supports large embedding capacity while maintaining the stego images quality. Firstly, the cover image is partitioned into non-overlapping blocks. The AC coefficients obtained after applying the DCT to each block are exploited to hide the secret message because modifying AC coefficients will not significantly affect the perceptual quality of the image as the core energy of the image is concentrated in the DC coefficient and the remaining information, or energy in the AC coefficients. Then, a fragile watermark logo is inserted in the stego image using simple LSB substitution to test the stego image's authenticity. The authenticity of the stego image is tested by extracting the watermark before extracting the message bits. If the extracted watermark matches the original one, the stego image is authentic, and the secret message can be perfectly reconstructed. If the extracted watermark is distorted, the stego image is unauthentic, indicating the image was attacked during its transmission. If the stego image is unauthentic, the message bits would also be erroneous, showing that the received message is corrupted. The simulation results show that our scheme gives better performance in payload capacity and imperceptibility as compared to the other state-of-the-art steganographic techniques. The proposed technique also can detect tamper or, alter and hence can be effectively used for content authentication.

The main contributions of this work are as follows:

1. Implementation of a high capacity steganographic technique without sacrificing the quality of the stego image.
2. Exploitation of AC coefficient of DCT to embed the secret message to maintain the good visual quality of the stego image.
3. Use of fragile watermark for tamper or alter detection and image authentication at the receiver. The proposed scheme also maintains the reversibility for authentic stego images.

4. Performance evaluation and verification of the proposed scheme without attack and with different image processing and geometrical attacks.

The remainder of the paper is structured in the following order: Sect. 2 presents the literature survey. The embedding and extraction procedures are explained in detail in Sect. 3. The simulation results in terms of payload capacity, imperceptibility, image authentication and fragility analyses are described in Sect. 4. Finally, the proposed scheme is concluded in Sect. 5.

2 Literature Survey

Several spatial and frequency domain steganography techniques have been studied in the past. The secret message in the spatial domain steganographic methods [17, 18] has been embedded directly into the LSBs of the cover image pixels. The method is simple with low computational complexity, but the embedding capacity needs improvement. In [19], a data hiding technique based on PVD was proposed. The technique provides a better quality stego image but has a lesser payload. To achieve a better payload, steganography based on PVD and modulus function was presented in [8] but resulted in a PSNR value of about 36 dB. A high capacity reversible steganographic technique based on the pixel to block conversion and the Intermediate Significant Bit (ISB) substitution for data embedding was proposed by [12], which provides good imperceptibility but the payload is reduced. The data hiding technique proposed in [7] uses image resizing and pixel permutation to embed the secret message. The method offers a satisfactory data payload but requires more processing time.

The frequency domain steganographic technique proposed in [9] embeds the message bits in the cover image's coefficients generated by IWT. The scheme results in a PSNR value of about 36 dB but has a low embedding capacity. To improve embedding capacity, [10] presented a steganography technique based on block partitioning and IWT. The method achieves high embedding capacity and a PSNR value of about 40 dB. An adaptive data hiding technique based on DWT [20] suffers from embedding errors due to its floating point operations. A similar IWT-based adaptive steganography technique using a lifting scheme was proposed in [21] to minimize the embedding errors, but it provides a low PSNR value of about 31 dB. [22] presented a DCT based steganography scheme to hide the information. The scheme does not offer a large payload and increasing the payload results in a low PSNR value of about 35 dB. The steganographic method based on a chaotic map presented in [23] used DCT coefficients to hide the message bits, resulting in low PSNR values of about 34 dB and 30 dB for (8×8) and (4×4) block sizes.

The block-based watermarking technique proposed in [24] results in a watermarked image of high quality and detects tampering correctly while a robust fragile watermarking scheme presented in [25] could locate the attacked blocks efficiently and shows high reliability. A DWT-based reversible fragile watermarking scheme proposed in [26] demonstrate that it can resist various attacks while a DWT and Schur decomposition-based watermarking technique [14] needs improvement in embedding capacity and robustness against high density geometric and signal processing attacks.

3 Proposed Steganographic Technique

This section explains the system and embedding & extraction procedures of the proposed reversible steganography method with authentication capability using a fragile watermark. The proposed technique generates a stego image by embedding the secret message in the original image called a cover image using a DCT-based steganography technique. Then, a watermarked image is generated by inserting a fragile watermark in the stego image using LSB substitution to check the authenticity of the stego image. The embedding procedure at the transmitter and an extraction procedure at the receiver are explained below:

3.1 Embedding Procedure

The block diagram of the proposed embedding scheme is depicted in Fig. 1. Firstly, the cover image of size (M × N) is partitioned into (8 × 8) blocks and DCT is applied to each block resulting in one DC and 63 AC Coefficients. Out of 63 AC coefficients, k AC coefficients are utilized to hide k bits of the message sequence. That is, a maximum of one bit per AC coefficient is used to embed the message. The message bits are read sequentially to hide the bits, and the AC coefficients are scanned from bottom to top in a zig-zag manner. For the bit '1', the value of the coefficient is incremented by '1', and for bit '0', the value of the coefficient is decremented by '1'. Once complete k bits are embedded, the IDCT is applied to the block and referred to as the stego image block. The procedure is repeated with all (8 × 8) blocks and the remaining message bits. Finally, the stego image blocks are merged to form the stego image.

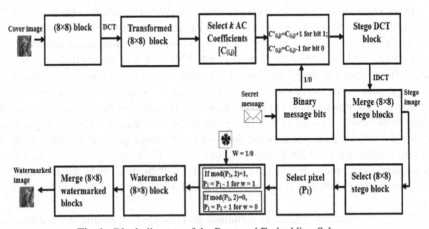

Fig. 1. Block diagram of the Proposed Embedding Scheme

The binary watermark is then embedded in the (8 × 8) block of the stego image as follows: The first pixel, P_1, is selected from the stego image block. For watermark bit '0', the value of pixel P_1 is incremented by 1 if mod(P_1, 2) = 0. For watermark bit '1', the value of pixel P_1 is decremented by 1 if mod(P_1, 2) = 1. The procedure is repeated with all (8 × 8) stego image blocks and the remaining watermark bits. Finally, the watermarked blocks are merged to form the watermarked image.

The maximum message bits (i.e., max capacity) which can be hidden using the proposed method is:

$$C_m = \frac{(M \times N)}{(8 \times 8)} \times k \tag{1}$$

The maximum size of the binary watermark logo is:

$$C_w = \frac{(M \times N)}{(8 \times 8)} \tag{2}$$

3.2 Extraction Procedure

The block diagram of extraction procedure is shown in Fig. 2. Firstly, the watermark from the watermarked image is extracted to check whether the stego image is authentic. The received image is partitioned into (8 × 8) blocks for watermark extraction. The first pixel of each block is examined to get an embedded watermark bit. To extract watermark bit '0', $\text{mod}(P_1, 2) = 1$, while for the extraction of watermark bit '1', $\text{mod}(P_1, 2) = 0$. After processing all the blocks, the binary watermark logo is recovered and the quality of the extracted watermark will be estimated for authentication.

If the estimated quality of the extracted watermark is very high, the received image is not tampered indicating that the hidden message is not corrupted. Otherwise, the received image has been tampered and the message is corrupted. The message is extracted at the receiver by comparing the stego and cover images as shown in Fig. 2. Both cover and the received images are partitioned into (8 × 8) blocks of pixels. Then, the DCT is applied to each (8 × 8) block of both images. The k AC coefficients from the blocks of both images are compared to get back the hidden message bits. When the AC coefficient of the watermarked image is equal to or less than the corresponding cover image AC coefficient, message bit '0' is extracted; otherwise, message bit '1'. The process is repeated until all the hidden message bits are recovered.

4 Simulation Results

The proposed scheme has been simulated and tested using the MATLAB 2019b platform. The standard 8-bit grayscale general and medical images of (512 × 512) pixel resolutions shown in Figs. 3 (a)-(h) have been used as cover images, while a binary watermark of size (64 × 64) pixel used for authentication is shown in Fig. 3 (i). The secret message of size $64 \times 64 \times k$ is generated and kept the same for obtaining the results for various cover images. The payload, imperceptibility, authentication and fragility analysis are used to evaluate the performance of the proposed scheme.

The payload is the ratio of the total number of bits embedded, n, to the size of cover image pixels, and it can be calculated by using Eq. (3) [27]:

$$Payload = \frac{n}{(M \times N)} \tag{3}$$

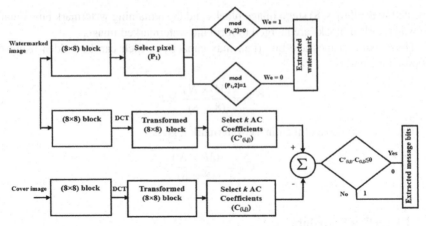

Fig. 2. Block diagram of the Extraction Process

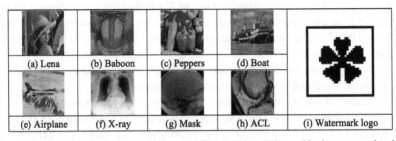

(a) Lena	(b) Baboon	(c) Peppers	(d) Boat	
(e) Airplane	(f) X-ray	(g) Mask	(h) ACL	(i) Watermark logo

Fig. 3. (a)-(h) Standard 8-bit grayscale images of size (512 × 512) used in the proposed technique as cover images. (i). Original binary Watermark of size (64 × 64).

Embedding capacity includes message bits and watermark bits. The quality of the watermarked images on the subjective ground is evaluated by the human visual system (HVS). The objective quality of the watermarked images is measured by various similarity metrics such as peak signal-to-noise ratio (PSNR) and structural similarity index measure (SSIM) [28]. The performance metrics PSNR, MSE, and SSIM are defined by Eqs. (4) to (6):

$$PSNR(dB) = 10\log_{10}\frac{(255)^2}{MSE} \tag{4}$$

$$MSE = \frac{1}{(M \times N)} \sum_{i=0}^{M-1} \sum_{j=0}^{N-1} \left[(W_{(i,j)} - I_{(i,j)})^2 \right] \tag{5}$$

where (M × N) represents the cover & the watermarked image's dimensions, $I_{(i,j)}$ and $W_{(i,j)}$ denote the cover & the watermarked image pixel intensities in the ith column and j^{th} row.

$$SSIM = \frac{(2\mu_x\mu_y + c_1)(2\sigma_{xy} + c_2)}{(\mu_x^2 + \mu_y^2 + c_1)(\sigma_x^2 + \sigma_y^2 + c_2)} \tag{6}$$

where μ_x, μ_y, σ_x, σ_y & σ_{xy} represent the means, standard deviations & cross-covariance and c_1 & c_2 are the luminance and contrast constants.

The image authentication of the proposed method has been performed by evaluating the Normalized Cross-Correlation (NCC) between the cover & the watermarked images and the Bit Error Rate (BER) is also determined between embedded 'message and watermark' and extracted 'message and watermark' for no attack and under various attacks [12, 28]. Equations (7) and (8) define the NCC and BER (%) as given below:

$$NCC = \frac{\sum_{i=0}^{M-1} \sum_{j=0}^{N-1} \left[I_{(i,j)} W_{(i,j)} \right]}{\sum_{i=0}^{M-1} \sum_{j=0}^{N-1} \left[I_{(i,j)} \right]^2} \tag{7}$$

The percentage bit error rate between embedded bits (d) & extracted bits (d^*) is given as follows:

$$BER(\%) = \frac{1}{n} \left[\sum_{i=0}^{n-1} d(i) \oplus d^*(i) \right] \times 100 \tag{8}$$

4.1 Imperceptibility Analysis

In the proposed method, the payload includes the message and watermark bits. Embedding capacity is evaluated in terms of the bits or bits per pixel (bpp), while PSNR and SSIM measure the imperceptibility. The Imperceptibility in terms of PSNR and SSIM at $k = 63$ embedding capacity for different images is shown in Table 1.

The payload or the capacity includes $64 \times 64 \times 63 = 258048$ message bits and $64 \times 64 = 4096$ watermark bits. From Table 1, it can be seen that the PSNR is more than 45 dB and SSIM ranges from 0.91 to 0.99. These values indicate that the quality of the stego image is still as good as the original cover image. It signifies that though a large amount of payload (262144 bits or 1 bpp) is embedded in the cover image, the quality of the image is still imperceptible. Our scheme achieves a higher PSNR value while maintaining a higher data payload of 262144 bits or 1 bpp.

The graphs in Figs. 4 (a) & (b) compare the capacity and PSNR of the proposed method with the method presented in [23]. These figures depict that our scheme's capacity is higher by 98304 bits and PSNR is higher by 13.4 dB than [23]. Similarly, the capacity of the proposed scheme is higher as compared to [12] by 0.25 bpp (65536 bits) while maintaining the PSNR higher by 1.44 dB because the technique proposed by Parah et al. in [12] has an average PSNR value 46.36 dB for an embedding capacity 0.75 bpp. Thus, our scheme achieves high payload capacity and good imperceptibility.

The **performance comparison of the proposed approach with recent state-of-the-art approaches** is explained as follows:

The proposed technique achieves an average PSNR of 47.8 dB for an embedding capacity 1.0 bpp. These experimental results are compared with [1]. The technique proposed by Lin et al. in [1] has an average PSNR of 45.5 dB for an embedding capacity 0.5 bpp. Hence, the capacity and PSNR of our technique are higher by 0.5 bpp and 2.3 dB compared to [1]. Similarly, the proposed technique is more imperceptible by 2 dB for the same embedding capacity than the technique presented by Rostam et al. in [2], as the

Table 1. Imperceptibility and visual quality in terms of PSNR and SSIM at a given capacity for different images

Cover Images (512 × 512)	Block Size (8 × 8)			
	Capacity (bits)	PSNR (dB)	Capacity (bpp)	SSIM
Lena	262144	47.7882	1.0	0.9618
Baboon	262144	47.7866	1.0	0.9935
Peppers	262144	47.7924	1.0	0.9316
Boat	262144	47.7884	1.0	0.9818
Airplane	262144	47.7863	1.0	0.9137
X-ray	262144	47.7949	1.0	0.9584
Mask	262144	47.8941	1.0	0.9810
ACL	262144	47.8450	1.0	0.9602

average PSNR value of Rostam et al. is 45.8 dB. The embedding capacity (262144 bits) of our technique is also much higher compared to the scheme presented in [6] because the coverless image steganography proposed by Biswas et al. in [6] provides a capacity of 96 bits. Thus, the proposed scheme outperforms the recent state-of-the-art approaches in embedding capacity and imperceptibility.

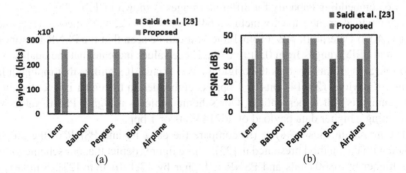

Fig. 4. (a). Capacity comparison with Saidi et al. (b). PSNR comparison with Saidi et al.

4.2 Authentication Analysis Without Attack

Table 2 shows the quality of various watermarked images and extracted watermarks on subjective and objective grounds. The extracted watermarks for different watermarked images under no attack condition resemble the original one, BER between embedded & extracted watermark (BER_w) equals 0, NCC approximately equals unity and BER between embedded & extracted message (BER_m) obtained also equals 0. The zero value of BER_w confirms that the extracted watermark is the same as the original one, the stego image is authentic and the hidden message is not corrupted due to zero value of BER_m. The authentic stego image also shows that the received image is not tampered and the hidden message can be perfectly reconstructed without any error under no attack conditions.

Table 2. Watermarked Images and Extracted Watermarks for No Attack

Images	Lena	Baboon	Boat	X-ray	Mask	ACL
Watermarked Images						
NCC	0.9998	0.9996	0.9998	0.9999	0.9996	0.9998
Extracted Watermarks						
BER_w (%)	0	0	0	0	0	0

Our proposed technique is reversible steganographic technique as the watermark bits and message bits extracted at the receiver are the same as the original watermark bits and message bits embedded at the transmitter for an authentic stego image under no attack conditions. The experimental results NCC approximately equals unity, BER_w equals zero and BER_m equals zero also support the statement. The cover image can also be completely recovered from the watermarked image after extraction of the watermark bits and message bits at the receiver if the received image is not tampered during transmission. Figure 5 depicts that the process is reversible due to the absolute black difference between the cover image and the recovered image.

4.3 Authentication and Fragility Analysis Under Various Attacks

The watermarked images have been subjected to different image processing and geometrical attacks to analyze the proposed method's fragility and authentication. Authentication parameters NCC and BER are evaluated to test the authentication and fragility of the proposed method. Table 3 shows the NCC and BER performance for attacks: i) Gaussian Noise ii) median filtering iii) rotation iv) JPEG compression.

Table 3 shows that when the watermarked images are attacked by Additive White Gaussian Noise (AWGN) with a variance equal to 0.02, NCC reduces to about 0.817, the average values of BER_w and BER_m are 50.46% and 46.59%. A high value of BER_w shows that the extracted watermark is completely destroyed. The visual quality of the extracted watermark and the low value of NCC also indicate that the received image is attacked, and around 47% of extracted message bits are corrupted. Compared with Parah et al., our technique is slightly more fragile. In our case, the BER_w is higher by 0.13% to 1% than [12].

Table 3 also shows the attack on the watermarked image by median filtering of the (3 × 3) kernel. The average values of NCC, BER_w and BER_m are found to be 0.998,

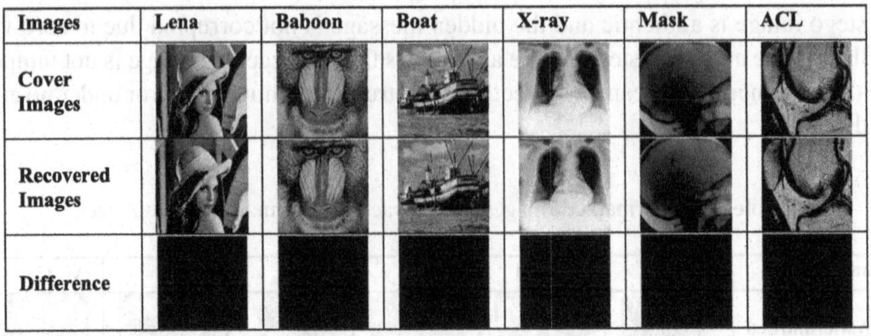

Fig. 5. Cover Images, Recovered Images and difference between two images.

46.20% and 40.83%, showing high fragility compared to the method [12] and on an average 40% of message bits are received in error. Similarly, subjecting watermarked images to rotation attack at an angle of $5°$ results in NCC = 0.626, BER_w = 51.93% and BER_m = 49.62%, while the average BER_w of the method [12] is 51.5%, respectively, showing that our scheme is more fragile to rotation attack and around 50% extracted message bits are in error. Likewise, NCC, BER_w and BER_m for JPEG compression having a quality factor of 90 are found to be 0.999, 46.12% and 42.18%, implying that the received watermark is destroyed and around 42% of message bits are received in error. It also shows that our scheme is more fragile to the JPEG attack than [12] due to high value of BER_w and can easily detect it.

The above results show that our proposed scheme is highly fragile and can detect various image processing attacks, geometrical attacks and erroneous message bits received at the receiver. The fragile watermark is destroyed with a slight alteration of the watermarked image, as evident from the NCC and BER_w values given in Table 3. Thus, it can be effectively used for tamper or, alter detection and image authentication.

Table 3. Performance comparison with Parah et al. [12] under various attacks.

Attacks	Images	Lena	Baboon	Boat	X-ray	Mask	ACL
AWGN (var=0.02)	Attacked Images						
	NCC	0.7999	0.7085	0.7895	0.8775	0.7996	0.8340
	Extracted Watermarks						
	BER$_w$ (%) (Proposed)	49.93	49.91	49.95	51.93	50.93	50.98
	BER$_w$ (%) [12]	49.80	N/A	N/A	50.85	50.37	50.51
Median Filtering (kernel size=3×3)	Attacked Images						
	NCC	0.9959	0.9199	0.9879	0.9997	0.9998	0.9993
	Extracted Watermarks						
	BER$_w$ (%) (Proposed)	47.21	49.32	48.48	46.78	45.85	45.19
	BER$_w$ (%) [12]	44.41	N/A	N/A	46.07	45.46	44.78
Rotation (angle=5°)	Attacked Images						
	NCC	0.5624	0.4117	0.5183	0.8146	0.8467	0.6896
	Extracted Watermarks						
	BER$_w$ (%) (Proposed)	51.90	50.09	50.15	51.97	51.78	51.95
	BER$_w$ (%) [12]	51.68	N/A	N/A	51.22	51.37	51.98
JPEG (quality factor=90)	Attacked Images						
	NCC	0.9987	0.9952	0.9980	0.9999	0.9997	0.9997
	Extracted Watermarks						
	BER$_w$ (%) (Proposed)	44.82	43.41	44.82	45.95	46.34	47.42
	BER$_w$ (%) [12]	42.68	N/A	N/A	45.75	45.90	47.05

5   Conclusion

This paper proposed a high capacity and reversible DCT-based steganographic technique with authentication capability for 8-bit grayscale general and medical images. The proposed approach utilizes selected AC coefficients out of 64 DCT coefficients per (8 × 8) block of the cover image to embed the message. The binary watermark is inserted in the first pixel of all stego image blocks to authenticate the stego image. The performance of the proposed technique was evaluated in terms of payload, perceptual imperceptibility, fragility, and image authentication analyses. Simulation results show that our proposed scheme provides high imperceptibility, a PSNR of 47.80 dB, and a large embedding capacity of 262144 bits or 1 bpp. Furthermore, our method outperforms the state-of-the-art techniques in payload and visual quality of the stego image.

The fragility and authentication analysis confirm the effectiveness of the proposed scheme with the stego image being authentic when the extracted watermark closely resembles the original one and BER_w equals zero, while the high value of BER_w shows that the extracted watermark is completely destroyed and stego image is unauthentic. For authentic stego image, zero value of BER_m and high value of NCC confirm that the extracted message bits are exactly the same as the hidden message bits and message can be perfectly reconstructed without any error for no attack. When the stego image is unauthentic, high value of BER_m and low value of NCC indicate that the message bits are received in error and are not the same as the hidden message bits, showing that the message has been corrupted as the stego image has been intentionally or, unintentionally attacked. The proposed method has practical applications in e-voting and e-healthcare, as it efficiently facilitates tamper or, alter detection and image authentication.

References

1. Lin, C.-C., Chang, C.-C., Kao, W.-J., Chang, J.-F.: Efficient electronic patient information hiding scheme with tamper detection function for medical images. IEEE Access. **10**, 18470–18485 (2022). https://doi.org/10.1109/ACCESS.2022.3144322
2. Rostam, H.E., Motameni, H., Enayatifar, R.: Privacy-preserving in the Internet of Things based on steganography and chaotic functions. Optik (Stuttg). **258**, 168864 (2022). https://doi.org/10.1016/j.ijleo.2022.168864
3. Atta, R., Ghanbari, M., IEEE, L.F.: A high payload data hiding scheme based on dual tree complex wavelet transform. Optik (Stuttg). **226**, 165786 (2021)
4. Rout, S., Mohapatra, R.K.: Hiding sensitive information in surveillance video without affecting nefarious activity detection. In: 2022 2nd International Conference on Artificial Intelligence and Signal Processing (AISP), pp. 1–6 (2022). https://doi.org/10.1109/AISP53593.2022.9760607
5. Debnath, S., Mohapatra, R.K.: A study on secret data sharing through coverless steganography. In: 2022 2nd International Conference on Artificial Intelligence and Signal Processing (AISP), pp. 1–6 (2022). https://doi.org/10.1109/AISP53593.2022.9760680
6. Biswas, S., Debnath, S., Mohapatra, R.K.: Coverless image steganography based on DWT approximation and pixel intensity averaging. In: 2023 7th International Conference on Trends in Electronics and Informatics (ICOEI), pp. 1554–1561. IEEE (2023)
7. Loan, N.A., Hurrah, N.N., Parah, S.A., Sheikh, J.A.: High capacity reversible stenographic technique based on image resizing and pixel permutation. In: 2017 Fourth International Conference on Image Information Processing (ICIIP), pp. 1–6. IEEE (2017)
8. Sahu, A.K., Swain, G.: Pixel overlapping image steganography using PVD and modulus function. 3D Res. **9**, 1–14 (2018)
9. Xuan, G., Zhu, J., Chen, J., Shi, Y.Q., Ni, Z., Su, W.: Distortionless data hiding based on integer wavelet transform. Electron. Lett. **38**, 1646–1648 (2002)

10. Seyyedi, S.A., Ivanov, N.N.: High payload and secure steganography method based on block partitioning and integer wavelet transform. Int. J. Secur. Appl. **8**(4), 183–194 (2014)
11. Bhalerao, S., Ansari, I.A., Kumar, A.: A secure image watermarking for tamper detection and localization. J. Ambient. Intell. Humaniz. Comput. **12**, 1057–1068 (2021). https://doi.org/10. 1007/s12652-020-02135-3
12. Parah, S.A., Ahad, F., Sheikh, J.A., Bhat, G.M.: Hiding clinical information in medical images: a new high capacity and reversible data hiding technique. J. Biomed. Inform. **66**, 214–230 (2017)
13. Mohammed, A.O., Hussein, H.I., Mstafa, R.J., Abdulazeez, A.M.: A blind and robust color image watermarking scheme based on DCT and DWT domains. Multimed. Tools Appl. **82**, 32855–32881 (2023). https://doi.org/10.1007/s11042-023-14797-0
14. Soualmi, A., Alti, A., Laouamer, L.: A blind image watermarking method for personal medical data security. In: 2019 International Conference on Networking and Advanced Systems (ICNAS), pp. 1–5. IEEE (2019)
15. Ernawan, F., Kabir, M.N.: A robust image watermarking technique with an optimal DCT-psychovisual threshold. IEEE Access **6**, 20464–20480 (2018)
16. Winarno, A., Arrasyid, A.A., Sari, C.A., Rachmawanto, E.H.: Image watermarking using low wavelet subband based on 8 × 8 sub-block DCT. In: 2017 International Seminar on Application for Technology of Information and Communication (iSemantic), pp. 11–15. IEEE (2017)
17. Chutani, S., Goyal, H.: LSB embedding in spatial domain-a review of improved techniques. Int. J. Comput. Technol. **3**, 153–157 (2012)
18. Chakraborty, S., Jalal, A.S., Bhatnagar, C.: LSB based non blind predictive edge adaptive image steganography. Multimed. Tools Appl. **76**, 7973–7987 (2017). https://doi.org/10.1007/ s11042-016-3449-4
19. Shen, S.-Y., Huang, L.-H.: A data hiding scheme using pixel value differencing and improving exploiting modification directions. Comput. Secur. **48**, 131–141 (2015)
20. Lai, B.-L., Chang, L.-W.: Adaptive data hiding for images based on harr discrete wavelet transform. In: Chang, L.-W., Lie, W.-N. (eds.) PSIVT 2006. LNCS, vol. 4319, pp. 1085–1093. Springer, Heidelberg (2006). https://doi.org/10.1007/11949534_109
21. El Safy, R.O., Zayed, H.H., El Dessouki, A.: An adaptive steganographic technique based on integer wavelet transform. In: 2009 International Conference on Networking and Media Convergence, pp. 111–117. IEEE (2009)
22. El_Rahman, S.A.: A comparative analysis of image_steganography based on DCT algorithm and steganography tool to hide nuclear reactors confidential information. Comput. Electr. Eng. **70**, 380–399 (2018)
23. Saidi, M., Hermassi, H., Rhouma, R., Belghith, S.: A new adaptive image steganography scheme based on DCT and chaotic map. Multimed. Tools Appl. **76**, 13493–13510 (2017). https://doi.org/10.1007/s11042-016-3722-6
24. Sumalatha, L., Rosline, K.G., Vijaya, K.V.: A simple block based content watermarking scheme for image authentication and tamper detection. Int. J. Soft Comput. Eng.(IJSCE) **2**, 2231–2240 (2012)
25. Shehab, A., et al.: Secure and robust fragile watermarking scheme for medical images. IEEE Access. **6**, 10269–10278 (2018). https://doi.org/10.1109/ACCESS.2018.2799240
26. Nguyen, T.-S., Chang, C.-C., Yang, X.-Q.: A reversible image authentication scheme based on fragile watermarking in discrete wavelet transform domain. AEU-Int. J. Electron. Commun. **70**, 1055–1061 (2016)
27. Atta, R., Ghanbari, M.: A high payload steganography mechanism based on wavelet packet transformation and neutrosophic set. J. Vis. Commun. Image Represent. **53**, 42–54 (2018)
28. Parah, S.A., Ahad, F., Sheikh, J.A., Loan, N.A., Bhat, G.M.: A new reversible and high capacity data hiding technique for E-healthcare applications. Multimed. Tools Appl. **76**, 3943–3975 (2017). https://doi.org/10.1007/s11042-016-4196-2

Rough Spatial Ensemble Kernelized Fuzzy C Means Clustering for Robust Brain MR Image Tissue Segmentation

Amiya Halder[(✉)], Rudrajit Choudhuri, and Arinjay Bhowmick

St. Thomas College of Engineering and Technology, 4 D. H. Road, Kolkata, India
amiya.halder77@gmail.com

Abstract. Image segmentation is a crucial step in image processing having various applications in biomedical image analysis. Segmentation of the magnetic resonance images of the brain is one such key area in biomedical image analysis that segments various tissues in the brain and detects tumor regions. In this paper, an unsupervised rough spatial ensemble kernelized fuzzy clustering segmentation algorithm is presented for automated segmentation of magnetic resonance images of the brain. The proposed algorithm is an integration of Rough Fuzzy C Means clustering and the kernel method with a novel ensemble kernel being a combination of spherical kernel, Gaussian, and Cauchy kernels, which improves the performance of the segmentation algorithm. The proposed algorithm performs better than the existing clustering algorithms across a wide range of magnetic resonance images of the brain along with visual indications obtained from the results.

Keywords: Iterative Optimization · Magnetic Resonance Imaging · Image Segmentation · Rough Set · Kernel Method

1 Introduction

Segmentation of medical images has an important application in biomedical image processing and computer vision which helps in quantification of various regions, tissue partitioning, and computer integrated surgery. Automated biomedical image analysis along with radiological imaging aid in successful diagnostic process of a patient by speedy detection of various abnormalities in different organs of the human body. Segmentation of brain tissues and tumor [2,17] detection is one vital area that requires quick and accurate identification for appropriate diagnosis of the patient.

Conventional intensity based FCM algorithm proposed by Pham et al. [14] has limitation of noise sensitivity, which is frequently present in brain MR images. To enhance the performance of FCM algorithm, different modified fuzzy clustering approaches have been presented in the past [3,13]. Chen et al. [4] proposed vFCM, which clusters the data points by varying the fuzziness parameter without considering any local neighbourhood information. Krinidis and Chatzis proposed

© The Author(s), under exclusive license to Springer Nature Switzerland AG 2024
H. Kaur et al. (Eds.): CVIP 2023, CCIS 2011, pp. 350–363, 2024.
https://doi.org/10.1007/978-3-031-58535-7_29

one parameter free algorithm FLICM [10] where fuzzy factor is defined to help the membership of local neighbour pixels to converge into one similar value. But using Euclidean distance measure makes this algorithm perform poorly in MR images of the brain. To overcome this problem, Gao et al. [7] proposed ARFCM which clusters data points based on adaptive elastic distance between local membership values. Zhang et al. [20] proposed NLFCM by considering pixel relevance into the fuzzy factor which could estimate the damping extent of neighbourhood pixels accurately. Other fuzzy clustering algorithms [1, 8, 18] have focused at local spatial information to handle region correlations and aberrations present in images. They perform fairly well but lack performance in highly correlated tissue regions infected by intensity inhomogeneity.

Zhang et al. proposed a kernelized version of clustering algorithm KFCM [19] to incorporate non linearity in data point mapping. Maji et al. [11] proposed RFCM incorporating advantages of both fuzzy and rough sets, which was further modified by clustering algorithms [12, 16] for effective MR image segmentation. Densely induced noise as such in some brain MR images degrade their performance. Halder and Talukdar proposed KRFCMSC [9] integrating rough fuzzy c-means with kernel having spatial constraints. Roy and Maji proposed sRFCM [15] which combines the merits of rough-fuzzy clustering and local neighbourhood information. R. Choudhuri and A. Halder proposed ARKFCM [5] which uses a circular kernel to account local spatial information and compensating inhomogeneity.

A rough spatial ensemble kernelized fuzzy set based c-means clustering algorithm is proposed for robust brain MR image segmentation. It integrates kernel induced distance metric [19] with the foundations of rough fuzzy c-means clustering algorithm [11] to form a reliable clustering algorithm. The novel kernel used in the proposed algorithm is an ensemble of spherical kernel, Gaussian and Cauchy kernels with respective weightages to compensate for intensity inhomogeneity and high correlations in brain MR image. It is shown that the proposed algorithm has better segmentation results on brain MR images corrupted by noise, inhomogeneity and other artefacts than the other existing algorithms.

The main contributions of the paper are:

– A Rough Spatial Ensemble Kernelized Fuzzy C Means (RSEKFCM) clustering algorithm is proposed.
– Extensive experimentation is performed across different types of brain MR images to compare and validate the abilities of existing methods.

The rest of the paper is organized as follows. Section 2 introduces basic concepts about fuzzy c-means, rough c-means and kernel methods. In Sect. 3, the proposed algorithm for brain MR image segmentation is derived. Experimental results are compared in Sect. 4. Finally, Sect. 5 presents the conclusion.

2   Background

2.1   Fuzzy C Means Clustering

Fuzzy C Means is an iterative optimization algorithm that clusters data points incorporating fuzzy set logic in order to calculate membership degrees that are needed to assign a category to a data point. Consider $P = (P_1, P_2, ..., P_n)$ to be an image consisting of n pixels which are to be segmented into C clusters. The cost function that is intended to be optimized is defined in Eq. 1.

$$J_{FCM} = \sum_{k=1}^{C} \sum_{i=1}^{n} \mu_{ki}^q \|P_i - v_k\|^2 \tag{1}$$

where μ_{ki} represents the membership value of pixel P_i corresponding to the kth cluster, v_k corresponds to the kth cluster centroid.

$$\mu_{ki} = \frac{1}{\sum_{j=1}^{C} \left(\frac{\|P_i - v_k\|}{\|P_i - v_j\|}\right)^{\frac{2}{q-1}}} \tag{2}$$

$$v_k = \frac{\sum_{i=1}^{n} \mu_{ki}^q P_i}{\sum_{i=1}^{n} \mu_{ki}^q} \tag{3}$$

FCM starts off with an initial assumption for each cluster centroids, and iteratively converges to give solutions for v_k which represents a saddle or a minima point of the defined cost function. The data points or pixels are thus segmented into C clusters.

2.2   Rough Fuzzy C Means Clustering

Rough Fuzzy C Means clustering is the amalgamation of the fuzzy C-means and rough C-means clustering algorithms. The RFCM algorithm adds the concept of fuzzy membership of fuzzy sets, and lower and upper approximations of rough sets into this algorithm. Consider $P = (P_1, P_2, ..., P_n)$ to be an image consisting of n pixels which are to be segmented into C clusters, where corresponding to the kth cluster, L(k) and U(k) denote the lower and upper approximation rough set respectively. Another rough set $B(k) = \{U(k) - L(k)\}$ denote the boundary region of kth cluster. The algorithm achieves convergence by minimizing the cost function described in Eqs. 4–6.

$$J_{RFCM} = \begin{cases} w \times J_L + \hat{w} \times J_B & \text{if } L(k) \neq \phi \text{ and } B(k) \neq \phi \\ J_L & \text{if } L(k) \neq \phi \text{ and } B(k) = \phi \\ J_B & \text{if } L(k) = \phi \text{ and } B(k) \neq \phi \end{cases} \tag{4}$$

$$J_L = \sum_{k=1}^{C} \sum_{P_i \in L(k)} \mu_{ki}^q \|P_i - v_k\|^2 \tag{5}$$

$$J_B = \sum_{k=1}^{C} \sum_{P_i \in B(k)} \mu_{ki}^q \|P_i - v_k\|^2 \tag{6}$$

where μ_{ki} represents the membership value of pixel P_i corresponding to the kth cluster, v_k corresponds to the kth cluster centroid, $\|.\|$ signifies the Euclidean norm function, and q is a fuzziness control parameter for the resultant partition. All the pixels in lower approximation take the same weight $w \in [0, 1]$ while all the pixels in boundary take another weight $\hat{w}$ uniformly. The parameter w and $\hat{w} = 1 - w$ correspond to the relative importance of lower approximation and boundary region.

Computation of the centroid is modified to include the effects of both fuzzy memberships and lower and upper regions. The modified centroid calculation for the RFCM is obtained by solving partial derivative of Eq. 4 with respect to v_k as described by Eqs.7–9.

$$v_k = \begin{cases} w \times \rho_L + \hat{w} \times \rho_B & \text{if } L(k) \neq \phi \text{ and } B(k) \neq \phi \\ \rho_L & \text{if } L(k) \neq \phi \text{ and } B(k) = \phi \\ \rho_B & \text{if } L(k) = \phi \text{ and } B(k) \neq \phi \end{cases} \quad (7)$$

where

$$\rho_L = \frac{\sum_{P_i \in L(k)} P_i}{|L(k)|} \quad (8)$$

and

$$\rho_B = \frac{\sum_{P_i \in B(k)} \mu_{ki}^q P_i}{\sum_{P_i \in B(k)} \mu_{ki}^q} \quad (9)$$

The process starts by randomly choosing k data points as the centroids of the C clusters. After calculating membership values μ_{ki} for every pixel using Eq. 2, the values of μ_{ki} are sorted for each pixel P_i. Let μ_{ki} be maximum and μ_{ji} be second maximum membership values of pixel P_i. If $|\mu_{ki} - \mu_{ji}| \leq \delta$ for some predefined threshold δ, then $P_i \in U(k)$ and $P_i \in U(j)$. Additionally, P_i is not part of any lower approximation set. Otherwise, $P_i \in L(k)$ since μ_{ki} is maximum and memberships are set as $\mu_{ki} = 1$ and $\mu_{ji} = 0$ for all $j \neq k$. Membership values for pixels not belonging to lower approximation of any cluster remain unchanged. Thereafter, cluster centroids are computed using Eq. 7. The above steps are iteratively repeated until cluster centroids converge in successive iterations.

2.3   Kernel Methods and Functions

Kernel methods are a particular category of algorithms used in pattern recognition. The main idea behind the approach is to easily structure or separate the data points by mapping them to a higher dimensional space. This is a powerful trick and it bridges the gap between linearity and non-linearity for any algorithm which can be defined in terms of scalar products between two vectors. A kernel function represents a scalar product in a feature space and is of the form defined in Eq. 10.

$$K(x, y) = \langle \Psi(x), \Psi(y) \rangle \quad (10)$$

where $\langle \Psi(x), \Psi(y) \rangle$ represents the scalar product between the vectors. Commonly, the cluster centroids are represented as a sum of a linear combination of all $\Psi(P_i)$, which basically implies that all centroids lie in the feature space.

3 Proposed Methodology: Rough Spatial Ensemble Kernelized Fuzzy C Means Clustering Algorithm (RSEKFCM)

In this section, rough spatial ensemble kernelized fuzzy C means clustering algorithm (RSEKFCM) is proposed. The proposed approach considers spatial information around an image pixel along with its intensity value as a feature. For achieving the same, a 3×3 window centred at a concerned pixel (P_i) is extracted and the average intensity value (S_i) of the window is computed and used as a data point for clustering. This compensates for inhomogeneity and correlations in images leading to efficient segmentation.

The proposed method uses a combinational approach where the data point mapping is based on spherical kernel, and outlier inclusion is handled using Gaussian and Cauchy Kernels. The combinational kernel used in the proposed approach is defined as follows:

$$K(x,y) = W1 * K1(x,y) + W2 * K2(x,y) + W3 * K3(x,y)$$

$$K1(x,y) = 1 - \frac{1}{2}\left(\frac{\|x-y\|}{\sigma_1}\right)^2 - \frac{1}{2}\left(\frac{\|x-y\|}{\sigma_1}\right)^3$$

$$K2(x,y) = \exp\left(-\frac{\|x-y\|^2}{2\sigma_2{}^2}\right)$$

$$K3(x,y) = \frac{1}{1+\left(\frac{\|x-y\|}{\sigma_2}\right)^2}$$

where K1, K2, and K3 represent spherical, Gaussian, and Cauchy kernels respectively. W1, W2, and W3 are kernel relevance control parameters that manage the influence of a particular kernel in the combinatorial kernel mapping scenario. σ_1 and σ_2 represents tuning parameter for adjusting kernel widths.

Since, we use the spherical kernel as the base kernel due to its ability in seamless mapping of highly correlated brain image regions and the Gaussian and Cauchy Kernels for outlier inclusion, therefore the tuning parameter W1 is always set higher than $(3 \times max(W2, W3))$.

The amalgamation of the above ensemble kernel with rough and fuzzy sets aid in effective tissue segmentation. While the membership values of fuzzy set enables effective handling of homogeneous regions commonly found in dense tissue regions of the brain, the lower and upper approximation rough sets deal with uncertainty, vagueness, and incompleteness in cluster region to determine the fine boundaries of tissue regions keeping into account the noise induced during image acquisition. This enables the proposed approach to perform better at obtaining consistent tissue segments when compared to other existing state of the art techniques.

In the proposed method, the membership values of pixels in lower approximation are $\mu_{ki} = 1$, while only pixels in boundary are fuzzified. Also incorporating the novel kernel, the objective function of the proposed algorithm is defined as follows in Eqs. 11–13.

$$J_{RSEKFCM} = \begin{cases} w \times J_1 + \hat{w} \times J_2 & \text{if } L(k) \neq \varnothing \text{ and } B(k) \neq \varnothing \\ J_1 & \text{if } L(k) \neq \varnothing \text{ and } B(k) = \varnothing \\ J_2 & \text{if } L(k) = \varnothing \text{ and } B(k) \neq \varnothing \end{cases} \tag{11}$$

$$J_1 = \sum_{k=1}^{C} \sum_{S_i \in L(k)} \mu_{ki}^q \|\Psi(S_i) - \Psi(v_k)\|^2 + \sum_{k=1}^{C} \lambda \sum_{S_i \in L(k)} (1 - \mu_{ki}) \tag{12}$$

$$J_2 = \sum_{k=1}^{C} \sum_{S_i \in B(k)} \mu_{ki}^q \|\Psi(S_i) - \Psi(v_k)\|^2 + \sum_{k=1}^{C} \lambda \sum_{S_i \in B(k)} (1 - \mu_{ki}) \tag{13}$$

where Ψ represents a non-linear mapping, S_i represents the immediate spatial neighbourhood information around the pixel P_i, and λ is a cluster influence control parameter. L(k) and B(k) are lower and boundary sets of kth cluster respectively. Simplifying the Euclidean norm term using the kernel substitution mapping we get,

$$\|\Psi(S_i) - \Psi(v_k)\|^2 = K(S_i, S_i) - 2K(S_i, v_k) + K(v_k, v_k)$$

Using the kernel, we get $K(m, m) = 1$ and also $\mu_{ki} = 1$ for $(S_i \in L(k))$. The objective function can be simplified as (Eq. 14 and Eq. 15):

$$J_1 = 2 \sum_{k=1}^{C} \sum_{S_i \in L(k)} (1 - K(S_i, v_k)) \tag{14}$$

$$J_2 = 2 \sum_{k=1}^{C} \sum_{S_i \in B(k)} \mu_{ki}^q (1 - K(S_i, v_k)) + \sum_{k=1}^{C} \lambda \sum_{S_i \in B(k)} (1 - \mu_{ki}) \tag{15}$$

For optimization, equating the partial derivative of the objective function with respect to the membership function to zero we get (Eq. 16):

$$\frac{\partial J_2}{\partial \mu_{ki}} = 0$$

$$\Rightarrow 2 \times q \times \mu_{ki}^{q-1} (1 - K(S_i, v_k)) - \lambda_i = 0 \tag{16}$$

$$\Rightarrow \mu_{ki} = \left(\frac{\lambda_i}{2q}\right)^{\frac{1}{q-1}} \times \left[\frac{1}{1-K(S_i, v_k)}\right]^{\frac{1}{q-1}}$$

As $(\sum_{j=1}^{C} \mu_{ji} = 1)$ is a boundary constraint,

$$\sum_{j=1}^{C} \left(\frac{\lambda_i}{2q}\right)^{\frac{1}{q-1}} \times \left[\frac{1}{1-K(S_i, v_j)}\right]^{\frac{1}{q-1}} = 1$$
$$\Rightarrow \left(\frac{\lambda_i}{2q}\right)^{\frac{1}{q-1}} = \frac{1}{\sum_{j=1}^{C} \left(\frac{1}{1-K(S_i, v_j)}\right)^{\frac{1}{q-1}}} \tag{17}$$

The membership function obtained is defined in Eq. 18:

$$\mu_{ki} = \frac{(1 - K(S_i, v_k))^{\frac{-1}{q-1}}}{\sum_{j=1}^{C} (1 - K(S_i, v_j))^{\frac{-1}{q-1}}} \tag{18}$$

Again, for optimizing the centroid values, the partial differentiation of the objective function with respect to the centroid computation function is equated to zero and we get the centroid function:

$$
v_k = \begin{cases} w \times \rho_1 + \hat{w} \times \rho_2 & \text{if } L(k) \neq \varnothing \text{ and } B(k) \neq \varnothing \\ \rho_1 & \text{if } L(k) \neq \varnothing \text{ and } B(k) = \varnothing \\ \rho_2 & \text{if } L(k) = \varnothing \text{ and } B(k) \neq \varnothing \end{cases} \tag{19}
$$

where

$$
\rho_1 = \frac{\sum_{S_i \in L(k)} S_i \cdot K(S_i, v_k)}{\sum_{S_i \in L(k)} K(S_i, v_k)} \tag{20}
$$

and

$$
\rho_2 = \frac{\sum_{S_i \in B(k)} \mu_{ki}^q \cdot S_i \cdot K(S_i, v_k)}{\sum_{S_i \in B(k)} \mu_{ki}^q \cdot K(S_i, v_k)} \tag{21}
$$

Given the computation functions for the pixel membership values and the centroids, the proposed algorithm iteratively converges to obtain optimum cluster centroids which represent a saddle point for the defined cost function, thereby segmenting the input image pixels into the required number of clusters. In subsequent iterations, the change noticed in the membership and centroid values highlight the convergence of the algorithm. The proposed algorithm is summarized in Algorithm 1.

Algorithm 1: PROPOSED ALGORITHM: RSEKFCM

Input: Brain MR Image (I)
Output: Tissue Segmented Brain MR Image

1 Assign number of clusters(C), maximum iterations (M), iterator (R), fuzziness control parameter (q), rough boundary threshold δ and convergence threshold $T \approx 0$.
2 Create empty sets L(k) for lower, U(k) for upper and B(k) for boundary, for each cluster k among C.
3 Compute mean vector S_i around 3×3 neighborhood of $P_i, \forall i = 1 : N$ pixels in input image.
4 Set initial membership values μ^0 as 0.
5 Set random initial centroids v_k^0 and set R as 1.
6 **while** $R < M$ **do**
7   Compute membership values μ_{ki}^R for every cluster k with respect to each S_i using Eq. 18.
8   **for** *each point S_i, i=1:N* **do**
9   Find the maximum membership value μ_{ki}^R and second maximum membership value μ_{ji}^R of S_i for some k, $j \in 1, C$ and $k \neq j$.
10   **if** $|\mu_{ki} - \mu_{ji}| < \delta$ **then**
11             $S_i \in U(k)$ and $S_i \in U(j)$
12   **else**
13             $S_i \in L(k)$ and $S_i \in U(k)$.
14   Set $\mu_{ki}^R = 1$ and $\mu_{ji}^R = 0, \forall j \neq k$.
15   Compute cluster centroids v_k^R based on Eq. 19.
16   **if** $|v_j^R - v_j^{(R-1)}| < T, \forall j \in 1, C$ **then**
17   break.
18     $R = R + 1$

19 After iterative optimization, each S_i is assigned a cluster k among C and the pixel intensity at spatial coordinate of S_i is set to the value of the corresponding cluster centroid v_k.

---

4   Results

In this section, the performance of the proposed rough spatial ensemble kernelized fuzzy c means clustering algorithm is evaluated on different types of real magnetic resonance images of brain obtained from the Brain Web image dataset [6]. These include T1-weighted, T2-weighted and proton density (PD) MR images of brain. Each volume consists of 51 slice images from slice number 50 to 100, and are contaminated with 7% noise and 40% inhomogeneity. The collected images have resolution of $181 \times 217 \times 181$ voxels and have a fixed size of $1\,mm \times 1\,mm \times 1\,mm$. The numbers of clusters is considered to be four (4) namely cerebrospinal fluid (CSF), gray matter (GM), white matter (WM) and background. The results obtained are compared against the following segmentation algorithms namely FCM, vFCM, FLICM, ARFCM, NLFCM, RFCM, KRFCMSC, sRFCM, ARKFCM. The mentioned algorithms along with the proposed algorithm were implemented in C using Dev C++ as the developing environment on a single CPU machine with 8GB RAM and an Intel i5 processor.

For comparing the segmentation algorithms, evaluation metrics including Partition Coefficient (V_{pc}), Partition Entropy (V_{pe}), Segmentation Accuracy (SA) are used. Partition coefficient is an important indicator of fuzzy partition and provides best performance with less fuzziness when V_{pc} takes its optimal value as 1, with higher values being better. It is defined in Eq. 22.

$$V_{pc} = \frac{1}{n} \sum_{k=1}^{C} \sum_{i=1}^{n} \mu_{ki}^2 \qquad (22)$$

Partition entropy is another important indicator of fuzzy partition and provides best performance when V_{pe} is minimal and its value is 0, with lower values being better. It is defined in Eq. 23.

$$V_{pe} = \frac{1}{n} \sum_{k=1}^{C} \sum_{i=1}^{n} -\mu_{ki} \log \mu_{ki} \qquad (23)$$

Segmentation accuracy is defined as the sum of the correctly classified pixels divided by the sum of total number of pixels in the image, given in Eq. 24.

$$SA = \frac{\sum_{i=1}^{n} card\,(P_i \cap G_i)}{\sum_{i=1}^{n} card\,(P_i)} \qquad (24)$$

Table 1, 2, 3, 4, 5 and 6 presents the quantitative evaluation metrics for performance comparison between the existing methods and the proposed segmentation technique. As noticed from the table, the partition coefficient for the proposed method is higher than the other methods in all different types of MR images, signifying its reliability and accuracy across use cases in brain tissue segmentation. Furthermore, the partition entropy is the lowest for the presented algorithm. Segmentation accuracy of different tissue segments in brain across different types of MR images show the effectiveness of the proposed approach. Qualitative indications suggested in Fig. 1 and 2 also highlight the robustness of the algorithm. Overall, the algorithm has a straightforward implementation and the performance is better than the compared algorithms across various brain MR image test cases.

Table 1. Vpc values of T1-Weighted Brain MR Image using different methods

Algorithm	50	60	70	80	90	95	100
FCM	0.910075	0.892448	0.893726	0.894631	0.905601	0.91364	0.913437
vFCM	0.910046	0.892312	0.893602	0.894472	0.905746	0.913535	0.913273
FLICM	0.912738	0.896885	0.897589	0.898437	0.908884	0.917727	0.920061
ARFCM	0.930684	0.910474	0.915192	0.907025	0.912305	0.926805	0.921446
NLFCM	0.944819	0.925179	0.925007	0.93029	0.932022	0.945663	0.939243
RFCM	0.927123	0.912714	0.914117	0.915202	0.927727	0.932961	0.931149
KRFCMSC	0.940119	0.92458	0.926181	0.926834	0.935982	0.944084	0.943738
sRFCM	0.945105	0.936132	0.941387	0.939261	0.949689	0.953861	0.956124
ARKFCM	0.961666	0.952791	0.953901	0.954366	0.960338	0.965062	0.964991
RSEKFCM	0.973362	0.968485	0.962603	0.963464	0.973168	0.977247	0.976523

Table 2. Vpe values of T1-Weighted Brain MR Image using different methods

Algorithm	50	60	70	80	90	95	100
FCM	0.170279	0.203997	0.202061	0.201489	0.181494	0.166955	0.166464
vFCM	0.170331	0.20424	0.202277	0.201663	0.181296	0.167135	0.166737
FLICM	0.168113	0.19767	0.19613	0.194925	0.174961	0.158398	0.154144
ARFCM	0.132823	0.171615	0.162796	0.178635	0.167772	0.140704	0.149876
NLFCM	0.103828	0.139398	0.139538	0.129751	0.126274	0.10118	0.11291
RFCM	0.130644	0.156038	0.153363	0.15179	0.129123	0.120092	0.12333
KRFCMSC	0.105095	0.131951	0.128741	0.128311	0.11197	0.097793	0.098756
sRFCM	0.094744	0.110043	0.100464	0.104527	0.086523	0.079344	0.075305
ARKFCM	0.063449	0.077825	0.075805	0.075431	0.065243	0.057546	0.057723
RSEKFCM	0.042333	0.049836	0.059718	0.058597	0.042343	0.035875	0.037157

Table 3. Vpc values of T2-Weighted Brain MR Image using different methods

Algorithm	50	60	70	80	90	95	100
FCM	0.909288	0.883077	0.882594	0.881061	0.888524	0.895752	0.896223
vFCM	0.909299	0.882986	0.882621	0.881077	0.888498	0.895784	0.896281
FLICM	0.913073	0.874428	0.908097	0.899501	0.894308	0.909134	0.90786
ARFCM	0.91695	0.924845	0.929846	0.901344	0.902693	0.92033	0.908539
NLFCM	0.940847	0.939411	0.932681	0.947255	0.954453	0.963313	0.967164
RFCM	0.922915	0.897374	0.898556	0.898226	0.903176	0.911518	0.912925
KRFCMSC	0.936893	0.917855	0.92936	0.926689	0.93637	0.944412	0.945246
sRFCM	0.932212	0.917876	0.917667	0.925318	0.928953	0.934878	0.938275
ARKFCM	0.963336	0.947048	0.956527	0.954663	0.958941	0.963989	0.964374
RSEKFCM	0.974488	0.964167	0.963207	0.970247	0.972604	0.975445	0.974912

Table 4. Vpe values of T2-Weighted Brain MR Image using different methods

Algorithm	50	60	70	80	90	95	100
FCM	0.169674	0.219748	0.219731	0.223214	0.20951	0.195812	0.194991
vFCM	0.169667	0.219856	0.219789	0.223253	0.209536	0.195813	0.194922
FLICM	0.169183	0.235961	0.18198	0.196364	0.200804	0.174401	0.176519
ARFCM	0.162447	0.150744	0.13971	0.193791	0.18938	0.156107	0.178307
NLFCM	0.109076	0.113944	0.125256	0.101133	0.087337	0.070982	0.063294
RFCM	0.136575	0.182964	0.179861	0.18052	0.172492	0.15636	0.154672
KRFCMSC	0.110661	0.142712	0.124499	0.128788	0.111123	0.097116	0.095444
sRFCM	0.117682	0.142199	0.141962	0.127929	0.121809	0.111382	0.105502
ARKFCM	0.060585	0.086075	0.071234	0.074158	0.06677	0.058338	0.057755
RSEKFCM	0.03996	0.055941	0.057088	0.046426	0.042721	0.03807	0.039043

Table 5. Segmentation accuracy in different tissues of T1-weighted brain MR images

ALGORITHM	CSF	GM	WM
FCM	0.966418	0.941212	0.962115
vFCM	0.966418	0.941212	0.962115
FLICM	0.968659	0.943988	0.962981
ARFCM	0.958635	0.943478	0.956208
NLFCM	0.973241	0.945617	0.963337
RFCM	0.966902	0.943478	0.962981
KRFCMSC	0.965807	0.944573	0.963439
sRFCM	0.96652	0.948163	0.963337
ARKFCM	0.967666	0.946508	0.967869
RSEKFCM	0.97579	0.947024	0.968302

Table 6. Segmentation accuracy in different tissues of T2-weighted brain MR images

ALGORITHM	CSF	GM	WM
FCM	0.964839	0.838633	0.852458
vFCM	0.964839	0.838633	0.852458
FLICM	0.964839	0.838633	0.852458
ARFCM	0.921413	0.853021	0.89462
NLFCM	0.971357	0.881228	0.89462
RFCM	0.973343	0.890037	0.898159
KRFCMSC	0.974209	0.88133	0.885098
sRFCM	0.973267	0.894977	0.900043
ARKFCM	0.962854	0.893627	0.901876
RSEKFCM	0.974998	0.895562	0.906637

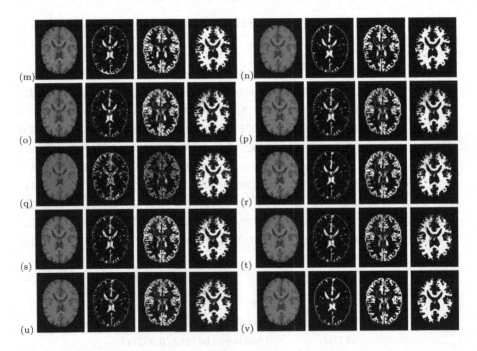

Fig. 1. Qualitative results of segmentation output of T1 - Weighted Brain MR Image with tissue segmentation of original image, CSF, GM, and WM (from left to right) using (n) proposed method (o) vFCM (p) FLICM (q) ARFCM (r) NLFCM (s) RFCM (t) KRFCMSC (u) SRFCM (v) ARKFCM and (m) original image, CSF ground truth, GM ground truth, WM ground truth images.

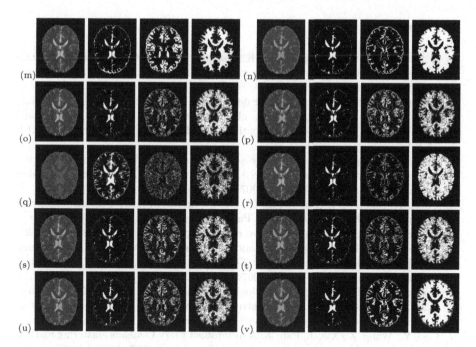

Fig. 2. Qualitative results of segmentation output of T2 - Weighted Brain MR Image with tissue segmentation of original image, CSF, GM, and WM (from left to right) using (n) proposed method (o) vFCM (p) FLICM (q) ARFCM (r) NLFCM (s) RFCM (t) KRFCMSC (u) SRFCM (v) ARKFCM and (m) original image, CSF ground truth, GM ground truth, WM ground truth images.

5   Conclusion

In this paper, a rough spatial ensemble kernelized fuzzy c means clustering algorithm is proposed for unsupervised tissue segmentation of magnetic resonance images of human brain. The proposed novel ensemble kernel performs seamless mapping of homogenous regions commonly found in brain tissue, along with outlier inclusion to retain fine boundaries of tissue regions. This dramatically improves the performance of the clustering algorithm and moreover leads to faster convergence.

Experimental results prove the robustness and the efficiency of the proposed approach in the domain biomedical image segmentation. The algorithm is simple, has low computation power requirement, and is scalable across domains of medical image segmentation.

References

1. Adhikari, S.K., Sing, J.K., Basu, D.K., Nasipuri, M.: Conditional spatial fuzzy C-means clustering algorithm for segmentation of MRI images. Appl. Soft Comput. **34**, 758–769 (2015)
2. Ahmmed, R., Hossain, M.F.: Tumor detection in brain MRI image using template based K-means and fuzzy C-means clustering algorithm. In: 2016 International Conference on Computer Communication and Informatics (ICCCI), pp. 1–6. IEEE (2016)
3. Chen, S., Zhang, D.: Robust image segmentation using FCM with spatial constraints based on new kernel-induced distance measure. IEEE Tran. Syst. Man Cybern. Part B (Cybern.) **34**(4), 1907–1916 (2004)
4. Chen, Y., Zhou, S., Zhang, X., Li, D., Fu, C.: Improved fuzzy C-means clustering by varying the fuzziness parameter. Pattern Recogn. Lett. **157**, 60–66 (2022)
5. Choudhuri, R., Halder, A.: Adaptive rough-fuzzy kernelized clustering algorithm for noisy brain MRI tissue segmentation. In: Raman, B., Murala, S., Chowdhury, A., Dhall, A., Goyal, P. (eds.) CVIP 2021. CCIS, vol. 1567, pp. 561–573. Springer, Cham (2021). https://doi.org/10.1007/978-3-031-11346-8_48
6. Collins, D.L., Zijdenbos, A.P., Kollokian, V., Sled, J.G., Kabani, N.J., Holmes, C.J., Evans, A.C.: Design and construction of a realistic digital brain phantom. IEEE Trans. Med. Imaging **17**(3), 463–468 (1998)
7. Gao, Y., Wang, Z., Xie, J., Pan, J.: A new robust fuzzy C-means clustering method based on adaptive elastic distance. Knowl.-Based Syst. **237**, 107769 (2022)
8. Gong, M., Liang, Y., Shi, J., Ma, W., Ma, J.: Fuzzy C-means clustering with local information and kernel metric for image segmentation. IEEE Trans. Image Process. **22**(2), 573–584 (2012)
9. Halder, A., Talukdar, N.A.: Brain tissue segmentation using improved kernelized rough-fuzzy C-means with spatio-contextual information from MRI. Magn. Reson. Imaging **62**, 129–151 (2019)
10. Krinidis, S., Chatzis, V.: A robust fuzzy local information C-means clustering algorithm. IEEE Trans. Image Process. **19**(5), 1328–1337 (2010)
11. Maji, P., Pal, S.K.: Maximum class separability for rough-fuzzy C-means based brain MR image segmentation. Trans. Rough Sets IX 114–134 (2008)
12. Maji, P., Roy, S.: Rough-fuzzy clustering and unsupervised feature selection for wavelet based MR image segmentation. PLoS ONE **10**(4), e0123677 (2015)
13. Pal, N.R., Pal, K., Keller, J.M., Bezdek, J.C.: A possibilistic fuzzy C-means clustering algorithm. IEEE Trans. Fuzzy Syst. **13**(4), 517–530 (2005)
14. Pham, D.L., Prince, J.L.: Adaptive fuzzy segmentation of magnetic resonance images. IEEE Trans. Med. Imaging **18**(9), 737–752 (1999)
15. Roy, S., Maji, P.: Medical image segmentation by partitioning spatially constrained fuzzy approximation spaces. IEEE Trans. Fuzzy Syst. **28**(5), 965–977 (2020)
16. Sarkar, J.P., Saha, I., Maulik, U.: Rough possibilistic type-2 fuzzy C-means clustering for MR brain image segmentation. Appl. Soft Comput. **46**, 527–536 (2016)
17. Vishnuvarthanan, G., Rajasekaran, M.P., Subbaraj, P., Vishnuvarthanan, A.: An unsupervised learning method with a clustering approach for tumor identification and tissue segmentation in magnetic resonance brain images. Appl. Soft Comput. **38**, 190–212 (2016)
18. Wu, C., Yang, X.: Robust credibilistic fuzzy local information clustering with spatial information constraints. Digit. Signal Process. **97**, 102615 (2020)

19. Zhang, D.Q., Chen, S.C.: A novel kernelized fuzzy C-means algorithm with application in medical image segmentation. Artif. Intell. Med. **32**(1), 37–50 (2004)
20. Zhang, X., Sun, Y., Wang, G., Guo, Q., Zhang, C., Chen, B.: Improved fuzzy clustering algorithm with non-local information for image segmentation. Multimed. Tools Appl. **76**, 7869–7895 (2017)

One Shot Learning to Select Data Augmentations for Skin Lesion Classification

Avani Tiwari[1] ⓘ, Prasad Kanhegaonkar[2](✉) ⓘ, and Surya Prakash[2] ⓘ

[1] Computer Science, New York University, Abu Dhabi, Abu Dhabi, United Arab Emirates
at4535@nyu.edu
[2] Department of Computer Science and Engineering, Indian Institute of Technology, Indore, Indore 453552, India
{phd2101201007,surya}@iiti.ac.in

Abstract. Skin cancer is a highly prevalent and malignant skin disease that is usually diagnosed by visual inspection by expert doctors or dermatologists and confirmed through several supporting methods including pathological examination, medical image processing, and artificial intelligence-based techniques. Researchers and developers have been trying to leverage deep learning for the detection and classification of various forms of skin diseases. Most deep learning pipelines include data augmentation techniques to improve the overall performance of the underlying model. Selecting the right and most relevant augmentation techniques during training deep learning models is essential to achieve better performance from the underlying model. Picking up the not-so-useful augmentation methods may negatively affect the performance and computational complexity of the underlying model. In this paper, we propose a novel one-shot learning-based method to optimally pick the most relevant and useful data augmentation methods that contribute to increased model performance. The paper also focuses on designing a lightweight model, which can be easily deployed in edge networks. We train a Siamese neural network to calculate the similarity scores of 15 data augmentation techniques on images from the HAM10000 dataset. The similarity scores are used to select the most relevant data augmentation methods. Further, the experimental results confirm the increased skin lesion classification performance for the designed lightweight classification model which is trained using the augmented data, where the augmented data is generated using these selected data augmentation techniques only.

Keywords: Skin Lesion Classification · Data Augmentation · Contrastive Loss · One Shot Learning · Siamese Network · EfficientNet

1 Introduction

Skin cancer is one of the most prevalent forms of cancer. Melanoma is the most life-threatening type of skin cancer. If left untreated or not diagnosed in its

H. Kaur et al. (Eds.): CVIP 2023, CCIS 2011, pp. 364–374, 2024.
https://doi.org/10.1007/978-3-031-58535-7_30

early stages, it can penetrate rapidly to other organs. It makes early diagnosis of Melanoma an essential requirement when combating skin cancer. Dermatologists diagnose Melanoma by visual inspection of dermoscopic images of the skin lesions. However, different classes of cancerous skin lesions look similar. It is very likely to miss the early diagnosis of Melanoma by patients or doctors due to multiple factors. Moreover, all people do not have access to advanced medical facilities and expert dermatologists. These reasons contribute to the late or missed diagnosis of Melanoma. The deep learning community is trying to address this problem by designing Convolutional Neural Networks (CNN) based solutions. Dermatologists can make use of such Artificial Intelligence (AI) based solutions or techniques to support and benefit their skin disease diagnosis tasks. These techniques can be deployed to edge devices and networks and can be used for the initial diagnosis or classification of skin lesions.

CNNs are widely adopted to design skin lesion classification models. They can learn image features in a meaningful and hierarchical manner. Convolutional layers use kernels or filters which slide all over the image. The dot product of the filter and the image intensity values generate feature maps. Feature maps store crucial information about image features. Fully connected layers at the end of the model use this information to classify the input data. CNNs are primarily used with image data and they are most suitable for skin lesion datasets consisting of dermoscopic images.

Many skin lesion datasets are available to use for building classification models. However, the available data in these datasets is insufficient to produce viable results. Data augmentation techniques can be applied to increase the available data for training the underlying model. Additionally, these methods add variation to the data and prevent overfitting, thus allowing the model to learn better and result in better accuracy. Image classification model architectures often make use of data augmentation techniques during preprocessing. Top teams in the ISIC 2018 competition task 3 leaderboard include data augmentation techniques like changing brightness, contrast, saturation, etc. These models usually select data augmentation techniques without a proper study or reasoning for their effectiveness in model training. This leads to the selection of multiple and perhaps less relevant data augmentation techniques thereby resulting in inefficient utilization of computational resources, as many of the applied augmentations fail to contribute to the model's learning process.

This paper aims to select the best augmentation techniques for skin lesion image datasets by introducing a novel systematic augmentation selection pipeline. This pipeline leverages the relationship between the augmented and original data in terms of similarity. The first part of the pipeline consists of a one-shot learning network to quantify this relationship by generating similarity scores. The augmentation selection uses similarity score ranking and this ranking is used to select the data augmentation techniques. The next stage of the pipeline uses the selected data augmentations only. This stage consists of a classification model that handles the class imbalance and classifies skin lesion images. The set of data augmentations that results in the highest classification accuracy on this model is considered the best and the data augmentation techniques from this set are the most relevant for the skin lesion classification task. The main contributions of this paper are as follows:

- Introducing a novel systematic data augmentation selection pipeline for skin lesion classification problem.
- Use this pipeline on a curated skin lesion dataset extracted from HAM10000 to estimate the most relevant set of data augmentations.
- Build a lightweight model for one-shot learning based on a Siamese network with EfficientNetB0 used for embedding as well as classification.

The rest of the paper is organized as follows. Section 2 describes the related work. Section 3 describes the proposed method. Section 4 describes the results. Finally, Sect. 5 concludes the paper.

2   Related Work

Since their introduction in 1993, Siamese networks have been utilized to solve a variety of image similarity estimation tasks [1]. The first use case of the Siamese networks is signature verification for signs on pen-input tablets [2]. This paper introduced the Siamese network as a novel technique with two identical subnetworks joined at the end. These subnetworks learn the structure of input data and generate embeddings. The distance between the embeddings of the verified stored signatures is compared with that of the unverified signature. If the distance is less compared to that of the verified signature, then the signature is accepted as real, otherwise, it is considered forgery. Other matching problems like image retrieval and object detection also employ Siamese networks [1]. We use a Siamese network in the first part of the augmentation selection pipeline. Our Siamese network architecture is similar to the one proposed in [3] that uses Siamese networks for image matching. Siamese networks can learn using triplet loss [4] or contrastive loss [5]. As explained in [3], contrastive loss works better for our purpose as it reduces the distance between similar images and has a minimum distance equal to the hyperparameter margin between dissimilar images.

The classification of skin lesions has attracted interest over time, leading to the creation of well-known peer-reviewed datasets like HAM10000. The International Skin Imaging Collaboration (ISIC) held annual competitions to encourage the community to come together and solve the problem of reliable classification of skin lesion images. Top teams in the ISIC 2018 Task 3 leaderboard like [6,7], and [8] use data augmentation techniques to increase the performance of their proposed techniques. The selection of these techniques is often arbitrary without a systematic study. Many of the selected augmentation techniques do not have a significant impact on the performance of the model. The extra augmentation techniques lead to inefficient utilization of resources and slow down the training process.

Table 1. Data augmentations with their respective parameter values

No	Augmentation	Parameter
1	Edge Enhance	–
2	CLAHE	–
3	Vignette	–
4	Gaussian Blur	Kernel size - 3
5	Optical Distortion	0.1
6, 7	Flip	Horizontal & Vertical
8, 9	Contrast	0.8 & 1.2
10, 11	Sharpness	0.8 & 1.2
12, 13	Brightness	0.8 & 1.2
14, 15	Saturation	0.8 & 1.2

3   Proposed Method

This section describes the proposed method, the dataset used, the one-shot learning framework, and the classification network.

3.1   Proposed Method

Our goal is to choose the most pertinent set of data augmentation strategies for classifying skin lesions that perform better than the set of data augmentation techniques that were chosen at random. Transfer learning [9] is used in the Siamese network and classification network. Transfer learning allows the model to initialize the weights of the model trained on the ImageNet dataset and fine-tune the corresponding weights on the skin lesion dataset. So, models need not start learning from scratch and hence converge faster. The one-shot learning framework uses 15 augmented images to create pairs of images such that the original image is paired with its augmented image. The data augmentation techniques used by Yao et al. [10] are used as the base to select the full set of augmentations in this paper to train our one-shot learning Siamese network. The proposed method returns a similarity score for each of the data augmentation techniques. Table 1 shows the data augmentations with their respective parameter values.

The second stage of the pipeline uses a classification model to assess the relevance of the augmentation approaches selected based on their similarity scores by comparing the accuracy using this subset with that of the entire set of augmentations. In the classification network, the dataset is used once without any augmentations, once with all 15 augmentations, and then with different subsets of the augmentations that are selected based on similarity scores to find the most relevant set. Both stages use EfficientNetB0 [11] as the CNN architecture. EfficientNetB0 uses compound scaling along with an inverted residual bottleneck block (also called an MBConv block) and Squeeze and Excitation (SE) [12] block. The inverted residual bottleneck blocks use depthwise separable convolutions thereby allowing them to incur very few parameters and FLOPs and making the model suitable for resource-constrained environments. The SE block applies attention to different channels and increases the accuracy of the model. EfficientNetB0 performs better than state-of-the-art models like ResNet and Inception while having a small number of parameters.

Table 2. HAM10000 Dataset

Class	AKIEC	BCC	BKL	DF	MEL	NV	VASC	Total
Images	327	514	1099	115	1113	6705	142	10015

Table 3. Classification Dataset

	AKIEC	BCC	BKL	DF	MEL	NV	VASC	Total
Train	90	159	439	51	360	3713	70	4882
Val	19	34	94	11	77	795	14	1044
Test	19	34	94	11	77	795	14	1044

3.2 Dataset

The HAM dataset ("Human Against Machine with 10000 training images") [13] is a widely accepted and popular dataset used for skin lesion segmentation and classification problems. The dataset serves as a benchmark for developing and evaluating algorithms for automated skin cancer diagnosis and classification. It is a collection of good-quality dermoscopic images of pigmented skin lesions collected from different populations. The dataset contains 10015 images divided into 7 classes - AKIEC (Actinic Keratoses and Intraepithelial Carcinoma), BCC (Basal Cell Carcinoma), BKL (Benign Keratosis), DF (Dermatofibroma), NV (Melanocytic nevi), MEL (Melanoma), and VASC (Vascular skin lesions). Table 2 shows the class-wise distribution of the HAM10000 dataset.

We have split the dataset into two subsets out of which one is used for training and testing the one-shot learning model and another for the classification model. The first step is removing the duplicate images (multiple images belonging to the same Lesion ID) from the HAM10000 dataset which are identified from the available metadata. From the unique images after removing duplicates, 100 images per class are randomly selected for the one-shot learning network. Out of these 100 images, 70 images per class are used for training while 15 images each per class are used for validation and testing respectively. All remaining images other than those used for one-shot learning are used for the classification dataset. The classification dataset has 4882 train images and 1044 images each for validation and testing. Table 3 describes the class-wise distribution of the classification dataset. We also tried to prevent overlap between images selected for the one-shot learning network and the classification network, however, the small size of DF and VASC classes made it inevitable to have some images common in both datasets (Fig. 1).

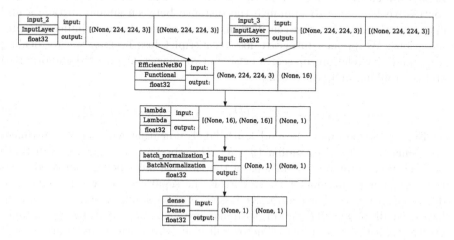

Fig. 1. One-shot learning framework used in the proposed method

3.3   One Shot Learning Framework

Based on the similarity between the augmented and original images, this paper seeks to find the most pertinent data augmentations for skin lesion image datasets. We have used similarity as a metric to rank data augmentation techniques using a Siamese network with contrastive loss to calculate the image similarity [5]. The first step is calculating the similarity between the augmented and original images. It is measured using the Euclidean distance between the feature vectors of the images through supervised one-shot learning. The classification network uses these subsets of data augmentations one at a time for training and prediction of the class labels.

Network Architecture: We use a Siamese network to do one-shot learning. The Siamese architecture contains two branches. These two branches are identical in architecture and weight information. We use EfficientNetB0 [11] for these branches as it is an efficient and lightweight CNN architecture with a small number of parameters and good results on image datasets. We also leverage transfer learning and pre-train the branches on ImageNet data [7]. The base network is followed by global average pooling, batch normalization, dropout, and softmax layer. We use this as the branch network that outputs the embeddings of the input images. These embeddings are passed to a layer to calculate the Euclidean distance between them. This data is normalized using a batch normalization layer and then passed on to a sigmoid layer. The sigmoid layer outputs the similarity scores used to rank the data augmentation techniques.

Loss Function: We have used the contrastive loss which is given in 1. The contrastive loss aims to minimize the distance between similar instances and maximize the distance between dissimilar instances to learn meaningful representations. We prefer contrastive loss over triplet loss because we are dealing with similarity relationship scores between two images (augmented and original) and not ranking in a triplet sample.

$$\mathcal{L}_{\text{contrastive}} = (1 - y) \cdot \frac{1}{2}(D_w)^2 + (y) \cdot \frac{1}{2}\max(0, m - D_w)^2 \tag{1}$$

Here, y is the binary ground truth label indicating whether the instances are similar ($y = 0$) or dissimilar ($y = 1$). D_w represents the Euclidean distance between the vector representations of the two instances being compared. m is the margin hyperparameter that controls the separation between similar and dissimilar instances. The contrastive loss encourages similar instances ($y = 1$) to have a small distance (D_w) and dissimilar instances ($y = 0$) to have a distance greater than the margin (m). The overall goal is to learn representations that effectively distinguish between similar and dissimilar instances.

$$D_w(x, y) = \sqrt{\max\left(\sum_{i=1}^{n}(x_i - y_i)^2, \epsilon\right)} \tag{2}$$

The Eq. 2 is the Euclidean distance formula. x and y are representations (vectors) of the two instances being compared, n represents the dimensionality of the vectors, x_i and y_i are the components of vectors x and y respectively, and ϵ (epsilon) is a constant used to avoid taking the square root of very small values. The equation computes the squared Euclidean distance between the vectors, sums the squared differences, takes the maximum of the sum and ϵ, and returns the square root of the maximum value.

Training: The Siamese network is trained for 50 epochs using the Adam optimizer with an initial learning rate of 0.00005. Early stopping is employed, with a patience of 10 epochs. The margin for contrastive loss is 1. All the hyperparameters are selected experimentally. The network outputs a similarity score which is used to rank the data augmentations in the next part of the pipeline.

3.4   Classification Network

The second part of the data augmentation selection pipeline consists of a classification network to determine the most relevant augmentation methods. The model is used with no augmentations, all augmentations, and selected augmentations. The augmentations from the class with the best similarity score are selected as the most relevant set.

Network Architecture: The classification network uses EfficientNetB0 [11] as the base model followed by batch normalization, global average pooling, dropout, and fully connected layers. The EfficientNetB0 base model is pretrained on the ImageNet [7] dataset. Using EfficientNetB0 also helps to keep the model light with less number of parameters and Floating Point Operations (FLOPs).

Loss Function: The classification network uses focal loss. Focal loss helps the model deal with class imbalance present in the dataset. It allows the model to focus more on hard examples and less on easy examples thereby handling the class imbalance problem. To achieve this a modulating term is added to the cross-entropy loss.

$$\text{Focal Loss}(p_t) = -(1 - p_t)^\gamma \cdot \log(p_t) \tag{3}$$

In the Eq. 3, p_t is the prediction probability of the sample. $(1 - p_t)$ is the modulating term that helps down weight the rightly classified sample and γ is the focusing parameter.

Training: The classification network is trained for 200 epochs. Early stopping regularization monitors the validation accuracy with a patience of 20. The initial learning rate is 0.00005. The batch size is 16 and the dropout rate is 0.3. Training of the model employs Adam Optimizer and a step-decay learning rate schedule. All the hyperparameters are chosen experimentally. The classification network is trained on non-augmented data, data with all augmentations, and data with selected augmentations. The selection of data augmentation depends on the ranking based on similarity scores from the one-shot learning model.

4   Experimental Analysis

This section describes the experimental analysis conducted and the results obtained.

4.1   Performance Evaluation Methods

The one-shot learning network is evaluated using the keras evaluate method which returns the scalar value of test loss. The Siamese network used here uses Euclidean distance between image pairs to calculate similarity scores. We have used the accuracy and the balanced accuracy for the classification network for different augmentation methods to evaluate the model performance.

4.2   Siamese Network Scores

In the Siamese network, the test accuracy is 98.94%. Table 4 presents the sum of predicted similarity score values for all 100 test images and the 15 augmentations.

4.3   Classification Scores

The accuracy of the classification network is measured using the test accuracy and balanced accuracy score. We have tested the skin lesion classification network for the three cases, namely training without any data augmentation, training with the use of all 15 augmentations, and training using only selected 4 augmentations (Fig. 2).

The selected augmentations mentioned in Table 5 are Gaussian Blur, Optical Distortion, CLAHE, and Vignette as their similarity scores are the highest than

Table 4. Sum of the similarity scores on images with different augmentations

Augmentation	Score	Augmentation	Score
Horizontal Flip	10.66	Contrast Increase	10.66
Vertical Flip	10.67	Sharpness Increase	10.81
Brightness Increase	10.81	Saturation Decrease	10.94
Saturation Increase	11.04	Contrast Decrease	11.37
Edge Enhance	11.41	Sharpness Decrease	11.41
Brightness Decrease	11.41	Gaussian Blur	12.14
Optical Distortion	12.97	CLAHE	13.62
Vignette	13.8		

Table 5. Classification Results

	Accuracy	Balanced Accuracy
No Augmentations	83.04	55.04
All Augmentations	**85.34**	54.87
Selected Augmentations	84.96	**55.72**

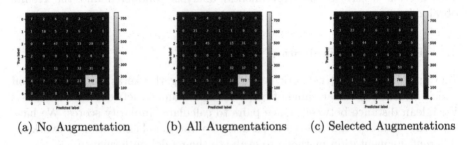

(a) No Augmentation   (b) All Augmentations   (c) Selected Augmentations

Fig. 2. Confusion matrices of classification for different augmentation cases

others. The test accuracy with these four augmentations is quite comparable to that of all augmentations. Moreover, the balanced accuracy of the selected augmentations is better as compared to all augmentations.

5   Conclusion

In this paper, we have designed a novel technique based on one-shot learning to optimally select the relevant data augmentation techniques. We have used a Siamese network structure to rank the data augmentation techniques based on their similarity scores. The classification results show an improved performance of the classification model which is trained with images produced using selected augmentation techniques. The need for computational resources that result from employing random augmentation approaches is reduced when just applying the chosen augmentation techniques. Future work involves experimenting with diverse and larger skin lesion datasets and testing more augmentation techniques for skin lesion classification.

References

1. Li, Y., Chen, C., Zhang, T.: A survey on siamese network: methodologies, applications and opportunities. IEEE Trans. Artif. Intell. 1–21 (2022)
2. Bromley, J., Guyon, I., LeCun, Y., Säckinger, E., Shah, R.: Signature verification using a "siamese" time delay neural network. In: Proceedings of the 6th International Conference on Neural Information Processing Systems (NIPS), pp. 737–744 (1993)
3. Melekhov, I., Kannala, J., Rahtu, E.: Siamese network features for image matching. In: Proceedings of 23rd International Conference on Pattern Recognition (ICPR), pp. 378–383 (2016)
4. Schroff, F., Kalenichenko, D., Philbin, J.: FaceNet: a unified embedding for face recognition and clustering. In: Proceedings of IEEE Conference on Computer Vision and Pattern Recognition (CVPR), pp. 815–823 (2015)
5. Hadsell, R., Chopra, S., LeCun, Y.: Dimensionality reduction by learning an invariant mapping. In: Proceedings of IEEE Conference on Computer Vision and Pattern Recognition (CVPR), vol. 2, pp. 1735–1742 (2006)
6. Gessert, N., et al.: Skin lesion diagnosis using ensembles, unscaled multi-crop evaluation and loss weighting (2018)
7. Russakovsky, O., et al.:. ImageNet large scale visual recognition challenge (2015)
8. Zhuang, J., et al.: Skin lesion analysis towards melanoma detection using deep neural network ensemble. ISIC Challenge **2018**(2), 1–6 (2018)
9. Weiss, K., Khoshgoftaar, T.M., Wang, D.D.: A survey of transfer learning. J. Big Data **3**(1), 9 (2016)
10. Yao, P., et al.: Single model deep learning on imbalanced small datasets for skin lesion classification. IEEE Trans. Med. Imaging **41**(5), 1242–1254 (2022)
11. Tan, M., Le, Q.: EfficientNet: rethinking model scaling for convolutional neural networks. In: Proceedings of the 36th International Conference on Machine Learning (ICML), vol. 97, pp. 6105–6114 (2019)

12. Hu, J., Shen, L., Sun, G.: Squeeze-and-excitation networks. In: Proceedings of IEEE/CVF Conference on Computer Vision and Pattern Recognition (CVPR), pp. 7132–7141 (2018)
13. Tschandl, P., Rosendahl, C., Kittler, H.: The HAM10000 dataset, a large collection of multi-source dermatoscopic images of common pigmented skin lesions. Sci. Data 5(1), 180161 (2018)

Improved Image Captioning Using GAN and ViT

Vrushank D. Rao$^{(\boxtimes)}$, B. N. Shashank, and S. Nagesh Bhattu

Department of Computer Science and Engineering, National Institute of Technology
Andhra Pradesh, Tadepalligudem, India
`mtcs2108@student.nitandhra.ac.in`

Abstract. Encoder-decoder architectures are widely used in solving image captioning applications. Convolutional encoders and recurrent decoders are prominently used for such applications. Recent advances in transformer-based designs have made SOTA performances in solving various language and vision tasks. This work inspects the research question of using transformer-based encoder and decoder in building an effective pipeline for image captioning. An adversarial objective using a Generative Adversarial Network is used to improve the diversity of the captions generated. The generator component of our model utilizes a ViT encoder and a transformer decoder to generate semantically meaningful captions for a given image. To enhance the quality and authenticity of the generated captions, we introduce a discriminator component built using a transformer decoder. The discriminator evaluates the captions by considering both the image and the caption generated by the generator. By training this architecture, we aim to ensure that the generator produces captions that are indistinguishable from real captions, increasing the overall quality of the generated outputs. Through extensive experimentation, we demonstrate the effectiveness of our approach in generating diverse and contextually appropriate captions for various images. We evaluate our model on benchmark datasets and compare its performance against existing state-of-the-art image captioning methods. The proposed approach has achieved superior results compared to previous methods, as demonstrated by improved caption accuracy metrics such as BLEU-3, BLEU-4, and other relevant accuracy measures.

Keywords: Vision Transformers · Data2Vec · Image Captioning

1 Introduction

Image captioning, the task of generating descriptive and contextually relevant captions for images, has witnessed significant advancements in recent years. Traditional approaches have relied on recurrent neural networks (RNNs) and convolutional neural networks (CNNs) to encode images and generate captions [20]. However, these methods often suffer from limitations such as generating repetitive or generic captions. To address these challenges, recent research has

H. Kaur et al. (Eds.): CVIP 2023, CCIS 2011, pp. 375–385, 2024.
https://doi.org/10.1007/978-3-031-58535-7_31

explored the potential of transformer-based models in the field of image captioning [21–23]. Transformers, initially introduced for natural language processing tasks, have demonstrated remarkable performance in capturing long-range dependencies and modelling complex linguistic structures. Leveraging the success of transformers, we propose a novel approach that combines the power of the Vision Transformer (ViT) and language transformer architecture to generate diverse and semantically meaningful captions for images.

Our approach is inspired by TransGAN [4], a state-of-the-art generative model that utilizes transformers for image generation. We adopt the TransGAN framework to the task of image captioning by employing a transformer-based generator and discriminator. The generator consists of a ViT encoder followed by a transformer, responsible for generating captions based on the visual input. By leveraging the ViT [2] encoder, our model can effectively encode and process the visual features of the input image. During the training process, we employ cross-entropy loss at the generator to optimize its performance. This loss encourages the generator to generate captions that accurately describe the image content. Additionally, we introduce a discriminator built using a transformer decoder to evaluate the authenticity and quality of the generated captions. The discriminator takes both the image and the generated caption as input and classifies whether the caption is real or fake. By training the generator-discriminator architecture, we aim to enhance the overall quality of the generated captions.

The key contribution of our research lies in the ability to generate diverse and semantically meaningful captions for a given image. By combining the ViT encoder with the transformer-based generator, our model can capture both the visual and linguistic information, leading to more contextually relevant and diverse caption generation. The discriminator component adds a layer of sophistication, ensuring that the generated captions are coherent and indistinguishable from real captions. To evaluate the effectiveness of our approach, we conduct extensive experiments on benchmark datasets for image captioning. We compare the performance of our model against existing state-of-the-art methods and demonstrate superior results in terms of caption diversity and semantic relevance. Through quantitative metrics and qualitative analysis, we showcase the strengths of our approach and provide insights into the quality of the generated captions. We investigate the accuracy and diversity of captions, examining their linguistic variations and ability to capture different aspects of the images.

Overall, this research aims to advance the field of image captioning by harnessing the capabilities of transformer-based generative models. The contributions of the proposed work are:

- By incorporating the ViT encoder and transformer decoder based generator, we achieve significant improvements in generating diverse and semantically meaningful captions.
- The integration of the discriminator ensures the authenticity and coherence of the generated captions.

– Through empirical evaluations and in-depth analysis, we contribute to the understanding and development of state-of-the-art techniques in image captioning.

2   Related Work

Transformers, originally introduced in the field of machine translation, have shown their effectiveness in capturing long-range dependencies and generating coherent sequences of text. In the context of image captioning, transformer-based architectures have been adapted to leverage both visual and textual information, resulting in improved caption generation capabilities.

The Show, Attend, and Tell (SAT) architecture introduced the concept of using transformers in image captioning [3]. It combined a CNN-based image encoder, such as a convolutional neural network (CNN) or an encoder-decoder architecture like the VGG [25] or ResNet [24], with a transformer-based caption decoder [1]. The image encoder extracts high-level visual features from the input image, which are then passed through the transformer decoder to generate captions. The transformer decoder attends to different image regions while generating each word, allowing it to focus on relevant visual information during the caption generation process.

The Image Transformer (IT) architecture extended the transformer-based approach by incorporating spatial positional encodings and positional embeddings to maintain spatial information [18]. Similar to SAT, IT employed a CNN backbone to extract image features. However, in IT, the image features were reshaped into a grid-like structure to preserve their spatial relationships. The positional encodings were then added to the input image features before passing them through the transformer layers for caption generation. By considering the spatial layout of the image features, IT aimed to improve the alignment between the generated captions and the corresponding image regions.

Another approach to transformer-based image captioning is to combine a transformer-based caption decoder with a CNN-based image encoder [19]. In this setup, the image encoder is responsible for extracting visual features, while the transformer decoder generates captions. The choice of CNN backbone architecture can vary, including popular ones such as ResNet or VGG. The image features obtained from the CNN backbone are typically flattened or pooled into a fixed-size representation before being fed into the transformer decoder. This architecture allows for the incorporation of both visual and textual information through the transformer decoder's self-attention mechanism.

3   Methodology

Our proposed model architecture is based on the TransGAN framework, adapted for image captioning. The architecture comprises a generator and a discriminator, both utilizing transformer-based components. The generator consists of a ViT encoder followed by a transformer. The ViT encoder processes the input image and extracts high-level visual features, which are then passed to the transformer. The transformer generates captions based on the encoded visual features, capturing the contextual and semantic information of the image. The discriminator is built using a transformer decoder. It takes both the image and the generated caption as input and learns to classify whether the caption is real or fake. The discriminator plays a crucial role in training the generator to produce authentic and coherent captions. The architecture is presented in Fig. 1.

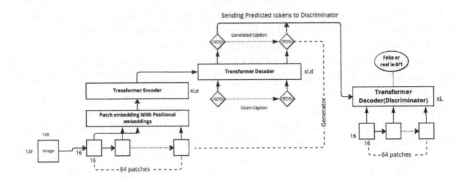

Fig. 1. Proposed GAN based architecture for Image Captioning (Proposed-model-1)

$$\min_G \max_D \mathbb{E}_{C \sim GT_i}[\log D_\theta(I, C)] + \mathbb{E}_{z \sim \mathcal{N}(\mu, \sigma)}[1 - \log D_\theta(G_\pi(I, z)] \qquad (1)$$

$$\min[1 - \log D_\theta(G_\pi(I, z)] \longleftrightarrow \max[\log D_\theta(G_\pi(I, z)] \qquad (2)$$

The learning objective of the Discriminator is as shown in Eq. 1 where:

- $\mathbb{E}_{(I,C) \sim G_i}[\log D_\theta(I, C)]$ represents the expected value of the log-probability that the discriminator assigns to a real image-caption pair (I, C) when sampled from ground truth GT_i.
- $\mathbb{E}_{z \sim \mathcal{N}(\mu, \sigma)}[1 - \log D_\theta(G_\pi(I, z)]$ represents the expected value of the log-probability that the discriminator assigns to the data generated by the generator, where z is a noise vector sampled from a normal distribution with mean μ and standard deviation σ.

The discriminator's goal is to find the optimal parameters θ that maximize this objective, which means it aims to become better at distinguishing real image-caption pairs from fake data produced by the generator. For the Generator, the objective function is shown in the Eq. 2 where $\log D_\theta(G_\pi(I, z)$ represents the log probability that the discriminator assigns to the fake data produced by the generator. The generator's goal is to find the optimal parameters π that maximize this log-probability, meaning it aims to produce image-caption pairs that are so convincing that the discriminator cannot distinguish them from real image-caption pairs.

The mathematical framework for the loss functions and optimization steps used in training:

1. **Discriminator Loss** (L_D): The Discriminator, D, aims to distinguish real captions from the ones generated. The loss function is binary cross-entropy.
   - Real Caption Loss (L_D^{real}): This term represents the loss when real captions are classified by D. It is defined in the Eq. 3

$$L_D^{real} = -\frac{1}{N} \sum_{i=1}^{N} y_i \log(D(x_i, y_i)) \tag{3}$$

   - Fake Caption Loss (L_D^{fake}): This term represents the loss when generated (fake) captions are classified by D. It is defined in the Eq. 4.

$$L_D^{fake} = -\frac{1}{N} \sum_{i=1}^{N} (1 - y_i) \log(1 - D(x_i, G(x_i))) \tag{4}$$

   - Gradient Penalty (L_D^{gp}): This term is used to stabilize the training of D by limiting its gradients. It is defined in Eq. 5.

$$L_D^{gp} = \lambda \mathbb{E}\hat{x} \sim p\hat{x}[(||\nabla_{\hat{x}} D(\hat{x})||_2 - 1)^2] \tag{5}$$

   - Total Discriminator Loss (L_D): This term sums up the aforementioned components to form the total loss for D, defined as in in Eq. 6

$$L_D = L_D^{real} + L_D^{fake} + L_D^{gp} \tag{6}$$

2. **Generator Loss** (L_G): The Generator, G, aims to create captions that are close to real captions. The loss function is cross-entropy.
   - Generator Loss (L_G): This term calculates the loss based on the difference between the generated captions and the actual ones. It is defined in Eq. 7.

$$L_G = \frac{1}{N} \sum_{i=1}^{N} \sum_{j=1}^{T} [-y_{i,j} \log(\hat{y}_{i,j})] \tag{7}$$

   - Total Generator Loss (L_{total}): This term sums the generator loss and a weighted version of the fake loss from D. It is defined in Eq. 8

$$L_{total} = L_G + \alpha L_D^{fake} \tag{8}$$

In the above, N is the batch size, y_i represents the actual label (1 for real, 0 for fake), x_i denotes the image, G is the generator network, $\hat{x}$ is a sample from the interpolated distribution between the real and fake data, λ is the weight of the penalty term, $p_{\hat{x}}$ is the distribution of $\hat{x}$, T is the caption length, $y_{i,j}$

is the actual word index, $\hat{y}_{i,j}$ is the predicted probability distribution over the vocabulary, and α is a hyper-parameter for balancing the losses.

The training process involves optimizing the generator and discriminator components using the loss function mentioned above. We feed the images through the ViT encoder during generator training to obtain visual features. The transformer then generates captions based on these features. The cross-entropy loss is computed between the generated captions and the ground truth captions from the dataset. The generator's parameters are updated using back-propagation and gradient descent optimization. The discriminator is trained to distinguish between real and generated captions. We provide pairs of real image-caption samples and generated image-caption pairs as input to the discriminator. The discriminator is optimized to minimize the adversarial loss, encouraging it to accurately classify the authenticity of captions.

Data2Vec is a versatile framework that employs a unified learning approach applicable to various domains such as speech, natural language processing (NLP), and computer vision. At its core, Data2Vec operates on the principle of predicting latent representations of complete input data by leveraging a masked perspective of the input within a self-distillation framework which is accomplished through the utilization of a standard Transformer architecture. In addition to the proposed architecture, a variation of the architecture where the ViT encoder in the generator is substituted with the Data2Vec [8] encoder (referred to as Proposed-model-2) is explored.

4   Results and Discussion

4.1   Dataset

We conducted our experimentation using three popular and widely used datasets: MS-COCO, Flickr8k, and Flickr30k. Each dataset provides a diverse collection of images with corresponding textual descriptions, making them suitable for various computer vision and natural language processing tasks.

Table 1. Dataset statistics

Dataset Name	Size		
	Train	Validate	Test
Flickr30k [11]	28000	1000	1000
Flickr8k [12]	6000	1000	1000
MS-COCO [13]	82783	40504	40775

The Microsoft Common Objects in Context (MS-COCO) dataset is a widely recognized benchmark for image captioning and object detection tasks. It contains a large-scale collection of images, comprising 80 object categories and around 82,783 training images with five captions per image. The dataset is well-annotated, providing bounding box annotations for object detection and accurate sentence-level descriptions for image captioning. MS-COCO has become a standard dataset for evaluating models' performance on visual recognition and language understanding tasks. The Flickr8k dataset is another popular dataset used for image captioning research. It consists of 8,000 images, where each image is associated with five descriptive captions written by different human annotators. The dataset covers a wide range of scenes, objects, and activities, offering a diverse set of visual content. Flickr8k has been extensively used in various studies to evaluate the quality of generated captions and to train models for image captioning tasks. Flickr30k is an extended version of the Flickr8k dataset, containing a larger collection of images with their associated captions. It comprises of images, each accompanied by five textual descriptions, resulting in a total of approximately 158,915 captions. Like Flickr8k, Flickr30k covers diverse visual content and provides multiple captions per image to capture different perspectives and variations in language. The data split of the datasets used is displayed in Table 1.

4.2   Experimental Setup

In the experimental setup, two Nvidia T4 GPUs were combined to leverage their collective processing power. This configuration enabled the distribution of workloads across both GPUs, harnessing their parallel processing capabilities. The experimentation was conducted in a cloud-based environment specifically designed for computational tasks.

4.3   Evaluation Metrics

Various accuracy metrics are employed to evaluate the quality of captions, with a specific focus on n-gram matching, unigram precision and recall, sentence structure, and TF-IDF cosine similarity. These metrics include BLEU score [14], METEOR [15], ROUGE [16], and CIDEr [17]. The BLEU score measures the extent of n-gram overlap between the generated caption and the ground truth caption. METEOR combines unigram precision and recall, giving more weight to recall [15]. ROUGE uses the Longest Common Subsequence (LCS) to more accurately capture sentence structure, instead of solely relying on n-grams [16]. CIDEr calculates the cosine similarity of TF-IDF vectors between the generated and reference sentences [17].

In addition to accuracy metrics, diversity metrics are also considered. These metrics include n-gram diversity, novel captions, and distinct captions. N-gram diversity refers to the ratio of distinct n-grams per caption to the total number of words generated per image. A sentence is considered novel if it does not exist in the training set. Distinct captions are calculated as the ratio of unique sentences to the total number of sentences generated.

4.4   Results

Table 2 and Table 3 show the accuracy and diversity metrics results, respectively. All the results are done with top-1 accuracy.

Table 2. Comparison of model performance

	model	Bleu				Meteor	Rouge	Cider	Spice
		Bleu-1	Bleu-2	Bleu-3	Bleu-4				
Flicker30k	NIC [9]	0.62	0.42	0.27	0.18				
	NIC [3]	0.66	0.43	0.29	0.19	0.18			
	SubGc [6]	0.69	0.51	0.37	0.27	0.21	0.48	0.58	0.28
	Proposed-Model-2	0.32	0.26	0.22	0.21	0.25	0.40	1.25	0.28
	Proposed-Model-1	0.54	0.49	**0.45**	**0.43**	**0.55**	**0.62**	**3.72**	**0.5**
Flicker8k	NIC [9]	0.61	0.41	0.27					
	NIC [3]	0.67	0.45	0.31	0.21	0.20			
	Proposed-Model-2	0.43	0.35	0.27	0.24	0.45	0.29	0.98	0.19
	Proposed-Model-1	0.56	**0.52**	**0.49**	**0.48**	**0.62**	**0.69**	**4.3**	**0.26**
MS-COCO	NIC [9]	0.62	0.46	0.32	0.24				
	NIC [3]	0.71	0.50	0.35	0.25	0.23			
	SubGc [6]	0.77	0.6	0.46	0.34	0.26	0.56	0.20	
	Proposed-Model-2	0.79	**0.67**	0.59	0.54	0.73	0.57	4.05	0.39
	Proposed-Model-1	0.66	0.65	**0.62**	**0.6**	**0.75**	**0.64**	**4.25**	**0.88**

Table 3. Diversity Metric Comparison

	Model	Distinct Caption	1-gram	2-gram
Flickr30k	Sub-GC [8]	69.2%	0.32	0.42
	Proposed-Model-2	35%	0.06	0.36
	Proposed-Model-1	24%	0.12	**0.54**
Flick8k	Proposed-Model-2	33%	0.013	0.21
	Proposed-Model-1	**35%**	**0.13**	**0.47**
MS-COCO	Sub-GC [8]	96.2%	0.39	0.57
	Proposed-Model-2	30%	0.01	0.25
	Proposed-Model-1	34%	0.07	0.33

Proposed-Model-1 refers to the architecture presented in Fig. 1. Proposed-Model-2 refers to the architecture where ViT encoder in the generator is replaced with Data2Vec transformer encoder. The Proposed-Model-1 has a good recall and outperforms other models with respect to a few accuracy metrics highlighted in the table. The Proposed-Model-1, with a consistent Bleu score, has higher scores for Meteor, Rogue, Cider and Spice scores for all the 3 datasets considered. In Table 2, we observe that the architecture employing the Data2Vec encoder within the generator demonstrates comparable caption generation performance as the volume of training data increases. Specifically, on the extensive MS-COCO dataset, the Proposed-model-2 excels in generating captions. However, its performance falters when applied to smaller datasets such as Flickr8k and Flickr30k.

Fig. 2. Attention-Visualization-examples.

Visualizing the attention weights in this manner provides valuable insights into the image regions that capture the model's focus during each step of the decoding process. These insights shed light on how the model constructs the caption and offers potential areas for enhancement, as demonstrated in example 1 of Fig. 2. In the example considered, the concentration of yellow, blue, and red dots primarily around the female figure, with a few dots on the bowling lane1, suggests the model's understanding of the scene. This spatial distribution of attention indicates that the model recognizes the presence of a bowling lane. Furthermore, as depicted in example 2 of Fig. 2, the image vividly illustrates the model's attention directed towards the bowling pins. This attention pattern allows the model to make accurate predictions regarding the bowler's position.

5   Conclusion

In the proposed work, we introduced a novel approach to image captioning based on the TransGAN framework, incorporating transformer-based models for both the generator and discriminator components. Our proposed model leverages the power of the Vision Transformer (ViT) encoder and transformer architecture to generate diverse and semantically meaningful captions for images. Through extensive experimentation and evaluation, we demonstrated the effectiveness of our approach in generating high-quality captions. Our model outperformed state-of-the-art baseline methods in terms of caption accuracy, as measured by metrics such as BLEU, METEOR, CIDEr, and ROUGE. The integration of the ViT encoder and language transformer-based generator enabled our model to capture both the visual and linguistic aspects of the images, leading to more contextually relevant and diverse caption generation. The discriminator component played a crucial role in enhancing the authenticity and coherence of the generated captions. By training the generator-discriminator architecture, we ensured that the generated captions were indistinguishable from real captions, contributing to the overall quality of the outputs.

References

1. Vaswani, A., et al.: Attention is all you need. In: Advances in Neural Information Processing Systems, vol. 30 (2017)
2. Dosovitskiy, A., et al.: An image is worth 16×16 words: transformers for image recognition at scale. arXiv preprint arXiv:2010.11929 (2020)
3. Xu, K., et al.: Neural image caption generation with visual attention. In Proceedings ICML, pp. 2048–2057 (2015)
4. Jiang, Y., Chang, S., Wang, Z.: TransGAN: two pure transformers can make one strong GAN, and that can scale up. In: Advances in Neural Information Processing Systems, vol. 34, pp. 14745–14758 (2021)
5. Dai, B. Fidler, S., Urtasun, R., Lin, D.: Towards diverse and natural image descriptions via a conditional GAN. In: 2017 IEEE International Conference on Computer Vision (ICCV), Venice, Italy, pp. 2989–2998 (2017). https://doi.org/10.1109/ICCV.2017.323
6. Zhong, Y., Wang, L., Chen, J., Yu, D., Li, Y.: Comprehensive image captioning via scene graph decomposition. In: Vedaldi, A., Bischof, H., Brox, T., Frahm, J.-M. (eds.) ECCV 2020. LNCS, vol. 12359, pp. 211–229. Springer, Cham (2020). https://doi.org/10.1007/978-3-030-58568-6_13
7. Kiros, R., Salakhutdinov, R., Zemel, R.: Multimodal neural language models. In: Proceedings of the 31st International Conference on International Conference on Machine Learning (ICML 2014), vol. 32, pp. II-595–II-603. JMLR.org (2014)
8. Baevski, A., Hsu, W.N., Xu, Q., Babu, A., Gu, J., Auli, M.: Data2vec: a general framework for self-supervised learning in speech, vision and language. In: International Conference on Machine Learning, pp. 1298–1312 (2022)
9. Vinyals, O., Toshev, A., Bengio, S., Erhan, D.: Show and tell: a neural image caption generator. In: 2015 IEEE Conference on Computer Vision and Pattern Recognition (CVPR), Boston, MA, USA, pp. 3156–3164 (2015). https://doi.org/10.1109/CVPR.2015.7298935

10. Wang, Y., et al.: 3D conditional generative adversarial networks for high-quality PET image estimation at low dose. Neuroimage **174**, 550–562 (2018)
11. Plummer, B.A., Wang, L., Cervantes, C.M., Caicedo, J.C., Hockenmaier, J., Lazebnik, S.: Flickr30k entities: collecting region-to-phrase correspondences for richer image-to-sentence models. In: Proceedings of the IEEE International Conference on Computer Vision, pp. 2641–2649 (2015)
12. Rashtchian, C., Young, P., Hodosh, M., Hockenmaier, J.: Collecting image annotations using amazon's mechanical turk. In: Proceedings of the NAACL HLT 2010 Workshop on Creating Speech and Language Data with Amazon's Mechanical Turk, pp. 139–147 (2010)
13. T-Y, L., et al.: Microsoft COCO: common objects in context. In: Fleet, D., Pajdla, T., Schiele, B., Tuytelaars, T. (eds.) ECCV 2014. LNCS, vol. 8693, pp. 740–755. Springer, Cham (2014). https://doi.org/10.1007/978-3-319-10602-1_48
14. Papineni, K., Roukos, S., Ward, T., Zhu, W.-J.: BLEU: a method for automatic evaluation of machine translation. In: Proceedings of the 40th Annual Meeting of the Association for Computational Linguistics, pp. 311–318 (2002)
15. Banerjee, S., Lavie, A.: METEOR: an automatic metric for MT evaluation with improved correlation with human judgments. In: Proceedings of the ACL Workshop on Intrinsic and Extrinsic Evaluation Measures for Machine Translation AND/OR Summarization, pp. 65–72 (2005)
16. Lin, C.-Y.: ROUGE: a package for automatic evaluation of summaries. In: Text Summarization Branches Out, pp. 74–81 (2004)
17. Vedantam, R., Lawrence Zitnick, C., Parikh, D.: CIDEr: consensus-based image description evaluation. In: Proceedings of the IEEE Conference on Computer Vision and Pattern Recognition, pp. 4566–4575 (2015)
18. Parmar, N., et al.: Image transformer. In International Conference on Machine Learning, pp. 4055–4064 (2018)
19. Wang, X., Girshick, R., Gupta, A., He, K.: Non-local neural networks. In: Proceedings of the IEEE Conference on Computer Vision and Pattern Recognition, pp. 7794–7803 (2018)
20. Wu, J., Hu, H.: Cascade recurrent neural network for image caption generation. Electron. Lett. **53**(25), 1642–1643 (2017)
21. Cornia, M., Stefanini, M., Baraldi, L., Cucchiara, R.: Meshed-memory transformer for image captioning. In: Proceedings of the IEEE/CVF Conference on Computer Vision and Pattern Recognition, pp. 10578–10587 (2020)
22. Liu, W., Chen, S., Guo, L., Zhu, X., Liu, J.: CPTR: full transformer network for image captioning. arXiv preprint arXiv:2101.10804 (2021)
23. Luo, Y., et al.: Dual-level collaborative transformer for image captioning. In: Proceedings of the AAAI Conference on Artificial Intelligence, vol. 35, no. 3, pp. 2286–2293 (2021)
24. He, K., Zhang, X., Ren, S., Sun, J.: Deep residual learning for image recognition. In: Proceedings of the IEEE Conference on Computer Vision and Pattern Recognition, pp. 770–778 (2016)
25. Simonyan, K., Zisserman, A.: Very deep convolutional networks for large-scale image recognition. arXiv preprint arXiv:1409.1556 (2014)

Robust CNN-Based Segmentation of Infrastructure Cracks Segregating from Shadows and Lines

Amit Patel and Tushar Sandhan[✉]

Electrical Engineering, IIT Kanpur, Kanpur, U.P., India
{amitpatel21,sandhan}@iitk.ac.in

Abstract. Detecting cracks early in various structures is crucial not only for preserving the integrity of these structures but also for safeguarding lives, especially in environments like coal mines, bridges, and buildings. However, employing deep learning(DL) and computer vision for crack identification in mines poses significant challenges. These challenges arise from the presence of intensity inhomogeneity in cracks and the intricate nature of the background such as elements, shadows, lines, and water-dripping patterns, which can resemble more like cracks. Moreover, these techniques often struggle to detect extremely small cracks, further complicating the detection process. Manually inspecting these extensive structures is highly arduous. Utilizing DL techniques in conjunction with image processing can prove immensely beneficial in the early identification of these cracks. In this study, we improve the performance of TernausNet with modified loss functions. The encoder component of TernausNet is substituted with various networks, including VGG-16 [19], Resnet34 [7], and Resnet101 [7]. Additionally, the study investigates the utilization of pre-trained weights from ImageNet [16] for the encoder component and compares it against training from random initialization for crack detection using TernausNet.

Keywords: Crack Segmentation · Convolution neural networks · Deep feature representation · Crack detection

1 Introduction

In the world, a substantial number of coal mines exist, according to the global coal mine tracker, which includes 70 nations and tracks 4300 active coal mines through 2023. The presence of cracks on the walls within these coal mines poses a significant threat to the safety of workers inside coal mines [21]. It is, therefore, crucial to detect and address any developing cracks promptly, through necessary repairs, to prevent the occurrence of catastrophic incidents, particularly in mines and bridges where the risk of collapse due to such cracks is higher [2]. Cracks serve as early indicators of structural damage, emphasizing the importance of early detection to avert complete structural failure.

© The Author(s), under exclusive license to Springer Nature Switzerland AG 2024
H. Kaur et al. (Eds.): CVIP 2023, CCIS 2011, pp. 386–396, 2024.
https://doi.org/10.1007/978-3-031-58535-7_32

There are two viable options for inspecting structures to identify cracks. The first approach involves manual inspection conducted by human observers. However, this method proves exceedingly challenging, depending on the size and location of the structures. For instance, underground coal mines and tunnels can extend several kilometers, necessitating surveyors to physically traverse the mine in search of cracks. These surveyors often move between different mine areas, thereby exposing themselves to hazardous conditions arising from cracks and water accumulation [10]. [14] As a result, manual inspection becomes highly impractical. Additionally, the accuracy of the inspection process may vary considerably, as it primarily relies on the knowledge and health of the inspector. Factors such as inexperience or fatigue can easily lead to erroneous reporting of damage.

The alternative option involves employing image processing techniques in conjunction with DL architectures, which offers a more feasible solution. This approach allows the utilization of cameras, robots, and drones to inspect extensive tunnels and coal mines efficiently. However, detecting cracks in mines using computer vision presents a considerable challenge [23], primarily due to the irregular shapes that cracks can assume. Furthermore, extrinsic factors, including outdoor conditions such as lighting variations, occlusions, complex backgrounds, and variations in pixel intensities [20], further complicate the crack detection process.

Nevertheless, these methods for crack identification emerge as a more realistic and practical strategy considering the inherent challenges associated with the manual inspection of structures.

In the dataset, we encounter images that contain actual cracks 2 and images without cracks 2, but where shadows may create an illusion of a crack.

Successful crack recognition relies on deep features that possess both strong representational capabilities and discriminative properties, which are fundamental for distinguishing cracks from shadows and line patterns. In our study, we embrace a crack detection approach that supports convolutional neural networks (CNN) to learn discriminative features from raw image patches directly. By training the CNN on our dataset, we aim to develop a robust model capable of accurately distinguishing between genuine cracks and instances where shadows might give the false impression of a crack.

enhance the performance of TernausNet [4,8] for crack detection. Specifically, we investigate the impact of replacing the encoder component of TernausNet with three different models ResNet101 [7], ResNet34 [7], and VGG16 [19]. These models have been pre-trained on ImageNet [16] weights, and we also explore the option of training them from random initialization(scratch). We modify the loss functions for crack segmentation, aiming to optimize the performance of TernausNet.

To conduct our experiments, we utilize the Crack segmentation dataset, which comprises 12 distinct subsets. During the training phase, we employ this dataset to train our model as well as, to evaluate its performance, we conduct tests on the CRWK100 [27] dataset and another Crack dataset.

We aim to assess the effectiveness of various encoder models and loss functions in enhancing the crack detection capabilities of TernausNet 1. This investigation will provide valuable insights into the optimal DL configuration for accurate and reliable crack segmentation.

In this manuscript, Sect. 2 provides an overview of related work 2, Sect. 3 gives insights into the methods 3 used, and Sect. 4.1 experimental results gives insights into Dataset 4.1, quantitative analysis 4.3 and qualitative analysis 4.4 and Sect. 5 contain the conclusion 5 of the work.

2 Related Work

The detection of cracks demands high-quality image data, as it becomes crucial to differentiate between genuine cracks and visual artifacts caused by shadows or water droplets. Previous endeavors have delved into this field, aiming to develop effective methodologies to overcome these obstacles and enhance the accuracy of crack identification.

To solve the problem of shadows in pavement images, Q. Zou et al. [26] presented a method by introducing Geodesic shadow reduction. They originally presented a crack detection approach based on the Crack Tree [26]. A crack's intensity may exceed the background pavement intensity due to variations in the fracture curve. Due to this, classic local intensity-based methods are used this method might detect insufficient crack segments. To get around this, the researchers created a threshold technique and a local intensity-difference measure that reliably detects cracked pixels. They then used a tensor voting approach to create a map that shows the likelihood of fracture presence, which improved pavement crack identification.

Zhang et al. [24] utilized a deep-learning approach to identify road cracks. Unlike traditional methods that require manual feature engineering, they grasp the power of automatic feature learning from images and compare the performance of SVM and boosting algorithms. The findings revealed that the CNN exhibited superior performance in crack detection compared to SVM and boosting methods.

Sharma et al. [17] presented a novel attention-based model called SCNet [17] for crack fault segmentation, using the UNet [15] segmentation model. SCNet utilizes a semantic segmentation-based hierarchical architecture, incorporating scale-space attention in both the decoder and encoder modules. To address the challenge of per-pixel classification with class imbalance, they employed binary focal loss. The model was trained using publicly available datasets, namely Deepcrack [11], CODEBRIM [13], METU, and CrackForest [18]. Notably, SCNet demonstrated superior performance compared to the baseline model HCNN [25].

A hierarchical convolutional-based design called DeepCrack [27]network, which is based on the SegNet [3] was introduced by Zou et al. [27]. SegNet uses an encoder-decoder architecture and the final pixel-wise classification layer. However, the outputs are sparse because there are no linkages between the encoder and decoder features in the original SegNet architecture. DeepCrack incorporates continuous and sparse feature maps at each size to resolve this issue.

For training the DeepCrack [27] network, the researchers used the Crack-Tree260 dataset [26], while the CRKWH100 [27], CrackLS315 [27], and Stone331 [27] datasets were utilized for testing. Notably, DeepCrack outperformed other networks such as SegNet, UNet, RCF [12], HED [22], SRN [9], SE [5], and CrackTree [26] when evaluated on the provided dataset. These results demonstrate the superior performance of DeepCrack in the context of pavement crack detection.

The researchers used a combination of the Jaccard loss [8] and binary cross-entropy, as their loss function to train the model in their study. For evaluation purposes, they conducted tests on the UAV75 [4] dataset, comparing their results against the DeepCrack methods proposed by Zou et al. [27] and Liu et al. [11] These approaches utilize the crack-as-line concept, which can result in significant false positives when encountering images with prominent planking patterns.

Iglovikov et al. [8] introduced the TernausNet network, a variant of UNet that incorporates transfer learning techniques. Unlike UNet, which heavily relies on data augmentation methods, By substituting a pre-trained VGG16 [19] model from ImageNet [16] for the encoder component of UNet, TernausNet improves UNet. This approach offers the advantage of using pre-existing weights, necessitating training solely on the decoder portion. Benz et al. [4] further utilized TernausNet for crack segmentation on unmanned aircraft systems-based images through transfer learning. The specific dataset used in their study is UAV75, consisting of images with planking patterns. Notably, TernausNet outperformed DeepCrack in terms of performance on this dataset.

3   Method

The TernausNet [8] network is built upon the widely recognized UNet [15] architecture.

UNet: The proposed UNet [15] architecture includes both encoder and decoder components, each of which has a specific function. While the encoder part seeks to capture a wider context, the decoder part concentrates on localizing information. The feature maps are decreased while the channels are increased in the encoder portion. The use of alternating convolutional layers, followed by 2×2 max-pooling layers, results in a reduction in the size of the feature maps. In contrast, the decoder portion uses convolutional layers first, then alternates between up-convolution layers of size 2×2. A skip connection is utilized to integrate the feature maps to guarantee flawless integration between the encoder and decoder. The output of the UNet, which enables pixel-wise categorization, ultimately assigns a class label to each pixel.

TernausNet: A straightforward VGG11 [19] Network replaces the UNet encoder in the TernausNet [8] Network, which is based on the UNet design. The fully linked layers are taken out and replaced with a single 512-channel convolutional layer to produce an encoder from VGG11. This redesigned encoder serves as a link between the network's encoder and decoder components. Convolution layers are alternated with max-pooling in Fig. 1's encoder, which results in a decrease in feature maps and an increase in channels. Pre-trained weights from the Imagenet dataset are used by the encoder. The network's decoder portion is the only one that receives training. Up-sampling and convolution layers are combined in the decoder, resulting in an increase in feature maps and a decrease in channels. For precise localization, high-resolution feature maps are combined with feature maps from the decoder layers.

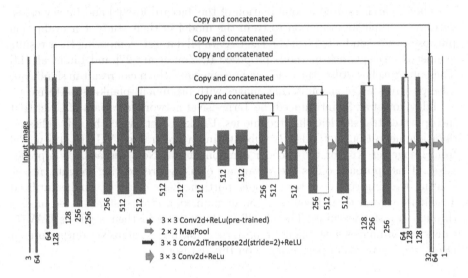

Fig. 1. TernausNet [8] Architecture.

Loss Function: The Loss function is chosen as a combination of the Jaccard loss [8] and BCE_logistic loss.

Jaccard index [8]: It measures the similarity between two sets, it is determined by dividing the size of the sets' union by the size of their intersection.

Jaccard index is described by Eq. 1 and is

$$\mathcal{J} = \frac{1}{m}\left(\sum_{k=1}^{m}\frac{y_k\hat{y}_k}{y_k + \hat{y}_k - y_k\hat{y}_k}\right) \tag{1}$$

where y_k determines the class membership of the pixel, while $\hat{y}_k$ signifies the probability estimated by the model for that particular pixel.

BCE_logistic loss: The binary cross-entropy logistic loss, is commonly used for binary classification problems. It measures the dissimilarity between the predicted probabilities obtained by applying the sigmoid function to the logits and the true labels.

The BCE logistic loss is as follows:

$$\ell(y,\hat{y}) = L = \{l_1,\ldots,l_N\}^\top, l_n = -w_n(y_n \cdot \log\sigma(\hat{y_n}) + (1 - y_n)\cdot\log(1 - \sigma(\hat{y_n}))) \tag{2}$$

where L represents the overall loss for a batch of samples, and it is a vector with N elements. l_n represents the individual loss for each sample in the batch, and it is calculated separately for each sample. $\hat{y}_n$ represents the predicted logit (score) for the n-th sample. y_n represents the true label or target value for the n-th sample. w_n represents the weight assigned to the n-th sample. It is a scalar that can be used to assign different importance or priority to different samples. $\sigma(\cdot)$ represents the sigmoid function, which maps the predicted logit $\hat{y}_n$ to a value between 0 and 1, interpreting it as a probability.

Regularization procedures are used to reduce overfitting and enhance the model's performance.

L1 regularization aims to incorporate a penalty term into the loss function of a model, which encourages sparsity in the coefficients of the model. This regularization technique is beneficial in feature selection, as it helps identify and prioritize the most important features for prediction or classification tasks.

L2 regularization introduces a penalty term into the loss function that promotes smaller and more evenly distributed coefficient values. By doing so, it discourages the model from relying too heavily on a small set of features and encourages a more balanced utilization of all the available features. This regularization technique is particularly useful in preventing overfitting when a model is too closely matched to training data and struggles to generalize to novel, unseen data.

The model's ability to generalize and generate precise predictions on new data is improved by using L1 or L2 regularisation. Regularisation assists in managing the model's complexity by achieving a balance between accurately fitting the training data and preventing overfitting.

L1 regularization is given as

$$R_{L1}(\omega) = \lambda \sum_{k=1}^{m} |\omega_k| \tag{3}$$

where m is the parameter count for the model, $|\omega_k|$ is the absolute value of the k-th parameter, and λ is the regularization parameter that controls the strength of the regularization.

L2 Regularization is given as

$$R_{L2}(\omega) = \lambda \sum_{k=1}^{m} \omega_k^2 \tag{4}$$

where m is the parameter count for the model, ω_k is the k-th parameter, and λ is the regularization parameter that controls the strength of the regularization.

In this paper, we used modified loss functions such as

$$L_1 = BCE\_logistic\ loss \tag{5}$$

$$L_2 = BCE\_logistic\ loss + \beta R_{L1}(\omega) \tag{6}$$

$$L_3 = BCE\_logistic\ loss + \beta R_{L2}(\omega) \tag{7}$$

$$L_4 = BCE\_logistic\ loss - \log J + \beta R_{L2}(\omega) \tag{8}$$

$$L_5 = BCE\_logistic\ loss - \log J + \beta R_{L1}(\omega) \tag{9}$$

4   Experimental Results

We employed a model, which is an encoder-decoder-based architecture, for our training purposes. In accordance with [4] the encoder of TernausNet is replaced by different networks such as VGG16, ResNet34, and ResNet101.

TernausNet training was conducted using two approaches. In the first approach, the encoder utilized pre-trained weights from the ImageNet dataset [16], while only the decoder was trained. The second approach involved training both the encoder and decoder from random initialization. Additionally, various loss functions were employed during training, and their performance was compared.

4.1   Dataset

For our work, we utilized the Crack Segmentation Dataset, which comprises 12 distinct subsets, namely Cracktree200 [26], GAPS384 [6], Crack500 [24], CFD [18], DeepCrack [27], Sylvie-Chambon [1], Crackforest [18], non-crack, Rissbildes-for-Florian, Volker, Nohra, and Eugen Muller.

The crack segmentation dataset contains 11,200 images and their corresponding masks. To ensure balanced representation, the dataset is separated into train and test sets. The train set includes 9,603 images, whereas the test set includes 1,695 images. Each image has dimensions of 448 × 448 pixels.

During training, a random split is applied, where 85% ofthe training data (8,162 images) is used for training, and the remaining 15% (1,441 images) is reserved for validation to prevent overfitting and assess model performance on unseen data.

For evaluation, both the CRKWH100 dataset [27] and the test set of the crack segmentation dataset are utilized. The CRKWH100 dataset serves as an external benchmark to evaluate the model's generalization and performance across various crack segmentation tasks.

4.2   Evaluation

We have utilized TernausNet, an advanced model based on semantic segmentation, for our image analysis. The approach involved treating the crack segmentation task as a binary classification problem by classifying pixels as crack or non-crack.

To evaluate the efficacy of different network architectures, we conducted experiments by replacing the encoder in TernausNet. Performance metrics such as F1 score, Average Precision (AP), and accuracy were used to compare the performance of each network.

Furthermore, we explored various loss functions and assessed their impact on performance. The outcomes of these experiments were recorded and included in Table 1.

4.3   Quantitative Analysis

In this section, we have undertaken a rigorous examination of the TernausNet network's performance by substituting the encoder with diverse networks. Our experimental investigations were focused on three distinct scene categories.

In the first scenario, we replaced the encoder with Resnet and conducted training in two ways: utilizing pre-trained Imagenet weights for the encoder and training only the decoder and training both the encoder and decoder from random initialization(scratch).

Shifting to the second case, we replaced the encoder with VGG16 and again followed two approaches: using a pre-trained VGG16 model for the encoder and training only the decoder and training both the encoder and decoder from scratch.

To evaluate performance, we employed various loss functions and conducted a comprehensive comparison of their efficacy using the CRWK100 dataset. This analysis aimed to gain valuable insights into the relative performances of these models.

In Table 1, the model represents the network that is used as an encoder of TernausNet. J is representing Jaccard index, $R_{L2}(\omega)$ is representing L2 regularization.

Table 1. Performance comparison of TernausNet with Various encoder and Loss function with CRKWH100 [27] Dataset.

Model	Loss Function	Test Data	F1 Score	AP	Accuracy
Resnet34(pretrained)	$BCE\_logistic$	CRKWH100	0.324	0.24	0.894
Resnet101(pretrained)	$BCE\_logistic$	CRKWH100	0.42	0.58	0.92
Resnet101(Scratch)	$BCE\_logistic$	CRKWH100	0.24	0.22	0.85
VGG16(pretrained)	$BCE\_logistic$	CRKWH100	0.42	0.58	0.92
VGG16(Scratch)	$BCE\_logistic$	CRKWH100	0.53	0.64	0.92
Resnet101(pretrained)	$BCE\_logistic-\log J + \beta R_{L2}(\omega)$	CRKWH100	0.342	0.311	0.89
Resnet101(pretrained)	$BCE\_logistic+\beta R_{L2}(\omega)$	CRKWH100	0.25	0.21	0.86

In Table 2 the best performance is given by the Resnet101 pre-trained model as an encoder for the loss function $BCE\_logistic + \beta R_{L2}(\omega)$.

Table 2. Performance comparison of TernausNet utilizing a ResNet101 (pre-trained) encoder, and various loss functions using the Crack segmentation dataset.

Model	Loss Function	Test Data	F1 Score	AP	Accuracy
Resnet101	$BCE\_logistic-\log J + \beta R_{L1}(\omega)$	Crack segmentation	0.429	0.421	0.602
Resnet101	$BCE\_logistic-\log J + \beta R_{L2}(\omega)$	Crack segmentation	0.775	0.826	0.966
Resnet101	$BCE\_logistic+\beta R_{L1}(\omega)$	Crack segmentation	0.789	0.826	0.89
Resnet101	$BCE\_logistic+\beta R_{L2}(\omega)$	Crack segmentation	0.795	0.846	0.907

4.4   Qualitative Analysis

We have acquired a set of three test images extracted from the crack segmentation dataset, accompanied by their corresponding outputs pertaining to diverse loss functions, as illustrated in Fig. 2.

According to Fig. 2, the image labeled as "img_a1" represents a cracked image. The model that exhibits superior performance in accurately detecting the crack utilizes a combination of loss functions, namely BCE_logistic, Jaccard, and L2 regularization. It demonstrates flawless detection of the crack. Conversely, the model employing the loss function BCE_logistic - $\log J$ + L1 regularization demonstrates subpar performance, providing less accurate results.

For non-crack image img_$a2$ model with loss function BCE_logistic - $\log J$ + L2 regularization is not detecting any crack, model with loss function BCE_logistic - $\log J$ + L1 regularization is wrongly detecting crack for non-crack images.

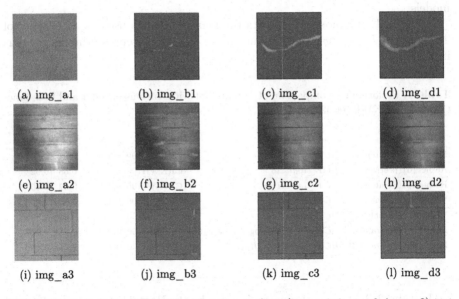

(a) img_a1	(b) img_b1	(c) img_c1	(d) img_d1
(e) img_a2	(f) img_b2	(g) img_c2	(h) img_d2
(i) img_a3	(j) img_b3	(k) img_c3	(l) img_d3

Fig. 2. Test output for different loss functions, where (img_a1, img_a2, img_a3) test images, (img_b1, img_b2, img_b3) test output for loss function BCElogistic - $\log J + \beta$ L1 Regularization, (img_c1, img_c2, img_c3) test output for loss function BCElogistic -$\log J + \beta$ L2 Regularization, (img_d1, img_d2, img_d3) test output for loss function BCElogistic $+\beta$ L2 Regularization.

5   Conclusion

We conducted training using TernausNet [8] with various network encoders to determine the optimal combination of encoder and loss function for enhancing the performance of TernausNet. The training process was carried out in two ways: first, by utilizing pre-trained network weights for the encoder, and second, by training the encoder from scratch.

For the CRWKH100 dataset, we observed that TernausNet performed the best when VGG16 was used as the encoder, BCE_logistic as a loss function, and trained from scratch. In this configuration, we achieved an F1 score of 53%, an average precision of 64%, and an accuracy of 92%. Since we had a large dataset, training from scratch yielded superior results for the CRWKH100 dataset. The second-best performance was obtained when using the pre-trained models of ResNet101 and VGG16 as the encoder, again with the BCE_logistic loss.

In Table 2, we compared the performance of TernausNet on the crack segmentation test set, using the pre-trained ResNet101 as the encoder, with different loss functions. From the table, we observed that the best performance was achieved with the BCE_logistic loss and L2 regularization, resulting in an F1 score of 79.5%, average precision of 84.6%, and accuracy of 90.7%. On the other hand, the combination of BCE_logistic, Jaccard, and L1 regularization showed the poorest performance.

The results indicate that for the CRWKH100 dataset, training TernausNet from scratch with VGG16 as the encoder yielded the best performance. For the crack segmentation testing dataset, using the pre-trained ResNet101 as the encoder with the BCE_logistic loss and L2 regularization resulted in the highest performance.

Acknowledgement. This work is supported by IIT Kharagpur AI4ICPS I Hub Foundation, a.k.a AI4ICPS under the aegis of DST.

References

1. Amhaz, R., Chambon, S., Idier, J., Baltazart, V.: Automatic crack detection on two-dimensional pavement images: an algorithm based on minimal path selection. IEEE Trans. Intell. Transp. Syst. **17**(10), 2718–2729 (2016)
2. As'ad, S., Sukiman, M., et al.: Investigation on wall crack damage and its proposed repair method. Procedia Eng. **54**, 165–175 (2013)
3. Badrinarayanan, V., Kendall, A., Cipolla, R.: SegNet: a deep convolutional encoder-decoder architecture for image segmentation. IEEE Trans. Pattern Anal. Mach. Intell. **39**(12), 2481–2495 (2017)
4. Benz, C., Debus, P., Ha, H.K., Rodehorst, V.: Crack segmentation on UAS-based imagery using transfer learning. In: 2019 International Conference on Image and Vision Computing NeGitHuband (IVCNZ), pp. 1–6. IEEE (2019)
5. Dollár, P., Zitnick, C.L.: Fast edge detection using structured forests. IEEE Trans. Pattern Anal. Mach. Intell. **37**(8), 1558–1570 (2014)
6. Eisenbach, M., et al.: How to get pavement distress detection ready for deep learning? a systematic approach. In: 2017 International Joint Conference on Neural Networks (IJCNN), pp. 2039–2047. IEEE (2017)
7. He, K., Zhang, X., Ren, S., Sun, J.: Deep residual learning for image recognition. arXiv preprint arXiv:1512.03385 (2015)
8. Iglovikov, V., Shvets, A.: TernausNet: U-net with vgg11 encoder pre-trained on ImageNet for image segmentation. arXiv preprint arXiv:1801.05746 (2018)

9. Ke, W., Chen, J., Jiao, J., Zhao, G., Ye, Q.: SRN: side-output residual network for object symmetry detection in the wild. In: Proceedings of the IEEE Conference on Computer Vision and Pattern Recognition, pp. 1068–1076 (2017)
10. Liu, H., Zhang, M., Su, L., Chen, X., Liu, C., Sun, A.: A boundary model of terrain reconstruction in a coal-mining subsidence waterlogged area. Environ. Earth Sci. **80**, 1–15 (2021)
11. Liu, Y., Yao, J., Lu, X., Xie, R., Li, L.: DeepCrack: a deep hierarchical feature learning architecture for crack segmentation. Neurocomputing **338**, 139–153 (2019)
12. Liu, Y., Cheng, M.M., Hu, X., Wang, K., Bai, X.: Richer convolutional features for edge detection. In: Proceedings of the IEEE Conference on Computer Vision and Pattern Recognition, pp. 3000–3009 (2017)
13. Mundt, M., Majumder, S., Murali, S., Panetsos, P., Ramesh, V.: Meta-learning convolutional neural architectures for multi-target concrete defect classification with the concrete defect bridge image dataset. In: Proceedings of the IEEE/CVF Conference on Computer Vision and Pattern Recognition, pp. 11196–11205 (2019)
14. Pan, J.S., Yuan, S.X., Jiang, T., Cui, C.H.: Experimental study on crack characteristics and acoustic emission characteristics in rock-like material with pre-existing cracks. Sci. Rep. **11**(1), 23790 (2021)
15. Ronneberger, O., Fischer, P., Brox, T.: U-net: convolutional networks for biomedical image segmentation. In: Navab, N., Hornegger, J., Wells, W.M., Frangi, A.F. (eds.) MICCAI 2015, Part III. LNCS, vol. 9351, pp. 234–241. Springer, Cham (2015). https://doi.org/10.1007/978-3-319-24574-4_28
16. Russakovsky, O., et al.: ImageNet large scale visual recognition challenge. Int. J. Comput. Vision **115**, 211–252 (2015)
17. Sharma, H., Pradhan, P., P, B.: SCNet: a generalized attention-based model for crack fault segmentation. In: Proceedings of the Twelfth Indian Conference on Computer Vision, Graphics and Image Processing, pp. 1–9 (2021)
18. Shi, Y., Cui, L., Qi, Z., Meng, F., Chen, Z.: Automatic road crack detection using random structured forests. IEEE Trans. Intell. Transp. Syst. **17**(12), 3434–3445 (2016)
19. Simonyan, K., Zisserman, A.: Very deep convolutional networks for large-scale image recognition. arXiv preprint arXiv:1409.1556 (2014)
20. Takarli, F., Aghagolzadeh, A., Seyedarabi, H.: Combination of high-level features with low-level features for detection of pedestrian. Signal Image Video Process. **10**(1), 93–101 (2016)
21. Tang, C., et al.: Inspection robot and wall surface detection method for coal mine wind shaft. Appl. Sci. **13**(9), 5662 (2023)
22. Xie, S., Tu, Z.: Holistically-nested edge detection. In: Proceedings of the IEEE International Conference on Computer Vision, pp. 1395–1403 (2015)
23. Yu, X., Yang, J., Lin, Z., Wang, J., Wang, T., Huang, T.: Subcategory-aware object detection. IEEE Signal Process. Lett. **22**(9), 1472–1476 (2014)
24. Zhang, L., Yang, F., Zhang, Y.D., Zhu, Y.J.: Road crack detection using deep convolutional neural network. In: 2016 IEEE International Conference on Image Processing (ICIP), pp. 3708–3712. IEEE (2016)
25. Zhu, Q., Phung, M.D., Ha, Q.: Crack detection using enhanced hierarchical convolutional neural networks. arXiv preprint arXiv:1912.12139 (2019)
26. Zou, Q., Cao, Y., Li, Q., Mao, Q., Wang, S.: CrackTree: automatic crack detection from pavement images. Pattern Recogn. Lett. **33**(3), 227–238 (2012)
27. Zou, Q., Zhang, Z., Li, Q., Qi, X., Wang, Q., Wang, S.: DeepCrack: learning hierarchical convolutional features for crack detection. IEEE Trans. Image Process. **28**(3), 1498–1512 (2018)

A Natural Language Processing-Based Multimodal Deep Learning Approach for News Category Tagging

Bagesh Kumar[2(✉)], Alankar Singh[2], Vaidik Sharma[1], Yuvraj Shivam[1], Krishna Mohan[1], Prakhar Shukla[1], Tanay Falor[1], and Abhishek Kumar[1]

[1] Indian Institute of Information Technology, Allahabad, India
{iib2020024,iib2021006,iit2022119,iit2022122}@iiita.ac.in
[2] Manipal University, Jaipur, India
bagesh.kumar@jaipur.manipal.edu, alankar.229311098@muj.manipal.edu

Abstract. With the rise in the amount of news available today, the need for its classification has emerged. In this paper, we present methods for tagging news categories using different deep learning models along with a comparison of their effects. These models include single-channel CNN model, multichannel CNN model, and multimodal CNN model. This study involves integration of natural language understanding with convolutional methods that understands descriptions, titles, and tags to enhance news ranking. The novel part of this approach is to find out using natural language understanding with the transfer learning from the supplemental external features that are associated with images. The accuracy of the single-channel model was found to be 81.30%, of the multi-channel model was 85.98% and that of the multi-modal model was 85.39%. We have used the N24 news dataset for the validation of the models.

1 Introduction

One of important and crucial work in news research is News Classification. The data provided is used to classify news into different categories. Earlier study in this subject involved only the processing of the text but not the image involved with it. However, a major portion of the news today contains images along with the text, therefore in this work we have used both texts and images to classify news into different groups.

Multimodal methods are needed to mix together heterogeneous information extracted from images and texts. Various types of information can be simultaneously processed by multimodal methods and are being used in news studies before to classify fake news which is more elaborated in the literature review.

The field of image classification and natural language understanding (NLU) has developed many different types: image processing with deep links and NLU with deep links. Traditionally, the fields of image classification and natural language understanding (NLU) have followed separate paths, with deep convolutional networks dominating image processing and deep sequence-based networks

H. Kaur et al. (Eds.): CVIP 2023, CCIS 2011, pp. 397–410, 2024.
https://doi.org/10.1007/978-3-031-58535-7_33

prevailing in NLU. However, the emergence of robust, transferable models for analyzing both image and text data has fostered a surge of interest in multimodal deep learning. This exciting approach aims to leverage the power of interconnected deep representations, enabling the exploration of joint information from diverse data types such as images and text. By integrating these modalities, researchers can unlock new possibilities and advance the frontiers of knowledge in various domains. This research paper introduces a novel architectural approach for acquiring deep representations of both images and text. It demonstrates that the integration of multiple models can enhance image classification performance. In order to combine the extraction of features from images and text, the proposed model includes separate inputs for images and associated metadata text. Parallel rounds of deep convolution and sequence networks are employed to initially process the images and text, respectively. The initial layers capture the distinctive attributes relevant to each data type. These extracted features are then flattened and merged into a single feature vector, maintaining the separation of image and text attributes. Then, a Dense Neural Network is employed to predict the class based on the combined feature vector.

2 Literature Review

Over the last decade, there has been a substantial improvement in the performance of different methods of visual content classification, largely driven by the advancements in deep learning. Notably, the field of computer vision has focused on deepening models to explore the spatial properties of images more effectively. The development of more efficient architectures has significantly enhanced the ability to extract and utilize these spatial characteristics, resulting in notable strides in image classification accuracy. [1]

At the same time, NLU has grown enormously. Progress with the coming of enormous corpora, models that preserve order data about bigger sections of content, and methods that exploit lexical knowledge and semantic representations [2,3]. Language learning models have evolved from analysis of word coincidences to word incorporation on the positional information obtained by analyzing the encyclopedic volumes of Corpus [4]. To enhance sequence models, one approach is to enhance the Long-Short-Term Memory (LSTM) networks [5] by increasing their size. By incorporating multiple weights and activations, these enlarged networks introduce a cellular state that can effectively preserve and propagate a greater amount of contextual information.

Multimodal deep learning [6] can take advantage of various kinds of features like speech, text, and image, to achieve optimum performance. Today, multimodal methods are being used for various tasks such as multimodal translation [8], multimodal question response [2], multimodal sentiment analysis [7], and multimodal emotion recognition [9].

Generally, a multimodal architecture uses multiple layers of models to process the information contained in the input data. For example, get text features first using a text classifier and then image features using image classifier and then merging them before further processing. Feature fusion is a crucial component in multimodal deep learning. Recent research proposes several methods for feature fusion. [13]

Nowadays, multimodal methods are also being incorporated in the study of news. Earlier, detecting fake news used to be the main focus in multimodal news surveys. A Reddit multimodal fake news dataset having six categories based on the extent and kind of fake news in the news was proposed by [12]. Word2vec was used by [13] in order to extract features from news text and five different image models were used for extracting features from news images. Fake news detection is also a common variation of news category tagging where there are only two tags available i.e. real or fake or we can say true or false. An antagonist neural network was used [14] to detect fake news on social media platforms. The task to categorize into two categories is quite simpler compared to broader classification involving multiple classes. Less number of studies have been made on the use of multimodal classification dealing with real world news.

3 Proposed Methodology

3.1 Dataset Description

N24 News Dataset [15] is a dataset which the authors have extracted from New York Times using the API. This dataset has 24 categories of news (health, science, travel, dance, movies, etc.). Each data point is a combination of image and a text article. Link

3.2 Text Preprocessing

- Stemming
  Stemming plays a crucial role in linguistics by reducing a word to its base or root form, which is known as the lemma. This process involves the identification and removal of affixes from the word, enabling it to be mapped back to its essential linguistic root. Stemming proves to be valuable in various applications such as text analysis and information retrieval, as it simplifies words to their fundamental structures. By employing stemming techniques, researchers and practitioners can gain deeper insights and facilitate efficient language processing tasks. [3]
- Lemmatization
  Lemmatization is a methodical process that ensures tasks are performed correctly by utilizing morphological analysis. It involves removing inflectional endings and obtaining the base or dictionary form of words, known as the lemma. This approach enhances consistency and comprehension in text analysis [20].

3.3   Text Vectorization

– Count Vectorization

In count vectorization, unique words are extracted from all the available documents i.e. a vocabulary is created. Each doc is shown as a vector of size which is the same as the size of vocabulary where each dimension corresponds to a word/token in vocabulary, and the value at that index is equal to the number of occurrences of that word/token in that document.

For example, let us consider the following documents:

Doc1: hello friend

Doc2: my friend is a good person, his friend is my friend

Doc3: day is good

So, the vocabulary we have is: {hello:1, my:2, friend:3, is:4, a:5,good:6, person:7, his:8, day:9}

And the vector representations are:

Doc1=(1,0,1,0,0,0,0,0,0)

Doc2=(0,2,3,2,1,1,1,1,0)

Doc3=(0,0,0,1,0,1,0,0,1)

– TF-IDF Vectorization

TF is the ratio of a word(w)'s occurrence in the document to the total number of words in the doc(d) or we can say a measure of the repetition of a word (w) in a document (d). TF-IDE

$$TF(w,d) = \frac{occurrences\ of\ w\ in\ document\ d}{total\ times\ w\ in\ the\ doc\ d} \tag{1}$$

IDF (Inverse Document Frequency) serves as a metric for assessing the significance of a word. It assigns a weight to each word according to its frequency within the corpus, D. By employing IDF, the importance of a word can be determined, considering its distribution across the document collection. This weighting scheme proves valuable in various natural language processing tasks, aiding in the identification and prioritization of key terms within the corpus.

$$IDF(w,D) = ln(\frac{Total\ docs\ (N)\ in\ corpus\ D}{no.\ of\ docs\ containing\ w}) \tag{2}$$

The product of TF and IDF is called TF-IDF. More frequent words are given more importance while less frequent words are given less importance in this model. It is based on the BOW model.

$$TFIDF(w,d,D) = TF(w,d) * IDF(w,D) \tag{3}$$

– Word Embedding

It is a learned technique where the words having the same meaning have similar representations.It is created using a neural network with one input,one hidden and one output layer. It is basically done to boost generalization and performance of NLP models. It represents implicit relationships between training and word embeddings. Word Embeddings

3.4   CNN Models

- BACKGROUND OF CNN

Artificial neural networks are used in deep learning here. One of the most effective deep learning used models networks is the Convolutional Neural Network. CNN (Convolutional Neural Network) stands out for its superior accuracy in image classification compared to other algorithms. What sets CNN apart is its ability to automatically learn relevant features from the images, eliminating the need for manual feature extraction. This is achieved through multiple layers, including the convolutional layer. In this layer, a kernel moves across the image, employing a 2D matrix for representation. By performing element-wise multiplication with a specific region of the matrix, the convolutional layer captures and stores the resulting values in another matrix. This process enables CNN to effectively extract and utilize important visual information for accurate classification. [19]

Convolution consists of following mathematical formula, (the size of filter = $(2a + 1) \times (2b + 1)$)

The dimension of the output matrix can be calculated by an equation. We can see an equation below where:

O - Dimension of output, N - Dimension of input, F - Size of Window, S - Stride, P - Padding

$$O = [\frac{N - F + 2P}{S}] + 1 \qquad (4)$$

In Convolutional Neural Networks (CNNs), the pooling layer serves two key purposes: memory reduction and computational efficiency. Typically positioned adjacent to the convolutional layer, this layer plays a crucial role in downsampling feature maps. Among the various pooling techniques used in CNNs, Max pooling is widely adopted [19] (Fig. 1).

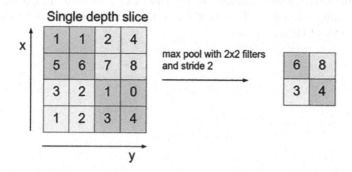

Fig. 1. Max pooling with 2 ×2 filter with stride 2

This method involves constructing a kernel and selecting the maximum value within each array. Subsequently, a fully connected layer takes the 2D or 3D array from the previous layer as input and transforms it into a 1D array.

The output layer of a CNN displays the probabilities associated with different classes. These probabilities are computed using the "SoftMax" function, which normalizes the outputs and represents the relative likelihood of each class. [18]

$$\sigma(X_i) = \frac{e^{X_i}}{\sum_j e^{X_j}} \tag{5}$$

- DATA PREPROCESSING
    - The dataset is split into training and testing datasets, with 80% for training and 20% for testing. Stratification is used to maintain proportional representation of both classes in both sets.
    - The document is encoded as a sequence of integers for the Keras Embedding layer. Each integer corresponds to a token and has a real-valued vector representation within the embedding. These vectors start as random values but become meaningful during training.
    - An instance of a class is constructed and trained on all the articles in the training dataset. This process builds a vocabulary of tokens and establishes a consistent mapping from words to unique integers.
    - To conceal the reviews in the training dataset, words are mapped to integers using the texts to sequences() function. To ensure uniform document length, all texts are padded to match the length of the longest review in the training dataset. The max() function is used to find the longest text, and the Keras pad sequences() function adds 0 values at the end for padding.
    - The vocabulary size, dimension of the real-valued vector space, and maximum length of input documents are specified for the Embedding layer. The vocabulary size is determined by the total number of words in the vocabulary, including an extra slot for unavailable words.
    - The word index attribute of the Tokenizer stores the mapping of words to unique integers. The vocabulary size can be computed by finding the length of this attribute.

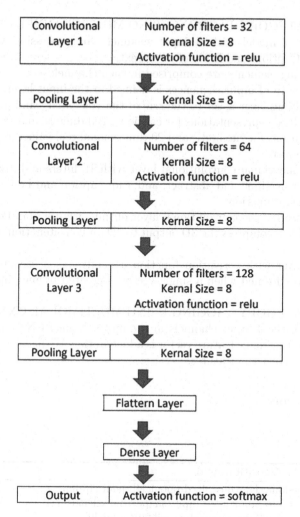

Fig. 2. Proposed Model

- NEWS CATEGORY TAGGING USING SINGLE-CHANNEL CNN
  Our model has 9 layers. We have used a 100-dimensional vector space. There are 3 convolutional layers after the embedding layer:
  • First layer has 32 filters, kernel size = 8 and 'relu' as activation function.
  • Second layer has 64 filters, kernel size = 8 and 'relu' as activation function.
  • Third layer has 128 filters, kernel size = 8 and 'relu' as activation function.

  In addition, we have used three max-pooling layers, each having a kernel size of two, each after every convolution layer. Then there is a flatten layer in the model. A dense layer is present in the end and has an activation function as 'relu'.'softmax' is used as the activation function in the final output (Fig. 2).

– NEWS CATEGORY TAGGING USING MULTICHANNEL CNN

We define a model with 4 input channels for processing the Headline, Abstract, Caption, and Body of news text.

The following elements are comprised in each channel:

- The length of input sequences is defined in the input layer.
- Embedding layer is set to the size of the vocabulary and 50-dimensional real-valued representations for captions, 100-dimensional real-valued representations for the body, and 20-dimensional real-valued representations for the rest.
- One-dimensional convolutional layer with 16 filters and a kernel size set to 8 for headline and abstract, and 4 for caption and body, having 'relu' activation function.
- To compress the convolutional layer output, we use Max Pooling layer.
- In order to compress the 3D output to 2D for concatenation, we use flatten layer.

A dense layer with activation function as 'softmax' is used to process the single vector formed when a single vector is created by merging all the four channels.

– NEWS CATEGORY TAGGING USING MULTIMODAL CNN

Apart from the 4 input channels in the multi-channel CNN, an extra input channel for the image feature vector is added in this. We have used the VGG19 model to extract the features.

3.5 Algorithm

Algorithm 1. Algorithm used
---
input_[4], embedding_[4], conv_[4], dropout_[4], pool_[4], flat_[4]

for $i = 0$ to $i = 3$**do** input_[i] ← Input(shape=(max_length[i],))

embedding_[i] ← Embedding(vocab_size[i],20)(input_[0])

conv_[i]   ←   Conv1D(filters   =   16,   kernel_size   =   8,   activation   = 'relu',padding='same')(embedding_[i])

dropout_[i] ← Dropout(0.5)(conv_[i])

pool_[i] ← MaxPooling1D(pool_size=2)(dropout_[i])

flat_[i] ← Flatten()(pool_[i])

3.6 Training the Models

Adam optimizer compiles all our models. 51k news articles with 3k per class and 17 classes are used in our dataset. We have divided the dataset as 80% training dataset for and 20% testing dataset. The networks are trained for 6 epochs.

– News Category Tagging using single-channel CNN

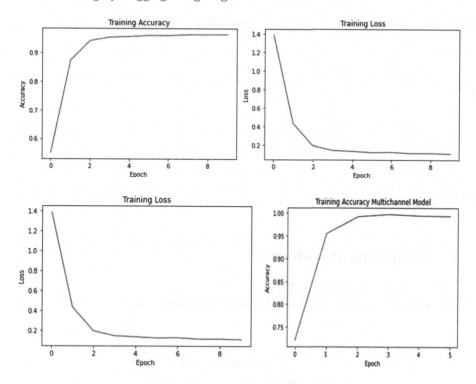

– News Category Tagging using Multichannel CNN

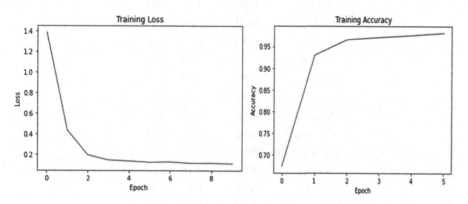

– News Category Tagging using Multimodal CNN

4   Comparing the Models

– Comparison on different Metrics
  • News Category Tagging using single-channel CNN

	precision	recall	f1-score
Art & Design	0.86	0.82	0.84
Books	0.82	0.78	0.8
Dance	0.83	0.97	0.89
Fashion	0.79	0.8	0.8
Food	0.89	0.84	0.86
Health	0.79	0.89	0.84
Media	0.82	0.84	0.83
Movies	0.55	0.76	0.63
Music	0.88	0.85	0.87
Opinion	0.82	0.82	0.82
Real Estate	0.91	0.91	0.91
Science	0.86	0.76	0.81
Sports	0.97	0.9	0.94
Technology	0.82	0.91	0.86
Television	0.88	0.7	0.78
Theater	0.94	0.74	0.83
Travel	0.84	0.81	0.83

- News Category Tagging using Multichannel CNN

	precision	recall	f1-score
Art & Design 0.8571	0.84	0.8485	
Books	0.7507 0	.8497	0.7972
Dance	0.9314	0.95	0.9406
Fashion	0.87	0.806	0.8368
Food	0.922 0	.8896	0.9055
Health	0.8336 0	.8698	0.8513
Media	0.7426	0.875	0.8034
Movies	0.7549 0	.8367	0.7937
Music	0.9202 0	.8267	0.8709
Opinion	0.81 0	.8028	0.8064
Real Estate	0.9186 0	.9247	0.9217
Science	0.8404	0.825	0.8326
Sports	0.9538	0.93	0.9418
Technology	0.8706	0.875	0.8728
Television	0.9061	0.773	0.8342
Theater	0.9186	0.86	5 0.891
Travel	0.8807 0	.8748	0.8777

- News Category Tagging using Multimodal CNN

	precision	recall	f1-score
Art & Design	0.8586	0.86	0.8593
Books	0.8148	0.8297	0.8222
Dance	0.8286	0.975	0.8959
Fashion	0.7174	0.8746	0.7882
Food	0.8764	0.9247	0.8999
Health	0.8664	0.8447	0.8555
Media	0.8783	0.7817	0.8272
Movies	0.7386	0.89	0.8073
Music	0.9641	0.76	0.85
Opinion	0.8361	0.8064	0.821
Real Estate	0.9089	0.9181	0.9135
Science	0.8222	0.84	0.831
Sports	0.8807	0.9717	0.9239
Technology	0.9225	0.7933	0.853
Television	0.9218	0.8063	0.8602
Theater	0.9367	0.765	0.8422
Travel	0.8574	0.8731	0.8652

– Comparison of accuracy, precision, recall and f1-score between different models

	Avg. Precision	Avg.Recall	Avg. f1-score	Accuracy
Single channel CNN	0.84	0.81	0.82	0.8130
Multichannel CNN	0.8638	0.8598	0.8605	0.8598
Multimodal CNN	0.8607	0.8539	0.8540	0.8539

5 Limitations

Due to memory constraints we couldn't load the image dataset into the memory as it was a very large size. So we had to take the help of feature extraction for reduction of dimensionality of image dataset so that it can be loaded into the memory. Due to this, the image channel couldn't be trained as robustly as it should be on our dataset. If we overcome this problem we can have a custom image channel instead of the pre-trained vgg19 model so that we can get better results in the multi-modal CNN model.

6 Future Work

The application of multi-modal architecture is not only limited to News Category tagging but also we can use it directly in social media and image sharing websites, as social media is full of posts containing texts as well as images, this model can be used to automatically classify posts of social media and image sharing sites [16] .

This model can be very useful in improving search and query results involving images and texts [17].

7 Conclusion

Natural Language Processing (NLP) and Deep Learning can be used to analyze the text and associated image of any given news item to apprehend what it is about, and enable appropriate tagging as a result. This article proposes a natural language integration method understanding of image classification to boost classification accuracy of news by using the associated metadata. Three different models were used for the purpose of classification which include single-channel CNN model, multichannel CNN model, and multimodal CNN model.The multi-channel CNN model's accuracy was higher than that of the single-channel CNN model' s accuracy by a significant margin, while it came out to be close to that of the multi-modal CNN model. The accuracy of the single-channel model, the multi-channel model and the multi-modal model was found to be 81.30%, 85.98% and 85.39% respectively. This improved accuracy can be used for better and more accurate news tagging. This could further be improved if the image dataset could be loaded into the memory without reduction in its dimensionality.

References

1. Simonyan, K., Zisserman, A.: Very deep convolutional networks for large-scale image recognition (2014). arXiv:1409.1556
2. Cer, D., et al.: Universal Sentence Encoder for English. In: Proceedings of the 2018 Conference on Empirical Methods in Natural Language Processing: System Demonstrations, pp. 169–174. Brussels, Belgium. Association for Computational Linguistics (2018)
3. Tai, K.S., Socher, R., Manning, C.D.: Improved semantic representations from tree-structured long short-term memory networks. In: Proceedings of the 53rd Annual Meeting of the Association for Computational Linguistics and the 7th International Joint Conference on Natural Language Processing (Volume 1: Long Papers), pp. 1556–1566. Beijing, China. Association for Computational Linguistics (2015)
4. Frome, A., et al.: DeViSE: a deep visual-semantic embedding model (2013)
5. Hochreiter, S., Schmidhuber, J.: Long short-term memory. Neural Comput. **9**(8), 1735–1780 (1997). https://doi.org/10.1162/neco.1997.9.8.1735
6. Ngiam, J., Khosla, A., Kim, M., Nam, J., Lee, H., Ng, A.: Multimodal deep learning. In: Proceedings of the 28th International Conference on Machine Learning, ICML 2011, pp. 689–696 (2011)
7. Soleymani, M., et al.: A survey of multimodal sentiment analysis. Image Vision Comput. (2017). https://doi.org/10.1016/j.imavis.2017.08.003
8. Sanabria, R., et al.: How2: a large-scale dataset for multimodal language understanding (2018). arXiv:1811.00347
9. Tzirakis, P., Trigeorgis, G., Nicolaou, M., Schuller, B., Zafeiriou, S.: End-to-end multimodal emotion recognition using deep neural networks. IEEE J. Select. Top. Sign. Process. (2017)
10. Yagcioglu, S., Erdem, A., Erdem, E., Ikizler-Cinbis, N.: RecipeQA: a challenge dataset for multimodal comprehension of cooking recipes. In: Proceedings of the 2018 Conference on Empirical Methods in Natural Language Processing, pp. 1358–1368. Brussels, Belgium. Association for Computational Linguistics (2018)
11. Zhang, C., Yang, Z., He, X., Deng, L.: Multimodal intelligence: representation learning, information fusion, and applications. IEEE J. Select. Top. Sign. Process. **14**(3), 478–493 (2020)
12. Nakamura, K., Levy, S., Wang, W.: r/Fakeddit: A New Multimodal Benchmark Dataset for Fine-grained Fake News Detection (2019)
13. Giachanou, A., Zhang, G., Rosso, P.: Multimodal fake news detection with textual, visual and semantic information. In: Sojka, P., Kopeček, I., Pala, K., Horák, A. (eds.) TSD 2020. LNCS (LNAI), vol. 12284, pp. 30–38. Springer, Cham (2020). https://doi.org/10.1007/978-3-030-58323-1_3
14. Wang, Y., et al.: EANN: event adversarial neural networks for multi-modal fake news detection. In: KDD 2018: Proceedings of the 24th ACM SIGKDD International Conference on Knowledge Discovery & Data Mining, pp. 849–857 (2018)
15. Wang, Z., Shan, X., Zhang, X., Yang, J.: N24News: A New Dataset for Multimodal News Classification. arXiv:2108.13327 (2021)
16. Miller, S.J., Howard, J., Adams, P., Schwan, M., Slater, R.: Multi-modal classification using images and text. SMU Data Sci. Revi. **3**(3), 6 (2020)
17. Gomez, R., Gomez, L., Gibert, J., Karatzas, D.: Self-Supervised Learning from Web Data for Multimodal Retrieval (2019)

18. Foysal, M.F.A., Islam, M.S., Karim, A., Neehal, N.: Shot-Net: a convolutional neural network for classifying different cricket shots. In: Santosh, K.C., Hegadi, R.S. (eds.) RTIP2R 2018. CCIS, vol. 1035, pp. 111–120. Springer, Singapore (2019). https://doi.org/10.1007/978-981-13-9181-1_10
19. Albawi, S., Mohammed, T.A., Al-Zawi, S.: Understanding of a convolutional neural network. Int. Conf. Eng. Technol. **2017**, 1–6 (2017). https://doi.org/10.1109/ICEngTechnol.2017.8308186
20. Kwak, N.: Introduction to Convolutional Neural Networks (CNNs) (2016)

Enhanced Heart Disease Classification Using Parallelization and Integrated Machine-Learning Techniques

Subham Panda[1], Rishik Gupta[2], Chandan Kumar[1], Rashi Mishra[1],
Saransh Gupta[1], Akash Bhardwaj[1], Pratiksh Kumar[1], Prakhar Shukla[1],
and Bagesh kumar[2(✉)]

[1] Indian Institute of Information Technology, Allahabad, Prayagraj, India
{iit2021144,iit2021209,iit2021240,iit2021163,iit2021019}@iiita.ac.in
[2] Manipal University Jaipur, Jaipur, India
rishik.209301615@muj.manipal.edu, bagesh.kumar@jaipur.manipal.edu

Abstract. The progressive application of machine learning in disease prediction within the realm of medical diagnosis is witnessing notable advancements. This remarkable evolution can be predominantly attributed to the substantial enhancements in disease identification and recognition systems, which furnish invaluable data facilitating the early detection of perilous ailments. Consequently, this pivotal development has yielded a momentous upsurge in the survival rates of patients. To augment disease prognosis, our study employs a diverse array of algorithms, each harnessing unique advantages, across three distinct disease databases sourced from the esteemed UCI repository. Complementing this methodology, we employ a meticulous feature selection process, leveraging backward modeling and rigorous statistical tests for each dataset. The empirical results derived from this study unequivocally reinforce the efficacy of machine learning in early disease detection. Notably, our system manifests the convergence of a support vector machine, KNN and an artificial neural network, both adeptly trained on comprehensive datasets replete with spectral information and meticulously engineered algorithms with parallel processing techniques to reduce training time for quick results Within the realm of data processing, the prediction of heart disease emerges as an intricate and riveting pursuit. The inherent scarcity of specialized medical professionals compounded by a disconcerting prevalence of erroneous diagnoses necessitates the development of an expeditious and efficient detection system. Intriguingly, prior systems have demonstrated the immense potential of amalgamating clinical decision support with computer-based patient records, thus engendering a tangible reduction in medical errors and concomitantly refining patient safety.

Keywords: Classification · Heart disease · Support vector machine · Disease prediction · UCI

H. Kaur et al. (Eds.): CVIP 2023, CCIS 2011, pp. 411–422, 2024.
https://doi.org/10.1007/978-3-031-58535-7_34

1   Introduction

The field of medical diagnosis has witnessed a revolutionary transformation with the progressive application of machine learning techniques. These powerful algorithms have demonstrated significant advancements in disease prediction, particularly in the realm of cardiovascular health. By leveraging the vast potential of machine learning, researchers and medical practitioners have been able to make great strides in the early identification and prognosis of heart disease, ultimately leading to improved patient outcomes and increased survival rates.

Heart disease stands as a major global health concern, responsible for a substantial number of deaths worldwide. The accurate and timely identification of heart disease is critical in effectively managing the condition and implementing appropriate treatment strategies. Traditional diagnostic approaches often face challenges in comprehensively assessing the complex interplay of various risk factors associated with heart disease. Furthermore, limited availability of specialized medical professionals and the occurrence of misdiagnosed cases further complicate the landscape of heart disease identification.

In light of these challenges, there is an urgent need to develop innovative and efficient systems that can facilitate the early detection of heart disease. Machine learning has emerged as a promising approach to address these complexities and enhance disease prognosis. By leveraging the advancements in disease identification and recognition systems, machine learning algorithms can analyze vast amounts of patient data, extracting valuable insights and patterns that aid in accurate disease prediction.

This research paper aims to delve into the potential of machine learning classification algorithms for the identification of heart disease. By harnessing the power of diverse machine learning algorithms, each offering unique advantages, we seek to enhance the accuracy and effectiveness of disease prognosis. The datasets used in this study are sourced from the esteemed UCI repository, renowned for its comprehensive and reliable collection of disease data.

In addition to utilizing various machine learning algorithms, we employ a meticulous feature selection process to identify the most informative and relevant features for accurate disease prediction. By leveraging backward modeling techniques and rigorous statistical tests, we ensure that the selected features provide meaningful insights into the complex nature of heart disease. This feature selection process enhances the efficiency of our disease prediction models and enables medical experts to make more informed decisions based on the identified risk factors [1].

Through the empirical results derived from this study, we aim to unequivocally reinforce the efficacy of machine learning in the early detection of heart disease. The findings of this research contribute to the growing body of knowledge on machine learning-based approaches for heart disease identification and prognosis. By providing valuable insights and tools, our research endeavors to empower medical professionals with enhanced capabilities to detect heart disease at its early stages, leading to improved patient outcomes and a higher overall survival rate for individuals affected by this pervasive health condition.

2   Problem Definition

Cardiovascular diseases, including heart disease, are a major global health concern, contributing to a significant number of deaths worldwide. The accurate and timely identification of heart disease is of paramount importance in improving patient outcomes and reducing mortality rates. However, traditional diagnostic approaches have limitations, often leading to delayed diagnoses and suboptimal treatment strategies [2].

One of the challenges in heart disease diagnosis is the complexity of the underlying factors and the interplay between various risk factors. Additionally, the shortage of specialized medical professionals and the prevalence of misdiagnosed cases further exacerbate the problem. To address these challenges, there is a pressing need to develop a rapid and efficient detection system that can leverage advanced technologies such as machine learning to improve the accuracy and timeliness of heart disease identification.

The objective of this research paper is to explore the potential of machine learning classification algorithms in the identification of heart disease. By harnessing the power of machine learning and leveraging the rich datasets available in the UCI repository, we aim to enhance disease prognosis and enable early detection of heart disease. Additionally, we seek to employ a meticulous feature selection process, utilizing backward modeling and rigorous statistical tests to identify the most relevant and informative features for accurate disease prediction [3].

By addressing these research objectives, we aim to contribute to the existing body of knowledge on machine learning-based approaches for heart disease identification. Ultimately, our goal is to provide valuable insights and tools that can assist medical professionals in making informed decisions, leading to improved patient outcomes and a higher overall survival rate for individuals affected by heart disease.

3   Literature Review

The identification and diagnosis of heart disease have long been critical challenges in the field of healthcare. With the emergence of machine learning techniques, particularly classification algorithms, significant advancements have been made in improving the accuracy and efficiency of heart disease detection. In this literature review, we focus on the utilization of K-Nearest Neighbors classification in the identification of heart disease.

KNN is a popular machine learning algorithm known for its simplicity and effectiveness in classification tasks. It belongs to the family of instance-based or lazy learning algorithms, as it makes predictions based on the similarity of instances in the feature space. Several studies have demonstrated the successful application of KNN in heart disease detection, leveraging its ability to capture complex relationships between input features and the target variable [4].

One notable study by S. Rajathi; G. Radhamani (2016) employed KNN for the identification of heart disease using a comprehensive dataset of patient records. Their findings revealed that KNN achieved a high accuracy rate in distinguishing between different heart disease categories. Furthermore, the study highlighted KNN's capability to handle noisy and incomplete data, making it a suitable choice for real-world clinical settings [5].

Another significant contribution by M. Akhil jabbar a, B.L. Deekshatulu (2013) focused on enhancing the performance of KNN in heart disease identification by incorporating feature selection techniques. By selecting relevant features and reducing dimensionality, their study demonstrated improved classification accuracy and reduced computational complexity. This highlights the importance of feature engineering and optimization in harnessing the full potential of KNN for heart disease detection [6].

While KNN has exhibited promising results in heart disease identification, it is important to consider the limitations and challenges associated with its application. KNN's performance heavily relies on the quality and representativeness of the training data. Adequate sample size, balanced class distribution, and careful feature selection are crucial to mitigate bias and enhance the reliability of the classification results. Additionally, the choice of distance metric and its impact on the KNN model's performance should be carefully considered based on the characteristics of the heart disease dataset [4].

In summary, KNN has demonstrated its efficacy in heart disease identification, offering simplicity, flexibility, and interpretability. Integration with data preprocessing techniques, ensemble learning, and interpretability methods has further improved its performance and understanding. However, ensuring the quality and representativeness of the training data, addressing the challenges associated with feature selection, and carefully selecting distance metrics are critical for harnessing the full potential of KNN in accurate heart disease detection. Future research should focus on addressing these challenges and exploring novel techniques to further enhance the capabilities of KNN for cardiac healthcare applications.

4   Problem Definition

Cardiovascular diseases, including heart disease, are a major global health concern, contributing to a significant number of deaths worldwide. The accurate and timely identification of heart disease is of paramount importance in improving patient outcomes and reducing mortality rates. However, traditional diagnostic approaches have limitations, often leading to delayed diagnoses and suboptimal treatment strategies [7].

One of the challenges in heart disease diagnosis is the complexity of the underlying factors and the interplay between various risk factors. Additionally, the shortage of specialized medical professionals and the prevalence of misdiagnosed cases further exacerbate the problem. To address these challenges, there is a pressing need to develop a rapid and efficient detection system that can leverage advanced technologies such as machine learning to improve the accuracy and timeliness of heart disease identification [8].

The objective of this research paper is to explore the potential of machine learning classification algorithms in the identification of heart disease. By harnessing the power of machine learning and leveraging the rich datasets available in the UCI repository, we aim to enhance disease prognosis and enable early detection of heart disease. Additionally, we seek to employ a meticulous feature selection process, utilizing backward modeling and rigorous statistical tests to identify the most relevant and informative features for accurate disease prediction.

By addressing these research objectives, we aim to contribute to the existing body of knowledge on machine learning-based approaches for heart disease identification. Ultimately, our goal is to provide valuable insights and tools that can assist medical professionals in making informed decisions, leading to improved patient outcomes and a higher overall survival rate for individuals affected by heart disease.

5 Proposed Methodology

The proposed methodology encompasses a comprehensive framework for the identification of heart disease utilizing advanced machine learning classification techniques. This section presents an elaborate and meticulously designed strategy that integrates multiple stages, including robust data preprocessing, sophisticated feature selection, astute algorithm selection, meticulous model training, and comprehensive performance evaluation [9].

5.1 Enriching Data Integrity and Cohesion

The proposed methodology for the identification of heart disease using machine learning classification unveils a comprehensive framework that harnesses the power of the K-Nearest Neighbours (KNN) algorithm, renowned for its simplicity, efficiency, and efficacy in handling classification tasks. With the objective of revolutionizing the field of cardiovascular disease diagnosis, this section delves into the intricate details of the proposed methodology, elucidating the core components, functionalities, and methodologies involved.

Data preprocessing assumes a pivotal role in fortifying the accuracy and coherence of the classification system. In this stage, a rigorous preprocessing pipeline is employed to address various data challenges, including missing values, outliers, and noise. Leveraging cutting-edge techniques, such as imputation, smoothing, and normalization, the proposed methodology strives to refine the raw dataset, ensuring its adherence to a standard format and optimal quality. Additionally, feature scaling methodologies, such as z-score normalization and robust scaling, are meticulously applied to mitigate the influence of disparate feature scales and enhance the effectiveness of subsequent analyses. Through these meticulous data preprocessing steps, the proposed methodology aims to cultivate a dataset that epitomizes integrity, reliability, and harmonization [10].

The proposed methodology commences its workflow by importing a wide range of essential libraries and modules, meticulously chosen to augment the system's processing capabilities and enable seamless data manipulation. These sophisticated tools encompass cutting-edge technologies such as pandas, numpy, matplotlib, and scikit-learn, which collectively empower the system with the prowess required for parallel processing, data exploration, feature engineering, and visualization. By leveraging these libraries, the system is equipped with an extensive arsenal of functions and methods that facilitate efficient data handling, statistical analysis, and machine learning model development.

5.2   Feature Selection

At the core of the proposed methodology lies the CustomKNN class, a meticulously designed entity imbued with an intricate set of methods engineered to unleash the system's predictive power. This subsection delves deep into the inner workings of the CustomKNN class, elaborating on its pivotal role in data preprocessing, feature extraction, model training, prediction, and evaluation. By encapsulating these crucial functionalities within a single class, the proposed methodology achieves modularity, extensibility, and code reusability, paving the way for seamless integration and experimentation. It extract the knowledge based on the samples Euclidean distance function d(x_i,x_j) and the majority of k-nearest neighbors [11].

$$d(x_{i,x_i}) = \sqrt{(x_{i,1} - x_{j,1})^2 + \ldots + (x_{i,m} - x_{j,m})^2}$$

Feature selection serves as a crucial facet in curtailing the dimensionality of the dataset while identifying the most influential and discriminative features. The proposed methodology orchestrates an exhaustive exploration of cutting-edge feature selection methodologies, encompassing both filter and wrapper approaches. Sophisticated techniques, including mutual information, Fisher score, and embedded feature selection algorithms, are deployed to excavate the intrinsic patterns and relevancy of each feature. By judiciously curating a subset of salient features, the proposed methodology endeavors to amplify the efficiency and interpretability of the ensuing classification model, empowering it to capture the essence of the underlying data characteristics.

5.3   Algorithm Selection

To overcome the challenges associated with handling large datasets and optimize computational efficiency, the proposed methodology integrates the splitlist function. This function leverages sophisticated algorithms to divide a given list into more manageable portions, thus facilitating streamlined data segmentation and enhancing parallel processing capabilities. By distributing the computational load across multiple subsets, the proposed methodology harnesses the power of parallel computing, enabling accelerated data processing and reducing the overall computational burden [12].

To ensure accurate measurement and tracking of the system's performance metrics, robust mechanisms for initialization and tracking are seamlessly integrated into the proposed methodology which serve as the cornerstone for tracking prediction accuracy, enabling comprehensive performance evaluation and facilitating insights into the system's efficacy (Fig. 1).

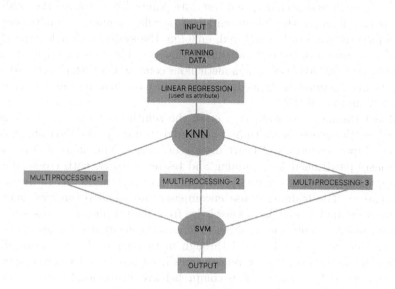

Fig. 1. Flowchart of Proposed Algorithm

The predict method, a pivotal component of the proposed methodology, unlocks the system's predictive capabilities by harnessing the intrinsic power of the KNN algorithm. This sophisticated method undertakes a complex set of operations, commencing with the calculation of the Euclidean distance between the input data point and each training data point. By leveraging proximity-based classification, the method identifies the k nearest neighbours, unravels the most prevalent class among them, and resolves any voting ties using advanced techniques such as linear Support Vector Machine (SVM) classification. This intricate process culminates in precise predictions, empowering the system to accurately classify and diagnose heart disease cases [13].

Algorithm selection entails meticulous deliberation to ascertain the most apt machine learning algorithm that aligns with the inherent intricacies of heart disease classification. A comprehensive evaluation is conducted, exploring an array of state-of-the-art algorithms, such as ensemble methods, support vector machines (SVM), deep learning architectures, and gradient boosting techniques. Each algorithm undergoes rigorous scrutiny based on a multitude of metrics, encompassing accuracy, precision, recall, and F1-score. The objective is to identify an algorithm that not only exhibits formidable predictive prowess but also accords with interpretability, scalability, and robustness in the context of heart disease classification [14].

5.4   Model Training and Evaluation

The proposed methodology's robustness and generalizability are meticulously evaluated using the comprehensive testing method integrated within the system. By leveraging inputs from both the test set and the training set, this method orchestrates a rigorous evaluation process, delving deep into the system's performance across diverse scenarios and test data points. To accelerate the prediction process and leverage the full potential of parallel computing, multiprocessing techniques are seamlessly employed, enabling the system to predict the classes of multiple subsets of the test data simultaneously. Through a meticulous analysis of the anticipated classes and a meticulous comparison with the ground truth, the system's accuracy is derived, offering invaluable insights into its reliability, precision, and recall [15].

Model training and evaluation mark the zenith of the proposed methodology, where the chosen algorithm is harnessed to unravel the intricate interplay between input features and heart disease outcomes. The annotated dataset is judiciously partitioned into training and testing subsets, with cross-validation techniques employed to ensure the reliability and generalizability of the model's performance. The training phase encompasses an iterative process where the classification model assimilates knowledge from the training data, discerning the intricate patterns and relationships that underlie heart disease instances. The model's efficacy is then assessed through meticulous evaluation using diverse metrics, including accuracy, precision, recall, F1-score, and receiver operating characteristic (ROC) curves. This comprehensive evaluation provides a holistic understanding of the model's predictive power, enabling a comprehensive assessment of its performance and real-world viability [16].

5.5   Algorithm

Algorithm 1. Pseudo code of Proposed Algorithm

---
input
for *group* = 1 *to all : data for allFeatures* ← *data[group] Euclidean_Distance* ← *append Distributions //append : [Euclidean dist, group, features]*
sort distributions ← *euclidean_distance*
k neighbors ← *nearest*
// find the most common class among neighbors
final prediction ← *linear_SVM classifier*
return result
for *frames* = 1 *to all*
(data ← *parallelize)* ← *multiprocessing*
//predictions, accuracy increment
return accuracy

5.6   Model Validation and Performance Optimization

To fortify the credibility and reliability of the proposed methodology, a rigorous validation process is undertaken using independent datasets or employing robust cross-validation strategies. This validation endeavors to affirm the generalizability and robustness of the classification model beyond the confines of the training dataset. Furthermore, if warranted, optimization techniques, including grid search, evolutionary algorithms, or Bayesian optimization, are employed to fine-tune the model's hyperparameters and optimize its performance. By leveraging the confluence of validation and optimization, the proposed methodology aims to propel the classification model towards the pinnacle of accuracy, ensuring its resilience and adaptability in diverse real-world scenarios [17].

The system's performance and generalizability are meticulously analyzed, scrutinizing its accuracy, precision, recall, F1-score, area under the receiver operating characteristic (ROC) curve, and other comprehensive metrics. Comparative analyses may be conducted to benchmark the proposed methodology against existing approaches, unveiling its strengths, limitations, and potential applications in clinical settings. The findings of this rigorous evaluation provide invaluable insights into the methodology's performance, reliability, and potential breakthroughs, paving the way for future advancements in heart disease identification using machine learning classification [18]. A critical component lies in the meticulous preprocessing of the input dataset, aimed at fortifying data integrity and ensuring consistency. The proposed methodology integrates cutting-edge techniques such as imputation, normalization, outlier handling, and feature scaling to address data imperfections and enhance the robustness of subsequent analyses. By replacing missing values, transforming skewed distributions, and eliminating noise, the proposed methodology achieves a refined dataset that serves as a solid foundation for accurate heart disease identification and classification [?].

6   Comparing the Models

In order to assess the effectiveness and suitability of different machine learning models for the detection of heart disease, we conducted a comprehensive comparative analysis. Various performance metrics were employed for evaluation, including accuracy, classification error, precision, F-measure, sensitivity, and specificity. The models considered for comparison encompassed Naive Bayes, Linear Model, Regression Model, SVM Model, and KNN Model (Fig. 2).

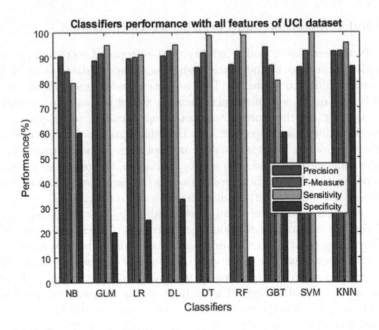

Fig. 2. Performance Comparison with Other Models

A meticulously curated dataset tailored for heart disease diagnosis served as the basis for training and testing these models. The results of our experiments, showcasing the performance of each model across the aforementioned metrics, are presented in the ensuing table. This comparative analysis provides valuable insights into the capabilities of each model for heart disease detection, empowering clinical decision-makers with informed choices [19] (Table 1).

Table 1. Accuracy improvement table of Proposed work

Models	Ace	CE	Pre	FM	SE	SP
Naive Bayes	75.8	24.2	90.5	84.5	79.8	60.0
Logistic Reg	82.9	17.1	89.6	90.2	91.1	25.0
Decision Tree	85	15	86	91.8	98.8	0.0
DeepLearning	87.4	12.6	90.7	92.6	95	33.3
Linear Model	85.1	14.9	88.8	91.6	94.9	20.0
RandomForest	86.1	13.9	87.1	92.4	98.8	10.0
SVM	86.1	13.9	86.1	92.5	98.8	100.0
KNN	90.25	9.75	85.2	93.7	98..8	99.6

– *Acc* : Accuracy of Model
– *CE* : Classification Error of Model
– *Pre* : Precision of Model

- FM : F-Measure of Model
- SE : Sensitivity of Model
- SP : Specificity of Model

7 Conclusion

In conclusion, the proposed methodology represents a pioneering advancement in the field of heart disease identification, leveraging the power of machine learning classification and the sophistication of the KNN algorithm. By seamlessly integrating various methodologies, algorithms, and techniques, the proposed methodology showcases remarkable potential in accurately diagnosing and classifying heart disease cases. The experimental evaluation reinforces the methodology's effectiveness, robustness, and reliability, igniting new possibilities for cardiovascular disease research and clinical practice. As the field of machine learning continues to evolve, future research endeavors can explore avenues such as ensemble techniques, hybrid models, explainable artificial intelligence, and deep learning architectures to further enhance the methodology's performance, interpretability, and applicability in real-world scenarios. Through such pioneering efforts, the proposed methodology sets the stage for groundbreaking advancements in heart disease identification, catalyzing the transformation of healthcare and fostering improved patient outcomes on a global scale.

References

1. Gjoreski, M., Simjanoska, M., Gradišek, A., Peterlin, A., Gams, M., Poglajen, G.: Chronic heart failure detection from heart sounds using a stack of machine-learning classifiers, pp. 14–19 (2017)
2. Li, J., Haq, A., Swati, S., Khan, J., If, A., Saboor, A.: Heart disease identification method using machine learning classification in e-healthcare. IEEE Access **8**, 107562–107582 (2020)
3. Ramaraj, M., Thanamani, A.S.: A comparative study of CN2 rule and SVM algorithm and prediction of heart disease datasets using clustering algorithms. Netw. Complex Syst. **3**, 1–7 (2014)
4. Mohan, S., Thirumalai, C.S., Srivastava, G.: Effective heart disease prediction using hybrid machine learning techniques. IEEE Access 1 (2019)
5. Ramalingam, V.V., Dandapath, A., Raja, M.: Heart disease prediction using machine learning techniques: a survey. Int. J. Eng. Technol. **7**, 684 (2018)
6. Patel, B., Sengupta, P.: Machine learning for predicting cardiac events: what does the future hold? Expert Rev. Cardiovasc. Ther. **18**, 02 (2020)
7. Olaniyi, E., Oyedotun, O., Khashman, A.: Heart diseases diagnosis using neural networks arbitration. Int. J. Intell. Syst. Appl. **7**, 75–82 (2015)
8. Dwivedi, A.: Performance evaluation of different machine learning techniques for prediction of heart disease. Neural Comput. Appl. (2018)
9. Yadav, S., Jadhav, S., Nagrale, S., Patil, N.: Application of machine learning for the detection of heart disease, pp. 165–172 (2020)

10. Nashif, S., Raihan, R., Islam, M.R., Imam, M.: Heart disease detection by using machine learning algorithms and a real-time cardiovascular health monitoring system. World J. Eng. Technol. **06**, 854–873 (2018)
11. Sinha, R., Aggarwal, Y., Das, B.: Backpropagation artificial neural network classifier to detect changes in heart sound due to mitral valve regurgitation. J. Med. Syst. **31**, 205–209 (2007). PMID: 17622023
12. Enriko, I.K., Suryanegara, M., Gunawan, D.: Heart disease prediction system using k-nearest neighbor algorithm with simplified patient's health parameters, vol. 8, pp. 59–65 (2016)
13. Ansarullah, S., Kumar, P.: A systematic literature review on cardiovascular disorder identification using knowledge mining and machine learning methods. Int. J. Recent Technol. Eng. **7**, 1009–1015 (2019)
14. Li, J.P., Haq, A.U., Din, S.U., Khan, J., Khan, A., Saboor, A.: Heart disease identification method using machine learning classification in e-healthcare. IEEE Access **8**, 107562–107582 (2020)
15. Shamrat, F.M.J.M., Raihan, M.A., Rahman, A.S., Mahmud, I., Akter, R.: An analysis on breast disease prediction using machine learning approaches (2020)
16. Mienye, D., Sun, Y., Wang, Z.: An improved ensemble learning approach for the prediction of heart disease risk. Inform. Med. Unlock. **20**, 100402 (2020)
17. Manur, M., Pani, A., Kumar, P.: A prediction technique for heart disease based on long short term memory recurrent neural network. Int. J. Intell. Eng. Syst. **13**, 31–39 (2020)
18. Yekkala, I., Dixit, S., Akhil, J.: Prediction of heart disease using ensemble learning and particle swarm optimization, pp. 691–698 (2017)
19. Shah, D., Patel, S., Bharti, D.: Heart disease prediction using machine learning techniques. SN Comput. Sci. **1**, 11 (2020)

Free Space Detection for Autonomous Vehicles in Indian Driving Scenarios

Haseeb Khan and Ram Prasad Padhy$^{(\boxtimes)}$ ⓘ

Indian Institute of Information Technology, Design and Manufacturing,
Kancheepuram, Chennai 600127, India
rampadhy@ieee.org

Abstract. This paper aims to address the problem of free space detection and safe path estimation for an autonomous vehicle by performing semantic segmentation on the road image data, captured from the front facing camera of a vehicle. The potential for accidents and economic losses can be significantly reduced by analyzing the road surface for obstacles and identifying safe directions for the vehicle to navigate. This involves the use of advanced algorithms for detecting and classifying objects on the image plane, and then determining the safest direction for the vehicle to proceed. The proposed work has significant implications for the development of autonomous driving technology, and its potential to revolutionize transportation by improving safety and reducing traffic congestion. This paper focuses on detecting free space for an autonomous vehicle by utilizing different state-of-the-art deep learning architectures, namely SegNet and UNet. The goal is to locate a path that is free of obstacles and can be used for safe autonomous navigation. The proposed method provides accurate and efficient detection of free road surfaces and obstacles, making it a valuable tool for autonomous driving technology. Moreover, this paper mainly focuses on complex driving scenarios of the Indian roads.

Keywords: Semantic Segmentation · Autonomous Vehicle · Free Space Detection · Path Estimation

1 Introduction

Semantic segmentation offers a wide range of applications, including autonomous navigation, scene interpretation, and inference of supporting relationships between objects [13,15]. Recently, popular machine learning algorithms have replaced the traditional techniques that relied on low-level visual signals. Due to the extremely complex environment in which the intelligent vehicles must operate, their perception tasks pose significant challenges (e.g. urban streets). In this

---

1. Grant Number SRG/2021/002399, funded by SERB - DST, Government of India.
2. Grant Number TiHAN-IITH/03/2022-23/180, funded by TiHAN - IIT Hyderabad, India.

context, camera sensors have become more important in the community as a result of the amazing developments in the computer vision sector [5,7,14]. The images represent a rich multi-dimensional signal that has to be processed using complex vision algorithms. The development of specific methods for recognition of traffic features, such as road surfaces, pedestrians, automobiles, or traffic signals was the primary focus of traditional vision-based technologies. However, recent developments in deep learning have made it possible to combine all of these classification issues into a single task, commonly known as semantic segmentation [2].

Fig. 1. Free space detection and finding safe direction on IDD dataset [17].

The goal of this work is to use semantic segmentation on the vehicle's front facing camera image data to find free space for it to operate safely on roads. After free space detection, the algorithm helps in finding the safe drivable direction for the vehicle. If a certain patch on the available road surface does not have any obstacle, then the free space is available. The goal is to predict whether or not an autonomous vehicle can move in that open region, and if so, determine the direction in which it can move safely without colliding with others on the road.

For our work, we have mainly focused on the Indian roads due to their complex nature of traffic. For Indian scenarios, the proposed algorithm is trained and tested on the India Driving Dataset (IDD) [17]. Figure 1 shows few example images from the IDD dataset, and the corresponding free space and safe path. We have also tested our algorithm on the real-world road images of our campus at the Indian Institute of Information Technology, Design and Manufacturing, Kancheepuram (IIITDM Kancheepuram, India).

2   Literature Survey

As discussed in the previous section, the proposed task is two-fold: (1) Semantic segmentation on the image data to find the road surface, (2) Finding the safe direction on the segmented data for the autonomous vehicle to navigate. Accordingly, the literature survey contains studies for both the sub-tasks.

2.1   Semantic Segmentation

Semantic segmentation algorithms associate a label or category with every pixel of an image. One such popular algorithm is SegNet [2], which is widely used by the computer vision community. It is an Encoder-decoder deep neural network architecture. The system is made up of an encoder network that extracts high-level features from the input image and a decoder network that upsamples these features to produce segmentation maps. SegNet has been successfully used by many semantic segmentation tasks in the past. The algorithm is effective in terms of computational complexity and accuracy.

Another famous deep architecture for semantic segmentation on images is UNet [1,8,12]. It is a convolutional neural network architecture that has now been used for several image segmentation tasks. A bottleneck layer connects the encoder and decoder blocks that make up the UNet. The decoder upsamples the feature maps back to their original size while decreasing the number of channels, while the encoder gradually decreases the spatial resolution of the input image. The bottleneck layer allows for accurate segmentation of the items of interest by capturing the image features in their most compacted form. UNet is often utilized in medical imaging applications including tumor identification, organ segmentation, and cell counting.

ERFNet [11] is another widely used network for image segmentation. This architecture's core layer employs factorized convolutions and residual connections to maintain efficiency while preserving remarkably accurate results. The architecture's primary component is a brand-new layer design that makes use of skip connections and convolutions with 1D kernels. It has two advantages, it enables the deeper layers to absorb more information (for better classification), and adds to the processing efficiency.

2.2   Safe Path Finding

This is the process of determining the safe path for the vehicle to operate on the road without colliding with other entities. One such algorithm is proposed by Pizzati et al. [10]. A three-step procedure is used by this method to tackle the issue: (1) Images are pre-processed to remove noise, (2) A Convolutional Neural Network (CNN) model is trained to distinguish between pixels from various lane borders, (3) Post-processing is performed on the CNN's output by extracting the convex hull for each of the two classes and clustering the detected points for each of them. Each cluster represents a lane's worth of drivable space.

Another algorithm for free space detection on roads using deep neural networks is proposed by Pazhayampallil *et al.* [9]. In this study, the network was trained to recognize open road surfaces in highway environments using a modified GoogLeNet architecture [16]. This architecture is used to localize free space on the image by running 1×1 convolution across the image feature activation volume.

Contrary to the above methods, our proposed method tries to first segment the road image to find the road surface, and then run the safe path finding algorithm on the output segmented images. As a major contribution of the work, the algorithm works on complex Indian roads, where the traffic is very congested most of the time.

3   Proposed Methodology

The proposed method first tries to perform binary semantic segmentation on the road image taken from the front facing camera of the vehicle. Then, it tries to find the safe drivable path for the vehicle using the road pixels on the segmented map. Both of theses sub-tasks are delineated in details in further subsections.

3.1   Encoder Decoder Model for Binary Segmentation

We are focusing only on binary segmentation as the algorithm needs only the road pixels to find the drivable free space. We have considered road as one class and all other entities, such as greenery, cars, bicycle, sky, buildings, humans *etc.* as another class. We have considered state-of-the-art encoder-decoder models, such as SegNet [2] and UNet [12] deep neural network architectures to perform the segmentation task. Both of these networks follow encoder-decoder strategy for performing segmentation. Encoder blocks generally use a series of convolution layers to down-sample the input feature maps, whereas the decoder blocks try to upsample the feature maps to the size of the target outputs.

Although SegNet was originally designed for a 12-class segmentation task, we have modified the last layer of the architecture to work for our binary segmentation problem. A 2-class softmax classifier is given to the final decoder output to create class probabilities for each pixel separately. Apart from that, the model architecture remains the same. The architecture is shown in Fig. 2.

In Fig. 3, the UNet network architecture is shown. There are two parts to it: an encoder and a decoder. The encoder component adheres to the standard convolutional network architecture. It is made up of applying 3×3 convolutions repeatedly. Each convolution is followed by a rectified linear unit (ReLU) and a down-sampling process using a 2×2 max pooling operation with stride 2. We quadruple the number of feature channels with each down-sampling step. Every step in the decoder part consists of up-sampling blocks, followed by two 3×3 convolutions, each followed by a ReLU, a concatenation layer, which is added with the corresponding convolution layer with cropped feature map from the encoder part, and a 2×2 convolution, also known as UpConvolution, which

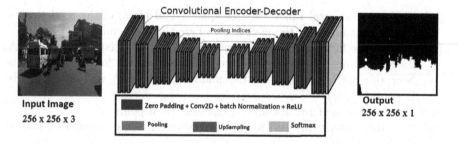

Fig. 2. SegNet based binary segmentation model [2]

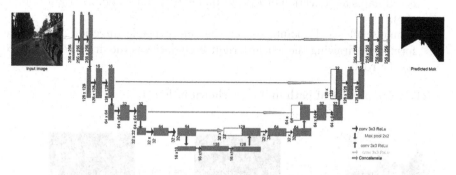

Fig. 3. UNet based binary segmentation model [12]

subtracts half of the number of feature maps at each step. Cropping is necessary because of the loss of boundary pixels in each convolution. Each component feature vector is transferred to the required number of classes in the final layer using a 1×1 convolution. In our problem statement, we have only 2 classes for segmentation. There are total of 23 convolutional layers in the network, including the encoder and decoder parts.

The output of the binary segmentation method is forwarded to the next step for safe direction estimation.

3.2 Finding the Safe Navigation Direction

The second part of the algorithm is to find the safe path for the vehicle from the available road surface. We have used a very simple, yet effective method to tackle this problem. The algorithm makes use of the binary segmentation map obtained using the first part of the proposed algorithm (Sect. 3.1). The segmented image contains two kinds (binary) of pixels: (1) road pixels having value of 1 or 255, and (2) all other pixels with a value of 0. The steps for safe path finding are described as follows:

(i) Take the predicted segmentation map of road segmentation model as input.
(ii) Start from the bottom left of the predicted segmentation map.

(iii) Find the first pixel where the free space (road pixel) of the road started, and in the same row, the next pixel where the road ends.

(iv) Assume the first pixel is P_1 as (x_1, y_1) and last pixel is P_2 as (x_2, y_1). As the row is same, hence the ordinate y_1 doesn't change for both the points.

(v) Now the path pixel will be the middle point of P_1 and P_2, given by $P = \left(\frac{x_1 + x_2}{2}, y_1\right)$.

(vi) Jump to the next row for finding the next path point.

(vii) Run above steps (iii)–(vi) for n times, where n is the number of rows in the image matrix.

(viii) Now we have path coordinates as collection of P points, and boundary coordinates as collection of P_1 (left boundary) and P_2 points (right boundary).

(ix) Connect all the P points to get the safe drivable direction. The space formed by drawing the left and right boundaries is the drivable free space on the road.

The enire process of path finding is shown in Fig. 4.

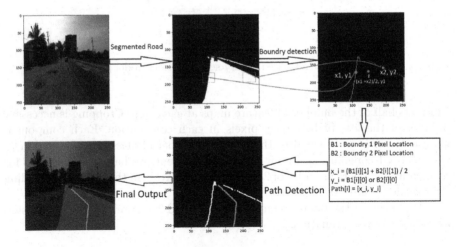

Fig. 4. Finding the Safe Navigation Direction

4 Experimental Results

4.1 Binary Segmentation

We used the KITTI [6], CamVid [3] and IDD [17] datasets for the task of segmentation. The datasets were individually trained with both the SegNet and UNet models. The input to the models is a color image with 3 channels (RGB), where as the output segmentation map is a binary image (black and white) with only one channel. The models were trained for 100 epochs with a batch size of 12. Initial learning rate is set to 0.001. Adam is used as the optimizer.

Dataset: Although we have used the KITTI, CamViD, IDD datasets to verify our segmentation algorithm, our aim was to emphasize on the Indian scenarios. Hence, for the task of path finding, we have used the IDD dataset only. The car that collected the IDD dataset, was driven around Hyderabad, Bangalore cities of India. The photos in the collection are taken from a front-facing camera mounted on the vehicle. Although the majority of the photographs have 1080p quality, there are also a few with 720p and lower resolutions. From 182 driving sequences on Indian highways, 10,004 images have been classified with 34 classes. Furthermore, it displays label distributions for road scenes that are substantially unlike those in the datasets that are already accessible [4], with most classes displaying higher within-class variation. Additionally, it finds categories that are compatible with actual driving patterns, such as drivable off-road sites.

Loss Function: Binary cross entropy (BCE) is used as the loss function to train the segmentation models.

$$L_{BCE} = -\frac{1}{N} \sum_{i=1}^{N} y_i \log(p_i) + (1 - y_i) \log(1 - p_i), \tag{1}$$

where y_i is the ground truth label for pixel i (either 0 or 1) and p_i is the predicted probability of pixel i belonging to the positive class (also between 0 and 1). N denotes the total number of pixels.

Accuracy Metrics: Root Mean Squared Error (RMSE) and Dice Coefficient (DiceCoef) are used as the accuracy metrics for the segmentation task.

$$RMSE = \sqrt{\frac{1}{n} \sum_{i=1}^{n} (y_i - \hat{y}_i)^2}, \tag{2}$$

$$DiceCoef = \frac{2 \sum_{i=1}^{n} y_i \hat{y}_i}{\sum_{i=1}^{n} y_i + \sum_{i=1}^{n} \hat{y}_i}, \tag{3}$$

where n is the number of samples, y_i is the binary ground truth label of the i-th sample, and $\hat{y}_i$ is the binary predicted label of the i-th sample.

Table 1 shows the accuracy metrics of both the SegNet and UNet models with different datasets.

4.2 Finding Safe Navigation Direction

Although we have used the KITTI, CamViD, and IDD datasets to verify our segmentation algorithm, our aim was to emphasize on the Indian scenarios. Hence, for the task of finding a safe navigation direction, we used the IDD dataset only. Once the segmentation maps are obtained, we used the method as described in Sect. 3.2 to obtain the safe navigation direction. We utilized UNet model segmentation map for the safe direction estimation, as the RMSE accuracy metric

Table 1. Accuracy metrics of SegNet [2] and UNet [12] models on the IDD, KITTI and CamVid datasets

Model	Dataset	RMSE	DiceCoef
SegNet	IDD	0.1824	0.9338
	KITTI	0.1532	0.6402
	CamVid	0.1590	0.9470
UNet	IDD	0.0771	0.8855
	KITTI	0.1146	0.9727
	CamVid	0.1467	0.9622

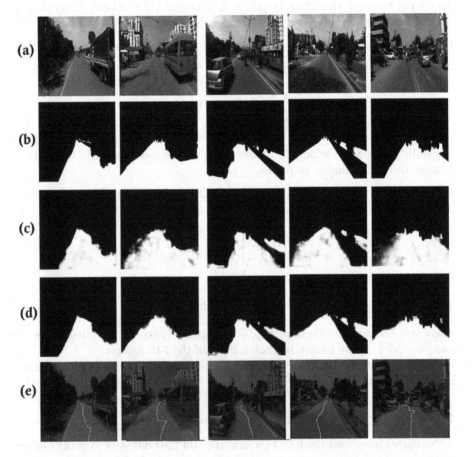

Fig. 5. Qualitative Output: (a) Input image, (b) Ground truth as road mask, (c) Predicted mask by the SegNet model [2], (d) Predicted mask by the UNet [12] model, (e) Final Output showing the free space and safe navigation direction (On UNet segmentation output).

Fig. 6. Qualitative Output in IIITDM Kancheepuram (India) Real-world Environment

for this model was better than the SegNet model for the IDD dataset. Also, the qualitative output of the UNet model is more distinct than the SegNet model near the road boundary pixels. This helps in finding accurate free space boundaries and the safe path estimation. The qualitative output of the segmentation models and the safe direction estimation on few of the samples of the IDD dataset (using UNet model segmentation map) are shown in the Fig. 5.

4.3   Experiment on Real-World Environment

We have collected the images and video data from our campus at the Indian Institute of Information Technology, Design and Manufacturing, Kancheepuram (IIITDM Kancheepuram, India) and tested the model. The results are shown in the Fig. 6. From the figure, it can be deduced that the model works well for real-world scenarios. It is able to segment the scenario to find the road pixels, and from there it can estimate the safe direction for navigation.

5   Conclusion and Future Work

This paper presented a method to detect free space on the Indian roads from the image data, and estimating a safe direction for an autonomous vehicle to navigate. State-of-the-art segmentation models, such as SegNet and UNet were utilized for binary segmentation of the road traffic images. Once the segmentation map is obtained, an effective method is used to find the safe direction for the vehicle using the segmented out road pixels. Segmentation model was trained on different datasets such as KITTI, CamVid and IDD, however the IDD dataset was given more emphasis for safe direction estimation on Indian roads. The segmentation model efficacy was verified, qualitatively as well as quantitatively. The safe direction estimation method accuracy was verified through qualitative results on IDD dataset as well as real-world environments.

Future research might look at domain adaption and transfer learning approaches to enhance the algorithm's generalization skills. In future work, we will try to estimate the road width to map pixel values. Also, depth estimation methods can be used to detect the distance from a particular object on the road. To allow the safe and effective operation of autonomous systems, future research can examine the integration of free space detection with decision-making algorithms, such as path planning and collision avoidance of autonomous vehicles.

Acknowledgments. The proposed work is partially supported by
1. Grant Number SRG/2021/002399, funded by SERB - DST, Government of India.
2. Grant Number TiHAN-IITH/03/2022-23/180, funded by TiHAN - IIT Hyderabad, India.

References

1. Abderrahim, N.Y.Q., Abderrahim, S., Rida, A.: Road segmentation using U-Net architecture. In: 2020 IEEE International Conference of Moroccan Geomatics (Morgeo), pp. 1–4. IEEE (2020)

2. Badrinarayanan, V., Kendall, A., Cipolla, R.: SegNet: a deep convolutional encoder-decoder architecture for image segmentation. IEEE Trans. Pattern Anal. Mach. Intell. **39**(12), 2481–2495 (2017)
3. Brostow, G.J., Fauqueur, J., Cipolla, R.: Semantic object classes in video: a high-definition ground truth database. Pattern Recogn. Lett. **30**(2), 88–97 (2008)
4. Cordts, M., et al.: The cityscapes dataset for semantic urban scene understanding. In: Proceedings of the IEEE Conference on Computer Vision and Pattern Recognition, pp. 3213–3223 (2016)
5. Farabet, C., Couprie, C., Najman, L., LeCun, Y.: Learning hierarchical features for scene labeling. IEEE Trans. Pattern Anal. Mach. Intell. **35**(8), 1915–1929 (2012)
6. Geiger, A., Lenz, P., Urtasun, R.: Are we ready for autonomous driving? The KITTI vision benchmark suite. In: 2012 IEEE Conference on Computer Vision and Pattern Recognition, pp. 3354–3361. IEEE (2012)
7. Höft, N., Schulz, H., Behnke, S.: Fast semantic segmentation of RGB-D scenes with GPU-accelerated deep neural networks. In: Lutz, C., Thielscher, M. (eds.) KI 2014. LNCS (LNAI), vol. 8736, pp. 80–85. Springer, Cham (2014). https://doi.org/10.1007/978-3-319-11206-0_9
8. Hou, Y., Liu, Z., Zhang, T., Li, Y.: C-UNet: complement UNet for remote sensing road extraction. Sensors **21**(6), 2153 (2021)
9. Pazhayampallil, J., et al.: Free space detection with deep nets for autonomous driving (2014)
10. Pizzati, F., García, F.: Enhanced free space detection in multiple lanes based on single CNN with scene identification. In: 2019 IEEE Intelligent Vehicles Symposium (IV), pp. 2536–2541. IEEE (2019)
11. Romera, E., Alvarez, J.M., Bergasa, L.M., Arroyo, R.: ERFNet: efficient residual factorized convnet for real-time semantic segmentation. IEEE Trans. Intell. Transp. Syst. **19**(1), 263–272 (2017)
12. Ronneberger, O., Fischer, P., Brox, T.: U-Net: Convolutional Networks for Biomedical Image Segmentation. In: Navab, N., Hornegger, J., Wells, W.M., Frangi, A.F. (eds.) MICCAI 2015, Part III. LNCS, vol. 9351, pp. 234–241. Springer, Cham (2015). https://doi.org/10.1007/978-3-319-24574-4_28
13. Simonyan, K., Zisserman, A.: Very deep convolutional networks for large-scale image recognition (2014). https://doi.org/10.48550/ARXIV.1409.1556. https://arxiv.org/abs/1409.1556
14. Socher, R., Lin, C.C., Manning, C., Ng, A.Y.: Parsing natural scenes and natural language with recursive neural networks. In: Proceedings of the 28th International Conference on Machine Learning (ICML-2011), pp. 129–136 (2011)
15. Szegedy, C., et al.: Going deeper with convolutions (2014). https://doi.org/10.48550/ARXIV.1409.4842. https://arxiv.org/abs/1409.4842
16. Szegedy, C., et al.: Going deeper with convolutions. In: Proceedings of the IEEE Conference on Computer Vision and Pattern Recognition, pp. 1–9 (2015)
17. Varma, G., Subramanian, A., Namboodiri, A., Chandraker, M., Jawahar, C.: IDD: a dataset for exploring problems of autonomous navigation in unconstrained environments. In: 2019 IEEE Winter Conference on Applications of Computer Vision (WACV), pp. 1743–1751. IEEE (2019)

EUWOD-16: An Extended Dataset for Underwater Object Detection

P. Vignesh[1]([⊠]) [iD], A. Shrihari[1] [iD], and Prithwijit Guha[1,2] [iD]

[1] Centre for Intelligent Cyber Physical Systems, Indian Institute of Technology
Guwahati, Guwahati, India
vignesh99ps@gmail.com, {a.shrihari,pguha}@iitg.ac.in
[2] Department of Electronics and Electrical Engineering, Indian Institute
of Technology Guwahati, Guwahati, Assam 781039, India

Abstract. Remotely Operated Vehicles (ROVs) along with vision based
underwater object detection techniques can assist underwater exploration and research by identifying specific objects, such as shipwrecks,
marine life, and man-made debris. These object detection algorithms
require large datasets for training. Since there are very few datasets
available for underwater objects, in this paper, an Extended Underwater Object Detection dataset with 16 object categories (EUWOD-16)
was constructed. This was achieved by building a new annotated dataset
consisting of divers, artifacts and various marine species, and merging
it with existing underwater object detection datasets by redefining their
annotations. Later, the dataset was evaluated by a modified YOLOv5n
architecture with GhostNet. This method involved the selective additions
of ghost blocks in appropriate places to decrease the number of network
parameters and FLOPs without a significant decrease in performance,
and a Bi-FPN connection for a refined feature fusion pathway. The proposed model achieved higher accuracy at a comparatively lower number
of parameters (and FLOPs) than both YOLOv5n and GhostNet.

Keywords: YOLOv5 · GhostNet · Bi-FPN · Divers · Artifacts

1 Introduction

The tasks of underwater exploration, marine ecosystem study, seafloor mapping,
historical wreck or artifact investigation, and underwater surveillance provide
crucial insights into marine biodiversity and help in understanding the impacts
of human activities on the oceans over time [1,15]. This would help in developing
effective strategies for preserving and conserving the oceans [7].

When it comes to object detection, the use of deep learning models is found
to be effective across multiple domains [21]. However, underwater object detection is challenging due to the factors such as low visibility, high noise, and color
deviation, which could make it difficult to identify and track objects [7]. Another
set of challenges includes the requirement of accurate and stable detection models that could operate under resource constraints in real time. This is because

H. Kaur et al. (Eds.): CVIP 2023, CCIS 2011, pp. 434–445, 2024.
https://doi.org/10.1007/978-3-031-58535-7_36

underwater environments often have limited computational resources and data transmission capabilities. In addition to the aforementioned factors, the diversity and comprehensiveness of datasets are also crucial in building robust object detection models. The ability of the model to accurately classify a wide range of objects in practical scenarios is largely dependent on the diversity and number of classes present in the dataset. The existing datasets for underwater object detection mostly consist of aquatic creatures such as fish, echinus, holothurians, starfish, and scallops.

In [3], a large-scale real-world underwater dataset (RUOD) was built containing 14,000 images of 10 categories. This included divers, corals, jellyfish, along with a few marine species, in diverse environmental challenges. They also compared the performances of the existing state-of-the-art object detection networks with their dataset. But these efforts have typically overlooked the identification of underwater artifacts such as statues, shipwrecks, and other objects of significance [11,17]. Also, lightweight and efficient object detectors are crucial for real-world underwater applications [19].

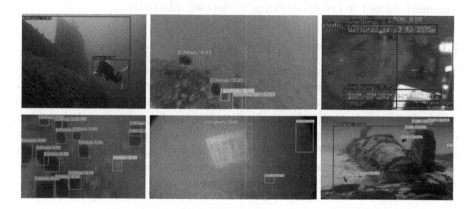

Fig. 1. Example detection results from YOLO-CSGB model

The contributions of this study, to address the above challenges, can be summarized as follows:

- A new dataset named UDAD is been proposed to include divers, underwater artifacts, fish, and other marine species. Also, several existing datasets such as DUO [13], UODD [9], Trash-ICRA19 [4] and the Brackish Dataset [16] have been merged with the proposed UDAD dataset to provide a diverse range of objects and underwater environments, forming a comprehensive dataset EUOD16.
- A modified YOLO-v5n (nano) model has been proposed. The proposed model, termed as YOLOv5-CSGB (Selective Ghosted Convolution with Bi-FPN), consists of GhostNet convolutions and Bi-FPN connection for creating more feature maps with less parameters and aggregating contextual information

from multiple levels of the feature pyramid, respectively. Quantitative analysis was performed and compared with the existing YOLOv5n and GhostNet models. The YOLOv5-CSGB achieves 4.1% increase in mAP@0.5–0.95 metrics in the EUOD16 dataset and 11.8%, 13%, and 7.9% increase in mAP@0.5–0.95 in the classes divers, artifact, and ROVs, respectively.

Figure 1 shows example results of the YOLOv5-CSGB model which is able to detect a variety of objects in the underwater scene, including divers, artifacts, fishes, and echinus even in challenging lighting conditions and cluttered backgrounds.

2   Dataset Preparation

Different underwater datasets with various classes of objects were combined. Their annotated labels were modified to provide common class names across the dataset, and new annotations for chosen categories of objects were added. Then, a new dataset of diver, artifact, ROV, fish and other-bio was added to the combined dataset to create an extended dataset, EUOD16.

2.1   Existing Datasets

The **DUO** (Detecting Underwater Objects) [13] dataset comprises 7782 images of four classes - holothurian, echinus, scallop, and starfish. These images were sourced from the URPC competition. On the other hand, **UODD** (Underwater Object Detection Dataset) [9] contains 3194 images of three classes - holothurian, echinus, and scallop, sourced from the RUIE image enhancement dataset. The DUO and UODD dataset pose challenges for object detection models due to small, cluttered objects such as holothurians, echinuses, scallops, and starfish, as well as varying lighting and greenish scenes.

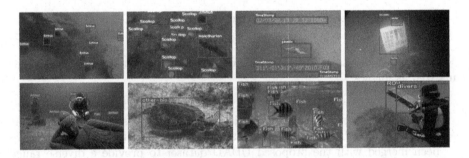

Fig. 2. Example images from the EUOD16 Dataset where the first row images belongs to existing Datasets and the last row images belong to UDAD Dataset

The **Trash-ICRA19** [4] Dataset was created from the J-EDI dataset of marine debris and contains 5,700 images labeled with bounding boxes on instances of trash, biological objects, and ROVs. The Trash-ICRA19 Dataset classifies trashes into plastic, metal, glass, and cloth, etc. However, objects other than plastic are comparatively fewer in number, and thus, they have been combined into a single category referred to as "non-plastic". Additionally, the biological objects present in the dataset, such as fish, crabs, and shrimp, which were named bio has been renamed to their respective categories to avoid inconsistencies with other datasets. The remaining categories of biological objects were placed in a separate category named "other bio".

Table 1. Distribution of Objects in the EUOD16 Dataset

Class	Train	Val	Test
Holothurian	9228	1569	1818
Echinus	44928	8932	9424
Scallop	2511	348	480
Starfish	16440	3306	2831
Crab	10205	1189	1343
Fish	17174	2819	2831
Jellyfish	528	56	62
Shrimp	547	76	85
Small_fish	8655	1148	965
other-bio	1109	51	188
non-plastic	12029	1491	1520
plastic	4580	854	938
ROV	1931	176	349
TimeStamp	12341	2335	2442
artifacts	666	103	96
divers	1305	207	168
Total	**125927**	**24190**	**25232**

The **Brackish** [16] dataset comprises 14,676 images of marine organisms such as fish, crabs, shrimp, jellyfish, and starfish, captured in Limfjorden, Denmark, 9m below the surface. The images are of poor quality with low visibility and small objects that are sometimes difficult to discern. Nonetheless, the dataset includes an extensive collection of bounding boxes that can be utilized for helping the object detector predict objects in the extensive noise in the background.

2.2 Extended Dataset for Underwater Object Detection(EUOD16)

A new dataset named **UDAD**(Underwater Divers and Artifacts Dataset) containing examples of artifacts and divers captured under different scenes and varying qualities is proposed. This dataset contains five distinct classes: ROV, artifact, diver, fish, and other-bio.

Table 2. Underwater Divers and Artifacts Dataset(UDAD)

Category	Occurrences
Diver	1689
Artifacts	867
Fish	18828
ROV	151
Other-bio	341
Total	**21776**

The dataset comprises a total of 2,697 images collected from three different sources: The first source is the UIEB [12], an image enhancement dataset, which consists of 890 images depicting various scenes with statues, shipwrecks, and divers. However, only 671 images were selected out of that dataset, and remaining images with many clustered fishes were ignored, since the focus is on divers and artifacts. The second source is the SUIM [6], an underwater segmentation dataset, which contains 1,525 train and 110 test images with segmentation labels. From this dataset, total 1,533 images were selected and over-crowded fish images were discarded. The third source is a YouTube video from the channel Guillaume Néry[1], from which 493 frames were generated and selected where a diver was thoroughly or appropriately present. All the selected images are annotated using labelImg[2] software, resulting in a total of 2,697 annotated images. The details of the UDAD dataset are shown in the Table 2.

The existing datasets were merged by refining the labels to form the combined dataset. Then the combined dataset is extended with the UDAD dataset to form EUOD16(Extended Underwater Object Detection) with 16 different classes. Figure 2 shows the example images from the EUOD16 Dataset. The distribution of the classes in the EUOD16 dataset is shown in Table 1.

3   Proposed Methodology

The proposed architecture uses YOLOv5n (nano), a lightweight deep learning model with 3.8 MB size and 0.45 ms detection speed [10]. The backbone of the YOLOv5 model is CSPDarknet-53, which is made up of repeating blocks of Cross Stage Partial Network (CSP) bottleneck, C3 layers and normal convolution layers. As shown in Fig. 5 the C3 module consists of CSP bottleneck with 3 convolution layers. The head of the YOLOv5 model consists of three convolution blocks for detecting small, medium and large-sized objects. Each of the blocks predicts the class probabilities, bounding box coordinates, and confidence score with the help of anchor boxes. The hidden layers in the YOLOv5 model use the SiLU [2] activation function to smoothen the gradient and to prevent the vanishing gradient problem. The SiLU activation function is defined as $SiLU(x) = x \cdot \sigma(x)$

---

[1] Guillaume Néry, https://www.youtube.com/watch?v=uQITWbAaDx0.

[2] labelImg, https://github.com/heartexlabs/labelImg.

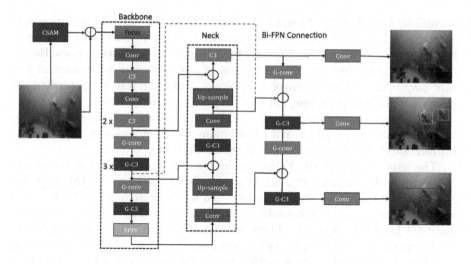

Fig. 3. Architecture of the proposed YOLOv5-CSGB

where $\sigma(x)$ is the sigmoid function applied on the input x. The loss function used is Focal Loss to focus more on hard examples by which class imbalance problems and background-foreground imbalance problems can be tackled. The focal loss function can be expressed as $FL(p_t) = -\alpha_t(1 - p_t)^\gamma \log(p_t)$ where α_t is the focal loss factor, p_t is model's estimated probability of the prediction and γ is tunable focusing parameter. The loss function used for bounding box prediction is Complete Intersection of Union(CIoU) [22] Loss. The CIOU loss function is defined as the difference between the Intersection of Union (IOU) of the predicted and ground truth bounding boxes and a regularization term that penalizes the difference between the aspect ratios and centre points of the bounding boxes R_{reg}.

$$CIOU = 1 - \frac{IOU - R_{reg}}{1 - IOU + R_{reg}} \tag{1}$$

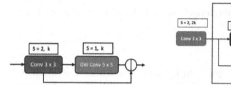

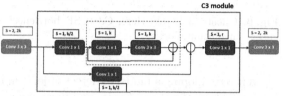

Fig. 4. Ghost Convolution Block

Fig. 5. C3 (CSP Bottleneck with 3 convolution layers) Block

GhostNet is a cost-effective alternative to traditional convolutional blocks, characterized by a reduction in both the number of weights and floating-point operations (FLOPs) [5]. Figure 4 and Fig. 6 show the ghost convolution and ghost-C3 blocks, respectively. It has been demonstrated that traditional convolutions generate a significant amount of redundancy in the feature maps. Hence, this method advocates for the generation of only a certain percentage of feature maps via traditional convolution blocks, while the rest are generated via inexpensive linear operations, aided by Depthwise convolutions.

The proposed architecture uses Ghost Convolutions and Ghost-C3 blocks. Instead of converting all normal convolutions to Ghost modules, only specific convolutions were converted, called *Selective Ghosting*.

The nano version of the YOLO model uses 32 filters in shallow layers and 256 filters in deep layers (32–256), which can be increased to 40–320 or 48–384 filters while keeping the size and computation within reasonable limits. It can be achieved by replacing the convolution and C3 blocks with ghost convolutions and ghost-C3 blocks, respectively. These modifications also reduces redundancy in the feature map [5]. However, when experimented with 40–320 filters, increasing the ghost modules did not provide the expected improvement, and 48–384 filters modification gave sufficient improvement but increased the size and computation significantly. It was found that just adding more filters using ghost convolutions did not significantly improve performance in the noisy underwater images.

To address these issues, *selective ghosting* was employed. Selective ghosting involves keeping normal convolution blocks in the crucial parts of the model and replacing the convolution blocks in the less crucial parts with ghost convolution blocks. This allowed the model to capture more features from the images without increasing the size or computation of the model.

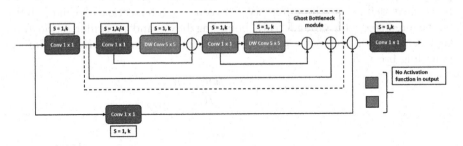

Fig. 6. Ghost-C3 Block. Here, C3 (CSP bottleneck layers) have been replaced with ghost convolution blocks.

When developing a model to detect objects in underwater images, it is important to address the issue of noise and fuzziness in the images [8]. To address this issue, it is better to build to a strong shallow part of the backbone network that has a large receptive field. This allows the network to get a global view of the input features and produce output features of good quality. Additionally, since the number of channels are less on the initial layers of the backbone, it carries less weight than the deeper layers, so they can be kept as normal convolution blocks without converting them to ghost blocks. This means that the first two normal convolutions and the first two C3 blocks can be kept without change, while the remaining blocks can be replaced by ghost blocks. This selective ghosting technique allows the number of filters to be increased without increasing the parameters in the backbone, resulting in more channels that can capture more features. The reliable convolution blocks from the shallow layers would provide less-noisy and dependable features of better quality, which can be combined and refined in the deeper ghost layers to form more complex and abstract representations of the input which could help in handling overfitting.

Similarly, the first two convolution blocks and an C3 block are retained in the neck part of the model before the small-scale detection head. This is because the EUOD16 dataset has numerous small objects merged with the background seabed, such as scallops. This change in the neck architecture benefits and helps in not only the detection of small objects but also large and medium-scale objects since the output of these blocks is combined with blocks corresponding to medium and large objects of the neck using the PANet [14] architecture.

Channel Sharpening Attention Module (CSAM) [9] is a channel-wise attention mechanism introduced to enhance the expressiveness of the YOLOv5 model in object detection tasks, particularly in challenging underwater environments where stacking, blurring, and unclear edges can occur between objects due to the opacity of the water and shooting angles. The CSAM module incorporates a sharpening convolution operation based on the Laplace Operator to improve edge information and enhance the contrast of underwater objects. The sharpening convolution operation enhances the discrimination of underwater objects from the surrounding environment, thereby improving the accuracy of object detection.

Bidirectional Feature Pyramid Network (Bi-FPN) [18] is a feature fusion method that combines multi-scale features from different levels of the backbone and neck of the model. BiFPN enhances the detection of objects at various scales by allowing the features to flow both up and down through the network. In the YOLOv5 model, the features from the backbone are fused with the neck section of the model which will results in better detection of the objects in multiple scales.

So, the proposed model YOLOv5-CSGB uses selective ghosting to get higher number of feature without increasing model size and uses BiFPN for improving multi-scale detection capability and CSAM to improve the sharpness of the images at the input.

4   Experiments

The proposed model, YOLOv5-CSGB, is compared with other modified YOLOv5 models, such as YOLOv5-GhostNet-BiFPN(YOLOv5-GB) and YOLOv5-Ghost Net-Neck(YOLOv5-GN) (also mentioned as YOLOv5-Ghostnet-Head) [20] models with different width multiples by training on the EUOD16 dataset and testing on both EUOD16 and UDAD datasets.

Table 3. Comparison of the other equivalent models with the proposed model

Model	BiFPN	Width multiple	Parameter	GFLOPs	mAP@E[1]	mAP@U[2]
YOLOv5n	✗	0.25	1.78 M	4.2	0.866	0.54
YOLOv5-GB	✓	0.3125	1.51 M	3.7	0.868	0.541
YOLOv5-GB	✓	0.375	2.16 M	5.1	0.873	0.576
YOLOv5-GN	✗	0.25	1.44 M	3.6	0.867	0.542
YOLOv5-GN	✗	0.3125	2.23 M	5.6	0.879	**0.598**
MobileNet-YOLO	✗	0.3125	1.84 M	4.3	0.615	0.215
YOLOv5-CSGB	✓	0.3125	1.6 M	4.9	**0.882**	0.583

[1] mAP@E - mAP @ IOU = 0.5 for the EUOD16 dataset
[2] mAP@U - mAP @ IOU = 0.5 for the UDAD dataset

4.1   Experimental Setup

The system used for the conducted experiments has linux operating System with NVIDIA Tesla V100 32 GB memory with CUDA 10.2. The programming language and framework used are python 3.9 and pytorch 1.8.0 respectively. All the models during the experiments were trained with batch size 8 and the learning rate starting at 0.01 for 200 epochs with SGD Optimizer. The dataset and the code are available at GitHub[3].

Fig. 7. Qualitative results of YOLOv5n vs YOLOv5-GB(0.375) vs YOLOv5-GN(0.3125) vs YOLOv5-CSGB

The evaluation metric used in the experiment is mAP @ IOU = 0.5. The mAP(mean Average Precision) @ IOU = 0.5 is a widely used metric in object detection. It measures the average precision of predicted bounding boxes with

---

[3] https://github.com/Vignesh048/EUOD16-An-Extended-Dataset-for-Underwater-Object-Detection/.

an IOU threshold of 0.5 or higher. The procedure involves calculating the area under the curve for precision and recall values obtained by varying the confidence score threshold.

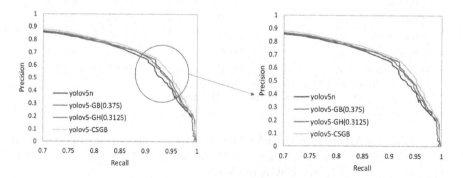

Fig. 8. Precision-Recall Curve @ IOU = 0.5 for YOLOv5n vs YOLOv5-GB(0.375) vs YOLOv5-GN(0.3125) vs YOLOv5-CSGB

4.2 Results and Discussion

From Table 3 it can be concluded that the YOLOv5-CSGB outperforms all the models except the YOLOv5-GN(w = 0.3125) where the proposed model performs equally but with 28% fewer parameters and 14% less FLOPs. The proposed model YOLOv5-CSGB scored 1.5% and 10% more compared to YOLOv5n on the EUOD16 dataset and the UDAD dataset, respectively. It can be concluded that, by comparing YOLOv5-CSGB and YOLOv5-GB that instead of adding more filters, the selective ghosting gives better performance with fewer filters, fewer parameters, and fewer FLOPs and By comparing YOLOv5-CSGB and YOLOv5-GN instead of entirely leaving the backbone with normal convolution and only ghosting in the neck, which results in a drastic increase in parameters and FLOPs, selective ghosting can fetch the same performance with fewer parameters.

Figure 7 and Fig. 8 show the qualitative results and Precision recall curve comparisons respectively on YOLOv5n, YOLOv5-GB(0.375), YOLOv5-GN(0.3125) and YOLOv5-CSGB.

4.3 Ablation Study

Selective ghosting technique was used to obtain the YOLOv5n-SG model, which is 10% lighter with 25% more number of filters in each block. This model was trained on the EUOD16 dataset and evaluated using mAP@0.5, yielding 1.2% and 7.14% improvements on the EUOD16 and UDAD datasets, respectively, when compared to YOLOv5n. Next, the effectiveness of the BiFPN feature fusion technique was assessed by integrating it into YOLOv5n, resulting in YOLOv5n-B. The evaluation of YOLOv5n-B on the dataset showed an increase of 0.5%

Table 4. Ablation study

Model	Selective Ghosting	Bi-FPN	Parameters	GFLOPs	mAP@E[1]	mAP@U[2]
YOLOv5n			1.78 M	4.2	0.866	0.54
YOLOv5n-B		✓	1.8 M	4.3	0.871	0.553
YOLOv5-SG	✓		1.58M	4.8	0.876	0.577
YOLO-v5-SGB	✓		1.6M	4.9	0.874	0.563
YOLO-v5-CSGB	✓	✓	1.6 M	4.9	0.882	0.583

[1] mAP@E - mAP @ IOU = 0.5 for the EUOD16 dataset
[2] mAP@U - mAP @ IOU = 0.5 for the UDAD dataset

and 1.35% in mAP@0.5 for the EUOD16 and UDAD datasets, respectively. In the ablation study, CLAHE enhancement has been used for the YOLOv5n-B, YOLOv5-SG and YOLOv5-CSGB models.

Finally, the proposed YOLOv5-CSGB model is evaluated on the datasets. The results indicated that the addition of BiFPN in YOLOv5-SG leads to nearly three times the accuracy improvement observed when BiFPN was combined with YOLOv5n. The Table 4 shows the ablation study results.

5 Conclusion

The contributions of the work include creating a new dataset that includes divers, artifacts, and marine species and curating a diverse range of existing datasets, by standardizing labels, and adding new labels to them to form a extended dataset EUOD16, which helped in creating the robust object detector capable of identifying a wide range of objects in different underwater settings. And, the YOLO-v5n model was modified to get improved performance with less complexity by selectively ghosting convolutions and introducing a refined feature fusion pathway. The YOLOv5-CSGB achieved a 4.1% increase in mAP@0.5-0.95 metrics, compared to YOLOv5n, and outperformed the YOLOv5-GhostNet-Bi-FPN (YOLOv5-GB) models on both the EUOD16 dataset and the UDAD dataset, being 35% lighter and 4% faster than YOLOv5-GB(w-0.375) and performing as equal as YOLOv5-GN(w-0.3125) but having 28% less parameters and 14% less FLOPs.

References

1. Barrett, N.S., Buxton, C.D.: Examining underwater visual census techniques for the assessment of population structure and biodiversity in temperate coastal marine protected areas (2002)
2. Elfwing, S., Uchibe, E., Doya, K.: Sigmoid-weighted linear units for neural network function approximation in reinforcement learning (2017)
3. Fu, C., et al.: Rethinking general underwater object detection: datasets, challenges, and solutions. Neurocomputing **517**, 243–256 (2023)

4. Fulton, M.S., Hong, J., Sattar, J.: Trash-ICRA19: a bounding box labeled dataset of underwater trash (2020)
5. Han, K., Wang, Y., Tian, Q., Guo, J., Xu, C., Xu, C.: Ghostnet: more features from cheap operations. CoRR **abs/1911.11907** (2019)
6. Islam, M.J., et al.: Semantic segmentation of underwater imagery: Dataset and benchmark. CoRR **abs/2004.01241** (2020)
7. Jesus, A., Zito, C., Tortorici, C., Roura, E., De Masi, G.: Underwater object classification and detection: first results and open challenges. OCEANS 2022-Chennai, pp. 1–6 (2022)
8. Jian, M., Liu, X., Luo, H., Lu, X., Yu, H., Dong, J.: Underwater image processing and analysis: a review. Signal Process. Image Commun. **91**, 116088 (2021)
9. Jiang, L., et al.: Underwater species detection using channel sharpening attention. In: Proceedings of the 29th ACM International Conference on Multimedia, pp. 4259–4267 (2021)
10. Jocher, G., et al.: ultralytics/YOLOv5: v7.0 - YOLOv5 SOTA Realtime Instance Segmentation, November 2022
11. Lazar, I., Ghilezan, A., Hnatiuc, M.: Development of tools and techniques for monitoring underwater artifacts. In: Advanced Topics in Optoelectronics, Microelectronics, and Nanotechnologies VIII, vol. 10010, pp. 244–249. SPIE (2016)
12. Li, C., et al.: An underwater image enhancement benchmark dataset and beyond. IEEE Trans. Image Process. **29**, 4376–4389 (2019)
13. Liu, C., et al.: A dataset and benchmark of underwater object detection for robot picking. In: 2021 IEEE International Conference on Multimedia & Expo Workshops (ICMEW), pp. 1–6. IEEE (2021)
14. Liu, S., Qi, L., Qin, H., Shi, J., Jia, J.: Path aggregation network for instance segmentation. In: Proceedings of the IEEE Conference on Computer Vision and Pattern Recognition, pp. 8759–8768 (2018)
15. Molina Molina, J., Salhaoui, M., González, A., Arioua, M.: Autonomous marine robot based on AI recognition for permanent surveillance in marine protected areas. Sensors **21**, 2664 (2021)
16. Pedersen, M., Bruslund Haurum, J., Gade, R., Moeslund, T.B.: Detection of marine animals in a new underwater dataset with varying visibility. In: Proceedings of the IEEE/CVF Conference on Computer Vision and Pattern Recognition Workshops, pp. 18–26 (2019)
17. Soreide, F., Jasinski, M.: Ormen lange: investigation and excavation of a shipwreck in 170 m depth. In: Proceedings of OCEANS 2005 MTS/IEEE, pp. 2334–2338 Vol. 3 (2005)
18. Tan, M., Pang, R., Le, Q.V.: Efficientdet: scalable and efficient object detection. In: Proceedings of the IEEE/CVF Conference on Computer Vision and Pattern Recognition, pp. 10781–10790 (2020)
19. Xu, S., Zhang, M., Song, W., Mei, H., He, Q., Liotta, A.: A systematic review and analysis of deep learning-based underwater object detection. Neurocomputing (2023)
20. Zhang, Y., Cai, W., Fan, S., Song, R., Jin, J.: Object detection based on yolov5 and ghostnet for orchard pests. Information **13**(11) (2022)
21. Zhao, Z.Q., Zheng, P., Xu, S.T., Wu, X.: Object detection with deep learning: a review. IEEE Trans. Neural Netw. Learn. Syst. **30**(11), 3212–3232 (2019)
22. Zheng, Z., Wang, P., Liu, W., Li, J., Ye, R., Ren, D.: Distance-iou loss: faster and better learning for bounding box regression (2019)

Low-Light Image Enhancement Using Zero-DCE and DCP

Kumar Rajnish[✉] and Tushar Sandhan

Department of Electrical Engineering, Indian Institute of Technology Kanpur,
Kanpur 208016, India
{krajnish,sandhan}@iitk.ac.in

Abstract. In this paper, a new low-light enhancement technique is proposed to enhance the performance of images. This technique is obtained by fusing zero-reference deep curve estimation (Zero-DCE) and dark channel prior (DCP). We calculate image-specific parameter curves using convolutional neural networks (CNNs), which enhance the low-light image pixel-wise. The proposed method follows a spatial attention mechanism to emphasize appropriate regions. This method is simple and effective for low-light enhancement. Further, the performance of the proposed method is validated and compared in terms of peak signal to noise ratio (PSNR), structural index similarity (SSIM) and run time (RT) with other existing methods. The qualitative and quantitative results show the superior performance of the proposed method compared to other existing methods.

Keywords: Convolutional Neural Network CNN · Dark Channel Prior DCP · low-light image enhancement curve · Zero-DCE

1 Introduction

The development of digital media, such as videos, animations, mobile apps, and television, has accelerated in recent years. These technologies rely significantly on images, which play a vital role in the delivery of visual experiences. However, obtaining images in low-light conditions presents significant difficulties, resulting in diminished perceptual visibility, compromised aesthetics, and loss of informational detail. Insufficient lighting, underexposure during image capture, objects situated against backlighting, and unbalanced lighting conditions can also cause noise in low-light images. The presence of disturbance in these images further exacerbates their flaws. Low-light images have an impact beyond the domain of visual media. They have a significant impact on the accuracy of computer vision algorithms, as inadequate illumination reduces the visibility of image contents. Consequently, tasks related to computer vision, such as identifying objects in images, recognition, image classification, and segmentation, struggle to produce accurate and dependable results. These duties are hindered by the limited information contained in low-light images. In this research paper, we utilized

© The Author(s), under exclusive license to Springer Nature Switzerland AG 2024
H. Kaur et al. (Eds.): CVIP 2023, CCIS 2011, pp. 446–457, 2024.
https://doi.org/10.1007/978-3-031-58535-7_37

the Zero-DCE model as a foundation and extended its capabilities by introducing the Dark Channel Prior (DCP) technique. By incorporating DCP into the model, we introduced spatial attention, which significantly improve the overall performance of the image enhancement process.

Low-Light Image   Enhanced Image

Fig. 1. Visual comparisons of a low-light image and enhanced image obtained through Zero-DCE

2 Related Work

Since decades researchers have been invented many techniques and methods to enhance the low-light effected images for handling the performance of the computer visions task. In general, these image enhancement models are classified as histogram-based approach, fusion-based approach, Retinex-based approach, Defogging-based approach, and data-driven-based approach. The histogram equali- zation (HE) based method is used for image enhancement, it was widely used technique for improving image contrast it was first developed by Jain [1]. It enhances contrast but is less successful when the contrast characteristics vary across the image. This problem is fixed by adaptive HE (AHE) [2,3], which generates the mapping for each pixel from the histogram in the adjacent window. The drawback of AHE is that, the amount of contrast enhancement cannot be controlled [4]. A partially overlapped sub-block histogram-equalization (POSHE) technique was introduced by Kim, et al. [5] to address the shortcomings of the AHE method. This technique can produce a similar contrast enhancement effect while significantly reducing computational complexity and removing blocking effects. However, this method often results in an over-enhancement effect, which amplifies noise in some areas. Contrast-limited adaptive histogram equalisa- tion (CLAHE) [6,7] was proposed to mitigate the blocking effects and noise amplification by breaking the image into numerous non-overlapping sub-blocks, then enhancing each sub-block separately.

Later, various image enhancement models have been developed based on the Retinex theory [8]. According to this, an image is built from the reflectance and illumination part, out of these parts, the reflectance part is considered as consistent in any lighting situation. So, the image enhancement method gets reduced to illumination enhancement problems. Diverse methods have been developed to separate the illumination part from the image. However, these algorithms use a Gaussian convolution template for illumination estimation and do not have the ability to preserve the edges.

Further, Kaiming et al. [9] proposed the dark channel concept to defog images, later gain popularity and became widely accepted technique in image enhancement. Dong et al. [10] suggested a low-light enhancement algorithm based on defogging theory, commonly known as a bright channel prior approach [11]. The fundamen- tal premise of this method is that when an RGB photograph taken in a dark environment is inverted, the resulting visual impression resembles an image captured during daylight in a foggy setting. So, similar to defogging using dark channel prior algorithm the inverted low-light image can be processed and then converted back to generate enhanced image.

In recent years the data-driven approach has become very popular to use because of its excellent performance on the image enhancement task. The deep learning model is core of these data-driven methods. various deep learning models have been proposed to enhance the low-light images. Most CNN-based approaches rely on paired training data. Several models for CNN-based image enhancement have been put forth lately [12–15]. EnlightenGAN [16] is an unsupervised GAN-based approach that learns to improve low-light photos utilizing unpaired low/normal light data. Yang et al. [17] suggested a two-stage semi-supervised low-light picture enhancement model by combining both CNN and GAN methods. In stage one, paired data is used to infer band signals from a coarse-to-fine band representation. In stage two semi-supervised learning can increase deep model generalization, but it risks overfitting on paired training data and has a high memory footprint.

In this study, we used the famous LOL dataset consisting of 500 image pairs, where one image in each pair represents a low-light photograph and the other image represents a normal-light photograph. The low-light photographs were captured under different exposure times and ISO settings while keeping other camera settings constant. The image pairs were taken from real scenes for low-light improvement.

In this paper, we followed a fusion-based approach to enhance images by combining two different methods, first one is a CNN-based model called zero-reference deep curve estimation (Zero-DCE) and the second one is dark channel prior (DCP), we use this DCP to modify the image enhancement Curve to perform better in the pixel adjustments task.

3   Proposed Methodology

The proposed technique is obtained by using DCP [9] and Zero-DCE [25]. In this method, we find DCP of low light image and applies to the light enhancement equation of Zero-DCE. DCP introduces spatial attention in the model to improve the enhancement of the low-light images appropriately.

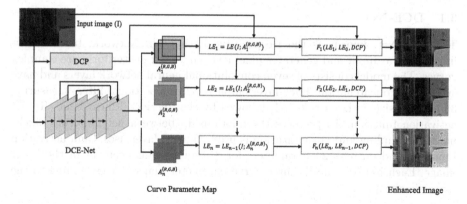

Fig. 2. The architecture of the proposed method to set the best-fitting light-enhancement parameter map. Using these parameter maps the proposed or modified light enhancement curve has formed as Eq. (10), which iteratively enhances the given input image. The function F_n is given by $F_n(LE_n, LE_{(n-1)}, DCP) = LE_{(n-1)} + (LE_n - LE_{(n-1)}) \times DCP$

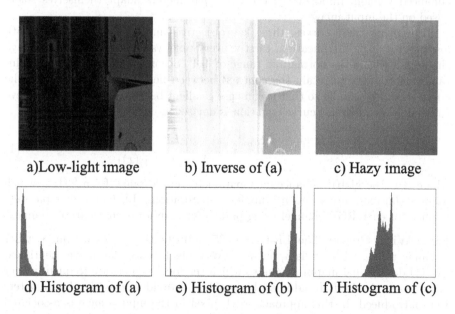

Fig. 3. Comparing the histogram of low-light, inverted, and foggy images

Figure 2 shows the proposed framework, model uses a CNN called DCE-Net to estimate the LE-Curve parameters maps. The Light Enhancement Curves(LE-Curves) are applied recurrently to all the pixels to each channel of the input image, generating the enhanced image.

3.1   DCE-Net

The DCE-Net, known as the Deep Curve Estimation Network, takes a low-light image as input and generates pixel-level curve parameter for more complex curves. The model consists of seven convolutional neural network layers and have symmetric concatenation. Each layer employs 32 convolutional filters measuring 33 units in size with a stride of 1, followed by the Rectified Linear Unit (ReLU) activation function. To preserve the relationship between neighbouring pixels, no downsampling and normalization is used. Output layer uses Tanh activation function, and outputs 24 parameters for 8 iterative enhancement of the input image. Each iteration needs three curve parameter maps, corresponding to the three channels.

3.2   Light-Enhancement Curve (LE-Curve)

This channel serves as a guide for the zero-DCE, enabling the generation of a specific curve capable of automatically transforming a low-light image into an enhanced version. Importantly, the curve parameters adapt themselves solely based on the input image.

In crafting these curves, three key objectives must be met to avoid data loss due to overflow truncation. Firstly, every pixel value in the improved image should fall within the normalized range of [0,1]. Second, the curve should maintain monotonicity to retain the contrast between neighboring pixels. Last, the curve should be simple so that it can ease gradient backpropagation. To achieve these aims, a quadratic curve equation is devised as follows,

$$LE_n(x) = LE_{(n-1)}(x) + \alpha_n LE_{(n-1)}(x)$$
$$(1 - LE_{(n-1)}(x)) \tag{1}$$

where α is the global enhancement parameter/curve range from $[-1, 1]$ which adjusts the exposure level, n= number of iterations. LE-Curve is separately applied for each RGB channel using parameter map for each separate channel.

Pixel-Wise Curve: The LE-Curve [25] adjusts the curve within a wider dynamic range, where it is applied to every pixel. Since the above mentioned Eq. (1) does global mapping, due to which the local regions are frequently over or under-emphasized. To address this problem, individual pixel-level parameters were introduced. In this approach, each pixel in the input image is associated with its unique curve that optimally adjusts the dynamic range, given by

$$LE_n(x) = LE_{(n-1)}(x) + A_n LE_{(n-1)}(x)$$
$$(1 - LE_{(n-1)}(x)) \tag{2}$$

where A is the local enhancement parameter curve/maps. LE-Curve is separately applied for each RGB channel. n = number of iterations.

3.3   Non-reference Loss Function

The Zero-DCE model [25], introduced four non-reference loss functions to assess the quality of the output image. Those loss functions are: Spatial Consistency Loss L_{spa}, Exposure Control Loss L_{exp}, Color Constancy Loss L_{col}, Illumination Smoothness Loss $L_{tv,A}$. The four loss functions are combined to obtain an overall evaluation.

Spatial Consistency Loss(L_{spa}): encourages spatial harmony in the improved image by maintaining the distinctions between neighboring areas of the initial and enhanced images.

$$L_{spa} = 1/K \sum_{k=1}^{K} \sum_{j \in (i)} (|(Y_i - Y_j)| - |(I_i) - I_j|)^2 \qquad (3)$$

K = number of local regions and (i) = adjacent area centered on i (top, down, left, right). Y and I are average intensity value in the output and low-light image, respectively.

Exposure Control Loss(L_{exp}): control exposure and counter over/under exposure to the output image. This loss is calculated as the difference between a region's average intensity value and a predefined well-exposedness level (E), set at 0.6. However, it's worth noting that performance remains largely consistent across a range of E values between 0.4 and 0.7, as observed in investigations [25].

$$L_{exp} = \frac{1}{M} \sum_{k=1}^{M} |Y_k - E|, \qquad (4)$$

M denotes the count of distinct, non-overlapping local regions, each measuring 16×16 units. Meanwhile, Y_k signifies the mean intensity value found within one of these local regions within the enhanced image.

Color Constancy Loss(L_{col}): This loss aims to rectify any possible color discrepancies in the improved image and establish coherence among the three adjusted channels.

$$L_{col} = \sum_{\forall (p,q) \in \epsilon} (J^p - J^q)^2, \epsilon = (R,G), (R,B), (G,B), \qquad (5)$$

where J^p stands for the mean intensity value of the p channel in the enhanced image, while (p,q) refers to a combination of two channels

Illumination Smoothness Loss($L_{tv,A}$): The model employs an illumination smoothness loss for each curve parameter map A, ensuring that the monotonic relationships between adjacent pixels are maintained

$$L_{tv_A} = \frac{1}{N} \sum_{n=1}^{N} (|\nabla_x A_n^c| + |\nabla_x A_n^c|)^2, \xi = (R,G,B), \qquad (6)$$

where N stands for the count of iterations, while ∇_x and ∇_y are horizontal and vertical gradient operators, respectively.

Total Loss: The total loss is a weighted sum of individual loss, can be expressed as:

$$L_{total} = W_{spa} \times L_{spa} + W_{exp} \times L_{exp} + \\ W_{col} \times L_{col} + W_{tv_A} \times L_{tv_A} \tag{7}$$

, where W_{spa}, W_{exp}, W_{col} and W_{tv_A}.

3.4 Dark Channel Prior (DCP)

This is one of the most famous techniques used to enhance foggy images [12]. This method reveals the presence of dark pixels within an image patch, where the intensity values are exceedingly near zero in at least one color channel, as demonstrated in Fig. 4. This observation leads to the following expression to identify this dark channel,

$$DCP = I^{dark}(x) = \min_{y \in \Omega(x)} (\min_{c \in (r,g,b)} I^c(y)) \tag{8}$$

where I^c represents the intensity value of a specific color channel, denoted as $c \in \{r, g, b\}$, referring to the RGB image. Additionally, $\Omega(x)$ designates a local patch centered around the pixel x, according to the Eq. 8, the dark channel denoted as $I^{dark}(x)$ is determined as the minimum value among all three channels within the $\Omega(x)$ region.

3.5 Proposed Light Enhancement Equation

The modified Light Enhancement equation after introducing DCP in the prior Eq. (2) is given by

$$LE_n^{dcp}(x) = LE_{(n-1)}^{dcp}(x) + A_n LE_{(n-1)}^{dcp}(x) \\ (1 - LE_{(n-1)}^{dcp}(x)) \times (1 - I^{dark}). \tag{9}$$

Rewriting the image enhancement Eq. (5) in terms of LE_n, LE_{n-1} and DCP

$$F_n(x) = LE_{(n-1)}^{dcp}(x) + (LE_{(n)}^{dcp} - LE_{(n-1)}^{dcp}) \times DCP \tag{10}$$

The DCP part acts as a spatial attention mechanism in the method to provide appropriate attention to the different intensity regions in the input image.

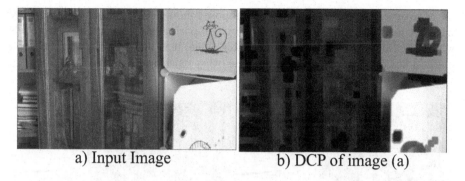

a) Input Image   b) DCP of image (a)

Fig. 4. Image and its dark channel prior (as per Eq. (8)) with patch size of 15.

4   Results

Experimental Setting: We used LOL dataset to train the model for 60 iterations. We resize the images to a size of $512 \times 512 \times 3$. For data preprocessing, the training images are normalized to $[0, 1]$. For the loss function, we used the loss function mentioned in the Zero-DCE model, the weights of $w_{spa}, w_{exp}, w_{col}$ and w_{tv_A} are set to 1.0, 20.0, 10.0 and 400.0 respectively. We use Adam optimizer with default parameters and a learning rate of 1×10^{-3} for network optimization with a batch size of 4. This method is implemented using the Pytorch framework.

Dataset: The LOL (Low-Light) dataset serves as a benchmark dataset specifically created to tackle the practical difficulty of enhancing low-light images. The dataset has a total of 500 pairs of images, with each pair consisting of a low-light image and a normal-light image. These pairs are further divided into 485 training pairs and 15 testing pairs. Visual Enhancement in the Low-Light Condition (VE-LOL) is a large-scale low-light image dataset for low/high-level vision with diverse settings and contents and complex deterioration in real scenarios.

Visual Comparison on LOL Dataset: We have examined the proposed method both qualitatively and quantitatively. Figure 5 shows the comparison of the proposed model with the zero-DCE model. From this comparison, it is observed that our proposed method 5(a) is giving comparatively better image enhancement than the zero-DCE method 5(b).

Visual comparison on VE-LOL dataset: Further, to verify the performance of the proposed method, we used a publicly available VE-LOL dataset. Figures 6, 7, and 8 show the qualitative results. Figures 6(a), 7(a), and 8(a) are the ground truth images, Figs. 6(b), 7(b), and 8(b) are the zero-DCE model images and finally, Figs. 6(c), 7(c) and 8(c) are the proposed method images. It is observed that the zero-DCE method over-enhances the brighter or whiter regions, whereas the proposed method is giving appropriate weightage to each region to enhance the image appropriately. From this observation, it is clear that the proposed method is giving better enhancement than the other model.

Moreover, the performance of the proposed model is evaluated quantitatively with the help of PSNR, SSIM and RT by comparing with other existing models which are tabulated in Table 1. From this table, it is noticed that the proposed method obtained better results than the other existing methods.

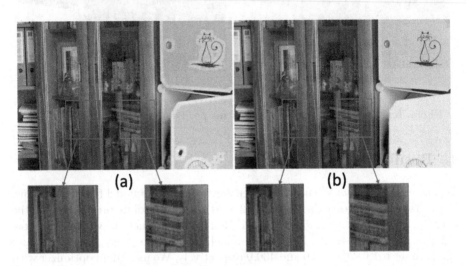

Fig. 5. Comparison of the enhancement regions of (a) proposed method with DCP method and (b) Zero-DCE

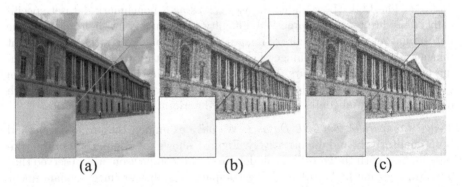

Fig. 6. Comparison of cloud regions (a) Ground truth (GT), (b) Zero-DCE (c) Proposed method

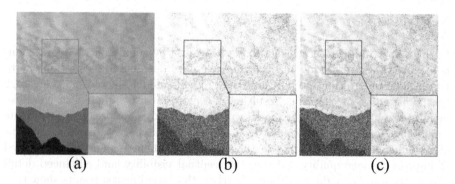

Fig. 7. Comparison of (a) Ground truth GT, (b) Zero-DCE (c) Proposed method

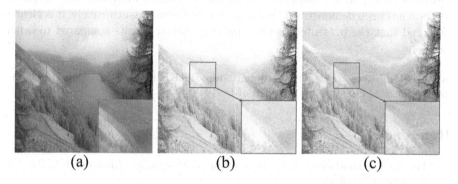

Fig. 8. Comparison of (a) Ground truth GT, (b) Zero-DCE (c) Proposed method

Table 1. Qualitative comparison of proposed and other models in terms of PSNR, SSIM and RT on the lol dataset

Methods	PSNR	SSIM	RT(sec)
EnlightenGAN [16]	9.08	0.220	0.0078
SRIE [20]	8.07	0.201	12.1865
LIME [21]	9.06	0.213	0.4914
Li et al., [22]	8.50	0.201	90.7859
Retinex Net [23]	8.95	0.198	0.1200
Wang et al., [24]	7.57	0.183	0.0210
Zero-DCE [25]	9.28	0.220	0.0025
Proposed Method	10.11	0.250	2.6715

5   Conclusion

In this paper, a fusion-based method is presented by combining the dark channel prior (DCP) technique and the zero-reference deep curve estimation (Zero-DCE). The integration of DCP into the previous model allowed us to leverage spatial attention mechanisms, resulting in a more precise and efficient enhancement of low-light images. The model was able to make more precise adjustments to the image's brightness, contrast, and other visual characteristics as a result of its enhanced understanding of the image's pertinent regions. This resulted in improved image quality, enhanced perceptual visibility, and enhanced detail preservation in low-light conditions. Further, the experimental results show that a low-light image enhancement equation equipped with DCP improves the performance of the model compared to the prior models. Moreover, the proposed method has been demonstrated both qualitatively and quantitatively, it is clearly observed that the presented method provides better results compared to other methods.

Acknowledgment. This work is supported by IIT Kharagpur AI4ICPS I Hub Foundation, a.k.a AI4ICPS under the aegis of DST.

References

1. Jain, A.K.: Fundamentals of Digital Image Processing. Englewood Cliffs, NJ, Prentice-Hall (1989)
2. Ketcham, D.J., Lowe, R., Weber, W.: Seminar on image processing. In: Real-Time Enhancement Techniques, 1976
3. Pizer, S.M., et al.: Adaptive histogram equalization and its variations. Comp. Vis. Graph. Image Process. **39**(3) (1987)
4. Liu, J., Zhou, C., Chen, P., Kang, C.: An efficient contrast enhancement method for remote sensing images. IEEE Geosci. Remote Sens. Lett. **14** (2017)
5. Kim, J.Y., Kim, L.S., Hwang, S.H.: An advanced contrast enhancement using partially overlapped sub-block histogram equalization. IEEE Trans. Circuits Syst. Video Technol. **11** (2001)
6. Reza, A.M.: Realization of the contrast limited adaptive histogram equalization for real-time image enhancement. J. VLSI Signal Process. Syst. Signal Image Video Technol. **38** (2004)
7. Zuiderveld, K.: Contrast Limited Adaptive Histogram Equalization. Graphics Gems IV; Academic Press Professional Inc., San Diego, CA, USA (1994)
8. Land, E.H., McCann, J.J.: Lightness and retinex theory. Josa **61**(1) (1971)
9. He, K., Sun, J., Tang, X.: Single image haze removal using dark channel prior. IEEE Trans. Pattern Anal. Mach. Intell. **33**(12) (2011)
10. Dong, X., Wang, G., Pang, Y., et al.: Fast efficient algorithm for enhancement of low lighting video. In: IEEE International Conference on Multimedia (2011)
11. Li, G., Li, G.J., Han, G.L., et al.: Illumination compensation using Retinex model based on bright channel prior. Opt. Precis. Eng. **26**(5) (2018)
12. Yuki, E., Yoshihiro, K., Jun, M.: Deep reverse tone mapping. ACM Trans. Graph. **36**(6) (2017)

13. Ha, E., Lim, H., Yu, S., et al.: Low-light image enhancement using dual convolutional neural networks for vehicular imaging systems. In: IEEE International Conference on Consumer Electronics (ICCE) (2020)
14. Ma, H., Ma, S., Xu, Y., et al.: Low-light image enhancement based on deep convolutional neural network. Acta Opt. Sin. **39**(2) (2019)
15. Kim, M.: Improvement of low-light image by convolutional neural network. In: IEEE International Midwest Symposium on Circuits and Systems (2019)
16. Jiang, Y., et al.: EnlightenGAN: deep light enhancement without paired supervision. IEEE Trans. Image Proc. **30** (2021)
17. Yang, S., Wang, Z., Wang, Z., Xu, N., Liu, J., Guo, Z. : Controllable artistic text style transfer via shape-matching GAN. In: CVPR (2019)
18. Wei, C., Wang, W., Yang, W., Liu, J.: Deep retinex decomposition for low-light enhancement. In: CVPR (2018)
19. Fu, X., et al.: A retinex-based enhancing approach for single underwater image. In: Proceedings of the International Conference on Image Processing (ICIP) (2014)
20. Fu, X., Zeng, D., Huang, Y., Zhang, X.P., Ding, X.: A weighted variational model for simultaneous reflectance and illumination estimation. In: CVPR (2016)
21. Guo, X., Li, Y., Ling, H.: LIME: low-light image enhancement via illumination map estimation. IEEE Trans. Image Proc. **26**(2) (2017)
22. Li, M., Liu, J., Yang, W., Sun, X., Guo, Z.: Structure-revealing low-light image enhancement via robust retinex model. IEEE Trans. Image Proc. **27**(6) (2018)
23. Wei, C., Wang, W., Yang, W., Liu, J.: Deep retinex decomposition for low-light enhancement arXiv, 2018
24. Wang, R., et al.: Underexposed photo enhancement using deep illumination estimation. In: CVPR (2019)
25. Guo, C., et al.: Zero-reference deep curve estimation for low-light image enhancement. In: CVPR (2020)
26. Mertens, T., Kautz, J., Van Reeth, F.: Exposure fusion. In: PCCGA (2007)
27. Mertens, T., Kautz, J., Van Reeth, F.: Exposure fusion: a simple and practrical alternnative to high dynamic range photography. Comput. Graph. Forum **28**(1), 161–171 (2009)
28. Buchsbaum, G.: A spatial processor model for object colour perception. J. Frankl. Inst. **310**(1), 1–26 (1980)

A Comparative Study on Performances of Adaptive and Nonadaptive Sparse Solvers for Electrical Impedance Tomography

Shantam Gulati$^{(\boxtimes)}$ ⓘ, Phanindra Jampana ⓘ, and C. S. Sastry ⓘ

Indian Institute of Technology, Kandi, Sangareddy, Hyderabad 502285, India
{ma19resch11005,pjampana,csastry}@iith.ac.in

Abstract. In electrical impedance tomography (EIT), one reconstructs the electric impedance of a part of an object or human body from its surface measurements of voltages. Applications of EIT are far and wide in several fields, including medical imaging, nondestructive testing and process tomography. Reconstruction in EIT in practical settings usually deals with a finite number of voltage differences, which is one of the standard problems in EIT. Of late, sparsity-based optimization techniques have been shown to provide economic descriptions in the sense that reconstruction of the underlying signal (or image) can be made from a few of its linear measurements. The adaptive sparse solvers are proven to be even more effective. Driven by the recent surge in nonconvex minimization, we deploy several solvers in the reconstruction of EIT and then compare and contrast the significance of adaptive minimization against standard solvers in EIT reconstruction.

Keywords: Electrical Impedance Tomography · Reconstruction · Adaptive sparse solvers

1 Introduction

Inverse problems in tomography continue to be a keen area of interest due to their wider applications in medical and industrial domains. Electrical impedance tomography (EIT) is one such problem that leverages the electrical properties for reconstruction from the surface measurements of voltages. Surface measurements are recorded from multiple electrodes attached to the surface from which small currents are applied, the range of current and voltages used mainly depend on the application. EIT has applications in lung imaging [1] and multiphase flow visualization [4], to mention a few.

Since a few voltage measurements are available for reconstructing a continuous conductivity distribution, the mathematical formulation of EIT results in an under-determined linear system. As the difference of conductivity profiles possesses many zero components [4], sparsity-driven optimization techniques have

H. Kaur et al. (Eds.): CVIP 2023, CCIS 2011, pp. 458–467, 2024.
https://doi.org/10.1007/978-3-031-58535-7_38

become natural tools for EIT. In Compressed Sensing (CS), one uses the sparsity promoting the ability of ℓ_1-norm and its variants, and solves the ill-posed problems that arise in inverse problems such as EIT and X-ray CT [4] [13]. Existing algorithms for EIT have been built upon optimizing a data fit and a regularization term, which is used to steer the optimization to acceptable solutions. The Gauss-Newton [9], total variation algorithms, a regularization involving combinations of l_1 and l_2 norms [3,14] have been used for analysis in medical and process tomography. Recently, new algorithms such as monotonicity [2], factorization [10] and D-Bar [11] algorithms have also been developed. It can be noted that these algorithms do not include partial prior knowledge of the support of conductivity distribution. To our knowledge, information priors have yet to be incorporated into the known CS and EIT-based methods. The classical CS solvers that use ℓ_1-norm based penalty function work very well when the underlying system matrix is highly incoherent [15] (that is, the maximum off-diagonal entry in the gram matrix of sensing or system matrix remains closer to 0). In the coherent cases, however, the nonconvex penalty functions like ℓ_{1-2} (which is $\ell_1 - \ell_2$) are effective.

Driven by the afore-stated points, the current work aims at incorporating information-prior into sparse reconstruction algorithms involving ℓ_1 and ℓ_{1-2} cost functions. While comparing and contrasting the simulation results, we single out the scenarios where the adaptive and convex solvers stand out in faithfully recovering the conductivity distribution. In particular, we demonstrate that the prior information can reduce reconstruction errors significantly.

This paper is organized through several sections. We discuss the linearization of EIT problem in Sect. 2. While in Sect. 3, we provide a brief account of compressed sensing and sparse solvers. In Sect. 4, we present the simulation results. The paper ends with some concluding remarks and a discussion in the last section.

2 Linearized EIT Problem

Let Ω be a domainin in $\mathcal{R}^2$, $\partial\Omega$ its boundary and $e_l, l = 1, 2, \cdots, L$, be the area occupied by the electrodes on the boundary, where L stands for the number of electrodes deployed. The complete electrode model (CEM) for EIT is given by

$$\nabla \cdot \sigma \nabla u = 0 \quad \text{in } \Omega,$$
$$\sigma \frac{\partial u}{\partial \nu} = 0 \text{ in } \Omega \backslash \cup_{l=1}^L e_l,$$
$$\int_{e_l} \sigma \frac{\partial u}{\partial \nu} = I_l \text{ for } l = 1, 2, \cdots, L, \tag{1}$$
$$u_l + \sigma z_l \frac{\partial u}{\partial \nu} = U_l (= \text{constant}) \text{ on } e_l, \text{ for } l = 1, 2, \cdots, L.$$

where e_l is the lth electrode, I_l is the current injected through the lth electrode, σ is the conductivity profile of the domain Ω and u is potential inside the domain Ω. Here by CEM, one means the set of equations in (1) that incorporate the electrode data with a combination of there surface impedance. In the adjacent stimulation pattern used in practice, current is sent through adjacent electrodes and the voltage differences at adjacent electrodes are measured. This results in an $L \times L$ voltage matrix where each column corresponds to a current pattern. The weak form of (1) has been discussed in Somersalo [5]. The map $F : L^\infty(\Omega) \to \mathbb{R}^{L \times L}$, providing the forward solution of (1), connects the conductivity distribution to the voltage matrix. Linearizing this map F using Frechet derivative implies that

$$F(\sigma) \approx F(\sigma_0) + F'(\sigma_0)(\sigma - \sigma_0) \text{ where } F'(\sigma_0) = \left(\int_\Omega \nabla u_{\sigma_0}^l \cdot \nabla u_{\sigma_0}^k \right)_{l,k=1,2,\cdots,L}.$$

In the above equation, $u_{\sigma_0}^j$ is the voltage solution vector for the current pattern j and conductivity σ_0, and the integral can be computed numerically using the finite element method. In (2), V and ΔV respectively represent the measured potential and the change in potential at the elctrodes. In practice, the conductivity is represented using finite elements resulting in a linear system of equations of the form

$$J(\sigma - \sigma_0) = \Delta V, \tag{2}$$

where, for a given number, N, of mesh cells, the sizes of the matrix J (the Jacobian or sensitivity matrix given by $F'(\sigma_0)$) and the vector $(\sigma - \sigma_0)$ are $L^2 \times N$ and $N \times 1$ respectively. One may use the EIDORS MATLAB software [4] for generating the discrete system in (2).

As stated in previous section, the vector $(\sigma - \sigma_0)$ has a few nonzero components and, as a result, the sparsity-promoting optimization techniques from compressed sensing provide a way out for recovering it from a few surface measurements of voltages (that is, for a small number L of electrodes).

3 Adaptive and Nonadaptive Sparse Solvers

In this section, we provide a brief account of sparsity-driven optimization techniques and their adaptive versions.

In compressed sensing (CS), for finding a sparse approximation of $b = Ax + \eta$ with $\|\eta\|_2 \leq \epsilon$, where $A \in \mathbb{R}^{m \times n}$ with $m < n$, one poses [7] the ℓ_1 minimization problem as

$$(\mathcal{P}_1) : \quad \min_{x \in \mathbb{R}^n} \|x\|_1 \text{ subject to } \|Ax - b\|_2 \leq \epsilon. \tag{3}$$

The recovery guarantees [7] of the afore-stated ℓ_1-norm problem are available in terms of coherence, Restricted Isometry Property (RIP) etc. The total variation problem [13] is posed as follows:

$$\min_x \left[\|x\|_{TV} + \lambda \|Ax - y\|_2^2 \right], \tag{4}$$

where $||x||_{TV}$ is the $TV-$norm that is defined as follows:

$$||x||_{TV} = \sum_{i,j} \sqrt{(x_{i,j} - x_{i-1,j})^2 + (x_{i,j} - x_{i,j-1})^2}.$$

In inverse problems, the TV-norm based optimization problem has been used successfully for recovering the underlying image from a few samples [4] [13]. Notwithstanding their potential for applications, the ℓ_1 and TV minimization problems per se do not take into account any prior information about the associated signal to be reconstructed.

3.1   Adaptive ℓ_1-Norm Based CS

The weighted CS techniques are signal adaptive as they incorporate prior partial support information of the signal into the recovery process. For instance, in interior tomography, one's target remains reconstructing interior portion accurately irrespective of how bad the reconstruction quality outside that region is, which amounts to retaining the support corresponding to the pixels in the target interior portion. In CS setting, however, this requirement translates to less-penalizing interior-centric pixels through an appropriate choice of weights. To accommodate prior information (like target support), recent results ([8] and the references therein) have proposed the following weighted ℓ_1 minimization problem, which is referred to as $\ell_{1,w}$ problem:

$$(\mathcal{P}_{1,w}): \quad \min_{x\in\mathbb{R}^n} ||x||_{1,w} \text{ subject to } ||Ax - b||_2 \leq \epsilon, \tag{5}$$

where $||x||_{1,w} = ||wx_T + x_{T^c}||_1$ with $w \in [0,1]$, and T is the prior partial support information. Here wx_T denotes the point-wise multiplication of the scalar w and the vector x_T (which is x restricted to T), and $x_{T^c} \in \mathbb{R}^n$ is x restricted to T^c in line with the definition of x_T.

3.2 ℓ_{1-2} Based Compressed Sensing

The authors of [6] [7] have observed that the level curves of the ℓ_{1-2} function via $(||.||_1 - ||.||_2)$ result in more pronounced sparsity than the conventional ℓ_1-norm. In view of this, they have considered the following nonconvex minimization problem:

$$(\mathcal{P}_{1-2,1}): \quad \min_{x\in\mathbb{R}^n} [||x||_1 - ||x||_2] \quad subject\ to \quad ||Ax - b||_2 \leq \epsilon. \tag{6}$$

Its unconstrained form is provided as

$$\min_{x\in\mathbb{R}^n} \left[\frac{1}{2}||Ax - b||_2^2 + \lambda(||x||_1 - ||x||_2)\right]. \tag{7}$$

The stable recovery guarantees of the afore-stated problem have been established in [15]. The popularity of ℓ_{1-2} minimization may be attributed to (i) its ability in accommodating highly coherent matrices and (ii) the availability of efficient solvers.

3.3 Adaptive ℓ_{1-2} Based Compressed Sensing

In [12], for $w \in [0,1]$, the authors have analyzed and studied the following weighted ℓ_{1-2} (for brevity, $\ell_{1-2,w}$) minimization problem for its applicability and the relevance of general weights:

$$(\mathcal{P}_{1-2,w}): \quad \min_{x \in \mathbb{R}^n} \left[\|x\|_{1,w} - \|x\|_{2,w}\right] \quad \text{subject to} \quad \|Ax - b\|_2 \leq \epsilon. \quad (8)$$

In particular, while establishing the convergence of the solver, they have shown that the general weights in $(0,1)$ attain prominence when we do not have completely accurate or completely corrupt information about the signal's support information.

3.4 Numerical Schemes for Weighted ℓ_{1-2} Minimization

In this section, we discuss briefly the 2 numerical schemes, one for solving (8) and another for estimating the optimal weights iteratively. The equation in (8) is in general solved via the following unconstrained problem [16]:

$$\min_{x \in \mathbb{R}^n} \left[\frac{1}{2}\|Ax - b\|_2^2 + \lambda(\|x\|_{1,w} - \|x\|_{2,w})\right]. \quad (9)$$

The algorithm [12] for solving the above problem may be summarized in Algorithm 1.

The step 3 of Algorithm 1 is in turn executed using *Alternating Direction Method of Multipliers* (ADMM) as given in Algorithm 2. For the afore-stated solver, a discussion on the choice of parameters such as c, λ has been provided in [15]. An iterative scheme [12] for designing the optimal weight is summarized as follows:

Given a weight function $w(t)$ (such as $\frac{1}{|t|+1}$, $1 - tanh(|t|)$) at the kth iteration, the weight w in the prior support set T may be updated as $w(x_*^{(k-1)})$, where $x_*^{(k-1)} = \max_{i \in T} |x_i^{(k-1)}|$ with all components of $(x_*^{(k-1)})_T$ being equal to the maximum component (in magnitude) of $(x^{(k-1)})_T$.

4 Simulation Results

We begin with a setup in circular domain with 16 equidistant electrodes placed at the edges and consider standard current patterns of injecting currents from the adjacent electrodes. Further, for the forward model, we have deployed the finite element model for which EIDORS packages [4] can be used. In our coding work, we have performed the phantom simulations on conductivity profiles with disturbance placed at the center of the domain. Here, the phantoms have been designed to replicate target as shown in Fig. 1, where the radius of the phantom is varied from 0.1 units to 0.5 units with 0.05 increment. We reconstruct the conductivity profile using the TV norm, GN one step method ([4] and the references therein), $l_1 - l_2$ and the weighted l_1 solvers and compare the results.

Algorithm 1: Algorithm for solving (9)

---

1   Define $\epsilon_0 > 0$. Initialize $x^0 = 0$.

2   **for** $k = 0, 1, \cdots, M_1$ **do**

3     $x^{k+1} = \arg\min_x \left[\frac{1}{2}\|Ax - b\|_2^2 + \frac{c}{2}\|x\|_2^2 + \lambda\|x\|_{1,w} - \langle x, \lambda e_w^k \rangle \right]$;

4   **end**

5   M_1: Maximum number of iterations for DCA.

Algorithm 2: ADMM for Step 3 of Algorithm 1

---

6   Initialize x^0, z^0 and y^0.

7   **for** $l = 0, 1, \cdots, M_2$ **do**

8     $x^{l+1} = (A^T A + (c + \delta)I)^{-1}(A^T b - v + \delta z^l - y^l)$

9     $z^{l+1} = \mathcal{S}(x^{l+1} + y^l/\delta, \lambda_w/\delta))$

10   $y^{l+1} = y^l + \delta(x^{l+1} - z^{l+1})$

11   **end**

12   M_2: Maximum number of iterations for ADMM.

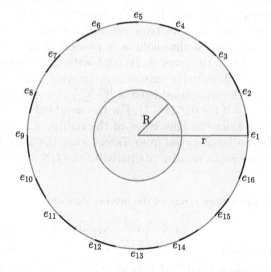

Fig. 1. Experimental set up depicting a centrally located phantom of radius R where the 16 electrodes (that is, $L = 16$) are placed along the circular boundary of radius r.

The forward and inverse meshes are shown in Fig. 2. The numbers of elements are 6400 and 47243 for the inverse and the forward meshes respectively. The inverse mesh is chosen to be different from the forward mesh to avoid an "inverse crime". The objective behind the simulations is to identify a method that sees the difference in the reconstructed profile well and predicts the correct radius of the phantom. In Fig. 3, we show the reconstructed images where the graphs show the errors obtained via different methods, for a specific radius of 0.5.

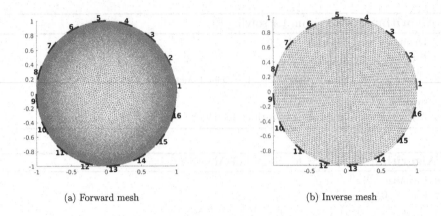

(a) Forward mesh   (b) Inverse mesh

Fig. 2. Meshes for the forward and inverse problems

It can be observed from the Fig. 3 that the TV, weighted $l_1 - l_2$ and weighted l_1 solvers provide a crisp interface whereas the GN method provides a diffuse reconstruction. Even though the TV norm results are close to the weighted solvers, the TV method results in large errors for small radius phantoms. To obtain a final radius value, a threshold is implemented on the radial profiles. The threshold is chosen in the range [0.01, 0.99] with the increment of 0.01. The optimum threshold is calculated by minimizing the error between the predictions and the true radius. The error considered is $\frac{100}{N} \sum_{i=1}^{N} |r_i - \hat{r}_i|$, where $N = (0.5 - 0.1)/0.05 + 1$ and $r_i = 0.1 + 0.05(i - 1)$. For the weighted $l_1 - l_2$ and l_1 solvers we deduce the prior from the knowledge of the radius. The prior is chosen as $r_0 = r - 0.55r$. It can be observed from Table 1 that the error from the $\ell_{1-2,w}$ and $\ell_{1,w}$ methods are much smaller compared to the GN and TV methods.

Table 1. Average percentage errors of the inverse algorithms on the various radius.

	GN	TV	Weighted $l_1 - l_2$	Weighted l_1
Optimal Threshold	0.54	0.98	0.90	0.82
Average Percentage Error	35.63	42.48	6.26	4.35

The simulation results reported herein primarily take into account the prior information (which is incorporated through weights in the sparse solver) about the phantom image. The methods proposed in the literature (such as the stated GN and TV) do not incorporate any prior information. As a result, the weighted solvers provide less reconstruction error without any compromise on any other front.

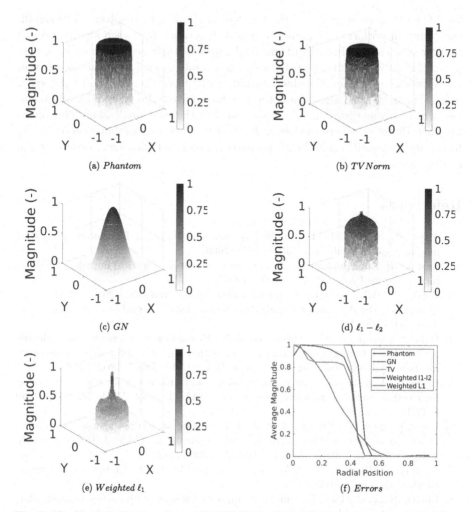

(a) *Phantom*

(b) *TVNorm*

(c) *GN*

(d) $\ell_1 - \ell_2$

(e) *Weighted ℓ_1*

(f) *Errors*

Fig. 3. For the test phantom image (surface) shown in (a), the images shown in (b) to (e) are the reconstructions provided by different solvers when radius is 0.5. The plots in (f) are the radial profiles, obtained using averaging along the radial position. In (f), the error so reported primarily reflects the representation of the deviation from the original radial profile.

5   Conclusion and Discussion

In this paper we have compared different minimization algorithms for the reconstruction of conductivity profile from the boundary voltage and current data. From the results, we observe that $\ell_1 - \ell_2$ and weighted ℓ_1 methods result in an order of magnitude less error than the standard solvers GN and TV norm. Therefore, it is evident that the sparsity framework holds great promise in reconstruction in electrical impedance tomography. The use of prior information is the key idea where we start to see the true use of the weighted solvers. The significant jump in performance points to a new direction where such algorithms can be paired with existing algorithms and improve their performance in a post processing case. We have recently seen such combinations with the use of Neural Networks and other Machine Learning (ML) algorithms as a post-processor units. Unlike the ML algorithms, the weighted solvers do not require any training, which means they can be simply added in the post processing. This opens up a new direction where the use of different weights, the combinations or priors from various algorithms and the guarantees associated with such reconstruction can be explored.

References

1. Adler, A., et al.: GREIT: a unified approach to 2D linear EIT reconstruction of lung images. Physiol. Meas. **30**(6), S35 (2009)
2. Bastian, H.: Interpolation of missing electrode data in electrical impedance tomography. Inverse Probl. **31**(11), 115008 (2015)
3. Borsic, A., Adler, A.: A primal-dual interior-point framework for using the ℓ_1 or ℓ_2 norm on the data and regularization terms of inverse problems. Inverse Probl. **28**, 095011 (2012)
4. Diddi, S., Jampana, P.V., Mangadoddy, N.: Evaluation of two noniterative electrical resistance tomography (ERT) reconstruction algorithms for air-core measurements in hydrocyclone. Ind. Eng. Chem. Res. **61**(49), 18017–18029 (2022)
5. Erkki, S., Margaret, C., David, I.: Existence and uniqueness for electrode models for electric current computed tomography. SIAM J. Appl. Math. **52**, 1023–1040 (1992)
6. Esser, E., Lou, Y., Xin, J.: A method for finding structured sparse solutions to non-negative least squares problems with applications. SIAM J. Imaging Sci. **6**, 2010–2046 (2013). https://doi.org/10.1137/13090540X
7. Foucart, S., Rauhut, H.: A Mathematical Introduction to Compressive Sensing. Birkhäuser Basel (2013)
8. Liu, H., Song, B., Tian, F., Qin, H.: Compressed sensing with partial support information: coherence-based performance guarantees and alternative direction method of multiplier reconstruction algorithm. IET Signal Proc. **8**(7), 749–758 (2014)
9. Margaret, C., David, I., Jonathan, C.N.: Electrical impedance tomography. SIAM Rev. **41**, 85–101 (1999)
10. Martin, B., Martin, H.: Numerical implementation of two non-iterative methods for locating inclusions by impedance tomography. Inverse Probl. **16**(4), 1029–1042 (2000)
11. Mueller, J.L., Siltanen, S.: The d-bar method for electrical impedance tomography—demystified. Inverse Probl. **36**(9), 093001 (2020)
12. Najiya, K.Z., Sastry, C.S.: Analysis of general weights in weighted 12 minimization through applications. Digit. Signal Process. **133**, 103833 (2023)
13. Theeda, P., Kumar, P., Sastry, C.S., Jampana, P.V.: Reconstruction of sparse-view tomography via preconditioned radon sensing matrix. J. Appl. Math. Comput. **59**(1), 285–303 (2019)

14. Theertham, G.T., Varanasi, S.K., Jampana, P.: Sparsity constrained reconstruction for electrical impedance tomography. IFAC-PapersOnLine **53**(2), 355–360 (2020)
15. Yin, P., Lou, Y., He, Q., Xin, J.: Minimization of ℓ_{1-2} for compressed sensing. SIAM J. Sci. Comput. **37**, A536–A563 (2015)
16. Zhang, J., Zhang, S., Wang, W.: Robust signal recovery for ℓ_{1-2} minimization via prior support information. Inverse Prob. **37**(11), 115001 (2021)

Face Detection in Challenging Scenes with a Customized Backbone

Yogesh Aggarwal[1]([✉]) [iD], Pankaj Choudhury[2] [iD], and Prithwijit Guha[1,2] [iD]

[1] Department of Electronics and Electrical Engineering,
Indian Institute of Technology Guwahati, Guwahati, Assam, India
{yogesh_aggarwal,pguha}@iitg.ac.in
[2] Centre for Linguistic Science and Technology, Indian Institute of Technology
Guwahati, Guwahati, Assam, India
pankajchoudhury@iitg.ac.in

Abstract. Existing works in deep network-based face detection have mostly used pre-trained backbone networks like ResNet-50/101/152 and VGG16/19. These networks are trained on large image collections and can produce rich image representations. Only a few works have attempted the development of customized backbones for the face detection task. The first contribution of this work proposes a novel backbone network with 7.5M parameters and 43 GFLOPs. The overall face detector is motivated by the RetinaFace architecture. The second contribution proposes a detector head considering the imbalance in face and non-face. The proposed face detector is benchmarked on the WIDER FACE and FDDB dataset and is observed to provide competitive performance against state-of-art approaches.

Keywords: Face Detection · Customized Backbone · Detector Head · Challenging scenes

1 Introduction

Face detection is a necessary prerequisite for several computer vision tasks like face tracking, alignment, recognition, pose identification, gender categorization and expression classification. A face detection system aims to accurately identify and locate faces in a given image. The task becomes harder in crowded situations and under challenging conditions like face pose variations, low illumination, occlusions, and poor image region quality (blur or small faces). An ideal face detector should be able to localize faces in an image with high accuracy and low computation cost.

Classical approaches to face detection used hand-crafted features with sliding window techniques [24]. The Viola-Jones face detector [22] is one of the most successful among the traditional approaches, known for its accuracy and fast execution. This method uses the Haar features and a cascade of detectors trained using the AdaBoost algorithm. Most recent face detectors are benchmarked on the widely used WIDER FACE dataset [25] which consists of images with different challenging scenarios like blur, pose variations, illumination changes and occlusions. This dataset also has annotations for easy, medium and hard face detection tasks. However, the Viola-Jones detector could not achieve very high performance on the WIDER FACE dataset.

Recent approaches to face detection are formulated in the deep learning framework owing to their higher accuracy compared to the traditional ones. These approaches use different convolutional neural network (CNN) architectures for visual feature extraction, attention modules and detection mechanism. Such proposals have shown significantly higher performance on the WIDER FACE dataset. The cascade CNN [10], RCNN series [23], single-shot face detectors [14,27], and RetinaFace [3] face detectors are examples of such systems. The Cascade face detector utilizes multiple convolutional networks with sliding window techniques. This approach offers a more efficient improvement over traditional face detection methods. However, this network has shown lower face detection performance in densely populated scenes compared to state-of-art approaches (like [3]). Taking inspiration from recent progress of deep learning based generic object detection methods [13,17], face detection techniques have also achieved significant improvement in performance [14,21,23,26]. However, this performance improvement has come at the cost of increased computations (FLOPs) required to employ these face detectors. The requirement for more computations is due to the use of standard CNN backbones like ResNet50/101/152 [5], VGG16 [19], and DenseNet121 [8]. It can be observed from Fig. 1 that these methods have almost comparable accuracies with small differences. Increasing accuracy further requires the use of heavier, and more complicated backbones, which is both difficult and impractical. A better balance between accuracy and computation cost is essential for applying face detection to more practical applications. This motivated the researchers to focus on creating customized backbones for face detectors. Although the previous attempts [4,6] to develop customized backbones with fewer parameters reduced the computations, they also resulted in a decrease in accuracy.

A CNN backbone is employed in computer vision applications to extract task-specific features. Existing face detectors have used popular CNN backbones for feature extraction. This include VGG16 [14,27], ResNet-18/34/50/101/152 [3, 26], Darknet-53 [2] and DenseNet-121 [28]. These backbones achieved impressive accuracy at the cost of high computations. A simple exchange of backbones in the state-of-the-art [11,15] face detectors have consistently achieved no significant performance enhancements (Average Precision $AP < 0.9$ on challenging datasets like WIDER FACE [25] validation hard set). Several researchers have created lightweight face detectors by utilizing lightweight feature extractor backbones [7] or customized backbones [6]. However, these face detectors have achieved significantly lower accuracy.

This work attempts to reduce the computation cost without significantly sacrificing the accuracy. The architecture of the proposed face detector is motivated by that of RetinaFace [3]. It consists of a backbone network, feature pyramid network, context modules and detector heads. This work proposes a customized

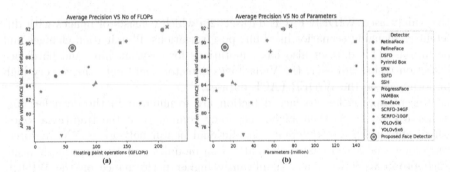

Fig. 1. Face detection performance (Average Precision) of state-of-art models on *Hard* subset of WIDER FACE validation dataset. The Average Precision is plotted with respect to (a) floating point operations (GFLOPs) and (b) model parameters in millions (M). Note the performance of the proposed face detector – 89.3% AP with 12.4M parameters and 62 GFLOPs.

backbone (7.5M parameters and 43 GFLOPs) for the face detector. Additionally, two detector heads are used for face classification while considering the imbalance in the training set. The proposed face detector is also evaluated on challenging scenarios involving blur, occlusion, illumination, expression, and pose variations. This proposal achieved an Average Precision of 89.3% on the hard set of the WIDER FACE dataset with 12.4M parameters and 62 GFLOPs. The main contribution of this paper can be briefly summarized as follows:

- A customized backbone network with 7.5M parameters and 43 GFLOPS is proposed.
- The proposed architecture has two detector heads. One is trained with binary cross-entropy loss. The other is trained with weighted binary cross-entropy loss while considering the imbalance in face and non-face training instances.
- The proposed face detector is evaluated on the WIDER FACE (validation) and FDDB datasets. Additionally, the face detector is also evaluated on individual challenging scenarios.

2   Proposed Face Detector Network

The overall architecture of the proposed face detector and its components are described in this section. The architecture of the proposed detector is motivated by that of RetinaFace [3]. It consists of (a) a *Customized Backbone* for image feature extraction, (b) *Feature Pyramid Network* (FPN) [12], (c) *Context Module* [14], and (d) the *Detection Head*. The customized backbone (explained in Subsect. 2.1) is employed to extract spatial features from an input image (W × H × 3). Initial convolutional layers of the backbone network extract low level features. On the other hand, the deeper convolutional layers of the backbone network extract more semantic features. This work has used the FPN architecture proposed in [12]. The FPN takes spatial features as input from different convolutional layers of the backbone network and provides more semantic information to feature maps obtained from lower-level layers. Such semantics refers to sets of edges and corners that define the structural information of the outline of objects [12]. The output feature maps P_i ($i \in \{1, 2, 3\}$ signifies the detection layers) of FPN are provided as input to the ith context module CM_i. The context module architecture used in [14] is adopted for this work. The context modules CM_i enhance the model's capacity to detect small faces. Finally, the output feature maps from the context modules are utilized in the detector head D_i. The detector head (explained in Subsect. 2.2) consists of four sub-networks – (a) Two heads for face classification, one trained with cross-entropy loss and another trained with weighted cross-entropy loss, (b) One head for face bounding box localization, and (c) one head to localize five facial landmarks.

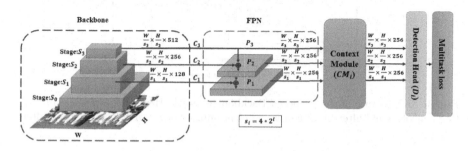

Fig. 2. Overview of the proposed face detector

2.1   Customized Backbone

The proposed backbone of the face detector consists of four stages (Fig. 3). In stage S_0, there are four CBNR (Convolution + Batch Normalization + LeakyReLU) layers, one layer with 7×7 filter and the rest of the three layers with 3×3 filters. The output feature map of S_0 is provided as input to stage S_1. The stage S_1 consists of one DSU (Down Sampling Unit) and three MFR (Multi-scale Feature Refinement) networks. In stage S_2, the features acquired from S_1 are passed through one DSU followed by two MFR blocks. The stage S_3 has a max-pooling and one group-convolution layer (with two groups) as shown in Fig. 3. Finally, the respective output feature maps C_1, C_2 and C_3 of stages S_1, S_2 and S_3 are fed to the FPN network to extract features from a given image as shown in Fig. 2.

In the proposed backbone, the MFR block is inspired by the inception module architecture [20]. The use of multi-scale filters in a convolutional neural network gives ability to the network to recognize patterns at various resolutions. Thus, in the MFR network, multi-scale filters have been applied and the resultant features are accumulated through depth concatenation.

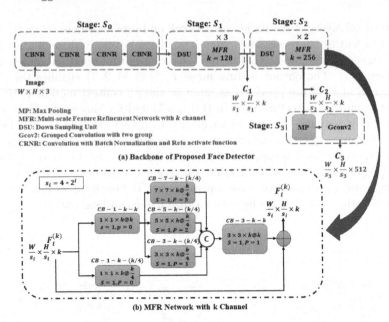

(a) Backbone of Proposed Face Detector

(b) MFR Network with k Channel

Fig. 3. Architecture of the proposed Backbone network. Here, $CB - n - k - m$ refers to a convolutional filter block consisting of m number of $n \times n \times k$ convolution filters.

The input feature map $F_i^{(k)}$ of the ith stage S_i is of size $\frac{W}{s_i} \times \frac{H}{s_i} \times k$. Here, $s_i = 4 \times 2^i$ is the down-sampling factor associated with each stage. Each stage enhances its input feature map and the input-output dimensions remain unchanged. The feature map $F_i^{(k)}$ is passed through two different 1×1 convolution layers $CB - 1 - k - k$ and $CB - 1 - k - (k/4)$ simultaneously[1]. The output of $CB - 1 - k - k$ is provided as input to three convolution layers ($CB - 7 - k - (k/4)$, $CB - 5 - k - (k/4)$, $CB - 3 - k - (k/4)$), each with $k/4$ number of filters. The 1×1 convolution layer $CB - 1 - k - (k/4)$ applies $k/4$ filters to the input feature map $F_i^{(k)}$. Furthermore, the output of $CB - 1 - k - (k/4)$ ($\frac{W}{s_i} \times \frac{H}{s_i} \times \frac{k}{4}$) is concatenated with the outputs of $CB - 7 - k - (k/4)$, $CB - 5 - k - (k/4)$, and $CB - 3 - k - (k/4)$ along channel dimensions to acquire a feature map of size $\frac{W}{s_i} \times \frac{H}{s_i} \times k$. The concatenated feature map is then refined by a $3 \times 3 \times k$ convolutional layer ($CB - 3 - k - k$). Finally, the feature map $F_i^{(k)}$ is added with the refined feature map through a residual connection to handle issues related to the vanishing gradient (Fig. 3).

---

[1] $CB - n - k - m$ refers to a convolutional filter block consisting of m number of $n \times n \times k$ convolution filters.

Table 1. Filters, parameters (in millions) and floating point operations (GFLOP) at each layer of the proposed backbone network. The floating point operations are calculated considering 640 × 480 input image size.

Layer or Stages	Filter Size, Stride, Padding	Output size of tensor	Parameters (M)	GFLOP
CNBR	$7 \times 7 \times 3@64$, 2, 3	$320 \times 320 \times 64$	0.01	1.47
CNBR	$3 \times 3 \times 64@64$, 1, 1	$320 \times 320 \times 64$	0.04	5.69
CNBR	$3 \times 3 \times 64@128$, 2, 1	$160 \times 160 \times 128$	0.07	2.85
CNBR	$3 \times 3 \times 128@128$, 1, 1	$160 \times 160 \times 128$	1.47	5.69
DSU	$3 \times 3 \times 128@128$, 2, 1	$80 \times 80 \times 128$	1.47	1.42
Stage 1	$MFR_k \times 3$ (with k = 128)	$80 \times 80 \times 128$	1.52	14.64
DSU	$3 \times 3 \times 128@256$, 2, 1	$40 \times 40 \times 256$	0.29	0.71
Stage 2	$MFR_k \times 2$ (with k = 256)	$40 \times 40 \times 256$	4.0	9.76
Maxpool	3×3, 2, 1	$20 \times 20 \times 256$	0.00	1.0
GC_2	$3 \times 3 \times 256@512$, 1, 1	$40 \times 40 \times 512$	1.18	0.71

2.2 Detector Head

The detector head plays the most significant role in face detection. This proposal contains four sub-networks as shown in Fig. 4. There are two classification heads – (a) classification head CLS trained with cross-entropy loss, and (b) classification head CLS_{WL} trained with weighted cross-entropy loss. In CLS_{WL} the weights are set to 7 : 1 for countering the imbalance of training instances of face and non-face. However, CLS does not use any weights. The third detector sub-network is used to localize the face bounding box coordinates. It is called the bounding-box regression head ($BBOX$). The fourth detector sub-network localizes the five facial landmark coordinates of detected faces. It is called the landmark regression head ($LANDM$).

The proposed model employs multi-task learning, which involves the integration of multiple tasks into a single model. The sliding anchor technique [17] is used for multi-task learning. The sliding anchor technique systematically slides a set of pre-defined bounding boxes called anchor boxes with different scales across an image. These anchor boxes serve as reference templates for covering faces of various sizes and aspect ratios. The sliding anchor technique reduces number of evaluations and improves face detection efficiency and accuracy. In multi-task learning, a convolutional (CNN) head is used for each task, and each layer of the context module output is connected to the corresponding layer of the multi-task heads. Finally, to reduce the multi-task loss $\mathcal{L}_{Total}$ for any given training anchor j (see Sect. 3), the following loss function is minimized.

$$\mathcal{L}_{Total} = \mathcal{L}_{cls}(p_j, \hat{p}_j) + \lambda_1 \mathcal{L}_{cls\_w}(p_j, \hat{p}_j) + \lambda_2 p_j \mathcal{L}_{box}(t_j, \hat{t}_j) + \lambda_3 p_j \mathcal{L}_{landm}(l_j, \hat{l}_j) \tag{1}$$

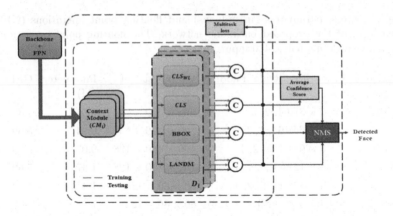

Fig. 4. Detector head of the proposed face detector

Here, $\mathcal{L}_{cls}$, $\mathcal{L}_{cls\_w}$, $\mathcal{L}_{box}$ and $\mathcal{L}_{landm}$ are the respective face classification loss (detector head $CL\overline{S}$), weighted face classification loss (detector head CLS_{WL}), bounding box regression loss and landmark regression loss.

The classification loss function $\mathcal{L}_{cls}(p_j,\hat{p}_j)$ compares actual label p_j of the anchor point j and predicted probability $\hat{p}_j$. If the anchor point is a positive example of a face, p_j is set to 1, and otherwise set to 0. The binary cross-entropy is used to compute classification loss $\mathcal{L}_{cls}$. The weighted classification loss $\mathcal{L}_{cls\_w}(p_j,\hat{p}_j)$ is defined as

$$\mathcal{L}_{cls\_w}(p_j,\hat{p}_j) = -\alpha p_j \log \hat{p}_j - (1-p_j)\log(1-\hat{p}_j) \qquad (2)$$

where the weight for face class is set to $\alpha = 7$.

The face bounding box regression loss for the jth positive anchor is denoted as $\mathcal{L}_{box}(b_j,\hat{b}_j)$ [3]. The variables $b_j = \{b_x,b_y,b_w,b_h\}$ and $\hat{b}_j = \{\hat{b}_x,\hat{b}_y,\hat{b}_w,\hat{b}_h\}$ represent the {center abscissa, center ordinate, width, height} of the ground-truth bounding box and predicted bounding box respectively. This work uses the bounding box regression loss proposed in [3].

The landmark regression loss $\mathcal{L}_{landm}(l_j,\hat{l}_j)$ is similar to $\mathcal{L}_{box}$ [3] with five landmark points. Here, $l_j = \{(l_j^{x1},l_j^{y1}),\ldots(l_j^{xm},l_j^{ym}),\ldots(l_j^{x5},l_j^{y5})\}$ and $\hat{l}_j = \{(\hat{l}_j^{x1},\hat{l}_j^{y1}),\ldots(\hat{l}_j^{xm},\hat{l}_j^{ym}),\ldots(\hat{l}_j^{x5},\hat{l}_j^{y5})\}$ are the respective coordinates of ground-truth and predicted facial landmark points. The facial landmark regression employs a target normalization approach based on the anchor center, similar to the bounding box center regression. This work uses the landmark regression loss proposed in [3]. The loss function weights are empirically selected as $\lambda_1 = 1$, $\lambda_2 = 2$ and $\lambda_3 = 1$.

3 Experimental Setup

Baseline Model – The performance of the proposed model is compared against 9 state-of-art models. These are RetinaFace [3], RefineFace [26], DSFD [11],

PyramidBox [21], SRN [1], SCRFD-34GF [4], SCRFD-10GF [4], YOLOv5l6 [16], YOLOv5x6 [16]. YOLOv5x6 has more parameters and requires more floating-point operations (FLOPs) than YOLOv5l6. The comparative performance analysis results are presented in Table 2.

Dataset – This proposal is validated on two widely used benchmark datasets, namely *FDDB* [9], and *WIDER FACE* [25]. The proposed face detector was trained and validated on *WIDER FACE*, whereas *FDDB* is only used for testing. The evaluation results on WIDER FACE are obtained through a multiscale testing strategy [14], whereas the performances on FDDB are assessed using the original images.

The WIDER FACE dataset comprises of 32,203 images and 393,703 annotated bounding boxes for faces. The images were randomly selected from 61 different scene categories. The dataset poses different challenging scenarios like pose, scale, occlusion, expression, and illumination variations. The dataset is divided into train, validation and test sets as 12883, 3226 and 16094 images, respectively. Additionally, five facial landmark points [3] were used in the training process. On the other hand, the FDDB dataset contains 2,845 images and 5,171 annotated bounding boxes for faces with poses and occlusions.

Anchor Setting – For every i^{th} detection layer ($i \in \{1, 2, 3\}$), three different anchor sizes are used at each location. The size of anchors is determined with respect to the original image as $2^i s_i$, $\frac{3}{2} \times 2^i s_i$, and $2^{i+1} s_i$. Here, $s_i = 4 * 2^i$ is the down-sampling factor of each detection layer. These anchors have a $1 : 1$ aspect ratio. As a result, the anchors cover areas ranging from 16×16 to 512×512 pixels in the input image.

During training, the anchors are categorized based on their overlap with the ground-truth boxes, specifically using the intersection over union (IoU) metric. If the IoU value exceeds a threshold (set to 0.35 here), then the anchors are labeled as face anchor. Otherwise, they are labeled as background (or negative). It is observed that most anchors (more than 99%) are categorized as negative. Thus, online hard example mining (OHEM) [18] is utilized to address the substantial imbalance between positive and negative examples during training. The negative anchors are sorted based on their loss and then the highest-ranking anchors are chosen. This selection process ensures that the ratio between negative and positive samples is maintained at a minimum of $7 : 1$.

Training Details – The proposed face detector was trained with the SGD optimizer with an initial learning rate of 1×10^{-3}, momentum factor of 0.9, and weight decay of 5×10^{-4}. The model was trained for 140 epochs. However, the learning rate is reduced by a factor of 10 at 100 and 120 epochs. The model was trained on NVIDIA Tesla V100 GPUs with a batch size of 8.

Testing Details – The standard practices described in [14] are adopted to evaluate the performance of this proposal on the WIDER FACE dataset. Specifically, the images are resized so that the shortest side is 1200 pixels while maintaining the aspect ratio and ensuring that the longest side is no more than 1600 pixels. The images of FDDB are used in their original size to evaluate the proposed model's performance. Within the detector head, the face confidence scores are obtained for all anchors from both the classification sub-networks. Subsequently, the average confidence score for each anchor is computed (Fig. 4). Now, those anchors are selected for the face detection process for which the confidence scores are higher than the threshold of 0.02. Finally, the non-maximum suppression (NMS) algorithm is employed with a Jaccard overlap of 0.4 [3]. This algorithm allows the generation of the final results by selecting the top 750 [26] highly confident detections for each image. The implementation of this proposal is available at: https://github.com/yogesh0757/Face_Detection_Challenging_Scenes.

4   Results and Discussion

This section presents a thorough evaluation of the proposed face detector. The performance of the proposed model is compared against state-of-art models on two benchmark datasets (WIDER FACE and FDDB). Additionally, an ablation study is included in the evaluation to analyse the contributions of individual components and techniques utilized in the model. Furthermore, the model's performances in different challenging scenarios such as occlusion, blur, illumination, pose and expression are separately evaluated.

4.1   Results on WIDER FACE Dataset

The performance of the proposed face detector is compared against 9 baseline algorithms (Sect. 3). The following observations can be made from the results presented in Table 2 and Fig. 5.

- The proposed model achieves the respective average precision (AP) scores of 94.8%, 93.5% and 89.3% in Easy, Medium and Hard subsets of the WIDER FACE validation set.
- The proposed model outperforms Yolovl6 [16], Yolovx6 [16], SCRFD-34GF [4], and SCRFD-10GF [4] in terms of performance on the hard set of the WIDER FACE validation dataset with comparable number of computations.
- The performance of the proposed model falls short compared to RetinaFace [3], RefineFace [26], SRN [1], and DSFD [11] face detectors. However, these state-of-art face detectors require much higher computations (GFLOPs) compared to the proposed face detector. As a result, the proposed face detector achieves faster processing speed while maintaining competitive accuracy levels.

The proposed face detector achieved a competitive performance with 62G FLOPS and 12.4 M parameters, which is much less compared to the state-of-the-art models.

4.2   Results on FDDB Dataset

The proposed model is also validated on the FDDB dataset. Table 3 shows the True Positive Rate (TPR) of the state-of-art models and the proposed model when the number of False Positives equal to 1000. The proposed model is found to achieve competitive results in comparison to the state-of-art models.

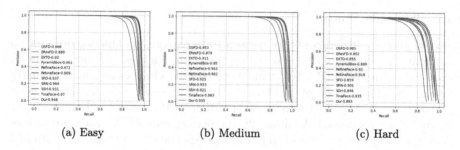

| (a) Easy | (b) Medium | (c) Hard |

Fig. 5. Precision-Recall graph of proposed face detector on Easy, Medium and Hard set of WIDER FACE validation dataset.

Table 2. Performance comparison of proposed model with state-of-art face detectors on WIDER FACE validation set. Here, AP implies Average precision

Detector	Backbone	Easy AP (%)	Medium AP (%)	Hard AP (%)	Param (M)	Flops (Giga)
RetinaFace [3]	ResNet152	96.9	96.1	91.8	70	208
RefineFace [26]	ResNet152	97.2	96.2	92.2	76	210
DSFD [11]	VGG-16	96	95.3	90	140	140
PyramidBox [21]	VGG-16	95.6	94.6	88.7	57	236
SRN [1]	ResNet50	96.4	95.3	90.2	54	160
SCRFD-34GF [4]	ResNet50	96.6	94.9	85.3	9.8	34
SCRFD-10GF [4]	ResNet34	95.1	93.9	83.1	3.8	10
YOLOv5l6 [16]	YOLOv5-CSPNet	96.4	94.9	85.88	76.7	45.3
YOLOv5x6 [16]	YOLOv5-CSPNet	96.7	95.8	86.55	141.16	88.6
Proposed	Proposed	94.8	93.5	89.3	12.4	62

Table 3. Performance comparison of proposed face detector with state-of-art face detectors on FDDB validation set. Here, TPR (True Positive Rate) for 1000 false positives is used for performance comparison.

Detector	Backbone	TPR (%)	Parameters (million)	FLOP (Giga)
RefineFace [26]	ResNet152	99.1	76	150
DSFD [11]	VGG16	99.1	140	140
Pyramid Box [21]	VGG16	98.7	57	236
SRN [1]	ResNet50	98.8	54	150
Proposed	Proposed Backbone	98.5	12.4	62

4.3   Ablation Study

Several ablation experiments are performed to explore the functionalities of the different components of the proposed face detector. All these ablation studies are executed on the WIDER FACE validation dataset. These experiments primarily involve the modification of backbone's structure to assess its impact on model performance. The optimal number of repetitions of the MFR blocks in stages S_1, S_2, and S_3 are examined. Additionally, the performance of the group convolution operation GC_2 against that of MFR blocks (specifically in stage S_3) is studied. The results of the ablation study are presented in Table 4.

Initially, a single MFR network block is applied within the proposed backbone in both stages S_1 and S_2. However, this led to a decline in accuracy across all subsets of the WIDER FACE validation dataset. Through multiple iterations, the optimal MFR block repetition values for stage S_1 and stage S_2 are determined as 3 and 2, respectively. By adopting these optimized values, a competitive accuracy is achieved while maintaining lower computations.

The group convolution technique effectively extracts more enhanced visual features from images with lesser parameters and lower computations. Thus, this technique is implemented initially. Subsequently, a performance evaluation of GC_2 and the MFR network block in stage S_3 is conducted. The use of MFR block slightly improves the accuracy, however it highly increases the computational FLOPs. Thus, GC_2 is used in the final backbone model of the proposed face detector.

Table 4. Ablation Study for the performance of various backbones (varying MFR blocks in stages) on WIDER FACE Validation dataset. The performance is measured in terms of Average Precision (AP). The parameter counts (in millions) and computations (in GFLOPs) are reported. The floating point operations are computed for 640×480 input images. Here, ZERO in third column (S_3) indicates no usage of MFR block and deployment of Group Convolution (GC_2).

No. of MFR Blocks In Stage			Weighted Loss	Easy in AP (%)	Medium in AP (%)	Hard in AP (%)	Params (Million)	FLOP (Giga)
S1 $K = 128$	S2 $K = 256$	S3 $K = 512$						
1	1	0	Yes	0.945	0.93	0.888	9.38	47.5
2	1	0	Yes	0.946	0.933	0.889	9.89	52.4
3	1	0	Yes	0.945	0.932	0.891	10.40	57.3
4	1	0	Yes	0.946	0.934	0.891	10.90	62.1
4	2	0	Yes	0.946	0.933	0.893	12.94	67.0
3	2	0	Yes	**0.948**	**0.935**	**0.893**	**12.43**	**62.1**
3	2	1	Yes	0.948	0.937	0.894	20.56	67.0
3	2	2	Yes	0.947	0.935	0.892	28.69	72.0

(a) Blurred Faces

(b) Occluded Faces

(c) Illumination variations

(d) Facial pose variations

(e) Facial expressions

Fig. 6. Qualitative results of the proposed face detector performance in different challenging scenes from WIDER FACE dataset.

4.4   Face Detector Performance in Challenging Scenes

The robustness of the proposed model is also validated by testing its performance on specific challenging scenarios. The WIDER FACE dataset has challenging scenario annotations for blur, occlusions, illumination changes, pose variations and facial expressions. First, the model is tested with the ResNet50 backbone. Next, the proposed detector is tested with the customized backbone. It is observed that the proposed model has comparable results (96.75%) for the challenges involving expressions. However, when the proposed model is trained with weighted classification loss along with other losses, the performance improved for challenging cases – blur (89%), occlusion (81.9%), illumination (95.1%), pose (89.3%) and expression (98%). The results of these experiments are reported in Table 5.

Table 5. Recall in (%) on Challenging condition on WIDER FACE Validation dataset

Backbone	Blur (%)	Occlusion (%)	Illumin. (%)	Pose (%)	Expres. (%)
ResNet50	88.7	81.2	93.6	88.3	96.7
proposed detector	87	78.3	92.8	86.7	96.75
proposed model + weighted loss	89.3	81.9	95.1	89.3	98

The qualitative results of face detection for different challenging scenarios are shown in Fig. 6. The proposed face detector is also found to fail in certain hard cases arising out of the challenging scenarios. Such cases include very tiny faces (lesser than 8×8 pixels), oriented profile faces, very high image blur, and low illumination. Figure 7 illustrates a few such failure cases.

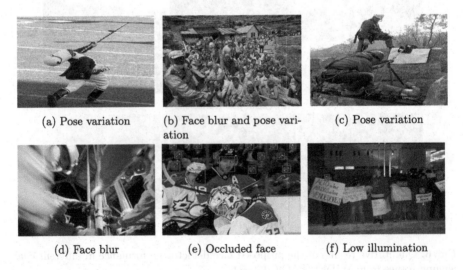

(a) Pose variation   (b) Face blur and pose variation   (c) Pose variation

(d) Face blur   (e) Occluded face   (f) Low illumination

Fig. 7. Illustrating failure cases for some challenging scenarios in images from the WIDER FACE dataset.

5   Conclusion

This work presented a face detector with a novel backbone and a combination of two classification sub-networks in the detector head. The proposal was validated on two standard datasets (WIDER FACE and FDDB) and benchmarked against nine state-of-art approaches. The proposal achieved competitive accuracy with a much lesser number of network parameters (12 M) and computations (62 GFLOP). The proposal is also validated on challenging scenes involving blur, occlusions, illumination changes, pose variations, and facial expressions. Compared to state-of-the-art heavy networks, the present work has significantly reduced the network size and the number of computations. However, a reduction in accuracy (by 2–3% with respect to the top-performing model) is also witnessed. This reduction is attributed to the false positives and the hard cases posed by challenging scenes. Accordingly, the future extension aims at improving the accuracy while further reducing the network size and floating point operations. This might be achieved by a proposal with better attention modules and task specific loss functions.

References

1. Chi, C., Zhang, S., Xing, J., Lei, Z., Li, S.Z., Zou, X.: Selective refinement network for high-performance face detection. In: Proceedings of the AAAI Conference on Artificial Intelligence, vol. 33, pp. 8231–8238 (2019)
2. Chun, L.Z., Dian, L., Zhi, J.Y., Jing, W., Zhang, C.: YOLOv3: face detection in complex environments. Int. J. Comput. Intell. Syst. **13**(1), 1153–1160 (2020)
3. Deng, J., Guo, J., Ververas, E., Kotsia, I., Zafeiriou, S.: RetinaFace: single-shot multi-level face localisation in the wild. In: Proceedings of the IEEE/CVF Conference on Computer Vision and Pattern Recognition, pp. 5203–5212 (2020)
4. Guo, J., Deng, J., Lattas, A., Zafeiriou, S.: Sample and computation redistribution for efficient face detection. arXiv preprint arXiv:2105.04714 (2021)
5. He, K., Zhang, X., Ren, S., Sun, J.: Deep residual learning for image recognition. In: Proceedings of the IEEE Conference on Computer Vision and Pattern Recognition, pp. 770–778 (2016)
6. He, Y., Xu, D., Wu, L., Jian, M., Xiang, S., Pan, C.: LFFD: a light and fast face detector for edge devices. arXiv preprint arXiv:1904.10633 (2019)
7. Howard, A.G., et al.: MobileNets: efficient convolutional neural networks for mobile vision applications. arXiv preprint arXiv:1704.04861 (2017)
8. Huang, G., Liu, Z., Van Der Maaten, L., Weinberger, K.Q.: Densely connected convolutional networks. In: Proceedings of the IEEE Conference on Computer Vision and Pattern Recognition, pp. 4700–4708 (2017)
9. Jain, V., Learned-Miller, E.: FDDB: a benchmark for face detection in unconstrained settings. Technical report, UMass Amherst technical report (2010)
10. Li, H., Lin, Z., Shen, X., Brandt, J., Hua, G.: A convolutional neural network cascade for face detection. In: Proceedings of the IEEE Computer Society Conference on Computer Vision and Pattern Recognition, pp. 5325–5334 (2015)
11. Li, J., et al.: DSFD: dual shot face detector. In: Proceedings of the IEEE/CVF Conference on Computer Vision and Pattern Recognition, pp. 5060–5069 (2019)

12. Lin, T.Y., Dollár, P., Girshick, R., He, K., Hariharan, B., Belongie, S.: Feature pyramid networks for object detection. In: Proceedings of the IEEE Conference on Computer Vision and Pattern Recognition, pp. 2117–2125 (2017)

13. Lin, T.Y., Goyal, P., Girshick, R., He, K., Dollár, P.: Focal loss for dense object detection. In: Proceedings of the IEEE International Conference on Computer Vision, pp. 2980–2988 (2017)

14. Najibi, M., Samangouei, P., Chellappa, R., Davis, L.S.: SSH: single stage headless face detector. In: Proceedings of the IEEE International Conference on Computer Vision, pp. 4875–4884 (2017)

15. Najibi, M., Singh, B., Davis, L.S.: FA-RPN: floating region proposals for face detection. In: Proceedings of the IEEE/CVF Conference on Computer Vision and Pattern Recognition, pp. 7723–7732 (2019)

16. Qi, D., Tan, W., Yao, Q., Liu, J.: YOLOv5Face: why reinventing a face detector. In: Karlinsky, L., Michaeli, T., Nishino, K. (eds.) ECCV 2022, Part V. LNCS, vol. 13805, pp. 228–244. Springer, Cham (2023). https://doi.org/10.1007/978-3-031-25072-9_15

17. Ren, S., He, K., Girshick, R., Sun, J.: Faster R-CNN: towards real-time object detection with region proposal networks. IEEE Trans. Pattern Anal. Mach. Intell. **39**(06), 1137–1149 (2017)

18. Shrivastava, A., Gupta, A., Girshick, R.: Training region-based object detectors with online hard example mining. In: Proceedings of the IEEE Conference on Computer Vision and Pattern Recognition, pp. 761–769 (2016)

19. Simonyan, K., Zisserman, A.: Very deep convolutional networks for large-scale image recognition. arXiv preprint arXiv:1409.1556 (2014)

20. Szegedy, C., et al.: Going deeper with convolutions. In: Proceedings of the IEEE Conference on Computer Vision and Pattern Recognition, pp. 1–9 (2015)

21. Tang, X., Du, D.K., He, Z., Liu, J.: PyramidBox: a context-assisted single shot face detector. In: Proceedings of the European Conference on Computer Vision (ECCV), pp. 797–813 (2018)

22. Viola, P., Jones, M.: Rapid object detection using a boosted cascade of simple features. In: Proceedings of the 2001 IEEE Computer Society Conference on Computer Vision and Pattern Recognition, CVPR 2001, vol. 1, p. I. IEEE (2001)

23. Wang, H., Li, Z., Ji, X., Wang, Y.: Face R-CNN. arXiv preprint arXiv:1706.01061 (2017)

24. Wu, H., Chen, Q., Yachida, M.: Face detection from color images using a fuzzy pattern matching method. IEEE Trans. Pattern Anal. Mach. Intell. **21**(6), 557–563 (1999)

25. Yang, S., Luo, P., Loy, C.C., Tang, X.: WIDER FACE: a face detection benchmark. In: Proceedings of the IEEE Computer Society Conference on Computer Vision and Pattern Recognition, pp. 5525–5533 (2016)

26. Zhang, S., Chi, C., Lei, Z., Li, S.Z.: RefineFace: refinement neural network for high-performance face detection. IEEE Trans. Pattern Anal. Mach. Intell. **43**(11), 4008–4020 (2020)

27. Zhang, S., Zhu, X., Lei, Z., Shi, H., Wang, X., Li, S.Z.: S3FD: single shot scale-invariant face detector. In: Proceedings of the IEEE International Conference on Computer Vision, pp. 192–201 (2017)

28. Zhang, Y., Xu, X., Liu, X.: Robust and high performance face detector. arXiv preprint arXiv:1901.02350 (2019)

A Comprehensive Study on Pre-trained Models for Skin Lesion Diagnosis in a Federated Setting

C. Siddarth⬤, Ajay Kumar Reddy Poreddy⬤, and Priyanka Kokil^(✉)⬤

Advanced Signal and Image Processing (ASIP) Lab, Department of Electronics and Communication Engineering, Indian Institute of Information Technology, Design and Manufacturing, Kancheepuram, Chennai 600127, India
{edm18b009,edm20d012,priyanka}@iiitdm.ac.in

Abstract. Privacy has been one of the main concerns when it comes to the application of deep learning in the medical domain. Medical institutes prioritizing the privacy of their patients do not make their data public, making it difficult to build better models to diagnose rare diseases. But, after the advent of federated learning, there have been immense improvements toward building better models that employ patient's private data without compromising their privacy. In this paper, we comprehensively study multiple models to diagnose skin lesions in a federated setting. Replicating real-life scenarios, we experiment in different settings where the number of clients or hospitals that participate varies. Further, we explore if the pre-trained weights obtained from natural image datasets could assist in building a better model for diagnosing skin lesions.

Keywords: Federated Learning · Transfer Learning · Skin Lesion

1 Introduction

As a result of ever-increasing air pollution, the ozone layer is depleting at an alarming rate, posing harm to humankind. This depletion, in turn, causes poor protection from the ultraviolet-B-radiation (UAB Radiation), which is a vital cause for melanoma and non-melanoma skin cancer development [1,2]. Though the worldwide mortality rate due to melanoma, a lethal skin cancer, has been decreasing, the number of cases is increasing at an alarming rate [2,3]. More than two U.S. residents die of skin cancer every hour. Each year in the United States, more people are diagnosed with skin cancer than with all other cancers aggregated [4]. Although it is known to be a life-threatening disease, early diagnosis and treatment of melanoma could save the life at threat. The five-year survival rate for

This work was funded by the Department of Science and Technology (DST) under the Fund for Improvement of S&T Infrastructure (FIST), Govt. of India [Grant no. SR/FST/ET-I/2020/578], and Science and Engineering Research Board (SERB) [Grant no. EEQ/2021/000804].

patients diagnosed with early-stage melanoma is around 99%. When cancer is detected late and spreads to lymph nodes, the survival rate drops to 68% [4].

There is no prognostic marker in clinical use for melanoma, and clinical features for skin lesions are subjective and imprecise. Thus, melanoma diagnosis seems to be based on the histopathologic gold standard, necessitating the use of experienced clinicians [5]. The diagnosis begins with a visual examination by the dermatologist. Though studies show that diagnostic accuracy strongly correlates with work experience, they commonly have an accuracy between 65% to 80% [6]. With an additional visual inspection of a dermatoscopic image, the absolute melanoma detection accuracy increases to 75%–84% [7].

With time, computers naturally solved the skin cancer detection problem. The initial approaches towards the diagnosis of skin cancer used hand-modeled features and image processing techniques [8–11]. Later approaches employed deep learning-based methods to diagnose melanoma [12–15]. This study will restrict ourselves to the approaches that employ transfer learning to identify melanoma (Table 1).

Table 1. Models and total number of trainable parameters

Model	Parameters (M)
ResNeXt [16]	25
ConvNeXt [17]	88
ViT-B 16 [18]	86
ViT-B 32 [18]	88

Transfer learning refers to re-using an existing and pre-trained model to solve a new and different problem. This allows us to impart knowledge from previous tasks and obtain better-performing models. Transfer Learning is generally used when the task doesn't have sufficient training samples, which could assist with features learned from a different problem [19–22]. Multiple works of literature in the past have considered models such as VGG [23], ResNet [24], and AlexNet [25] for transfer learning [26–28]. Though they perform well, there has been much improvement over them in terms of architecture and optimization. Hence, for this study, we consider newer architectures incorporating state-of-the-art techniques, namely ResNeXt, ConvNeXt, and two versions of Vision Transformers.

1. ResNeXt [16] - ResNeXt is an improved version of the popular model ResNet. It's formed by reiterating a basic structure combining a collection of transformations with the same configuration. For the first time, the paper investigates a new dimension known as 'cardinality,' which refers to the size of the set of transformations. Furthermore, it was observed that increasing cardinality, rather than going deeper or wider, is a more effective way of gaining accuracy. For this work, we employ the ResNeXt-50 (32x4d) model.

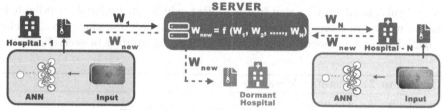

Fig. 1. Overview of Federated Learning

2. ConvNeXt [17] - ConvNeXts are known as the 'modernized ResNets.' They are pure convolutional models (ConvNet) inspired by the design of Vision Transformers and are shown to outperform transformer-based vision models. This study employs the convnext Base model, represented as ConvNeXt-B in [17].

3. Vision Transformers [18] - Also known as ViT, these transformer-based models changed the perspective of convolution filters. Till 2018, CNNs were the de facto model for visual data, which ViTs completely broke. ViT employs a Transformer-like architecture that inputs patches of the images, which are linearly embedded with positional embedding. Though very new, ViTs have found tremendous applications in the medical domain. In this study, we employ two versions of ViTs, namely ViT-B 16 (represented as ViT_16) and ViT-B 32 (represented as ViT_32).

This choice of models is to observe and compare the performance and efficacy of 2 different purely convolution-based models and two transformer-based models. This paper's convolution-based models collectively refer to ResNeXt and ConvNeXt, whereas transformer-based models refer to ViT_16 and ViT_32.

As mentioned before, the accuracy of dermatologists diagnosing skin lesions increases with their work experience. Similarly, the larger and more varied their training set for AI algorithms, the better their predictions. However, such data sets have traditionally proved hard to acquire, especially in the case of melanoma. Hence, hospitals have to rely on their data set, which could be highly biased; if trained, such models would be unable to generalize. Or the hospitals could gather the required data from other hospitals to account for a large data set with a variety. However, due to privacy concerns of the patients, many institutions do not share their data with others, making it difficult to train a generalized model.

Federated learning is a method of privacy-preserving computation that has arisen recently to meet this difficulty. Federated learning allows building such models without sharing the data among institutions. Instead, the hospitals share trained weights, fine-tuned iteratively Fig. 1. Over the course of multiple iterations, also known as communication rounds, the shared model gets exposed to a large variety of samples, which in turn results in a better model.

In this study, we employ Federated Averaging (FedAvg) [29], the foremost introduced algorithm that, to date, performs well and serves as the baseline for other federated learning algorithms. In every communication round, FedAvg produces a global model by taking the weighted average of every client's local model. This global model is sent to every client, which gets updated by individual clients, which are then again weighted average to update the global model. The weighted average is based on the number of training samples of each client.

Algorithm 2. Federated Averaging

1: Initialize W_G, CR and C
2: **for** communication_round $cr \in \{0, 1, 2, ..., CR\}$ **do**
3:     $W_{clients} \leftarrow [\ ]$
4:     **for** each client $c \in C$ **do**
5:         $W_c \leftarrow W_G$
6:         Update W_c via training on client data
7:         Append W_c to $W_{clients}$
8:     **end for**
9:     $W_G \leftarrow F(W_{clients})$
10: **end for**

---

where W_G, CR, and C denote the Global weights, total communication rounds, and participating clients, respectively. It is to be noted that not all clients who have enrolled should participate in the training process. This may be attributed to no or very few training samples or poor infrastructure at the client end. Such clients who do not participate are dormant, whereas others are known as participating clients.

This work explores four existing models in multiple scenarios where the number of participating clients varied. Further, we study the efficacy of pre-trained weights via another set of experiments. This experiment aims to study the diagnosis of skin lesions in a federated setting and the efficacy of transfer learning.

2   Dataset

We use the HAM10000 dataset [30,31], which stands for 'Human against the machine with 10000 training images'. The dataset, containing 10015 images, was acquired from various dermatoscopy types from various sites and institutions. Table 2 represents the number of images present in the HAM10000 dataset [30, 31] for each class. Sample images for each class can be found in Fig. 2. Each lesion is diagnosed as one of the following:

1. **AKIEC: Actinic keratosis/Bowen's disease**
   Actinic keratosis, commonly known as Bowen's disease, is an early stage of skin cancer that is easily cured. The main indication of Bowen's disease is a red scaly patch, which grows very slowly. Though the chances of it turning fatal are less, leaving it untreated could lead to a serious type of cancer.
2. **BCC: Basal cell carcinoma**
   Basal cell carcinoma is a type of skin cancer that develops in the lower part of the outer layer of skin, commonly exposed to the sun. It can be a small white or flesh-colored bump that grows slowly and bleeds. They are the most common form of skin cancer.

3. **BKL: Benign keratosis**
   Seborrheic keratoses are noncancerous skin growths that are commonly found in older adults. They are commonly found on the chest or back, with a scaly and elevated appearance. Seborrheic keratoses do not require any treatment and are easily removable.

4. **DF: Dermatofibroma**
   Dermatofibromas, or histiocytomas, are common noncancerous skin growths commonly found on the skin of the lower leg of adults. They are commonly skin-colored or slightly darker. Usually, without any symptoms, they may last long and could be cured as depressed scars.

5. **MEL: Melanoma**
   Melanoma, also known as 'black tumor,' is potentially the most severe type of skin cancer. Prevalent among white-skinned adults, the skin patch may be of various colors, including blue and red. It usually begins as a small mole but grows a few centimeters in diameter before diagnosis.

6. **NV: Melanocytic nevus**
   Melanocytic nevi is a common tumor that occurs in childhood and early adolescence. The size of such tumors increases with time, but they are easily diagnosed and treated in an early stage. They are commonly found to have any shade of brown and may appear reddish in very complex patients.

7. **VASC: Vascular lesion**
   Vascular lesions, also known as birthmarks, are common abnormalities of human skin and the underlying tissues. They could be found in a newborn infant and disappear in early childhood.

Table 2. Class wise distribution

Diagnosis	Sample Count
AKIEC (class 0)	327
BCC (class 1)	414
BKL (class 2)	1099
DF (class 3)	165
MEL (class 4)	1113
NV (class 5)	6705
VASC (class 6)	192
Total	10015

3 Experimental Setup

All the images are pre-processed before training and evaluation. Each image is center-cropped to a size of 224 × 224 and normalized according to the mean

488   C. Siddarth et al.

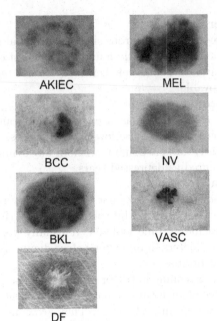

AKIEC   MEL

BCC   NV

BKL   VASC

DF

Fig. 2. Illustration of sample images from each class in HAM10000 dataset [30,31].

and standard deviation from Table 3. More information on the choice of values in Table 3 could be found here[1]

Table 3. Mean and Standard Deviation for pre-processing data

Channel	Mean	Std_Dev
Red	0.485	0.229
Green	0.456	0.224
Blue	0.406	0.225

Four different architectures, namely ResNeXt, ConvNeXt, ViT_16, ViT_32, were trained and evaluated with a various number of participating clients $\in \{5, 10, 25, 50, 100\}$. These were done in two different situations, with and without pre-trained weights, accounting for 40 experiments (= 4 models × 5 clients settings × with/without pre-trained weights). The different number of participating clients is done to replicate the real-life scenario. While five clients could represent five hospitals in a small town associating to learn a global model, 100 clients could represent a state-level collaboration.

The training set was split into three parts, 80% accounting for training and the remaining 20% for validation. The training samples were randomly split

---

[1] https://pytorch.org/vision/stable/models.html.

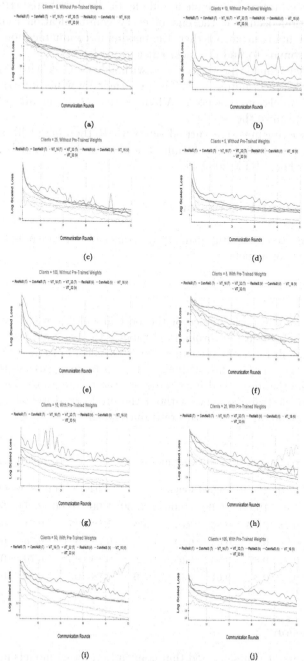

Fig. 3. Illustration of Log Scaled loss for different Communication Rounds.

among clients, imitating independent and identically distributed (IID) data. The model evaluation occurs at the end of every communication round, and the best set of weights is saved. Further, the maximum communication rounds were limited to 50 rounds to find the most efficient model.

Every model's final layer was replaced with a dense layer with 7 output nodes corresponding to each unique class. The pre-trained weights were obtained from training the models on ImageNet. Adam, with a learning rate of 0.001, was employed to optimize the weights.

All the experiments were carried out with Python-based libraries, mainly PyTorch [32], for building and training the models. These models were trained on Nvidia's GeForce RTX 2080 Ti.

4   Results and Discussion

In this section, we outline the primary outcomes of our research before delving deeply into the consequences.

4.1   Results

The F1-score of the performance of the best models from each experiment is shown in Table 4. Figure 3a through 3j visualize the log scale loss and the communication rounds for one to ten experiments (= 5 clients setting × with/without pre-trained weights). The dashed lines in Fig. 3a to 3j represents the validation loss, whilst the the un-dashed lines represent the training loss. Figures 3a to 3e correspond to the training curve without the pre-trained weights, Figs. 3f to 3j correspond to training curve with pre-trained weights.

Table 4. F1-Score of all the 50 experiments. The best result in each case is bolded.

	Without Pre-trained weights					With Pre-trained weights				
Client Count	**5.00**	**10.00**	**25.00**	**50.00**	**100.00**	**5.00**	**10.00**	**25.00**	**50.00**	**100.00**
ResNeXt	**0.78**	**0.75**	**0.72**	0.64	**0.69**	0.78	0.74	0.74	0.69	0.68
ConvNext	0.71	0.65	0.63	0.64	0.64	0.70	0.70	0.76	0.69	0.69
ViT_16	0.65	0.67	0.66	0.65	0.62	**0.81**	0.74	0.70	**0.74**	**0.76**
ViT_32	0.67	0.67	0.61	0.66	**0.66**	0.78	**0.75**	**0.76**	0.72	0.75

4.2   Discussion

From the results, it is understood that convolution-based models perform better when there are no learned weights available. This is clearly understood from comparing the effects of convolution-based models with transformer-based models in the two different settings, i.e., with and without pre-trained weights. This could be attributed to transformer-based models' Inductive Bias (IB). As the transformer-based models treat any image as a 1-D sequence of discrete visual tokens, they lack intrinsic IB in comprehending local visual clues and objects at different scales [33]. The convolution-based models intrinsically learn due to their sliding filters, traversing the complete image.

Also, a common trend found in most models is their performance drop when the number of clients increases as shown in Figs. 3a to 3j. It is to be noted that as the total training set size is constant, increasing the number of clients leads to a lesser data count per client. Hence, this trend could be attributed to the high variance among the client's weights. As each client's model was trained on a very small data set, this could have led the client's model to overfit on their small data set. The aggregation of such models with high covariance causes poorer results when compared to the aggregation of models with lesser covariance.

5   Conclusion and Future Scope

This paper illustrates the benefits of federated learning in enhancing the precision of diagnostic models by facilitating collaboration among medical institutions, thereby enabling the exchange of valuable insights while upholding the confidentiality of patient data. This approach can enhance skin lesion diagnosis accuracy and apply to other medical areas where privacy concerns have impeded advancement.

Our study encompassed an extensive examination of prevailing models within a federated framework for categorizing diverse skin lesion images. We conducted a comparative analysis between convolution-based and transformer-based models and delved into the utility of transfer learning. Additionally, we investigated the impact of the quantity of participating clients on model performance.

In the future, we aim to expand this research to encompass the diagnosis of various medical conditions and formulate resource-efficient models that maintain their effectiveness.

References

1. Sample, A., He, Y.Y.: Mechanisms and prevention of UV-induced melanoma. Photodermatol. Photoimmunol. Photomed. **34**(1), 13–24 (2018)
2. Fabbrocini, G., et al.: Epidemiology of skin cancer: role of some environmental factors. Cancers **2**(4), 1980–1989 (2010)
3. Brinker, T.J., et al.: Skin cancer classification using convolutional neural networks: systematic review. J. Med. Internet Res. **20**(10), e11936 (2018)
4. Bhattacharya, A., Young, A., Wong, A., Stalling, S., Wei, M., Hadley, D.: Precision diagnosis of melanoma and other skin lesions from digital images. AMIA Summits Transl. Sci. Proc. **2017**, 220 (2017)
5. American Cancer Society: Cancer Facts & Figures 2022. American Cancer Society, Atlanta (2022)
6. Argenziano, G., Soyer, H.P.: Dermoscopy of pigmented skin lesions-a valuable tool for early. Lancet Oncol. **2**(7), 443–449 (2001)

7. Ali, A.R.A., Deserno, T.M.: A systematic review of automated melanoma detection in dermatoscopic images and its ground truth data. In: Medical Imaging 2012: Image Perception, Observer Performance, and Technology Assessment, vol. 8318, pp. 421–431 (2012)

8. Sarrafzade, O., Baygi, M.H.M., Ghassemi, P.: Skin lesion detection in dermoscopy images using wavelet transform and morphology operations. In: 17th Iranian Conference of Biomedical Engineering (ICBME), pp. 1–4. IEEE (2010)

9. Fatichah, C., Amaliah, B., Widyanto, M.R.: Skin lesion detection using fuzzy region growing and ABCD feature extraction for melanoma skin cancer diagnosis. In: International Workshop on Advanced Computational Intelligence and Intelligent Informatics, IWACIII 2009 (2009)

10. Chiem, A., Al-Jumaily, A., Khushaba, R.N.: A novel hybrid system for skin lesion detection. In: 3rd International Conference on Intelligent Sensors, Sensor Networks and Information, pp. 567–572. IEEE (2007)

11. Cula, G.O., Bargo, P.R., Kollias, N.: Imaging inflammatory acne: lesion detection and tracking. In: Photonic Therapeutics and Diagnostics VI, vol. 7548, pp. 120–126. SPIE (2010)

12. Yuan, Y.: Automatic skin lesion segmentation with fully convolutional-deconvolutional networks. arXiv preprint arXiv:1703.05165 (2017)

13. Li, Y., Shen, L.: Skin lesion analysis towards melanoma detection using deep learning network. Sensors **18**(2), 556 (2018)

14. Goyal, M., Oakley, A., Bansal, P., Dancey, D., Yap, M.H.: Skin lesion segmentation in dermoscopic images with ensemble deep learning methods. IEEE Access **8**, 4171–4181 (2019)

15. Bissoto, A., Perez, F., Valle, E., Avila, S.: Skin lesion synthesis with generative adversarial networks. CoRR abs/1902.03253 (2019)

16. Xie, S., Girshick, R., Dollár, P., Tu, Z., He, K.: Aggregated residual transformations for deep neural networks. In: Proceedings of the IEEE Conference on Computer Vision and Pattern Recognition, pp. 1492–1500 (2017)

17. Liu, Z., Mao, H., Wu, C.Y., Feichtenhofer, C., Darrell, T., Xie, S.: A ConvNet for the 2020s. In: Proceedings of the IEEE/CVF Conference on Computer Vision and Pattern Recognition, pp. 11976–11986 (2022)

18. Dosovitskiy, A., et al.: An image is worth 16×16 words: transformers for image recognition at scale. arXiv preprint arXiv:2010.11929 (2020)

19. Pratap, T., Kokil, P.: Computer-aided diagnosis of cataract using deep transfer learning. Biomed. Sig. Process. Control **53**, 101533 (2019)

20. Pratap, T., Kokil, P.: Deep neural network based robust computer-aided cataract diagnosis system using fundus retinal images. Biomed. Sig. Process. Control **70**, 102985 (2021)

21. Krishna, T.B., Kokil, P.: Automated classification of common maternal fetal ultrasound planes using multi-layer perceptron with deep feature integration. Biomed. Sig. Process. Control **86**, 105283 (2023)

22. Krishna, T.B., Kokil, P.: Automated detection of common maternal fetal ultrasound planes using deep feature fusion. In: 19th India Council International Conference (INDICON), pp. 1–5. IEEE (2022)

23. Simonyan, K., Zisserman, A.: Very deep convolutional networks for large-scale image recognition. arXiv preprint arXiv:1409.1556 (2014)

24. He, K., Zhang, X., Ren, S., Sun, J.: Deep residual learning for image recognition. In: Proceedings of the IEEE Conference on Computer Vision and Pattern Recognition, pp. 770–778 (2016)

25. Krizhevsky, A., Sutskever, I., Hinton, G.E.: ImageNet classification with deep convolutional neural networks. In: Advances in Neural Information Processing Systems, vol. 25 (2012)
26. Jain, S., Singhania, U., Tripathy, B., Nasr, E.A., Aboudaif, M.K., Kamrani, A.K.: Deep learning-based transfer learning for classification of skin cancer. Sensors **21**(23), 8142 (2021)
27. Hosny, K.M., Kassem, M.A., Foaud, M.M.: Classification of skin lesions using transfer learning and augmentation with AlexNet. PLoS ONE **14**(5), e0217293 (2019)
28. Gouda, N., Amudha, J.: Skin cancer classification using ResNet. In: 5th International Conference on Computing Communication and Automation (ICCCA), pp. 536–541. IEEE (2020)
29. McMahan, B., Moore, E., Ramage, D., Hampson, S., Aguera y Arcas, B.: Communication-efficient learning of deep networks from decentralized data. In: Artificial Intelligence and Statistics, pp. 1273–1282. PMLR (2017)
30. Tschandl, P., Rosendahl, C., Kittler, H.: The HAM10000 dataset, a large collection of multi-source dermatoscopic images of common pigmented skin lesions. Sci. Data **5**(1), 1–9 (2018)
31. Codella, N., et al.: Skin lesion analysis toward melanoma detection 2018: a challenge hosted by the international skin imaging collaboration (ISIC). arXiv preprint arXiv:1902.03368 (2019)
32. Paszke, A., et al.: PyTorch: an imperative style, high-performance deep learning library. In: Advances in Neural Information Processing Systems, vol. 32 (2019)
33. Xu, Y., Zhang, Q., Zhang, J., Tao, D.: ViTAE: vision transformer advanced by exploring intrinsic inductive bias. In: Advances in Neural Information Processing Systems, vol. 34, pp. 28522–28535 (2021)

Author Index

H. Kaur et al. (Eds.): CVIP 2023, CCIS 2011, pp. 495–499, 2024.
https://doi.org/10.1007/978-3-031-58535-7

Printed in the United States
by Baker & Taylor Publisher Services